# The Edinburgh Companion to the First World War and the Arts

# The Edinburgh Companion to the First World War and the Arts

Edited by Ann-Marie Einhaus and Katherine Isobel Baxter

EDINBURGH
University Press

Edinburgh University Press is one of the leading university presses in the UK. We publish academic books and journals in our selected subject areas across the humanities and social sciences, combining cutting-edge scholarship with high editorial and production values to produce academic works of lasting importance. For more information visit our website: edinburghuniversitypress.com



Edinburgh University Press Ltd
13 Infirmary Street, Edinburgh, EH1 1LT

First published in hardback by Edinburgh University Press 2017

Typeset in 10/12 Adobe Sabon by
IDSUK (DataConnection) Ltd, and
printed and bound in Great Britain by
CPI Group (UK) Ltd, Croydon CR0 4YY

A CIP record for this book is available from the British Library

ISBN 978 1 4744 0163 0 (hardback)
ISBN 978 1 3995 4675 1 (paperback)
ISBN 978 1 4744 0164 7 (webready PDF)
ISBN 978 1 4744 2572 8 (epub)



Published with the support of the University of Edinburgh Scholarly Publishing Initiatives Fund.

# Contents

**VI. Publishing and Material Culture**

# List of Illustrations

## Figures

## Plates

The Plate Section can be found between pages 148 and 149.

# Acknowledgements

The editors would like to thank Edinburgh University Press and particularly Jackie Jones for the opportunity to edit this volume, which has been an exciting journey. We would also like to thank Adela Rauchova for unceasingly excellent support and patience throughout the editorial process, Rebecca Mackenzie for the beautiful cover design, and of course all our wonderful contributors for the hard work they put in to make this volume happen. Special thanks go to Kate Macdonald and Andrew Maunder for shouldering the additional burden of reading and commenting on the introduction and the chapter on short fiction respectively, and we are immensely grateful to Matthew Potter for stepping in at the eleventh hour to provide an excellent chapter on First World War painting. Our gratitude moreover goes to our anonymous readers for their kind and valuable feedback on the proposal, and to our colleague Victoria Bazin for sharing her expertise on early-twentieth-century magazine culture. In addition to thanks expressed by individual contributors for kind assistance by a number of individuals and institutions, our gratitude goes to copyright holders for granting permission to reproduce illustrations; and, in particular, our thanks to the British Library, the Bridgeman Art Library, the Imperial War Museum, Getty Images and the Literary and Philosophical Society of Newcastle upon Tyne for reducing or waiving copyright fees in the light of the academic nature of this volume. In a small number of instances, contributors were unable to contact the copyright holders despite all reasonable attempts being made.

# Introduction

*Ann-Marie Einhaus and Katherine Isobel Baxter*

The First World War affected most aspects of public and private life in many of the combatant nations, and its impact was felt worldwide. Unsurprisingly, this global, total war also made itself felt across a wide range of media and areas of cultural production. Some of these cultural and artistic responses are well known, particularly literary portrayals of the war, and its representation in fine art and sculpture. Others have become notorious, such as the war's treatment in the press and in the medium of recruitment and propaganda posters. But cultural and artistic responses to the First World War were not limited to these, and they were not confined to the war years and the war's immediate aftermath. This volume's use of 'the Arts' is in the broadest possible sense, including any area of cultural production, from fine art to literature, performance, film and broadcasting, and curatorial and publishing practice. This introduction outlines the scope and coverage of the volume, reflects on the First World War centenary commemorations to date, and establishes a contextual understanding of the role of cultural and artistic production in commemorating the First World War today.

## Commemoration

Centenary commemorations differ significantly from country to country in line with different national experiences of the war. While the major European participants and many former colonies began commemorating the centenary in 2014 – with a significant run-up period in 2013 in a number of countries, particularly Belgium – the official centennial commemorations in the USA commence in 2017. The centenary of the Battle of Verdun in 1916 was one of the most significant moments of remembrance for both France and Germany, while the 'Somme 100' commemorations were a centrepiece of British commemoration, and Gallipoli formed a key focus for Australian commemorative efforts. The memory of the Dardanelles campaign takes on yet another political significance in Turkey.[1] There is, moreover, plenty of evidence that the memory of the war – and by extension the 'best' or 'right' way to commemorate it – continues to be contested. Why and how should the First World War continue to be commemorated at a time when it is finally slipping from living memory altogether? Although there seems to be broad international agreement that its continued commemoration is important, there is no consensus as to the means and motivations of remembrance beyond a generalised obligation to the dead and a desire to avoid future world wars.

In the run-up to the centenary, for instance, Britain experienced a minor row about the commemoration of the First World War, as the then Secretary of State for Education, Michael Gove, criticised the 'left-wing' view he felt historians and educators were promoting, that the First World War was about 'lions led by donkeys', allegedly inspired by the 1989 BBC TV series *Blackadder Goes Forth*.[2] Revisionist historians, with Gary Sheffield in the vanguard, responded by arguing that their view was, in fact, the very opposite of the lions-led-by-donkeys myth, and sought to promote a measured understanding of the war that went beyond simplistic notions of either patriotic sacrifice or futile slaughter. Sheffield, with other historians, subsequently criticised the government's commemorative programme for being overly focused on defeats and not sufficiently ambitious.[3]

A further, international controversy was sparked by the German government's commemorative plans, which were critiqued as insufficient by commentators in Britain, France, Australia and Germany itself. Foreign commentators particularly highlighted the small budget allocated to commemorative efforts, which contrasted with far more generous allocations in other combatant nations, especially Australia. Internal criticism in Germany, voiced by historian Gerd Krumeich, partly centred on the nature of commemorative events and a bias towards commemorating the war on the Western front, and partly chastised the 'fundamental lack of interest' on the part of the German government in commemorating the war.[4] The lower expenditure and lack of official planning, however, may reflect the traditionally stronger focus on the Second World War and the Holocaust in German war commemorations.

Controversy aside, the centenary commemorations of the First World War have involved a plethora of artistic activities. In part, these activities centred on earlier artistic responses to the war, revived or restored for the centenary. The years leading up to 2014 saw the restoration and cleaning of war memorials across different combatant nations, and the British government, for instance, pledged £5 million towards the preservation of war memorials in 2013.[5] In 2014, the Volksbund Deutsche Kriegsgräberfürsorge (the German equivalent of the British Commonwealth War Graves Commission, the American Battle Monuments Commission and the French National Commission for French Military Graves) arranged for specially commissioned replicas of Käthe Kollwitz's memorial sculpture *The Grieving Parents* to travel from Vladslo in Belgium to the peace park at Rzhev in Russia in a bid to commemorate the dead of both world wars.[6] Exhibitions of war art have been a global feature of centenary commemorations. The Canadian War Museum/Musée Canadien de la Guerre in Ottawa – like the Imperial War Museum London – has long held an extensive collection of war art, the Beaverbrook Collection of War Art, which comprises over 13,000 drawings, paintings, prints and sculptures. A selection of twelve sculptures from the Beaverbrook Collection were exhibited as part of the special exhibition 'Ordinary Canadians in Extraordinary Times' between July 2014 and February 2017. In the USA, a major exhibition of American war art, 'World War One and American Art', ran at the Palmer Museum of Art at Penn State University from 4 November 2016 to 9 April 2017 before touring a number of other museums, marking the centenary of America's entry into the war. This exhibition was conceived to acknowledge and showcase '[t]he war's impact on art and culture', since 'nearly all of the era's major American artists interpreted their experiences, opinions and perceptions of the conflict through their work'.[7]

The centenary has also, however, sparked new artistic production in many former combatant nations. In Britain, one of the first and most widely reported commemorative activities was the art installation *Blood Swept Lands and Seas of Red* by artists Paul Cummins and Tom Piper, which had 888,246 ceramic poppies gradually filling the Tower of London's moat between July and November 2014, representing the number of British fatalities during the war. This installation, as well as a wide range of other individual commissioned artworks, performances and exhibitions, was part of '14–18 NOW', an initiative funded collaboratively by a large number of arts organisations as well as the British government's Department for Culture, Media and Sport, the British Council and the European Union. In addition to national events such as these, which have drawn widespread media attention, the centenary in Britain has also seen the opening of a new First World War gallery at the Imperial War Museum, the publication of a large number of books – including many novels, volumes of poetry and stories – on the subject of the war, and a host of smaller-scale local initiatives. These initiatives frequently endeavour to put local experiences or the marginalised war stories of particular groups (women, children, colonial soldiers, conscientious objectors) back on the commemorative map. An example of this kind of commemorative activity is the crowd-funded WW1 Sikh Memorial Fund, which raised £22,000 to commission a memorial for the 130,000 Sikh men who fought in the war, unveiled in the National Memorial Arboretum on 1 November 2015.

In the USA and Canada, art likewise plays a significant role in the official centennial commemorations. As in Britain and elsewhere, memorials and public sculptures are an important part of commemoration and remembrance in North America, exemplified by the Canadian National War Memorial in Ottawa – designed by artist Vernon March – which was inaugurated in 1939, as well as the continued cultural significance of the Canadian memorial at Vimy Ridge (completed and dedicated in 1936). The continued importance of sculpture is also visible, for instance, in the drive to erect a new National WWI Memorial in Pershing Park, Washington, DC. This project, which relies entirely on private donations for its realisation, is part of the commemorative initiative of the US Foundation for the Commemoration of the World Wars and the US World War One Centennial Commission. The architect and artist behind the memorial, Joe Weishaar and Sabin Howard, received their commission in January 2016 following an international design competition. The memorial will take the form of murals and a number of sculptures, and will be the first national memorial to American participation in the First World War since the inauguration of the National World War One Memorial in Kansas City in 1926 – another memorial entirely funded by private donations, in this case raised by the citizens of Kansas City.

Performance and theatre have been a recurring feature of centenary commemorations. A high-profile commemorative event that formed part of the British '14–18 NOW' programme was the nationwide live performance event *We're here because we're here*, which was conceived and created by artist Jeremy Deller in collaboration with Rufus Norris, Director of the National Theatre. The performance event, which took place in locations across the UK on 1 July 2016 to commemorate the centenary of the first day of the Battle of the Somme, was commissioned by '14–18 NOW', and produced by Birmingham Repertory Theatre and the National Theatre in collaboration with twenty-seven local or regional organisations. Volunteers dressed as First World War soldiers gathered in public spaces, silent except for occasional renditions of the soldier's song 'We're Here Because We're Here' (discussed in this volume in George Simmers's chapter), and handing out cards with the details of men who died on 1 July 1916. In Germany, the Hamburg-based drama company Axensprung developed *Weltenbrand* ('World on Fire'), a collage performance for three actors which combines readings from the work of expressionist writers and soldiers, Edlef Köppen and August Stramm, with extracts from official war documents, fragments from newspaper reports and projections of photographs, field postcards and artwork by Otto Dix, accompanied by a specially arranged composition of war sounds and music. This show has toured a variety of public venues – from schools and museums to theatres – since April 2014, and is available with French and English subtitles.[8]

Art as commemoration is, of course, hardly a centennial phenomenon, and a number of chapters in this volume demonstrate that artworks have been created by individuals and commissioned by official organisations in the name of remembrance ever since the conflict. French historian Annette Becker has discussed among others a particularly interesting site of artistic commemoration, the Chemin des Dames in France, for which the then Prime Minister, Lionel Jospin, commissioned original artwork for the 1998 commemorations. This includes, in the midst of a memorial arboretum, a sculpture by artist Haïm Kern, *Ils n'ont pas choisi leur sépulture* ('They did not choose their tomb'), which represents faces of soldiers caught in a metal mesh in honour of those who do not have a known grave.[9] This sculpture sparked some controversy, as its perceived links with the 1917 mutinies in the French army have polarised pacifist and militarist-patriotic opinion in France, leading to the sculpture being 'vandalized several times by partisans of military order and/or from the extreme right, who see the sculpture – which shows only the suffering of the war – as a three-dimensional rejection of heroism and patriotism'.[10] Kern's sculpture offers an excellent example of the continuing relevance and potential explosiveness of art as commemoration, not least as its mixed reception also speaks to tensions between pacifist and patriotic-heroic modes of remembrance outside of France.

## Context

This collected volume brings together, for the first time, literary, musical, artistic and journalistic responses to the First World War from 1914 to the present day as well as essays reflecting on the impact of the war on material culture. The emphasis in this volume is two-fold: cross-disciplinary and developmental. On the one hand, each contribution scrutinises responses to the war distinct to a particular medium or genre, and is placed in relation to cognate media or genres through the organisation of this volume into broader sections. On the other hand, wherever possible, essays explore their chosen subject not simply in terms of immediate responses to the First World War, but also with regard to developments in or uses of their particular genre over time. The underlying critical assumption of this volume is that literary and artistic responses to the war are often, if not always, closely linked with the war's evolving memory and its perception in the popular imagination, and that the two frequently influence each other over time. Each individual chapter provides a research-informed, original discussion of its particular genre or medium, drawing on the specific expertise of our contributors and situating each medium in its wider historical context as far as possible.

In writing about the legacy of the First World War today, it is vital to acknowledge research on the First World War and colonialism as a particularly vibrant current trend, thanks to the work of scholars such as Alison Fell, Santanu Das and Richard Smith. Projects such as the Humanities in the European Research Area (HERA)-funded 'Cultural Exchange in a Time of Global Conflict: Colonials, Neutrals and Belligerents during the First World War' have moved First World War studies beyond analyses of traditional media by scrutinising the manifold cultural traces of the war in former colonies, particularly in South Asia. This new research is in many instances based on an understanding of the war as a series of cultural encounters of different kinds, a way of reading the war that tallies closely with the interest of this volume in the cultural and artistic dimension of the First World War and its impact specifically on forms of cultural expression.

Many of the chapters included in this volume also adopt a comparative approach and scrutinise multiple countries. However, where this was not possible due to limitations of space, they present a deeper investigation of the British experience. An example of the latter category is Clara Dawson's chapter on war poetry, which was challenged by the need to give even weight to canonical and non-canonical war poets in Britain alone. Much could have been said about the contrasting career and reception of major poets who wrote about the war outside Britain, such as Anna Akhmatova, Filippo Tommaso Marinetti, Guillaume Apollinaire, August Stramm, Gottfried Benn or Alan Seeger. However, the editors felt that to do justice to the very different poetic traditions and trajectories of poetic commemoration of the war would require more room than one poetry chapter could provide. Readers interested in looking beyond British poetic responses to the First World War can turn to the forthcoming *Cambridge History of First World War Poetry*, edited by Jane Potter, whose broader scope covers poetic responses to the war from around the globe. In addition, a number of other volumes offer further reading on some of the topics covered in this Companion: Santanu Das's *The Cambridge Companion to the Poetry of the First World War* (2013) covers English-language war poetry in great depth, while Vincent Sherry's *The Cambridge Companion to the Literature of the First World War* (2005) looks at a wide variety of literary responses to the war, including cinema and the writing of the European avant-gardes. Kate McLoughlin's *The Cambridge Companion to War Writing* (2009) and *The Edinburgh Companion to Twentieth-Century British and American War Literature* (2012), edited by Adam Piette and Mark Rawlinson, also include some chapters on the impact of the First World War in literature. For a wide-ranging historical account of the impact of the war, John Horne's *A Companion to World War I* (2010) – which includes chapters on 'Intellectuals and Writers', 'The Visual Arts' and 'Film and the War' – and the online encyclopaedia *1914–1918 online* (launched in 2014) offer a wide array of chapters covering the war on a truly international scale.

## Content

The volume is split into six sections, each comprising between four and six chapters. **Section I: Literature** examines a range of literary genres, including prose, poetry, drama and short fiction as well as letters and (colonial) memoirs, as examples of autobiographical writing. The rationale behind this selection is to allow genres traditionally associated with the First World War, such as poetry and novels, to be read alongside less explored literary forms like drama and the short story, contrasting both kinds of responses. In her chapter on war novels, Marie Stern-Peltz looks at a selection of British and Irish novels about the First World War written from the war years to the present. Rather than approaching these novels as part of distinct phases or categorising them as either pro-war or anti-war, Stern-Peltz reads them through the lens of their emphasis on uncertainty and transformation, arguing that it is this very engagement with uncertainty that makes the novel a powerful and enduring medium in which to write about the war. Clara Dawson's chapter on First World War poetry, by contrast, limits itself to poetry written by six British writers who witnessed the war at first hand: Siegfried Sassoon, Wilfred Owen, Jessie Pope, Vera Brittain, Edward Thomas and Ivor Gurney. Dawson's chapter uses these English-language poets to trace the reception of war poetry across the century since it was first published as a way of exploring some of the questions raised within the war poetry genre. Her choice of poets reflects the desire to include established canonical poets alongside two women whose war poetry has been either habitually reviled as callous propaganda (Pope) or overshadowed by their longer prose (Brittain).

Following these initial chapters on novels and poetry, Ann-Marie Einhaus explores a less widely known genre of First World War writing, the short story, as it appeared in periodicals and anthologies during and after the war. Focusing on Britain, the USA and Germany, Einhaus traces the publication of short stories about the war from the war years to the centenary, and offers an overview of how these stories fit into changing literary and political contexts. Her chapter is followed by Andrew Maunder's exploration of theatre and plays, another genre of war writing that has hitherto received little attention. Maunder uses British drama about the war from the war years to explore a genre that continues to feature significantly in the way the First World War is publicly remembered, and traces this significance from the inter-war stage hit *Journey's End* (1928) to the international success of the stage adaptation of *War Horse* (2007) and other modern plays.

Two further chapters complete this section by looking at examples of life writing during the First World War. Alice Kelly's chapter on letters makes a case study of the correspondence of Vera Brittain and Roland Leighton, Wilfred Owen, and Ivor Gurney. Kelly treats the 'war letter' as a genre in its own right and argues that epistolary conventions were stretched, even distorted, in wartime as letter-writers were faced with challenges ranging from templates for war letters, rhetorical conventions of the 'break-the-news' letter notifying the recipient of a loved one's death, to censorship and self-censorship of correspondence. Anna Maguire's chapter on colonial life writing during the First World War expands this section beyond the white European experience, as Maguire traces the war experience of West Indian volunteers as represented and recorded in three different genres of colonial life writing. She explores how the First World War, as a time of global mobilisation, created new spaces for encounter, exchange and transnationalism that reverberated through colonial life writing long after war's end.

**Section II: Visual Arts** devotes chapters to painting, sculpture, memorials, posters and advertising. Similar to the section on literature, the aim here is to encompass both established and new visual media, and to contrast traditional and popular forms. Separate chapters on sculpture and memorials were commissioned to prevent a conflation of these forms, and to ensure that a wide variety of sculptures, including those not designed as public memorials, are given equal treatment. Matthew Potter's chapter on painting opens the section with a look at one of the most prominent forms of artistic response to the First World War. He revisits the notion that innovative responses to the war were the prerogative of the avant-garde, and explores the war art of a number of 'establishment' artists who responded to their war experiences in ways that are not always formally innovative, but push the boundaries of the traditional artist's toolbox. Potter also looks at First World War painting in the wake of the war's centenary. In the subsequent chapter, Laura Brandon shows that Western First World War sculpture encompasses numerous smaller public and private commissions that were not overtly commemorative. Her chapter examines British, Australian, European and North American sculpture, arguing that, like its art, the sculpture associated with the conflict is simultaneously contradictory in terms of approach and broadly cohesive in terms of meaning. Brandon contends that the unprecedented casualties of 1914–18 provided a tragic focus that ensured that artist and viewer alike, by and large, worked and observed in a context centred on memory. Brandon's chapter is complemented by Laura Wittman's chapter on memorials, whose exploration of memorialisation includes sculpture, but also moves beyond it to include memorials as wide-ranging as landscaped gardens and parks, and memorial books. Wittman's particular focus is on the ideas of embodiment and time as expressed in a diverse array of case studies from Italy, France and Germany. The final chapter in this section – James Thompson's essay on posters – offers an examination of the response to the First World War in the advertising produced both at the time and subsequently. The posters and advertising of the First World War have often been taken to mark the emergence of state propaganda in a modern sense. Thompson argues that there are, however, problems with existing accounts, which have tended to neglect continuities with pre-war practices in party political campaigning. This chapter addresses the place of posters and advertising in how the war has come to be understood, not least the way in which visual appeals to patriotic duty came to be incorporated into retrospective critical narratives about the war.

**Section III: Music** similarly incorporates a range of traditional and popular chapters, covering music hall and musical theatre, soldiers' songs, as well as requiems, memorial music and the legacy of the war in popular music from the 1960s onwards. These popular and canonical responses to the war are examined in their own time and by their adaptation, quotation or recreation in later media. Robert Dean's opening chapter to this section looks at the role of music hall acts in recruitment throughout the First World War, exemplified by the case study of Paul A. Rubens's song 'Your King and Country Want You' (1914), commissioned by the *Daily Mail* and performed by a wide range of music hall stars (including Vesta Tilley) throughout the war. Dean showcases this song as a particular form of gendered propaganda and explores its incorporation alongside other recruitment tactics into music hall programmes throughout the First World War. His chapter further considers how this strategy was subsequently represented in later dramatic texts including *Cavalcade* (Coward 1931/1933) and *Oh, What a Lovely War!* (Littlewood 1963/Attenborough 1969). George Simmers's chapter on soldiers' songs discusses their links to popular music hall tunes of the day and the hymns soldiers had learned in their youth. Simmers explores how songs could make long marches more bearable, enliven formal and informal gatherings, and offer a means of social bonding. Contemporary references are used to assess the range of soldiers' songs during the First World War, and to place them in their social context, as well as exploring later usage of war songs in *Oh, What a Lovely War!* and Max Arthur's *When this Bloody War Is Over* (2001).

Peter Grant's chapter on the First World War in international popular music scrutinises the appearance of First World War themes and ideas in music composed and recorded since the 1960s. Grant explores how popular songs (and in some cases whole albums) follow or reconstruct both aurally and visually the various 'myths' that have grown up about the First World War. From early examples in French *chanson*, folk/protest songs and 'progressive rock', the discussion moves through to the present day. Grant particularly notes the rapid increase in songs about the war since roughly the mid-2000s, almost entirely within heavy metal and the related genres of martial industrial and neo-folk. Popular music, Grant argues, nearly always utilises some of the myths of the war, but uses these as shorthand to develop new artistic agendas.

The final chapter in this section looks at requiems and memorial music inspired by the First World War. Kate Kennedy's contribution approaches the music discussed as a barometer of the times, serving a public need as well as being a vehicle for private emotion. Kennedy argues that as the war progressed, people's emotional needs changed, and by the end of the conflict music was required most to express people's grief and to serve as a memorial to the dead. The chapter discusses a number of composers of war requiems and memorial music, particularly Edward Elgar, Arthur Bliss, Ivor Gurney and Benjamin Britten.

**Section IV: Periodicals and Journalism** scrutinises popular and 'little' magazines, coverage of the war in newspapers and pamphlets, as well as the still relatively young art of war reporting. The essays in this section acknowledge that responses to the war in public media are governed not only by ideological approaches, but by practical restrictions. Kate Macdonald traces – for the first time – the extent to which the periodical market in Britain was affected by the war's effects at home, ranging from the impact of the Defence of the Realm Act on what was considered publishable, to the physical limitations imposed by paper rationing. She explores the principal categories of magazines published in Britain during the First World War that catered for leisure interests as well as for information and instruction, and considers how the ebb and flow of titles in different categories reflected the population's reading requirements.

Christopher La Casse's chapter offers a material historical analysis of the war's impact on the production and circulation, as well as the political, cultural and aesthetic agendas, of the non-commercial publications that laid the foundations for the modern literary 'renaissance'. The vibrant pre-war, counter-cultural space in which little magazines such as *Poetry* and *Blast* first emerged was rife with fringe politics and experimental modes of expression. Wartime paper shortages, rising production costs and the withdrawal of financial support from pro-war patrons, however, ended many little magazines' print runs, as did political repression. La Casse provides a broad survey of Anglo-American modernist little magazines in the pre-war years and the material and political disruptions of war.

Magazines and periodicals were not, of course, the only print medium to respond to and be affected by the war. Matthew Shaw's chapter, which scrutinises the understudied modern pamphlet, traces the role of political pamphlet publication and the official distribution as well as censorship of pamphlets during and after the First World

War. Shaw offers a fascinating insight into pamphlets as a form of mass medium and public communication that made use of cheap print and paper, responded to the increasing literacy of soldiers and on the home front, and operated within the sophisticated networks of postal and commercial distribution.

The final chapter is by Jo Laycock, who develops a new perspective on First World War journalism by addressing the British response to the war on the Eastern front and in the Middle East. Laycock's chapter focuses on the reporting of violence in the borderlands of the Russian and Ottoman Empires in the British press, with particular emphasis on the representation of the deportation and massacre of the Ottoman Armenian population as a 'war atrocity'. The chapter addresses both the networks of humanitarians, journalists, politicians and scholars involved in disseminating information about these events to the press, and the ways in which violence and atrocity in this region were represented, focusing on the extent to which older narratives of imperial decline and images of the violent unruly borderlands of Europe were reframed in the context of war. Laycock moreover reflects on the ways in which violence and atrocity in the 'East' were connected to the conflict on the Western front and made to 'matter' to British audiences.

Moving on from print, **Section V: Film and Broadcasting** is dedicated to media that were in their infancy or still in the early phases of their development during the war, as well as television drama. The inclusion of a chapter on official British war films, using the example of the game-changing *The Battle of the Somme* (1916), distinguishes between the use of film in wartime, and the changing uses to which such material has been put subsequently. Toby Haggith's chapter looks at British official filmmaking during the First World War and, besides providing a general overview of British filmmaking activities at that time, concentrates on a study of the first of four big campaign films, *The Battle of the Somme*, as it has been the most significant in terms of its impact upon audiences, filmmakers and historical memory.

Michael Paris's contribution turns to feature films. Filmmakers, as Paris shows, recorded the Great War from the very beginning, from the militaristic displays in the last years of peace, through newsreel shots of distant battle, to the early imaginative interpretations in feature film. Even in the twenty-first century, cinema is still interrogating the meaning of the war. Paris argues that, given the popularity of the moving image, cinema has helped to shape and continues to influence the public memory of the First World War, notwithstanding the critically privileged position of war literature in the cultural canon of the Great War. This chapter focuses on British feature films of the war, and outlines their similarities with European and American contemporary films, from the patriotic flag-wavers of the war years and after to the bitter, anti-war films which began to emerge in the late 1920s.

Emma Hanna's chapter showcases the rich array of responses to the First World War in the realm of British television drama. Hanna provides a detailed analysis of the ways in which British television dramas have represented the First World War since the 1960s, and argues that the production, broadcasting and reception of these programmes adds significance to discussions about representations of 1914–18 in contemporary Britain, particularly for the centenary period. Hanna examines a range of dramatic programmes, from *Upstairs, Downstairs* (LWT, 1974) to *Peaky Blinders* (BBC, 2013) and a number of new BBC productions for the centenary, in terms of their cultural and historical significance for Britain's modern memory of 1914–18.

Concluding this section, Richard Hand's contribution takes us from the moving image to the spoken word and recorded sound as he discusses the First World War and sound, analysing a variety of relevant audio and radio dramas from the contemporaneous to the present day, including an account of the development of the BBC's ambitious 'real-time' epic serial *Tommies*, which will run from 2014 to 2018. Hand shows that the First World War was also a conflict of terrifyingly new and intense sounds, a cacophony of mechanised war and its human suffering from bombardments to music hall tunes. Although public radio broadcasting began only in the 1920s, by 1914 wireless was already an indispensable communication tool for the military. Hand discusses examples of what one might call 'pre-radio drama' such as 'In the Trenches' (1917), an extraordinary studio recording which attempts to capture, along with vivid dialogue and sound effects, the 'sound' of the frontline during an intense attack, as well as post-war radio plays about the conflict.

**Section VI: Publishing and Material Culture** explores how the publishing industry and the still relatively new medium of photography, as well as museums, exhibitions and the games industry, responded to the war, and acknowledges the impact of the war beyond the aesthetic into the tangible and practical. This section also acknowledges the early drive to collect, preserve and display the war in a chapter on exhibition practices, using the Imperial War Museum in London as a case study. Jane Potter's opening chapter offers an overview of the many challenges the British publishing industry faced during the First World War. Loss of staff to the forces, paper rationing and rising costs of production were among the more practical hardships. The commitment of British publishers to the war effort, their patriotism, and, for some, an uncertain confidence in if not antipathy to 'the Cause' affected the businesses they strove to keep afloat. Potter analyses the state of British publishing between 1914 and 1918, highlighting key publishers, both pro-war and pacifist, who produced the books and magazines that enlightened, encouraged and entertained a wartime reading public.

Moving from the printed page to the photographic image, J. J. Long's chapter investigates wartime photography and its role in establishing – and, especially in Germany, contesting – the memory of the First World War in the inter-war period. Long takes stock of the state of development of photography as a technology and a process, investigating the prevalence of cameras on the frontline, the production and consumption of photographs in the trenches, as well as strategic and tactical military uses of photography within the emerging field of aerial reconnaissance. He also looks at the development of photojournalism during the First World War, and considers the afterlives of First World War photography. The approach taken by this chapter is comparative, with Britain and Germany being the main focal points.

Photographs form part of the collection discussed in the subsequent chapter by Alys Cundy, whose contribution traces the history of the Imperial War Museum (founded in 1917) as an example of the role museums and collections played in the negotiating of the war's legacy. As Cundy argues, the question of the appropriate 'afterlife' of the material culture of the conflict became a pertinent topic in the final years of the First World War, a question that was nowhere more evident than in museums. By focusing on a small number of case studies of particular objects or collections of objects, this chapter traces the different values that the IWM has ascribed to exhibits and the way that these values have been communicated to the viewing public through display policy and practice. In doing so Cundy considers what the IWM's treatment of its objects over nearly a century can tell us about museums and the material response to the First World War.

The final chapter of this section, and indeed the volume, moves us firmly into the material culture of the present, with Chris Kempshall's exploration of the war's treatment in computer games, which build on a longer tradition of First World War games in other formats and a close relationship between war and play generally. Kempshall's chapter explores the question of how suitable the First World War is for games and play to begin with, given its brutality and relative lack of movement. Kempshall shows that the First World War quickly inspired toys and games, and has been the recurring subject of computer games since the early days of the genre. The chapter argues that it is the lack of a clear moral narrative for the war that allows games makers to reimagine the war in innovative ways for a growing audience of players.

No single volume can hope to offer a comprehensive account of international artistic responses to the First World War. We nevertheless hope our readers will find this Companion a useful and representative selection of essays covering not only some widely known genres in which the experience of the war was reflected, but also some lesser-known and under-researched areas of cultural production. This cultural production spans the entire century from 1914 to the present day. As centenary commemorations approach the one hundredth anniversary of the Armistice and as we enter the second century since the war's end, the evidence gathered in this volume suggests that we can safely expect artistic engagement with the First World War to continue likewise.

## Notes

1. For an excellent overview of commemorative activities in different countries in the wake of the centenary, see Bart Ziino (ed.), *Remembering the First World War* (London and New York: Routledge, 2015).
2. Michael Gove, 'Why Does the Left Insist on Belittling True British Heroes?', *Daily Mail*, 2 January 2014, <http://www.dailymail.co.uk/debate/article-2532930/MICHAEL-GOVE-Why-does-Left-insist-belittling-true-British-heroes.html> (last accessed 12 October 2016).
3. Jasper Copping, 'Historians Complain Government's WW1 Commemoration "Focuses on British Defeats"', *Daily Telegraph*, 5 May 2013, <http://www.telegraph.co.uk/history/britain-at-war/10037507/Historians-complain-Governments-WW1-commemoration-focuses-on-British-defeats.html> (last accessed 12 October 2016).
4. Klaus Wiegrefe, 'Weltkriege und Mauerfall: Gauck muss das Super-Gedenkjahr retten', *Der Spiegel*, 9 November 2013, <http://www.spiegel.de/politik/deutschland/gauck-bundespraesident-rettet-super-gedenkjahr-a-932405.html> (last accessed 12 October 2016).
5. Prime Minister's Office, 'Millions of Pounds to Support Restoration and Repair of First World War Memorials', 19 December 2013, <https://www.gov.uk/government/news/millions-of-pounds-to-support-restoration-and-repair-of-first-world-war-memorials> (last accessed 12 October 2016).
6. A. Kockartz, 'Kollwitz-Replik aus Vladslo reist nach Rshew', *Flanderninfo.be*, 14 June 2015, <http://deredactie.be/cm/vrtnieuws.deutsch/landundleute/1.1997400> (last accessed 12 October 2016).
7. 'World War One and American Art', Philadelphia Academy of the Fine Arts (PAFA) website, <https://www.pafa.org/WW1> (last accessed 12 October 2016).

8. For detailed information (in German), see project website: <http://weltenbrand14.de/das-projekt> (last accessed 12 October 2016).
9. Annette Becker, 'Museums, Architects and Artists on the Western Front: New Commemoration for a New History?', in Ziino (ed.), *Remembering the First World War*, pp. 92–5.
10. Ibid., p. 93.

# I.

# Literature

# 1

# The Uncertain War a Century on: The First World War in British and Irish Fiction

*Marie Stern-Peltz*

## Introduction

In Frances Hardinge's 2014 children's novel *Cuckoo Song*, a young girl struggles to discover who – and indeed what – she is, in a family riven by the loss of a son in the First World War who nonetheless keeps sending letters. During her strange journey between worlds, she meets a mysterious man who tells her that it is the war which has caused the uncertainty of self from which she is suffering, and uncertainty of death which is afflicting her brother:

> The War crushed *faith*. All kinds of faith. Before the War, everybody had their rung on the ladder, and they didn't look much below or above it. But now? Low and high died side by side in Flanders Fields, and looked much the same face down in the mud. [. . .] And the women! Once they kept to their pretty little path [. . .] But those that worked in the farms and the factories during the War have a taste for running their own lives now, haven't they? So all their menfolk are panicking. Frightened. *Uncertain*.[1] (italics in original)

This is a striking expression of the myth of the First World War: that it was a war which fundamentally changed the way society worked, thought and was organised, a war which upset the class structure and disrupted gender norms, turned heroes into traumatised men alienated from the home front, leaving Britain's status uncertain, society transformed, and its closest colony – Ireland – in turmoil.[2] Despite the efforts of revisionist historians such as Brian Bond and Gary Sheffield, this myth is still alive and well in British fiction, rooted in the combat memoirs of Edmund Blunden, Robert Graves and their fellow poets, and reimagined and reiterated in contemporary novels from Pat Barker's *Regeneration* (1991) and Alan Hollinghurst's *The Stranger's Child* (2011) to children's books such as Michael Morpurgo's *Private Peaceful* (2002) and Hardinge's novel cited above. It is too easy to say that the appeal of this myth is its simplicity; to dismiss the representation of the war in *Cuckoo Song* as a reiteration of the myth of the (futile, hellish) war is wilfully to misread it. At the end of the novel, the protagonist, Tris, finds herself drawing a different conclusion from the one presented earlier: 'All was *perhaps*. Nothing was certain. And that, that was wonderful.'[3] The post-war world is uncertain and in-between; it is also full of possibilities. In the century's worth of British novels about the First World War, the war and its aftershocks are represented as ambivalent, ambiguous; the war is a site of horror and futility, but it also brings about transformation and with it the potential for hope.

Published a century after the outbreak of the First World War, *Cuckoo Song* illustrates the central idea of this chapter: that it is the war's ambivalence and duality which is at the heart of its continued appeal to readers and to British and Irish societies both grappling, albeit in very different ways, with ongoing questions of national identity. The myth of the war is at the heart of their representation, even if the Irish narratives necessarily wrestle with the attendant mythology of the Easter Rising and the ensuing civil war in Ireland. This chapter centres around two main ideas: that the war's continued appeal comes from uncertainty, and that reading these novels through uncertainty as a paradigm nuances our understanding of the representational meaning of shell shock, gender, sexuality and memory, particularly in the novels of the past twenty-five years. This chapter argues that the power of these novels lies in their inability to be entirely anti-war or pro-war. I contend that it is the representation of uncertainty and transformation which gives this literature its power, both in the initial responses to the war, and in the post-1990 novels which respond to and rearticulate the initial novels of the war.[4] While this chapter focuses on British and Irish novels, the same sense of a grappling with uncertainty also informs war novels in other languages, from Sébastien Japrisot's *Un long dimanche de fiançailles* (1991; published in translation as *A Very Long Engagement* in 1993) to Elisabeth Zöller's recent young adult novel *Der Krieg ist ein Menschenfresser* (2014). Tris's family's sense of transformation, fear of the future, anger at and simultaneous nostalgia for the war, and ultimately ambiguous view of the future, moreover, finds its precedents in characters such as Christopher Tjetens and Valentine Wannop in Ford Madox Ford's *Parade's End* (1924–8), George Sherston in Siegfried Sassoon's *Sherston Trilogy* (1928–36) and Lily Briscoe in Virginia Woolf's *To the Lighthouse* (1927). And it is this sense of the endless, transformative war which continues to influence and shape the literature of the First World War, even into the next century – in Britain, and in Ireland.

In this chapter, I document the changing meaning and importance of the First World War across the century in adult, young adult and children's fiction, through readings of representative British and Irish novels. In arguing that, despite the variety and diversity of First World War representations across genres, the twin themes of transformation and haunting recur and have become increasingly dominant, I am not attempting to synthesise the literature of the First World War into a single narrative. Nor am I setting out to create a complete narrative of a century's worth of literature; such a project is well beyond the scope of this chapter.[5] Instead, I look at representative novels in which I trace these themes, arguing that they are the reason for the enduring literary appeal of the First World War: as a cataclysmic event, an ongoing crisis, a catalyst for change, and a site for transformation.

## Continuities and Disruptions on the Home Front

The outbreak of war provoked mixed responses. The mythical understanding of an innocent and patriotic nation marching gladly to war is, as myths often are, a simplification. Adrian Gregory convincingly documents that even those who did have a simple response to the war – either for or against – ultimately felt some ambivalence about their positions.[6] This is reflected in the literary response; novels which celebrate the war as a chance to reiterate British superiority nonetheless betray a fear that the war may leave the Empire and the nation transformed and insecure. In John Buchan's second Richard Hannay novel, *Greenmantle* (1917), Hannay observes:

> I never could stand London during the war. It seemed to have lost its bearings and broken out into all manner of badges and uniforms which did not fit in with my notion of it. One felt the war more in its streets than in the field, or rather, felt the confusion of war without feeling its purpose.[7]

Buchan is writing in the past tense, from a (fictional) future where the war is over; there is an implied temporariness assigned to this loss of bearings. Yet the transitory nature of this disruption cannot be guaranteed. The possibility of return to the normative nation is a concern which informs many of the ostensibly pro-war texts of the period, from the writings of Rudyard Kipling to the novels of Mrs Humphry Ward.[8] In this context, it is significant that when Hannay returns to Britain after the war, he is immediately married off.[9] As Sarah Cole suggests, heterosexual activity in war novels often signifies 'normalcy and a return to healthy masculinity', allowing the male hero 'to exit the war domain and re-enter a productively civilian one'.[10] The establishment of heterosexual family units shores up any further concerns about national stability; as long as the family unit is secured, so is the nation, and the disruption of the war can be safely dismissed.[11] The heterosexual imaginary, which asserts the stability and constancy of the nuclear family, also stabilises discourses surrounding Empire, nation, and Edwardian and Georgian ideals. If the family survives, so do these structures.[12]

Buchan assumes that the uncertainty which the war exposes is to be rejected and that the certainty of heteronormative society is a necessary correction to any doubts brought about by the First World War. Rebecca West's *The Return of the Soldier* (1919), however, represents this correction as both troubling and, ultimately, destructive. The double meaning of the title – a soldier's return home, and Chris Baldry's being returned to the state of a soldier – suggests the possibility of a return to 'normality'. Yet the novel itself, with its dual traumas (the loss of a child, the horror of war), questions whether this is desirable. These returns may in fact just reiterate a repressive system. As a result of his concussion, Chris disappears back into an idyllic time when he was in love and spent most of his time in the woods surrounding his ancestral home. This return to the past renders the future uncertain; it also presents a challenge to the norms of class, gender and social expectation. Chris returns to a time when he was romantically involved with a woman of a lower class than his own, spending a lot of time away from his home and free from the responsibilities of the gentry. His return to this time period, then, presents a significant challenge to social norms. Chris's cousin Frank writes that he 'never realised the horror of warfare until [he] saw [his] cousin [. . .] wantonly repudiating his most sacred obligations'.[13] The disgust this cousin feels is not directed at the injury itself, but rather its consequences: Chris's rejection of his marriage and, through that, his rejection of the obligations of class and landownership. Fear of the war's ability to undo the presumed certainty created through societal pressures and norms dominates his cousin's letter.

The value of these norms is constantly challenged in the novel, by Chris, by Jenny, and later by Margaret, as well as by Dr Anderson. When Chris is finally diagnosed, the doctor is blunt: 'Quite obviously he has forgotten his life here because he is discontented with it.'[14] He has forgotten the war, true, but Chris has also forgotten his ultimate accession to social and class norms and responsibilities. Beyond that, he has forgotten the traumatic loss of his son; significantly, it is by forcing Chris to remember his son that normative order is restored. Marina MacKay argues that in the novel 'rural seclusion and modern warfare create parallel, and not contrasting, landscapes [. . .] the domestic beauty of Baldry Court is not a contrast to the grimness of war, redemptive femininity opposed to masculine sterility'; both the war and the norms which sustain Baldry Court are corrupt and limiting.[15] It is only through the war that the failures of Baldry Court, and heteronormative domesticity, are exposed. Jenny reflects that she 'knew that one must know the truth. I knew quite well that when one is adult one must raise to one's lips the wine of the truth, [and] celebrate communion with reality.'[16] The war exposes the constraints of normative Edwardian and Georgian society, as well as its repressive and oppressive potential. Writing in 1918, West refuses to predict change. *The Return of the Soldier* ends with Chris restored to normality, his marital, heteronormative and privileged class position recovered as he returns to the war. Continuity is supposedly assured, as Chris returns to the front. Yet there is an implicit promise of change: Jenny and Margaret have both been disturbed by the experience, and have come to question what they before assumed was true and certain.

This questioning of the value and certainty of heteronormativity in relation to the war is also present in R. H. Mottram's *The Spanish Farm* (1924). His protagonist, the French-Flemish Madeleine, is compared to the titular farm; like it, Madeleine embodies 'the implacable spirit of that border-land so often fought over, never really conquered'.[17] Thus she cannot be truly displaced by the war. Rosa Maria Bracco argues that the 1920s was a period in which authors attempted 'to rescue the war from futility not through a defunct rhetoric of glory and honour, but by describing for its readers the link between the suffering and the lessons of war, and an uninterrupted pattern of historical [. . .] significance'.[18] It is easy to read Madeleine as an example of this; she appears to be part of an unbroken line, carrying on an established historical norm. However, her position at the end of the war is more complicated. Through the novel, Madeleine negotiates her affairs with, respectively, the son of her landlord, and a British officer. The freedom of the war allows her to reject provincial norms, and the limitations of normative discourse; however, the war also takes away the possibility of a union with the landlord's son, ultimately leaving Madeleine alone, facing an uncertain future where only her farm remains unchanged. At the end of the novel, although she is nominally a sign of continuity, she is also 'a portent' who inspires 'fear in statesmen' and 'makes philosophers shudder'.[19] Madeleine may symbolise the certainty of the rural, but through her wartime transformation, and her rejection of normativity, she also represents unstable and uncertain nationhood. Madeleine's ever-adaptable, flexible heterosexuality proves able to sustain her through the war, symbolising an ability to survive and adjust to uncertainty and crisis, and, implicitly, thrive in that uncertainty, as opposed to the gentry and the urban philosophers and statesmen.

In Sebastian Barry's *A Long Long Way* (2005), the questions of heterosexuality and nation become even more entangled in the Irish question: Willie Dunne's fate is sealed when he discovers that the woman he loved, Gretta, has not been faithful, having found a new lover. The severance of this heterosexual connection comes alongside the end of his belief in the righteousness of British rule in Ireland. Gretta's behaviour is a betrayal of faith, not unlike that of the British rulers of Ireland. Shortly after these twin losses of certainty, Willie is killed in battle – he does not belong in the new world, his only real place is on the battlefield, among the other men who have been made exiles. He has no place in the hegemonic masculine space of the new Ireland, ready for the real battle beyond the false war against Germany.

Barry's insistence on the heteronormative union as central to sustaining national identity – loyalist or Irish – reiterates heteronormativity's cultural importance as a sign of stability; the new nation to come will need that connection to survive. The uncertainty of the Easter Rising must be balanced by some form of continuity. However, in Jamie O'Neill's *At Swim, Two Boys* (2001), national turmoil is presented alongside queer uncertainties, suggesting a commonality between the transforming country and the flexibility and fluidity of sexual identity. Focusing on the love story of two young boys, Jim and Doyler, set against the backdrop of the Easter Rising, the novel sends its main representative of normative masculine heterosexuality, Jim's older brother Gordie, to the front to die. Gordie dies unburied and unnamed on the shores of Gallipoli. His death is discovered through a newspaper headline: 'the British had evacuated from Gallipoli [. . .] But Gordie they left behind.'[20] His bold heterosexual masculinity cannot save him; at the moment of his death he is rejected as no longer belonging to the British nation. Gordie's death is an ending for a certain kind of Irish masculinity, implicated in a vision of a loyalist, heteronormative Ireland. His very stability as a sign dooms him. By contrast, when Doyler falls in the Battle of O'Connell Street, Jim is able to find his body and mourn him properly. Doyler's death also becomes a spur to further action, making the desire for change *more* pressing: 'this wasn't the end but the beginning. But the wars would end one day and Jim would come there then, to the island they would share.'[21] As Jodie Medd argues, '[l]ike Jim, Ireland is in the process of its own becoming, and its destination is not yet determined.'[22] The queerness of Jim, Doyler and their sometime lover, the Anglo-Irish aristocrat MacMurrough, allows them to reconfigure themselves as Irishmen, irrespective of the normative demands of Empire, nation and society. Their queerness allows them to embrace the uncertainty of the Ireland to come in a way which is not possible for Gordie – even if their queer narrative will eventually find itself erased from the national narrative, just as Gordie's has already been.

In these novels, socio-cultural disruptions are bound up with the war; it is the war which opens the space for uncertainty and, for West and O'Neill in particular, for questioning the value of social norms and ideals. Hannay's heterosexual union closes down any potential uncertainty caused by the war. In *The Return of the Soldier* and *The Spanish Farm*, the war exposes the flaws of heteronormative sexuality, and heteronormativity in turn symbolises the inflexible norms which in West's reading cause the war, and in Mottram's reading are shaken and potentially destroyed by the war. For Barry and O'Neill both, heteronormativity is bound up with the crisis brought about by Irish participation in the (British) war. For all of these novels, their representation of sexuality suggests the power of the war to disturb and disrupt; the cataclysmic power of the First World War both makes insecure those institutions which appear most solid and exposes their repressive and limiting function. However, as *At Swim, Two Boys* suggests, in the new millennium, this exposure and insecurity is as potentially transformative as it is troubling.

## Despair, Determination and the Gendered Trenches

Away from the home fronts of Britain and Ireland in the trenches of France and Belgium, the transformative power of the war is even more pressing and immediate. Critics such as Elaine Showalter and Sandra Gilbert argue that the war feminised the soldiers who fought. They point to the prevalence of shell shock (or neurasthenia) in the literature of the war, arguing that trench warfare destroyed the manliness of war, reducing men to hysterics. Gilbert further argues that this transformation of masculinity is matched by an empowerment of women brought about by increased mobility through work and occupation of social space.[23] The myth of the First World War has, in the last thirty years, expanded to include women's empowerment, usually through nursing and political involvement, a narrative which coincides with a critical reappraisal of Vera Brittain's *Testament of Youth* (1933) and Mary Borden's *The Forbidden Zone* (1929), among others.[24] The themes of shell shock and female empowerment are more complex, however, than this gendered analysis necessarily implies. Peter Leese argues that shell shock is also intimately bound up with the war's modernity: 'Shell shock is modern because surrounding it are scientific and bureaucratic procedures designed to manage human emotions and behaviour and direct them towards mass, state-controlled activity, in this instance, making war.'[25] The war is about control, establishing security and continuity; shell shock, then, is a reaction to this, and can function as a critique – not dissimilar to the nurse's potential, particularly in post-1990 young adult fiction, to illuminate the ambivalent relationship between individual, community and state. In this version of the myth, the experience of the war is potentially transformative – individually and nationally.[26]

Shell shock is particularly associated with the combatant novels published in the war books boom of the 1920s and 1930s, a period crucial to the shaping of the myth of the First World War. In doing so, these books also codified the exemplary First World War soldier, described by Gail Braybon as soldiers who 'fought on the Western Front [. . .] young, straight from school or university, and idealistic [. . .] primarily middle or upper class [. . .] and highly literate [. . .] white [. . .] the victims of politicians and generals who exploited their idealism'.[27] These soldiers are ideal sites of disruption: their gender, class and age mark them out as the inheritors of power and authority, representing national and social continuity. For Edmund in *Undertones of War* (1928) and George Sherston in *Memoirs of an Infantry Officer* (1930) and *Sherston's Progress* (1932), as well as for Winterbourne in Richard Aldington's *Death of a Hero* (1929) and other novels by combatants in particular, the war and the trauma it inflicts make this continuity impossible and, more importantly, undesirable. The war becomes all-encompassing, transformative, and even if there is pride, heroism and even occasional enjoyment to be found in it, the war is primarily disruptive and alienating.

Nowhere is this clearer than in *Death of a Hero*, which ends with the death of Winterbourne. The last thing Winterbourne hears is his second runner saying, 'I can't stand it. The agony. *Kill* me.'[28] The runner implicitly voices Winterbourne's own thoughts, worn down by the horror of the war, unable to get back to the pleasure-loving, artistic and heroic self of the first half of the novel. Instead, by the end, he is transformed: a man who can no longer see a world beyond the war, and feels no connection to the home front. Winterbourne is a particularly powerful example: as a character, he encompasses both a sense of continuity and the possibility of social change. He is already critical of his patriotic middle-class upbringing before the war, and rejects social norms such as monogamous marriage, but nonetheless feels a social and national obligation to join the war and sustain the nation through his service. His shell shock suggests the hollowness of the latter ideology, and the war's destruction of any sense of purposeful future; his death marks the end of the potential for change that he embodied.

A similar connection between shell shock, disillusionment with patriotism and sense of futurelessness is mapped out in Sebastian Faulks's much later novel *Birdsong* (1993). Early on in the novel, his protagonist, Stephen Wraysford, speaks of his fear of 'being reduced to numbers, to ranks of nameless people who were not valued in the eyes of another individual'.[29] Inevitably, as he is drawn into the war, this happens: he becomes a creature of the war, a cog in the army machine, any ideological, social or heroic potential erased. He necessarily breaks down. He finds himself having 'lost all connection with any earthly happiness that might persist beyond the sound of guns'.[30] For Stephen the war is *only* destructive; its transformation provides no hope; he is an heir of Winterbourne's despair and distrust of any sense of continuity or historical belonging. In *Death of a Hero*, Aldington has Winterbourne ponder the continuity with the Edwardian past, ultimately concluding that the past can hold no value and the norms of the past cannot be preserved.[31] However, the solution for Winterbourne is death, whereas *Birdsong* allows for some potential hope, in the form of Stephen's daughter – a link to the future, despite his initial rejection of the possibility of any future at all.

For both Aldington and Faulks, the war breeds uncertainty in its exposure of the meaninglessness of nationalism and continuity; both use shell shock in order to explore this sense of futility further. Here shell shock functions as a marker of the war's horror, and the uncertainty it engenders is ultimately negative and unproductive. However, this is not always the case; for Robert Graves, in *Good-Bye to All That* (1929), shell shock also allows for a kind of freedom, giving him a new critical perspective and willingness to leave behind norms which have outlived their usefulness. Even more strikingly, in post-1990 novels, shell shock can suggest regenerative critical uncertainty. In Pat Barker's *Regeneration Trilogy*, trauma does indicate the horror and inhumanity of the war. However, the trilogy extends the critical potential of shell shock beyond the futility myth: its protagonists, from the historical figures of W. H. R. Rivers, Siegfried Sassoon and, to a lesser extent, Wilfred Owen, to the invented characters of Sarah Lumb, Charles Manning and Billy Prior, undergo several changes and transformations through the trilogy, and although some are negative, they also offer possibilities. One such example is Rivers's shift from a (somewhat reluctant) model of Edwardian masculinity to someone who believes he may be changed for the better. Early on, Rivers observes that '[i]n advising his young patients to abandon the attempt at repression and let themselves *feel* the pity and terror their war experiences inevitably evoked, he was excavating the ground he stood on'.[32] The class, gender and sexual mores which scaffolded and supported Rivers's identity are transformed by his patients. In treating them, he moves towards embracing a model of self which does not aspire to a single unified sense of self, and faces a productively uncertain future where the limitations of class, gender and family structures may be reimagined or re-examined. Barker is not just writing about shell shock in relation to the war; the productive uncertainty of the trilogy has as much to do with post-Cold War Britain and with the challenges to (working-class) identity after Thatcher as it does with the experience of warfare.[33] This context makes the trilogy's use of shell shock as a symbol of instability and uncertainty even more pressing. These novels are a call to memory, but they are also a call for a new way of thinking; and for a new vision of what it means to be masculine, privileged and empowered.

This desire for a new way of thinking is also evident in the rising interest in nursing narratives. The nurse is the female equivalent of the soldier in the myth of the war, although there are notable exceptions: Sarah Lumb, in the *Regeneration Trilogy*, works in a munitions factory; and, indeed, in the literature of the immediate post-war period women were allowed a much wider range of occupations, most prominently ambulance drivers, as in Helen Zenna Smith's *Not So Quiet* (1930). However, the nurse remains the primary object of mythical focus. The iconic model is, of course, Vera Brittain, whose *Testament of Youth* presents the reader with the quintessential female coming-of-age story: it follows her claiming independence from her family to go to university, then becoming a nurse when war breaks out, falling in love, and losing her innocence through her experiences and the loss of her lover and brother. This narrative is often repeated and reworked in contemporary young adult fiction in particular. Esther MacCallum-Stewart argues that these young adult writers, by 'simply sending the heroine to the fight (nursing) and often making them suffer a bereavement (their first lover)', allow 'both reader and heroine the opportunity to experience the hell of war and to undergo the traditional process of disillusion'.[34] However, just as it is too easy to dismiss Brittain's nuanced memoir as a proto-romance novel, this reading also underestimates the importance of female inclusion in recent First World War novels written for teen readers.

In novels such as Linda Newbery's *Some Other War* (1990), Theresa Breslin's *Remembrance* (2002) and Kate Saunders's *Five Children on the Western Front* (2014), nursing becomes emblematic of a complicated relationship to participatory citizenship as the female characters simultaneously desire to be part of the national narrative and become sceptical of authorities. Alice, in *Some Other War*, is emblematic in this way: through nursing, she develops a strong friendship with her fiancé's sister, Lorna, a suffragette who goes from supporting Emmeline Pankhurst to working with Sylvia Pankhurst in the East End of London. Alice reflects that Lorna symbolises a new engagement with the nation: '[w]hen the war was over, young women who had proved that they could cope with all kinds of demanding work would be unwilling to return to lives confined to the kitchen, nursery and drawing-room.'[35] What nursing provides for Alice and Lorna is a chance to negotiate their ambivalent societal position, as they have to make the argument repeatedly that they belong in the narrative even as Alice and Lorna reconsider whether they want to be part of its power structure. In *Some Other War*, as in similar novels, nursing also comes to symbolise young people's negotiations with an increasingly uncertain adult world. These novels present a model of adolescence that operates between the dichotomies of continuity and disruption, at once wanting to be part of an adult world and wanting to transform it. The insecurity of the nursing role, then, is also bound up with the uncertainty of coming of age.

The nursing role becomes another way in which the war is transformative, bringing instability which has the potential to create a new world. In some ways, after 1990, the (empowered) nurse is the inverse of the (shell-shocked) soldier. Stephen is unable to reintegrate into society in *Birdsong*, Billy Prior dies at the end of the *Regeneration Trilogy*; even contemporary children's novels which deal primarily with male experiences of the war, such as Michael Morpurgo's *Private Peaceful* (2002), present a bleak vision of the world to come. Yet these shell-shocked soldiers also present a critique of the world which led to the war, and suggest the impossibility of re-establishing continuity with the Edwardian and Victorian past. Through the symbolic value of the nurse, too, after 1990 the war becomes not the first catastrophe of the twentieth century, but an end and culmination of the restrictive and potentially destructive continuity of the nineteenth century. The twentieth century is chaotic, violent and horrifying – and after it, there is no hope of returning to the supposed stability of before. However, with that uncertainty comes possibility.

## The Uncertain Post-War

Early on in *Brideshead Revisited*, there is a brief reference to the First World War, when, seeing his scout's displeasure at having women in the college, the novel's protagonist, Charles, observes 'this was 1923, and for Lunt, as for thousands of others, things could never be the same as they had been in 1914'.[36] Charles has just missed the war and he seems unconcerned by it. Yet the world in which Charles comes of age, eventually ending up in his own war, is obviously and consistently presented as a post-war world, marked by the war, even if Charles and Sebastian choose not to acknowledge this. The first section, 'Et in Arcadia Ego', in particular is marked by a sense of renewal, of a breakdown of norms and order which defines the uncertain post-war. Famously, *Brideshead Revisited* is in part about a fear of losing continuity after the Second World War; its anxiety is a mirror image of that of the inter-war years. And yet contemporary depictions of the post-war present a more ambiguous engagement with questions of disruption and continuity – and with questions of how the war is remembered.[37] It is not just a question of memorialisation, memory and post-memory; for the novels of the immediate post-war and the novels which re-present and remember the war seventy-five or one hundred years on, there is also a concern with the transformation and potential for change evoked by the war.

Ross J. Wilson argues that '[t]he ability of the war to be evoked within society to alter or to comment on its ideals is one which is rarely considered within discussions of the memory of the First World War'.[38] Yet it is evident particularly in the novels of the post-war, from the 1920s onwards, that this is a central concern of representations of the war. These novels trace the psychic and social transformations wrought by the war, both as a historical and as a political event. In doing so they seek to understand the war's power and potential: as warning, as critique and as haunting reminder of the precarious position of that which is otherwise seen as certain. Virginia Woolf's *Mrs Dalloway* (1922) captures this concern with the war's power to critique. *Mrs Dalloway* takes place in the 1920s, but the war remains ever present. Despite Clarissa's assertion 'The War was over', she cannot even finish the sentence before she has to amend it to exempt those who have lost sons in the war.[39] As she walks through London, it becomes increasingly evident that this is not the only change. Even looking for gloves brings up the war, disrupting Clarissa's sense of continuity. The 'glove shop where, before the War, you could buy almost perfect gloves' is associated with Uncle William, who 'had turned on his bed one morning in the middle of the War'.[40] What is mourned here – the loss of the perfect gloves, the death of Uncle William, the loss of the familiar and expected – is not directly linked to the war, yet the war colours them. *Mrs Dalloway* weaves the war in as a backdrop, a constant haunting reminder, not just in the explicit trauma represented by Septimus Smith's shell shock, but throughout all the narratives of the text, appearing even in the relatively peaceful and domestic observations of the people who comprise the stream of consciousness of *Mrs Dalloway*'s narrative.

These recurring interruptions of post-war normality function as a critique of a world which has moved on too fast from the war, a critique which is especially evident in the representation of Doctor Bradshaw and Doctor Holmes, with their demands of conventionality and desire to hide away anything which does not conform to their pantomime of social norms (Septimus is meant to 'lie in a bed in a beautiful house in the country', where his potential for critique can be safely hidden from the national narrative).[41] Yet the war and its effects refuse to be dismissed or to be forgotten, and so even as Septimus kills himself, he disrupts the appearance of the return to normality: 'in the middle of my party, here's death [. . .]'.[42] It is not just death which has arrived at the party – it is the other and the erased, those who have been repressed and rejected, who nonetheless demand their place at the party and in British society. The recurring war, Septimus's inescapable memories and obsessive returns suggest the limitations of normality and the impossibility of continuity. Remembering the war, then, in *Mrs Dalloway* is to reject the impetus to go on as normal – it is to accept that society has been fundamentally changed by the war. Furthermore, the war has revealed the uncertainties of social and individual experience.

This desire to remember the war and learn from it is at the heart of the discussions of memory and post-memory in relation to contemporary representations of the First World War. From the debates surrounding the accuracy of the myth and the desire of revisionist historians to bolster the historical record of the war, to the arguments over the centennial commemorations and whether these were too patriotic, too ideological, too anti-war or too celebratory of the heroics of soldiering, it is clear that there is no consensus except for the importance of remembering in itself and the certainty, alternately implicit and explicit in all these discussions, that there is some lesson to be learnt, some conclusion to be drawn from the war.[43] Yet as *Mrs Dalloway* suggests, following *The Return of the Soldier* and *The Spanish Farm*, what makes the war powerful is not any lesson about war itself, but rather the way in which the war keeps disrupting constructions of family, society, nation and Empire, and in doing so exposes insecurities and uncertainties where there was an assumption of stability and continuity. There are multiple examples of this in the contemporary landscape of First World War representations. Linda Newbery's *The Shell House* (2002) is a novel that is particularly illustrative of this approach: focused on two young men, a young upper-class officer during the war and a working-class teenager living in the present, it appears to set out to reiterate the myth. However, *The Shell House* uses the myth to expose the shortcomings of heteronormativity (the officer, Edmund, is involved in a homosexual love affair; contemporary teen Greg has a homoerotic flirtation with a classmate), ongoing class conflict, and the ambivalent politics of the heritage industry which sustains the eponymous shell house, despite Edmund's desire to destroy it. *The Shell House* illustrates how the myth distorts and closes down possibilities of understanding the past, as Greg's commitment to the myth hinders him from ever discovering what happened to Edmund. Newbery uses the myth to challenge the reader, to disturb their certainty about what they can access in the past, and to encourage an uncertainty which opens up new, non-mythical and previously invisible narratives.

The most obviously erased narrative of the First World War is the colonial narrative: T. E. Lawrence and, less well known in Britain, Mulk Raj Anand aside, there is little reference and few canonical works which engage with the colonial experience of the First World War. As I explore above, the Irish case is particularly interesting in this context. The historic political ambivalence around Irish participation in the war and its relationship to the Easter Rising means that questions of memory and Ireland are fraught. There has been a tendency, recently changing, to ignore those soldiers who fought in the war entirely. As Eugene McNulty argues,

> [w]hile in the British canon of war writing [the soldiers] are men *who will have died* but *never be forgotten*; in the context of Southern Irish soldiers the tense needs some adjusting – these are men *who will have died* and *will have been forgotten*.[44]

Writing Irish fiction about the First World War, then, is a conscious political project of remembering and rewriting national history. Jennifer Johnston's 2001 novel *This Is Not a Novel* elegantly interweaves three generations of Anglo-Irish family history, tracing the trauma of war and the civil war which followed, through the Troubles and up to the present. The novel uses recognisable signifiers of the First World War narrative, echoing *Birdsong*'s recovery plot in its protagonist's recreation of her family history. Here too are gay soldiers, the trauma of the front, the horror at the loss of a son. But these features are contextualised through the question of Irish identity, rather than as part of the British mythology, particularly focusing on the increased marginalisation of the Anglo-Irish, as well as the liminal place of women and gay men in the Irish national identity. Protagonist Imogen's grandmother writes in 1917: '*New world. I want a new world for this child. I have lived for over half a century and I do not like it.*'[45] Yet her words disappear into a trunk and are forgotten; it is only ninety years on that the truth of her son's death in the war comes out, through Imogen's publication of her memoirs. It is only then, too, that Imogen – and by proxy Ireland – can begin to come to terms with the war and the secrets it has helped conceal. The myth adds to the sense of uncanny resurfacing, as the myth is present, but subverted, rewritten and reappropriated for an Irish, queer and feminist understanding of the twentieth century.

This rewriting and reappropriation of the myth in service of forgotten narratives is also evident in Kamila Shamsie's 2014 novel *A God in Every Stone*. The novel's Pashtun soldier, Qayyum, experiences the classic trench narrative: he wants to serve heroically, yet finds himself in 'a devil-made world in which men had to run across a field without any cover [. . .] and when the tattered remnants of one division reached the enemy lines [. . .] a yellow mist entered their bodies and made them fall'.[46] The imagery here evokes the poetry of Owen, and the novel functions as an engagement with Owen's demand at the end of 'Dulce et Decorum Est'. Yet Shamsie's response to Owen is necessarily ambivalent. Dying in a trench in France may not be good and sweet, but there is a glory in fighting for independence, for the nation to come; in Qayyum's case, Pakistan, and more specifically Peshawar, is worth sacrificing himself for. Even as he is warned that an independent nation is an uncertain proposition, he moves forward, and slowly but surely the characters of the novel, British and Pashtun both, converge, presenting a hesitant optimism which contrasts with the futility myth of the British (and indeed Irish) First World War.

Perhaps that is what the cultural discourse of the First World War, with its twin themes of disruption and transformation, has to offer the present: an old context for new arguments, a way of thinking about the modern world, the twentieth and twenty-first centuries, and contemporary British, Irish and postcolonial identity. These novels ground the debates of the present in the past and remind us that there is always ambiguity and ambivalence to be found, and always another way of understanding the past. The post-1990 novels of the First World War suggest the continuing power of the war to make us face up to the possibilities of multiple narratives and visions of the past – and encourage us to revisit the classic narratives of the war in order to map out the origin of this power and to re-read and re-remember these texts through the framework of uncertainty, ambiguity and, ultimately, possibility.

## Notes

1. Frances Hardinge, *Cuckoo Song* (London: Macmillan Children's Books, 2014), p. 230.
2. I use the phrase 'myth of the war' to indicate the popular understanding of the war documented by Samuel Hynes in *A War Imagined* (1990; London: Pimlico, 1992) and Dan Todman in *The Great War: Myth and Memory* (London: Hambledon, 2005), among others.
3. Hardinge, *Cuckoo Song*, p. 417.
4. In doing so, I am drawing on the work of James Campell in 'Interpreting the War', in Vincent Sherry (ed.), *The Cambridge Companion to Literature of the First World War* (Cambridge: Cambridge University Press, 2005), pp. 261–79, and Stephen Heathorn in 'The Mnemonic Turn in the Cultural Historiography of Britain's Great War', *The Historical Journal*, 48.4 (2005), 1,103–24. I treat 1914–39 as one wave, and 1971–2014 as the second, reflecting the major periods of publication of fictional representations of the First World War.
5. For useful overviews see for example Paul Edwards, James Campbell and Sharon Ouditt in Sherry (ed.), *The Cambridge Companion to Literature of the First World War*, George Parfitt's *Fiction of the First World War* (London: Faber, 1988), and Virginie Renard's *The Great War and Postmodern Memory* (Brussels: Peter Lang, 2013).
6. Adrian Gregory, *The Last Great War* (Cambridge: Cambridge University Press, 2008), pp. 21–3, 28–30.
7. John Buchan, *Greenmantle* (1917; Amazon eBooks, 2011), location 1,525.

8. See for example Humphry Ward's *Missing* (1917), which deals with the possible loss of a son in the war, and implicitly considers how society will cope without a generation of men.
9. John Buchan, *Mr Steadfast* (1919), *Three Hostages* (1926).
10. Sarah Cole, 'People in War', in Kate McLoughlin (ed.), *The Cambridge Companion to War Writing* (Cambridge: Cambridge University Press, 2009), pp. 25–37 (p. 33).
11. See conclusion to Rosa Maria Bracco, *Merchants of Hope: British Middlebrow Writers and the First World War* (Providence, RI: Berg, 1993).
12. This definition of the heterosexual imaginary draws on the work of Chrys Ingraham, particularly in *White Weddings* (New York: Routledge, 1999).
13. Rebecca West, *The Return of the Soldier* (1918; Project Gutenberg eBooks, 2011), location 299.
14. Ibid., location 1,122.
15. Marina MacKay, 'The Lunacy of Men, the Idiocy of Women: Woolf, West, and War', *NWSA Journal*, 15.3 (Fall 2003), 124–44 (133).
16. West, *The Return of the Soldier*, location 1,272.
17. R. H. Mottram, *The Spanish Farm* (1924; London: Endeavour Press, 2014), location 2,608.
18. Bracco, *Merchants of Hope*, p. 1.
19. Mottram, *The Spanish Farm*, location 2,608.
20. Jamie O'Neill, *At Swim, Two Boys* (2001; London: Scribner, 2002), p. 354.
21. Ibid., p. 641.
22. Jodie Medd, '"Patterns of the Possible": National Imaginings and Queer Historical (Meta) Fictions in Jamie O'Neill's *At Swim, Two Boys*', *GLQ: A Journal of Lesbian and Gay Studies*, 13.1 (2007), 1–15 (14).
23. Sandra M. Gilbert, 'Soldier's Heart: Literary Men, Literary Women and the Great War', *Signs*, 8.3, special issue on Women and Violence (Spring 1983), 422–50.
24. See, for example, Campbell, 'Interpreting the War', pp. 268–72.
25. Peter Leese, *Shell Shock: Traumatic Neurosis and the British Soldiers of the First World War* (Basingstoke: Palgrave Macmillan, 2002), p. 4.
26. I treat these memoirs as novels, following an established tradition. See for example John Onions in *English Fiction and Drama of the Great War, 1918–1939* (Basingstoke: Macmillan, 1990), pp. ix, 2–3; Hynes, *A War Imagined*, pp. 424–5.
27. Gail Braybon, 'Winners or Losers', in Braybon (ed.), *Evidence, History and the Great War* (New York: Berghahn Books, 2005), pp. 86–7.
28. Richard Aldington, *Death of a Hero* (1929; London: Hogarth Press, 1984), p. 372.
29. Sebastian Faulks, *Birdsong* (1993; London: Vintage, 1996), p. 87.
30. Ibid., p. 125.
31. Aldington, *Death of a Hero*, pp. 259–60.
32. Pat Barker, *Regeneration* (London: Penguin, 1991), p. 48.
33. For a more in-depth analysis, see Marie Cecilie Stern-Peltz, 'Coming of Age: The First World War in British Fiction after 1989', unpublished thesis, Newcastle University, 2014, chapter 1.
34. Esther MacCallum-Stewart, '"If they ask us why we died": Children's Literature and the First World War, 1970–2005', *The Lion and the Unicorn*, 31.2 (2007), 182–3.
35. Linda Newbery, *Some Other War* (1990; London: Barn Owl Books, 2002), pp. 137–8.
36. Evelyn Waugh, *Brideshead Revisited* (1945; London: Penguin, 2000), p. 24.
37. Hynes convincingly argues that Waugh was interested in creating a myth of his generation in response to his understanding of the First World War. See Hynes, *A War Imagined*, pp. 388–9.
38. Ross J. Wilson, *The Cultural Heritage of the First World War* (Farnham: Ashgate, 2013), p. 176.

39. Virginia Woolf, *Mrs Dalloway* (1922; London: CRW Publishing, 2003), pp. 6–7.
40. Ibid., pp. 13–14.
41. Ibid., p. 108.
42. Ibid., p. 204.
43. For an overview of the focus on memory and a brief recap of the debates, see Heathorn, 'The Mnemonic Turn in the Cultural Historiography of Britain's Great War'; see also Graham Galer, 'Myths of the Western Front', *Global Society*, 18.2 (2004), 175–95. Gary Sheffield's *Forgotten Victory* (London: Headline, 2001) remains the central revisionist text, and invokes, in its introduction, the problem with learning 'the wrong thing' from the past. For the recent centennial debates, Michael Gove's argument about how the war should be commemorated in school is exemplary for the celebratory response ('Why Does the Left Insist on Belittling True British Heroes', *Daily Mail*, 2 January 2014), as is Michael Morpurgo's argument on behalf of the futility narrative ('Teachers Should Cry in Class', *Daily Telegraph*, 30 June 2014). See also Helen Amass, 'When the Tragedy of War Can Inspire Peace', *Times Educational Supplement*, 1 August 2014.
44. Eugene McNulty, 'Incommensurate Histories: The Remaindered Irish Bodies of the Great War', in Petra Rau (ed.), *Conflict, Nation and Corporeality in Modern Literature* (London: Palgrave Macmillan, 2010), p. 73.
45. Jennifer Johnston, *This Is Not a Novel* (London: Headline, 2001), p. 115; italics in original.
46. Kamila Shamsie, *A God in Every Stone* (2014; London: Bloomsbury, 2015), p. 61.

# 2

# Poetry of the First World War in Britain

*Clara Dawson*

In 1918 John Middleton Murry wrote that 'it is the fact, not the poetry of Mr Sassoon that is important [. . .] Mr Sassoon's verses [. . .] are not poetry [. . .] He gives us only the data.'[1] Nearly a century later, Andrew Motion posited that 'it wasn't just the quality of their work which made them special, it was the fact that they had been there – fought, suffered and in many cases died. Their value as witnesses [. . .] became inseparable from their role as makers.'[2] Both elements of the genre classification of war poetry – the facts and the form – have been fiercely contested in the century following the end of the First World War. Must a poet have been to war before he (and I use the masculine pronoun deliberately) can be designated a *war* poet? Equally, how can the boundaries between poetry and verse be suitably maintained when thousands of soldiers and non-combatants alike turned their hand to verse to document their experience? Can anyone who writes about war in verse forms be a war *poet*? The academy has often proved itself disquieted by poetry or verse which has a mass appeal and, as my discussion of Siegfried Sassoon and Jessie Pope demonstrates, an impulse to police the borders of poetry itself is one feature of the criticism of war poetry. Poetry and truth, poetry and pity, poetry and data, poetry and protest, poetry and politics: these are some of the pairings which make war an uneasy bedfellow for poetry and seem to perturb an idea of poetry existing in and of itself. The anthology has been the primary medium of war poetry and this mode of dissemination has contributed to a sense that theme has more significance than poetic skill within the genre. As Hibberd and Onions remind us, 'most Great War anthologies have been designed to reinforce one view or another of the war; few, if any, have been based exclusively on aesthetic criteria'.[3]

Notably, it is the Romantics to whom critics appeal when staking their claims for which side of the poetry-border a war poet occupies. Wordsworth's dictum, that poetry 'takes its origin from emotion recollected in tranquillity',[4] is often used; for Murry, reviewing Owen in 1921, Owen is a poet because he 'has, at whatever cost, mastered his experience; his emotion has become tranquil'.[5] Elsewhere, critics point to the influence of Keats and other Romantic poets on both Owen and Sassoon as a way of locating them firmly within the English poetic tradition. This orientation towards the Romantics also signals an occlusion of modernism which adds another layer of complication to the reception of war poetry. 'Few soldier-poets were in touch with *avant-garde* movements in the arts,'[6] write Hibberd and Onions in their 1986 anthology. War poets such as Owen, Rosenberg and Thomas, who all died in the war, have come to represent for some critics the ghost-possibility of an English poetic tradition which might have flourished in opposition to an American-inflected modernism had these poets lived.

Alongside these critical debates, anthologies such as Andrew Motion's *First World War Poems* (2003), Jon Stallworthy's *Anthem for Doomed Youth: Twelve Soldier Poets of the First World War* (2003) and Tim Kendall's *Poetry of the First World War: An Anthology* (2013) are testament to the continuing appeal of the soldier-poet to the British public. A series of audio recordings of war poems compiled by the British newspaper *The Mirror* in 2014 presents an eclectic mix of male and female, soldier and non-combatant, protest and patriotic poets. Yeats, Kipling and Housman mix with Sassoon, Owen, Thomas and Gurney, as well as Jessie Pope, Charlotte Mew and May Herschel-Clarke. Their selection reflects the sheer diversity of war poetry in more recent anthologies, returning to the wide range of poets published during and just after the Great War itself. This chapter will give an account of the reception of six poets across the century since their work was published as a way of exploring some of the questions raised within the war poetry genre. Wilfred Owen and Siegfried Sassoon are the two poets who have come to define our idea of the war poet, a role which comes with its own problems. Jessie Pope and Vera Brittain represent two different non-combatant roles: the newspaper propagandist assigned to cheer up the troops and the nation, and the auxiliary nurse, confronting the consequences of technological warfare on bodies first-hand. Edward Thomas and Ivor Gurney exist on the borders of the war poetry genre in a number of ways: between modernism and Georgianism, between beauty and disillusionment, and between war poetry and nature poetry.

## Wilfred Owen and Siegfried Sassoon

Geoff Dyer determines Owen's prominence in British myths and memories of the war when he describes how Owen 'succeeded [. . .] in memorialising the war in the image of his poems [. . .] It is impossible to read about the First World War except through their words.'[7] Owen's assimilation into the industries of memorialisation has meant that his poetry has always been in danger of losing itself in an existence as cultural artefact. 'Some body has put his worst and most famous poem in a glass-case at the British Museum,'[8] sniffed Yeats, as if the glass-case somehow snuffed out any possibility of aesthetic value. Dan Todman's book *The Great War: Myth and Memory* argues that the vision of war presented by war poets such as Owen and Sassoon has muddied historical perception and has created a partial view of the miseries of war. Mark Rawlinson succinctly diagnoses the effects of Owen's 'cultural prominence', whereby his 'normative status' as 'an accessible modern, and an absolute historical witness [. . .] threatens to reduce his poems to convergent paraphrases and memorable epigrams'.[9] Rawlinson argues that a more rigorous reading of Owen's poems is necessary in order to move beyond the platitudinous, and when Owen's reception is traced back to its origins in the early 1920s, it is evident that a concern about his poetic substance has always been at issue.

Owen's regular presence in anthologies of war poetry from 1923 onwards has ensured a steady interest in the poet's work, but the publication of single-volume editions in 1920 (ed. Sassoon), 1931 (ed. Edmund Blunden) and 1963 (ed. Cecil Day-Lewis) generated clusters of reviews and reassessments of his work. The reception of his work reflects the wider questions at stake in assessments of war poetry: the friction between poetic truth and reportage, the role of the poet in protesting against war, the fabrication of an English poetic tradition, and the aesthetic value of war poetry. The most notorious incident in Owen's posthumous career was his overt rejection from Yeats's 1936 edition of *The Oxford Book of Modern Verse*. Whilst illustrating the unresolved contention over poetry and verse which haunts the genre, Yeats's editorial ruling also exemplifies the continuing split between the modernist and the Georgian tradition which has been maintained across the twentieth century. Several critics have speculated about a phantom English tradition that would have reinvigorated the Georgian tradition and rivalled the American modernist tradition if Owen, Thomas and Rosenberg had lived. In 1919, the modernist periodical *Wheels* (a journal edited by the Sitwell siblings which saw itself in contention with the Georgian tradition) dedicated an issue to Owen. Such an instance evokes the possibility that Owen's poetry might have bridged the division between Georgian and avant-garde poetry had he lived. However, Dennis Welland, Owen's first major critic, sustains the division when he points out that 'it was not from the War but from Pound [. . .] that Eliot learnt how to write' and in his inclusion of a chapter on the impact of the war on Owen's poetry.[10] More recently, *The Oxford Handbook of British and Irish War Poetry* and *The Cambridge Companion to the Poetry of the First World War* each have a chapter dedicated to modernist poetry and the First World War which foregrounds the engagement of modernist poets such as Ezra Pound, David Jones, T. S. Eliot and W. B. Yeats with the war, but neither situates these poets in relation to the more traditional war poets. Vincent Sherry states that Jones's work *In Parenthesis* 'is really the only modernist poem to come out of the actual experience of combat'.[11]

Part of what motivates this split tradition of poetry written in English in the twentieth century is an idea of poetic genius as a phenomenon which is created not by circumstance but by innate talent. In a review of the 1960 edition of Owen's poetry, Philip Larkin writes that we withhold the highest praise from war poets 'on the grounds that a poet's choice should seem an action not a reaction [. . .] the first-rank poet should ignore the squalid accident of war: his vision should be powerful enough to disregard it'.[12] In the first major critical study of Owen's poetry (1960), Dennis Welland felt that Owen must be defended from such a charge, arguing that 'it is grotesquely untrue if it is used [. . .] to imply that it was only the War that made him a poet'.[13] In 1964, Ted Hughes supported Welland's view when he wrote that Owen's purpose in exposing the realities of trench warfare gave him an 'urgent, defined, practical purpose [. . .] which perhaps explains his extraordinary detachment from the agony, his objectivity'.[14] Welland's study aims to show that Owen was a poet as well as a war poet by tracing his poetic development back before the war, with a chapter on 'Owen's early ideas of poetry' preceding a chapter on 'The impact of the war on Owen's poetry'. Indeed, almost all critics of Owen's work draw attention to his half-rhymes as his most important formal innovation. Dominic Hibberd takes a similar approach when he traces Owen's poetic evolution in the pre-war period, eschewing the belief that 'front-line experience alone had created Owen's mature style'.[15]

Although critics have had, at times, to excavate Owen's poetry from its status as artefact, if we take a brief look at the reception of one of Owen's most famous and, indeed, finest poems, the constants in those who appreciate his poetry become apparent. 'Strange Meeting' was first published in *Wheels* and was reviewed as part of this volume in 1919. In its first notice in *The Athenaeum*, John Middleton Murry singles out 'Strange Meeting' as the strongest poem in the volume and writes that it will remind the reader 'that poetry is rooted in emotion, and that it grows by mastery of the emotion, and that its significance finally depends upon the quality and comprehensiveness of the emotion'.[16] This evaluation is significant in that it touches on one of the demarcations of poetry which is essential to Owen criticism, that of mastering an emotion and transforming it from the personal to the comprehensive. In reviews of the 1931 Blunden edition, reviewers singled out the role that Owen's command of emotion played in elevating his work. Dilys Powell comments that 'it is this note of pity which transmutes his terrible scenes to poetry' and thus argues against treating Owen's poems as journalistic protest.[17] In *The Athenaeum* Murry also writes that 'the creative impulse is that of Keats [. . .] it touches great poetry by more than the fringe'[18] and that it is equally Owen's transmutation of his Romantic touchstones, Keats and Shelley, which defines his achievement. Owen's Romantic legacies are by no means passive and critics have recognised that Owen produces something singularly his own from them. Harold Bloom writes of 'Strange Meeting' that 'it is an example of how Owen's connection to the Romantic tradition could produce a powerfully lyric and yet unmistakably modern poem'.[19] For Sandra M. Gilbert, the 'fixed stare' in 'Strange Meeting' is redolent of Keats and shows that Owen is 'still engaged in his struggle with Keatsian Romantic tradition'.[20]

Although the poem powerfully evokes the physical and moral horrors of war (as Harold Bloom writes, it 'is terrifying in its representation of the ultimate retrogression of humanity and its disintegration of values'),[21] the poem is as much about poetry itself and the fate of poetic voice. For Mark Rawlinson, 'the poem's central concern is the fate of the poetic vision, which is here to be interred far from mortal sight', signalling that Owen's poetry is not just documenting the war, but exploring the nature of poetic vision itself.[22] For Alan Tomlinson, 'Owen is both the dreaming narrator of "Strange Meeting" and the ghost who has shared his poetic vocation and now seeks to explain its nature and purpose to him.'[23] Owen's reworking of Romantic ideas about poetry and battle make this poem part of a larger examination of poetry and politics. Dominic Hibberd sums up the way in which it transcends any particular interpretation: 'the event in Owen's poem cannot be reduced to a meeting between a man and his double [. . .] but neither is it concerned with the immediate divisions suggested by "German" [. . .] or "British" [. . .] The poem is larger and stranger than that.'[24]

As well as Owen's turn to Romantic poets, his place in English poetry is defined by his effect on poets who came after him. Alongside Owen's critical reception runs his influence on other poets of the twentieth century, another reason why proponents of a reinvigorated English pastoral tradition lament his early death. Owen's poetry has become a touchstone for generations of poets who seek to engage with contemporary politics. Anthony Cronin writes that 'Owen was for the 1930s a sort of avatar'[25] and Janet Montefiore elaborates on this connection, arguing that 'the widely copied "Audenesque style" partly draws its characteristic imagery of derelict industrial landscapes and its consciously youthful, rebellious stridency from the war poetry of Owen and Sassoon'.[26] Michael O'Neill and Gareth Reeves's book on 1930s poets Auden, MacNeice and Spender draws out connections with Owen's poetry: Auden's dramatic character John Nower is an 'intermittent descendant' of the 'strange friend' in Owen's 'Strange Meeting'; MacNeice's 'An Eclogue for Christmas' and Spender's Spanish Civil War poem 'Two Armies' echo Owen's 'Anthem for Doomed Youth'.[27] What both Reeves and O'Neill emphasise is that these poets learn from Owen the 'pitfalls' of 'pity as a poetic emotion': Reeves argues that Owen's pararhyme has 'quizzical gravity' and 'resists full-throated heroics' and O'Neill that Owen's 'Insensibility' spells out 'the tendency [of pity] to exploit suffering for the sake of a poetic effect'.[28] This sense of the difficulty of responding to political violence has also made Owen an important figure for Irish poets, particularly Seamus Heaney, Michael Longley and Derek Mahon. Fran Brearton points out that 'acknowledging the link between art and violence means also to experience the temptation and pressure to compromise the former in the face of [. . .] the latter',[29] and that Owen, along with other Great War poets, provides a model for Irish poets to resist this temptation.

Hibberd and Onions discuss the pairing of Owen and Sassoon in the popular imagination and argue that 'no other poets of the Great War have surpassed them as its spokesmen. This success has had the side-effect of obscuring their uniqueness and the differences between them.'[30] Owen and Sassoon are inseparable in the public mind. However, their status in the academy resolutely has Owen (along with Thomas, Rosenberg and Gurney) as the finer poet and critics have a strong sense of their differences. Jon Stallworthy claims that 'as imaginative and musical structures, [Owen's poems] are more complex and reverberant than Sassoon's'.[31] Owen's poetic talent was signalled by, amongst other things, a clear formal innovation in his development of half-rhyme or consonantal rhyme. Sassoon lacked such an original poetic feature and in the reception of his poetry there is greater anxiety about the blurring of poetry and reportage. Philip Larkin neatly sums up this distinction when he writes that 'Sassoon concentrated on the particular [. . .] Owen deliberately discarded all but generalities [. . .] in the end Owen's war is not Sassoon's war but all war, not particular suffering but all suffering'.[32] Larkin's distinction between the general and the particular reflects the judgement that poetry must aspire to the universal and transcend the particular. Owen's ability to transform experience into the 'universality of poetic truth'[33] has been recognised by many critics and reviewers, but Sassoon's claim to aesthetic over political value, or what Day-Lewis called 'poetical truth' over 'common honesty',[34] has been disputed. When Philip Hobsbaum writes that 'Sassoon's poems certainly include much first-hand reaction to experience. But I am not so sure that his technique is equal to his sensibility',[35] the implication is that the content is of greater significance than the form. Donald Davie calls 'The Show' 'amateurish writing' and argues that its interest lies in the British obsession with trench warfare, implying that the poem's value, 'for a British reader, has really nothing to do with [its] very dubious status as poetic art'.[36]

Yet this mid-century critical viewpoint does not correspond with the promise of Sassoon's poetic career during and just after the war itself. The high point of Sassoon's poetic career was from 1917 to 1920 when, as Paul Fussell describes, 'he became the talk of literary London'.[37] Hibberd informs us that Sassoon's publication in journals meant that 'by mid 1917 he was beginning to acquire the status he held between 1918 and the publication of Owen's poems in 1920 as the most impressive new poet of the war'.[38] In a review of his first single volume, *The Old Huntsman and Other Poems*, Virginia Woolf places him first among the war poets when she writes that he makes the reader feel the 'sordid and horrible experiences' of the war 'in a measure which no other poet of the war has achieved'.[39] Woolf also credits Sassoon with a genuine poetic gift and she portrays him as a promising young poet, hoping 'to see what Mr Sassoon does with his gift'.[40] However, even in the 1920s, when Sassoon's star was relatively high, he was defined by his documentary quality, as a reviewer in *The Spectator* demonstrates: 'these verses may not be great poetry, yet some of them may live, for they say neatly and incisively what some people feel.'[41] As for later critics, the content of the poems is valued more highly than their poetic qualities.

While critics speculate about the state of the English poetic tradition if Owen and Thomas had lived, Sassoon's post-war writing had little impact. In his critical reception, Fran Brearton notes, Sassoon 'remained trapped in the mode of "war poet"' and his 'new lyrical poems from the 1930s to the 1950s cast few ripples on the water'.[42] By the 1930s, as Sassoon continued to publish a mixture of new and old poems, his critical cachet was dropping. When reviewing a new collection, *Vigils*, in 1935, Edmund Blunden described the volume as 'the inner experience of a modern Vaughan'.[43] However, other reviewers found his poetry fundamentally weakened. In 1934, a reviewer describes the 'faint sarcasms' of his verse, in which Sassoon 'seems annoyed rather than roused in passionate protest'.[44]

In assessments of Sassoon in the 1960s, the consensus was also that his post-war poetry failed to live up to his promise. In 1966, Michael Thorpe writes that it was the lack of commitment that caused Sassoon's satiric mode to degenerate: 'there is no thoroughgoing hatred [. . .] no reforming purpose, no passionate conviction.'[45] Although he writes a broadly sympathetic essay, Bergonzi comments that 'when Sassoon attempted to write straightforward poems on subjects remote from the war, he dwindled to the stature of a minor Georgian survival'.[46] In the major war poetry anthologies such as Nichols's in 1943 and Gardner's in 1964, it is his satirical and protest poems which are selected for publication, poems such as 'Blighters', 'The General', 'Counter-attack' and 'Remorse'. The selection of his poems published in the anthology *Georgian Poetry 1916–1917* – 'A Letter Home', 'The Kiss', 'In the Pink' and 'Haunted' – show a different side to his work. These poems lack the realistic detail, bitterly conveyed in the anti-war poems of 1917, and have a more pastoral, musing quality. More recently, critics have tried to bring some of these other poems to light and to demonstrate Sassoon's varied registers. Fran Brearton analyses some of the poems written before and after the satiric war poems: she writes of 'A Letter Home' that, 'as with many of Sassoon's poems, [it] indulges Marvellian pastoral and seeks out Miltonic "pastures new" for the dead [. . .] it is also a poem of aesthetic idealism'.[47] Sarah Cole acknowledges that Sassoon's protest leads to readings of his work as 'a body of verse that installs dissent against the war at its center'.[48] Yet she also points to the poetry's 'quieter currents [. . .] its meditations and its metaphysics' and argues that his post-war poetry was 'attuned to the tense, swirling issues surrounding the war's remembrance'.[49] These critics are attentive to the singularities of Sassoon's poetry in order to counter 'the "one size fits all" approach to war poetry still found in circulation'.[50]

While Owen and Sassoon differ in their critical reception, they are still secure in their place as the most important poets of the Great War. As soldiers who wrote directly from their experience in the trenches, they have become cultural as well as poetic icons. More recently, however, social historians and literary critics have become interested in excavating the poetic work of non-combatants in the war, particularly of women. Jessie Pope documented the experience of women in Britain during the war, as well as writing jingoistic and imperially minded poetry. Vera Brittain's poetry was more lyrical and literary, and many of her poems address the situations of nurses (she worked as an auxiliary nurse) and of women who have lost loved ones.

## Jessie Pope and Vera Brittain

'Englishmen play the game!';[51] 'smash it by clean British Cricket':[52] in 1914, Kipling, Hardy, Chesterton and others summoned by the British government complied, despite private qualms, with the government's request for patriotic poetry which would encourage men to join up. Yet it is often Jessie Pope who bears the weight of vilification for the kind of ideologically charged lines above. She fulfils two targets at once: the female non-combatant and the imperially minded purveyor of public-school masculinity. It may have been this combination which inspired Wilfred Owen to dedicate a draft version of 'Dulce et Decorum Est' 'To Jessie Pope, etc.',[53] bestowing on Pope a notoriety which has caused her to become 'the war poet students love to hate'.[54] As Tim Kendall points out, 'scholars encouraged by that initial judgement have taken the opportunity to present Pope as the epitome of civilians' ignorance.'[55] Though immensely popular during her lifetime, Pope's work largely disappeared after her death, and her volumes of war poetry have not been reprinted. She has been making a slow but steady reappearance through limited selections in war poetry anthologies, particularly as interest in women writers of the war increases and as critics redress the invisibility of women writers of the war. Simon Featherstone writes of the significance of military experience: 'the hostility of the poets and the neglect of the anthologists are both the result of the great emphasis placed upon the "experience" of war.'[56] Both Jessie Pope and Vera Brittain have thus been rehabilitated as critics have become more interested in expanding the war poetry canon beyond the male anti-war poet exemplified by Owen and Sassoon. Although Pope's poetry may not represent the realism of the trenches, critics such as Nosheen Khan, Argha Banerjee and Claire Buck have found her poetry illustrative in regard to the civic role of female writers in the war.

Taking stock of Pope's reputation in the centenary of the First World War, however, it becomes clear that Pope is still attracting censure. The BBC News online magazine piece quoted above investigates her parlous reputation amongst GCSE and A-level students: in the classroom, she is taught alongside Owen and Sassoon in order to compare her jingoistic support of the war unfavourably with their anti-war stance. Her depiction in other public media tends to concur with this binary attitude. The British Library entry on Pope encourages this view, describing her poems as a 'blatant attempt to cajole men into doing their bit' and suggesting that they 'contrast greatly with the brutal imagery of the later war poets such as Owen and Sassoon'.[57] The contrast with Owen and Sassoon certainly perpetuates the division between the combatant poet and the female non-combatant (the charged diction of 'blatant' and the not-so-casual gesture of 'such as' belie the ideological positioning here). The British Library has selected three of Pope's poems: 'The Silent Camp', 'The Blackest Lie' and 'No!'. 'No!' refers to the 'bull-dog pluck' of the Tommies and each of the three verses ends with the refrain 'Are we down-hearted? No!', meant to illustrate the warmongering of which Pope stands accused. There is certainly a blasé attitude to the dead soldiers in the lines 'There are some who stand and some who fall / But how does the chorus go–'. 'The Silent Camp' imagines a 'black, solemn peace' over the camp at night, where soldiers in 'sleep's maternal arms' lie 'like children once again', demonstrating the idealising propensities of the female non-combatant far from the gruesome realities of trench warfare. *The Guardian* also indulges in some bantering mockery when it offers up a headline knowingly playing off its own historic rivalry with the *Daily Mail*: 'Jessie

Pope: The Daily Mail's favourite first world war poet'. Here, the contrast between Pope – with her 'blast of doggerel' – and Owen, Sassoon and Thomas – 'the secular saints of [the] conflict' – is set up along the lines of their own political opposition to the *Daily Mail*.[58] Her association with that particular publication is blamed for giving a vast readership to her 'tub-thumping, eerily jolly exhortations to fight'.[59]

Both *The Guardian* and the British Library ignore Pope's poems dealing with women's experience of the home front and those attacking war profiteers, as do several academic anthologies. *The Norton Anthology of English Literature: Twentieth Century* selects 'The Call' as 'the best-known example of Jessie Pope's jingoistic war poems, exhorting young men to enlist and save England, or be labeled cowards'.[60] Dominic Hibberd and John Onions include two poems in *Poetry of the Great War: An Anthology* (1986) which focus on a patriotic ideal of men fighting for their country, 'Cricket' and 'The Beau Ideal' (they cut 'Cricket' for the 2007 re-edition). There is a clear distinction between selections of her work in anthologies of women writers of the war, however, and in these more general poetry anthologies. *Lines of Fire: Women Writers of World War I*, edited by Margaret Higonnet, selects 'Socks', a poem which explores the mental anguish of the women left at home, knitting socks for the war effort while waiting for news. There are five four-line stanzas, and the last line of each stanza is a direction for a knitting pattern, such as 'Slip 1, knot 2, purl 14', illustrating that the woman is thinking as she works.[61] The lines 'Shining pins that dart and click / In the fireside's sheltered peace' make it clear that the woman is physically comfortable and safe, yet the frequent use of dashes demonstrates the way in which she has to continually check her thoughts. The penultimate line, 'He'll come out on top, somehow –', shows the fear that the woman cannot name, that her loved one will be killed. Higonnet's choice of this poem supports her desire to show the way that female poets 'trace relationships between the politicized masculine domain of death in the frontlines and an obscured domain "behind" the lines, where women were supposed to remain, concealed and silent'.[62] In *Scars Upon My Heart* (1981), the first major anthology of women's First World War poetry, edited by Catherine W. Reilly, there is a balanced selection: two poems which present an idealised view of masculine combat, 'The Call' and 'The Nut's Birthday', and two which deal with women's experience, 'Socks' and 'War Girls'.

In *Not With Loud Grieving: Women's Verse of the Great War* (1994), edited by Nosheen Khan, 'Cricket', the call to arms, is accompanied by 'Come into the 'Lotment, Maud' and 'A Zeppelin Show'. 'Come into the 'Lotment, Maud' is a parodic riff on Tennyson's famous lyric from *Maud*, 'Come into the Garden, Maud'. It styles itself as a rallying cry to women, who, now that men are fighting, are required to do agricultural and farming work. The actions of the gardener are militarised and performed against an enemy – 'the slugs in their snug retreat / Are squirming and turning pale' – and there is imagery satirically resonant of the trenches in the lines 'And the clods shall blossom, beneath her feet, / In onions and curly kale'.[63] Khan's selections show a wider range of subject matter, but Khan also defends Pope by pointing out that 'while [her] light-hearted appreciation of an object which inflicted damage to life and property [in 'A Zeppelin Show'] may cause offence, her attitude was in no way singular'.[64]

Jessie Pope is no exception to the way in which war poets trouble the categories of verse and poetry and provoke the need to defend their inclusion in anthologies or their worthiness for academic study. When her poetry is discussed, critics are quick to note that they see her aesthetic limitations. Tim Kendall writes that 'Pope was no poet, but she wrote fairly accomplished verse',[65] while W. G. Bebbington writes that 'she has no place in the history of literature'.[66] Bebbington is concerned with the wide readership she held under her sway when he writes: 'the type of broadsheet "simple rhymes" which she contributed to the *Daily Mail* and the *Daily Express*, being the voice of the masses, does have a mass appeal, however, and can have a good or a bad influence.'[67] Kendall writes that '"War Girls" does merit attention on sociological grounds, for the skilled way in which it responds to contemporary anxieties',[68] and Banerjee argues that it is important 'to explore a few of her celebrated war poems as spontaneous extensions of the socio-cultural milieu in which they were written; and not as isolated poetic specimens for arbitrary comparison with the male canon'.[69] Pope is thus embedded in a critical impulse to open up war poetry beyond the traditional anti-war protest poet.

Vera Brittain's renaissance has also been part of a feminist project to bring to visibility female poets of the war, though her dramatic life story has produced more public interest and sympathy than Pope holds. Public interest in Brittain tends to coalesce around her memoir, *Testament of Youth*, which became a best-seller when it was published in 1933. The republication of her memoir in 1978 by Virago and BBC film adaptations in 1979 and 2014 have given her prose a wide circulation. Mark Bostridge's edition, *Because You Died: Poetry and Prose of the First World War and After* (Virago, 2008), is the only reprint of the full selection of her war poems, *Verses of a V.A.D.* (1918). Both Pope and Brittain demonstrate a trajectory of women's poetry which was recognised during the war itself but disappeared in the following decades, to be resurrected with the growth of feminist criticism from the 1970s onward. In 1918, *The Bookman* commented that 'the "Verses of a V.A.D." have grown out of what a girl in khaki has seen of the war and suffered from it',[70] acknowledging the authenticity of Brittain's poetry. The more recent growing interest in Brittain's work is illustrated in the increased selection from Hibberd and Onions's 1986 anthology, *Poetry of the Great War: An Anthology*, to their 2007 update, *The Winter of the World: Poems of the First World War*. 'Hospital Sanctuary' in 1986 is joined by 'August 1914', 'The Lament of the Demobilised' and 'The Superfluous Woman'. More recently, critics have begun to engage with the formal and political aspects of Brittain's poetry rather than treating her work as being primarily of sociological interest. Gill Plain analyses 'Sic Transit' and 'Roundel', arguing that the juxtaposition of 'short monosyllabic lines against heavier Latinate syntax [. . .] can be seen as an attempt, through formal experiment, to augment the sense of fragmentation and dislocation'.[71] Claire Buck explores the ways in which her 'poems do the women's work of mourning' and offer 'feminist criticism an alternative model of women's war poetry'.[72]

Reilly's anthology, *Scars Upon My Heart*, 'fills a poignant gap' in this invisible history of women war poets.[73] Where the focus of other war anthologies had been on the suffering of male soldiers, Reilly's anthology, according to Judith Kazantzis' preface, acts as a corrective by illuminating the suffering of women, including the 'endlessly repeated tragic [experience] of bereavement'.[74] Reilly selects 'Perhaps', a poem written about the loss of Brittain's fiancé, and 'To My Brother' to illustrate this experience. It is from Brittain's poem 'To My Brother' that the title of the anthology is taken. The opening line of the poem, 'Your battle-wounds are scars upon my heart', conflates the physical wounds of the soldier with the emotional injuries of the woman waiting for loved ones. The third poem by Brittain presented here is 'The Lament of the Demobilised', where the men who have survived the war express disillusion about the way they are treated once the war has ended. The cynical tone of this poem supports Reilly's argument that 'the received view of "women at home" as ignorant and idealistic is quite false'.[75] In *The Forgotten Army: Women's Poetry of the First World War* (1991), editors Nora Jones and Liz Ward select Brittain's 'Hospital Sanctuary' to highlight the war work undertaken by women. As the title of their anthology suggests, they wish to emphasise women's first-hand experience of the war, arguing that women's poetry 'was not "emotion recollected in tranquillity" but more an immediate expression of exceptional circumstance'.[76] It is worth noting that while Owen is praised for his Wordsworthian qualities, women's poetry is valued for the very documentary quality for which Sassoon was deemed second rate.

Margaret Higonnet also emphasises the first-hand experience of women through her selection of Brittain's poetry in *Lines of Fire*, counteracting the view that 'women's writing was understood to be "inauthentic" and unrealistic, since they stood – even if only symbolically – outside the line of fire'.[77] Both poems by Brittain have a subheading stating the place that they were written: 'August 1914' in Somerville College, Oxford, and 'Sic Transit' in London, June 1917. In one sense, these places draw attention to the fact that they take place behind the frontline. Yet both poems display the desolation and suffering which women experience. 'Sic Transit' describes a soldier nursed by Brittain, and in this poem imagery of a beautiful sunset is mixed with hints of death and blood: 'The dying sun incarnadines the West / And every window with its gold is fired'.[78] The energising rhymes of 'fired', 'desired' and 'aspired' are framed by the two short lines at beginning and end: 'I am so tired', illustrating the despair and exhaustion that characterises the life of the nurse who mourns the loss of everything she loved and to which she aspired.

Nosheen Khan selects 'August 1914', 'A Military Hospital', 'Roundel' and 'The Superfluous Woman' in her 1994 anthology of women's war poetry. 'A Military Hospital' shows Brittain's distress at the 'mass of human wreckage' and 'The Superfluous Woman' evokes 'Ghosts crying down the vistas of the years'.[79] Brittain confirms the superfluous position of women, but at the same time evokes the pathos of women left behind. 'August 1914' was written before the war started, and gives an example of an early protest poem. It is a notable absence that none of these anthologies publish the poems from *Verses of a V.A.D.* specifically addressing her fellow female nurses. In the slim volume, there are poems addressed and dedicated to individual soldiers and collective groups, but there are also four poems specifically dedicated to her female colleagues: 'The Sisters Buried at Lemnos', 'To my Ward-Sister', 'To Another Sister' and 'Vengeance Is Mine'. 'The Sisters Buried at Lemnos' refers to the sinking of the HMHS *Britannic*, which was used as a military hospital. Therein Brittain celebrates the contribution of nurses, writing 'Poets praise the soldier's might and deeds of War, / But few exalt the Sisters, and the glory / Of women dead beneath a distant star'.[80] However, the work done by the critics and anthologists mentioned in this section, as well as the publicity created by Brittain's memoir, have contributed to a renewed interest in women's war writing. The Royal College of Nursing Library and Heritage Centre, for instance, held an event in July 2015 on 'Women's Poetry in the Great War' which celebrated women's experience of nursing and endeavoured to bring these female poets to a wider audience.

## Edward Thomas and Ivor Gurney

Edward Thomas and Ivor Gurney have not attracted popular attention to the same degree as Sassoon and Owen. For some critics, this is precisely to their advantage. The poet C. H. Sisson, reviewing Kavanagh's edition of Ivor Gurney in 1982, comments that 'we are [. . .] far from Sassoon's showing off and "protesting" [. . .] Gurney was far too from Owen's pretentious moralities'.[81] While Owen and Sassoon have become somewhat solidified as cultural icons, Gurney and Thomas enable critics to have a freer hand in speculating on the genre of war poetry. For Edna Longley, Thomas and Gurney 'set the war itself in long perspectives' and show that war poetry 'belongs to a larger poetic field'.[82] For Andrew Motion, Thomas's poetry 'loosened-up my idea of what war poetry can be'.[83] Their more marginal position enables critics of war poetry to resist what Longley elsewhere calls the 'subject-matter fallacy',[84] where the theme of the trenches is used to define the genre, and also to enlarge critical views on war poetry and modernism.

Where Thomas diverges from Gurney (and converges with Owen) is his significance within the poetic tradition and his influence on other poets, particularly in England. Ted Hughes famously called him the 'father of us all' during a speech at the unveiling of the War Poets Memorial in Westminster Abbey in 1985. Andrew Motion, while acknowledging Gurney's 'distinct poetic personality', places him secondary to Thomas when he writes that 'Gurney was more strongly influenced by Thomas than by any other writer',[85] and Edna Longley refers to Thomas as Gurney's muse.[86] Yet in other ways their reputation across the twentieth century converges. Both faded from view after the 1920s, and though they make the occasional appearance in war poetry anthologies (both have two poems in Brereton's *An Anthology of War Poems* in 1930, neither appears in Nichols's 1943 *Anthology of War Poetry 1914–1918*, and Thomas has one poem in Gardner's 1964 *Up the Line to Death* anthology), it is not until the early 1980s that they become prominent again with new editions of their work. Gurney published two volumes of poetry in his lifetime, *Severn and Somme* (1917) and *War's Embers* (1919). Further editions were published by Edmund Blunden in 1954 and Leonard Clark in 1973, but it was not until Patrick Kavanagh's edition in 1982, widely reviewed, that Gurney's reputation was lifted. 'Before then', writes John Lucas, 'he was typically dismissed as a minor Georgian poet whose survival depended on a few, regularly anthologized poems.'[87] Gurney is well represented in recent anthologies, with a substantial selection of poems in Simon Featherstone's *War Poetry: An Introductory Reader* (1995), Andrew Motion's *First World War Poems* (2003), Hibberd and Onions's *The Winter of the World: Poems of the First World War* (2007) and Tim Kendall's *Poetry of the First World War* (2013). Thomas's poetry was published in several volumes, including *Last Poems* in 1918 and *Collected Poems* in 1920, which were well reviewed, but after the 1920s he had to wait until 1978 before Oxford University Press published a new edition of his poems. Like Gurney, Thomas is now a regular presence in the modern war poetry anthology. He is well represented in the Hibberd and Onion and the Motion anthologies and is also one of the six poets in Adrian Barlow's *Six Poets of the Great War* (1995). Matthew Hollis's biography, which won the Costa Biography Award in 2011, also brought Thomas to a wider audience.

Since the revival of Gurney and Thomas in the late 1970s, their poetry has inspired critics to rethink the division between war poetry and modernist poetry. In my discussion of Owen, I pointed out that critics speculate on the possibility that Owen would have turned the direction of English poetry had he lived, finding a middle ground between these two segregated traditions. Critics similarly see Gurney and Thomas as poised between the Georgian lyrics of poets such as Rupert Brooke and Wilfrid Gibson and the modernist works of Pound and Eliot. Reviewing Kavanagh's 1982 edition, Motion writes of Gurney's poetry written after 1919 that 'predominantly Georgian qualities are consistently pressed out of shape [. . .] Gurney never departs from orthodoxy altogether, but challenges and buckles and reinvents it'.[88] Nicholas Freeman describes Thomas as a 'cultural diplomat seeking a negotiated solution to an increasingly vicious struggle between aspects of late Victorian and self-consciously modern literary practice'.[89] This sense of Thomas as operating between two extremes is reflected in the first publication of his poems in *An Annual of New Poetry* in spring 1917, which Jacek Wiśniewski notes 'was perceived by many critics and readers as rival to Edward Marsh's Georgian volumes'.[90] It is partly the fact that Gurney and Thomas wrote many of their poems away from the trenches (indeed Thomas writes very little poetry whilst in the trenches) and about other subjects that broadens the scope of their poetry and by extension the genre of war poetry itself. The emphasis on the theme of the trenches when categorising war poetry is deprecated by Banerjee, who includes Thomas and Gurney in his chapter on pastoral war poetry, and argues that 'experimentations within the pastoral mode in war poetry did pave the way for modernist lyrical revisions'.[91]

This somewhat looser relation to literary history which Thomas and Gurney bring to the war poetry genre is also evident in the contradictory ways in which both poets are defined against it. Thomas's classification as within or without the war poetry genre has fluctuated throughout the decades, and this fluctuation is illustrated in part by Faber's recent oscillations. In Faber's 2004 edition of Thomas's collected poems, the dust jacket notes that

> though sometimes classified with Owen, Rosenberg, and Sassoon as a 'war poet', he was rather a poet who died tragically in the war, and whose main subjects were the English countryside and its people, and the solitude of the observing self.[92]

In 2014, as part of centenary celebrations, however, Faber released an edition of Thomas's *Selected Poems* as part of a series of six books entitled Poets of the Great War. Elsewhere critics have debated how far to see Thomas as a war poet. Andrew Motion argues that 'because all [Thomas's] poetry was written after the outbreak of war, it is all, in an important sense, war poetry'.[93] For Motion, 'whether mentioned or not', the war could always be read in the poetry. Nicholas Freeman reproaches those who have followed Motion and taken a 'critical *carte blanche* to transport Thomas's poems to the Western front and enshrine them in the canon of anthems for doomed youth'.[94] While critics acknowledge the oblique way in which the war is present in Thomas's poetry, its extent is still a contentious question. Hibberd and Onions write that Thomas 'seldom wrote directly about the war although all his poetry was affected by it', a position also held by both Edna Longley and Tim Kendall.[95]

However, these views have a counterpoint in Thomas's reception after the war. Thomas's entry on the Poetry Foundation website claims that he 'only wrote one war poem per se'[96] ('This is no case of petty right or wrong'), and in reviews written just after the war, Thomas is not treated principally, or even at all, as a war poet. In a review of *The Last Poems of Edward Thomas* in *The Bookman* in 1919, John Freeman omits any mention of the war or of Thomas's career as a soldier, instead praising the 'English spirit', the 'singularly absorbed and unconscious presentation of the poet's own mind', and the depiction of the English countryside.[97] Another review of *Last Poems* in 1919 similarly disregards the war; the reviewer quotes from 'The New House' and writes that 'the "feel" of houses [. . .] is a thing to which Edward Thomas seems to have been specially sensitive'.[98] Aldous Huxley ascribes 'the secret of Thomas's influence' to the fact that he is a 'nature poet', a poet who has 'felt profoundly and intimately those particular emotions that nature can inspire'.[99] However, Thomas is included in the war poetry anthologies published in the early 1920s. 'Lights Out' was published in the 1920 edition of Jacqueline Trotter's *Valour and Vision* and 'The Trumpet' in the 1923 edition, though Thomas is absent from Osborn's 1917 war poetry anthology *The Muse in Arms*, in which Sassoon and Gurney are present.

Gurney's poetry has also proved resistant to a classic war poetry narrative in that recent critics have argued that it disrupts the oft-restated narrative of disillusion to protest. During and just after the war, when Gurney published two volumes, his poetry was placed alongside the work of other war poets who progressed, like Sassoon and Owen, from an illusion of glory to bitter protest. In a lengthy article entitled 'Poets in Khaki', written a month after the end of the war, the anonymous critic describes how 'Gurney has felt the uplift of the rapt idealism', but argues that there is now 'a realisation of the madness and crime that war is which grows in power and volume in the later verse of the soldier poets'.[100] The four poems selected by Osborn for his 1917 anthology fit with the tropes of the war poem, especially with the close bonds between the soldiers. Osborn includes 'To Certain Comrades', a poem which displays the comradeship also depicted by Sassoon and described by Osborn in his introduction as 'the secret of our victorious warfare'.[101] Here, Gurney is co-opted in the service of patriotism, but Simon Featherstone writes about the difficulty of classifying Gurney's ideological tendencies. In 'Strange Service', Featherstone argues that 'Gurney is already writing in a way which cannot be classified as pro- or anti-war. It doesn't reject the language of nationalism, but [it is] never allowed to rest.'[102] However, as with Osborn, Gurney's publication in anthologies has often resulted in his poetry being used to support a tradition of protest poetry. 'To His Love' is the only Gurney poem selected by Hollis and Keegan in *101 Poems Against War* (2003). 'To His Love' could in one sense be classified as an anti-war poem, for the poem mourns the loss of an unnamed soldier, who will 'walk no more on Cotswold'. The final stanza reads:

> Cover him, cover him soon!
> And with thick-set
> Masses of memoried flowers –
> Hide that red wet
> Thing I must somehow forget.[103]

The shock of 'Thing' as it comes after the line break conveys at once the horror and the banality of a soldier's corpse, reduced to an anonymous piece of material which bears no resemblance to the man who rowed 'on Severn river' and thus could be read as exposing war's horrors. Yet the poem could equally be sharply critical of the memorialising industry of which the anthology forms a part, which buries and covers over the horrors of war with its mass of 'memoried flowers'. Indeed, Robert Hemmings argues that, despite its frequent anthologisation, the poem 'embraces an ambiguity that is unsettling and ultimately resistant to any patriotic commemorative co-opting'.[104] When Gurney's poetic career is taken as a whole, it becomes clear that he has a complicated, even tormented relationship with memory and memorialising which shifts over time. Kendall describes how, between 1919 and 1922, Gurney's poetry ignores the war, attempting to forget its horrors, but in 1922 he returns to the war with an 'increasingly angry disillusionment with the nation'.[105]

Another way in which Thomas and Gurney's poetry differs from the protest and pity of Owen and Sassoon's work is their celebration of beauty, even in dire circumstances. Vivien Noakes argues that some poets found in the war a source of beauty, 'that, for all its horror, there was in war a vitality, even a beauty, that could transcend the immediate experience'.[106] She singles out Isaac Rosenberg, David Jones and Gurney: 'what sets these three writers apart [. . .] is that they did not move from the war to the poetry. Poetry, as a way of thought and expression through which they could search for abstract, universal beauties, was their starting-point.'[107] Through this argument, she refutes for Gurney the accusation made often of Owen and Sassoon, that the poetry has less aesthetic value because the war rather than the poetry is their starting point. Critics have also noted the appreciation of beauty in Thomas's poems. Jon Stallworthy writes that 'his awareness of the natural world, its richness and beauty, is now intensified by a sense of impending loss and the certainty of death – his own and others''.[108] Thomas's depiction of the countryside and the natural world have also drawn attention in regard to his relation to England. His occupation of a middle ground between modernism and the Georgians has also led to debate about the nature of national identity and his relation to Englishness. Piers Gray argues that the 'voices of the native sons', including Edward Thomas and Ivor Gurney, were 'profoundly alienated' by modernists such as Eliot as '*English* English writing comes to be seen as somehow provincial'.[109] However, Stan Smith takes to task those critics who have too neatly placed Thomas's work in a native counter-tradition to the modernist cosmopolitanism of Eliot, Pound or Yeats.[110] Smith argues that Thomas's poetry instead demonstrates that England can only ever exist as 'an ideological construct'.[111] Other critics have been drawn to Thomas precisely because of his portrayal of the complexities of English identity. Tom Paulin describes his attempt to formulate a cultural identity as 'his mystic introverted patriotism'.[112]

As each of these poets demonstrates, the genre of war poetry, despite emerging from the boundary-wars of the modern nation-state, itself has permeable boundaries. It opens up beyond the trenches and political protest to take in propaganda, the experience of women tending broken bodies, complex explorations of national identity, negotiations with modernist technique, the formation of cultural icons, and the processes of the memorialisation industry, to mention only a few. For those who feel that truth-telling in poetry risks falling into journalistic data, Owen's doubling of truth ('That is why true Poets must be truthful')[113] in his much-quoted preface is significant, and a gloss from Cecil Day-Lewis is helpful here: 'there is poetical truth, and there is common honesty; they are very distant relations.'[114] What Day-Lewis saw as inspiring for a post-war generation was that Owen's poetry brought the two together, celebrating the achievements of the poetry that was produced by the Great War generation.

## Notes

1. John Middleton Murry, 'Mr Sassoon's War Verses', *The Nation*, 13 July 1918, p. 398; reprinted in Dominic Hibberd (ed.), *Poetry of the First World War: A Casebook* (London: Macmillan, 1981), pp. 47–51 (p. 48).
2. Andrew Motion (ed.), *First World War Poems* (London: Faber & Faber, 2003), p. xi.
3. Dominic Hibberd and John Onions (eds), *Poetry of the Great War: An Anthology* (Basingstoke: Macmillan, 1986), p. 3.
4. William Wordsworth, 'Preface', in *Wordsworth and Coleridge: Lyrical Ballads*, ed. R. L. Brett and A. R. Jones (London: Methuen, 1963; repr. 1971), p. 266.
5. John Middleton Murry, 'The Poet of the War', *The Nation and Athenaeum*, 19 February 1921, p. 678; reprinted in Hibberd (ed.), *Poetry of the First World War*, pp. 60–4 (p. 62).
6. Hibberd and Onions (eds), *Poetry of the Great War*, p. 16.
7. Geoff Dyer, 'Stained Stones Kissed by the English Dead', *The Independent*, 13 March 1993, p. 30.
8. W. B. Yeats, *Letters on Poetry from W. B. Yeats to Dorothy Wellesley* (Oxford: Oxford University Press, 1940), p. 124.
9. Mark Rawlinson, 'Wilfred Owen', in Tim Kendall (ed.), *The Oxford Handbook of British and Irish War Poetry* (Oxford: Oxford University Press, 2007), pp. 114–33 (p. 114).
10. Dennis Welland, *Wilfred Owen: A Critical Study* (London: Chatto & Windus, 1960; repr. 1978), p. 12.
11. Vincent Sherry, 'The Great War and Modernist Poetry', in Kendall (ed.), *The Oxford Handbook of British and Irish War Poetry*, pp. 190–207 (p. 191).
12. Philip Larkin, 'The War Poet', *The Listener*, 10 October 1963, p. 562.
13. Welland, *Wilfred Owen*, p. 14.
14. Ted Hughes, 'The Crime of Fools Exposed', *New York Times Book Review*, 12 April 1964, p. 4.
15. Dominic Hibberd, *Owen the Poet* (Basingstoke: Macmillan, 1986), p. 55.
16. John Middleton Murry, 'The Condition of English Poetry', *The Athenaeum*, 5 December 1919, p. 1,285.
17. Dilys Powell, 'The Poet of Pity', *Sunday Times*, 10 May 1931, p. 10.
18. Murry, 'The Condition of English Poetry', p. 1,284.
19. Harold Bloom, *Poets of World War One: Wilfred Owen and Isaac Rosenberg* (Philadelphia: Chelsea, 2009), p. 24.
20. Sandra M. Gilbert, 'Wilfred Owen', in Santanu Das (ed.), *The Cambridge Companion to the Poetry of the First World War* (New York: Cambridge University Press, 2013), pp. 117–28 (p. 125).
21. Bloom, *Poets of World War One*, p. 23.
22. Rawlinson, 'Wilfred Owen', p. 129.
23. Alan Tomlinson, 'Strange Meeting in Strange Land: Wilfred Owen and Shelley', *Studies in Romanticism*, 32 (Spring 1993), 75–95 (79).
24. Hibberd, *Owen the Poet*, p. 177.
25. Anthony Cronin, 'Hero-Poet of Anti-War', *Times Literary Supplement*, 18 November 1960, p. 742.
26. Janet Montefiore, *Men and Women Writers of the 1930s* (London: Routledge, 1996), p. 116.
27. Michael O'Neill and Gareth Reeves, *Auden, MacNeice, Spender: The Thirties Poetry* (Basingstoke: Macmillan, 1992), pp. 13, 65, 230.
28. Ibid., pp. 38, 13, 38.
29. Fran Brearton, *The Great War in Irish Poetry: W. B. Yeats to Michael Longley* (Oxford: Oxford University Press, 2000), p. 161.

30. Hibberd and Onions (eds), *Poetry of the Great War*, p. 30.
31. Jon Stallworthy, in Tim Cross (ed.), *The Lost Voices of World War I: An International Anthology of Writers, Poets and Playwrights* (London: Bloomsbury, 1988), p. 77.
32. Larkin, 'The War Poet', p. 562.
33. Basil de Selincourt, 'Wilfred Owen', *Times Literary Supplement*, 4 June 1931, p. 443.
34. Cecil Day-Lewis, *A Hope for Poetry* (Oxford: Oxford University Press, 1934), pp. 14–17; reprinted in Hibberd (ed.), *Poetry of the First World War*, pp. 76–9 (p. 77).
35. Philip Hobsbaum, 'The Road Not Taken', *The Listener*, 23 November 1961, pp. 860–3; reprinted in Hibberd (ed.), *Poetry of the First World War*, pp. 101–8 (p. 103).
36. Donald Davie, 'In the Pity', *New Statesman*, 23 August 1964, p. 282; reprinted in Hibberd (ed.), *Poetry of the First World War*, pp. 108–13 (p. 111).
37. Paul Fussell, *The Great War and Modern Memory* (Oxford: Oxford University Press, 1975; repr. 2000), p. 103.
38. Hibberd, *Owen the Poet*, p. 97.
39. Virginia Woolf, 'Mr Sassoon's Poems', *Times Literary Supplement*, 31 May 1917, p. 259.
40. Ibid.
41. Unsigned book review, *The Spectator*, 29 May 1926, p. 913.
42. Fran Brearton, 'A War of Friendship: Robert Graves and Siegfried Sasson', in Kendall (ed.), *The Oxford Handbook of British and Irish War Poetry*, pp. 208–26 (p. 220).
43. Edmund Blunden, 'The Watch-Tower', *The Listener*, 27 November 1935, p. 984.
44. George Henry Perrott Buchanan, 'Some Recent Poetry', *Times Literary Supplement*, 15 March 1934, p. 190.
45. Michael Thorpe, *Siegfried Sassoon: A Critical Study* (Oxford: Oxford University Press, 1966), p. 53.
46. Bernard Bergonzi, *Heroes' Twilight* (London: Constable, 1965), pp. 102–8; reprinted in Hibberd (ed.), *Poetry of the First World War*, pp. 188–96 (p. 195).
47. Brearton, 'A War of Friendship', p. 213.
48. Sarah Cole, 'Siegfried Sassoon', in Das (ed.), *The Cambridge Companion to the Poetry of the First World War*, pp. 94–104 (p. 95).
49. Ibid., pp. 95, 102.
50. Brearton, 'A War of Friendship', p. 209.
51. Jessie Pope, 'Play the Game', in *Jessie Pope's War Poems* (London: Grant Richards, 1915), p. 11.
52. Jessie Pope, 'Cricket', in Hibberd and Onions (eds), *Poetry of the Great War*, p. 58.
53. W. G. Bebbington, 'Jessie Pope and Wilfred Owen', *Ariel*, 3 (1972), 82–93 (82).
54. Marek Pruszewicz, 'The WW1 Poet Kids Are Taught to Dislike', 1 May 2015, <http://www.bbc.co.uk/news/magazine-32298697> (last accessed 18 October 2016).
55. Tim Kendall (ed.), *Poetry of the First World War: An Anthology* (Oxford: Oxford University Press, 2013), p. xxvi.
56. Simon Featherstone, *War Poetry: An Introductory Reader* (London: Routledge, 1995), p. 95.
57. 'Jessie Pope's War Poems', British Library World War One website, <http://www.bl.uk/collection-items/jessie-popes-war-poems> (last accessed 18 October 2016).
58. Lindesay Irvine, 'Jessie Pope: The Daily Mail's Favourite First World War Poet', *The Guardian*, 11 November 2008, <http://www.theguardian.com/books/booksblog/2008/nov/11/jessie-pope-first-world-war-poetry> (last accessed 18 October 2016).
59. Ibid.
60. Jessie Pope, 'The Call', in *The Norton Anthology of English Literature: Norton Topics Online*, <http://www.wwnorton.com/college/english/nael/20century/topic_1_05/jpope_call.htm> (last accessed 18 October 2016).

61. Jessie Pope, 'Socks', in Margaret Higonnet (ed.), *Lines of Fire: Women Writers of World War I* (New York: Plume, 1999), p. 478.
62. Higonnet (ed.), *Lines of Fire*, p. xxxii.
63. Jessie Pope, 'Come into the 'Lotment, Maud', in Nosheen Khan (ed.), *Not With Loud Grieving: Women's Verse of the Great War* (Lahore: Polymer Publications, 1994), pp. 74–5.
64. Khan (ed.), *Not With Loud Grieving*, p. 98.
65. Tim Kendall, 'Jessie Pope: "War Girls"', <http://war-poets.blogspot.co.uk/2010/11/jessie-pope-war-girls.html> (last accessed 18 October 2016).
66. Bebbington, 'Jessie Pope and Wilfred Owen', p. 92.
67. Ibid.
68. Kendall, 'Jessie Pope: "War Girls"'.
69. Argha Banerjee, *Women's Poetry and the First World War* (New Delhi: Atlantic, 2014), p. 326.
70. A. St John Adcock, 'Poets in Khaki', *The Bookman*, 55 (December 1918), 83–100 (96).
71. Gill Plain, '"Great Expectations": Rehabilitating the Recalcitrant War Poets', *Feminist Review*, 51 (Autumn 1995), 41–65 (50).
72. Claire Buck, 'First World War English Elegy and the Disavowal of Women's Sentimental Poetics', *English Literature in Transition, 1880–1920*, 53 (2010), 431–50 (439).
73. Judith Kazantzis, 'Preface', in Catherine W. Reilly (ed.), *Scars Upon My Heart: Women's Poetry and Verse of the First World War* (London: Virago, 1981), p. xv.
74. Ibid., p. xxiii.
75. Catherine W. Reilly, 'Introduction', in *Scars Upon My Heart*, p. xxxv.
76. Nora Jones and Liz Ward (eds), *The Forgotten Army: Women's Poetry of the First World War* (Beverley: Highgate Publications, 1991), p. v.
77. Higgonet (ed.), *Lines of Fire*, p. xxiii.
78. Vera Brittain, in Higgonet (ed.), *Lines of Fire*, p. 516.
79. Vera Brittain, in Khan (ed.), *Not With Loud Grieving*, pp. 135–6.
80. Vera Brittain, *Verses of a V.A.D.* (London: Erskine Macdonald, 1918), p. 29.
81. C. H. Sisson, 'Book Review', *PN Review*, 1 January 1982, p. 62.
82. Edna Longley, 'Edward Thomas and Ivor Gurney', in Das (ed.), *The Cambridge Companion to the Poetry of the First World War*, pp. 129–43 (p. 129).
83. Andrew Motion, 'War Poetry: A Conversation', in Das (ed.), *The Cambridge Companion to the Poetry of the First World War*, pp. 257–68 (p. 259).
84. Edna Longley, *Poetry in the Wars* (Newcastle upon Tyne: Bloodaxe, 1986), p. 12.
85. Andrew Motion, *Times Literary Supplement*, 15 October 1982, p. 1,121.
86. Longley, 'Edward Thomas and Ivor Gurney', p. 130.
87. John Lucas, *Times Literary Supplement*, 25 October 1991, p. 3.
88. Motion, *Times Literary Supplement*, 15 October 1982, p. 1,121.
89. Nicholas Freeman, 'Edward Thomas, Swinburne, and Richard Jefferies: "The dead oak tree bough"', *English Literature in Transition, 1880–1920*, 51 (2008), 164–83 (165).
90. Jacek Wiśniewski, *Edward Thomas: A Mirror of England* (Newcastle upon Tyne: Cambridge Scholars, 2009), p. 239.
91. Argha Banerjee, *Poetry of the First World War 1914–1918: A Critical Evaluation* (New Delhi: Atlantic, 2011), pp. 169–70.
92. *Edward Thomas: Collected Poems* (London: Faber & Faber, 2004), dust jacket.
93. Andrew Motion, *The Poetry of Edward Thomas* (London: The Hogarth Press, 1991), p. 92.
94. Freeman, 'Edward Thomas, Swinburne, and Richard Jefferies', p. 164.
95. Hibberd and Onions (eds), *Poetry of the Great War*, p. 6; Longley, *Poetry in the Wars*, p. 12; Tim Kendall, *Modern English War Poetry* (Oxford: Oxford University Press, 2004), p. 74.

96. 'Edward Thomas', Poetry Foundation website, <http://www.poetryfoundation.org/bio/edward-thomas> (last accessed 18 October 2016).
97. John Freeman, *The Bookman*, 56 (April 1919), 22–3 (22).
98. A.E., *English Review*, March 1919, p. 271.
99. Aldous Huxley, *The Athenaeum*, 24 September 1920, p. 406.
100. St John Adcock, 'Poets in Khaki', p. 98.
101. E. B. Osborn (ed.), *The Muse in Arms: A Collection of War Poems* (London: John Murray, 1917), p. xxiii.
102. Featherstone, *War Poetry*, p. 31.
103. *Ivor Gurney: Collected Poems*, ed. P. J. Kavanagh (Manchester: Fyfield Books, 2004), p. 21.
104. Robert Hemmings, 'Of Trauma and Flora: Memory and Commemoration in Four Poems of the World Wars', *University of Toronto Quarterly*, 77 (2008), 738–56 (746).
105. Kendall, *Modern English War Poetry*, p. 90.
106. Vivien Noakes, 'War Poetry, or the Poetry of War? Isaac Rosenberg, David Jones, Ivor Gurney', in Kendall (ed.), *The Oxford Handbook of British and Irish War Poetry*, pp. 174–89 (p. 175).
107. Ibid., p. 189.
108. Stallworthy, in Cross (ed.), *The Lost Voices of World War I*, p. 63.
109. Piers Gray, *Marginal Men: Edward Thomas; Ivor Gurney; J. R. Ackerley* (Basingstoke: Macmillan, 1991), p. 13.
110. Stan Smith, *Edward Thomas* (London: Faber & Faber, 1986), p. 11.
111. Ibid., p. 20.
112. Tom Paulin, 'Thomas the Rhymer', *Sunday Times*, 13 September 1981, p. 42.
113. Wilfred Owen, *Poems by Wilfred Owen* (London: Chatto & Windus, 1920), p. vii.
114. Day-Lewis, *A Hope for Poetry*, p. 77.

# 3

# First World War Short Fiction

*Ann-Marie Einhaus*

In literary terms, the First World War is associated primarily with its poetry (especially in Britain) and with soldier novels and memoirs (in Germany, France and the USA), whereas the short story in this period is regarded largely as a civilian and particularly a modernist form. However, the First World War coincided with a heyday for newspapers and magazines that published short fiction, meaning short stories appeared in vast numbers across a wide range of publications. Published in avant-garde literary magazines as well as newspapers and popular fiction periodicals, short stories, sketches and prose vignettes were written both for and by civilians and combatants and addressed virtually all aspects of the war: in Britain, professional soldiers like 'Sapper' H. C. McNeile penned frontline tales for the wide, civilian readership of the *Daily Mail*, while civilian writers like D. H. Lawrence used the short story genre to imagine combatant reality in the pages of the literary periodical *The English Review*, while others, such as Annie Edith Jameson (writing as J. E. Buckrose), captured the more mundane aspects of war from rationing to letter-writing. In the USA, civilian writers traced the effects of war on a home front physically remote from the fighting, and veterans – including the modernist giant William Faulkner and the Harlem Renaissance writer Claude McKay – scrutinised the lot of soldiers returning from overseas. Yet while poetry and longer prose are the texts usually remembered – from Wilfred Owen, Siegfried Sassoon and Robert Graves in Britain, to Henri Barbusse in France and Erich Maria Remarque or Ernst Jünger in Germany – it is usually forgotten what a lively and varied market for short fiction there was in most, if not indeed all, countries which participated in the war. This includes the USA, where short fiction generally receives far more critical attention, but where, some better-known stories by Willa Cather, William Faulkner and Edith Wharton aside, the war is still remembered via longer prose, such as Ernest Hemingway's *A Farewell to Arms* (1929) or Dalton Trumbo's *Johnny Got His Gun* (1939).

Although the 'golden age' of short fiction was arguably over by the late 1940s, short story writers after the Second World War continued to engage with the First through the short form, from Muriel Spark to Julian Barnes and Anne Perry in Britain, and Richard Brautigan in the USA; moreover, the First World War is currently experiencing something of a revival in the themed story anthology. This chapter will draw on a range of short stories by British, American and German writers to explore how short prose fiction was adapted to reflect a wide variety of responses to the war and its aftermath from 1914 to 2014. Given the short story's close relationship to its media of dissemination, this chapter is divided into two distinct sections that broadly correspond to the wartime and inter-war period on the one hand (looking primarily at short stories published in magazines), and the inter-war and post-war period on the other (looking at a selection of war story anthologies). Naturally, these are not neat divisions, but splitting the chapter into these two modes of publication nevertheless provides a useful organising principle. The main focus of this chapter is on English-language short fiction by British and American authors, with some comparative references to Germany as a non-English-language example.

## First World War Short Stories in Magazines

The British and American magazine markets at the time of the First World War and in the inter-war period were remarkably similar and frequently interlinked. A number of highly successful commercial magazines published fiction for mainstream audiences on both sides of the Atlantic: among these magazine giants of the fiction market were *The Strand Magazine* (1891–1950), *The Cornhill* (1860–1975) and *Blackwood's* (1817–1980) in Britain, and the *Saturday Evening Post* (1821–1969), *Cosmopolitan* (1886–present) and *Collier's* (1888–1957) in the USA. At the same time, an array of smaller, artistic and/or avant-gardist magazines catered to coterie audiences. In Britain, these ranged from established literary journals like *The Athenaeum* (1828–1921) and longer-lived new publications such as *The English Review* (1908–37) to the short-lived and more radical *Rhythm* (1911–13) and *Blast* (1914–15); in the USA, such 'little' magazines included *The Little Review* (1914–29), *The Smart Set* (1900–30) and the more political *The Masses* (1911–17). The boundaries between different kinds of periodicals were fluid and magazines like *Scribner's* (1887–1939) in the USA or *The New Age* (1907–22) in Britain offered a meeting point for literary experimentation and more traditional writing. Last but not least, the overlap in terms of contributors and contributions between British and American magazines, whether popular, mainstream or avant-garde, was often significant. Authors as varied as Rudyard Kipling, John Galsworthy, James Joyce, H.D., Marianne Moore, P. G. Wodehouse, E. Phillips Oppenheim, Edith Wharton and Amy Lowell published their work in periodicals in both countries, sometimes simultaneously. In Germany and Austria-Hungary, the market for short fiction was equally split between politically and/or aesthetically radical periodicals – such as the satirical magazine *Die Fackel* (1899–1936), the expressionist journal *Die Aktion* (1911–32), and *Der Sturm* (1910–32) – and more mainstream outlets, including the *Vossische Zeitung*, which first published Remarque's *All Quiet on the Western Front* in serialised form in 1928.

Magazines across the spectrum responded to the outbreak of war in August 1914 relatively quickly, although monthly magazines took a little longer to include short stories and serials that addressed the war, as fiction contributions were planned weeks or months in advance. Whereas stories and serials were mainstays of popular and mainstream magazines, most of the little magazines of the period only included fiction on an occasional basis alongside poetry, letters, reviews, comment pieces, essays, short plays and various other contributions. The war consequently took its time to invade the periodicals in the form of fiction, although it quickly began to dominate the letter pages, comment pieces and editorials of magazines across the spectrum on both sides of the Atlantic. 'We are all soldiers now and literature, for the time, has disappeared,' proclaimed E. Buxton Shanks in his 'London Letter' in the *Little Review* of November 1914, dismissing the poetic war efforts of the British literary establishment as fundamentally un-literary.[1] This is by no means to suggest that short story writers did not quickly begin to tackle the war in their work, and by early 1915 the magazines had caught up and most British and American publications began to feature at least some war-related short fiction – provided short stories were in their repertoire. Newspapers, used to much shorter turnaround times, were faster to respond to the war in their fiction contributions, and Arthur Machen's story 'The Bowmen' appeared in the *Evening News* on 29 September 1914. Precisely how short fiction responded to or portrayed the war, however, was not only dependent on the socio-political outlook of individual magazines and their target readership, but also reflected national and/or regional concerns.

In Britain, short stories about the war ranged from popular genre fiction to modernist prose. Popular and mainstream fiction magazines like *Blackwood's* and *The Strand Magazine* published the greater proportion of war stories throughout the conflict compared to highbrow literary magazines. This was partly due to the larger proportion of short fiction published by popular magazines in general. However, it is also possible that the war sat somewhat uneasily with writers who eschewed the popular formulae of romance, detection and adventure that accommodated the war so readily. A number of modernist writers in particular were torn between conflicting desires to ignore, oppose and at the same time portray the effects of war, exemplified by Virginia Woolf's 'The Mark on the Wall' (1917). The narrator's internal monologue in Woolf's story seems to skirt around the war, but her reflections and observations are nevertheless permeated by the war's reach into everyday life and everyday thought. The narrator describes the present moment as 'since the war', and the war has become a natural way for the narrator to date her experiences when she reflects on changes to what she perceives as real or normal. The war also intrudes on the only brief section of dialogue at the end of the story, where the ongoing conflict is seen to dominate the newspapers. Woolf's story acknowledges the presence and pervasive effects of war, if obliquely, and although war is openly damned by the narrator's interlocutor, it is at the same time implicitly invoked as a force for positive change that may see the old, stuffy certainties of Victorian reality 'laughed into the dustbin where the phantoms go, the mahogany sideboards and the Landseer prints, Gods and Devils, Hell and so forth, leaving us all with an intoxicating sense of illegitimate freedom – if freedom exists'.[2]

Woolf was not the only author of short stories to address the war in a roundabout fashion, if she was perhaps unique in her way of doing so. Particularly in the early stages of the war, British short fiction frequently turned its gaze on France and on pre-war Germany, expressing sentiments that were variously wistful or foreboding. Charles Oliver, a regular contributor to *Blackwood's Magazine*, published a French and a German tale in quick succession in January and February 1915. In both stories, his well-travelled British narrator recalls encounters with notable characters whose national characteristics he explores in light of the ongoing conflict. The first of these, 'Old Pipriac', is both a wistful portrayal of a thriving and hospitable farm in Brittany, and an atrocity story in support of British morale. Its narrator encounters a curious Frenchman, deaf due to an accident though only about thirty years old. Although the story initially reads like an affectionate portrait of the French countryside and its curious characters, it takes a darker turn when the narrator inquires about Old

Pipriac's plans. Pipriac tells him of a farm on which he used to work, burned down by the Prussians along with most of the livestock, and he hints at an even more heinous though unspecified crime, possibly the burning of a woman or child, which is left for the reader to imagine. Pipriac is determined to make his way to the front despite his deafness in order to find and kill the perpetrator of this crime, offering a gentle prompt for male readers of military age who might still have been undecided as to whether they ought to volunteer. In the second story, 'The Old Junker: A Souvenir', the narrator recalls a pre-war sojourn in Germany and particularly his acquaintance with a Prussian Junker in whose house – turned into a boarding-house by his kind and enterprising wife – he spent several months before the war. Oliver's story paints a partly damning, partly sympathetic and on the whole surprisingly nuanced picture of what he perceives to be the Prussian national character. He clearly separates pre-war Prussian Junkerdom from its more brutal manifestations that, in the narrator's view, have brought about the war. Other stories were less subtle: R. S. Warren Bell's 'Master and Pupil', which appeared in *The Strand Magazine* in March 1915, is a rather more ham-fisted attempt to champion French resistance and condemn German aggression than Oliver's stories in which a retired English public-school master narrowly escapes the old grudge a former pupil – now a German officer – bears him. Where Oliver's stories remain somewhat ambiguous in their judgement of the enemy, atrocity tales such as Bell's present the Germans as unambiguously evil and barbaric.

As the war progressed, atrocity and propaganda stories continued to appear, but just as the war became part of everyday life, so too it became part of everyday plots. Romance, comic, adventure and mystery stories had been a staple of magazines before the war; now dashing officers fitted effortlessly into the part of romantic hero, dastardly Germans slipped with equal ease into the part of the criminal spy and saboteur, salt-of-the-earth 'Tommies' provided Kiplingesque humour, and the war's toll on human life and the eerie environment of the trenches provided fertile ground for tales of mystery and the supernatural, from Machen's early 'The Bowmen' (1914) to Kipling's 'A Madonna of the Trenches' (1926).[3] The quickly rising death toll not only encouraged a surge in Spiritualism, it also prompted authors to envision communion with realms beyond the earthly, as in a short story by German-Czech writer Max Brod, 'Die Erste Stunde nach dem Tode: Eine Gespenstergeschichte' ('The First Hour after Death: A Ghost Story'; 1916). In Brod's tale, an influential and self-assured politician is shaken by a ghostly encounter with the inhabitant of another realm, which briefly causes him to reassess his glib political outlook. Besides incorporating the war into popular formulae, short stories also started to respond to wartime worries that became reality for thousands: how to deal with the loss of a loved one, the loss of limbs, disfigurement, food shortages, or anxious weeks and months of separation.

In the USA, we see many similarities with British wartime short fiction, in that the war also began to be incorporated in genre fiction, inspired stories that addressed particular wartime concerns, and invaded highbrow and popular publications alike. The scope of the market and the nature of these concerns differed from the British context, however. American periodicals such as the weekly *Saturday Evening Post* covered the First World War for millions of readers in various formats, from reportage, editorials and comment pieces to short fiction.[4] Along with its sister publication, the *Ladies' Home Journal*, the *Post* was arguably one of the most 'established and influential social institutions in American popular culture' by the time the First

World War broke out.[5] As a high-profile, commercially successful weekly, the *Saturday Evening Post* published a wide range of writers, from canonical authors such as Edith Wharton and William Faulkner to contemporary best-sellers like Pearl S. Buck, E. Phillips Oppenheim and the British comic writer P. G. Wodehouse, whose stories were a regular feature of the *Post*. Although the *Post*'s short fiction contributions have been collected over the years in a host of anthologies, from 'best of' selections to themed anthologies on sport, Westerns, fantasy and, amongst others, the Second World War, no dedicated anthology of First World War fiction appears to have been compiled from amongst its pages. This absence presumably reflects a perceived lack of public interest in a First World War story anthology, as there is certainly more than enough material available to fill such a collection, and the 1954 *Saturday Evening Post Treasury* (ed. Roger Butterfield) does indeed include a number of First World War-related contributions, though largely of a journalistic, non-fictional nature.

In the period between August 1914 and December 1920, each issue of the *Saturday Evening Post* generally included between four and ten stories, one or two of which were parts of a serial, alongside a hefty dose of commercial advertising, some political reportage, business advice and general interest articles. Most of the stories included in this period were written by American contributors and represented a mix of adventure, mystery and crime fiction, with some romance stories thrown in for good measure. The paper at first adopted a relatively neutral stance on the war, but gradually began to take an anti-German view and printed articles by British and French authors rather than German or German-American authors. The *Post*'s flagship war reporter on the Western front, Irvin S. Cobb, likewise endeavoured to remain neutral during the first months of the war, condemning the war in the abstract rather than condemning the Germans specifically. In his short story 'Field of Honor' (13 May 1916), Cobb outlined the sufferings caused by war in France, Germany and among European immigrants in New York. Cobb's story shows the same concern with the humanitarian crisis brought on by the war that is visible in his non-fiction contributions, and he retained his relative neutrality until the US entered the war.

The first few war-related stories that appeared in the *Saturday Evening Post* give a flavour of the magazine's cagey engagement with war in its early stages, and also illustrate how the war was frequently addressed as part of particular subgenres. The first fiction contribution that addresses the war at all appeared in the issue of 31 October 1914, and perhaps surprisingly casts a Belgian as the villain of the story, albeit in the light of a perhaps justifiable thirst for revenge: in Melville Davisson Post's 'The Miller of Ostend', a Belgian peasant refugee takes care of four shot-down Zeppelin crew-members and, pretending at first to help them, ties them to the four arms of an old windmill to die and present a horrible greeting to the advancing German Uhlans.[6] From 14 November 1914, Arthur Train's science fiction serial story 'The Man Who Rocked the Earth' also addressed the war.[7] Set in July and August 1915, its protagonist causes the earth to change its orbit and threatens to wreak further havoc on the planet if the devastating hostilities do not stop. Where Train offers early science fiction, C. J. Cutcliffe Hyne's 'The Mine Layer' falls back on popular adventure formulae, as his protagonists, the seafaring Shepherd brothers, hit a mine with their trawler, have to fly to safety in a life-boat whilst dodging German mines and mine-layers, and manage to survive an English attack on the German fleet.[8] After a gap of several months in which no war-related fiction appeared (although the magazine ran regular war reportage), the next war story also took the form of genre fiction (in this case a mixture of melodrama and romance) and resolutely encouraged readers to concern themselves with American affairs rather than with events on the European front. Calvin Johnston's 'Redcrossie' revolves around a little girl whose socialite mother is cured of the fashionable charity craze when she finds an orphaned little American boy doing Red Cross work for the war, which makes her decide to take care of her own poor instead of righting the wrongs of Europe.[9] Much to her daughter's delight, the mother is reconciled with her husband and the family move to the countryside.

Whereas the first war stories to be published in the *Saturday Evening Post* centred on the USA, subsequent stories began to offer American readers rather more encouragement to turn their thoughts to Europe. Popular British writer George A. Birmingham contributed a selection of sketches, 'Our Town in Wartime', to one of the March 1915 issues: one set in a village assembly, earnest in its gentle and distinctly non-militarist patriotism and eager to help out 'little Belgium'; another in a rural post office where an upright young man waits for news about his commission, from which he is never to return; a third in the house of a poor but honest working woman whose husband has gone to the front and who is humanely helped out of her difficulties by wealthy benefactors; and finally a London gentlemen's club where some gruff old men display their readiness to 'see things through' and their belief in the inevitability of the present war, noting that they 'don't really believe in civilization by bureaucracy' as they observe: 'We value men, character, the individual, more than the doing of this or that. [The Germans] look at things the other way. There are two quite different ideas and they had to clash.'[10]

As late as 14 April 1917, *Post* stories championed the merits of not becoming involved in the war as a combatant and doing one's bit in other ways, as in Earl Derr Biggers's rather odd story 'Each According to His Gifts', in which a frail French designer resident in New York makes the world a better place by designing a magical dress when he is rejected for active service in the French army. This story potentially tackles the frustrations felt by some American men at being unable to take an active part in the European theatre of war just as the country entered into the hostilities and the route to straightforward war service in the US army opened up. The locations and protagonists of *Saturday Evening Post* war stories were also remarkably varied: Thomas H. Uzzell's 'Ivan Revolts' (3 June 1916) described the atrocious situation of Russian soldiers fighting Germany under cruel officers and with inadequate equipment; Herbert D. Ward's 'The Lion's Eyes' (9 December 1916) revolved around a young British lieutenant stationed at Aden – a kind of proto-Lawrence of Arabia – who is sent on a dangerous mission into the midst of the Turkish and Arab position and manages to escape from captivity by setting free and befriending a lion, while Arthur Train's 'Helenka' (27 January 1917) is a story of love and narrowly avoided betrayal set in wartime Warsaw.

Once war had been declared and the USA joined the war, the *Saturday Evening Post* stepped up the pace at which war stories appeared in its pages and ran a number of stories by well-known British authors (including stories about Indian soldiers by Rudyard Kipling and vociferously anti-German stories by Frederick Britten Austin). Other stories addressed potential qualms about enlisting on the part of particular groups of American citizens, such as established adventure writer Peter B. Kyne's 'Saint

Patrick's Day in the Morning' (19 May 1917), in which a young Irishman has joined the British Army, much to the annoyance of his patriotic Irish family, to go looking for adventure. A later story – Donn Byrne's 'Sweet Honey in All Mouths' (13 April 1918) – tackled the anti-war sentiments of the Jewish-American community by showing a group of Jewish-Americans realising the need to fight for America.

The first story that actually featured an American on active service appeared in the *Post* on 30 June 1917, but (in keeping with the experience of volunteers at this stage) does not move beyond training camp. The narrator of George Pattullo's 'Fall In! Fall Out' is a young man who has volunteered for the US army and writes a long letter to his uncle that describes the enriching (if often taxing) life in training camp. Pattullo – though Canadian himself – subsequently supplied the majority of *Saturday Evening Post* stories about the exploits of American 'doughboys' in Europe, alongside regular non-fiction contributions on various aspects of the Canadian, British and American war effort. Yet Pattullo's story did not usher in a flood of stories about young American soldiers: subsequent war stories in the pages of the *Saturday Evening Post* returned to exploring the war primarily from the non-combatant perspective: enterprising women, American civilians in France, and a movie director and his producer, who have been tasked with making an epoch-making war movie in H. C. Witwer's 'Warriors All' (14 July 1917).

As a country with a sizeable population of German immigrants, the USA was placed in a somewhat awkward position once it had declared war on Germany, and it is not surprising that the widespread debates on so-called hyphenated Americans of German extraction that surfaced elsewhere in the press and public discourse also manifested themselves in the shape of short stories. Some stories – such as Constance Skinner's love story 'Contraband of War' (12 June 1915), in which a young German-American couple fall in love despite their reluctance to comply with their parents' wishes – presented German-Americans sympathetically and defended them against potential slurs by portraying them as upright American citizens. Similarly, in Thane Miller Jones's 'Invaders of Sanctuary' (8 September 1917), an American lawyer begins to doubt his German-born colleague's integrity when it comes to judging fellow German-Americans, but finds in the end, much to his relief, that he has been very much mistaken.

The positive effect of such forgiving stories about German-Americans was counteracted nonetheless by the publication of openly anti-German atrocity stories, mostly by British authors such as Perceval Gibbons, whose story 'Plain German' (29 September 1917) appeared both in the *Post* and in the British *Strand Magazine* in December of the same year. Subsequent stories about German-Americans in the pages of the *Post* were as likely to promote suspicion as conciliation. On the one hand, Melville Davisson Post's 'The Pacifist' (29 December 1917) relates the cautionary tale of an American senator who is tricked by a German-born friend into passing on information about the routes of US troop ships to the German navy on the pretext of supporting the American war effort. On the other hand, Booth Tarkington's 'Captain Schlotterwerz' (26 January 1918) portrays a devoted German-American father's disenchantment with his strong patriotic allegiances to the country of his birth when he and his daughter – who is thoroughly American to begin with – meet a German relative and are both horrified to find that the young man claims to love war for war's sake only. A somewhat ambiguous story by Irvin S. Cobb also showed the potential consequences of pro-German sympathies: in 'The Thunders of Silence' (9 February 1918) a middle-aged Congressman ruins his brilliant political career by displaying violent pro-German sympathies and opposing America's entry into the war. His punishment is absolute silence in the press: no paper or magazine will print his name any longer, refusing him any publicity whatsoever in an unprecedented union, causing his eventual suicide. Throughout 1918, at least every other issue included a story on German-Americans, veering from outright condemnation of hyphenated Americans as unpatriotic and treacherous to some more moderate and sympathetic portrayals.

As magazines like the *Post* targeted a largely civilian readership, its stories about army life, even when they finally do start to appear, are balanced by plenty of war stories that look at men unable to fight and at men and women who contribute to the American war effort in all manner of weird and wonderful ways. This did not mean, however, that 'shirkers' got off any more lightly than they did in mainstream British magazines. William Hamilton Osborne's 'Infamous Inoculation' (9 March 1918), for instance, roundly condemns both a physically fit young man who tries to avoid conscription, and the doctor who gives him and other young men an injection that will spare them being sent to the front. In another parallel to British magazines, the war was frequently shown through the lens of romance as allowing women to demonstrate their patriotism by marrying disabled and/or socially inferior men as a reward for their military service. For instance, in John Colton's 'Oh, This War!' (10 August 1918), a beautiful and coquettish New York debutante shocks her family and friends by choosing for her husband simple Seaman Scudder, instead of one of the three most eligible society bachelors competing for her hand in marriage.

While war fiction (as opposed to reportage and comment pieces) had been slow to take hold in the *Saturday Evening Post*, by August 1918 most issues featured between two and four short stories that explicitly dealt with the war in various ways, which carried on well into 1919. While a large number of stories still looked back at the war itself, some tackled the transition back to peace and the war's social and economic fall-out at home. In Mildred Cram's 'A Man's Job' (15 February 1919), up and coming young journalist Joe Garrison returns to New York after the war and is surprised and a little disappointed to find everything unaltered at first sight. His disappointment turns into rage, however, when he finds his old job occupied by a woman, and none other than beautiful and well-bred Dora Whittlesey, formerly his boss's secretary, with whom he had fallen in love before the war. Before long, however, everything goes back to rights when Dora and he renew their love and get engaged, and Dora does not even have to leave her new job for him because he is offered a superior position with a more important magazine: male superiority is safely re-established. Cram and other contributors addressed concerns as to whether men who had gone to fight for their country would return to find their lives altered for the worse, and their tales of loyal and loving women who welcome back their men with open arms – even if shell-shocked, disabled or disfigured – seek to put such fears to rest. Nevertheless, as late as 28 August 1920, Boice Dubois's story 'The Come-Back of a Send-Off' shows that returning to the US was not necessarily an easy task for American doughboys after the Armistice, as the first employee of a big American corporation to enlist for the war, seen off with a banquet and magnificent farewell, finds settling back in rather more troublesome than setting out. Although all eventually ends well for Dubois's protagonist, the story picks up on very real underlying concerns.

Although most of the stories that appeared in the *Post* were genre fiction written by authors now mostly forgotten, and war stories formed no exception, some stories were contributed by more canonical authors. Edith Wharton's 'The Marne' is one such example and appeared on 26 October 1918, by which point Wharton had already contributed articles and reportage on the war for several years. Her story revolves around the war service of a wealthy young New Yorker, Troy Belknap, who has spent his summers in France ever since he can remember, and is surprised there in 1914 by the outbreak of the war. Horrified at the attack on 'his' France, and the atrocities suffered by people he knows and loves, he is detained in Paris, not yet old enough to enlist. He returns to France as an ambulance driver after three years of war when he is finally eighteen and his loyalty to France is repaid when a French soldier saves his life on the battlefield. Although America had by this point entered the war and contributed significantly to its imminent conclusion, Wharton – as a lifelong Francophile and indefatigable wartime aid-worker in France – clearly seized the opportunity to take to task what she saw as the tardiness of her mother country in coming to the aid of France. Wharton was also quite capable of comedy, however, and her post-war contribution 'The Refugees' (18 January 1919) is a delightfully tongue-in-cheek take on the wartime charity craze among well-meaning, wealthy British ladies.

As this brief survey of the *Saturday Evening Post* shows, short stories about the First World War most often adopted well-established subgenres such as romance, detective or adventure fiction. The *Post*, with its wide circulation and transatlantic contributors, offers an excellent example of how mainstream magazines incorporated short fiction about the war into their offerings to the reading public. War stories in the magazines appeared alongside responses to the war in other genres, from journalism and comment pieces to illustrations and poetry. On both sides of the Atlantic, short fiction about the war responded to changing concerns and experiences conditioned by the particular situation of the country of publication – *Saturday Evening Post* stories about German-Americans are a case in point, as are stories published in both Britain and the USA that address topics such as recruitment, voluntary work, war aims or pacifism. What characterises magazine stories is thus (often if not always) their relative topicality and time-bound nature, which might explain why the majority of these stories are forgotten today.

## First World War Story Anthologies

Outside of magazines and periodicals, short stories about the First World War appeared – and continue to appear – in three additional media: author collections of short stories, general short story anthologies, and themed anthologies of war stories. While the inclusion of war-themed stories in author collections or general anthologies is usually incidental – a number of collections with extended or exclusive war content aside, such as D. H. Lawrence's *England, My England and Other Stories* (1922), and Paul Alverdes's *Die Pfeiferstube* (*The Whistler's Room*; 1929) – anthologies of war stories are interesting because they provide a focused platform for war stories and arguably confer a greater degree of visibility and durability on stories included. The remainder of this chapter offers an overview of a selection of representative war story anthologies published during the war, in the inter-war period, and in the late twentieth and early twenty-first century.

Wartime anthologies tended to take the form of either 'true story' volumes rather than compilations of actual short stories – such as the anonymously authored and edited *Wonderful Stories: Winning the V.C. in the Great War* (1917) – or gift books used to raise funds for charity, which collated stories donated by well-known writers towards helping with the war effort, such as *The Queen's Gift Book in Aid of Queen Mary's Convalescent Auxiliary Hospitals for Soldiers and Sailors Who Have Lost Their Limbs in the War* (1915). Such publications had their equivalent in Germany, where *Feldgrau Voran! Deutsches Heldenbuch 1914/15* ('Field Grey Forwards! German Book of Heroes 1914/15') collected soldiers' letters, real-life accounts from the fighting zone and short stories from the Eastern and Western fronts for audiences at home.

The inter-war period saw the development of three brands of war story anthology continuing into the present day: on the one hand, we can see a continuation of the 'true story' collection and collections of war stories through the ages, often beginning with classical antiquity and excerpts from Homer in translation. These anthologies increasingly included more modern conflicts and are by far the most common kind, but they are problematic to readers interested in short fiction as they frequently combine genuine short stories with excerpts from longer prose texts. On the other hand, we see the emergence of a small number of anthologies dedicated specifically to the First World War that usually adopt an international outlook and mainly collect short stories proper. The most prominent example of this final category is an anthology that appeared on both sides of the Atlantic, albeit with different editors and slightly different titles. In the USA, the volume appeared under the title *Best Short Stories of the War* (1931), edited and introduced by British journalist and writer H. M. Tomlinson. In Britain, the same anthology had been published the previous year under the title *Great Short Stories of the War* (1930), edited by Captain H. C. Minchin with a foreword by Edmund Blunden. Minchin's and Tomlinson's anthology exemplified the international outlook of world war writing that contributed to the worldwide success of novels such as Remarque's *All Quiet on the Western Front*, and although its interest is limited primarily to the USA and Western European nations, it can be seen as a precursor for the global scope of more recent anthologies, and more recent criticism. It collected sixty-six war stories by authors of mixed nationality, including German writers, ranging from well-known names such as Joseph Conrad, French soldier-novelist Henri Barbusse and Ernest Hemingway, to lesser-known writers like Laurence Stallings or the German writer and philosopher Fritz von Unruh.

In the USA, one further anthology of First World War stories is noteworthy, in that it is drawn, in the editor's words, from 'a score or more of national publications',[11] and thus constitutes a selection from wartime and inter-war magazines. This anthology – James Dunton's *C'est la Guerre! The Best Stories of the World War* (1925) – appears to be the only other dedicated to First World War stories in inter-war America, and is intriguing not least because it offers a specifically North American counterpoint to British narratives. Authors included were Stephen Morehouse Avery, Eugene Cunningham and the Canadian James Warner Bellah, who had served with the British Royal Flying Corps during the war. In Germany, perhaps predictably, the rise to power of the Nazis prompted a spate of nationalist, revisionist short story anthologies that sought to emphasise to young readers in particular the heroism of a German army purportedly unbeaten in military terms. Anthologies such as *Vier Nächte beim Franzmann und andere Erzählungen* ('Four Nights with the Frenchies and Other Stories'; 1935), part of a series of story anthologies published by Stuttgart-based publisher Kohlhammer, sought to foster a sense of war as adventure and arguably aimed to counter the effect of anti-war novels and stories published in the late 1920s. These kinds of anthologies, allegedly inspired by real-life events, are relatively rare, however, and in both Germany and the USA most short stories about the First World War appeared in single-author collections rather than dedicated multi-author anthologies, collections that were, moreover, outnumbered by memoirs and novels.

Following the outbreak of the Second World War, war story anthologies took a broader approach and rarely focused on the First World War specifically. In 1942, mid-way through the Second World War, Ernest Hemingway edited and introduced the anthology *Men at War: The Best War Stories of All Time*, which saw seven reprints and new editions between 1952 and 1979, the later ones edited by Fred Urquhart. The rationale behind this volume, whose contents changed gradually in the course of its multiple editions, combined Hemingway's disdain for warmongering politicians with an acceptance that war is part of human life, and a grudging admiration for feats of arms.[12] The contents of Hemingway's anthology ranged from stories about prehistoric battles to modern warfare, and stories about the First World War formed only a very small proportion of contributions, particularly as most of the texts included were extracts from longer prose works. The *Men at War* anthology aside, few war story anthologies appeared in this period between the Second World War and the 1980s. The only anthology of specifically First World War stories was George L. Bruce's *Short Stories of the First World War* (1971), a small but expensively produced anthology of twelve stories, some of which were again extracts from longer novels and memoirs. It was not until the 1980s and 1990s – possibly sparked by the war's approaching eightieth anniversary – that a number of new anthologies appeared.

In Britain, the majority of war story anthologies published since the 1980s have been aimed at either young readers, war enthusiasts, or a combination of both, and rely largely on either extracts from well-known longer prose texts or custom-written fiction for children and young adults. Examples of adult anthologies include Jon E. Lewis's *Mammoth Book of Modern War Stories* (1993) and *The Vintage Book of War Stories* (1999), the latter edited by Jörg Hensgen with an introduction by Sebastian Faulks. Both of these volumes collate writing about a range of different conflicts with only a small number of First World War stories. A number of modern anthologies primarily for young readers are made up of specially commissioned work by contemporary authors. These include Tony Bradman's *Gripping War Stories* (1998), Michael Morpurgo's *War: Stories about Conflict* (2005), and the more recent *The Great War: Stories Inspired by Objects from the First World War* (2014), which includes stories by well-known writers such as Morpurgo, David Almond, Tracy Chevalier and A. L. Kennedy. The e-book anthology *The Clock Struck War: An Anthology of Conflict Stories* (2014), unusually, is made up of the winning entries of a short story competition. Where anthologies do not rely on purpose-written work, however, they usually fall back on well-known authors and texts and extracts from longer prose works. By contrast, at least some more recent publications have the aim of recovering lesser-known First World War short stories for a modern audience interested specifically in short fiction. In Britain, these include Trudi Tate's *Women, Men and the Great War* (1995), *The Penguin Book of First World War Stories* (2007), edited by Barbara Korte and Ann-Marie Einhaus, and most recently Andrew Maunder's *British Literature of World War I: The Short Story and the Novella* (2011). In the USA, Margaret Higonnet's *Lines of Fire: Women Writers of World War I* collected writing by women from Africa, Belgium, France, Germany, Hungary, Italy, India, the United Kingdom, the USA, Turkey and the Middle East, although contributions included in this volume are once again for the most part not short stories, as the emphasis is on women's war experience rather than short fiction. Indeed, in both the USA and Germany dedicated anthologies of First World War short stories appear to be an altogether centennial phenomenon.

While it is perhaps less surprising that short stories about the war should experience a modest renaissance in the United Kingdom, a country with an enduring culture of commemorating the First World War, it is striking to see short story collections about the war surface in the USA and Germany, where there has been a notable absence of anthologies on the subject of the First World War until the approach of the centenary. Alexandra Rak's young adult anthology *Mitten im Leben sind wir vom Tod umfangen: Erzählungen über den Ersten Weltkrieg* ('In the Midst of Life We Are in Death: Stories about the First World War') appeared in 2014, seeking to appeal to young Germans whose knowledge of the conflict is most likely eclipsed by its successor. Two recently published anthologies for adult readers – one (Swiss-)German, one American – are likewise particularly noteworthy because the First World War has traditionally been of far less import in these countries and increased remembrance has only been sparked by the approaching centenary. The (Swiss-)German anthology *Über den Feldern: Der Erste Weltkrieg in den großen Erzählungen der Weltliteratur* ('Above the Fields: The First World War in Great Narratives of World Literature'; 2014) adopts an international approach of unprecedented scope and collects not only German-language short stories and novellas but Armenian, Bulgarian, Czech, Danish, English, Farsi, French, Italian, Japanese, Polish, Russian, Serbo-Croat, Spanish and Turkish works in translation. The range of writers included is equally impressive, stretching from Ernest Hemingway and Virginia Woolf to Marcel Proust and Guillaume Apollinaire, Joseph Roth and Bertolt Brecht, Gabriele d'Annunzio and Jorge Luis Borges, as well as authors markedly less well known to German- and indeed English-speaking audiences, such as the Turkish writer Yakup Kadri or Armenian Axel Bakunts. In a note at the end of the book, the editor Horst Lauinger comments on the remit of the volume:

> Es ist der Vorzug eines weltliterarischen Panoramas, eine Vielzahl an Perspektiven mit einbeziehen und unterschiedlichste Kriegsrealitäten miteinander kontrastieren zu können. Die Texte sind in der Mehrzahl während der Kriegsjahre oder unmittelbar danach entstanden, somit deutlich vor den Weltkriegsromanen der späten 1920er-Jahre.
>
> (It is the advantage of a panorama of world literature to be able to offer a variety of perspectives and contrast diverse realities of war. The majority of the texts included were written during the war or immediately after its end, notably earlier than the war novels of the late 1920s.)[13]

Lauinger's concept of a 'panorama of world literature' is effective not only in exposing the global reach of the First World War, but in demonstrating that there is no such thing as 'the' experience or 'the' short story of the First World War. The stories he collects are as different as their writers and cultural backgrounds, and range from the classic Western front trench narrative (as in Georges Duhamel's field hospital story 'La troisième symphonie'; 1917) to the ripples of war in faraway Japan, as portrayed by Akutagawa Ryūnosuke in his story 'Monkey' (1916).

Whereas Lauinger's *Über den Feldern* takes a global approach, casting its editorial net beyond national boundaries, Scott D. Emmert and Steven Trout take the opposite approach of zooming in on rather than out of national boundaries in their collection *World War I in American Fiction: An Anthology of Short Stories* (2014). In a country as proud of its short story tradition as the United States, the relative neglect of short stories about the First World War has so far been a striking lacuna, which Emmert and Trout seek to remedy with their anthology. Their selection is exceptionally balanced, and while it does include some well-known names – Willa Cather, F. Scott Fitzgerald and Edith Wharton, to name but three – the stories included cover the widest possible range of perspectives and styles. The experiences of men and women are represented in equal depth, as is the specific and doubly traumatic war and post-war experience of African-American veterans, in stories by Carita Collins, Claude McKay and Langston Hughes, whilst a popular magazine story by Hugh Wiley illustrates the ingrained racism that black servicemen faced during their service and upon their return. Stories included range from the wartime popular fiction produced by Wiley, Edna Ferber and others to retrospective experimental fiction such as Richard Brautigan's 1971 story 'The World War I Los Angeles Airplane', which closes the volume.

As this brief survey shows, some anthologies are more varied than others in terms of their scope of authors and topics, and the greater number of post-war anthologies in particular rely heavily on extracts from longer prose works and texts about other conflicts. There are also differences in terms of the geographical spread of authors represented within a particular volume and the balance between male and female, popular and 'literary' writers represented. The main difference in outlook, however, is determined by the way in which their content is framed by introductions, prefaces and presentation. Anthologies of specifically women's writing aside, the majority of volumes published between the end of the Second World War and the centenary include similar kinds of stories, with an emphasis on combatant experience on the Western front. While virtually all war anthologies share an emphasis on the suffering of war in their selection of stories, they do differ markedly in the degree of pacifist sentiment expressed in the preliminary matter. Perhaps understandably, anthologies such as *The Great War* – written for young readers – take a more didactic approach and seek to emphasise the desirability of not repeating the mistakes of the past; Faulks and Hensgen highlight the horrors of war, but also show a sense of fascination with the experience of armed conflict visible in both the introduction and the selection of content. Anthologies like the *Mammoth Book*, on the other hand, often refrain from framing their content in an explicitly anti-war manner and instead foreground the extraordinary nature of war as a unique human experience.

## Conclusions

Short stories of the First World War have been eclipsed to varying extents by war writing in other genres in Britain, the USA and Germany. While British war stories have been experiencing a tentative revival since the 1990s in the form of a limited number of specialised anthologies, driven by academic interest, such anthologies have only just begun to appear in Germany and the USA. Yet the output of short stories in the latter countries was comparable to that in Britain during and after the war, as thriving international and national magazine markets encouraged literary expression of war experience in short prose forms, from sketch to narrative. While it would be impossible and somewhat futile to determine typical features of First World War short fiction, one can note its extreme diversity. Short story writers tackled the manifold aspects of war experience in a wide range of modes and subgenres, from psychological sketches to detective fiction, ghost stories and melodrama. Although 'the' First World War short story does not exist, and would in any case be nationally and culturally determined, the brief overview of short stories in magazines and anthologies offered in this chapter demonstrates some transnational themes, such as death, mourning, coming to terms with loss or injury, coping with wartime hardships at home, and questioning as well as affirming reasons to fight. Often hailed, whether appropriately or not, as a quintessentially modern form, the short story certainly rose to the occasion in offering expression to a diverse range of wartime experience, most often by embedding the war into existing generic conventions. Moreover, centenary anthologies such as *The Great War* demonstrate that short fiction about the First World War has not yet ceased to play its part and continues to engage with the way in which the war is remembered in the present.

## Notes

1. E. Buxton Shanks, 'London Letter', *The Little Review*, 1.8 (November 1914), 45–7 (45).
2. Virginia Woolf, 'The Mark on the Wall', in *The Norton Anthology of English Literature*, vol. 2, 8th edn (London and New York: W. W. Norton, 2006), pp. 2,082–7 (p. 2,084).
3. See, for example, Jane Potter on the adaptability of popular fiction in *Boys in Khaki, Girls in Print: Women's Literary Responses to the Great War 1914–1918* (Oxford: Oxford University Press, 2005), p. 55.
4. To mark the war's centenary, the *Saturday Evening Post* webpages feature a WWI blog that allows readers to rediscover articles and cover art of the period; see <http://www.saturdayeveningpost.com/sections/history/ww1-blog> (last accessed 19 October 2016).
5. Helen Damon-Moore, *Magazines for Millions: Gender and Commerce in the* Ladies' Home Journal *and the* Saturday Evening Post *1880–1910* (New York: State University of New York Press, 1994), p. 155.
6. Melville Davisson Post, 'The Miller of Ostend', *Saturday Evening Post*, 187.18 (31 October 1914), 3–4, 34.
7. Train's story was published in three instalments on 14, 21 and 28 November 1914, in volume 187, numbers 20–2 of the *Saturday Evening Post.*
8. C. J. Cutcliffe Hyne, 'The Mine Layer', *Saturday Evening Post*, 187.21 (21 November 1914), 16–17, 45–6.
9. Calvin Johnston, 'Redcrossie', *Saturday Evening Post*, 187.36 (6 March 1915), 15–17, 49–50.
10. George A. Birmingham, 'Our Town in Wartime. Four Scenes', *Saturday Evening Post*, 187.39 (27 March 1915), 6–7, 69 (69).

11. James G. Dunton (ed.), *C'est la Guerre! The Best Stories of the World War* (1925; Boston, MA: Stratford, 1927), p. xiv.
12. See Ernest Hemingway (ed.), *Men at War: The Best War Stories of All Time* (New York: Crown, 1942), p. xi. For a more detailed discussion of this anthology, see Ann-Marie Einhaus, *The Short Story and the First World War* (Cambridge: Cambridge University Press, 2013), pp. 60–1.
13. Horst Lauinger (ed.), *Über den Feldern: Der Erste Weltkrieg in den großen Erzählungen der Weltliteratur* (Zurich: Manesse, 2014), p. 777; my translation.

# 4

# Theatre: 1914 and After

*Andrew Maunder*

Robert Cedric Sherriff's *Journey's End*, premiered in 1928, contains typical features of a play about the Great War: a frontline dugout where tensions between protagonists are repressed beneath public-school gentility and a determination to carry on against the odds. A colonel orders a foolhardy raid on a German trench; seven men die. There are brave young officers, and there are good-humoured working-class soldiers – but it is left to an alcoholic captain, a former captain of 'rugger', to reflect on the horror before leading his men out to die against the *Friedensturm* (the German offensive of March 1918). The play has been described as 'old-fashioned' and its social attitudes can seem so. But, nearly ninety years on, its appeal remains.

If theatre has sometimes been neglected in surveys of the war and its cultural legacy, it is not because of a shortage of materials, but because for much of the twentieth century plays about the war were invariably perceived as limited, and therefore inadequate. Scripting and staging failed to capture the war experience with the same intensity that trench poetry, for example, managed, and certainly not as 'truthfully'. Indeed, the ink on the Versailles peace treaty of 1919 was barely dry before theatre's contribution to the conflict began to be questioned. In his preface to *Heartbreak House* (1919), George Bernard Shaw wrote of the 'childish antics' of the wartime entertainment industry, labelling its output shallow and meaningless. The 'higher drama' had been 'put out of action' by theatre managers whose aim was to 'exploit' the 'hyperaesthesia' of soldiers on leave, 'smiling men' who because they 'were no longer under fire' were ready to be pleased by anything.[1] In his reference to audiences being exploited Shaw sounded a theme which would be echoed many times. It is one taken up in Theatre Workshop's *Oh, What a Lovely War!* (1963; film 1969), where wartime theatre's 'complicity' (to draw on the terminology of new historicism) in the horrors of the conflict, its deceit towards the men who enlisted, is conveyed via recreations of music hall turns and recruiting sergeants.

In contrast, plays about the war which emerge *after* 1919 are invariably characterised by their sense of grief; they are often angry; they also emphasise the war's lasting and destructive legacy. As plays with a purpose, they tend to be notable for their accusatory tone, making things explicit, and concluding with a message that such things must never happen again. 'Every moment we see the countries of Europe arming themselves to the teeth as hard as they can go and that is why I wrote my play,' explained W. Somerset Maugham, defending *For Services Rendered* (1932) against charges of negativity, 'to try and protect the new youth of today from dying in the trenches or losing five years of their lives in a war that seems almost imminent.'[2] For many dramatists since, this has remained a powerful driver.

Attitudes towards the topic of theatre and the war have therefore never been straightforward. This chapter surveys some of the dramatic works brought about by the outbreak of war in 1914, as well as the uneasy relationships between playwrights, censors and theatre critics. In reality, the wartime theatre industry was a far more complex affair than is often suggested, involving different cultural fields and enterprises and a variety of subject positions. When the conflict came to be reappraised post-1919, the theatre changed too, representing the war in different ways for successive generations of audiences.

## 1914–1919

The impact of the war on the theatre industry of 1914–19 has long been acknowledged. So have attempts by some dramatists, notably Shaw, J. M. Barrie and John Galsworthy, but also Arnold Bennett, Harold Brighouse and Edward Knoblauch, to carve positions for themselves within it. Opinions about theatre's contribution to the war effort differ but most contemporary observers agreed that the theatre industry enjoyed 'a boom time'.[3] However, in his magisterial *History of English Drama* Allardyce Nicoll noted that 'playhouses for the most part sank into becoming the purveyors of the cheapest entertainment', adding that 'stage activities which had given distinction to the Edwardian and Georgian days were [. . .] rudely terminated'.[4] Nicoll's phraseology is of course significant here and the fate of drama during the war is quickly settled: serious work killed off by crude pieces only worth recognising in the context of the theatre industry's eye for the main chance. In contrast, recent critics have suggested that wartime theatre has a good deal to interest the historian of wartime culture. L. J. Collins notes that to study wartime theatre is to be faced with 'a myriad of over-lapping and different types of theatre provision', not only in London, and with 'a multiplicity of inter-related functions'.[5] There is certainly little doubt that wartime theatre was a vital, well-attended and profitable environment requiring a constant supply of new plays to sit alongside the inevitable revivals of Shakespeare and other patriotic crowd-pleasers: *The Scarlet Pimpernel* (1905), *The Flag Lieutenant* (1908) or *Drake* (1912). The cultural landscape included musicals and also revues, including *Odds and Ends* (1914), *Samples* (1915), *Shell Out!* (1915), *Now's the Time* (1915) and *5064 Gerard* (1915), reliable money-spinners which offered satiric sketches, risqué humour and catchy songs, enabling theatres to keep afloat during quiet periods. They had to compete with cinemas and also music halls and variety theatres, spaces Siegfried Sassoon recreated in '"Blighters"' (1917), in which a tank is imagined 'lurching' down the gangway of a raucous variety theatre to fire on its cackling audience and the 'harlots' in the chorus.[6]

Something of the extent of the theatrical landscape of 1914–19 can be found in the work of George Street, 'examiner' of plays for the Lord Chamberlain's Office, that representative in the Royal Household who, under the Stage Licensing Act, censored scripts before licensing them for public performance. In August 1914, Street read Edmund Goulding's *God Save the King*, in which a young man is bribed by his family's German lodger into taking photos of some coastal defences before changing his mind and strangling the German, but also dying himself. In his report on this 'play of the moment', Street took it as a test-case of 'how far it shall be permissible to vilify

Germany': 'Before the war it might have been injudicious to depict it in a play as offensive to a friendly power, but [. . .] that reason can hardly apply now [. . .] The public must, I think, be indulged with plays reflecting the national feeling.'[7] However, in other instances, Street despaired at the quality of plays submitted. Joseph Millane and Claire Shirley's *War and a Woman* (1915) was 'silly and ignorant'; *The Master Hun* (1915) was clearly 'the work of a lunatic'.[8] Occasionally Street was willing to be seduced by an exciting plot; in 1916 he admired Eva Elwes's *Heaven at the Helm*, whose heroine prevents an invasion by a flotilla of U-boats, and he was also moved by Ernest Temple Thurston's *The Cost* (1914), about the impact of war on a middle-class family. And while it is rare nowadays to hear Horace Annesley Vachell mentioned, he, too, won plaudits for *Searchlights* (1915) and its prescient, albeit very polite, representation of shell shock. But Street was also increasingly exasperated by 'silly trash' which took tabloid scare stories for source material.[9] As Street saw it, the ban on Horace Hunter's *Outraged Women* (1915) was entirely justified. Here, an English governess is raped by a German soldier, stands trial for the murder of the resulting baby, but is acquitted when the jury agree her defence that such children should not be allowed to live. The stage was 'entirely unfitted as a place for the discussion of this dreadful and difficult question, even apart from the violent and (as most people would think) wicked solution propounded by the author'.[10] For Street it was far better to be moved by Herbert Beerbohm Tree in *Henry IV, Part 1* (1914), Frank Benson in *Henry V* (1914–15) or even John Martin Harvey in *The Only Way* (based on *A Tale of Two Cities*). All had at least some claim to grandeur and sought to encourage higher feelings than mere hatred. Overall, Street's attitudes to the hundreds of plays he read remained ambiguous, fluctuating between appreciation of the patriotic sentiments behind them and ridicule for the crudity of the results. For him, as for others, they were salutary reminders of the coarsening of theatrical culture, and of the decline of the 'well-made' play.

In the years 1914–19 the notion that British dramatists were failing to meet the challenge of writing a serious war play was a common one. One of the ways in which this registered was in the press. *The Era*, *The Referee*, *The Bystander*, *The Sketch*, *The Illustrated Sporting and Dramatic News*, *The Stage* and *Tatler* all debated the issue at length. During the conflict, plays were variously written by leading performers, by theatre managers, by soldiers, by suffragettes, by pacifists. Nevertheless, there was a widespread sense that hardly any of them knew how to write about the war in any meaningful sense. They were 'afraid of khaki on the stage – properly handled', as *The Referee* put it in 1915, and this left a gap until Captain Bruce Bairnsfather's *The Better 'Ole* arrived in 1917.[11]

What plays *were* successful? One surprise hit was Thomas Hardy's verse drama about the Napoleonic wars, *The Dynasts*, staged in 1914 under the avant-garde director Harley Granville Barker. This was proper 'patriotism' from the elderly novelist, announced *Tatler*, 'not the kind you get in some places of alleged amusement where large nosed ladies shriek frantically, tearfully, hoarsely all sorts of ghastly doggerel about "the dear old flag"'.[12] Typical of the latter type, but enormously popular, was *England Expects* (1914), a collaboration between leading men of the theatre – Seymour Hicks, Charles Cochran and Edward Knoblauch – which included recitations, films and dramatic re-enactments of battles, performed three times a day, replete with recruiting sergeants. Most accounts, however, suggest it was not until December 1914 that a play

Figure 4.1 *Miriam* (Ruth Mackay): Whatever have you found? *Brent* (Dennis Eadie): A wireless up the chimney. Still from *The Man Who Stayed at Home*, Royalty Theatre London, December 1914. Author's collection.

appeared which struck a chord with critics *and* public. This was J. E. Harold Terry and Lechmere Worrall's *The Man Who Stayed at Home* (Figure 4.1), wherein a secret agent, posing as a 'silly ass' young waster, uncovers a nest of spies at a seaside boarding house. Dismissed by one critic as 'the ordinary stage detective story cast in a war setting to fit the moment',[13] *The Man Who Stayed at Home* helped encourage the belief that there *was* a market for literate drama, with melodramatic excess kept in check, protagonists who are by turns heroic, clever, comic but also ordinary, and villains who are evil, scheming, traitorous and yet prosaic.

So what else made *The Man Who Stayed at Home* popular? One reason had to do with the hero's display of calm determination and refusal to lose his cool, even when given a white feather by an ignorant young woman. Another was the play's exploitation of British paranoia about German spies shown using carrier pigeons and radio transmitters to communicate with enemy ships. 'These strange times of spying stress', as George Street described them, prompted an avalanche of espionage dramas.[14] Chester Bailey's *The Day Before the Day*, featuring a hoard of secret documents and a heroine who executes her former fiancé, a Prussian guardsman, after he is revealed to be a spy, premiered in June 1915, clearly striking the mood of the moment. One reviewer noted that the play 'emphasizes the alleged methods of the German spy in England, and lays the frightfulness on with a heavy trowel'. He also learned 'that it is quite the usual thing for German spies in this country to attend family parties in the suburbs with loaded revolvers in their pockets ready to shoot on sight anyone attempting to interfere with their sinister designs'.[15] Yet the cultural stereotyping of *The Day Before the Day* was the rule, not the exception. Other examples included Walter Howard's *Seven Days' Leave* (1917), E. D. Biggers's *Inside the Lines* (1917) and Walter Melville's *The Female Hun* (1918), in which a general shoots his traitorous wife, prompting great cheers in the audience.[16] The espionage craze reached its apogee in Laurence Cowan's *The Hidden Hand* (1918), about German agency in high places, wherein an MP, who is a German agent, attempts to introduce germ warfare via Zeppelins, but is foiled by the heroine and, in an example of the kind of rough justice which became typical, forced to shoot himself. All these plays suggest how playwrights took the familiar features of melodrama and developed them into a kind of sub-speciality, with plots mimicking the activities of real-life secret agents (as they were understood). While they are easy to dismiss, the popularity of such plays is not difficult to appreciate: as a form of drama which is really about the elemental struggle between good and evil, and which depicts upright British men and women re-installing order and expelling fiendish foreign undesirables, they had broad appeal.

The stage's sense of suburbanites as vigilantes was appealing, but so, too, were the details – accrued through successive plays – about the methods used to neutralise spies. All of it could seem ludicrous, of course, but for wartime audiences it does not seem to have mattered. A handsome agent besting a German spy who has been dropped off by a submarine ('No spy play is complete without this detail,' noted *The Bystander*) gave colour to war-weary lives.[17] This at least was one of the explanations suggested by Frank Vernon in his assessment of wartime theatre published in 1924. He also attributed the demand for such work to women, and in particular the 'flapper', 'an excited, uneducated young person who couldn't be bothered to listen to a play unless it had melodrama and jejune sentimentality in slabs'.[18] For some women who, thanks to wider employment opportunities, had more disposable income, going to the theatre was a form of freedom. Indeed, women, more so than soldiers, came to be seen as dictating what was staged and it was not only exotic musicals like *Chu Chin Chow* (1916) and *The Maid of the Mountains* (1917) which appealed. Spy plays, especially those featuring such self-confident heroines as Lady Mary who swims out to sea in *Seven Days' Leave* in order to flush out a German submarine, or the Red Cross nurses who find themselves combatants at the front in Andrew Emen's *For England, Home and Beauty* (1915), offered visions of what might be. This was all the more important given that with a few exceptions – Harold Brighouse's *Hobson's Choice* (1916) and John Galsworthy's *Foundations* (1917), for example – the wartime theatre often fell back on traditional representations of a woman's role: she was 'domestic, nurturing and nubile' or simply 'fallen'.[19]

Eagerness to glimpse into different wartime worlds was also catered for by J. M. Barrie, notably in *A Kiss for Cinderella* (1916) and *Dear Brutus* (1917), the latter a play of second chances in which eight people ('dwellers in darkness') disappear into a magical wood to live a different life for one night.[20] The appeal of both is not hard to understand: they go beyond concerns with the war to encourage an interest in what Barrie called 'the might have been'.[21] Other Barrie plays, *Der Tag* (1914) and *Rosy Rapture* (1915), were judged failures, but he was on surer ground in a series of one-act plays which focused on family relationships: *The New Word* (1915), *The Old Lady Shows her Medals* (1917) and *A Well-Remembered Voice* (1918). In the first and last of these, Barrie explores what Leonée Ormond describes as 'the problem of finding a language of feeling so that fathers and sons, normally emotionally restrained, can express their love'.[22] In *The New Word*, both John Torrance and his son, Roger, who is about to join his regiment, find attempts to confront the issue excruciating. 'Of course, you and I know', father tells son, 'that display of that sort is all bunkum – repellent even to our natures.'[23] But part of him would like it if his son *did* let his guard down. While this father and son remain distant, *A Well-Remembered Voice* shows a pairing who *are* brought together. After a seance held by Mrs Don in an attempt to contact her dead son, Dick, is judged unsuccessful, the lost son appears to his sceptical father. The reunion of father and son is hurried and unsatisfactory. 'Tell me, Dick, about the – veil. I mean the veil that is drawn between the living and the –,' Mr Don pleads.[24] But all that Dick chooses to report is that the other side is like a jolly boarding school where men who have crossed over – Germans included – have their 'fun' just as they always did.[25] Taken together, the play's different voices satirise the wartime craze for Spiritualism, but recognise an aching need on the part of those who are mourning to find out something beyond the official telegram. Barrie's attempts to come to terms with the death in Flanders, in 1915, of George Llewelyn Davies, one of the originals for the 'lost' boys of *Peter Pan*, also haunt both plays.

If J. M. Barrie's works represent one tradition of wartime theatre, those of Miles Malleson are another. Although often seen as the epitome of mild-mannered respectability, Malleson's plays *'D' Company* (1914) and *Black 'Ell* (1916) are examples of how dramatists walked a tightrope; they could be challenging, but should not be seen to be subversive. The setting for *'D' Company* is a barracks in Malta (where Malleson had served) occupied by Territorials of different social classes who bicker and joke. 'They jus' chucked us out 'ere,' complains one of them. 'Get sacked, out of our jobs or come 'ere and 'ave 'em kept.'[26] The men are cynical about the war, but George Street, in his role as censor, was very taken with this 'slice of daily life', noting how, despite the crudity of some of them, the soldiers 'are all good fellows in their different ways, and no intelligent spectator could fail to have an increased sympathy and pride in them and their like'.[27]

*Black 'Ell*, however, merited a much colder response. The play, which shoehorns sentiments from Malleson's pacifist tract, *Second Thoughts* (1916), that the British public was being 'disastrously prejudiced and misled, and [. . .] kept in ignorance of the real course and significance of events', was stopped in its tracks.[28] When it was published, the authorities, acting under the terms of the Defence of the Realm Act, raided the publishers' offices, carrying away all the available copies. The hero, Harold Gould, is haunted by his killing a German soldier in one-to-one combat (an event described in graphic detail) and he now queries the idea of self-defence upon which Britain has entered the war. Harold's well-meaning parents and fiancée cannot understand and Malleson stresses the distance between those who have seen and those who have not. The bitterest attack is reserved for a gung-ho, jolly-hockey-sticks young woman for whom war is a chance to dress up in quasi-military garb and pretend to do useful work while in reality having the time of her life. Meanwhile, Harold, the one person who has actually seen action, has been pushed to the position of an outsider, and in his expressions of admiration for the dead soldier's beauty reveals himself an aesthete who thumbs his nose at the idea that all Germans are baby-killers. War brings young men medals, Malleson explains, and their families get a share of the glory, but it brutalises everyone concerned. *Black 'Ell* ends in deadlock with Harold saying 'you can shoot me [. . .] because I'm not going back [. . .] I'm going to stop at home and say it's all mad [. . .] I'm going to keep on saying it [. . .] somebody's got to stop sometime [. . .] somebody's got to get me sane again'.[29] Although perhaps exaggerating the potential impact of such pieces, the banning of *Black 'Ell* was not surprising, and when questioned in the House of Commons, the Secretary of State for War remained implacable. The play was 'a calumny on the British soldier'.[30] It was not until 1926, a time when, as the Lord Chamberlain's Office noted, 'the views expressed have become a commonplace in many quarters', that *Black 'Ell* was awarded a performance licence.[31]

## Theatre after 1919

If 1914–19 represents one phase of First World War theatre, the years immediately following seemed to promise another. Ella Hepworth Dixon predicted 'an undercurrent of "war" sentiment', and of 'situations; arising out of the war, for many a long year to come. It has so profoundly changed our social life and smashed all our little social prejudices to bits that drama inevitably arises out of this new condition.'[32] The removal, in 1917, of the ban on Eugène Brieux's *Damaged Goods*, a play about venereal disease, on the grounds that it had importance for the health of the British nation also suggested that the war might just be ushering in a new kind of stage realism. In the event, this took time to materialise. J. E. Harold Terry's *General Post* (1917) centred on the new military (and social) phenomenon of 'temporary gentlemen' officers, and the implications for meritocracy in post-war society, but it did so in a cosy way, which was probably why it ran for 535 performances. Even after the Armistice, theatre managers continued to put on lurid melodramas about German spies including Louis N. Parker and George Sims's *The Great Day* (1919) and Guy Reeves's *Once a German . . . Always a German* (1919), the premise of which recalls *The Man Who Stayed at Home*, produced four years earlier. Some observers – George Bernard Shaw, St John Irvine, J. T. Grein, John Drinkwater – continued to shake their heads at the prurient philistinism and 'cynicism' of it all.[33] They continued to be irritated, too, about the 'banality' of the messages given to young people.[34] Drinkwater, whose historical plays, *X=O* (1917), set in the Trojan war, and *Abraham Lincoln* (1919), flagged up the pain and suffering of war, did have some success, but another pacifist playwright, Maude Deuchar (writing as 'Herbert Tremaine'), was unable to get *The Handmaidens of Death* performed in 1919. Here, a group of unmarried female munitions workers send personalised messages in the shells they make. When the bloodied German soldiers they have killed come back to haunt them, the audience realises the culpability of these women. They are life-takers rather than life-creators and they are doomed to remain unmarried and childless.

In the event it was a much more established figure, W. Somerset Maugham, who in articles and interviews became the most high-profile exponent of the post-1918 war play, and, convinced of its relevance to contemporary society, took up the cudgels on its behalf. Although it has been fashionable to ignore Maugham, a cocktail dramatist whose outlook, like that of his contemporaries Coward and Sherriff, can seem based on a narrow, hierarchical view of the world, his views are important in the reformulation of British theatre's attitudes to the conflict in the 1920s and 1930s. Theatre needed to be used,

Maugham argued, to make audiences reflect on what had been won, but also on what had been lost. Maugham's plays *Home and Beauty* (1919) and *The Unknown* (1919) are part of this idea. In the former, a vacuous, upper-class woman finds herself married to two husbands after believing the first to have been killed at Ypres. In the second, more outspoken play, a young officer, John Wharton, returns to the village where he has grown up and is struck by the continued religiosity of his family, fiancée and neighbours. When a woman who has lost two sons to the 'noble cause' loses her faith and asks 'who is going to forgive God', she is regarded as slightly mad.[35] She no longer attends church, telling the vicar 'it would bore me'.[36] His response is to tell her that her behaviour is 'a scandal'.[37] Yet John feels the same way. He scoffs when he hears that people have prayed for him and has no time for the idea that the war is something sent by God to be endured: 'I should like some of those people who talk about the purifying influence of suffering to have a mouthful of gas and see how they liked it.'[38] Having placed so much faith in a rational God, it is no surprise, Maugham's argument goes, that people found their beliefs destroyed by the war's irrational cruelties as well as the Church's complacency.

The most successful of the post-war writers, Sherriff, offered a more conventional picture. *Journey's End* (1928) introduced twenty-one-year-old Captain Dennis Stanhope, the former school prefect with a passion for discipline – and also whisky (Figure 4.2).

Figure 4.2 *Journey's End*, Savoy Theatre, January 1929, with Colin Clive (Captain Dennis Stanhope) and Maurice Evans (Lieutenant James Raleigh). Reproduced courtesy of Surrey History Centre.

The play ran for 594 performances in the West End, 485 on Broadway, was a worldwide hit, including in Berlin, and was also made into a successful film in 1930. An ex-soldier, Sherriff planned to write the story as a novel, feeling that this would give him more scope for elaborating on the central relationship between Stanhope and new young recruit James Raleigh, a former schoolfriend who loves him. Nonetheless, in 1929 the play was an enormous hit partly because Sherriff seemed to have found the 'perfect pitch' at which to represent the 'tragedy' of 1914–18.[39] *Journey's End* brought together key elements of an emerging mythology, including the idea of the lost generation. Having ambitions for the play to stand up to the scrutiny of veterans who knew the experience of war, Sherriff took pains to reproduce the humdrum character of life in a dugout as well as its pressure-cooker environment (Stanhope is on the verge of a breakdown; another officer feigns illness). Yet Sherriff's fondness for small details – his characters spend a lot of time eating meals – did not please everybody, and there was criticism of his reluctance to tackle wider issues.

Sherriff's play brought him a lot of money and legions of fans, but his meteoric success, which seemed to come with little dramatic ambition, prompted comment. In a letter, George Bernard Shaw called the play 'a "slice of life" – horribly abnormal life' and wrote that the play 'is, properly speaking, a document, not a drama. The war produced several of them. They require a good descriptive reporter with the knack of dialogue [. . .] I could give the author a testimonial as a journalist.'[40] But to criticise Sherriff on his inability to provide a more expansive, angrier theatrical experience was to miss the point. Richard Jennings, writing in *The Spectator*, suggested that 'one may compare *Journey's End*, which conveys no deliberate message, and attempts no propaganda, to the similarly faithful and quiet record of Mr Edmund Blunden's *Undertones of War*. This too, is written with the same unobtrusive art – tunnelling as it were, under the surface of sensational events.'[41] Sherriff's is not an anti-war play; instead it hymns the bravery of the young officers who died, glamorous representatives of an older England of cricket and chivalry which never really existed.

Other post-war works – and these could be duplicated at length – include John Galsworthy's *Loyalties* (1922; soldier struggles to adjust to the post-war world), Allan Monkhouse's *The Conquering Hero* (1923; sensitive young artist enlists), Henry Wall's *Havoc* (1924; two soldiers are in love with the same heartless woman; a trick by one causes the other to be blinded), Hubert Griffith's *Tunnel Trench* (1924; Flying Corps officers deal with the loss of comrades as well as the need to kill), Henrietta Leslie and Joan Temple's *Mrs Fischer's War* (1931; English woman married to a German is made a social outcast), Sean O'Casey's *The Silver Tassie* (1928; Irish footballers are left betrayed, scarred and disabled by their time in the trenches), Aimée and Philip Stuart's *Nine to Six* (1930; women's bereavement and their post-war survival as workers), and J. R. Ackerley's *The Prisoners of War* (1925; war-scarred officers interned in a Swiss hotel). The last was a curious success and has, since its first appearance, been a work liable to provoke a wide variety of responses. It has become commonplace to suggest that Ackerley created the play as a means of escaping his romantic frustrations as an army officer interned in a hospital in Switzerland in 1918, erotically obsessed with another inmate, who in turn became the model for the play's object of desire, Allan Grayle, a shallow Royal Flying Corps officer. Whether such writing was therapeutic or not, Ackerley attempts a claustrophobic, boarding-school-style world of squabbles, frustrations and subliminal homosexuality, in which Captain Jim Conrad (supposedly based on Ackerley himself) is driven mad by a series of events including a quarrel with Grayle, in which he strikes him, and the suicide of another officer, Lieutenant Adelby, whose wife has died. Finally, Conrad has a seizure and retreats into a twilight world. Stage directions show him staring at the mountains, '*a creature obscure, apart, with* [. . .] *his profile turned to catch the last rays of the setting sun*'.[42]

A modern reader can easily find the play melodramatic and its characters grating. Grayle's comment on Captain Rickman ('He *is* rather rough. He's rather a different class you know') also encapsulates a snobbery which the play shares with *Journey's End*.[43] Nonetheless, *The Prisoners of War* became an iconic work. In one exchange Madame Louis, a widow, tries to flirt with Conrad. 'I have heard you do not like much the fair sex,' she begins. 'The fair sex?' Conrad replies. 'Which sex is that?'[44] Some encouraging comments about the play from Siegfried Sassoon ('impressive' but 'painful', and its behaviour 'strange to watch, on the stage'[45]) impelled Ackerley to keep going. *The Prisoners of War* was eventually staged by a private drama club at the Court Theatre in 1925, before transferring to the West End and being hailed by some critics as 'the most important new play produced this year'; Ackerley's 'tragedy of disintegration' was seen to be worthy of Ibsen.[46] The majority, however, confessed to being shocked at this 'dreadful story' about the 'least understood of abnormalities'[47] and its run ended after only twenty-four performances. Arnold Bennett dismissed *Prisoners* as 'no good at all, quite untrue to life', and many were put off by its seemingly pathological characters and unrelieved 'morbidity'.[48]

If the idea of veterans of the war as damaged individuals was no longer outlandish, making them the main attractions in a play certainly still seemed to be so. As the 1930s approached this was challenged by Sherriff, but also by Somerset Maugham in *For Services Rendered* (1932). Here Maugham mourned the failure of the promise to build 'a land fit for heroes' (to borrow Prime Minister David Lloyd George's 1919 electioneering slogan) and offered a coruscating picture of post-war middle-class selfishness. The complacency and venality shown by the Ardsley family and their neighbours, combined with ongoing displays of greed, dishonesty, infidelity, forgery and profiteering, all taking place against a background of bourgeois respectability, creates a picture which many critics found upsetting in 1932. 'Should Maugham Get Away With It?' fumed the *Daily Express*.[49] In the *Saturday Review*, John Pollock was more sanguine, noting how the play 'seizes us by its closeness to our own lives' but warning that '[e]very Englishman should [. . .] fear [. . .] its indictment of our failure'.[50] Maugham's state-of-the-nation play attributes – or diagnoses – a new kind of meaninglessness to the war. Amongst the play's characters only the family's eldest son, a blind soldier, sees things for what they are. His unmarried sister, condemned to look after him, goes mad waiting for her soldier fiancé who will never return. Meanwhile their parents are too old or unwilling to understand what is going on. The play's diatribes against the false values of the post-war world and those in it (represented also by the play's audience) were one reason *For Services Rendered* only managed a short run. Another was Maugham's refusal to offer his protagonists redemption or happiness. He explained:

> The audience could have walked out of the theatre feeling that war was a very unfortunate business, but that, notwithstanding, God was in his heaven and all was right with the world; there was nothing to fash oneself about and haddock *à la crème* would finish the evening very nicely. But it would not have been the play I wished to write.[51]

Read in this light, it is not difficult to see how the plays of the 1920s and 1930s seemed to drift away from celebrating deeds of derring-do towards new dystopias of wrecked lives. Following Somerset Maugham and also Muriel Box, whose *Angels of War* (1935) represented female suffering, it is possible to discern an alternative version of the post-war, devoid of spiritual and moral values, in which protagonists live lives of repression and are scarred – even haunted – by their wartime experiences. It was a tendency encouraged by writers of clipped, sprightly plays such as Noël Coward, whose *Post-Mortem* (1930) features the ghost of a dead officer revisiting old haunts, disgusted by what he sees; and more confidently by J. B. Priestley in *Time and the Conways* (1937), which revisits the hopefulness of 1919, showing how it all went wrong for yet another middle-class family. In contrast, Coward's epic *Cavalcade* (1931), mixing tunes, cheerfulness and large-scale stage manoeuvres, had many more admirers because it showed that those who wanted to remember the war did not have to engage only with depressives or pacifists. Coward's extravaganza tells 'England's story' beginning with the Boer War, through the death of Queen Victoria and the Great War, and ending up in a night-club (a metaphor for the messiness of post-war life). The personal histories of the Marryot family and their servants celebrate good manners and gallantry and any darker implications tend to get hidden under all the pageantry and songs. Nonetheless, in 1931 the sections covering 1914–18 were still close enough to living memory to pack a punch. 'Drink to the war then if you want to,' says Jane Marryot bitterly. 'I'm not going to. I can't [. . .] drink to Victory and Defeat, and stupid tragic sorrow.'[52] A scene of soldiers crowding the stage, marching uphill '*endlessly*' into '*darkness*', likewise puts a check on the play's tendency to self-congratulation.[53] Like Sherriff, Coward toasts the bravery but also invites the audience to reflect on the waste.

It is interesting to try to chart the development of the First World War play *after* the 1930s. For one thing, it seems apparent that what hampered such work was not simply the passing of time. Instead, as Dan Todman has noted, the outbreak of a new world war, the shocks produced by the Holocaust and Hiroshima, 'disrupted' remembrance of 1914–18 and its victims to the extent that their 'prominence in public life' was 'reduced'.[54] While one post-war hit, Terence Rattigan's *The Winslow Boy* (1946), was a period piece, set before 1914, its message made all the more bitter by the knowledge that the real-life model, George Archer-Shee, died aged nineteen at Ypres, the new mood required plays which looked forwards. One such play was Daphne du Maurier's *The Years Between* (1945), whose heroine gave voice to the popular call 'to build a wiser, happier Britain'.[55] In 1951, the lack of interest in the London revival of *Journey's End* may well have had something to do with post-1945 disapproval of the play's officer favouritism, but the lukewarm response also seemed proof that remembrance of the Great War had 'a shelf-life'.[56] Most of the post-1918 plays had been written by those with a close link to the old war – the writing was forged by fighting in it or living through it – but these people were elderly and disappearing, while the 1939–45 war had also helped fracture some of the links.

The most influential post-1945 developments in staging the war were those initiated by Theatre Workshop, whose *Oh, What a Lovely War!* (1963) is regularly cited as kick-starting a new kind of representation. With the challenges of the post-World War Two world halting reflection about World War One, the prospects for this project seemed poor. 'I didn't relish the idea of a show about World War One,' recalled cast member Victor Spinetti. 'The thought of that war made me sick. Poppy day, the Last Post'; such symbols were the remnants of imperial power to which modern Britain was trying pathetically to cling.[57] Yet when the show finally opened in Stratford East in March 1963, followed by West End and Broadway transfers, it clearly resonated with large sections of the theatregoing public. Looking back with hindsight, it is not difficult to understand why. Every play carries some trace of the time in which it is written. *Oh, What a Lovely War!* is an example of a play about the Great War bound up with post-1945 cultural reorientation which, by 1963, included anti-war movements and shifting attitudes towards ideas of class deference. In the late 1950s a new generation of historians had also begun to validate the experiences of ordinary soldiers, some of whom were ready to talk. Charles Chilton's radio documentary *The Long, Long Trail* (1962), in which the comedian Bud Flanagan, himself a veteran, narrated stories about the frontline against the soundtrack of wartime songs, also struck a chord, not least with Gerry Raffles, one of the founders of Theatre Workshop. He pushed the revolutionary director Joan Littlewood to widen out Chiltern's concept into a show whereby the songs, cheerful but now full of irony, would be interspersed with the story of troops led to their deaths by incompetent generals – including villainous Douglas Haig – who were also members of the ruling class. Half a century later, it is striking that a piece by a theatre company whose vision was defiantly alternative and oppositional has come to be synonymous with modern orthodoxy, at least as regards what the Great War is said to have been like.

Inspired perhaps by the success of *Oh, What a Lovely War!*, the 1960s saw the emergence of other playwrights who also insisted that modern audiences forget the horrors of 1914–18 at their peril. Thus John Wilson's *Hamp* (1964), later filmed as *King and Country* (1967), took up the idea of the ordinary combatant as victim. Arthur Hamp, a former millworker, is court-martialled for desertion after crawling out of a shell hole at Passchendaele and walking away. He is the platoon's sole survivor, but his defence ('I never were a coward before, sir') cuts little ice and he is shot.[58] Part of the significance of *Hamp* is that it is an early example of writers reimagining the genre of the history play, showing large events impacting on so-called little people, something Peter Whelan would take up in *The Accrington Pals* (1981). Whelan described the histories of the 'Pals battalions', the units of friends from the same towns raised in response to Lord Kitchener's calls in 1914 for more volunteers, as 'like looking through a pinhole into the past and finding a whole vista of humanity revealed in a very unexpected way'.[59] In the resulting play there is no named villain, but the emphasis on the dishonesty of those in power is typical of Whelan's work and also of recent plays about the war more generally.

What Whelan also shares with several contemporaries who have emerged since the 1980s, including Frank McGuinness (*Observe the Sons of Ulster Marching Towards the Somme*; 1985), is the idea that the experience of war that involved fighting in the trenches was, for working-class people, only one of several battles which needed winning but the only one which could be won. Additionally, the label 'state of the nation' might usefully be given to some of these plays, not a tag likely to be given to Sherriff's *Journey's End*, but plausible here because of a tendency to connect the harsh lives of those living in 1914–18 to the present day. In *The Accrington Pals*, Whelan wanted to suggest parallels between the working classes of wartime Lancashire and the social impact of Thatcherism in the late 1970s. 'We are all crossing into no man's land now,' he explained.[60] More recently, Peter Gill has likewise argued for the necessity of drama to point to 'how we [in David Cameron's Britain] live now'.[61] His play *Versailles* (2014), about an upper-middle-class English family, the Rawlinsons, whose idealistic son is one of the participants at the Versailles peace conference, suggests how the issues debated then can still be relevant a century later. Gill's protagonists want retribution for the losses Britain has suffered, but the play also reveals an entrenched middle-class blindness about the state of society, together with widespread apathy and a refusal to grasp the nettle and change things.

Another notable feature of *Versailles* is the way in which it – like another contemporary play, Howard Brenton's *Doctor Scroggy's War* (2014) – comments knowingly on existing stories of the war (patriotism/propaganda leads to youthful volunteers which, when combined with idiots in charge, leads to meaningless slaughter) before finding new heroes or imposing different arcs on familiar narratives. In *Versailles*, a work referencing Shaw, Sherriff, Maugham and Priestley (amongst others), its young (secretly gay) protagonist Leonard Rawlinson occupies an uncertain position; he is not a Lieutenant Stanhope, and neither is he Sydney Ardsley, the blind ex-soldier in *For Services Rendered*. Yet he ends up rubbing shoulders with both; he admits the existence of things others refuse to see. 'We are still in thrall to the system that brought it [the war] about,' he announces. 'We're stuck.'[62] Similarly, *Doctor Scroggy's War* follows its author's practice of taking what he describes as 'a rooted, popular myth from the British national consciousness' in new directions.[63] Prior to the play's 2014 premiere at London's Globe Theatre, Brenton explained that he wanted to focus on Dr Harold Gillies, the father of plastic surgery, as a means of demonstrating that a war play can be 'life affirming'.[64] But in showing his soldier protagonists' enjoyment of the war experience, of explosions and killing, Brenton's play is a step removed from the sentimentality which overcomes most twenty-first-century war plays, typified perhaps by Phil Porter's *The Christmas Truce* (2014). The message of *Doctor Scroggy's War*, as discovered by Lieutenant Jack Twigg, the play's broken hero, is that 'mutilation is a great leveller'. Dr Gillies's hyperactive, kilt-wearing alter ego 'Doctor Scroggy' refuses to allow self-pity or survivor guilt and works to cheer up his inmates on the basis that 'we don't do glum here'.[65]

The desire to level out representations of the war experience remains an important impetus behind British theatre's approach to the conflict even as the cultural landscape shifts. The figure of the doomed young officer epitomised by Dennis Stanhope seems omnipresent – on film and television, as well as on stage – but what modern playwrights have increasingly wanted to do is to tell the stories that have not yet been told, often involving non-combatants or the so-called home front, something which the centenary commemorations beginning in 2014 have also thrown into sharp relief. *Conscientious Objector or Coward? The Story of Arthur Waterman*, by the fringe theatre company Twisted Events (2014), is a case in point: a play which uses tribunal records and diaries to recreate the experiences of a real-life marginalised figure. Yet there is still a sense that being an officer matters and, for playwrights, a sense that upholding the traditions of their stories matters as well. This is a feeling captured in Nick Stafford's long-running adaptation of Michael Morpurgo's *War Horse* (2007), which has had global appeal. The play's life-size horse puppets remain a draw, but so does its depiction of what Morpurgo describes as 'the universality of suffering' brought about by the First World War – and all wars since then.[66] Fashions are transient – as the forgotten reputations of people like Horace Annesley Vachell and Walter Melville attest – but the appeal of the war play remains constant, its complicated mixture of lofty idealism and harsh realism retaining an ability to speak to new generations of theatregoers.

## Notes

1. George Bernard Shaw, *Complete Prefaces, 1914–1929*, ed. Dan H. Laurence and Daniel J. Leary (London: Allen Lane, 1995), pp. 318–53 (pp. 344, 346).
2. 'Why Mr Maugham Wrote It', *Daily Express*, 3 November 1932, p. 11.
3. Gladys Cooper, *Gladys Cooper: An Autobiography* (London: Hutchinson & Co., 1931), p. 164.
4. Allardyce Nicoll, *English Drama 1900–1930* (Cambridge: Cambridge University Press, 1973), p. 3.
5. L. J. Collins, *Theatre at War, 1914–18* (Basingstoke: Macmillan, 1998), p. 219.
6. Siegfried Sassoon, *Collected Poems 1908–1956* (London: Faber & Faber, 1961), p. 21.
7. British Library, Lord Chamberlain's Plays collection, LCP 1914/27.
8. British Library, LCP 1915/2.
9. British Library, LCP 1916/3.
10. British Library, LCP 1915/5, 30 April 1915.
11. *The Referee*, 24 June 1915, p. 2.
12. 'The Letters of Eve', *Tatler*, 16 December 1914, p. 233.
13. Derek Ross, 'The Theatre', *The Herald*, 22 May 1915, p. 11.
14. British Library, LCP 1915/10.
15. 'A Drama of Spies and Spitefulness', *The Bystander*, 2 June 1915, p. 344.
16. 'The Female Hun', *The Bystander*, 23 October 1918, p. 149.
17. 'The Hidden Hand', *The Bystander*, 4 December 1918, p. 427.
18. Frank Vernon, *The Twentieth Century Theatre* (London: Harrap, 1924), pp. 118–19.
19. Sos Eltis, 'From Sex-War to Factory Floor': Theatrical Depictions of Women's Work during the First World War', in Andrew Maunder (ed.), *British Theatre and the Great War, 1914–1919* (London: Palgrave, 2015), pp. 103–20.
20. J. M. Barrie, *Dear Brutus*, in *Complete Plays*, ed. A. E. Wilson (London: Hodder & Stoughton, 1942), pp. 993–1,060 (p. 995).
21. Ibid., p. 1,040.
22. Leonée Ormond, *J. M. Barrie* (Edinburgh: Scottish Academic Press, 1987), p. 116.
23. J. M. Barrie, *The New Word*, in *Echoes of the War* (New York: Charles Scribner's Sons, 1918), pp. 65–107 (p. 101).
24. J. M. Barrie, *A Well-Remembered Voice*, in *Echoes of the War*, pp. 143–88 (pp. 165–6).
25. Ibid., p. 170.
26. Miles Malleson, *'D' Company and Black 'Ell* (London: Henderson, 1925), pp. 9–31 (p. 18).
27. British Library, LCP 1916/13.
28. Miles Malleson, *Second Thoughts* (London: National Labour Press, 1916), p. ii.
29. Malleson, *'D' Company and Black 'Ell*, pp. 35–64 (p. 64).
30. Malleson, 'Preface', in *'D' Company and Black 'Ell*, n.p.
31. British Library, LCP 1926/38.
32. Ella Hepworth Dixon, 'Woman's Ways', *The Sketch*, 29 December 1915, p. ii.
33. John Drinkwater, 'Introduction', in Vernon, *The Twentieth Century Theatre*, p. 1.
34. Ibid., p. 4.
35. W. Somerset Maugham, *The Unknown* (London: Heinemann, 1920), p. 97.

36. Ibid., p. 29.
37. Ibid., p. 84.
38. Ibid., p. 95.
39. Samuel Hynes, *A War Imagined: The First World War and English Culture* (London: Bodley Head, 1990), p. 439.
40. R. C. Sherriff, *No Leading Lady: An Autobiography* (London: Gollancz, 1968), p. 45.
41. Richard Jennings, '*Journey's End*', *The Spectator*, 2 February 1929, p. 154.
42. J. R. Ackerley, *The Prisoners of War* (London: Chatto & Windus, 1925), p. 109.
43. Ibid., p. 61.
44. Ibid., p. 68.
45. Siegfried Sassoon, *Diaries: 1923–25*, ed. Rupert Hart-Davis (London: Faber & Faber, 1985), p. 284.
46. John Shand, '*Prisoners of War*', *New Statesman*, 11 July 1925, p. 366.
47. James Agate, *The Contemporary Theatre, 1925*, quoted in Peter Parker, *Ackerley: A Life of J. R. Ackerley* (London: Constable, 1989), p. 100.
48. Arnold Bennett, quoted in Sassoon, *Diaries*, p. 284.
49. 'Should Maugham Get Away With It?', *Daily Express*, 17 November 1932, p. 10.
50. John Pollock, 'For Services Rendered', *Saturday Review*, 12 November 1932, pp. 502–3.
51. W. Somerset Maugham, 'Preface', in *Collected Plays* (London: Heinemann, 1960), p. iv.
52. Noël Coward, *Cavalcade*, in *Plays: Three* (London: Methuen, 1979), pp. 125–200 (p. 183).
53. Ibid., pp. 183–4.
54. Dan Todman, *The Great War: Myth and Memory* (London: Hambledon, 2005), p. 59.
55. Daphne du Maurier, *The Years Between* (London: Victor Gollancz, 1945), p. 75.
56. Todman, *The Great War*, p. 226.
57. Victor Spinetti, 'Afterword', *Oh What a Lovely War* (London: Bloomsbury, 2014), pp. 89–93 (p. 89).
58. John Wilson, *Hamp* (London: Evans, 1966), p. 28.
59. Peter Whelan, 'Preface', in *Plays: One* (London: Methuen, 2003), p. 3.
60. Ibid., p. 5.
61. Peter Gill, 'Nothing Happens Unless the Middle Classes Do It', *The Guardian*, 26 February 2014, <http://www.theguardian.com/stage/2014/feb/26/peter-gill-theatre-donmar-versailles-first-world-war> (last accessed 20 October 2016).
62. Peter Gill, *Versailles* (London: Faber & Faber, 2014), pp. 121, 123.
63. Howard Brenton, 'Preface', in *Plays: Two* (London: Methuen, 1989), p. 2.
64. Howard Brenton, '*Dr Scroggy's War* and an Arena of Opportunity', *The Independent*, 9 September 2014, <http://www.independent.co.uk/arts-entertainment/theatre-dance/features/howard-brenton-on-doctor-scroggys-war-and-an-arena-of-opportunity-9722094.html> (last accessed 20 October 2016).
65. Quoted in Michael Billington, 'Howard Brenton Explores Horror of Combat', *The Guardian*, 18 September 2014, <http://www.theguardian.com/stage/2014/sep/18/doctor-scroggys-war-review-howard-brenton-shakespeares-globe-london-first-world-war> (last accessed 20 October 2016).
66. Tom Brook, 'How War Horse Took on the World', *BBC News*, 13 June 2011, <http://www.bbc.co.uk/news/entertainment-arts-13746762> (last accessed 20 October 2016).

# 5

# Words from Home: Wartime Correspondences

## *Alice Kelly*

'"Mail's up!" The vast of night is over, / And love of friends fills all one's mind,' begins Ivor Gurney's poem 'Letters', recording the soldier's joy after the loneliness, uncertainty and fear of the night is relieved by news from home.[1] Wartime letters offered the soldier a mental release from the war and reminded him of the loved ones he had waiting at home for his return, 'His wife, his sister, or his lover'.[2] Many writers and artists stressed the importance of letters during the Great War, what Gurney described elsewhere as 'like stars in a dark night'.[3] The war memorial at Paddington Station, London, depicts a soldier, eyes downcast and a faint smile on his face, engrossed in reading a letter.[4] Popular songs exhorted women to

> Send him a cheerful letter,
> Say that it's all OK.
> Tell him you've ne'er felt better,
> Though it's all the other way.
> Don't send a word of sorrow,
> Send him a page of joy,
> And don't let your teardrops
> Fall upon the kisses
> When you write to your soldier boy.[5]

The 1915 American song 'Three Wonderful Letters from Home' notes that '[e]ach word was like a soft caress that soothed his aching heart'.[6] The soldier receiving a letter was a trope familiar enough for Charlie Chaplin to parody in his 1918 film *Soldier Arms*, when his character falls into a mock melancholia when he is the only one in his troop not to receive a letter – and when he does receive a parcel from home, it carries such a repellent Limburger cheese that he immediately has to hurl it over to the German lines.[7] The importance of letters has carried over into public memory of the war, demonstrated by over twenty thousand submissions received for one centenary project to write an imagined First World War soldier a letter.[8]

Letters, as reminders of home permitted to cross the boundary between the home front and the actual front during the First World War, occupied a uniquely important place in wartime culture. Working as both a lifeline for combatants and proof of their loved ones' safety for civilians, the intensely important role of wartime letters, in terms of both communication and morale, cannot be underestimated. This was recognised by the British, French and German governments, who prioritised the continuance of the post in wartime despite the demanding logistics and enormous financial costs this entailed, and provided an entirely free service for letters from the war zones to the home fronts.[9] With the telephone and telegram reserved for generals and staff to communicate movements of troops and urgent orders, the letter was the primary form of communication between civilians and soldiers and the primary means for civilians to know on a daily basis whether or not their loved one was still alive.

This chapter argues that the First World War letter was not qualitatively different from other forms of letters – following the same epistolary conventions of the place and date of writing, salutation, descriptive content, confirmation of affection or longing for the recipient, and sign-off – but that the letter took on a heightened significance in wartime because of its role in assuring survival or notifying of a death, as a form that could alternately bring intense joy or grief. Intrigued by Margaretta Jolly's premise that 'war letters by professional writers tend to show heightened awareness of the function of writing in such situations', I examine the genre through the letters of four British authors: Vera Brittain and Roland Leighton, Wilfred Owen, and Ivor Gurney.[10] This chapter focuses on letters from the early years of the war, 1914–16, as writers experimented with the opportunities and boundaries of this increasingly used literary form. Beginning with a review of the generic and historical contexts of First World War epistolary exchange, I then examine some common characteristics of war letters, and conclude with the rhetorical conventions of the 'break-the-news' letter and the use of letters as a memorial form.

## Keeping Open the Lines of Communication: Generic and Historical Contexts

Despite the continued popularity of anthologies and editions of First World War correspondence, the critical field on First World War letters, in English-language criticism at least, remains relatively nascent. Studies have focused on national epistolary traditions during the First World War, or how war letters articulate and inform gender, intimacy and class.[11] The recent critical move to theorise letters in terms of their 'letterness' and its attendant seriality can provide some useful insight on the war letter genre.[12] Letters, Liz Stanley argues, 'are characterized by temporal and spatial interruptions, are always "unfinished" in the sense of containing gaps, ellipses and mistakes, and also presume a response and thus an "after"'.[13] The implicit seriality of the wartime letter – that the outbound letter would be matched by an inbound one – therefore became a proof of survival in wartime: a unique means of marking time and attempting to ensure continuity. Letters, as a type of metronome for the chaotic and unpredictable nature of wartime life, could even be said to structure wartime experience, as time was measured by the spaces between letters. A 'processual dynamics' develops between correspondents:

> An economy of exchange and reciprocity is involved in long-term epistolary exchanges, with mutuality built in and giving rise to a processual dynamics in which there are distinctive (to the particular correspondence) interpretations of time and its passing ['by the time you receive this, I will . . .'] and space and its separations ['here I am . . . there you are . . .'].[14]

A letter from Roland Leighton in the trenches to his sweetheart Vera Brittain from April 1915 demonstrates this: 'This letter will have been carried under fire by the time it reaches you.'[15] Brittain's response to Leighton in turn demonstrates this temporal dislocation: 'I shudder to think that even as I read you may be in danger from those very guns which you heard thundering in the distance.'[16] Stanley's observation that 'letter writing is located *in* [and] *about* actual things' is clearly relevant for wartime letters, which frequently included the conditions of writing:

> Your two last letters came one last night and one the night before, and I read them by candlelight sitting on the little wooden bench outside my dug-out. I am sitting there now writing this, while the sun shines on the paper and a bee is humming round and round the bed of primroses in front of me.[17]

Many wartime letters fulfil Stanley's 'characteristics of metonymy and a simulacrum of presence', as letters came to stand in for the person. Brittain told Leighton in April 1915, '[s]ometimes even your existence seems a dream too, and I have to look at your letters & the things you have given me to make myself feel it is real . . .'[18] Because the bodies of British soldiers were not returned home from 1916, this quality became particularly explicit if the soldier didn't survive the war. In these cases, the soldier's letters functioned as a substitution for his corpse, and, when published in memorial volumes, as biographies.

The efficient delivery of the twelve and a half million letters that were sent from Britain every week to the Western front – over two billion letters during the course of the simultaneously chaotic and highly bureaucratic war years – was something of an administrative wonder.[19] Whereas '[i]n the early weeks of the war it could take up to ten days for a letter to arrive at the front', from December 1914 onwards letters sent from Britain would reach the front in only two or three days, meaning that even perishable food could be sent, alongside soap, buttons, socks and ointment.[20] Brittain wrote to Leighton in May 1915: 'I am glad my letters arrive so soon after I write them. I like to think of you receiving & reading them, & wonder what you feel when you see my writing on the envelope, and if it is anything like *I* feel when I see yours.'[21] This delivery speed was possible because of the static nature of trench warfare with established lines of communication, where units would be moved around, but addresses remained. Michael Roper notes the effect of this speed of delivery, where 'similar time zones, weather and seasons intensified the feeling of proximity' and allowed both writer and reader to 'imagine what the other was doing in the very instant of writing'.[22] For this reason, Brittain feared her brother Edward being sent to the Dardanelles, because 'it takes so long for news & letters to come'.[23]

Letters sent from the home front were addressed to the recipient and his military unit. Every morning the General Post Office received a report letting them know the current location of each unit. Letters arrived at the Home Postal Depot in London, which had been established in early August 1914. As demand increased, a second letter-sorting office was established in early 1915 on a different site, and in 1916 the original Home Postal Depot was moved to a purpose-built 200,000 square foot wooden structure in Regent's Park in London (making it the largest wooden structure in the world), with 2,500 employees. The first letter-sorting office was responsible for the BEF post, and the second processed letters to all other locations. In 1917, when the volume of letters was at its peak, some work was outsourced to offices in Birmingham, Bristol, Glasgow, Leeds, Manchester and Sheffield. From the Home Postal Depot the post was transported by army lorries to the embarkation ports at Folkestone or Southampton, and by ship to one of the sixteen Base Army Post Offices (BAPOs). The five BAPOs in France for letters to the British Expeditionary Force were in Le Havre, Nantes, Rouen, Boulogne and Calais. The mail was then sorted at the BAPO by the Royal Engineers Postal Section and carried by supply train through the night for transportation to the railhead. It was then transferred by lorry to the Refilling Points. Here, it was sorted by the Field Post Office staff, who distributed it to the Unit Post Orderlies, who delivered the mail to the men. Letters sent back to the home front were collected from the Field Post Offices and taken back to the BAPOs, where they would be sent back to the home front by ship and then put into the normal postal system for delivery. The importance of catching 'the last post' is demonstrated by the wartime postcard in Plate 1, which depicts British soldiers racing to post their letters on time.[24]

Civilians were encouraged, primarily through the popular press, to write regularly to their loved ones in the war zones and an important effect of the war was to make letter-writing a popular form of communication amongst all classes and age groups. The enormous number of letters sent during the war was in part due to the pre-war rise in literacy rates, a result of improved education provision since 1870.[25] However, these literacy rates were still largely class-dependent, as Michael Roper notes. Parents who had left school before the introduction of compulsory education had to learn the art of personal correspondence, including how to balance 'the difference between conversation and [. . .] formality' and how to address an envelope.[26] For the many rankers who 'had probably never even written a letter to a parent before joining the Army', the little instruction in composition they had received at school was matched by a lack of experience, having 'been neither taught nor encouraged to communicate their own thoughts and experiences in writing'.[27] Roper argues:

> These pre-war differences in writing habits were exacerbated by the conditions under which men on the Western Front wrote home. Officers, even when in trenches, could generally write at tables, lit by candlelight, their paper kept dry by a dug-out roof. Privates in the line were less well protected from the rain and cold. They lacked light and their conditions were more cramped. [. . .] The comparatively expansive style of officers' letters was not due only to their superior education and familiarity with letter-writing, but to their more comfortable conditions.[28]

For the privates, the development of the Field Service Postcard – a generic form where the soldier would delete pre-printed sentences as appropriate – was a very helpful means of efficiently communicating a message to home (and would be frequently parodied in the wartime and post-war years).[29]

A further epistolary wartime innovation was prompted by the Defence of the Realm Act (DORA), introduced in early August 1914, which resulted in the censorship of letters going from the war zones to the home front. This new culture of censorship meant that letters were no longer a private form but a public one, where every letter would be read initially by someone other than its intended recipient. Censorship of soldiers' letters was undertaken by junior officers, with content such as troop movements, battle plans, locations, criticism of superiors, or even the weather, censored in order to maintain morale at home. These censorship rules were frequently disregarded. Leighton wrote to Brittain in March 1915, before he left England: 'Havre is where we are to be landed (though I am not allowed to tell you this), and from there presumably we are sent up into the fighting line. I will try to send you a telegram when we get to Havre, if censors allow such things.'[30] Soldiers used various methods to evade the censor, such as sending letters home with returning comrades or using codes. Leighton wrote to Brittain, 'I have not forgotten our arrangement about putting small dots – in pencil – under certain letters, that you may know where I am.'[31] Wilfred Owen told his mother in January 1917, 'If on my Field Post Card I cross out "I am being sent down to the base" with a double line ══════ then I shall actually be at the Front.'[32] Without naming their location, the writer might give enough detail to make it obvious: 'We are holding the front edge of a wood – a wood very famous in the history of the war – and our support and reserve trenches are hidden away inside,' Leighton wrote to Edward Brittain in April 1915.[33]

The emotional labour of censorship for the officers who carried it out is often forgotten. Guy Chapman wrote of his deliberate attempt to avoid the personal in the letters he censored:

> I have an old platoon roll before me; three pages of names, numbers, trades, next-of-kin, religions, rifle numbers, and so forth. Faces come back out of the past to answer to these barren details, the face of this man dead, of that vanished for ever. [. . .] Did I know you? I censored your letters, casually, hurriedly avoiding your personal messages, your poignant hopes [. . .][34]

Leighton wrote in similar terms about censorship in response to a letter from Brittain: 'I cannot answer it now – not as I should like. For one thing I have a lot of men's letters to censor before the post goes – prosaic and unimaginative most of them, but a few make me feel like a Father Confessor.'[35] The phrase 'make me feel' demonstrates Leighton's sense of having involuntarily trespassed on his men's personal lives. Green envelopes provided the only legitimate means of circumventing the censor. Each soldier was given one green envelope per month, which was for a personal private letter which would not be censored, but contained a declaration that 'the contents refer to nothing but private and family matters'. Brittain wrote of the joy of receiving 'uncensored letters from Roland in green envelopes' in her summer 1915 term at Oxford, and the envelopes were enough of a phenomenon to be gathered into post-war anthologies.[36]

In this new era of mass letter-writing, there was an enormous boom in the wartime stationery industry, and the accompanying advertising provides a useful insight into wartime desires and fears. Soldiers were frequently the focus of adverts for writing tools that were suitable for use on active service. The Onoto pen in particular was marketed as 'The Perfect pen for soldiers'.[37] Showing a pen tucked neatly inside a military pocket, one 1915 advert stated: 'THE MILITARY SIZE Onoto Pen fills itself, never leaks, and exactly fits the uniform pocket.'[38] However, the majority of adverts were directed at civilians, instructing them on which pen their soldier friend would most appreciate: 'Do not make the mistake of sending the wrong kind of Pen to the front. Send an Onoto, the Pen the soldier wants' (Figure 5.1).[39] Another advert shows a disappointed soldier with the caption 'Pity she didn't send me an Onoto'.[40] These adverts also suggested that sending the correct pen would result in more letters being sent home, as a 1916 advert for Venus pencils shows: 'Send your friend in the trenches a package. You'll get an appreciative letter in return.'[41] An advert for the Swan service writing outfit explained how the kit worked and the consequences it would have for the civilian:

Figure 5.1 Advertisement for the Onoto Pen, *The Times*, 6 December 1915, p. 4. Private collection. Reproduced courtesy of Andrew McCarthy.

> All the soldier has to do is to fill his pen from his water bottle and drop a tablet in. The tablet dissolves quickly and makes perfect writing ink. Simple as A.B.C.
>
> Send your soldier or sailor friend this splendid writing outfit. It will both remind and enable him to write you frequently.[42]

A Waterman's Ideal fountain pen advert similarly suggested the pen as an ideal 'Parting Gift': 'Whenever he gets the opportunity to write he now has the means at hand to do so. Moreover Waterman's Ideal will be a daily encouragement to him to write.'[43] Another advert suggested that sending a Swan fountain pen would prompt correspondence: 'If you are not getting as many letters as you would like from your friend on Active Service, don't blame him. Send him a "Swan." You've no idea how it helps' (Figure 5.2).[44] Another strategy used was to make those on the home front feel guilty for not writing to their loved ones more regularly. One advert for Swan pens included an extract of an emotive article entitled 'Write Oftener' by John Oxenham:

> ONE of my padré friends at the front begs me to ask and ask and ask, and to keep on asking, all the folks at home to write and write and write, and to keep on writing to their men out there. He says no one knows how the letters are valued by them – no matter how simple they are, nor how small the thing they are written about. It is, after all, the small things that make up the greater part of life.
>
> He says he censors thousands of letters and nearly every one of them plaintively says, 'Why don't you write oftener?'[45]

The advert concludes: 'The "Swan" is the best means of meeting this big need.' Writing more letters was presented as an important morale-boosting role the civilian could play in wartime, which could be fulfilled with the pen they provided: 'Now, this is a matter in which every one of us can do our bit.' Just to push home the point, the extract ends: 'Every such letter – if it is a right letter – is to the men out there like a gleam of sunshine on a stormy day – like a glimpse of the far away home-light on a dreary night.'

Some adverts even suggested that purchasing their particular brand would ensure the continuance of a relationship. The longevity of the Waterman's Ideal pen was implicitly linked with lifelong romantic attachment:

Figure 5.2 Advertisement for the Swan Fount Pen, *Land & Water*, 10 August 1916, p. xxv. Private collection. Reproduced courtesy of Andrew McCarthy.

> Only the best is good enough for the man who is fighting out yonder. So send him not the second best or just a Fountain Pen, but a genuine Waterman's Ideal. Then he will have a pen which will hold a permanent place in his affections, a pen he can trust, a pen that is sure to write when he wants it to write, a pen that never goes wrong.[46]

The advert suggests that the woman, via the pen she gives to her soldier friend, 'will hold a permanent place in his affections'. Other adverts used war rhetoric to get the same message across (Figure 5.3):

> **The 'Swan' Fount Pen**
> **Keeps open the Lines of Communication.**
>
> When a 'Lull' comes and the RIFLE is laid down then is the time the soldier wants his 'LITTLE BLACK GUN.' He can 'FIRE' cheery messages telling of his safety. He just loves to scribble a few lines home, it seems to shorten the distance and ease his mind.[47]

The accompanying image shows parallel figures: a woman at a desk in London writing a letter, superimposed over a map of England, with the soldier writing a letter on

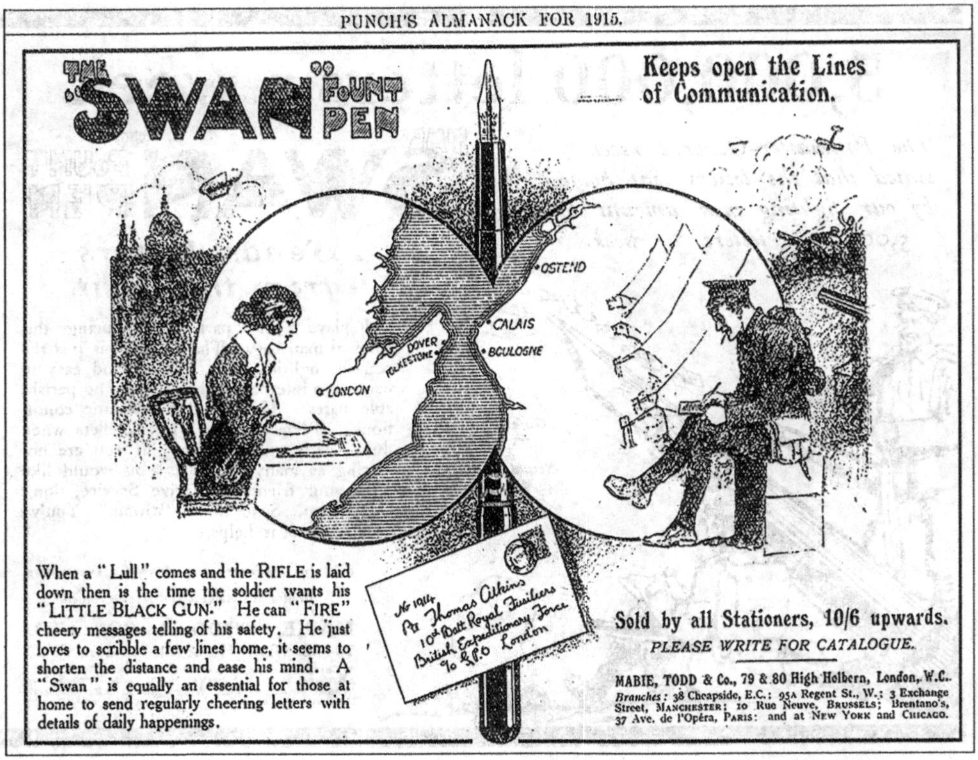


Figure 5.3 Advertisement for the Swan Fount Pen, *Punch's Almanack for 1915*, late 1914 (n.p.). Private collection. Reproduced courtesy of Andrew McCarthy.

his knee beside a row of tents, superimposed over a map of France, with a pen, in the middle, linking them – a testimonial to the importance of the mutual act of letter-writing for those at home and at the front.

## The Actualities of the War: Revelation and Concealment

Combatants frequently wanted to share their new experiences – air raids, the conditions of trench warfare, the sound of the war zones, the battles – with their loved ones. War letters therefore included extended descriptive passages, with accompanying illustrations, which attempted to bridge the distance between soldiers and civilians. Ivor Gurney described camp life to his friends, the Chapman family, in June 1915:

> We have been here in camp just over a week, and the whole time has been a rush, from 5 o'clock reveille to 9.45 Light out. The chief thing is attacks and all sorts of company and brigade actions; this is why we have come into camp. The roads are horrid, bristly with shingle and pebbles which raise blisters in record time. For breakfast we have as a rule bacon; for dinner either what they call shackles (stewed meat) or roast meat; for tea, bread, margarine, jam, and 'tea', made in the same dixie as the shackles – very different in every way to the dainty meal held about the same time at St Michael's High Wycombe.[48]

Gurney knew his daily schedule would be of interest to his civilian readers, writing similarly to Marion Scott that they had 'reveillé at 5. Breakfast at 6. Parade at 7. Dinner at 2. Tea somewhere about 4.30 – 5.30.'[49] Leighton writing to Brittain from his training camp in October 1914 told her, 'I have to get up at 5.45am and am kept hard at work with intervals for meals until 7.30pm. By that time I usually feel too tired to do anything but have some dinner and get to bed.'[50] War letters therefore function as useful historical eyewitness accounts, written in the immediacy of the moment or soon afterwards and unedited.

Sometimes the writer employed figurative language to liken their new experience to something the civilian reader would understand. Writing to Scott, Gurney described the immense noise accompanying the departure of one hundred men to the front: 'The only things that can give you an idea of that sound are either elemental sounds like the war of winds and waves or the greatest moment in music – the end of the development in the 1st movement of the Choral Symphony. Like the creative word of God.'[51] Leighton similarly compared a French landscape to 'the clear cut landscape in a child's painting book' and explained the explosion of a shell in domestic terms: 'When the shell hits the ground it makes a circular depression like a pudding basin about a yard and a half across by 18 inches deep.'[52] Conversely, the writer might note how unlike the experience was to what they had imagined. Leighton wrote to Brittain in April 1915: 'It is all as yet unrealisable. It seems very far from death and horror and fighting.'[53] Many writers gave a sense of their scene of writing. Leighton wrote, 'I am writing this in the kitchen of a French farm house about 3 miles south of B[éthune]', describing what he could see and hear around him: 'At night the flares sent up from the German trenches lighten the sky on two sides of us every four or five minutes.'[54] A few days later, he was 'writing this sitting on the edge of my bunk in the dug-out'.[55] He described his surroundings for Brittain:

> Our heavy artillery has been shelling a large disused brewery behind the German lines all the morning. The shells come straight over the trenches, and you hear first the dull boom as they leave the muzzle of the gun, & then the scream of the shell passing overhead, ending in a crash as it bursts. This is going on as I write now. I have just been outside the trench watching it all.[56]

Leighton's phrasing, that the shelling was going on as he wrote and that he had 'just' been outside, adds to the letter's sense of immediacy, what Stanley notes as the '"flies in amber" quality' of letters, being 'always "in the present tense"'.[57] Letters were particularly valuable in helping civilians to understand what war was like: 'Nothing in the papers, not the most vivid & heart-rending descriptions,' Brittain wrote to Leighton, 'have made me realise war like your letters.'[58] She told her brother that she wanted to 'tell [him] about some most thrilling letters I have had from R. all about what it is like out there'.[59] Combatant writers even went so far as to try to give readers an actual taste of the war zones, at least when military supplies were still plentiful at the war's beginning: 'You may expect an army biscuit by post soon [. . .] though they are terrifically hard, hot tea alters that,' Gurney told the Chapmans.[60] Leighton sent Brittain from Flanders 'a rather pathetic souvenir that I found among the rubbish [. . .] some pages from a child's exercise book'.[61]

Letters could also give civilians a private knowledge of what life was like in the military. Gurney noted: 'the details about army life are from the inside, and, chiefly, about the inside.'[62] The soldier writer often commented on the latest war rumour (true or otherwise), such as Gurney's comments on 'one or two very interesting discoveries' about a German spy captured in Epping: 'One was that his garden shone phosphorescent at night with an arrow pointing to London.'[63] More often than not, however, the soldier was as much in the dark as the civilian. Leighton wrote to Brittain in November 1914, '[w]e received a message from the War Office this morning asking if we were prepared to move out of Norwich, if required, at six hours' notice. It is rumoured that we shall probably be sent – if we do move – to take the place of some other more prepared battalion that has been hurried off to the coast.'[64] Gurney told Mrs Chapman of their 'hopelessly vague' arrangements: 'We are reported to be leaving here either on Sat: or Monday. [. . .] But nothing – nothing is certain, but uncertainty.'[65]

The war letter took on a moral dimension when combatants told civilians about their experiences in order to counteract the romantic and patriotic ideas of warfare on the home front. Owen described visiting a hospital in Bordeaux, complete with graphic illustrations, to his brother in September 1914:

> One poor [drawing] devil had his shin-bone crushed by a gun-carriage-wheel, and the doctor had to twist it about and push it like a piston to get out the pus. Another had a hole right through the knee; and the doctor passed a bandage thus: [drawing] Another had a head into which a ball had entered and come out again. [Two drawings] This is how the bullet lay in the Zouave. Sometimes the feet were covered with a brown, scaly, crust – dried blood. [Drawing] I deliberately tell you all this to educate you to the actualities of the war.[66]

This educative and moral dimension continued into the post-war period. The editor of the collection *Green Envelopes*, an anonymous soldier injured at Ypres, hoped that the letters might affect post-war policy:

> [T]he sentiments expressed in this series of letters from fighting men at the Front, are, taken as a whole, so noble, so inspiring, so wholesome, and so redolent of all that is greatest in our manhood, that to withhold them would be refusing to the rising generation an inspiration that, on the score of national policy alone, is of some importance.[67]

In *War Letters of Fallen Englishmen* (1930), the editor Laurence Housman argued for the moral education provided by war letters due to their veracity: 'If such letters bring home to us the dishonour vicariously borne by men of noble character, [. . .] they will teach better wisdom to the race than those [. . .] which extol the "fineness" of war.'[68]

However, many writers exercised self-censorship as a means of protecting those at home. Brittain was adamant that Leighton did not do this with her letters, considering her knowledge of his hardships a means of sharing them:

> You will tell me all you have to go through, won't you – at any rate as much as Censorship will allow. Please don't keep things back with a vague idea of sparing my feelings; I am not so weak that I fear to face in imagination what you have to endure in reality. [. . .] Why should you hesitate to tell me of these things? I can

> after all read about them in the papers, only without that personal element of yours which will make them specially mine. I shall not be afraid to know and confront the real; the imagined has far greater terror for me. Let me share your hardships – perhaps your sufferings – in the only way I can.[69]

She reiterated this a fortnight later, telling him, 'I hate to think of you wandering about in front of the trenches only 60 yards from the Germans & in full view of their fire. [. . .] (But don't on this account not tell me. I will be quite as wakeful if you don't.)'[70] She was pleased when he was able to use green envelopes, which meant his letters didn't have to be censored: 'Not that your *letters* ever suffered much from over-"reserve"! But it makes it easier to write to people, doesn't it, when your letters are not going beneath the eyes of someone intermediate, though impersonal.'[71] Interestingly, Roland did exercise a degree of self-censorship, seen in a letter to Edward Brittain where he reserved the most gruesome details for a parenthesis: 'The whole country is a muck-heap. (E.g. three days ago while digging a machine gun emplacement just to the front of my bit of trench we had to cut through 3 dead bodies to get there.)'[72]

Margaretta Jolly attributes the critical neglect of war letters as a genre until recently to the fact that letters are 'so often heavily *self*-censored in war', meaning that '[m]any of the most interesting or disturbing effects of war on personal identity [. . .] are precisely those that are downplayed'.[73] However, war letters seemed to provide a safe space for exercising experimental thoughts or fears. Leighton told Brittain that he feared the effect of army life on his mind: 'Even now in war time the Army means mental starvation. By the time this war ends I shall have become too commonplace and orthodox for you to care to talk to.'[74] Letters provided a useful means for women to measure how their men were being affected by war. Brittain wrote: 'I sit [. . .] thinking of you among barbed-wire entanglements at night, & of you suffering from the horrors of war & yet keeping your essential personality – as I see you are in your letters – untouched by them all.'[75] She repeated this sentiment twelve days later: 'Your letters, certainly, don't seem to illustrate you as fundamentally altering.'[76]

For civilians, the non-arrival of a letter could be a matter of a terrible agony, and numerous writers wrote about the particular experience of waiting for letters, and the fear that resulted when they were delayed. Speaking of his potential death, Brittain told Leighton: 'Every letter makes me realise how near you are to that great Fact.'[77] Many combatant letters therefore began with an apology for having not written sooner or only writing a short letter. Leighton told Brittain that he 'had no time to write till to-day' and later that 'this can only be a truncated and inadequate letter'.[78] Later in the war, after what was ostensibly a five-day break in their correspondence, he asked: 'Have you forgiven me for keeping you letterless so long?'[79]

Many combatant writers wrote of the cheering, even life-preserving, quality of letters. Leighton wrote to Brittain in April 1915: 'I must write if only two lines to thank you for your sweet letter [. . .] It is the first and only one I have received so far. I cannot tell you how much it has meant to me.'[80] Brittain replied: 'I can imagine a little what it must be to get them [. . .] I will write as often & as fully as I can.'[81] The following month, in a letter where Leighton told Brittain he had been taking the things out of the pockets of the first of his men to be killed to send home, he wrote: 'I should so like to write you a really long letter as an adequate recompense for letters that help me to live.'[82] Brittain replied: 'Do my letters really help you to live? I wish they could do more & ensure your life.'[83] Owen told his mother in April 1915 of the support her correspondence gave him: 'My chief Easter Joy was your postcard: the handwriting alone, comforting and reassuring.'[84]

Writers were highly aware of the power and function of their letters in wartime. Owen asked his mother in March 1915 to keep his letters as a means of recording the 'landmarks of one's Thoughts' in the absence of a diary.[85] He, in particular, had fun with the new military language in the first months of the war. In August 1914, he 'captured together' his mother's two recent mails.[86] In October he was 'positively fatigued after my heroic efforts', and he told his sister, undertaking nursing training, to 'make war on microbes!'.[87] In January he was able to 'preserve a strictly neutral attitude' in domestic matters in the French house where he was staying.[88] Likewise, Gurney notes the experiences in the war zones that were 'worth the writing about'.[89] Language was an explicit part of what writers were fighting for: Owen, writing to his mother in December 1914 about his anxieties at having not yet signed up, told her: 'Do you know what would hold me together on a battlefield?: The sense that I was perpetuating the language in which Keats and the rest of them wrote!'[90] Despite the difficulties of writing in wartime, letters home gave much information about writers' experiences of war and it is hardly surprising that they enjoyed the new opportunities offered by this omnipresent genre to describe and comment on what they saw and felt.

## Letters as a Memorial Form

Whereas in the Victorian and Edwardian period, the deathbed encouraged presence at the death of a loved one, or at least the breaking of news via a letter from a family member who was present, during the war the majority of families would learn of a death via a letter from a stranger. Michael Roper and Jessica Meyer have considered the particular format and role of notification and condolence letters.[91] The distinct hierarchy in communications meant that the family of the common soldier might learn of the death of their loved one in the newspapers before the official letter arrived. Roper notes that parents of officers received a notification via telegram, a letter from the commanding officer and at least one other officer, followed by one or more personalised letters from non-combatant officers, batmen and soldiers serving in the platoon.[92] The 'break-the-news' letter had a set format, which began:

> _______________ Record Office,
>
> _______________ Station,
>
> ___ ___, 191__.
>
> Sir,
>
> It is my painful duty to inform you that a report has this day been received from the War Office notifying the death of
>
> (No.) ____________________ (Rank) ____________________
>
> (Name) ____________________ (Regiment) ____________________
>
> __________ which occurred at ______ on the _____ of ______, and I am to express to you the sympathy and regret of the Army Council at your loss. The cause of death was ______________________________

Although more personalised, condolence letters also followed an implicit set of guidelines, which Jay Winter summarises: 'the man in question was loved by his comrades; he was a good soldier; he died painlessly'.[93] If it was impossible for the writer to conceal the actual nature of the man's injury, the writer would instead emphasise 'the personal qualities he had shown in bearing up to pain'.[94] Meyer notes the distinction between letters written by the civil community (family, friends and business associates) and those written by the military community (officers and men who formed the unit, platoon or even regiment in which the dead man had served), suggesting that, '[w]here civil mourners offered the consolation of a worthy cause and noble sacrifice, military letters of condolence were more likely to commemorate the qualities of the soldier, such as martial ability and bravery, that the individual was claimed to have embodied.'[95] She notes, however, that both types of letters 'construct[ed] the dead as specifically heroic'.[96] Occasionally these condolence letters arrived before the formal notification letter, meaning that these unofficial letters simultaneously functioned as 'break-the news' letters – a genre with particular conventions in which young men were not always well-versed. As families would often write to 'anyone remotely connected to the time and place of death', including soldier servants, platoon sergeants, chaplains, orderlies and nurses, the previously middle-class practice of writing letters of condolence spread to all different classes, as Meyer notes.[97]

As the war continued, letters played an increasingly large role in the memorialisation of a man after his death. The means by which men would convey their sympathies via letter included demonstrating personal knowledge of the man and his family, including the reaction of the other men to his death, conveying something of the dead man's character and showing sensitivity to what his family might be feeling, telling the family where the son was buried, and recounting actions or events in which their son took part.[98] It was difficult if the man had only been in the platoon for a short time, but even 'perfunctory condolence' was highly valued by families, who would often have these letters typed out.[99] In some cases, condolence letters from soldiers would lead to 'long correspondences with the families of their dead comrades', with soldiers 'receiving parcels and letters from them in place of the dead son or brother'.[100] Meyer notes that civilians didn't have to know the dead individual in order to write a condolence letter, giving the example of the father of one soldier, whose professional acquaintances 'wrote to condole [him] over the loss of a young man they had never met'.[101] However, numerous combatant writers wrote about the emotional labour of writing these memorial letters home. Roper notes that not all letter-writers were as conscientious, and there were a number of reasons why some men avoided writing these letters as far as possible. Sometimes men were too upset by certain deaths to write themselves, and asked family members on the home front to visit the bereaved family and break the news in person instead. The sheer numbers of deaths also made individual letters of condolence problematic: '[m]ass death strained to breaking point the whole idea of the personal letter of condolence.'[102]

Memorial volumes, posthumous collections of letters, became increasingly prevalent throughout the war. Enough of these were published to form a genre in their own right, although these were largely restricted to private printing by upper-middle- and upper-class families which were circulated to family and friends.[103] The man's letters, sometimes from school as well as the war, were collected alongside commentaries and testimonials from ministers, teachers, peers and men who served with him in the war, organised usually by his mother or wife. The enormous body of writing left by many combatants through letters formed ready biographies, a consolation of sorts to families in the absence of bodies and the breakdown of earlier commemorative forms.

## Conclusion

Letters were enormously important during and after the First World War. The commitment of the authorities of all involved nations and the huge logistical efforts they made to provide a reliable and efficient wartime postal service demonstrates the significant role letters played in wartime culture, and underlines their understanding that this was key to maintaining high morale and support for the war. Although the letter format was not qualitatively different from peacetime, the war brought a new era of mass letter-writing which spanned age and class divisions, and provoked accompanying epistolary innovations: the establishment and implementation of mass censorship under DORA (prompting new epistolary codes as a means of avoiding the censor), the development of new official formal genres of the Field Service Postcard and the 'break-the-news' letter, and the development of the condolence letter. Through their seriality, wartime letters provided a means of marking and structuring time, of keeping constant the survival or death of a loved one. As the war continued and the death toll rose, letters became increasingly important as a memorial genre, as a readily available means of commemorating one individual through his own words and those of his friends.

Our contemporary readings of these fragile and fleeting acts of writing are made all the more poignant by our knowledge of the end of the serial exchange. It makes us pause when we read Owen's note in a letter to his mother that he had seen a notice for the Artists' Rifles, of Brittain's excitement for the Christmas she would not eventually spend with Leighton in 1915, or hints of Gurney's increasing mental illness which would overwhelm him after the war. For writers in particular, the letter form offered new opportunities for expression, and writers understood the intense comfort and reassurance that words from home could bring. In its manifestations of presence and absence, the physical and metaphorical distance between civilians and combatants, and its power to break lives, the humble letter became the single most representative object of the war's impact on not only writers, but ordinary people.

## Notes

1. Ivor Gurney, 'Letters', in *Severn & Somme* (London: Sidgwick & Jackson, 1917), p. 30.
2. Ibid.
3. Gurney to the Chapman family, 20 March 1916, in *Ivor Gurney: Collected Letters*, ed. R. K. R. Thornton (Ashington and Manchester: Mid-Northumberland Arts Group and Carcanet Press, 1991), p. 74.
4. Dedicated to the memory of GWR employees who died during the war, the Great Western Railway War Memorial was unveiled on 11 November 1922.
5. R. P. Weston and Bert Lee, 'Send Him a Cheerful Letter' (London: Francis, Day & Hunter, 1917). Sung by Miss Maie Ash.
6. Words by Joe Goodwin and Ballard MacDonald, music by James F. Hanley, 'Three Wonderful Letters from Home' (New York: Shapiro, Bernstein & Co., 1918). Other songs were explicitly written as letters, such as 'When the War Is Over Maggie: A Soldier's Letter from the Front', words by Cyrus B. Cuyler, music by John Ashton (London: E. Osborne & Co., 1915).

7. Charles Chaplin (dir.), *Soldier Arms* (US: First National Pictures, 1918).
8. Kate Pullinger and Neil Bartlett's 'Letter to an Unknown Soldier' project in 2014 invited members of the British public to send a personal message to a First World War soldier, represented by the memorial at Paddington Station.
9. In Britain, letters and postcards were free to send to and from the war zones during the war, but parcels were not. In France and Germany it was free to send letters (*Feldpostbriefe* in German), postcards and parcels to and from the war zones. I am grateful to John Horne, Benjamin Ziemann and Jay Winter for this information.
10. Margaretta Jolly, 'War Letters', in Jolly (ed.), *Encyclopedia of Life Writing: Autobiographical and Biographical Forms* (London: Fitzroy Dearborn, 2001), pp. 927–30 (p. 928); Alan Bishop and Mark Bostridge (eds), *Letters from a Lost Generation: The First World War Letters of Vera Brittain and Four Friends: Roland Leighton, Edward Brittain, Victor Richardson, Geoffrey Thurlow* (London: Virago, 2008; anniversary edition); Wilfred Owen, *Collected Letters*, ed. Harold Owen and John Bell (London: Oxford University Press, c. 1967); and *Ivor Gurney: Collected Letters*. For an example of previous readings of some of these letters, see Carol Acton, 'Writing and Waiting: The First World War Correspondence between Vera Brittain and Roland Leighton', *Gender & History*, 11 (1999), 54–83.
11. French studies: Martha Hanna, 'A Republic of Letters: The Epistolary Tradition in World War I France', *American Historical Review*, 108 (2003), 1,338–61, and *Your Death Would Be Mine: Paul and Marie Pireaud in the Great War* (Cambridge, MA: Harvard University Press, 2006); Martyn Lyons, 'French Soldiers and their Correspondence: Towards a History of Writing Practices in the First World War', *French History*, 17 (2003), 70–95. German studies: Philipp Witkop, *German Students' War Letters*, trans. A. F. Wedd, foreword by Jay Winter (1929; Philadelphia: Pine Street Books, 2002); Dorothee Wierling, 'Imagining and Communicating Violence: The Correspondence of a Berlin Family, 1914–1918', in Christa Hämmerle, Oswald Überegger and Birgitta Bader Zaar (eds), *Gender and the First World War* (Basingstoke: Palgrave Macmillan, 2014), pp. 36–51. American studies: Anne Powell, 'Another Welcome Letter: Soldiers' Letters from the Great War', *Contemporary Review*, 265 (1994), 254–60. Indian studies: David Omissi, 'Introduction', in Omissi (ed.), *Indian Voices of the Great War: Solders' Letters, 1914–18* (Basingstoke: Macmillan, 1999), pp. 1–22. Gender and intimacy studies: Kate Hunter, 'More than an Archive of War: Intimacy and Manliness in the Letters of a Great War Soldier to the Woman He Loved, 1915–1919', *Gender and History*, 25 (2013), 339–54; Jessica Meyer, *Men of War: Masculinity and the First World War in Britain* (Basingstoke: Palgrave Macmillan, 2009); Michael Roper, *The Secret Battle: Emotional Survival in the Great War* (Manchester: Manchester University Press, 2009). Class studies: Lucie Matthews-Jones, '"I still remain one of the old Settlement boys": Cross-Class Friendship in the First World War Letters of Cardiff University Settlement Lads' Club', *Cultural and Social History* (2016), <http://dx.doi.org/10.1080/14780038.2016.1202011> (last accessed 21 October 2016). For French-language studies see, for example, Clémentine Vidal-Naquet, *Couples dans la Grande Guerre: Le tragique et l'ordinaire du lien conjugal* (Paris: Les Belles Lettres, 2014), and Vidal-Naquet (ed.), *Correspondances conjugales: 1914–1918: Dans l'intimité de la Grande Guerre* (Paris: Laffont, 2014). For German-language studies see, for example, Bernd Ulrich, *Die Augenzeugen: Deutsche Feldpostbriefe in Kriegs- und Nachkriegszeit 1914–1933* (Essen: Klartext, 1997); Aribert Reimann, 'Die heile Welt im Stahlgewitter: Deutsche und Englische Feldpost aus dem Ersten Weltkrieg', in Gerhard Hirschfeld, Hans P. Ullman, Gerd Krumeich and Dieter Langewiesche (eds), *Kriegserfahrungen: Studien zur Sozial- und Mentalitätsgeschichte des Ersten Weltkriegs* (Essen: Klartext, 1997), pp. 129–45; Hans-Joachim Anderson and Horst Borlinghaus, *Die Deutsche Feldpost im Ersten Weltkrieg 1914–1918: Handbuch und Katalog* (Münster: Geschäftsstelle der ArGe Dt. Feldpost 1914–1918, 2000); Veit Didczuneit, Jens Ebert and Thomas Jander (eds), *Schreiben im Krieg, Schreiben vom Krieg: Feldpost im Zeitalter der Weltkriege* (Essen: Klartext, 2011).

12. Liz Stanley, 'The Epistolarium: On Theorizing Letters and Correspondences', *Auto/Biography*, 12 (2004), 201–35; Margaretta Jolly and Liz Stanley, 'Letters as / Not a Genre', *Life Writing*, 2.2 (2005), 91–118; Sarah Poustie, 'Re-Theorising Letters and "Letterness"', *Olive Schreiner Letters Project: Working Papers on Letters, Letterness & Epistolary Networks*, 1 (2010), 1–50.
13. Stanley, 'The Epistolarium', p. 221.
14. Ibid., p. 214.
15. Leighton to Brittain, 12 April 1915, *Letters from a Lost Generation*, p. 80.
16. Brittain to Leighton, 15 April 1915, *Letters from a Lost Generation*, p. 81.
17. Stanley, 'The Epistolarium', p. 212; Leighton to Brittain, 20–21 April 1915, *Letters from a Lost Generation*, p. 86.
18. Brittain to Leighton, 17 April 1915, *Letters from a Lost Generation*, p. 83.
19. Roper notes: 'The volume of mail sent home by the British Army on the Western Front kept increasing during the war and by 1917 over eight million letters were being sent each week, an average of nearly one a day for each soldier based in France.' *The Secret Battle*, p. 50.
20. Ibid., p. 52.
21. Brittain to Leighton, 7 May 1915, *Letters from a Lost Generation*, p. 96.
22. Roper, *The Secret Battle*, p. 53.
23. Brittain to Leighton, 11 May 1915, *Letters from a Lost Generation*, p. 99.
24. My thanks to Tony Allen of ww1postcards.com for providing the image and information about this postcard.
25. See David Vincent, *Literacy and Popular Culture: England 1750–1914* (Cambridge: Cambridge University Press, 1989) and *The Rise of Mass Literacy: Reading and Writing in Modern Europe* (Cambridge: Polity Press, 2000), and Martyn Lyons, *The Writing Culture of Ordinary People in Europe, c. 1860–1920* (Cambridge: Cambridge University Press, 2013).
26. Roper, *The Secret Battle*, p. 56.
27. Ibid., p. 55.
28. Ibid., p. 57. There were few, if any, comprehensive letter-writing manuals published during the war in Britain. Wartime letter-writing guidance was therefore most likely obtained from magazine and newspaper articles and from other people. I am grateful to Eve T. Bannet for her advice on this topic.
29. See Peter Doyle, *British Postcards of the First World War* (Oxford: Shire, 2010), for contemporary parodies of the Field Service Postcard.
30. Leighton to Brittain, 26 March 1915, *Letters from a Lost Generation*, p. 62.
31. Ibid.
32. Owen to Susan Owen, 1 January 1917, *Collected Letters*, p. 421.
33. Leighton to Edward Brittain, 27 April 1915, *Letters from a Lost Generation*, p. 91.
34. Guy Chapman, *A Passionate Prodigality: Fragments of Autobiography* (London: Ivor Nicholson & Watson, 1933), pp. 59–60.
35. Leighton to Brittain, *Letters from a Lost Generation*, 26 March 1915, p. 62, and 29 April 1915, p. 93.
36. Vera Brittain, *Testament of Youth: An Autobiographical Study of the Years 1900–1925* (1933; London: Penguin, 2005), p. 151. *Green Envelopes*, ed. Anonymous (London: John Murray, 1929).
37. Onoto Pen, *Land & Water*, 30 March 1916, p. xv. I am very grateful to Andrew McCarthy for alerting me to these adverts and providing copies of them.
38. Onoto Pen, *Land & Water*, 6 November 1915, p. 20.
39. Onoto Pen, *The Times*, 6 December 1915, p. 4.
40. Onoto Pen, *Land & Water*, 27 November 1915, p. 23.
41. Venus Pencils, *Punch*, 27 September 1916, p. xxii.

42. Swan Fount Pen advert, *Land & Water*, 27 November 1915, outside back cover.
43. Waterman's Ideal Fountain Pen, *Punch*, 29 May 1916, p. xi.
44. Swan Fount Pen advert, *Land & Water*, 10 August 1916, p. xxv.
45. Swan Fount Pen advert, supplement to *Land & Water*, 11 April 1918, p. vi.
46. Waterman's Ideal Fountain Pen, *The Graphic*, 25 November 1916 (n.p.).
47. Swan Fount Pen advert, *Punch's Almanack for 1915*, published late 1914 (n.p.).
48. Gurney to the Chapman family, 29 June 1915, *Collected Letters*, p. 26.
49. Gurney to Marion Scott, 28 June 1915, *Collected Letters*, p. 25.
50. Leighton to Brittain, 18 October 1914, *Letters from a Lost Generation*, p. 33.
51. Gurney to Marion Scott, 28 June 1915, *Collected Letters*, p. 25.
52. Leighton to Brittain, 1–3 May 1915, *Letters from a Lost Generation*, pp. 94–5.
53. Leighton to Brittain, 3 April 1915, *Letters from a Lost Generation*, p. 71.
54. Leighton to Brittain, 7–9 April 1915, *Letters from a Lost Generation*, p. 73.
55. Leighton to Brittain, 12 April 1915, *Letters from a Lost Generation*, p. 77.
56. Leighton to Brittain, 12 April 1915, *Letters from a Lost Generation*, p. 78.
57. Stanley, 'The Epistolarium', p. 208.
58. Brittain to Leighton, 17 April 1915, *Letters from a Lost Generation*, p. 83.
59. Brittain to Edward Brittain, 18 April 1915, *Letters from a Lost Generation*, p. 84.
60. Gurney to the Chapman family, February 1915, *Collected Letters*, p. 15.
61. Leighton to Brittain, 1–3 May 1915, *Letters from a Lost Generation*, p. 94.
62. Gurney to the Chapman family, 9 March 1915, *Collected Letters*, p. 16.
63. Gurney to Mrs Voynich, late September 1915, *Collected Letters*, p. 44.
64. Leighton to Brittain, 16 November 1914, *Letters from a Lost Generation*, p. 36.
65. Gurney to Mrs Matilda Chapman, 21 April 1915, *Collected Letters*, p. 18.
66. Owen to Harold Owen, 23 September [1914], *Collected Letters*, p. 285.
67. *Green Envelopes*, pp. 5–6.
68. Laurence Housman (ed.), *War Letters of Fallen Englishmen* (1930; New York: E. P. Dutton, n.d.), p. 8.
69. Brittain to Leighton, 1 April 1915, *Letters from a Lost Generation*, p. 66.
70. Brittain to Leighton, 20 April 1915, *Letters from a Lost Generation*, p. 85.
71. Brittain to Leighton, 1 May 1915, *Letters from a Lost Generation*, p. 96.
72. Leighton to Edward Brittain, 13 May 1915, *Letters from a Lost Generation*, p. 101.
73. Jolly, 'War Letters', p. 928.
74. Leighton to Brittain, 14 December 1914, *Letters from a Lost Generation*, pp. 39–40.
75. Brittain to Leighton, 25 April 1915, *Letters from a Lost Generation*, pp. 88–9.
76. Brittain to Leighton, 7 May 1915, *Letters from a Lost Generation*, p. 96.
77. Brittain to Leighton, 7 May 1915, *Letters from a Lost Generation*, p. 97.
78. Leighton to Brittain, 30 November–3 December 1914, *Letters from a Lost Generation*, p. 37; Leighton to Brittain, 7 January 1915, *Letters from a Lost Generation*, p. 46.
79. Leighton to Brittain, 15 February 1915, *Letters from a Lost Generation*, p. 55.
80. Leighton to Brittain, 7 April 1915, *Letters from a Lost Generation*, p. 73.
81. Brittain to Leighton, 11 April 1915, *Letters from a Lost Generation*, pp. 75–6.
82. Leighton to Brittain, 9 May 1915, *Letters from a Lost Generation*, p. 98.
83. Brittain to Leighton, 13 May 1915, *Letters from a Lost Generation*, p. 101.
84. Owen to Susan Owen, 4 April 1915, *Collected Letters*, p. 329.
85. Owen to Susan Owen, 5 March 1915, *Collected Letters*, p. 326.
86. Owen to Susan Owen, 11 August 1914, *Collected Letters*, p. 275.
87. Owen to Susan Owen, 14 October 1914, *Collected Letters*, p. 287; Owen to Mary Owen, 29 October 1914, *Collected Letters*, p. 291.
88. Owen to Susan Owen, 8 January 1915, *Collected Letters*, p. 312.
89. Gurney to F. W. Harvey, February 1915, *Collected Letters*, p. 13.

90. Owen to Susan Owen, 2 December 1914, *Collected Letters*, p. 300.
91. See Roper, 'Love and Loss', in *The Secret Battle*, pp. 205–42, and Meyer, 'Remembering the Heroic Dead: Letters of Condolence', in *Men of War*, pp. 74–96.
92. Roper, *The Secret Battle*, p. 215.
93. Jay Winter, *Sites of Memory, Sites of Mourning: The Great War in European Cultural History* (1995; Cambridge: Cambridge University Press, 2008), p. 35.
94. Roper, *The Secret Battle*, p. 214.
95. Meyer, *Men of War*, p. 75.
96. Ibid., p. 96.
97. Ibid., p. 79.
98. Roper, *The Secret Battle*, pp. 210–11.
99. Ibid., p. 212.
100. Meyer, *Men of War*, p. 78.
101. Ibid., p. 76.
102. Roper, *The Secret Battle*, p. 212.
103. Ibid., p. 223. See, for example, Denis Oliver Barnett, *In Happy Memory: His Letters from France and Flanders, October 1914–August 1915* (Stratford-upon-Avon: Privately printed, 1915), of which 150 copies were printed; Charles Gordon Jelf, *Charles Gordon Jelf: Born June 8, 1886; Killed in Action October 13, 1915* (Oxford: Printed for private circulation, 1915); Harold Leslie Rayner, *Letters from France, July 26, 1915 to June 30, 1916*, selected by his mother (London: Printed for private circulation by John Bale, Sons & Danielsson, 1919).

# 6

# Transnational Lives: Colonial Life Writing and the First World War

*Anna Maguire*

> A regiment comes swinging up the narrow old street on its way to a forward area. British it obviously is, for the khaki is that of the soldiers who throng the streets, but there is an unusual aspect about them which renders them at once objects of interest to both the British Tommy and the French civilian, blasé as they are both apt to be to the presence of troops marching through their midst. They are coloured men.[1]

Remembering a small French village indelibly changed by the presence of war, army padre Reverend A. E. Horner set the scene for the main actors in his published account of his war experience: the West Indian men who served in his battalion of the British West Indies Regiment during the First World War. The First World War, and the Western front in particular, most popularly known in literature from the trench lyrics of the soldier-poets, also inspired expressions of war experience and war's memory from colonial authors.[2] Among these colonial troops were men from the West Indies, who filled the pages of Horner's memoir, and whose lives can be traced through his text and other occasions of life writing that offer glimpses into West Indian experiences of war.

Over four million non-white troops were mobilised by the Allied Forces during the First World War. Britain drew heavily from her Empire to fulfil the manpower demands of industrialised warfare, sending troops, nurses, doctors and padres across the world. India contributed the largest number of men, approximately 1.4 million. Another 1.3 million were recruited from the settled dominions – Australia, New Zealand, Canada, Newfoundland and South Africa – including their indigenous populations. More troops came from the West Indies and from China, as well as Africans mobilised as soldiers and labourers, or carriers during the fighting in German imperial territories. Colonial troops saw service on the Western front, in the Dardanelles, and in Salonika, Egypt, Palestine, and East and West Africa. On the war's outbreak, the West India Regiment, a professional unit, was stationed in Sierra Leone and Cameroon. Raised originally in 1795 from the slave population, the Regiment had served in many British campaigns, including the Napoleonic Wars.[3] During the First World War, many more West Indians wanted to volunteer their services, expressing loyalty to the Empire. Black West Indian intellectuals, like Theophilus Marryshow, felt black participation might contribute to political reforms and equality.[4] The British government was reluctant, however, to arm black troops, drawing on martial races theory and racialised assumptions about masculinity.[5] It was feared that deploying black men would imply equality with white men, since the black West Indians would be serving alongside them as equals and would be killing primarily a white enemy. Some West Indians travelled to Britain to enlist, with varying success. But demand from the West Indies and extensive losses necessitated further recruitment. After months of negotiations, including intervention by King George V, the British West Indies Regiment (BWIR) was established in October 1915.[6] Half of those who volunteered for the BWIR were dismissed as unfit. In the end around 16,000 men served in the BWIR, mostly from Jamaica.[7] They underwent military training but were not allowed to fight in Western Europe, where they served from 1916 to the end of the war. Instead the BWIR performed labour duties, though evidence suggests some were involved in active combat in Egypt, in 1916–17, and Palestine, in 1917–18, where their enemy was mostly men of colour, and therefore the BWIR's deployment was considered less challenging to a racially understood imperial authority.[8]

The vast colonial experience of the First World War has often been missing from remembered narratives in both academic investigation and public commemorations. Those from the white dominions who served have been more readily included than the Indians, Chinese or West Indians alongside whom they lived and worked. The number of archived collections of white dominion letters and diaries from the First World War, such as those held in the Imperial War Museum or in national collections, has inevitably increased the depth and variety of research into their experience. Seeking out West Indian evidence written by West Indians is considerably harder, with no archived collection of private papers available, resulting from racially biased collecting practices as well as lower literacy rates among non-white recruits. The BWIR was also a much smaller regiment than the ANZAC forces, who numbered hundreds of thousands. The paucity of letters and diaries written by non-white colonial troops and the predominant absence of published literary accounts requires casting a wide net to trace the lives of these West Indian men and to engage with their accounts of the war.

Though life writing remains 'a contentious term covering a wide range of texts and forms', its encompassing nature means the fragmented archive of West Indian war writings, and that of colonial troops more generally, can be drawn together to attempt to explore personal experiences of the First World War.[9] As readers, researchers and writers of lives, we can move across the 'generic borders' of these texts, just as many life writers have previously done, enabling us to locate aspects of colonial experience within letters, diaries, newspapers, published memoirs, biographies and autobiographies, and in fiction.[10] Frequently the traces of West Indian lives are transitional; the texts give very little sense of the whole life lived. Yet, as work on modernist autobiography has shown, framing this recovery work through periods of emotional intensity such as the First World War can help focus what is trying to be understood.[11] Drawing on the model of Santanu Das's recovery of the 'private, tremulous life of the sepoy' rather than the whole 'life trajectory of any particular sepoy or the collective biography of Indian war experience', this chapter investigates the personal experience of West Indian soldiers during the life-altering and potentially life-defining period of war.[12]

This chapter takes three case studies, two of which are largely unknown to the general reader, to investigate different genres of West Indian life writing during the war: the published account of army chaplain Alfred Horner, *From the Island of the Sea: Glimpses of a West Indian Battalion in France* (1919); newspaper extracts of published letters from men serving in the British West Indies Regiment, predominantly from 1916; and Claude McKay's novel *Banjo: A Story without a Plot* (1929). Of these three case studies, Horner's book and the letter extracts sit outside the literary canon, with little, if any, intention to be literary at all. The chapter will investigate the glimpses of West Indian war experience within these texts in what Hermione Lee has described as 'moments of intimacy, revelation or particular inwardness' that draw the reader into the life being written.[13] The First World War, as a time of global mobilisation, created new spaces for encounter, exchange and transnationalism that reverberated through colonial life writing long after the war's end. The implications for reconsidering other types of life writing of the First World War as sites of archived instances of colonial experience through the framework of encounter will be shown. This particularly relates to Horner's text, as an example of a white account informing us of black West Indian experience. The afterlife of these texts, including their accessibility for contemporary audiences, will be addressed, before an examination of Andrea Levy's short story *Uriah's War* (2014) as fiction built from fragments.

## Glimpsing a West Indian Battalion in France: Reading Encounters in Published Stories of War

Among the literary outpourings published immediately following the war were first-hand testimonies of experience, not restricted solely to those with combatant experience but including nurses and padres. Alfred Egbert Horner was the Senior Chaplain to the 9th Battalion of the British West Indies Regiment. He wrote *From the Island of the Sea*, a short pamphlet of sixty-eight pages, published by the Guardian Office, Nassau, in Barbados on 19 July 1919, to correspond with Peace Day, drawing on articles he had previously published in the *Nassau Tribune*. It would be fair to assume that the booklet had limited circulation and, as far as is known at present, it exists only in one edition. Horner had been born to Anglo-Irish parents, educated in the army, and was posted to the Bahamas as Rector of St John's.[14] Another West Indian padre, John Ramson, made reference in the introduction to his own book to fifty-four men from the Bahamas accompanied by their own padre, who was a combatant officer, suggesting he and Horner were on the same ship.[15] Horner borrowed material from Ramson's text and paid tribute to 'that excellent booklet "Carry On" from which some of my material has been gathered' (*FIS*, 4). While there was shared experience and intertextuality between the two chaplains' accounts, Ramson was more focused on his personal service, reflecting on his men circumstantially rather than as the central motivation we find in Horner's text.

*From the Island* falls somewhere between anthropological study, biography and autobiography, a collection of essays and observations, full of anecdotes and commentary about the West Indian men he served with and his own personal reflections. It included extracts not only from John Ramson, but quotes from various officers who served alongside the BWIR. Horner never intended his short book to have any great literary value. He prefaced the book with a disclaimer of sorts for the mismatched way in which the text had been constructed:

> These articles are the gathering together of various rough notes and letters, scribbled in all sorts of odd places and amidst many distractions. At the request of the *Nassau Tribune* I permitted them to be published serially, and now I have been requested to permit them to be published in book form. I have consented, but they must go as they are, with all their imperfections and lack of literary correctness. (*FIS*, 1)

The 'gathering together' of stories and reflections from odd places may well epitomise the activity of the literary biographer, but Horner did not categorise himself as such, and *From the Island* sits outside any recognised literary canon of war writing. But the window granted through the life writing of Alfred Horner does not necessitate literariness in its valuable representation of West Indians during the First World War. As one of the few places where these lives were written, its uniqueness demands its acknowledgement and inclusion in a cultural if not literary canon of war writing.

Horner was a mediator of West Indian experience in France, chaperoning his men in his capacity as army chaplain and negotiating how he in turn represented their experience to his readers. He was aware that he was distilling this information to numerous audiences and saw his role as a conduit; in his first pages he wrote that 'in presenting these few lines for what I may term Home consumption, I am immediately conscious the entire first chapter must be re-written' (*FIS*, 1). Horner perceived that the text would have to fulfil the expectations of both West Indian and British audiences in his descriptions of his West Indian battalion at war, and that these could be conflicting, as home pride met imperial control. Horner was also operating within his own internalised colonialism as a white British man who had travelled to the West Indies as a missionary. As a result, *From the Island* carefully negotiates between maintaining colonial preconceptions about West Indians and the relation of brave deeds and praise for the men, which challenged how they could be perceived. Tributes to the martial abilities of the men – 'do not think, though, for a single second that we had become mere labourers and had lost either our military style or our military bearing' (*FIS*, 39) – and praise of their 'splendid physical proportions' (*FIS*, 8) appear alongside lamentations about their lack of discipline, 'smartness, neatness, and above all, punctuality' as to be 'expected' (*FIS*, 7). Horner positions himself as the ultimate insider, moving between 'we' and 'they' in his reference to the men. He was close enough to the West Indians with whom he served to be immensely knowledgeable of their character, sentiments and experience, but sufficiently removed to make discerning, and at times racist, observations.

What is evidenced in the published memoirs of colonial troops and servicepeople while the war was ongoing and in its immediate aftermath is the bearing of war's global nature on their experience. Their texts offer an opportunity to explore the First World War as a moment of encounter, where the interactions and relationships, formed across divisions of race, ethnicity, nationality, class and gender, that war had occasioned were archived in written form. In *From the Island*, one of Horner's key themes is the presentation of the First World War as a period of transnationalism, when both he and the BWIR men encountered new peoples and places. His extensive descriptions of the charming way in which the West Indian men befriended other colonial troops, nurses and doctors in hospitals, and British and French civilians seem intended to please his West Indian audience, as well as negate any sense of threat that these men of colour might pose to the whiteness of Western Europe, particularly white women.

> Before night-fall the little estaminets and coffee-houses will be found to contain these men, fraternizing in a wonderful way with the French civilians, telling them of their sunny home in broken French, which they pick up quickly, making themselves useful, and generally, by their quiet and respectful demeanour, earning for themselves the sobriquet which I have mentioned above, 'the friendly (or amiables) coloured soldiers.' Nor is that all: there will be scarcely a canteen belonging to the troops quartered there which does not contain a few of our men establishing friendly relations and exchanging experiences. (*FIS*, 4)

The broader context of the booklet's publication after the return of the British West Indies Regiment, particularly following the Taranto Mutiny of 1918 and the various racial discriminations on individual and institutional levels to which the West Indians were subjected during the war, made the promotion of 'friendly relations' across races significant. Acts of racialised discrimination from the West Indian men were accounted for; Horner would highlight that 'with the ordinary native labour corps, particularly the Chinese, our men do not agree very well', but this was attributed to their comparative elite status as soldiers rather than labourers, of which fact they were proud (*FIS*, 51). Horner's representation, though, was of his battalion as transnational actors, comfortable in the new situations in which war placed them.

Colonial life writing from the midst of the conflict also reflected on the effect that the war would have on the future of the British Empire. Colonial troops would have been exposed to Horner's despatches from the frontline from which he later compiled his booklet, and these were frequently hopeful about new links that this international conflict would forge. Gratitude was expressed for how the West Indian men were received with welcome and friendship in the 'mother-country' of England:

> Women, daughters and men of England, on behalf of our dusky lads from over the seas a poor wanderer thanks and salutes you. Unknown to yourselves, on that day you forged another priceless link in that golden chain of affection which binds the Empire together. Through your deeds and cheers came the thanks of the great mother-land; and as I remember the gratitude, simple yet really true, of our West Indian lads which your sympathy evoked. (*FIS*, 14)

West Indian stretcher bearing on the Western front would in Horner's view strengthen the brotherhood of Empire, 'for possibly some lad from a far distant clime, of another race, may remember with sympathy and affection the day when our West Indian coloured lads carried him out of danger to life and to health' (*FIS*, 36). The friendship cemented between British Tommies and the West Indian men in the canteens and barracks he hoped would 'bring forth its fruit yet in the great reorganization of Empire which must take place after the war' (*FIS*, 21). In his representation of these encounters and his own reflections about the consequences, Horner was attempting to shape the future of the British Empire through his life writing. The promotion of friendship, tolerance and equality, as well as the predominance he allowed the West Indian men in their achievements and behaviour, spoke more of his own idealistic and privileged perceptions of the potential of war to destabilise and ultimately remove unequal imperial hierarchies than of realities.

*From the Island* not only traces the lives of West Indian men, but also allows Horner's experience of war to come to the fore in his choice of representation. Despite determinedly shifting the text's focus away from himself in the book's title and introduction, Horner's personal investment as author and life writer on behalf of these men is clear. As Max Saunders has reflected, to accept that 'no genre can escape the impress of the autobiographic means that no author can say a work isn't autobiographic'.[16] *From the Island* is subject to layers of projection and history in how its white British author chose to articulate his perceptions of the lives of these black men, separated from each other by race, age and colonial status, but brought together as they journeyed to and through the First World War. His life and lived experience of the war is the core around which the rest of the text is tethered; he was the named authority and storyteller acting as gatekeeper to these West Indian lives. His self-reflective subtitle, 'Glimpses of a West Indian Battalion in France', revealed the fragmented nature of the text, full of 'characteristic' anecdotes to exemplify the anonymised men, insightful but not comprehensive in its coverage. To use these glimpses to recover completely a single life trajectory of a member of the 9th Battalion, even just through the period of war, would be to misunderstand Horner's intention and scope. Rather, *From the Island* allows us to explore more fully how the West Indian experience of war impressed itself upon one of their companions through the conflict, and how he chose to record what happened.

## Lives Extracted: Newspaper Selections from West Indian Letters

Horner was not, of course, the only person serving with the British West Indies Regiment to try to communicate their experience in written forms. Diaries and letters written during the war have proved to capture vividly moments of emotional intensity or the everyday monotony of life at war. Collected letters written home from the frontline by men of the BWIR are distinctly absent from the archive, however. They must have been written, as glimpses of their epistles can be gleaned through their republication in newspapers. One can imagine and hope for careful stacks of old, yellowing envelopes, pencil fading on the outside, their contents cracking around edges folded long ago, in family homes. To find these would offer a more complete recovery of West Indian life writing. For now, however, I rely on the voices of West Indian men in the letters that they wrote that newspapers like the *Jamaica Times*, *The Daily Gleaner* (published in Kingston, Jamaica) and *The West Indian* (Grenada) chose to publish as part of their coverage of the events of the First World War.

The letters of the West Indian men published in West Indian newspapers pose problems for analysis. Including letters in the broader genre of life writing can be challenging in any case: as Margaretta Jolly and Liz Stanley's dialogue on letters suggests, letters can open up a new archive for those studying life writing, but present tension 'between the utilitarian and the aesthetic aspects of writing more generally'.[17] The letter-writer promises only to communicate with the reader, and a specific reader at that, the addressee, rather than the pact of 'truth' or sincerity agreed between the reader and writer of autobiography.[18] For many collections of archived letters, the conversation is preserved, or some sense is given in the extent of the letters held. The extracts from the West Indian newspapers remove many of the letters' functions in their selection for publication. The reciprocity of the correspondence is lost: there is no sense of the response to the letter, nor the person to whom it was addressed. Indeed, the intended reader becomes instead the person reading the newspaper rather than the recipient of the letter. The multi-purpose intent of these letters is reduced to single descriptions of certain aspects of these men's experience, which become artificially significant in their isolation as well as removing them from the structural convention of the letter.

Most problematic of all is the lack of a sense of the self divulged in this correspondence in its most basic terms. The men of the BWIR who wrote these letters are named, but very little autobiographical information is supplied. Moments, often solitary, of particular interest to the newspapers' readership, as decided by the respective editors, are all we are given to gain a sense of their person and voice. More than edited books of war letters where selections were made from a vast range, these letters were further reduced to quotations, read alongside another from a fellow regiment member, in the context of article columns usually named 'From Our Boys at the Front', collectivising and homogenising the experience. To try to make 'the whole figure out of body parts', to make any kind of coherent narrative for the men who often had only one letter published, is nearly impossible with so few documents existing.[19] The temporary and fleeting engagement that the newspapers enable us to have with these men, whose lives have been extracted in the selections of their letters, problematises their use as evidence in exploring the emotional experience of the war for the West Indian men.

The extracts chosen from the letters were often centred on key events that marked the induction of the British West Indies Regiment into the maelstrom of the global conflict. The West Indian newspapers all deemed that the arrival of the BWIR in England in early 1916 was of exceptional interest to their respective reading public, and the letters selected were often particularly reflective of the writer's reception by British people. In 'With Our Contingent Across the Ocean', Private G. J. Dadd of the First Contingent wrote at the very beginning of 1916 from Seaford, Sussex, where the men were encamped:

> As we passed the girls they cheered and threw kisses at us. The first place we stopped was North Tawton. The farmers ran out with bags of apples and gave us them. Each man had his hat and pockets filled. We passed other stations. Our next stop was at St David's Exeter, where we had free tea and cakes provided by the Mayor's wife. As she handed it she said, 'you are welcomed to England'.[20]

Private J. Gladstone, also quoted in the *Jamaica Times* slightly later in the year, echoed the welcome: 'The English folks do not know how to make enough of us they are so much infatuated. Soldiers have got an enormous amount of privileges.'[21] Private Alexander King wrote: 'one thing that strikes me is the manner in which we are appreciated and respected by the English people. You can just imagine how it makes us darkies feel at ease in our minds.'[22] The absence of racial tension and the open-hearted manner in which these men felt they were accepted appears repeatedly in the extracts: proof of the bond between imperial centre and colony, and assurance for those at home who were considering enlistment of their good treatment in the mother country. Unsurprisingly, extracts about time spent in London were equally full of praise; a second letter from Private Dadd in March 1916 named the city 'an earthly paradise', while Private Gladstone had proclaimed of London in February:

> Well, I must say that it is one of the God-blessed spots in this earth, the city of great scenes. Do you not feel that we Jamaicans have got and are still having fine opportunities? We used to sing of Tipperary and Piccadilly. It's a long way to Tipperary but thank God I've reached it.[23]

The overwhelming positivity of these selections, with complaints seemingly restricted to the cold British winter into which the men arrived, reveals more about editorial choices than the sincerity of the men; after all, they did not write with the intention of publication. The manipulation of these incomplete letters preserved by the press for purposes of propaganda and the reinforcement of colonialism can mar their reading, but the honest expressions of joy and relief, simply expressed or couched in language of biblically inspired reverence, cannot be disguised.

The complex emotional lives of these men were divulged in the short glimpses offered in the newspapers. Extracts, though incomplete, allow us to gain insight into instances of self-reflection and representation. The relief of acceptance in England speaks of apprehension, fear and anxiety in anticipation of arrival, of long, unsettled journeys full of waiting and imagining. There could also be disappointment and an opportunity to reflect on the imperially and racially determined inequalities in which the men operated. The diary of a Jamaican man of the Second Contingent was quoted from March 1916: 'Another thing which seems of great importance to a large proportion of the brave Jamaican boys, is that there are no black women in England, a probability to them which is some ways almost a fact (!) and which they dearly hoped for.'[24] Soldiers' appreciation and gratitude for the children in France who brought them news and 'come around and throw chocolates and cigarettes to the boys' was based on the fact that they were not allowed to go out of camp, an important disclosure about the racial discrimination they suffered that could be isolating and segregating.[25] The experience of their transnationalism and encounter with new and foreign peoples and places was communicated and reflected upon; Private A. Lester Sampson wrote that 'one hears all manner of tongues in Alexandria: Arabic, Maltese, Soudanise [*sic*], Persian, Italian and French, it makes one's ear ache to hear them at times.'[26] Lance-Corporal Cummins described his travels and exploration in Alexandria in May 1916: 'I have seen the River Nile and the catacombs and I know the place pretty well now.'[27] Rather than the generalising and homogenising 'boys' of Horner's writing, more sense of the men's agency as individuals, as people, can be found in the letter extracts.

## Transnational Spaces: Claude McKay's *Banjo: A Story without a Plot* (1929)

Claude McKay, the Jamaican poet and writer and seminal figure of the Harlem Renaissance, will be more familiar to the general reader than Alfred Horner or the various men of the BWIR who became published letter-writers in the newspapers of their homes. Born in Clarendon, Jamaica, in 1889, McKay was twenty-five years old and living in New York on the outbreak of war and did not experience war from the perspective of an enlisted soldier. His civilian status did not prevent him from being a global traveller, however, witnessing war's impact, and articulating how the global conflict shook the world. As McKay himself explained:

> The world was then a vast theatre full of dramatic events. The capital of the Empire was full of British and Allied officers and soldiers. And they and the newspapers impressed upon one the fact that the world was passing through a universal upheaval.[28]

His novels do not explicitly centre on the experience of the First World War, but McKay's writing, his languages of blackness, and the transnationalism of *Banjo* in the 'marvellous, dangerous, attractive, big, wide, open port' of Marseilles reverberate with what Michelle Ann Stephens has called 'the traces of discussions of nationality that were so prevalent in the discourse of modern political identity in the immediate period after World War I'.[29] His pioneering use of dialect gives an authentic sense of the West Indian voice often absent, or imitated by the likes of Alfred Horner, that more intensely evokes their lives.

McKay was a transnational and travelling black subject among the war's upheaval who was able to articulate the changing nationalist and internationalist cultures and politics of the early twentieth century from a unique position. He visited London in 1919, and in 1922 moved to Russia, where he spent six months. From Russia, he travelled to Germany and France, including a spell in Marseilles where he found casual work among the dockers, the society he would articulate so vividly in *Banjo*. McKay sought to combat empire and racism within his writings, though he must also be understood as a colonial Jamaican who had, to some degree, internalised colonialist discourse. The tensions in his Atlantic identity should be traced in his texts, registering 'the force and power of colonial discourse and race theory' at the same time as they are opposed in his writing.[30] Employing the 'explicitly transnational and intercultural perspective' of black Atlantic theory in the understanding of McKay's texts allows us to explore race and modernity in a way 'which renders the modern experience in new culturally contingent and, sometimes, inclusive forms'.[31]

*Banjo: A Story without a Plot* (1929) was McKay's second novel following *Home to Harlem* (1928). *Banjo* follows the lives of a group of unemployed black seamen in the major port of Marseilles in the 1920s, their camaraderie, their discussions of home and their encounters with the port's diverse and transient population. Amongst them is Ray, the war veteran wanderer from *Home to Harlem*, now come to Europe. Critics have appraised the novel as a considerable ideological move, in which the 'ambiguity that marked his affinity with his race in the earlier writings has [. . .] resolved into lucid race solidarity'.[32] Particularly of note is the way that the French people, including the police, treat the men of colour in the text. McKay's ideological evolution informed the modernist structure of the novel – without plot – and the views expressed by his characters. *Banjo* was not, however, a commercial success as *Home to Harlem* had been, perhaps a result of the unfamiliar locale of the book's setting and its technical faults as a novel.[33]

Reading *Banjo* as 'an alternative, lost story of global modernity', of the transnational story of black people, allows the implications of the First World War's travel, exploration, encounter and exchange to come to the fore through the fictionalised life writing of one West Indian traveller.[34] Like *From the Island of the Sea* and many of the letters of the West Indian servicemen, *Banjo*, too, offered a predominantly male, exclusive perspective (excepting the character Latnah), which 'characterizes the alternative, mobile, free community figured in McKay's motley and transnational black "crew"'.[35] If tracing male transnational lives in colonial life writing is problematic, then locating colonial women as actors within these narratives is almost impossible – a result of the gendered nature of combatant service for the West Indians writing home or, in McKay's case, part of the gendered context for the process of identity formation for the black diaspora, which Stephens has explored more fully.[36]

From the outset, the spaces of Marseilles – the beach, the Ditch, Boody Lane, the Bum Square – are presented as hubs of transnational activity as a result of the many different seamen, employed or not, who stopped on its streets, echoing the remnants of war's presence in the city.

> They were all on the beach, and there were many others besides them – white men, brown men, black men. Finns, Poles, Italians, Slavs, Maltese, Indians, Negroids, African Negroes, West Indian Negroes – deportees from America for violation of the United States immigration laws – afraid and ashamed to go back to their own lands, all dumped down in the great Provençal port, bumming a day's work, a meal, a drink, existing from hand to mouth, anyhow any way, between box car, tramp ship, bistro and bordel.[37]

Though the men were predominantly seamen looking for casual work, rather than veteran soldiers, this description could have been of the amassed troops of the British and French Empires who passed through the port on their way to and from the Western front: the Egyptian Labour Corps, the South African Native Labour Corps, the British West Indies Regiment. McKay's descriptions of bars where 'Senegalese, Sudanese, Somalese, Nigerians, West Indians, Americans, blacks from everywhere, crowded together, talking strange dialects' capture the sense of solidarity between these nationally diverse black men, while they simultaneously recall French estaminets and cafés where colonial troops mingled during the war. As Ray emerges in the book's second part, he perceives the ways of Marseilles as 'vividly significant of the great modern movements of life'.[38] As 'Europe's best back door', Marseilles was historically transnational for sailors and soldiers alike.[39]

While the First World War is never explicitly referenced, the way black men were treated during the conflict and in its aftermath is briefly touched on in *Banjo*. During his time in Marseilles, Ray makes the acquaintance of an unnamed white Englishman. In conversation with him, Ray describes going to Germany at a time when black French troops were stationed in the Ruhr:

> A big campaign of propaganda was on against them, backed by German-Americans, Negro-breaking Southerners, and your English liberals and Socialists. The odd thing about the propaganda was that it said nothing about the exploitation of primitive and ignorant black conscripts to do the dirty work of one victorious civilization over another, but it was all about the sexuality of Negroes – that strange, big bug forever buzzing in the imagination of white people.[40]

While this is part of a longer story about how Ray was received with kindness by the German people, the reference to exploitation and 'dirty work' carried out by black conscripts should be noted. This politically driven text, in which McKay's distinct racialised solidarity was elucidated, carries within it the traces of the deployment of colonial troops during the war: their participation and the coercion and discrimination they faced. Just as the transnationalism of the spaces in which the war operated, and which the war created with its mass mobilisation of colonial servicemen around the world, reverberated through the port of Marseilles, so too the colonial exploitation and racism exacerbated during the war solidified McKay's desire to speak out against inequality and empire. *Banjo* offers resonances of McKay's own life experience as a West Indian transnational, and once again the partially recorded traces of West Indian lives during and after the First World War.

## The Afterlife of Colonial Life Writing

McKay's *Banjo* is not usually thought of as an example of First World War literary life writing. It records transitory experience, the global mobility of the early twentieth century and the subsequent transnational spaces opened up in the upheaval of the war. The inclusion of *Banjo* here in life writing tracing the lives of West Indians during the war relates in part to its much longer afterlife compared to the other examples given. *Banjo*, despite its initial lack of commercial success, has had multiple editions and reprints throughout the twentieth century and into the twenty-first, and gained recognition during the Black Power movement.[41] Moreover, it has become a frequent object of study for academic researchers in the fields of literary studies, history and black studies, as well as for philosophers and theorists of black Atlanticism, liberalism, modernism and cosmopolitanism.

While McKay's intellectual and literary credentials have long been recognised and his works rightfully lauded and preserved for the reading public, Alfred Horner's booklet existed in just one contemporary edition and is now available in only one public location in the UK, the British Library. Historians like Richard Smith and myself have made use of this text, but critical engagement does not near the level afforded to McKay's work. Similarly, the newspapers containing the letter extracts of the West Indian men are held in the British Library's collections. Finding the extracted letters requires patience and perseverance, scrolling through tens, if not hundreds, of rolls of microfilm to find half a column in one or two issues a month of a daily published newspaper. These are not texts of great literary worth, nor are they enduring. They are held in privileged institutions that are not as publicly accessible as one would like to think. The time and effort required to piece together these fragmented lives should be acknowledged along with their limited afterlife in the memory of colonial participation during the First World War.

The interdisciplinary and inclusionary technique of life-writing scholarship, moving from genre to genre, allows the parts of these colonial lives to be included in our understanding of West Indian experience of the First World War. Challenging the bounds of what is covered by biography or autobiography, published collections of observations, letters that have been edited for publication, or modernist fiction based on experience of travel offer an opportunity to explore elements of colonial lives that would otherwise remain undiscovered. The occurrence of war as a time for transnationalism is embodied in the life writing: arriving in new lands, meeting and building relationships with new people, exploring spaces of national and ethnic diversity. While they cannot offer a generalised history of West Indian men during the war, these documents allow us to touch their lives briefly and intimately, just for a moment, before their story moves on.

## 'No rifle, no combat, but just as likely to die': Andrea Levy's *Uriah's War* (2014)

The centenary commemorations have seen concerted efforts to ensure that the experiences of West Indian men, and other colonial troops of colour, are included in the war's commemoration. Exhibitions, lottery-funded community projects and documentaries like David Olusoga's BBC2 series *Forgotten Soldiers* have gone some way towards sharing these neglected histories with a wider public. It was for these same reasons that author Andrea Levy wrote her short story *Uriah's War* (2014), available exclusively in digital format. Levy had been surprised to learn recently from a relative that her grandfather had served with the British West Indies Regiment on the Western front; she did not believe that it was true – she had never heard of Jamaicans taking part in that war – until she began to do her own research. In her introduction she writes:

> The centenary of the outbreak of World War One made me want to add the experiences of West Indian troops to the record. The more I researched, the more I was struck by the patriotism and courage of the West Indian men who volunteered to fight for the British Empire.[42]

In her short story, Levy constructs a fictionalised narrative of two West Indian soldiers, Uriah and his friend Walker, who served together in the 1st Battalion of the BWIR in Palestine and Egypt: in the words of Levy's narrator, Uriah, war was 'our chance to show the British what black men can do'.[43] The story follows the men from their arrival in Seaford, and their deployment to Egypt and Palestine, where they distinguish themselves, to Taranto and the mutiny which curtails Uriah's narrative. The story's epilogue, written from Walker's perspective, reflects on the unfair discrimination against West Indian men and how their patriotism was insulted when, as he accuses the assumedly (white) British reader, 'you have failed to recognise our contribution'.[44] This is an emotionally and politically driven work: why were men like Levy's grandfather forgotten, and what can be done to make up for this failure?

Levy acknowledges Richard Smith's book *Jamaican Volunteers in the First World War* (2004) as a key source in her research: 'without it I would still not believe that my grandfather was at the Somme.'[45] Levy uses traces from current historiography, which itself features examples from the official record and elements of life writing, to construct a fictional piece that exemplifies elements of First World War experience. The intertextual relationship between her fiction and that of the primary source material employed by Smith shows literature's capacity to make a whole from fragmented parts. Levy's text is a form of life writing by proxy, a first-person narrative that draws on many lives, in an attempt to recover what had been forgotten, lost or deliberately ignored. As the centenary commemorates the lives of the First World War, *Uriah's War* will enable many more to access those whose lives are not represented in memorial, exhibition, textbook or lyric poem.

## Notes

1. A. E. Horner, *From the Island of the Sea: Glimpses of a West Indian Battalion in France* (Nassau: Guardian Office, 1919), p. 1. All further references made are to the edition cited, referred to as *FIS*, and will be provided parenthetically.
2. Santanu Das, 'Touching Semiliterate Lives: Indian Soldiers, the Great War, and Life-"Writing"', in Maria DiBattista and Emily O. Wittman (eds), *Modernism and Autobiography* (Cambridge: Cambridge University Press, 2014), p. 128.
3. British and Caribbean Veterans Association, 'We Were There: West Indians in the British Armed Forces', <http://bcva.weebly.com/we-were-there.html> (last accessed 31 October 2016).
4. Glenford Deroy Howe, *Race, War and Nationalism: A Social History of West Indians in the First World War* (London: Ian Randle, 2002), p. 17.
5. Richard Smith, *Jamaican Volunteers in the First World War: Race, Masculinity and the Development of National Consciousness* (Manchester: Manchester University Press, 2004), p. 40.
6. Ibid., p. 55.
7. Glenford Howe, 'Military Selection and Civilian Health: Recruiting West Indians for World War', *Caribbean Quarterly*, 44.3 (1998), 42.
8. Smith, *Jamaican Volunteers*, p. 90.
9. Max Saunders, *Self Impression: Life-Writing, Autobiografiction, and the Forms of Modern Literature* (Oxford: Oxford University Press, 2010), p. 4.
10. Ibid., p. 6.
11. DiBattista and Wittman, *Modernism and Autobiography*, p. xi.
12. Das, 'Touching Semiliterate Lives', p. 130.
13. Hermione Lee, *Body Parts: Essays on Life-Writing* (London: Chatto & Windus, 2005), p. 3.
14. 'Sudden Death of Canon A. E. Horner', *Ashton-under-Lyne Reporter*, 7 November 1952, p. 5.
15. John Ramson, *Carry On: or Pages from a Life of a West Indian Padre in the Field* (Kingston: 1918), p. 5.
16. Saunders, *Self Impression*, p. 3.
17. Margaretta Jolly and Liz Stanley, 'Letters as / Not a Genre', *Life Writing*, 2.2 (2005), 92.
18. Ibid.
19. Lee, *Body Parts*, p. 8.
20. 'Letters from Our Soldiers', *Jamaica Times*, 1 January 1916, p. 17.
21. 'Letters from Our Soldiers', *Jamaica Times*, 26 February 1916, p. 10.
22. '"Advance Jamaica" News of Our Soldiers', *Jamaica Times*, 8 January 1916, p. 6.
23. 'Letters from Our Soldiers', *Jamaica Times*, 25 March 1916, p. 11; 26 February 1916, p. 10.
24. 'Diary of Second Contingent in England', *The Daily Gleaner*, 4 March 1916, p. 4.
25. Private Norris Roach, 'From Our Boys', *The West Indian*, 9 November 1917, p. 2.
26. 'Letters from Our Soldiers', *Jamaica Times*, 27 May 1916, p. 6.
27. 'Letters from Our Soldiers', *Jamaica Times*, 27 May 1916, p. 6.
28. Claude McKay, *A Long Way from Home* (New Brunswick: Rutgers University Press, 1937), p. 52.

29. Claude McKay, *Banjo: A Story without a Plot* (New York: Harper & Brothers, 1929), p. 13; Michelle Ann Stephens, *Black Empire: The Masculine Global Imagery of Caribbean Intellectuals in the United States, 1914–1962* (Durham, NC, and London: Duke University Press, 2005), p. 5.
30. Len Platt (ed.), *Modernism and Race* (Cambridge: Cambridge University Press, 2011), p. 11.
31. Ibid., p. 9.
32. Kotti Sree Ramesh and Kandula Nirupa Rani, *Claude McKay: The Literary Identity from Jamaica to Harlem and Beyond* (Jefferson, NC, and London: McFarland & Company, 2006), p. 112.
33. Ibid.
34. Stephens, *Black Empire*, p. 169.
35. Ibid., p. 163.
36. Ibid., p. 168.
37. McKay, *Banjo*, p. 6.
38. Ibid., p. 69.
39. Ibid.
40. Ibid., p. 146.
41. The latest edition I have been able to find is the 2008 publication by Profile Books.
42. Andrea Levy, 'Introduction', *Uriah's War* (London: Tinder Press, 2014), n.p.
43. Levy, *Uriah's War*, p. 2.
44. Ibid., p. 10.
45. Levy, 'Introduction', n.p.

# II.

# Visual Arts

# 7

# The 'abysmal inexcusable middle class', Painting, Commemoration and the First World War

*Matthew C. Potter*

## Introduction

This chapter seeks to map the theoretical foundations of and transformations within the practice of painting in the wake of the First World War. It explores the afterlife of the Great War in the specific realm of painting in order to supplement the commonly held view that the conflict should primarily be considered as a catalyst for formal innovation amongst avant-garde artists. Without rejecting the war as an aesthetic driver, this chapter examines how it also inspired painters with more conservative stylistic agendas to invent new ways to capture their experiences of modern warfare as both personal 'eye-witness' accounts and deliberate acts of commemoration. The chapter begins by constructing a theoretical framework for these discussions. It explores the narratives produced by art historians that centre on avant-garde and establishment divisions within artworks produced in response to the First World War. The function of memorialising the conflict through painting is then considered in order to open up the particular investigation of three examples of 'conservative' painters who reflected upon the war through recording and transforming their experiences. Finally, the effect of the Great War on painters today, who have no direct experience of the conflict one hundred years on, will be considered in order to better understand the interactions of avant-garde and establishment artistic practice within the realms of the painting and commemoration of the First World War.

## The First World War, Commemoration and the Art World: A Theoretical Framework

Rightly or wrongly, painting has long been privileged as the primary medium within the history and practice of the fine arts, reinforced by the apogee of Romantic cultural values in the nineteenth century.[1] The First World War rocked the foundations of such assumptions because every aspect of the status quo deemed responsible for the catastrophe was questioned.[2] Clement Greenberg's *The Avant-Garde and Kitsch* (1939) arguably set the parameters for thinking about the fracturing of the avant-garde in the modern era, based on the original role it played in subverting the bourgeois 'establishment', and the subsequent 'crisis' he identified in a faction who sold out to the establishment by settling for the production of recycled 'kitsch' the existence of culture instead of true and innovative art forms.[3] Greenberg's observation regarding the existence of true and false artistic avant-gardes has evolved into the conventional wisdom within histories of modern art, that even if the First World War did not lead to the immediate death of 'establishment' painting, it awakened the avant-garde to the creative bankruptcy of its recent practice.[4] A renewal of interest in the First World War in the 1960s brought a postmodern critical perspective capable of subverting the polarising Greenbergian turn by producing two contradictory avant-garde components termed by Hal Foster as 'resisting' (critiquing) and 'reactionary' (conservative) postmodernism.[5]

Artists function much like historians regarding the intellectual 'tidying up' that occurs in post-war eras. From an available field of historical facts they select which ones to preserve or obscure, drawn from their own personal recollections as well as other available sources, and are affected just as much by live issues (ideological presence) as by the distortions involved in the passage of time (historiographical distance).[6] The postmodern effect is that the communal memory of important events like the First World War is fractured and multivalent. Contrasting interpretations by artists from the establishment and the avant-garde 'proper' are thus reconcilable within this historical model and equally valid as responses to the war. Their real difference arguably exists not in their forms but in their dependence upon the presence or absence of an infinite set of variables (e.g. horror, trauma, frustration and/or creative impulse) which may connect artists from the different camps just as effectively as it potentially divides those within the same group.

Wartime conditions impacted severely on all artists: the art market crashed at the outbreak of war as dealers and buyers ceased their activities.[7] Without state patronage the memorialisation of war and the dead would have been impossible as war pictures generally did not sell well on the private market.[8] In the United Kingdom state-sponsored painting featured in the portfolio of Wellington House (established July 1916), then the Department, and later Ministry, of Information (February 1918), as well as the Imperial War Museum (March 1917), the British War Memorial Committee (February 1918) and the abortive Hall of Remembrance project.[9] The work of these agencies was intimately connected to the Imperial War Graves Commission (IWGC, established May 1917 and renamed as the Commonwealth War Graves Commission, in 1960), and also the individual organisations of the other Allied nations: for example, the Canadian War Records Office (CWRO, established January 1915), the associated Canadian War Memorials Fund (CWMF, established November 1916), and the Australian War Record (AWR, established 1917 under British control but transferred to Australia in 1925).[10] These agencies aimed at public memorialisation through varied media in order to promote 'memory, mourning and catharsis'.[11] The level of intervention by officials in the creative process varied. Often artists were given free rein; however, in other cases, such as the AWR, artists were forced to follow strict directives using verifiable historical records in order to produce 'correct' official accounts, and were forced to make constant corrections if their interpretations were challenged by trusted 'experts' even many years later, such as the 1933–4 repainting of Septimus Power's *Saving the Guns at Robecq* (1920).[12]

The immediate effect of war was universally felt by all artists, no matter what their stylistic associations. It often offered an impediment to artistic creativity both emotionally (through the psychology of trauma) and logistically (with sketching artists being mistaken for spies, the disruptions of active service, and the absence of painting equipment).[13] The death toll amongst artists was also high, especially in the years before the war artist commissions which invariably removed artists from the dangers of frontline service: fatalities included August Macke (1887–1914), Henri Gaudier-Brzeska (1891–1915), Isaac Rosenberg (1890–1915), Franz Marc (1880–1916), Umberto Boccioni (1882–1916), Antonio Sant'Elia (1888–1916), Guillaume Apollinaire (1880–1918) and Raymond Duchamp-Villon (1876–1918); the 1918–19 Spanish influenza pandemic also killed Harold Gilman, Gustav Klimt and Egon Schiele.[14] Artistic networks were systematically disrupted, bringing the end of groups like Die Brücke and Der Blaue Reiter.[15] Additionally, the war produced cultural backlashes especially against the 'violent' modernist German 'Kubism' or 'Junkerism', as well as merchants of art supplies who possessed German names, leading many in the art world to anglicise their names, including George Grosz, John Heartfield, Charles Wolston and Ford Madox Ford.[16]

Not all artists were commissioned to produce official work, and of those who were, some were too old to undertake active service or else held traditional views of the function of war art. Other artists failed the physical examination necessary for recruitment despite their willingness to enlist. The overall impression of war art is its 'selectiveness': commissioned artists were often products of academic training, and while the war at home was featured (e.g. George Clausen, *In the Gun Factory at Woolwich Arsenal* (1918); Anna Airy's *The 'L' Press Forging the Jacket of an 18-inch Gun, Armstrong-Whitworth Works, Openshaw* (1918); Randolph Schwabe's *Voluntary Land Workers in a Flax-field* (1919)), certain campaigns, such as the war at sea, were relatively under-represented compared to battles like Gallipoli and the Somme.[17] Innovation was not always most obvious in formal aspects, but often more in subject matter during the First World War. The aristocratic nature of naval painting (dominated by officer portraits) was in sharp contrast to the more democratic developments that emerged in depictions of the army: Eric Kennington's *The Kensingtons at Laventie* (1915) has been claimed as the first truly democratic picture of the British 'Tommies'.[18]

The war's fracturing effect on the European avant-garde is undeniable.[19] Artists belonging to Foster's 'resisting' avant-garde category continued their pre-war activities after 1914. Despite the recoil from aggressive modernism, Gino Severini produced his Futurist *Armoured Train in Action* (1915). The disestablishmentarian reaction to the war also encouraged new paths, such as André Breton's surrealist developments, which were based on his observations of the perception-altering post-traumatic stresses of soldiers in 1915, and Pablo Picasso's life-size nudes, which were fuelled by his anti-war rage.[20] Many British modernists embraced documentary remits (e.g. Wyndham Lewis's *A Battery Shelled* (1918) or William Roberts's *A Shell Dump, France* (1918–19)). Stylistically, C. R. W. Nevinson embraced a traditional manner, whilst others like Paul Nash altered their styles, for example, resulting in not only the terrifying *We Are Making a New World* (1918) but also his surrealist *Landscape at Iden* (1929) which transmogrified the war dead into felled trees.[21] The visionary art of Guillaume Apollinaire survived the First World War even if he did not, and frequently avant-garde paintings were retrospectively re-inscribed with memorial meanings, including Vassily Kandinsky's *Fragment 2 for Composition VII* (1913), Franz Marc's *Tierschicksale* (*Animal Destinies* or *Fate of the Animals*) (1913), and

Henri Matisse's *French Window at Collioure* (1914).[22] The resisting impulse was arguably also evident outside of professional practice in the world of 'trench art' (a subject beyond the parameters of this present chapter). This shared characteristics with bricolage (the assemblage of art from available materials, e.g. in the use of found war objects in the work of Gaudier-Brzeska and André Derain). Decorative pseudo-sculptural assemblages of spent bullets and shrapnel perform remembrance functions, via the creation and collection of such objects, and the spread of such techniques beyond the 'high art' world of museums into domestic spaces generated a different and more democratic role for such art forms. Despite its usual exclusion as 'kitsch' from accounts of First World War art, 'trench art' thus arguably represented a more authentic and personal form of artistic memorialisation than painting.[23]

Foster's 'reactionary' avant-garde may perhaps be seen most prominently in the embracing of traditional subject matter and form as constituted in the post-war neo-classical 'return to order', which in turn built on the foundations laid by the Fauve movement.[24] Similar developments were afoot in Germany, where women artists combined formal innovation with traditional practice in manners that defied simple categorisations as conservative or avant-garde.[25] Likewise, the Neue Sachlichkeit (New Objectivity) movement straddled such categories: retaining the social use demanded of art by Greenberg, but often reviving old techniques to do so. Its critique of the pre-war establishment allowed Neue Sachlichkeit to reconcile alternate styles and political positions, accommodating the 'return to order' neo-classical right wing (such as Georg Schrimpf) as well as the Verist left wing (personified in Otto Dix and Grosz).[26] The conservative style of Rudolf Schlichter's *Margot* (1924) and Georg Scholz's *Female Nude with Plaster Bust* (1927) could belie their radical socio-political message – both contain prostitutes who subvert the 'establishment' associations of the professional business persona of *Margot* and the neo-classical ideals present in the *Female Nude*.[27] References to art historical models existed both via emulation of historic artists (e.g. Hans Holbein and Philipp Otto Runge) and also in their revival of old-fashioned media (like egg tempera and the use of wooden supports for paintings), all of which opened the Neue Sachlichkeit artist up to being labelled as 'kitsch'.[28]

## Commemoration and the Afterlife of the Great War in Painting

In terms of commemorative activity, references to the First World War abound in the Neue Sachlichkeit oeuvre, most famously via imagery of invalided veterans, as in Grosz's *Grey Day* (1921) or Dix's *Metropolis* (1927–8) which memorialise survivors whilst chastising society for its neglectful behaviour towards such people. Dix's *The Match Seller* (1920) and *The Skat Players* (1920) had even more rhetorical impact with their stark depictions of the maimed and marginalised German veterans. Following the marking of the tenth anniversary of the Great War, Weimar Germany was thrown into disarray by the Wall Street Crash of 1929. With the gradual rise of the Nazi party, many felt a renewed unease about the possible return of military conflict. German artists naturally recalled the horrors of 1914–18. Barthel Gilles's *Self-Portrait with Gas Mask* (1930) includes a Janus-faced apocalyptic vision simultaneously retrospective and prophetic – the gas mask is both a death's head *memento mori* and an invocation of his war service, whilst the burning city of Cologne in the background to the left invokes a potential future catastrophe.[29]

Yet the commemorative function of Neue Sachlichkeit paintings is arguably greatest in scenes depicting the war dead. Dix's fifty-print cycle of etchings *The War* (1924), published ten years after the start of the Great War, sought to undermine the hawkish idealisation of soldiers by displaying the realities of death and injury in war.[30] The impact of such imagery was greater once introduced into monumental paintings, such as Dix's composition of the same title (1929–32) (Plate 2), where the apocalyptic views could have greater psychological effects of abjection, as in Nash's *We Are Making a New World*. The polyptych format of the piece allowed multiple aspects of combat to be shown simultaneously whilst also engaging with the Gothic traditions of the visionary artist Matthias Grünewald.[31] The bottom 'predella' panel invokes the function of Renaissance altar decoration. Those early paintings prompted priests and others at the base of the altar to undertake intimate self-reflection. In an analogous fashion Dix may have been recalling his memories of the coffin-like confinement offered to the soldiers at rest in their bunkers. The work's critical success no doubt encouraged his *Flanders* (1934–6).[32]

The avant-garde fractures manifested themselves in Britain with Vorticist attacks on their more conservative colleagues: Wyndham Lewis used *Blast* to label Frank Brangwyn as a representative of the 'abysmal inexcusable middle class', and Edward Wadsworth was dismissive of Stanley Spencer.[33] Moreover, the more conservative British avant-garde has been continually set apart by historians from its more progressive European counterpart.[34] Such views have perpetuated ideas of continuity amongst certain art historical accounts, tracing a tradition of compromised modernism from the Pre-Raphaelite Brotherhood to the outbreak of the First World War and beyond, taking in the Camden Town Group, the figurative register of Nash, the post-war portraiture of Wyndham Lewis, and the neo-humanism of the Euston Road Group.[35]

Art historians have tended to argue that the representation of war casualties was more common in European avant-garde circles than British 'establishment' war art. A few exceptions are usually granted, such as William Orpen's *Dead Germans in a Trench* (1918), but their deliberate transgressions are excused due to their exclusive focus upon enemy fatalities.[36] While the point is valid regarding European artists like Dix, Grosz and Max Beckmann, depictions of death as a largely futile sacrifice also existed amongst Allied artists from the 'establishment', for example in Charles Spencelayh's *Who Dies if England Live?* (1914), William Lionel Wyllie's *Gallipoli: V-Beach and the fort of Sedd-el-Bahr, seen from the 'River Clyde', 25 April 1915* (1915), Maurice Cullen's *Dead Horse and Rider in a Trench* (1918), Fred Varley's *For What?* (1917) and C. R. W. Nevinson's *Paths of Glory* (1917), which famously received censure for its bleak and relentless portrayal of the costs of war.[37] William Orpen's *To the Unknown Soldier in France* (1921–8) continued this genre of painting after the end of the war, transforming it from a petitioning to a memorialising mode – albeit with a satirical interlude which briefly included cherubs and dead semi-draped soldiers acting as guards of honour, before they were painted out.[38] Henry Tonks enlisted in the Royal Army Medical Corps (1916–17) after his service as a Red Cross Orderly, and before assuming a commission as a war artist.[39] Tonks produced *An Advanced Dressing Station, France, 1918* (1918) for the abortive Hall of Remembrance project. Guided by his sense of decorum regarding what could be depicted in a public painting, Tonks removed explicit reference to the horrific injuries sustained by British soldiers, although his earlier sketches of facial reconstructions meant he was well aware of such matters.[40]

## Commemoration and 'Establishment' Art of the First World War

The work undertaken by establishment artists seeking new ways to commemorate their war experiences engages with the challenge of what Sue Malvern has described as 'the impossible project of History Painting' following the First World War.[41] These works are problematic for, despite Laura Brandon's assertion that aesthetics are less important than the personal observations of artists for the memory-making capacity of war painting, there is a danger of such paintings being generally perceived as part of a wider quietist establishment cultural response to the horrors of war.[42] Yet there is a palpable difference between the distraction techniques evident in the 'Peace Pictures' of the first years of the war and the genuine attempts to provide consolation in the commemorative works of establishment artists focused on in the remainder of this chapter.[43]

### *George Clausen and the allegorical representation of mourning*

*Youth Mourning* (1916) by George Clausen (1852–1944) provides a stark contrast to much of his other work as a commissioned war artist – either in his realistic depictions of the munitions industries or in his quietist propaganda work.[44] The challenge his pre-war 'nostalgic' landscape paintings posed to inclusion in the modernist canon was considerable; nevertheless a subtle shift in emphasis occurred in his work so that 'by the eve of the Great War the labourer was simply an accessory, an attribute of the English landscape and no longer such an essential icon'.[45] War presumably inspired his *Renaissance* (1915, destroyed) which reintroduced the allegorical figure in order to challenge the jingoism of some works by contemporary artists.[46] Such experimentation was continued with *Youth Mourning*, which used a realistic representation of a battleground wasteland as a backdrop to an allegorical representation of a female figure mourning the dead of the Western front (Plate 3). The painting was reportedly triggered by the death in 1915 of Second Lieutenant Geraint Payne, the fiancé of Kit Clausen, the artist's daughter.[47] The present painting does not show its original configuration, but rather its 1928 reworking, as at first there had been fifty crosses depicted on a green field.[48] While many identify the intensification of mourning on the tenth anniversary of war's end as the chief cause of this alteration, Clausen may have also taken this as an opportunity to rework unsuccessful aspects of the composition.[49]

Clausen's increasingly Symbolist treatment of his subject arguably reinforced tendencies visible in his previous paintings, such as his moody landscapes which fed into the background of *Youth Mourning*, and the female nudes which became a feature of his oeuvre during 1914–18.[50] Whilst direct links are difficult to trace, formal and psychological affinities exist for Anna Ancher's *Sorrow* (1902) with the obscured face of the mourning naked female youth and its dream-like spirituality.[51] Ancher (1859–1935) studied under Pierre Puvis de Chavannes (1824–98), an artist whose work was coming back into fashion.[52] Further inspiration may have come from German Symbolists with their visions of Arcadian collapse, such as Oskar Zwintscher's *Grief* (1898) and *Dead Man by the Sea* (1913).[53] Such works in turn linked back to the traditions of Holbein's *Dead Christ* (1520–2).[54] While little evidence exists of Clausen's interest in historic or contemporary German art, he did sign the reciprocal letter from English artists triggered by the friendly communiqué from their German colleagues published in *The Times* in 1906.[55] The huge casualty lists of the First World War no doubt would have increased the relevance of Symbolist motifs for Clausen in 1916.

The manifestoes of early modernism are often taken as the register of artistic thought at the dawn of the modern age; however, it should be remembered that other theories continued to enjoy currency. The Symbolist and idealist systems of the late nineteenth century did not neatly expire and the lectures delivered by Clausen at the Royal Academy in 1905 and 1906 give the historian important clues to the values he took forward to evoke deeper meanings in his war paintings. *Youth Mourning* rebalances real and ideal elements in favour of the latter. It articulates in paint Clausen's earlier statement in his lectures that '[t]ruth of resemblance does not cover the whole ground of art; much of the finest work appeals on other grounds; through subject, or sentiment, and demands that the spectator be in sympathy and prepared to receive its message'.[56] Clausen argued for the primacy of imagination and 'dramatic insight' such that 'there must be a creative impulse of the artist; that his aim is to express something, not merely to copy', warning against superficiality and the 'ignoring of deeper truths'.[57] The allegorical representation of the eponymous *Youth Mourning* against the *vraisemblance* of the war-torn landscape arguably satisfied exactly the pictorial criteria that he had set out in his lectures.

Interestingly, the challenge of modernity also featured in his lectures. Clausen lamented that 'our life is too complicated' to sustain the ideals of Italian Renaissance historical painting, but that 'imaginative art is still possible, though its direction may be different'.[58] His *Renaissance* can be seen in such a capacity, as might *Youth Mourning*. G. F. Watts may also have provided inspiration for such a course of action. Watts's recent death in 1904 led Clausen to discuss his works in the lectures.[59] That artist's attempt at a reinvention of *memento mori* allegorical painting may have offered a further emulative model from the British tradition for Clausen.[60]

## *Spirituality and commemoration in the paintings of Stanley Spencer*

Many art historians have attempted to reclaim Stanley Spencer's art for modernism by finding crucial formal innovation in his war work, whilst others have divined Neue Sachlichkeit affinities in his realist revivalism.[61] However, like Clausen before him, Stanley Spencer (1891–1959) combined innovation and tradition to make sense of the First World War. Like Tonks and Nevinson, Spencer's war years were spent as a medical orderly, but he gained combat experience in 1918 and retold the excitement he felt in battle and on hearing accounts of Gallipoli, before finally being commissioned as a war artist.[62] The spiritual register of his war art emerged first through his discovery of the landscapes of war, especially the Vardar valley in Macedonia, which he noted 'became the goal & place wherein spiritually I was wanting to find the redeeming & delivering of myself in all the activities [the] unexpressed me had lived through & in'.[63] While religious themes were common in First World War artwork, investing the sacrifice of soldiers with theological and patriotic meaning, the propaganda function of works like James Clark's *The Great Sacrifice* (1914) or Frank Dicksee's *The Avenger*

(1916) are poles apart from the more thoughtful spiritual reflection of Spencer.[64] His religious war paintings read biblical associations into his personal recollections, and steered away from quasi-realist morphologies (such as apparitions of the crucified Christ on the battlefield) towards more subtle implications of religiosity, most notably resurrection themes. Such developments were presumably encouraged by changed expectations of the war, following the low points of the Gallipoli campaign (February 1915–January 1916) and the Somme offensive (July–November 1916).[65]

Commemorating the spiritual lives of common soldiers was the key drive of Spencer's war art. Writing in 1917 from the hospital in Salonica where he was based, Spencer noted how he was 'so keen on drawing patients that I spend my whole time on it [. . .] I do anything for these men. I do not know why but I cannot refuse them anything & they love me to make drawings of photos of their wives & children or a brother who has been killed'. In the same letter he recalls how he had been dragged into a discussion on the joyous and eternal afterlife in which these men were partaking.[66] Spencer completed *Travoys with Wounded Soldiers Arriving at a Dressing Station at Smol, Macedonia* (1919) in fulfilment of his official War Artists' Advisory Committee's (WAAC) (rather than the service of worship at the front suggested to him in April 1918) and also his personal desire to produce a religious war painting: it balanced his eye-witness account (albeit from memory, given the loss of his field sketches) of his 68th Field Ambulance Unit in action with an emphasis on peace in war, redemption over horror.[67]

Equally important amongst Spencer's war art were his paintings for the Sandham Chapel, Burghclere, for the Behrend family. Another commissioned war artist, Henry Lamb, introduced the Behrends to Spencer, who had come up with the scheme in 1923 at his friend's house as 'an Odyssey of my war experiences', deriving symbolic spiritual abstractions from his real experiences such that '[t]hey don't look like war pictures, they rather look like heaven'.[68] The freedom Spencer was given by his patrons is apparent in the fact that, although commissioned due to his experiences of Macedonia (where Lt Henry Willoughby Sandham – Mary Behrend's brother – had served and died), Spencer was at liberty to introduce scenes from his Bristol army hospital life.[69] The personal quality of the work was underlined by this direct connection, and Spencer insisted that all his figures were based on empathetic imaginings of how he would react to events, and in fact a self-portrait was included in the soldier picking litter with a bayonet in the *Camp at Karasuli* scene and autobiographic details in the *Bedmaking* canvas.[70] At the centre of the Sandham cycle was *The Resurrection of Soldiers* (1928–9) and unlike the staid *Travoys* or the sanitised sites of the IWGC's cemeteries, this painting offered restorative peace in a democratic and Protestant spirit to everyone via its Old Testament allusions, for, as Spencer remarked in his notebook: 'This picture is supposed to be a reflection of the general attitude & behaviour of men during the war. As soon as I decided in [*sic*] this it seemed that every army incident was a coin, the obverse of which was the Resurrection.'[71]

While *Travoys* was a success at the 1919 War Art exhibition at the Royal Academy, Tonks expressed disapproval, claiming Spencer had moved away from explicit war art.[72] Reflecting in 1945–7, Spencer noted his lasting regret at not having taken up the WAAC's suggestion of the 'service at the front', but wanted in his post-war life to recombine his spiritual commemorations with the nurturing locus of his Berkshire home. As Spencer admitted in his notebooks: 'I felt a wish to join that war-experience-hope felt in midst of war & war experience, to my Cookham love & home feeling & the religious feeling as well. This wish found for me considerable fulfilment in the "Unveiling a War Memorial" painting. The service was not at the front, but in Cookham' (Plate 4).[73] The critic R. H. Wilenski argued that the painting balanced specific (Cookham at the unveiling) and universal (spirituality) elements perfectly.[74] Historians have speculated that the civilians lying down in the bottom right corner symbolise fallen soldiers returned home.[75] Unlike *The Resurrection of the Soldiers*, this picture was factual, yet the use of Cookham inevitably ensured a spiritual register. The use of a vertiginous perspective also connects it to Spencer's psychology: the obscuring of the sky may equate to the excision of heavenly matters from the picture, locating spirituality within this world. The level of imaginative manipulation in Spencer's rendition of this commemorative event may be grasped by comparison to contemporary photographs of the unveiling event on 21 September 1919 (Figure 7.1).[76] Spencer's point of view was slightly to the right of that of the photographer, but crucially the photograph confirms that Spencer's seemingly symbolic devices were based largely on factual observation: the observers in the windows of nearby houses, and the Union Jack, are evident. Christian symbolism is clear in the prominence Spencer gave to the simple white Cornish granite Celtic cross and the girl attendants with their white costumes indicating virginal purity, as well as the daffodils referring to the

Figure 7.1 Thompson/Topical Press Agency/Getty Images, *The dedication of Cookham War Memorial in Berkshire* or *War Veterans* (21 September 1919), photograph, Hulton Archive no. 3163936, Thompson/Stringer. Reproduced courtesy of Getty Images.

promise of rebirth.[77] Potential clues exist for ascertaining Spencer's views on organised religion and the establishment more generally, for not only were the clergymen removed but so too were the praying servicemen. The latter edit reflected Spencer's decision to move away from military subjects. The result draws attention to the civilian population of his beloved Cookham and both the religious and social meaning for them of war commemoration.

## *Will Longstaff's ghost soldiers and Spiritualist painting as commemoration*

*Menin Gate at Midnight* (or *The Ghosts of Menin Gate*, 1927) by the Australian artist Will Longstaff (1879–1953) offers another deliberate attempt at invoking commemoration. AWR artists comprised those already in service and those specifically sent to paint, but in both cases establishment artists were exclusively represented, as AWR officials rejected modernist styles in favour of 'accurate' artistic records.[78] Longstaff belonged to the former group of artists – having seen action from October 1915 in the Australian Imperial Force, he was invalided out and reattached as part of the AWR scheme in June 1918.[79] *Menin Gate at Midnight* was, however, produced outside the AWR scheme and Longstaff was thus free in this painting from the realist constraints otherwise placed on commissioned Australian war artists (Figure 7.2). Longstaff was arguably continuing the intention of the Menin Gate memorial itself in

Figure 7.2 Will Longstaff, *Menin Gate at Midnight* (or *The Ghosts of Menin Gate*) (1927), oil on canvas, 137 × 270 cm. © Australian War Memorial (ART09807). Reproduced courtesy of Australian War Memorial, Canberra.

commemorating the British Empire war dead on the tenth anniversary of the renewed 1917 offensives on the Ypres Salient. Media coverage augmented the impact of the unsettling ghostly ranks of soldiers that inhabited the space before the monument in the painting. One contemporary Australian newspaper noted how Longstaff's painting fitted within the occult spirit of the age, and how the artist

> had doubts himself as to whether the spring of his inspiration was not in fact some occult force that had for the time possessed him. He confesses to having, while walking along the Menin Road at midnight following the unveiling of the Menin Gate Memorial, suddenly observed a phantom ghost of diggers, who had fallen in the terrible fighting on the Ypres salient, rising from the adjacent cornfields. The spectacle so unnerved him that he hurried back to his hotel.[80]

Notwithstanding this, the fact that Longstaff himself denied any spectral vision suggests that Symbolism, not Spiritualism, was his aim.[81] More worldly alternative inspiration was reported in a chance conversation from July 1927 between Longstaff and a Mrs Mary Horsburgh, who ran a British canteen in the First World War and claimed, 'I just want to be with my dead boys. I can feel them all round me.'[82] A further prompt may also have come from Arthur Conan Doyle's poem 'Those Others', published in *The Guards Came Through and Other Poems*.[83] The last two of the poem's six verses were reprinted in the AWR booklet:

> To each his dreams, and mine to me,
> But as the shadows fall I see
> That ever-glorious company –
>     The men who bide out there.
> Rifleman, Highlander, Fusilier,
> Airman and Sapper and Grenadier,
> With flaunting banner and wave and cheer,
>     They flew through the darkening air.
>
> And yours are there, and so are mine,
> Rank upon rank, and line on line,
> With smiling lips and eyes that shine,
>     And bearing proud and high.
> Past, they go with their measured tread,
> These are the victors, these – the dead!
> Ah, sink the knee and bare the head
> As the hallowed host goes by![84]

The pamphlet cited 'romantic inspiration and conception' and how Longstaff imagined 'a deathless army' at Hellfire Corner near the Menin Gate.[85] Whatever the origins, Longstaff was probably consciously engaging with a post-war Spiritualist revival, producing four further paintings featuring phantom armies.[86] When purchasing *The Rearguard* (or *The Spirit of ANZAC*, 1928), another canvas featuring ghost soldiers, this time from Gallipoli, Conan Doyle was quoted in the Australian newspapers stating that 'Mr. Longstaff says that he never professed to be a spiritualist; but he realises that behind his emotion there was a compelling psychic force'.[87] Doyle's Spiritualism was triggered by the 1918 death of his son, Kingsley, from influenza aggravated by wounds received at the Battle of the Somme, and the purchase of *The Rearguard* becomes a memorial act in such light.[88]

*Menin Gate at Midnight* fanned the flames of collective grief, using readily legible metaphorical language for the harvest of souls that Ypres represented with the prominent patches of poppies that populate its foreground.[89] The painting played an important role as an extension of the architectural monument itself, firstly, as a substitute for a site of mourning for relatives unable to visit European gravesites (due to their geographical remoteness, especially for Australians, or the absence of grave-markers for unretrieved bodies of some soldiers); secondly, as a sight of pilgrimage; and thirdly, as already noted, as an outlet for post-war Spiritualism.[90] Furthermore, the artwork and the account surrounding it function commemoratively in three ways: in remembering the war *in toto*; in displaying the personal trauma of Longstaff as a soldier-artist; and in marking the communal receptivity to such an account in London and the Australian cities where it was shown on the tenth anniversary of the Armistice (1929).[91]

The Sydney-based *Sun* reported that '[i]t is doubtful whether any artist has conveyed a greater suggestion on the legions of the dead'.[92] Art historians are, however, left with the task of ascertaining whether Longstaff's strategy was as manipulative as the Menin Gate scheme which was criticised by Siegfried Sassoon.[93] Longstaff's *Menin Gate* undeniably combined commemoration, patriotism and self-promotion (and, as seen, he repeated this strategy with similar success with *The Rearguard*).[94] Sir Dudley de Chair, the 25th Governor of New South Wales between 1924 and 1930, declared *Menin Gate* a fitting 'memorial to British courage and devotion' and described it as 'a worthy tribute of the Empire's gratitude to known and unknown heroes. He hoped that it would inspire all who saw it, not only to honour the memory of the fallen, but also to follow their example of service and self-sacrifice.'[95] The purchase of the canvas for 2,000 guineas by James Buchanan, Baron Woolavington, a Canadian-born British businessman, and his presentation of the painting to the Australian people 'as a tribute to the gallant Australians who served in the war, and also as a mark of my admiration of the Commonwealth' represents a desire to shore up an integrated vision of the British world in the wake of the trauma of the First World War.[96] Buchanan had supported Joseph Chamberlain's 1903 Tariff Reform policy which essentially aimed to convert the British Empire into a protectionist framework, and his whisky industry links (via the Buchanan Dewar Ltd Company, established in 1919) possibly stimulated his gift-giving: whisky was a key Australian import in the early twentieth century that was already being undercut by changing Australian drinking habits, so any additional advantage would have been welcome.[97]

## Recent Commemorative Paintings of the First World War

More recent artistic interventions need to be considered in order to take the narrative up to the modern day. With the 2014–19 centenary anniversaries it is not surprising to see First World War subjects featuring in contemporary practice; however, to a certain extent, the avant-garde versus establishment divisions have possibly returned, albeit in an altered state. With the removal of painting from its pedestal within contemporary art (despite Stuckism and other related 'revivalist' and revisionist interventions in the medium), recent commemorative events have placed more emphasis on experiential spaces (installations), photography, posters and performance. Photography is central to Helen Marshall's *The Face of World War One* (2014) with its digital mosaic of photographic portraits of First World War soldiers from the Imperial War Museum Collection, and Sandy Grant, Sig Bang Schmidt and Chris van Wierst use various forms of photographic techniques to recycle and invoke the First World War. Installations of three-dimensional objects form another important genre of works responding to the war. *Blood Swept Lands and Seas of Red* (2014) at the Tower of London saw artists Paul Cummins and Tom Piper progressively filling the Tower's moat with 888,246 ceramic poppies between July and November to represent the ever-mounting British fatalities during the war. Rob Heard's *The 19240 Shrouds of the Somme* project (2016) consisted of 19,240 hand-stitched shrouded effigies of the British soldiers killed on the first day of that battle installed on the lawns of Northernhay Gardens in Exeter. Christine Borland's artefact-led project ties into the sensibilities of found objects as 'war art' (2016 onwards). In other fields, designers like Vivienne Westwood and Roksanda Ilinčić took inspiration from the conflict for their 'Fashion and Freedom' exhibition (2016), and in *We're here because we're here* (2016) Jeremy Deller and Rufus Norris used performance to disrupt everyday life with the appearance on modern-day streets of British soldiers, like Heard's project representing the dead from the first day of the Battle of the Somme, who handed out biographical details on cards of the people they were portraying.

Painting only features as part of the monumental '14–18 NOW' project in a liminal form, in the series of 'dazzle ships' which recreate the Vorticist-inspired patterns used by Norman Wilkinson to camouflage British shipping from U-boat attacks.[98] The sequence so far includes: Carlos Cruz-Diez's *Chromatique à Double Fréquence pour l'Edmund Gardner Ship / Liverpool. Paris 2014* (Liverpool 2014); Tobias Rehberger's *Dazzle Ship* (London 2014); Sir Peter Blake's *Razzle Dazzle* (Manchester 2015); and Ciara Phillips's *Dazzle Ship* (Leith 2016).[99] Yet unlike Marshall's and Borland's use of authentic artefacts – albeit creatively repositioned – the '14–18 NOW' Dazzle Ships project is fundamentally anachronistic because the majority of the ships used – Cruz-Diez's *Edmund Gardner* (1953), Blake's *Snowdrop* (1959) and Phillips's *MV Fingal* (1963) – postdate the conflict; only Rehberger's *HMS President* (1918) hails from the period. Furthermore, the mostly bright pop-art colours used are antipathetic to the more subtle schemes evolved by the Royal Academy of Art for the government.[100]

There are significant numbers of paintings by modern artists taking the First World War as their subject, but in the majority of cases their works fall under the category of illustration. Graham Turner's award-winning depictions of the First World War in the air are accurate in their archaeological depictions but imitate or simulate rather than commemorate: *Into the Hands of Fate* (2013) approaches the art historical register of historical genre.[101] Symbolic devices – such as the poppy – perhaps connect more adequately with the post-war period, seen in Longstaff's *Menin Gate at Midnight*, for example. Charron Pugsley-Hill's *In Flanders Fields* (2015) creates a vibrant colour field of floral decoration that invokes John McCrae's poem and its evocation of the loss of life as remembrance but subverts his intention to spur on continued fighting.[102] The poppy and First World War combat also feature in the work of Jacqueline Hurley, for example in *Lest We Forget* (2015).[103] The artist and gravesite tour-guide Søren Hawkes uses war graves as inspiration, recalling his own family connections to the war (his great-uncle died at Ypres and was commemorated on the Menin Gate).[104] In *Ghost Soldier at the Menin Gate Viewing Tributes* (2015). Hawkes remembers Private S. Smalley of the Leicestershire Yeomanry whose ghost stands holding both a small commemorative wooden cross and a vivid red poppy in his left hand up against his name on the memorial (Figure 7.3).[105] The use of watercolour pigment as a supplement to the pencil outline and hatched shadows reproduces the provisional and ephemeral qualities of the eye-witness field sketches produced by war artists. The transparency of the soldier, whose form is violated by the lines where the granite slabs on the memorial intersect, is a stark reminder of the supernatural subject matter, again harking back to the commemorative and psychological devices employed by Longstaff.

Responding to the IWM's *'Truth and Memory' exhibition* (London, 19 July 2014 to 8 March 2015), the abstract figurative painter Hughie O'Donoghue commented upon the irony of war art and its connections to the art historical seam of Dadaism, and Marcel Duchamp's 'ready-mades' as a response to the nonsense of war.[106] In his series of paintings under the title *Seven Halts on the Somme* (2013–16) O'Donoghue visits and recreates images of places intimately connected with deadlocks in that particular First World War offensive. In *Trônes Wood* (2014), O'Donoghue channels

Figure 7.3 Søren Hawkes, *Ghost Soldier at the Menin Gate Viewing Tributes* (2015), watercolour and pencil on paper, 29.7 × 42 cm. © Søren Hawkes. Reproduced courtesy of the artist.

his personal memory of memorials to soldiers lost in the conflict (recalling a modest commemoration to one soldier, Joseph Partridge, consisting of a hand-written note and photograph pinned to a tree in the woods). The light beams simulate the daylight breaking through the regrown foliage; however, it also links art historically to Nevinson's various *Searchlights* compositions of 1916 and the apocalyptic landscapes of Nash. In his work, O'Donoghue engages with art history (Poussin, Goya, El Greco and in particular Titian), history painting and war art, and the *Seven Halts* series easily fits into the visceral journey through painting that he has undertaken, whereby a 'canvas becomes [. . .] a terrain over which a battle is fought'.[107] Yet for all the personal expressive potential here, the primary mode of action is mnemonic, for, as O'Donoghue explains:

> Our memory of the First World War is now cultural as opposed to personal, so my paintings are about remembering, putting flesh back on the bones of something, a creative act as opposed to simple recall. Remembering and painting are close companions; both seek equivalents for something profound, a calling to mind of something not to be forgotten.[108]

## Conclusions

This chapter has established the deep psychological and physical trauma and disruption caused by the First World War to painters who were either involved in the combat or have subsequently tried to use their work to make sense of the unfathomable. Whilst the resisting avant-garde have tended to be privileged in modernist accounts of war art, it is clear that 'establishment' artists were as keenly concerned with recording their experiences in ways that mixed the real with the ideal, and the old with the new. The methods they used – whether it be Clausen's allegorical expression, Spencer's spiritual community at Cookham, or Longstaff's spectral soldiers – all originated in distinctly canonical traditions, but pushed the parameters to break innovative ground.

According to Foster's categories the works analysed in this chapter may be seen as 'reactionary' or belonging to the values of Lewis's 'abysmal inexcusable middle class', yet such a label obfuscates the creative effort and flexibility involved. Establishment artists between 1914 and 1932 checked their methodological toolboxes as 'academic' artists and found them unfit for the task of painting the war. Making the best of their training, they put old artistic formulae to new uses. Rather than undertaking a reactionary attack on modernism itself, this chapter has sought to give due attention to neglected painterly responses to the challenge of commemorating the war dead in a meaningful albeit conservative fashion. Ultimately the paintings of the establishment artists surveyed in this chapter represent a middle-ground reaction to the genuine abysmal and inexcusable horrors of the First World War.

## Notes

1. Stephen Melville, 'What Was Postminimalism?', in Dana Arnold and Margaret Iversen (eds), *Art and Thought* (Malden, MA: Blackwell, 2003), p. 169. This bias has been reproduced in historiography of First World War art, although important work by historians, such as Carolyn Malone in the realms of decorative arts, pushes back such limits.

2. Paul Wood, 'Introduction', in Steve Edwards and Paul Wood (eds), *Art of the Avant-Gardes* (New Haven and London: Yale University Press, 2004), p. 1; Wendy Baron, *Perfect Moderns: A History of the Camden Town Group* (Aldershot: Ashgate, 2000), p. 78.
3. Clement Greenberg, *Art and Culture: Critical Essays* (Boston, MA: Beacon Press, 1961), pp. 3–5; Paul Wood, 'Introduction: The Avant-Garde and Modernism', in Wood (ed.), *The Challenge of the Avant-Garde* (New Haven and London: Yale University Press, 1999), pp. 7, 9–11, 13; David Cottington, *Cubism in the Shadow of War: The Avant-Garde and Politics in Paris 1905–1914* (New Haven and London: Yale University Press, 1998), p. 49.
4. Victor Burgin, *The End of Art Theory: Criticism and Postmodernity* (Basingstoke: Palgrave, 1986), p. 5; Cottington, *Cubism in the Shadow of War*, p. 9; David Peters Corbett, *The World in Paint: Modern Art and Visuality in England, 1848–1914* (Manchester: Manchester University Press, 2004), p. 251.
5. Hal Foster, 'Postmodernism: A Preface', in Foster (ed.), *The Anti-Aesthetic: Essays on Postmodern Culture* (Seattle: Bay Press, 1983), pp. ix–xi; Nicholas J. Saunders, *Trench Art: Materialities and Memories of War* (Oxford: Berg, 2003), p. 156; Hans Belting, *Art History after Modernism* (1987; Chicago and London: University of Chicago Press, 2003), pp. 28, 32; Martin Gaughan, 'Narrating the Dada Game Plan', in Edwards and Wood (eds), *Art of the Avant-Gardes*, p. 339; James Fox, 'Conflict and Consolation: British Art and the First World War, 1914–1919', *Art History*, 36.4 (2013), 811; David Cottington, 'Modernities and Avant-Gardes: London and Paris 1900–1914', in Trevor Harris (ed.), *Art, Politics and Society in Britain (1880–1914): Aspects of Modernity and Modernism* (Newcastle: Cambridge Scholars, 2009), pp. 23–7, on the historiography of avant-gardism, including Peter Bürger and Linda Nochlin.
6. Geoffrey Cubitt, *History and Memory* (Manchester: Manchester University Press, 2007), pp. 49, 51, 205–6, 236–9.
7. Kenneth E. Silver, *Esprit de Corps: The Art of the Parisian Avant-Garde and the First World War, 1914–1925* (Princeton: Princeton University Press, 1989), p. 2; James Fox, *British Art and the First World War* (Cambridge: Cambridge University Press, 2015), pp. 11–31.
8. Margaret Hutchison, '"Accurate to the Point of Mania": Eyewitness Testimony and Memory Making in Australia's Official Paintings of the First World War', *Australian Historical Studies*, 46.1 (January 2015), 41.
9. Sue Malvern, *Modern Art, Britain and the Great War: Witnessing, Testimony and Remembrance* (New Haven and London: Yale University Press, 2004), pp. 17–35, 69–89; Paul Gough, *A Terrible Beauty: British Artists in the First World War* (Bristol: Sansom & Company, 2010), pp. 28, 31, 197–8; George Robb, *British Culture and the First World War* (Basingstoke: Palgrave, 2002), p. 165; Fox, *British Art and the First World War*, pp. 56, 68, 87–8, 95–6, 91; Ulrike Smalley, 'How the British Government Sponsored the Arts in the First World War', Imperial War Museums, <http://www.iwm.org.uk/history/how-the-british-government-sponsored-the-arts-in-the-first-world-war> (last accessed 3 November 2016).
10. The German War Graves Commission was formed in late 1919, but painting was not part of its work (see K. Michael Prince, *War and German Memory: Excavating the Significance of the Second World War in German Cultural Consciousness* (Lanham, MD: Lexington Books, 2009), p. 44). Jonathan F. Vance, *Death So Noble: Memory, Meaning, and the First World War* (Vancouver: University of British Columbia Press, 1997), p. 164; Maria Tippett, *Art at the Service of War: Canada, Art, and the Great War* (Toronto: University of Toronto Press, 1984); Laura Brandon, *Art or Memorial? The Forgotten History of Canada's War Art* (Calgary: University of Calgary Press, 2006); Vera Blackburn, 'Australian War Memorial Library', *Military Affairs*, 23.2 (1959), 102.
11. Fox, *British Art and the First World War*, pp. 142–4.

12. Hutchison, '"Accurate to the Point of Mania"', pp. 28, 33–40.
13. Hilary Spurling, *Matisse the Master: A Life of Henri Matisse, The Conquest of Colour, 1909–1954* (New York and London: Knopf and Hamish Hamilton, 2005), pp. 167, 184; Alfred Munnings, *An Artist's Life* (London: Museum Press, 1951), p. 296; Tate Gallery Archives (TGA) 945.20: Spencer to Lamb, 23 November 1914, reproduced in Andrew Glew (ed.), *Stanley Spencer: Letters and Writings* (London: Tate Publishing, 2001), p. 50; Timothy Hyman, 'Stanley Spencer: Angels and Dirt', in Timothy Hyman and Patrick Wright (eds), *Stanley Spencer* (London: Tate Publishing, 2001), p. 19; Spencer to James Wood, 26 May 1916, reproduced in Glew (ed.), *Stanley Spencer Letters*, pp. 68–9; Spencer to Desmond Chute [28 October 1916], Chute Correspondence, Stanley Spencer Gallery, Cookham, reproduced in Glew (ed.), *Stanley Spencer Letters*, p. 77; Gough, *A Terrible Beauty*, pp. 35–41; Fox, *British Art and the First World War*, pp. 33–4.
14. Baron, *Perfect Moderns*, p. 76.
15. Jason Gaiger, 'Expressionism and the Crisis of Subjectivity', in Edwards and Wood (eds), *Art of the Avant-Gardes*, p. 13.
16. James Fox, '"Fiddling while Rome is Burning": Hostility to Art During the First World War, 1914–18', *Visual Culture in Britain*, 11.1 (March 2010), 49–65; Silver, *Esprit de Corps*, pp. 8, 11; Gaughan, 'Narrating the Dada Game Plan', p. 347; Gough, *A Terrible Beauty*, p. 28; Matthew C. Potter, 'Cambridge University and the Intellectual Bridge to Germany', in Grace Brockington (ed.), *Internationalism and the Arts in Britain and Europe at the Fin de Siècle* (Oxford, New York and Bern: Peter Lang, 2009), pp. 157–77; Gail Day, 'Art, Love and Social Emancipation: On the Concept "Avant-Garde" and the Interwar Avant-Gardes', in Edwards and Wood (eds), *Art of the Avant-Gardes*, p. 317; Fox, *British Art and the First World War*, pp. 32–8; Matthew C. Potter, *The Inspirational Genius of Germany: British Art and Germany, 1850–1939* (Manchester: Manchester University Press, 2013), pp. 245–6.
17. Christine Riding, 'Introduction: Art and the War at Sea, 1914–45', in Riding (ed.), *Art and the War at Sea, 1914–45* (London: Lund Humphries, 2015), p. 9.
18. Ibid., pp. 20–1; Gough, *A Terrible Beauty*, p. 20.
19. Charles Harrison, *English Art and Modernism, 1900–1939* (London and Bloomington, IN: Allen Lane and Indiana University Press, 1981); Peters Corbett, *The World in Paint*, p. 218; Wood, 'Introduction: The Avant-Garde and Modernism', pp. 22–4; Cottington, *Cubism in the Shadow of War*, pp. 11–12.
20. Spurling, *Matisse the Master*, p. 197; Fionna Barber, 'Surrealism 1924–1929', in Edwards and Wood (eds), *Art of the Avant-Gardes*, p. 428; Claudia Siebrecht, *The Aesthetics of Loss: German Women's Art of the First World War* (Oxford: Oxford University Press, 2014), pp. 15–16.
21. Francis Marshall, 'The Avant-Garde and Tradition', in Stephen Whittle (ed.), *Creative Tension: British Art 1900–1950* (London: Paul Holberton, 2005), pp. 72, 82; Mary Beal, '"For the fallen": Paul Nash's Landscape at Iden', *The Burlington Magazine*, 141.1150 (January 1999), 20–1, 23; Paul Gough, 'Paul Nash between the Wars', in Paul Gough and Gemma Brace (eds), *Brothers in Arms: John and Paul Nash and the Aftermath of the Great War* (Bristol: Sansom & Company, 2014), p. 85.
22. Adrian Hicken, *Apollinaire, Cubism and Orphism* (Aldershot: Ashgate, 2002), pp. 60, 79; Sir Michael Ernest Sadler, *Modern Art and Revolution* (London: Leonard and Virginia Woolf at the Hogarth Press, 1932), pp. 18–19; Joke Brouwer, *The Politics of the Impure* (Rotterdam: V2_ Publishing, 2010), pp. 166–7; Henry Adams, Margaret C. Conrads and Annegret Hoberg (eds), *Albert Bloch, the American Blue Rider* (Munich and New York: Prestel, 1997), p. 39; Louis Aragon, *Henry Matisse: A Novel*, trans. Jean Stewart (London: W. Collins, 1971), vol. 1, p. 303.
23. Saunders, *Trench Art*, pp. 6–7, 13–14, 83, 86, 112, 156, 166–7, 174, 222.

24. Cottington, *Cubism in the Shadow of War*, pp. 54–116; James D. Herbert, *Fauve Painting: The Making of Cultural Politics* (New Haven: Yale University Press, 1992), p. 145; Silver, *Esprit de Corps*, p. 11.
25. Siebrecht, *The Aesthetics of Loss*, p. 16.
26. Sergiusz Michalski, *New Objectivity: Painting, Graphic Art and Photography in Weimar Germany 1919–1933* (Cologne: Taschen, 1994), pp. 71–87; Jeanne Anne Nugent, 'Germany's Classical Turn from the Great Disorder to a Kingdom of the Dead', in Kenneth E. Silver (ed.), *Chaos and Classicism: Art in France, Italy, and Germany, 1918–1936* (New York: Guggenheim Museum, 2010), pp. 159–61; Olaf Peters, 'On the Problem of the Continuity of New Objectivity Painting during the Consolidation of the Third Reich: The Case of Rudolf Schlichter 1930–1937', *History of European Ideas*, 24.2 (1998), 93–112.
27. Michalski, *New Objectivity*, pp. 37, 41; Helen Hsu, 'Classical Bodies, New Humanity', in Silver (ed.), *Chaos and Classicism*, pp. 69, 74; James van Dyke, 'Ernst Barlach and the Conservative Revolution', *German Studies Review*, 36.2 (2013), 281–305.
28. Michalski, *New Objectivity*, pp. 59, 61: Dix was named 'Otto Holbein from Dresden'.
29. Ibid., p. 122.
30. Dagmar Grimm, 'Otto Dix', in Stephanie Barron and Peter W. Guenther (eds), *Degenerate Art: The Fate of the Avant-Garde in Nazi Germany* (Los Angeles: Los Angeles County Museum of Art; New York: H. N. Abrams, 1991), p. 224; Kenneth E. Silver, 'A More Durable Self', in Silver (ed.), *Chaos and Classicism*, p. 18.
31. Fred S. Kleiner, *Gardner's Art through the Ages: The Western Perspective* (Boston, MA: Cengage Learning, 2008), p. 718.
32. German Werth, 'Flanders 1917 and the German Soldier', in Peter Liddle (ed.), *Passchendaele in Perspective: The Third Battle of Ypres* (Havertown: Pen and Sword, 2014), p. 329.
33. Gillian Naylor, 'Introduction: Brangwyn Reviewed', in Libby Horner and Gillian Naylor (eds), *Frank Brangwyn 1867–1956* (Leeds: Leeds City Art Gallery, 2006), p. 15; Corinne Miller, 'Swiftness, Vigour and Exuberance', in Horner and Naylor (eds), *Frank Brangwyn*, pp. 102, 124; TGA 8116.39: Stanley Spencer to Jacques [Raverat] and Gwen [Darwin], 12–17 July 1914, reproduced in Glew (ed.), *Stanley Spencer Letters*, p. 49.
34. Harrison, *English Art and Modernism*, p. 86; David Peters Corbett, *The Modernity of English Art 1914–1930* (Manchester: Manchester University Press, 1997), pp. 6–7, 14; Janet Wolff, 'Modernism, Modernity and English Art: Review of David Peters Corbett: The Modernity of English Art 1914–1930', *Oxford Art Journal*, 21.2 (1998), 199–201; Lisa Tickner, *Modern Life and Modern Subjects: British Art in the Early Twentieth Century* (New Haven and London: Yale University Press, 2000), p. 1; Cottington, 'Modernities and Avant-Gardes', p. 23.
35. Peters Corbett, *The World in Paint*, pp. 10, 14; Wood, 'Introduction: The Avant-Garde and Modernism', pp. 43–9; Baron, *Perfect Moderns*, p. 78; Mark A. Cheetham, *Artwriting, Nation, and Cosmopolitanism in Britain: The 'Englishness' of English Art Theory since the Eighteenth Century* (Farnham: Ashgate, 2012), p. 102; Paul Edwards and Richard Humphreys, 'Contradict Yourself, In Order to Live, You Must Remain Broken Up', in Edwards and Humphreys (eds), *Wyndham Lewis Portraits* (London: National Portrait Gallery, 2008), p. 14.
36. Alan Kramer, *Dynamic of Destruction: Culture and Mass Killing in the First World War* (Oxford: Oxford University Press, 2007), pp. 170, 267.
37. Pieter van der Merwe, 'Pictorial Narratives of the War at Sea: Wyllie, Eurich and Wilkinson', in Riding (ed.), *Art and the War at Sea*, pp. 29, 35; Robert J. Blyth, 'The Sinking of the Lusitania', in Riding (ed.), *Art and the War at Sea*, p. 39; Kramer, *Dynamic of Destruction*, pp. 264–5; Laura Brandon, 'Above or Below Ground? Depicting Corpses in First and Second World War Official Canadian War Art', in Sherrill Grace, Patrick Imbert and Tiffany Johnstone (eds), *Bearing Witness: Perspectives on War and Peace from the Arts and Humanities* (Montreal: McGill-Queen's University Press, 2012); Fox, *British Art and*

*the First World War*, pp. 10, 118–23, 160; Robb, *British Culture and the First World War*, p. 166; Malvern, *Modern Art, Britain and the Great War*, pp. 37–67; Michael J. K. Walsh, *C. R. W. Nevinson: This Cult of Violence* (New Haven and London: Yale University Press, 2002), pp. 174–9.

38. Richard Cork, *A Bitter Truth: Avant-Garde Art and the Great War* (New Haven and London: Yale University Press, in association with the Barbican Art Gallery, 1994), pp. 266–7.
39. Julian Freeman, 'Professor Tonks: War Artist', *The Burlington Magazine*, 127.986 (May 1985), 285.
40. Gough, *A Terrible Beauty*, p. 38.
41. Malvern, *Modern Art, Britain and the Great War*, p. 91.
42. Fox, *British Art and the First World War*, pp. 36, 110–17, 160; Laura Brandon, 'The Canadian War Museum's Art Collection as a Site of Meaning, Memory and Identity in the Twentieth Century', PhD thesis, Carleton University, 2002, p. 24, referenced in Hutchison, '"Accurate to the Point of Mania"', p. 28.
43. Fox, 'Conflict and Consolation', pp. 812–18.
44. Kenneth McConkey, 'Clausen, Sir George (1852–1944)', *Oxford Dictionary of National Biography* (Oxford: Oxford University Press, 2004); online edition (October 2007), <http://www.oxforddnb.com/view/article/32435> (last accessed 3 November 2016); Fox, 'Conflict and Consolation', p. 816; Stuart Sillars, *Art and Survival in First World War Britain* (Basingstoke: Macmillan, 1987), p. 133; Sue Malvern, 'War Tourisms: "Englishness", Art and the First World War', *Oxford Art Journal*, 24.1 (2001), 51–2.
45. Ysanne Holt, *British Artists and the Modernist Landscape* (Aldershot: Ashgate, 2003), pp. 1, 2, 6, 12–13, 26–7.
46. Peter Harrington, 'Religious and Spiritual Themes in British Academic Art during the Great War', *First World War Studies*, 2.2 (2011), 151; Kenneth McConkey, *George Clausen and the Picture of Rural English Life* (Edinburgh: Atelier Books, 2012), pp. 167–8.
47. See <http://blog.nationalarchives.gov.uk/blog/my-tommys-war-youth-mourning> (last accessed 3 November 2016) for an account of the background to this painting by Bruno Derrick, great-grandson of George Clausen.
48. Kenneth McConkey, *Sir George Clausen, R.A. 1852–1944* (Bradford: Bradford Art Galleries and Museums and Tyne and Wear County Council Museums, 1980), p. 80; Cork, *A Bitter Truth*, pp. 129–30 (including an illustration of the original composition); Harrington, 'Religious and Spiritual Themes', pp. 155–6.
49. J[ames] B[one], 'The Academy in War Time: Second Article', *The Manchester Guardian*, 24 May 1916, p. 3, quoted in McConkey, *George Clausen and the Picture of Rural English Life*, p. 169.
50. McConkey, *George Clausen and the Picture of Rural English Life*, pp. 165, 176.
51. Lise Svanholm, *Northern Light: The Skagen Painters* (Copenhagen: Gyldendal, 2003), p. 162, citing Annette Johansen.
52. Aimée Brown Price, 'Catalogue', in Brown Price et al. (eds), *Pierre Puvis de Chavannes* (New York: Van Gogh Museum, 1994), p. 250.
53. Hans H. Hofstätter, 'Symbolism in Germany and Europe', in Ingrid Ehrhardt and Simon Reynolds (eds), *Kingdom of the Soul: Symbolist Art in Germany 1870–1920* (Munich: Prestel, 2000), p. 27.
54. Hans H. Hofstätter, 'Faith and Damnation: Religious Depictions in Symbolism', in Ehrhardt and Reynolds (eds), *Kingdom of the Soul*, pp. 138, 147; see also Rolf Günther, 'Under the Titan's Sway', in Ehrhardt and Reynolds (eds), *Kingdom of the Soul*, pp. 224, 230.
55. George Clausen, *Aims and Ideals in Art: Eight lectures delivered to the students of the Royal Academy by George Clausen A.R.A., R.W.S., professor of painting at the Royal Academy, with thirty-two illustrations* (London: Methuen & Co., 1906), p. 115. Clausen

contrasts the 'true to nature' observational character of the Germans with the Italians' augmentation of realism with aesthetic rules and ideals; Hannes Schweiger, 'Between the Lines: George Bernard Shaw as Cultural and Political Mediator', in Brockington (ed.), *Internationalism and the Arts*, p. 275; Grace Brockington, '"A Jacob's Ladder between Country and Country": Art and Diplomacy before the First World War', in Brockington (ed.), *Internationalism and the Arts*, p. 299.

56. Clausen, *Aims and Ideals in Art*, p. 6.
57. Ibid., pp. 10, 15, 27.
58. Ibid., pp. 39–40.
59. Ibid., pp. 44–52; Paul Wood, 'The Revolutionary Avant-Gardes: Dada, Constructivism and Surrealism', in Wood (ed.), *The Challenge of the Avant-Garde*, p. 233.
60. Matthew Potter, 'Materialism and the Mark of Modernity in the Work of G. F. Watts', *British Art Journal*, 7.3 (Winter 2006–7), 70–8.
61. Robert Upstone, 'Study for the Resurrection of the Soldiers, Burghclere', in Hyman and Wright (eds), *Stanley Spencer*, p. 129; Hyman, 'Stanley Spencer: Angels and Dirt', pp. 24, 26–9; Richard A. Lofthouse, *Vitalism in Modern Art, c. 1900–1950: Otto Dix, Stanley Spencer, Max Beckmann and Jacob Epstein* (Lewiston: Edwin Mellen Press, 2005), pp. 134–45.
62. TGA 945.27: Spencer to Henry Lamb, 19 July 1915, reproduced in Glew (ed.), *Stanley Spencer Letters*, p. 57; see also diary entry pp. 57–60; TGA 8116.56: Spencer to Jacques Raveat and Gwen Darwin, [December?] 1915, reproduced ibid., p. 65; TGA 733.2.25: Spencer, Numbered Writings (1936), reproduced ibid., pp. 94–6; Gough, *A Terrible Beauty*, p. 256; TGA 8116.61: Spencer to Jacques Raveat and Gwen Darwin, [June/July? 1916], reproduced in Glew (ed.), *Stanley Spencer Letters*, p. 72; TGA 945.40: Spencer to Henry Lamb, 3 June 1918, reproduced ibid., p. 92.
63. TGA 733.3.86: Spencer, Notebook (1945–7), reproduced in Glew (ed.), *Stanley Spencer Letters*, pp. 76–7.
64. Harrington, 'Religious and Spiritual Themes', pp. 146, 159.
65. Cork, *A Bitter Truth*, pp. 91–149.
66. Chute Correspondence, Stanley Spencer Gallery, Cookham: Spencer to Desmond Chute, 4 January 1917, Notebook (1945–7), reproduced in Glew (ed.), *Stanley Spencer Letters*, pp. 78–9.
67. Robert Upstone, '*Travoys with Wounded Soldiers Arriving at a Dressing Station at Smol, Macedonia*', in Hyman and Wright (eds), *Stanley Spencer*, pp. 102–3; see also Gough, *A Terrible Beauty*, pp. 270–2.
68. Duncan Robinson, 'Introduction', in *Stanley Spencer at Burghclere: The Oratory of All Souls Sandham Memorial Chapel, Hampshire* (London: National Trust, 1991), pp. 4, 7–8; TGA 825.14: Stanley Spencer to Florence Spencer, [September/October] 1923, reproduced in Glew (ed.), *Stanley Spencer Letters*, p. 124.
69. Ibid., pp. 4, 8–9.
70. TGA 825.14: Stanley Spencer to Peggy Andrews, [1928/29?], reproduced in Glew (ed.), *Stanley Spencer Letters*, p. 140; Patrick Wright, 'Purposeful Art in a Climate of Cultural Reaction: Stanley Spencer in the 1920s', in Hyman and Wright (eds), *Stanley Spencer*, pp. 51–2; Robinson, 'Introduction', p. 8.
71. Wright, 'Purposeful Art in a Climate of Cultural Reaction', pp. 44–6; TGA 733.3.86: Stanley Spencer, Notebook, 6 December 1947, reproduced in Glew (ed.), *Stanley Spencer Letters*, p. 142.
72. TGA 8116.87: Spencer to Jacques Raveat and Gwen Darwin, [4 November 1919], reproduced in Glew (ed.), *Stanley Spencer Letters*, p. 107; Gough, *A Terrible Beauty*, pp. 273–4; Upstone, '*Travoys*', p. 103.

73. TGA 733.3.86: Stanley Spencer, Notebook, 1945–7, reproduced in Glew (ed.), *Stanley Spencer Letters*, p. 111.
74. Malvern, *Modern Art, Britain and the Great War*, p. 162.
75. Andrew Causey, *Stanley Spencer: Art as a Mirror of Himself* (Farnham: Lund Humphries, 2014), pp. 52–4.
76. See <http://www.iwm.org.uk/memorials/item/memorial/7925> (last accessed 3 November 2016); the dedication occurred on 21 September 1919 (see also *Maidenhead Advertiser*, 24 September 1919, 8 September 1920, 19 June 1946).
77. Toby Thacker, *British Culture and the First World War: Experience, Representation and Memory* (New York: Bloomsbury, 2014), pp. 260, 320 n. 34.
78. Hutchison, '"Accurate to the Point of Mania"', pp. 29–30.
79. Anne Gray, 'Longstaff, William Frederick (Will) (1879–1953)', *Australian Dictionary of Biography*, National Centre of Biography, Australian National University, 1986: <http://adb.anu.edu.au/biography/longstaff-william-frederick-will-7231/text12521> (last accessed 3 November 2016); see <https://www.awm.gov.au/people/P10676718/#Art> (last accessed 3 November 2016) for a list of works produced by Longstaff for the AWR programme.
80. Anon., 'At Menin Gate: Longstaff's Picture: Was It Occult Inspired?', *Canberra Times*, 21 February 1929, p. 3, column d.
81. Jay Winter, *Sites of Memory, Sites of Mourning: The Great War in European Cultural History* (Cambridge: Cambridge University Press, 1995), pp. 60–1.
82. Anon., '"Menin Gate." Mr. Longstaff's Inspiration. LONDON, June 8', *Sydney Morning Herald*, 11 June 1932, p. 13, column b.
83. Arthur Conan Doyle, *The Guards Came Through and Other Poems* (London: John Murray, 1919).
84. Australian War Memorial, *'Menin Gate at Midnight' (Or 'The Ghosts of Menin Gate'): The Story of Captain Will Longstaff's Great Allegorical Painting* (Melbourne, 1929), p. 13: <http://nla.gov.au/nla.obj-35299942/view?searchTerm=woolavington+longstaff#page/n12/mode/1up> (last accessed 9 November 2016).
85. Australian War Memorial, *'Menin Gate at Midnight'*, p. 15.
86. See exhibition 'Will Longstaff: Art & Remembrance', 20 November 2001 to 10 February 2002, Australian War Memorial, Canberra. *Immortal Shrine* (or *Eternal Silence*, 1928) depicted ghost soldiers passing the Cenotaph on Remembrance Day 1928; *Ghosts of Vimy Ridge* (1931) portrayed the spirits of Canadian servicemen, and *Carillon* (1932) New Zealand soldiers, all as companion pieces to *Menin Gate at Midnight*. See also Anon., '"ETERNAL SILENCE." Will Longstaff's New Work', *The Register* (Adelaide), 22 November 1928, p. 9, column d; 'Eternal Silence' was Colonel Williams's suggestion (possibly Lt Col. Ernest Morgan Williams in the Australian Imperial Force) for the title: <https://www.awm.gov.au/people/rolls/R1536932> (last accessed 3 November 2016).
87. Anon., 'The Rearguard: Longstaff Picture Bought by Sir C. Doyle', *Barrier Miner* (Broken Hill, NSW), 10 May 1928, p. 4, column a; Michaela Boland, 'Gallipoli Painting Unearthed', *The Australian*, 29 April 2010: <http://www.theaustralian.com.au/arts/gallipoli-painting-unearthed/story-e6frg8n6-1225859609532> (last accessed 3 November 2016).
88. Owen Dudley Edwards, 'Doyle, Sir Arthur Ignatius Conan (1859–1930)', *Oxford Dictionary of National Biography*; online edition (April 2016), <http://www.oxforddnb.com/view/article/32887> (last accessed 3 November 2016).
89. John Stephens, '"The Ghosts of Menin Gate": Art, Architecture and Commemoration', *Journal of Contemporary History*, 44.1 (2009), 19.
90. Ibid., pp. 9–10.
91. K. S. Inglis and Jan Brazier, *Sacred Places: War Memorials in the Australian Landscape* (Carlton, Victoria: Melbourne University Press, 2008), p. 262.

92. Anon., 'Marching: Legions of Dead: Menin Gate: Longstaff's Triumph ("Sun" Special), LONDON, Friday Night', *The Sun* (Sydney), 3 December 1927, p. 1, column d.
93. Stephens, '"The Ghosts of Menin Gate"', p. 8.
94. Australian War Memorial, *'Menin Gate at Midnight'*, p. 4.
95. Anon., 'British Courage. "Menin Gate" is Memorial. Longstaff's Picture Unveiled. Sydney, March 26', *Queensland Times*, 27 March 1929, p. 8, column d.
96. Anon., 'Great Allegorical Painting offered to Canberra. London, Wednesday Night', *The Sun* (Sydney), 19 January 1928, p. 1, column f; Stephens, '"The Ghosts of Menin Gate"', pp. 24–5.
97. Ronald B. Weir, 'Buchanan, James, Baron Woolavington (1849–1935)', *Oxford Dictionary of National Biography*; online edition (January 2011), <http://www.oxforddnb.com/view/article/32151> (last accessed 3 November 2016); Gary B. Magee and Andrew S. Thompson, *Empire and Globalisation: Networks of People, Goods and Capital in the British World, c. 1850–1914* (Cambridge: Cambridge University Press, 2010), p. 156.
98. Riding, 'Introduction: Art and the War at Sea', p. 13; Fox, *British Art and the First World War*, pp. 78–80.
99. See <https://www.1418now.org.uk/dazzle-ship-scotland-remains-leith-dock-end-august> (last accessed 3 November 2016).
100. See <http://www.iwm.org.uk/collections/item/object/30019074> (last accessed 3 November 2016).
101. See <http://www.studio88.co.uk/acatalog/WW1_Albatros_painting.html> (last accessed 3 November 2016).
102. See <http://www.charronpugsleyhill.com/2015/06/14/in-flanders-fields-today-original-painting-by-peterborough-artist-charron-pugsley-hill> (last accessed 3 November 2016); James Fox, 'Poppy Politics: Remembrance of Things Present', in Constantine Sandis (ed.), *Cultural Heritage Ethics: Between Theory and Practice* (Cambridge: Open Book Publishers, 2014).
103. See <https://uk.pinterest.com/pin/556898310155036183> (last accessed 3 November 2016).
104. See <http://bellewaarde1915.co.uk/art/soren%20hawkes.htm> (last accessed 3 November 2016).
105. See <http://www.paoyeomanry.co.uk/PM/LYWW1.htm> (last accessed 3 November 2016).
106. Hughie O'Donoghue, 'Acts of Remembrance: Hughie O'Donoghue RA Contemplates Art of the First World War', *RA Magazine*, summer 2014, p. 20.
107. James Hamilton, 'The Work of Hughie O'Donoghue', *Irish Arts Review Yearbook* (1990–91), 144, 152.
108. O'Donoghue, 'Acts of Remembrance'.

# 8

# 'Varied to Infinity': The First World War and Sculpture

*Laura Brandon*

## Introduction

Practically and creatively, the First World War had a huge impact on sculptural work in the West. During the conflict, a growing creative divide, originating in the immediate pre-war artistic activity centred largely in Paris, continued. On the one hand, there were the established more representative but still relatively modern traditions (such as Impressionism) of the long-established Paris ateliers associated with celebrated psychologically deep Romantic sculptors such as Auguste Rodin (1840–1917). On the other hand, there were the burgeoning but publicly still little-appreciated avant-garde modernist and formalist movements associated with Cubism, Expressionism, Abstraction, Symbolism and other Post-Impressionist approaches. A growing interest in primitive and ancient art led by artists such as Spaniard Pablo Picasso (1881–1973) invigorated these new advances although, strictly speaking, their associated artists did not necessarily only self-identify as sculptors. Relatively absent in this period was any evolving neo-classical direction. To emerge so strongly immediately post-war, however, it had to have existed, probably in remembered traditional art training with its repetitive study of classical statuary, and through the work of established proponents such as Aristide Maillol (1861–1944). In such creatively divergent circumstances, Paris-trained American sculptor Jo Davidson (1883–1952) was recorded as claiming – and with no apparent irony – that the war had no influence on art, only on some of its themes.[1]

With few exceptions, art production dropped during the conflict. The events of August 1914 instigated a rapid exodus of artists from Paris in the direction of their homes or neutral countries, or for parts of France not in immediate danger. Many artists enlisted in their national armies or, ultimately, were conscripted. Pre-war colleagues found themselves uncomfortably on opposite sides. Indeed, numerous up-and-coming twentieth-century artists of many nationalities spent much of the war as soldiers and not as artists, assuming they survived. With difficulty, in many cases, they coped with a mechanised, industrialised conflict and its legacy of millions of dead alongside an unparalleled annihilation of the urban and rural landscape that had no precedent. Together with multiple deaths and injuries involving friends, family and collaborators, artists also saw and learned of sculptural loss in the widespread destruction of medieval European towns, villages and cathedrals as a result of bombing and shellfire. Furthermore, even their own art was not immune to destruction.

Ukrainian Cubist sculptor Alexander Archipenko's (1887–1964) *Family Life* (1912), for example, was demolished in Paris during a bombardment and is today known only through photographs.[2]

Those who did not participate in the conflict but continued to try to work were hampered by shortages of materials, commissions and sales, and curtailed travel and exhibiting opportunities. Some relief came with official assignments through various countries' official war art programmes, but these were scarce and often impossible to complete before the conflict's end. Some artists in exile, traumatised by unfamiliar and difficult circumstances, did little or no work at all. Belgian Symbolist sculptor George Minne (1866–1941), for instance, produced no notable work during his sojourn in Wales.

Picasso, perhaps the early twentieth century's most inventive artist, made no sculpture between 1915 and 1927. In consequence, much of the sculptural production associated with the conflict was completed years, and even decades, after 1914–18. Rarely, for example, were the great public and private war memorials that commemorate the dead conceived in wartime. Nevertheless, because sculptural practice had been exciting and divergent pre-war, some sculpture – Dada work, for example – was made during the conflict, and continued to challenge preconceptions as to what sculpture was or could be. If this work was not coloured necessarily by the grand themes of battle, it was driven by the inanity of war and it was the circumstances of conflict that brought many of the artists together. Furthermore, it certainly reflected and developed pre-war innovations and practices and incorporated a wide variety of subject matters.

For the purposes of clarity, this introduction to the First World War and sculpture in the West focuses on the war years and does not explore war memorials, as these are the subjects of Laura Wittman's chapter in this volume. Following a brief introduction to the state of sculpture internationally prior to the conflict's outbreak, it looks at the emergence of the Dada and Constructivist movements in the war years. The subsequent three sections are organised geographically, centring on three of the main combatant countries: France, Great Britain and Germany. The work of many other countries' sculptors is integrated into these where there are obvious intersections. Inevitably there are omissions, as this account cannot claim to be anything more than a brief general survey. The focus is the links between artists and movements in the period. Endnotes provide more details about works mentioned in the text, and, as the majority of the artists have well-established reputations, the internet affords a wealth of further information and imagery relating to them.

## Before the War

In Europe, by the end of the nineteenth century, improved transportation and also the social disruptions caused by conflicts such as the Franco-Prussian War (1870–1) had mobilised sculptors. North Americans, and other far-flung Western nationals too, were encouraged to study abroad, their international experience fostering growing reputations at home. Mobilisation brought the possibility of secure teaching positions in different countries as well as stable commissions, new markets and exhibition opportunities. It was a nation-building age and many countries (and their inhabitants) were eager to commission sculptures that reflected their histories and the men and women who made them. In the wake of exhibition opportunities, furthermore, emerged art critics who eagerly commented on new work to a growing educated and leisured middle class. Not only mobilisation but also industrial development brought easier access to materials and technology. Countering this rosy picture, however, was the fact that sculpture was an undeniably expensive creative medium. The result was that popular taste regularly drove commissions, which were nevertheless numerous, representational, mostly in bronze, and highly visible. If, in general terms, the plethora of public art held back artistic vitality, one notable exception was Rodin, who, perhaps in response to widespread mediocrity, successfully melded startling innovation with public expectations.

Change came gradually in the early twentieth century. Cubism, launched by Picasso and French painter Georges Braque (1882–1963) in Paris between 1907 and 1914, deconstructed traditional anticipated subjects and encouraged experimentation in form and materials that transformed painting, sculpture, photography and a host of other media. Expressed in sculptures or assemblages emphasising space and structure, Cubist approaches challenged representational art forms and inspired a new generation of artists. Nevertheless, it was Rodin and his successors Aristide Maillol and Antoine Bourdelle (1861–1929) who still dominated the field with their solid yet expressive and emotional compositions. Moreover, their reliance on extensive assistance ironically was to provide many in succeeding generations with the technical skills necessary to strike out as non-dependent sculptors. Shortly before war broke out, two new figures made an impact in Paris. The innovations of Italian Futurist Umberto Boccioni (1882–1916) and Romanian Constantin Brancusi (1876–1957) began to erode the sculptural status quo and influence the new generation. When war broke out in 1914, Paris was the centre for artists, a place where the established and the emergent could meet and exchange ideas in numerous studios, ateliers and cafés, and at exhibitions.

If any innovations can be considered to have matured in the war, it is those advanced by Boccioni and Brancusi. Influenced by Cubism, Boccioni decided to become a sculptor after he visited various avant-garde sculptors' and painters' studios in Paris in 1912. As a result, in his 1912 *Technical Manifesto of Futurist Sculpture* he advocated combining non-traditional materials including cement, glass, light, wood and textiles in sculpture. Using a more traditional material – plaster – in his dynamic *Unique Forms of Continuity in Space* (1913), the sculptor captured the essence of movement in time and space.[3] He also incorporated the Futurists' militaristic leanings in the figure's overall armoured appearance and seemingly helmeted face. After war was declared, Boccioni enlisted in the Italian army and was killed in 1916 following a fall from a horse. His pugnacity is remembered, however, in fellow Futurist Giacomo Balla's (1871–1958) bright red abstract sculpture *Boccioni's Fist – Lines of Force II* (1916–17).[4]

Like so many sculptors of the period, as a young man Constantin Brancusi spent a short time in Rodin's Paris studio. Disenchanted with the factory-like atmosphere of the studio and its use of moulds, however, he very quickly opted to make his way independently in his quest for pure form. From 1907, he often carved his materials directly, breaking with the traditional practice of modelling in clay for later enlargement in marble or stone by a specialist craftsperson. Even when he utilised traditional techniques, the critical response his abstract *Princess X* (1915) received underlined the

First World War era's prevailing conservative attitudes towards modern sculpture.[5] He showed this sculpture of Princess Marie Bonaparte in New York at the Society of Independent Artists in 1917 to generally negative reviews, but when the bronze version was exhibited in Paris in 1920 it was banned as being deliberately phallic. It was only reinstated as a result of a campaign led by Brancusi's friends and colleagues, who signed a manifesto, published in *Le Journal du Peuple* (25 February 1920). Later, in 1935, the by now acceptable Brancusi took a commission to design a powerful First World War memorial at Targu Jiu in Romania.

## The First World War

### *Dada*

The most startling sculptural art forms to emerge directly from the First World War were the assemblages and readymades associated with the pan-national Dada movement. Emerging as a literary and artistic movement in neutral Switzerland beginning in 1915, Dada exploited irrationality, nonsense, accident, travesty and incongruity to challenge contemporary conventional art and cultural values into the early 1920s in a number of European and American cities including Berlin and New York. It was profoundly anti-war, anti-bourgeois, and radically left wing. By 1924 it was over, but its impact was enormous and resonates in artistic and literary counter-establishment and postmodern movements to this day. Key artists associated with Dada who made sculptures include Jean (Hans) Arp (French, 1887–1966), Marcel Duchamp (French, 1887–1968), Max Ernst (German, 1891–1976), George Grosz (German, 1893–1959), John Heartfield (German, 1891–1968), Hannah Höch (German, 1899–1978), Marcel Janco (Romanian, 1895–1984), Man Ray (American, 1890–1976), Morton Livingston Schamberg (American, 1881–1918), Kurt Schwitters (German, 1887–1948), Sophie Taeuber-Arp (Swiss, 1889–1943) and Baroness Elsa von Freytag-Loringhoven (German, 1874–1927).

During the war, in Berlin Hannah Höch constructed and exhibited stuffed dolls with exaggerated and often abstract features that drew on her knowledge of the materials associated with women's work.[6] But the conflict shattered her worldview, leading her to create post-conflict photomontages that pieced together in more cynical form her newly devastated environment. In post-war Berlin, Dada exemplified the cynical reaction of many to the war's immense physical destruction, which left tens of thousands of severely damaged ex-soldiers. George Grosz and John Heartfield, both better known for their two-dimensional work, met as soldiers and, after the war, created the electro-mechanical performative piece *The Middle-Class Philistine Heartfield Gone Wild* (1920), now only known from photographs although it has been reconstructed.[7] The physical consequences of war are exemplified in this store-bought mannequin whose missing body parts are replaced with found objects including a light bulb and metal rod.

Former soldier Max Ernst, severely traumatised by his wartime experiences, produced work in post-war Cologne that envisaged the world as irrational. His most celebrated composition, *Celebes* (1921), a quasi-portrait of an elephant-like form made up of disparate 'found' items, may not be a sculpture per se, but was inspired by a three-dimensional object in the form of a Sudanese corn bin.[8] In 1915, Jean (Hans)

Arp, whose father was German, left Paris for Switzerland to take advantage of Swiss neutrality, where, following Futurist dictates about the use of new materials, he created colourful painted wooden reliefs inspired by forms in nature, and not war, such as *Hammer Flower* (1916).[9] There he met and married Swiss-born Sophie Taeuber, whose Dada heads made of carved wood, paint and found decoration are significant examples of immediate post-war Dada sculpture.[10] Romanian Marcel Janco also moved to Switzerland during the war, where his carved African-style masks played a vital role in early Dada performance art. Kurt Schwitters also served briefly in the German army but it was his country's post-war collapse and the influence of Jean Arp that most affected his art, resulting in the abstract collages he dubbed *Merz* – a part of the word 'Kommerz' (commerce). Between 1923 and 1933, he transformed his Hanover family home into a sculpted non-art total environment, the *Merzbau*, which was destroyed in 1943 and is now known only through photographs and reconstruction.[11]

Even if Cubism and Futurism clearly influenced Dada, there is no doubt that in the work of Marcel Duchamp, such influences were only the beginning. When war was declared, exempted from military service, he moved from Paris to New York. His Dada-inspired 'found art' or readymades include his famous 1917 *Fountain*, a urinal signed R. Mutt (now lost but replicated with the artist's permission in an edition of eight in 1964).[12] One of the most influential sculptures of the twentieth century, *Fountain* declares unequivocally that it is the artist who determines what is, and what is not, a work of art. In an era when sculptors depended on commissions for their livelihood, thus subjecting any evaluation of their work as art to the whims of popular taste, Duchamp's work resonated with artists first quietly, but ever more strongly as the years went by. Contemporary evidence suggests that Baroness Elsa von Freytag-Loringhoven, a German-born artist and poet who lived Dada (stamps stuck to her face and a birdcage with a live canary dangling from her neck), assisted in the creation of *Fountain* as it was more in line with her scatological interests than those of Duchamp.[13] She also possibly worked with pacifist Morton Livingston Schamberg to create *God* (c. 1917), an iron plumbing trap mounted upside-down on top of a wooden mitre box.[14] Apparently the piece and its title alluded to a comment made by Duchamp that extolled plumbing as America's greatest artwork. Man Ray also came into Duchamp's orbit and created readymades. *The Coat Stand* (1920), a photograph of a naked woman posed as half a coat stand, however, begs the question as to whether Ray saw her as a servile object or, by overtly presenting her as such, was in fact protesting her servility on her behalf.[15]

## Constructivism

Another unique product of the war, Constructivism, a Cubist offshoot, and one that encompassed more disciplines than sculpture alone, emerged in Russia. Its genesis lay in the work of a group of Russian artists forced back to their country by the circumstances of the conflict. Exciting and innovative between 1914 and 1922, its practitioners were ultimately discouraged from continuing their pioneering practices in the wake of the 1917 Bolshevik Revolution. Their ideas, however, continued to reverberate well into the twentieth century through the ongoing work of those who fled revolutionary Russia for other countries. One Constructivist, much inspired in Paris by Picasso's pre-war collages, assemblages and reliefs, was Vladimir Tatlin (1885–1953), whose wartime abstract corner reliefs explored space with arrangements of three-dimensional geometric forms in room corners.[16] Another important Russian artist associated with Constructivism, who returned to Russia from Paris, was Naum Gabo (1890–1977). *Head No. 2* (1916) exemplifies his early approach, which he termed the 'stereometric method', eschewing mass to demonstrate a sure facility with plane, surface, shape, space and angle in the construction of this female portrait bust.[17] Similarly isolated in Moscow by the war, Alexander Rodchenko (1891–1956) also worked in a Constructivist mode, creating complicated freestanding, and often kinetic, abstract structures out of metal and other materials, such as *Spatial Construction No. 12* (c. 1920).[18]

## *France*

Following the declaration of war on 4 August 1914, the elderly Rodin fled to Britain, where he gifted a collection of bronze, marble and terracotta sculptures to the Victoria and Albert Museum as a token of his admiration for the British and French soldiers participating in the conflict. Newspaper reports gave his donation greater import, however, viewing the gift as a kind of monument to Allied ideals. By 1915, he was in Italy, where he sculpted a bust of Pope Benedict XV. In 1916, he began his final work (which remained unfinished), a bust of Étienne Clémentel, the French Minister of Commerce, Industry, Posts and Telegraphs, who had played an important role in the founding of the Rodin Museum in Paris. These eclectic activities on the part of the world's then best-known sculptor provide telling evidence of the nature of traditional sculptural activity during the First World War. In his last years, which coincided with the conflict, Rodin fled his home country, accepted a commission (the papal bust), began a personally meaningful work (the Clémentel bust), and paid respect to those involved in the conflict, in his case with donated work.

Originally inspired by Rodin, but by now clearly in tune with Cubist and Futurist approaches, established French sculptor Raymond Duchamp-Villon (1876–1918) became a soldier in the French army. His major Cubist sculpture, *The Horse*, was incomplete when he died of typhoid fever in 1916.[19] The tightly orchestrated and dynamic arches, curves, hollows, spirals and straight lines of *The Horse* (1914) suggest both animal and mechanical parts at one and the same time. His brothers Jacques Villon (1875–1963) and Marcel Duchamp enlarged it and had it cast in 1930–1. Duchamp-Villon's Ukrainian associate Alexander Archipenko spent the war years in Nice, France, where he continued to create Cubist-inspired figurative sculptures such as *Woman Combing her Hair* (1915) using interlocking and overlapping solids and sculptural voids to show various views of the figure simultaneously.[20] Influenced by Rodin as well as Cubism and Futurism, Paris-based Russian Ossip Zadkine (1890–1967) also utilised dramatically expressive shapes and forms with concave contours and hollows in his sculptures. A Cubist sculptor who continued to work in Paris during the war was Lithuanian-born Jacob Lipchitz (1891–1973). His *Man with a Guitar* (1915) demonstrates the movement's enduring quotidian subject matter during the war years, at the same time that its overlapping geometric limestone forms belie his material's inherent solidity.[21] Another Cubist sculptor was Henri Laurens (1885–1954), who, exempted from war service for health reasons, made constructed sculptures and Cubist-style paper collages (now rare) in Paris after 1915. In *Bottle and Glass* (1917), a piece of newspaper indicates the here and now in an otherwise abstract composition.[22]

Older and established, Henri Matisse (1869–1954) wanted to enlist in the French army and purchased soldier's boots and took a medical examination, but a weak heart resulted in rejection. As the German army advanced on Paris he sold prints to buy food for French soldiers and refused to do solo shows while Frenchmen were fighting. Ultimately, he relocated from Paris to Nice in 1917. In the years before the war he had been struggling to respond to new sculptural idioms and African art in his work, but Rodin remained a dominant influence. He worked obsessively on *The Serf* (1900–8), using the same Italian model that Rodin hired for his *John the Baptist* (1878) and *Walking Man* (c. 1900). In Matisse's work, the transition to a more modern approach was lengthy and is best represented by the series of four *Back* sculptures completed between 1903 and 1931, as well as his five *Jeannette* heads (1910–16). Family members were also his subjects during the war years. With its powerful handling and abstracted elements, the bust of his daughter, Marguerite (1915), shows an artist who is still evolving.[23]

Given the legacy of war in France and Belgium, it is not surprising to learn that when it came to erecting war memorials more than 2,000 sculptors were associated with 'Les monuments aux morts'.[24] This suggests that sculpture in France survived the exigencies of conflict. One can cite sculptor Charles-Édouard Richefeu (1868–1945) as one example of this large, prolific but relatively unknown group, an example of whose work can be found in the Imperial War Museum's collection.[25] Better-known participants in the post-war monument-building enterprise are Rodin's disciples Bourdelle and Maillol, who completed a number of war memorial commissions following the cessation of hostilities.

## *Great Britain*

Rodin's immense popularity in Britain at the outbreak of war affected popular taste during and after the war and led to a preponderance of powerful, expressive and, at times, somewhat sentimental sculptural work in traditional materials. The need for vigorously emotive artworks during and after the conflict perhaps underlines the timing of the unveiling of Rodin's magisterial *The Burghers of Calais* (1889) in Victoria Tower Gardens, abutting London's Houses of Parliament, in July 1915. The story of the six besieged Calais citizens who turned themselves over to English King Edward III in 1347 in return for the city's salvation and were spared spoke to prevailing British wartime notions of self-sacrifice for the greater good. Calais, it should be noted, capitulated on 4 August 1347, the same day and month that the First World War began.

Not quite three months after the sculpture's unveiling, on 12 October 1915, a German firing squad executed Edith Cavell, head of a Brussels Red Cross hospital. Sir George Frampton (1860–1928) promptly offered to design a memorial without charging a fee, and the necessary funds were swiftly raised by subscription. It was not, however, unveiled until 1920 as the necessary marble and bronze were not easily available in wartime. The work is surprisingly modern with its geometric planes, and includes quasi-archaic Greek qualities, as in the mother and child figures on top.

Perhaps Frampton, despite his age and long career, was cognisant in designing it that sculpture was changing in Britain in the wake of Cubism and Futurism. Combined with a revival of interest in ancient Chinese, Egyptian, Assyrian and Greek precedents and new discoveries in Africa and Oceania, sculptural practice in his country was being transformed. With this memorial, Frampton became one of the first to try to reconcile these modernist tendencies in traditional commemorative sculpture.

Young British sculptors increasingly shunned the traditional studio practice that had allowed Rodin's craftspeople to replicate his clay and plaster studies in stone and bronze. They favoured personal involvement with the original material, direct carving being one notable route. Artist and critic Roger Fry (1866–1934) and critic Clive Bell (1881–1964) influenced a number of them in this direction with their adherence to the concept of Bell's term 'original form'. The pair's understanding of French painter Paul Cézanne's (1839–1906) handling of volume and space also provided young painters and sculptors with a new outlook on composition. The inclusion of some of Paul Gauguin's (1848–1903) woodcarvings in his posthumous 1906 Paris retrospective also had a notable impact on the British sculptural community. Furthermore, knowledge of Brancusi's rejection of Rodin's practice with early direct stone carvings such as *The Kiss* (1907–8), which has to be understood in the context of Rodin's smooth and luminous marble *The Kiss* (c. 1888–98), set a new direction for modern British sculptors that was in opposition to public taste of the time, which was definitely Rodinesque.[26] Another major influence on pre-war British sculpture in terms of direct carving was the pre-war work of the Paris-based Italian artist Amedeo Modigliani (1884–1920) in the form of elongated, simply carved portraits.

Direct carving was pioneered by three UK-based artists just prior to the First World War, namely Anglo-American Jacob Epstein (1880–1959), Eric Gill (1882–1940) and Frenchman Henri Gaudier-Brzeska (1891–1915). A slightly later adherent to the practice was Frank Dobson (1886–1963), whose *Kneeling Female Figure* (c. 1915) shows these artists' shared debt to the inspiration of the ancient global collections they could view so easily in the British or Victoria and Albert Museums and, before the war, in the Louvre in Paris.[27] Epstein claimed it was the British Museum that made him relocate from the United States to Britain in 1905, where in 1907 he became a citizen. Indeed, Epstein made his own impressive collection of primitive and ancient sculpture during his lifetime. Over time, however, Epstein's war work expressed divided loyalties, the later war busts of the rich and famous owing more to his earlier adherence to Rodin's approach than to that espoused by his modernist colleagues.

The somewhat serene classicism of Eric Gill's work before the war shows Maillol's influence. Although Gill never entirely gave up modelling, he used carving extensively to render his preferred erotic subjects. During the war, however, in conjunction with his own spiritual affiliations, his work was almost exclusively religious. His most important commission, which effectively occupied him for the entirety of the war, was his *Stations of the Cross* (1913–19) for the Catholic Westminster Cathedral in London. Clarity of line and simplicity of pattern enhance the narrative content of these low reliefs and they remain exemplars of the art of stone carving in early twentieth-century Britain.

It was in fact Gill who taught Epstein how to carve. In 1912, Epstein met Picasso and Brancusi in Paris and was further diverted towards more experimental sculpture.

The occasion was the unveiling of Epstein's controversial tomb of Oscar Wilde (1912) in the cemetery of Père Lachaise, which, despite its Assyrian sculptural influences, critics deemed indecent. Back home on the other side of the English Channel, Epstein responded with *Birth* (c. 1913), a small, audacious stone carving depicting parturition in relatively graphic detail.[28] His celebrated *Rock Drill* (1913–16) followed, now in complete form known only through photographs and reproductions (Plate 5).[29] Albeit now minus its drill, Epstein's menacing bronze today encapsulates the mechanistic nature of the Great War, whereas in 1913 it was its overt sexuality that drew critical reaction. In plaster, the machine-like torso, a foetus contained within it, stood astride a real, and phallic, pneumatic drill (probably one similar to those used to prepare suitable stone for carving). Describing it in his 1940 autobiography, with the Second World War under way, Epstein wrote: 'Here is the armed, sinister figure of to-day and to-morrow. No humanity, only the terrible Frankenstein's monster we have made ourselves into.'[30]

The *Rock Drill* connects Epstein to the incipient Vorticist art movement, founded in 1914, a British offshoot of Futurism that similarly focused on dehumanised mechanism. It also links him to Marcel Duchamp, who in 1913 unveiled in his Paris studio his first readymade – a bicycle wheel on a stool.[31] In 1915, Epstein reworked the *Rock Drill*'s figure, giving it arms, which seemingly protect the foetus while adding an overall sense of vulnerability, arguably appropriate to the circumstances of the conflict, which then concerned him with its growing casualty lists. In 1916, he revised the sculpture once more, removing one arm and both legs and deleting the drill entirely, suggesting an even greater vulnerability evocative of the very real carnage daily presented to him in war news and very present in the death of good friends and fellow artists.[32]

*Rock Drill*'s reincarnation was not Epstein's only anti-war response. In 1916, his abhorrence of conflict finally turned him away from Vorticism, Abstraction and direct carving, for the most part towards modelled portraiture in bronze. His rich and high-born clients included, rather surprisingly, Admiral of the Fleet Lord Fisher (1916), whose more traditional likeness still incorporates something of Epstein's modernist language.[33] His changed approach provided him with his first exhibition at the Leicester Galleries in 1917, where his work sold reasonably well. To avoid war service, *The Tin Hat* (1916), a portrait of an ordinary soldier, was an attempt to get him a commission with the British War Memorials scheme, run by Canadian expatriate newspaper baron Lord Beaverbrook, a plan that failed in part due to establishment sculptor George Frampton's negative intervention.[34] Frampton clearly did not believe that the Epstein of the *Rock Drill* was in any way reformed. His failure to obtain any official status in contemporary British sculptural circles probably also contributed to Epstein's failure to receive any post-conflict war memorial commissions. It forced him to enlist in 1917 and in 1918 he suffered an apparent nervous breakdown.

Under Epstein's influence, Gaudier-Brzeska was a constant visitor to the British Museum after his arrival in Britain in 1911 and he claimed that Epstein made him into a stone carver. Considered one of the finest practitioners of his generation, and a key member of the Vorticist group, Gaudier-Brzeska was given no opportunity to respond to the war in sculpture. In 1914, he enlisted in the French army, and he was killed the following year. Shortly after he enlisted, he carved a toothbrush out of bone for a comrade, and ornamented his wooden rifle butt with carvings. He also wrote an article, 'Vortex Gaudier-Brzeska', for the 1914 second issue of *Blast: Review of the Great English Vortex.* The following extract provides some inkling as to why his death was so mourned by his colleagues:

> My views on sculpture remain absolutely the same [. . .] I shall derive my emotions solely from the arrangement of surfaces [. . .] Just as this hill where the Germans are solidly entrenched gives me a nasty feeling, solely because its gentle slopes are broken up by earth-works, which throw long shadows at sunset. Just so shall I get feeling, of whatever definition, from a statue according to its slopes, varied to infinity.

As for direct carving, after the war it became an established British practice exemplified in the sculptures of artists such as Henry Moore (1898–1986) and Barbara Hepworth (1903–75).

If not all sculptors working in Britain shared Gaudier-Brzeska's tragic fate, war interrupted many promising careers. Gilbert Ledward (1888–1960) won a Royal Academy scholarship for arts students, the Prix de Rome for sculpture, in 1913 and subsequently served in the artillery until April 1918, when the Ministry of Information seconded him as a war artist to produce reliefs of soldiers in action. Post-war, as a representational sculptor, he was greatly in demand as a maker of war memorials. Interestingly, by the 1920s he had largely abandoned bronze casting in favour of direct carving. Late in the war, Charles Sergeant Jagger (1885–1934), who won the Prix de Rome the year after, also found employment through the Ministry of Information, subsequently creating some of Britain's most memorable memorial sculptures such as *No Man's Land* (1919–20) and the Royal Artillery Memorial at Hyde Park Corner, London (1925).[35] Like so many British sculptors caught up in the conflict, Philip Lindsey Clark (1889–1977) established his career, in part through war memorial commissions, only after distinguished service in battle. It seems clear that the authorities demonstrated minimal interest in employing sculptors in the official war art scheme. A survey of the Imperial War Museum's First World War collections lists work by eight sculptors mentioned elsewhere in this chapter and a further eighteen, several wartime and post-war refugees or expatriates resident in London, whose work – mostly portrait busts – was donated, most often by the sculptor in the years following the Armistice.[36]

Lord Beaverbrook not only ran the British War Memorials scheme, but also ran its Canadian equivalent, the Canadian War memorials.[37] As part of the British Empire, Canada was at war the moment Britain was. As a result, a number of British sculptors were commissioned to do work for the Canadians. Clare Sheridan (1885–1970) was one, producing a bronze portrait of Canadian air ace Billy Bishop (1918–19).[38] Only a handful of sculptors were active in Canada at the time, but two women (also partners in life) became significant figures in the field's post-war expansion as a result of a 1918 official commission for fourteen representative bronze figures of male and female munitions and farm workers. Florence Wyle (1881–1968) created nine of them and Frances Loring (1887–1968) five. Like almost all Canada's official war art, these are now in the collection of the Canadian War Museum.[39] Loring also created a large bronze frieze of factory workers on their lunchtime break, *Noon Hour in a Munitions Plant* (1918–19),[40] and, privately, a moving sculpture of a grieving woman entitled *Grief* (1918).[41] Canada's best-known wartime sculptor was then American resident and physician Robert Tait McKenzie (1867–1938), who served with the Royal Army Medical Corps during the war, completing a number of war memorials afterwards.

Canada's official war programme was also instrumental in acquiring a major sculpted frieze, *The Canadian Phalanx* (1918), from Croatian sculptor Ivan Meštrović (1883–1962).[42] Like so many modern sculptors, Meštrović had spent time in Paris, where he encountered the art of Rodin and Picasso. He then unexpectedly exploded on to the British sculptural scene with a wartime London exhibition in 1915. With the exception of Rodin's gift discussed above, he was the first living artist to be given an exhibition at the Victoria and Albert Museum. If Rodin's gift was given more import than the artist intended, the Meštrović exhibition was undeniably a political gesture on the part of Great Britain in support of Yugoslavia in its attempts to break away from the Austro-Hungarian Empire during the war. Indeed, the Yugoslav Committee for National Liberty was based in London for the duration of the conflict and Meštrović was its symbol. Furthermore, two rival Yugoslav groups wanted to support the show and promoted their desires to do so effectively, which provided the sculptor with unprecedented publicity. As for Meštrović, he was so distressed by the war that he returned to Croatia and started working on large low reliefs in wood, as there were no other materials. After the war, he designed a number of war memorials in Croatia. His skill as a carver made a huge impression on those sculptors already attuned to direct carving through their Paris experiences. Gill's wartime work in particular owes much to Meštrović's example. Equally, the Croatian's adherence to ancient precedents made him a compelling authority. *The Canadian Phalanx* shows these influences with its repetitive low relief carved automaton soldiers moving forward, reminiscent of the Assyrian style.

Controversy is also associated with another Canadian War Memorials sculptural commission, *Canada's Golgotha* (1918), by leading British sculptor Francis Derwent Wood (1871–1926).[43] During the Second Battle of Ypres, rumours circulated that a Canadian soldier had been crucified on a Belgian barn door, a story the Germans denounced as propaganda. Whether truth or fiction, *Canada's Golgotha* illustrates the intensity of wartime myths and imagery, even though the crucifixion remains unproven. Later, Wood acquired further notoriety for his elegant sculpture of a youthful David atop the Machine Gun Corps Memorial on Hyde Park Corner in London (1925). An adjacent biblical quotation referencing the tens of thousands David slaughtered suggested to many that David's presence on the memorial glorified war. Finally, the Canadian experience provides another daunting example of the critical nature of the alliance between patron, public and artist in the realisation of public sculpture. In 1925, established Canadian sculptor Emanuel Hahn (1881–1957) won the design for the Winnipeg Cenotaph, but in 1927, public opinion forced him to withdraw because of his German birth. If other more startling wartime sculptures such as *War the Despoiler* (1915), in which a war god tears its victims from the womb of a prostrate female nude, also did not find a public at the time, despite his various post-war setbacks Hahn's war memorial successes ultimately, and perhaps ironically, outstripped those of all other Canadian sculptors.[44]

## Germany

Perhaps the best-known German war sculpture is celebrated graphic artist Käthe Kollwitz's (1867–1945) powerful and personal memorial to her son, *The Grieving Parents*, in the Vladslo German war cemetery in Flanders. Even if it was not completed until 1931, seventeen years after he died in October 1914, its long genesis through the war and afterwards is testament to the indelibility of personal tragedy. In the somewhat aesthetically and geographically fragmented field that is First World War German sculpture, two other names predominate: Ernst Barlach (1870–1938) and Wilhelm Lehmbruck (1881–1919). Like so many early modern(ist) sculptors, Lehmbruck's exposure to Rodin and Maillol in Paris beginning in 1910 was critical. Later he made the acquaintance of Modigliani, Brancusi and Archipenko. Forced by the war to return to Berlin in 1914, where he served in a military hospital, by the time of his suicide in 1919, Lehmbruck, who had moved to Switzerland in 1917, was living once more in Berlin. Notable among a number of figurative and portrait works completed during the conflict are his two major war sculptures, the elegant but harrowing *The Fallen Man* (1915–16) and *Seated Youth* (1916).[45] In its time, *The Fallen Man* offered a radical counter image to that of the heroic soldier, then a popular subject in Germany's pre-war militarised society. At the point of death, Lehmbruck's soldier is thin and fragile; he crawls, head bowed, holding a broken sword in one hand. *Seated Youth* is an almost painterly portrayal of grief. Lehmbruck mourned his many friends and colleagues who died in the conflict, yet this sculpture captures not only his personal sadness, but also something of his response to his own war service, where he was daily exposed to death and dying. In both works, the figures' nakedness increases their searing vulnerability.

There is a late-Gothic sinuousness to Lehmbruck's work which combines with psychological insight, while Barlach's richly carved sculptures show a clear indebtedness to Expressionism and in their illustrative nature to earlier medieval Gothic precedents. Barlach also studied in Paris and spent time in Russia, where his interest in peasant subjects originated. Subsequently, unlike Lehmbruck, he rejected French influences in favour of a more traditional folk art-like approach. In 1910, he settled in the small town of Güstrow, from where Berlin dealer Paul Cassirer (1871–1926) purchased everything he created. Barlach's working style was by then rigorous and solid, distinguished by his adherence to woodcarving and an emphasis on hands and faces. His early support for the war is seen in *The Avenger* (1914), in which a truly vengeful cloak-garbed figure stretches forward, almost parallel to the ground, his large hands clasping a sword, which, like his flowing cloak, stretches out behind him.[46]

In 1915, Barlach volunteered for war service, but after three months he was demobilised due to a heart ailment. By 1916, war weary, he believed Germany faced defeat. *Shivering Girl* (1917) is a portrait of fear.[47] His post-conflict anti-war work, much of it installed in churches, destroyed his growing reputation. The best-known example is his life-size *Der Schwebende* (*The Hovering*, 1926). Güstrow commissioned it as a war memorial for its cathedral. It shows a mother floating horizontally in the air, not grief-stricken but at peace within the cathedral's Christian confines, looking towards the Western front, the source of the original pain of her son's death. Works like this were not popular with the Nazi regime. Barlach's work was included in the 1937 Degenerate Art exhibition (as was Lehmbruck's) and he was prevented from working thereafter, no doubt hastening his death the following year. As for *The Hovering*, the original bronze was taken down that same year and melted down by the Nazis during the Second World War. A copy of the original now hangs in the cathedral.

## Conclusion

The First World War destroyed empires and nations and tens of millions of human lives in one way or another. In the years following, it brought one kind of sculpture to the fore in the form of war memorials in a way that had not previously been experienced. When the thousands of monuments created between the First and Second World Wars are examined alongside post-war public and private work that does not have war obviously as its subject, a certain commonality is apparent. First, much of the memorial sculpture is figurative, and second, much of it, if not directly quoting classical precedents, certainly evokes that ancient world. In many respects, what followed the war was a resurgence of the classical beaux arts aesthetic that sculptors like Maillol had continued to interpret in their work. Alongside modernist approaches, the overtly sexual content advocated by many avant-garde pre-war sculptors is missing. Classically inspired and often monumental figures made of stone or bronze provided viewers with reminders of the sober, immutable heritage the conflict had not destroyed while acknowledging the fleeting nature of life that the war had so manifoldly demonstrated was humankind's lot. Maillol's *Grief*, the thoughtful and substantial seated figure on his war memorial in Céret, France (1921–3), is one such example.

If on visual evidence alone it can be argued that many in the avant-garde actually abandoned non-objectivity post-war, it is interesting to see how the figurative sculpture so common to war memorials, once eschewed by avant-garde sculptors, began also to populate paintings. Former Cubist Picasso, in *The Source* (1921), depicted a draped woman leaning in classical repose in an arid Mediterranean landscape languidly letting water pour from a jug lying on her lap.[48] Other members of the European avant-garde were not immune to using classical allusions, including Italian future Surrealist painter Giorgio de Chirico (1888–1978), whose *The Departure of the Argonauts* (1921) demonstrates his enthusiasm for classical themes and features.[49] Classical architecture, classical sculpture and classically inspired figures abound in this plaza scene depicting the legendary Greek hero and his team about to lead a perilous quest for the legendary Golden Fleece. Like so many artists discussed here, de Chirico had lived in Paris prior to the war, before returning to Italy after war broke out to enlist in the army.

A decade later, what American art historian Kenneth Silver terms the 'backward-looking avant-garde' is palpable in German sculptor Anton Hiller's (1893–1985) life-size *Female Wood Figure* (1932).[50] Combining the classical, clean-lined female form with a little of the vulnerable quality of Lehmbruck's immediate post-war sculptures and, in its material, referencing Barlach, this solitary form, carved the year before Hitler seized power in Germany in 1933, reminds us in a single work of the lives, cultures and heritage the First World War put at risk, and chillingly anticipates its successor.

Curiously, however, neo-classical and realist approaches did not long survive the Second World War. One of the most surprising aspects of First World War avant-garde sculpture is its largely post-Second World War resurrection. It survived to provide an alternative to the dominant nationalistic art of the 1920s and 1930s, now so closely associated with the rise of dictatorial states. With the post-Second World War renewal of interest in Abstraction and the recentring of the art world on New York came the unanticipated phenomenon of recasts and reconstructions of First World War material with the approval of the artists or their estates. The artwork endnotes in this chapter show how often this happened. The First World War may have destroyed much, but it did not destroy the will of a number of surviving sculptors to have their work recovered, unfettered by the kind of political considerations that in one momentous year – 1937 – had deemed so much art 'degenerate' and thus worthy of destruction.

## Notes

1. Lincoln Steffens, *The Autobiography of Lincoln Steffens* (New York: Harcourt, Brace and Company, 1931), cited in <http://spartacus-educational.com/Ajo_davidson.htm> (last accessed 4 November 2016).
2. See <https://en.wikipedia.org/wiki/File:Alexander_Archipenko,_La_Vie_Familiale,_Family_Life,_1912.jpg> (last accessed 4 November 2016).
3. Umberto Boccioni, *Unique Forms of Continuity in Space*, 1913, plaster, 43⅞ × 34⅞ × 15¾ ins, Museo de Arte Contemporânea, São Paulo, Brazil.
4. Giacomo Balla, *Boccioni's Fist – Lines of Force II*, 1916–17 (reconstruction 1956–8, cast 1968), painted brass, 33 × 31½ × 13 ins, Hirshhorn Museum, Washington, DC.
5. Constantin Brancusi, *Princess X*, 1915, marble, 22 × 11 × 9 ins; limestone base, 6⅜ × 6⅜ × 5½ ins, Sheldon Memorial Art Gallery and Sculpture Garden, University of Nebraska, Lincoln.
6. Hannah Höch, *Dada Puppe* (Dada Doll), 1916, fabric, yarn, thread, board and beads, 23⅝ ins (ht), Berlinische Galerie, Landesmuseum für Moderne Kunst, Berlin.
7. George Grosz and John Heartfield, *Der wildgewordene Spiesser Heartfield (Elektromechan. Tatlin-Plastik)* (The Middle-Class Philistine Heartfield Gone Wild (Electro-Mechanical Tatlin Sculpture)), 1920 (reconstructed 1988), tailor's dummy, revolver, doorbell, knife, fork, letter 'C' and number '27' signs, plaster dentures, embroidered insignia of the Black Eagle Order on horse blanket, Osram light bulb, Iron Cross, stand and other objects, including base, 86⅝ × 17¾ × 17¾ ins, Berlinische Galerie, Landesmuseum für Moderne Kunst, Berlin.
8. Max Ernst, *Celebes*, 1921, oil on canvas, 49½ × 42½ ins, Tate Gallery, London.
9. Jean (Hans) Arp, *Fleur Marteau* (Hammer Flower), 1916, oil on wood, 24⅜ × 19⅝ ins, Fondation Arp, Clamart, France.
10. See, for example, Sophie Taeuber-Arp, *Dada Head*, 1920, painted wood with glass beads on wire, 9¼ ins (ht), Museum of Modern Art, New York.
11. See, for example, <https://www.youtube.com/watch?v=4cF2Qb4bNm0> (last accessed 4 November 2016).
12. Marcel Duchamp, *Fountain*, 1917 (reconstructed 1964), glazed ceramic with black paint, 15 × 19¼ × 24⅝ ins, San Francisco Museum of Modern Art.
13. See <http://www.independent.co.uk/arts-entertainment/art/features/was-marcel-duchamps-fountain-actually-created-by-a-long-forgotten-pioneering-feminist-10491953.html> (last accessed 4 November 2016).
14. Morton Livingston Schamberg and Elsa von Freytag-Loringhoven, *God*, c. 1917, wood mitre box and cast iron plumbing trap, 12⅜ ins (ht); base, 3 × 4¾ × 11⅝ ins, Philadelphia Museum of Art.
15. Man Ray, *The Coat Stand* (Porte Manteau), 1920, published in *New York Dada*, Centre Pompidou, Paris.

16. Vladimir Tatlin, *Counter-Relief*, 1914–15, metal, wood, wire, 46½ × 28 ins, Russian State Museum, St Petersburg.
17. Naum Gabo, *Head No. 2*, 1916 (enlarged version 1964), steel, 69 × 52¾ × 48¼ ins, Tate Gallery, London.
18. Alexander Rodchenko, *Spatial Construction No. 12*, c. 1920, plywood, open construction partially painted with aluminium paint, and wire, 24 × 33 × 18½ ins, Museum of Modern Art, New York.
19. Raymond Duchamp-Villon, *The Horse*, 1914, plaster, 17½ × 17½ ins, Philadelphia Museum of Art.
20. Alexander Archipenko, *Woman Combing her Hair*, 1915, bronze, 13⅞ × 3⅜ × 3½ ins including base, Tate Gallery, London.
21. Jacob Lipchitz, *Man with a Guitar*, 1915, cast limestone, 38¼ × 10½ × 7¾ ins, Museum of Modern Art, New York.
22. Henri Laurens, *Bottle and Glass*, 1917, printed paper, graphite, oil paint, chalk on millboard, 15¼ × 11½ ins, Tate Gallery, London.
23. Henri Matisse, *The Artist's Daughter, Marguerite*, 1915, bronze, 12½ ins (ht), private collection.
24. See <http://monumentsmorts.univ-lille3.fr> (last accessed 4 November 2016).
25. Charles-Édouard Richefeu, *A French Soldier*, 1915, bronze, 8 ins (ht), Imperial War Museum, London.
26. Constantin Brancusi, *Le Baiser* (The Kiss), 1907–8, stone carving, 11 × 10 × 8½ ins, Muzeul de Arta, Craiova, Romania; Auguste Rodin, *The Kiss*, c. 1888–98, marble, 71½ × 44¼ × 46 ins, Musée Rodin, Paris.
27. Frank Dobson, *Kneeling Female Figure*, c. 1915, sandstone, 19¾ × 8 × 7¾ ins, Bradford Art Galleries and Museums.
28. Jacob Epstein, *Birth*, c. 1913, stone, 12 × 10½ × 4 ins, Art Gallery of Ontario, Canada.
29. See, for example, <https://www.youtube.com/watch?v=6S1Or9x1Pp0> (last accessed 4 November 2016).
30. Jacob Epstein, *Let There Be Sculpture: An Autobiography* (London: Michael Joseph, 1940), p. 56.
31. Marcel Duchamp, *Bicycle Wheel*, 1913 (later reconstruction), steel and painted wood, 49½ × 25 × 12½ ins, Israel Museum, Jerusalem.
32. Jacob Epstein, *Rock Drill*, 1913–16, bronze on stone base, 27¾ × 20¾ × 20 ins without base; overall measurement with base 35½ × 22¾ × 21½ ins, National Gallery of Canada, Ottawa.
33. Jacob Epstein, *Admiral of the Fleet, Lord Fisher*, 1916, bronze, 18½ × 13¼ × 11½ ins, Imperial War Museum, London.
34. Jacob Epstein, *The Tin Hat*, 1916, bronze, 23½ × 12 × 11 ins, Art Institute of Chicago. For more on the British official war art scheme, see Sue Malvern, *Modern Art, Britain and the Great War* (New Haven: Yale University Press, 2004).
35. Charles Sergeant Jagger, *No Man's Land*, 1919–20, bronze, 50 × 130 ins, Tate Gallery, London. The first sketch for this commissioned relief was begun in mid-1918 in Sheffield, where a seriously wounded Jagger was recovering. In 1919–20, while on a British School of Rome scholarship, the sculptor executed the final relief in London.
36. Frank Baxter (1865–1933), Benjamin Clemens (1875–1957), Kisfalud Sigismund de Strobl (Hungarian, 1884–1975), Robert Jackson Emerson (1878–1944), Agnes Freda Forres (c. 1880–1942), Richard R. Goulden (1876–1932), Herbert Haseltine (American, 1877–1962), Malvina Hoffman (American, 1887–1966), Charles d'Orville Pilkington Jackson (1887–1975), William Goscombe John (1860–1952), Kathleen Kennett (1878–1947), Bertram McKennell (Australian, 1863–1931), William McMillan (1887–1977), Georges Mallissard (French, 1877–1942), Avram Melnikoff (Israeli, 1892–1960), Albert

James Miller (1880–1955), Henry Alfred Pegram (1862–1937), Louis Frederick Roslyn (1878–1940).

37. For more on this programme, see Maria Tippett, *Art at the Service of War: Canada, Art, and the Great War*, 2nd edn (Toronto: University of Toronto Press, 2014).
38. Clare Sheridan, *Colonel W. A. Bishop, V. C.*, 1918–19, bronze, 26¾ × 17 × 11 ins, Canadian War Museum, Ottawa.
39. These can be found on the Canadian War Museum's website through a collections search using each artist's name.
40. Frances Loring, *Noon Hour in a Munitions Plant*, bronze, 35 × 73½ × 6 ins, Canadian War Museum, Ottawa.
41. Frances Loring, *Grief*, 1918 (cast 1965), bronze, 20 × 20 × 10½ ins, National Gallery of Canada, Ottawa.
42. Ivan Meštrović, *The Canadian Phalanx*, 1918, marble relief, 78¾ × 119 × 13½ ins, National Gallery of Canada, Ottawa.
43. Francis Derwent Wood, *Canada's Golgotha*, 1918, bronze, 32½ × 25 × 10 ins, Canadian War Museum, Ottawa. Wood was too old to enlist, but during the war in London he applied his plastic skills to the creation of painted face masks for severely facially injured soldiers.
44. Emanuel Hahn, *War the Despoiler*, 1915, painted plaster, 8¼ × 32¾ × 15 ins, National Gallery of Canada, Ottawa.
45. Wilhelm Lehmbruck, *Der Gestürzte* (The Fallen Man), 1915–16, stone cast, 30¾ × 94½ × 32½ ins; *Sitzender Jüngling* (Seated Youth), 1916, bronze, 40½ × 30¼ × 45¼ ins, both Lehmbruck Museum, Duisburg, Germany.
46. Ernst Barlach, *Der Rächer* (The Avenger), 1914 (later cast), bronze, 17¼ × 22¾ × 8 ins, Tate Gallery, London. The first version of this work was a slightly larger plaster made in September–October 1914, which served as the working model for the bronzes and a larger 1922 woodcarving. There is also a further version in stucco secretly made from the woodcarving in 1939, after the Nazis confiscated the latter.
47. Ernst Barlach, *Frierendes Mädchen* (Shivering Girl), 1917, oak, 30 × 8¼ × 8½ ins, Ernst Barlach House, Hamburg.
48. Pablo Picasso, *La Source* (The Source), 1921, oil on canvas, 25 × 35½ ins, Moderna Museet, Stockholm.
49. Georgio de Chirico, *La Partenza degli Argonauti* (The Departure of the Argonauts), 1921, oil on canvas, 21¼ × 28¾ ins, private collection.
50. Anton Hiller, *Weibliche Holzfigur* (Female Wood Figure), 1932, oak, 62¾ × 17¾ × 11 ins, Lehmbruck Museum, Duisburg, Germany. Kenneth E. Silver uses this term several times in his catalogue *Chaos and Classicism: Art in France, Italy, and Germany, 1918–1936* (New York: Guggenheim Foundation, 2010).

Plate 1 'The Last Post', British postcard (c. 1915). Private collection. Reproduced courtesy of Tony Allen (ww1postcards.com).

Plate 2 Otto Dix, *Der Krieg* (1929–32, 'The War'), mixed media on plywood, middle panel 204 × 204 cm, left and right panel 204 × 102 cm, predella 60 × 204 cm. Reproduced courtesy of bpk | Staatliche Kunstsammlungen Dresden | Elke Estel | Hans-Peter Klut.

Plate 3 George Clausen, *Youth Mourning* (1916), oil on canvas, 91.4 × 91.4 cm. © IWM (Art.IWM ART 4655). Reproduced courtesy of the Imperial War Museum.

Plate 4 Stanley Spencer, *Unveiling a War Memorial at Cookham* (1921), oil on canvas, 152.4 × 147.32 cm. Private collection. © The Estate of Stanley Spencer. Reproduced courtesy of the Bridgeman Art Library.

Plate 5 Photograph of Jacob Epstein, *Rock Drill* (1913–16, cast 1916), bronze on stone base, 70.5 × 53 × 50.8 cm without base; overall measurement with base 90.5 × 58 × 55 cm. Purchased 1956. © National Gallery of Canada. Reproduced courtesy of National Gallery of Canada, Ottawa.

Plate 6 Bernard Partridge, 'Take Up the Sword of Justice' (1915). Poster, lithograph. © IWM (Art.IWM PST 6092). Reproduced courtesy of the Imperial War Museum.

Plate 7 Film poster for *Bei unseren Helden an der Somme* (1917). Author's collection.

Plate 8 Film poster for Swedish release of *Westfront 1918* (1930, dir. G. W. Pabst). Author's collection.

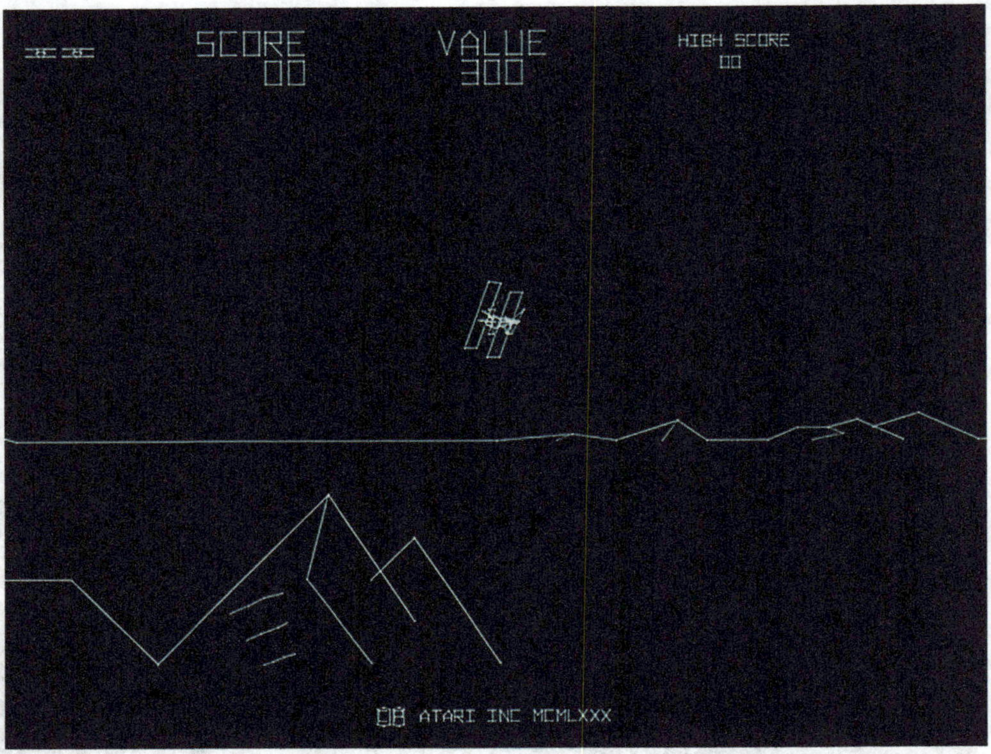


Plate 9 Gameplay screen for *Red Baron* (1980). © Atari.

Plate 10 Gameplay screen for *History Line: 1914–1918* (1992). © Blue Byte Software.

# 9

# Memorials: Embodiment and Unconventional Mourning

*Laura Wittman*

## Introduction

THE BEST-KNOWN WAR memorials from the Great War include those of local communities, most commonly lists of names without buried bodies, and the Unknown Soldier memorials that almost every combatant nation eventually created, in which a single nameless body stands for all the missing. To these we may add the vast military cemeteries that bury individual identity underneath identical grave markers, as well as ossuaries, in which the remains of many are gathered into one.[1] Striking in all these instances is a profoundly ambivalent, and mostly unacknowledged, relationship to the suffering body of the soldier: it is either rendered abstract by lists and repetition (communal lists, military cemeteries) or, when its physicality is foregrounded, its unique personhood is undercut by anonymity (Unknown Soldiers, ossuaries). Such ambivalence is clearly related to the unprecedented obliteration of combatants' bodies in the First World War, as well as to the widespread feeling that humans had been reduced to 'animals' and 'cannon fodder'.[2] In this chapter, I set aside these most visible (and well-discussed in scholarly literature) forms of commemoration, to examine the role of the body in a handful of emblematic non-canonical war memorials.

Do such memorials develop a different relationship to the body than their more famous counterparts? Even in the latter, embodied suffering suggests a pacifist message; is this more or less the case in the former? Given the great formal variety in the memorials I will consider (ranging from piles of broken earth to photographs), do we find that a particular medium is more suited to confronting the suffering body? Finally, what do such memorials reveal about our changing understanding of memory, history and embodiment over the past one hundred years? In his insightful discussion of our current 'memory boom', Jay Winter concludes that we should 'see the terms "history" and "memory" as describing a field in social thought and social action', and focus in particular on 'the overlaps and creative space between the two'. With awareness that memory is individual and psychologically complex, whereas history is social and politically complex, we can, Winter offers, counter the memory boom's tendency toward nostalgia and the replacement of historical and political awareness with a sort of cultural 'narcissism'.[3] Individuals experience and create memory, whereas history is a social and political construct, but we cannot forget how the two constantly engage with each other. My proposal is that embodiment plays a key role in this engagement, for at least two reasons that I hope this chapter will bear out.

First, as Winter also notes, 'whatever their condition is termed, the victims of traumatic memory are "witnesses" of a special kind', or, as he writes with great acuity, 'shell shock is a theater of memory out of control' in which the body performs the 'cognitive dissonance' caused by inassimilable war experiences.[4] In other words, via the body the inwardness of memory is externalised into a social event that, as Anne Harrington has argued, bears the promise of unique truthfulness – the body 'cannot lie'; the body is the special witness, or so it is hoped, whose story cannot be co-opted by ideology.[5] Second, as Edith Wyschogrod argues following Levinas, the suffering body of the witness constitutes a demand for the historian, akin to a categorical imperative.[6] It requires, if I may simplify her argument so brutally, that compassion be the foundation of the historian's pursuit of truth, with full awareness that no story, not even the body's, is fully exempt from some amount of 'lying'. In sum, then, embodiment calls us to make room for the whole person in both history and memorials, but it also warns us against believing we have fully succeeded in this endeavour.

The memorials considered in this chapter were chosen both to explore these issues and to give a small taste of the remarkable variety of media in which remembrance can take form. They include landscape and soil itself used as a memorial (the Trench of Bayonets at Verdun will be my example); memorial parks (such as Gabriele d'Annunzio's 'Vittoriale' gardens); sculptures (those of Käthe Kollwitz, the Péronne and Châteauroux war memorials); and a photo book (contemporary to the war, by Augusto Tognasso). There are many more – including collections of letters or memorabilia, personal museums, literary texts as memorials, films, and, in more recent times, exhibitions, re-creations, television and internet archives – which, for reasons of space, I cannot discuss. It is my hope, however, that my examples will give a good sense of how embodiment is a key intersection between memory and history, between preserving and betraying individual experience, and between pacifism and trauma, and as such speaks incisively to the current memory boom.

## Memorial Gardens

While the association of cemeteries with picturesque gardens dates from the nineteenth century, the idea of a memorial garden goes as far back as the ancient world. Parks and gardens as sites for First World War remembrance are very common throughout Europe and the United States, and they tend to have a contemplative quality, emphasising the passing away of suffering and return of new life evoked by natural cycles; this cyclical quality also explains the layering often found in such memorials, in which plaques, sculptures or new landscaping can be added to commemorate further wars.[7] In contrast, I will focus on two memorials that are far more emotionally raw as they engage with the landscape.

First is the famous 'Trench of Bayonets' at Verdun. Based on a real incident when after a particularly bloody battle in June 1916 machine guns were found sticking out of the ground, the monument was inaugurated in 1920. In the intervening years a legend, and a controversy, had begun that would shape commemorations at Verdun into the twenty-first century, pitting two very different notions of heroism against each other. The popular press claimed that the machine guns (subsequently transformed into more heroic bayonets) were those of soldiers who had been buried alive in their trench, and that their bodies were still standing underneath the earth, perpetually defending France. From this idea the memorial we still see today was created: a roof supported by columns and surrounded by barbed wire both marks and protects the filled-in trench, where the bayonets have been replaced by crosses to mark the location of each body.[8] To this were added, also at Verdun – seen as 'lieu national par excellence' – the 'Carré des soldats inconnus' (where the seven bodies not chosen to rest in the Unknown Soldier memorial under the Arc de Triomphe were buried, inaugurated in 1920 also), the museum in the Hôtel de Ville (inaugurated in 1927), and the Monument to Victory (representing a 'guerrier victorieux apaisé' defending the city's ramparts, inaugurated in 1929).[9]

The site's ideological trajectory, as can be evinced even from this short list, moved away from the concreteness of the battlefield and toward its spiritualisation in victory. It is notable that the 'undead' or 'perpetually mobilized' bodies of the first memorial are replaced by ones more properly buried (if still anonymous) and then finally rehabilitated by the victorious soldier who survived (of which there were so few at Verdun). Thus it is not surprising that by 1923, ceremonies at Verdun stopped incorporating the Trench of Bayonets, and moved toward greater and greater spiritualisation – not to say erasure – of suffering.[10]

The trench was, initially, the locus of more rebellious mourning in which veterans in particular could symbolically assert that they were still standing in the battlefield with their comrades. Notably, old postcards of the trench show both that the soil was still rough and unpacked (whereas now it is a smooth, shallow mound) and that at times there were machine guns sticking out as well as crosses.[11] Both these elements hark back to improvised battlefield commemorations: for example, the minimalist graves created on the battlefield, in which a soldier's weapon might support his helmet to mark the spot and his allegiance; but also, more disturbingly, the recurrent image in First World War testimony of a dead soldier's hand reaching out from the ground, in anger at not being heard or properly laid to rest.[12] In sum, then, the initial Trench of Bayonets highlights the gruesome image of being buried alive and insists that such trauma will prevent bodies from ever resting in peace, returning to the soil they defended (Figure 9.1).

However, the story of Verdun has many unexpected turns, and thus by 1930 a soldier was denouncing the false heroism of 'bayonets'. To be fair, already in 1920, the Veterans' Association and the military had pointed out that exhumations did not reveal any standing bodies, and that it was a common practice to use machine guns to mark mass graves – especially ones burying enemy soldiers.[13] But veterans only found the Trench of Bayonets truly objectionable once the iconography of the memorial as a whole shifted toward the image of an 'appeased and victorious soldier' and as its soil hardened into something that could be a more permanent memory. In reaction, from 1927 to 1932, the Ossuary of Douaumont was built, emphasising once again the concreteness of bodies, and seeking to create a memorial that could not be termed 'victorious'; it was based on the previous provisional ossuary in the same location, which was fronted by a statue of Silence, holding her index finger over her mouth, with the inscription below, 'Aux héros inconnus'.[14] I cannot discuss the ossuary further for lack of space, but will point out that its silence clearly implies that the soldiers' remains – in which suffering is inscribed in broken bones and unidentifiable bodies – speak for themselves. But Verdun was also a site honouring the great First World

Figure 9.1 Photograph of historical postcard of the Trench of Bayonets at Verdun. Author's collection.

War general, Pétain. When he became the incarnation of occupied France, after 1945, Verdun would undergo many ideological renovations (including a legal battle to transfer Pétain's ashes to the ossuary, a transfer that was ultimately deemed illegal).[15] In 1960 a 'Memorial' museum was created to accompany the ossuary, with its mission both to educate the young and to promote Franco-German rapprochement. This would perhaps finally lay to rest those soldiers who could not stop fighting – and perhaps enough time has passed for the museum to incorporate both appeasement and outrage.

If we look at this story from the perspective of unconventional mourning, however, we might provisionally observe that while it clearly involves a disturbing corporeality, it is not necessarily pacifist in its initial conception, or at least not in the same way we would define pacifism. As Winter has noted, this definition has changed considerably, since pacifism in the wake of the First World War for the most part still included raw anger, and the possibility of a just war (as the Great War remained for the Allies). In the Trench of Bayonets, especially as it was first imagined, rebellion against appeasing narratives that could justify the carnage is expressed via a graphic reminder both to the state and to future generations of the actual flesh that war destroys, as though asking them to use it far more carefully and parsimoniously. Moreover, in terms of form and materials, the Trench, in spirit at least, depends on arresting time: just as the landscape is supposed to remain torn up (both nature and culture prevented from taking their course), insistence on the bodies' verticality (however improbable) catches them in the instant of death. Finally, the need to reframe Verdun repeatedly reminds us that the idea that bodies speak for themselves is tremendously fragile, and that their power as a moral imperative depends on the vigilance of later generations.

My second example is a private landscape memorial, though it has now become a museum: the home and gardens of Gabriele d'Annunzio on Lake Garda, known as the 'Vittoriale'. D'Annunzio, already established as a major literary figure, became a First World War hero for his genuinely daring but also symbolically powerful battles, as well as his charismatic speeches. He led the occupation of the city of Fiume (September 1919–December 1920), deemed by many Italian veterans in particular to be due to Italy after the war. Following the Italian state's failure to support the occupation, d'Annunzio retired from public life, purchasing his villa on Lake Garda, which he would spend the rest of his life (he died in 1938) turning into a 'theater of memory' (in Re's words) celebrating both his literary oeuvre and his military *gesta*.[16] The specific memorial I want to focus on, within the large Vittoriale complex, is the 'Arengo', created in 1923–4 (Figure 9.2).

Very centrally located next to the main house and museum, it is a circular garden bordered by a stone bench and surrounded by columns celebrating twenty-seven 'victims' or 'victories' of Italy in the First World War and at Fiume. They are of different stones

Figure 9.2 Photograph of the 'Arengo' at the Vittoriale on Lake Garda. © The Estate of Gabriele d'Annunzio. Reproduced courtesy of Fondazione Il Vittoriale degli Italiani – Archivio Iconografico.

and styles, many with ornate capitals; the darkest and central one represents Caporetto and is surmounted by an urn filled with soil from the Carso.[17] There is a statue of Victory here, but she is crowned with thorns. Caporetto was, of course, a tremendous defeat for Italy, and the site of both major desertions and significant executions; it was considered the greatest carnage Italians suffered, as well as evidence of Italy's generals' incompetence. Elsewhere at the Vittoriale, and as its design evolved throughout the 1920s and 1930s, the more heroic victory it is presumably named after is more evident: for example, in the 'Pilo del Piave' surmounted by winged Victory, or in the *Nave Puglia* (a battleship partly preserved and ensconced in the hillside), or in the aeroplane used by d'Annunzio for his famous flight to drop leaflets on Vienna (in the museum).

Once again we see that later creations incorporate the rawness of death into a story of the victorious nation, and into a spiritualised vision of the war. In contrast, the Arengo was used by d'Annunzio to 'harangue' (hence its name) his soldiers who fought in the First World War and at Fiume; there he performed with them rituals on all the significant dates for 'their war', commemorating 'their dead' and keeping the concreteness of the battlefield alive. Though the iconography of the Arengo has been somewhat taken for granted, since columns to commemorate victory have been well known since Trajan's Column in Rome, a closer look shows us something less heroic. The columns themselves, as noted, represent defeats as well as victories. More importantly, they represent victims: they echo the ancient Greek association of columns with the human body, but as they are all of different materials and heights, and not organised into a temple or any symmetrical structure, the effect is to invoke ruins. They also recall a not entirely uncommon sculptural motif used in small town memorials: soldiers depicted still standing, or caught in their last act as they are shot down.[18] The soil from the Carso seeks to bring home the rawness of death on the battlefield. If this interpretation of the Arengo as a stylised representation of perpetually mobilised dying soldiers seems far-fetched, I hope it is made more plausible by its association with d'Annunzio's *Notturno*. Published in 1921, but begun in 1916 when the poet was convalescing from an aviation accident that blinded him in one eye, this novel is written in poetic prose and consists mostly in the evocation of d'Annunzio's dead comrades and the various ways in which he mourned them. Its 'nocturnal' quality has been much commented upon; one of its main features is d'Annunzio's obsession with the similarity between his convalescing body as he lay in bed and the recently dead bodies of the comrades he mourned and at times carried.[19] All of them are still in 'no man's land': both still at war, but also, as d'Annunzio imagined it, in a liminal space between life and death in which key spiritual insight is possible.[20] The rituals performed in the Arengo echoed the ones described in the *Notturno*, hence my 'nocturnal' reading of the space itself.

There are similarities here with the Trench of Bayonets, particularly the image of the standing soldier who remains caught between life and death, and the desire to commemorate defeat or, indeed, to remind future generations that victory was built on such defeats. But, just as the image of being buried alive in the Trench is replaced by the more aerial columns, we see in d'Annunzio's memorial a tendency to stylise death, to make it beautiful. I have proposed elsewhere that this impulse represses a terrifying awareness of the physicality of death on d'Annunzio's part, hence his recourse to a longer history. It is key that both memorials are ruins, presumably invoking the battlefield and seeking to keep its liminal status as well as invoking ruined bodies. But in d'Annunzio's case the ruin gestures toward ancient Greek and Roman ones, and is overlaid with modern Western culture's sense of these as sublime depictions of decay.[21] In this context, war becomes one of those blights that destroy human flesh and the denunciation expressed is far less raw than it is at Verdun. To borrow Re's well-chosen title, bodies speak in a 'theater' here, with less immediacy. To make another provisional conclusion: from the perspective of unconventional mourning, what we see in the Arengo is not so much that a particular style shifts us away from anger to beauty, but that the sense of time implicit in each memorial connects memory and history in a different way. The Trench of Bayonets began as a provisional memorial and has faced the ambiguous task of preserving a moment of shock, a traumatic memory, for history. The Arengo, already at its inception, saw itself as inserting the trauma of the First World War into a much longer temporality: its task is to disrupt the theatre of history enough to make embodied suffering live anew. Much, if not all, of this was done for d'Annunzio's Arengo via its active use as a commemorative place. This points to how scale also affects temporality and the connection it makes between memory and history: the national scale of Verdun means that memory, too, and its immediacy and preciousness, have to become somehow monumental; the semi-private scale of the Vittoriale allowed d'Annunzio to rely on a specific community to maintain the individuality of memory, for at least as long as the memorial remained active.[22]

## Sculpture

My next examples take us more directly to representations of the body, in memorials that include statues. While lists of names on obelisks, walls or other purely architectural elements dominate our vision of First World War memorials, sculptures of Victory, or of the soldier, alone or in a group, were not uncommon. I will consider three examples that depict mourning for the dead soldier – itself a less popular motif, which in these particular cases again manifests a rawness and urgency associated with a powerful physicality.[23] First is the Péronne war memorial, a sculpture by Paul Auban of the dead soldier with his mother, known as *Picarde maudissant la guerre*, inaugurated in 1926. Cited by scholars as an unusual example of a pacifist memorial, it depicts a mother crouching over her dead son's completely horizontal body, aiming her fist forward toward the viewer. Auban had previously sculpted two mourning mothers in similar poses, but as a war memorial his choice stands out, not only because it is the only example of pure outrage I have come across, but also because of its extreme horizontality – and therefore lack of transcendence.[24] In contrast, statues of the dead or dying soldier, whether alone, with Victory, or (more rarely) with his wife or mother, almost invariably emphasise verticality: he is often only half-prone, the mourning figures are standing, or Victory rises above him; predominantly, there are also large architectural elements that frame both soldier and mourner(s). As a result, these bodies – for the most part sculpted with representational realism – acquire more of a narrative quality and less of a physical presence. The theme of the 'last kiss' from a wife or mother accentuates this, but we are often encouraged to sketch a story, whether it is of a mother laying a wreath on a grave or helping to put her son in his coffin. In cases where there is only a mourning female figure and the soldier is not present, she is most commonly visiting his grave or sitting near it with wreaths or flowers. What is remarkable about Auban's sculpture, to my eyes, is thus how it interrupts the story, and the flow of time, with anger that has not yet turned into specific action or been appeased by mourning – it has no frame, and feels threatening to the viewer. Auban was a pacifist, but without that knowledge we could wonder whether this mother demands revenge rather than an end to war and justice from the state.

My other sculptural examples were both inaugurated in 1932 and are similar in idea if not in execution: both depict two mourning figures with no body or even tomb present, and almost no architectural support. The Châteauroux memorial, known as *Les pleureuses*, work of the architect L. Suard and the sculptor Ernest Nivet, consists of two women, one older, one younger, standing with heads bent and shadowed by hoods in an attitude of sombre contemplation. They are on a simple pedestal with three steps on either side, surrounded by a hedge, and look down over flowers and gravel. Though they are vertical, the lack of architectural framing emphasises their physicality, and their gaze into emptiness in particular undercuts the narrative impulse, in ways that recall the Péronne memorial. Notably, contemporary commentary imagined them to be in front of an open grave, watching an exhumation, or a burial.[25] This again emphasises the moment, the cry of grief, rather than its appeasement in the process of mourning; the ghostly image of exhumation not only brings back the gruesome physicality of death, but reminds us that for many, the bodies of dead loved ones were never retrieved and thus remained symbolically unburied. Time stops, here, in a way that is less obviously threatening, yet it is powerfully disturbing, for it implies a never-ending grief.[26]

*The Grieving Parents* by Käthe Kollwitz shows both figures kneeling but upright, each on a separate pedestal, backed by a hedge, and once again looking down at emptiness. The sculpture was intensely personal, as Kollwitz had lost her son, Peter, on the battlefield in 1914; his grave, with those of many of his comrades, lies before the statues, just a little further away, keeping the parents isolated in their despair, as they are also isolated from each other. Kollwitz had initially imagined a family, with the parents together, holding their dead son but after years of mourning came to this design, which recognises the community of young men of which Peter was a part, some of whom survived, and helped the parents keep their son's memory alive. This evolution also undercuts narrative framing in favour of raw physicality: the mother bends forward whereas the father seems to hold himself up; both have their arms around themselves as if trying to contain emotions that might destroy them; both emanate congealed grief.[27] Unlike previous examples, these sculptures tend toward Expressionism in their style: features and lines are spare, suggesting and magnifying bare emotion rather than offering a realistic portrait. (We may recall Munch's famous *The Scream* here for the dual quality of unbearable horror and silence.) But time seems to stop here, too, as in our previous examples.

Key in all three cases, I would propose, is the lack of architectural framing of any sort, not only because it emphasises the bodies, but because it transforms our sense of scale and our relationship to the sculptures. Because they lack a frame, we are pulled into their space; rather than looking at an image of mourning, we become part of a community of mourners.[28] This is all the more evident in the case of Kollwitz's memorial, given the presence of Peter's dead comrades, and the mourning community they invoke. Winter has commented that Kollwitz's memorial shows us that 'the smaller the canvas, the more continuous is the thread connecting topoi and experience, connecting sites of memory and the agents of remembrance'.[29] I would add that a smaller scale is also what transforms all three of these memorials' relationship to time (as opposed to their styles, which are different). We are drawn into the moment of grief, instead of seeing that moment as part of a longer journey. Recalling the poet Giuseppe Ungaretti's remark that during the Great War it was only possible to live in the instant, and the instant expanded to the point of feeling eternal, these sculptures stop before words can unfold.[30] They imply a community that does not need narrative to cohere, a community of shared experience in which 'topoi' do not need explanation or framing. Notably, in all three cases we need more historical information to interpret these memorials: to know Auban, and Picarde, are threatening but pacifist; to know survivors assisted at exhumations; to know Kollwitz's parents gaze at an emptiness full of youthful ghosts. Hence these pieces also warn us that the rejection of narrative and stopping of time will always eventually be incorporated into the interwoven frames of history and memory. In 2014, as part of the Great War's centenary, the Berlin War Graves Commission had replicas made of Kollwitz's *The Grieving Parents* that travelled from Belgium, all the way through Germany, Poland and Belarus.[31] This itinerary, and their separation from the graves of their son and his comrades, drastically changes the scale of Kollwitz's memorial: while the intent is evidently pacifist, we are removed from the raw grief of the original. Is such 'museumification' inevitable, or can we somehow recapture the powerful interruption of time that is at the core of these memorials?

## Photography

My last example is a book of photographs by Augusto Tognasso, the Italian lieutenant who oversaw the exhumations that would lead to the choice of one body to be buried in the Unknown Soldier memorial at the Vittoriano in Rome.[32] Tognasso's book *Ignoto Militi* was printed in 1922 in Milan for the Association of Mutilated Veterans, to benefit the ossuary on Monte San Michele in the Carso.[33] The book does not indicate the name of the photographer – a choice that already emphasises its celebration of anonymous sacrifice – but we gather from the brief preface that it was Tognasso himself, perhaps in collaboration with other soldiers, during the work of the Exhumations Commission. The preface presents Tognasso as mutilated veteran, and emphasises that the Unknown Soldier is the 'Son' and 'Daddy' ('Babbo') of all, uniting those who had been divided before the war; making up for the failures of the Risorgimento, and for divisions about whether to enter the war at all. The main part of the book consists of photographs accompanied by Tognasso's narrative, which gives the details of the various procedures that were followed in the exhumations, and also in the choice of eleven bodies that were taken to the Cathedral of Aquileia for a 'choosing ceremony', in which one among them would become *the* Unknown Soldier; it also briefly outlines the ceremonial transport of that body to Rome and its national burial in the Vittoriano, on 4 November 1921. My commentary on this text will be very limited, not least because the issue of texts as memorials opens a new field of inquiry.[34] I will focus instead on the photographs, which occupy rather more space than the narrative and seem very much to be allowed to speak for themselves, telling a slightly different, less official, story.

They begin with a photograph of the whole Commission, presumably out on the battlefield, with a truck behind them; we then see them carrying boxes, with a coffin in the background; the third photograph is of a skeleton and a small cross laid over many broken stones, and its caption reads: '. . . Una rozza croce, nascosta da una piccola parete di roccia, indicò l'esistenza della salma di un prode . . .' ('a rough cross, hidden by a small wall of rocks, indicated the existence of a valiant soldier's remains') (Figure 9.3). The series of photographs continues very much in the same way, alternating images of the Commission digging and of the landscape (perhaps one fifth of the photos are of this sort) with images of bones, usually but not always arranged into as human a form as possible, sometimes on a white shroud, sometimes in the open grave itself (these constitute the other four fifths). The captions tell a minimal and rather repetitive story, for example: '. . . and as were all the others, these [bones] were piously composed on the shroud . . .'; '. . . when behind a wall of rocks a wood cross was found'; 'The doctor reunited those relics on a shroud as nature indicated and science suggested . . .'. At the very end of the book there are a few more public images: of the crowds at Aquileia, where the Unknown Soldier was chosen by Maria Bergamas, from Bergamas herself, and of crowds kneeling at the Unknown Soldier's

Figure 9.3 Image from Augusto Tognasso, *Ignoto Militi* (Milan: Association of Mutilated Veterans, 1922). The caption reads: '. . . Una rozza croce, nascosta da una piccola parete di roccia, indicò l'esistenza della salma di un prode . . .' ('a rough cross, hidden by a small wall of rocks, indicated the existence of a valiant soldier's remains'). Reproduced courtesy of Stanford University Library.

passage and at other commemorative events in Rome for his burial. The book ends, however, back at Aquileia, as the Bishop of Fiume blesses the ten bodies that were not chosen to be buried in Rome, and finally as they are buried near the cathedral. These were described in the media as offering an even greater sacrifice and image of suffering than the Unknown Soldier himself, precisely because they did not receive a national tomb and honours.[35]

The thrust of this collection of images is thus very clear: to celebrate not only the ten who were not chosen, but the hundreds who were exhumed and reburied elsewhere, not to mention all those whose remains were never retrieved. The latter are further invoked because the bulk of the narrative is concerned with how the Commission chose sites for exhumation, and how carefully they investigated what minimal traces of a battlefield grave, such as little crosses, remained. The images of the Commission on the rocky landscape have the same intent, and emphasise in addition the care and concern of all those involved – and this is where Tognasso's status as a mutilated veteran (presumably not the most agile leader for this Commission) is key to establishing his moral stature and physical empathy with the dead. The captions, in their spare repetitions, often preceded and/or followed by ellipses, suggest how long, slow and painstaking the exhumations were, adding a pious tone but without emphasis (referring to the remains as 'relics', for example). The role of the doctor is clearly to reassure us that the bodies were properly recomposed. And, most striking of course, the images of the remains themselves insist on gathering what is left into something that speaks its own humanity, into what is clearly a skeleton, if often not a complete one. Here embodied suffering is made visible, as the images seem to admonish the viewer, 'This was once a living and complete human body! Do not forget!'

Tognasso's book is extraordinary from a number of perspectives. First, among the many nations that exhumed bodies to create an Unknown Soldier memorial, this is the only instance of this process becoming visible to the public. In fact, in all cases, journalists and the public were forbidden from attending.[36] Tognasso shows us broken skeletons whereas the state, overwhelmingly, wished to emphasise a body that was, often according to a Christological model, resurrected, spiritually returned to a wholeness that would also represent the healing of the nation into wholeness. Hence, second, Tognasso's book is remarkable for its rejection of narrative, and especially of the state's narrative about the Unknown Soldier. This is already expressed by the book's wider horizontal format, which privileges the photographs over the text, and undercuts the vertical transcendence of state scripts. Moreover, the latter took place entirely on the national stage, beginning quite remarkably with the choosing ceremony – and official language went so far as to imagine that the eleven bodies rose up from the battlefield of their own volition, completely eliding the messiness of exhumations. In contrast, Tognasso's text for the most part describes the exhumations, which took place on the small scale of the Commission, made up entirely of veterans; it is extremely repetitive, as are the photographs, and shows us a community experiencing and re-experiencing mourning, again and again, with every body that is found.

Nonetheless, third, Tognasso's book is also remarkable for what it does not show. His images make it easy to forget that photographs can not only at times lie, but also unavoidably compose and frame reality.[37] Most obviously, he never shows us a pile of rubble and bones *before* they are recomposed into a skeleton. He also does not show us the piles of bones that, inevitably, must have belonged to multiple soldiers and could never be separated properly, which would find their way into an ossuary. The images themselves seem very realistic, yet they avoid the details of torn uniforms or decaying leather that some witnesses during the war mention (only in one case do we see a metal helmet, which, in the spirit of recomposing, is placed over the dead soldier's skull). Moreover, by 1920–1, when the exhumations took place, some dry flesh should have remained on the skeletons, and they would have been fused into the earth – all of which we never see. On the contrary, Tognasso's images seek to distinguish the skeleton, with its implied individual personhood and wholeness, from its surroundings; this is of course all the more visible when it is placed on a shroud on the ground. Hence, though Tognasso's book resists state narratives of heroism, victory and resurrection, it supports the state's effort to transform a horrific mass of corpses into clean skeletons.

We know, however, that there was real anxiety about this among veterans and bereaved families: some wondered if the national origin of these corpses could really be known via torn uniforms, and a few others went so far as to say this was a good thing; some, though very few, voiced a more visceral fear of how the war exposed bodies to decay even before they were dead (becoming part of the mud of the trenches, which were filled with dead bodies, is a key image here), and how their dying lacked integrity and humanity (mass graves, no coffins, often no shrouds).[38] My sense is that Tognasso avoids the more grisly side of exhumations not for political reasons, but in order to spare the viewer from what Winter describes as the war's radical transformation of 'what was thinkable, what was imaginable, about human brutality and violence'.[39] As Eric Leed has shown, soldiers such as Tognasso feared their own transformation into 'animals' or something less than human because of their experience, and they often sought to protect their families from this.[40] Another way of putting this is that Tognasso's images emphasise the integrity of bodies in order to ensure empathy is still possible, and not overshadowed by horror.[41] From the perspective of unconventional memorials, and of memory's engagement with history, what we begin to see here is an insistence on embodied suffering in a more shadowy form, via what is not said or shown, yet is – more or less consciously – made implicit. For a veteran (and we must not forget that the book was printed by a veterans' association), the photographs would bring back actual experience of the dead and the dying, with the full senses of touch and smell in addition to sight. If we consider how common trauma (or what we now call PTSD) was, it is easy to see why Tognasso might have considered his work to be by far explicit enough. His book's repetition of similar gestures and images is thus key, as are the ellipses, for they invoke the broken temporality of trauma: a present that recurs and cannot be relegated to the past, and thus insists that even constant reframing cannot quite contain the truth of suffering.

What do these unconventional memorials, especially taken together, tell us about memory and history, and how remembrance articulates these terms? Embodiment is foregrounded in all my examples. Notably, however, making suffering as explicit as possible via representational realism is not its main manifestation; nor do we find that other styles, more minimalist, or more expressionistic, are required. Rather, embodiment – whatever its material support, and this chapter has touched upon a number of examples, but many more have been used in memorials – is most effective when it succeeds in arresting the flow of social and political time. Here personal time, and the time of small living communities, comes into a creative, often tense, engagement with history. If the body 'cannot lie', what it offers is not narrative closure, and certainly no 'grand récit'. We thus see that embodiment is key for its rawness, for its small scale, for its resistance to narration and dwelling in the unfinished instant of experience, and finally for its return to trauma and rejection of teleology. I would propose that what we have in all these very different instances is a visceral sense of time's incompleteness. We do not know the direction grief will take, and we experience our finiteness in the shadow of its power.

This is not to say that these monuments fail to console, drawing us into an endless mourning that is pathological. They do question an exceedingly quick return to health in the face of horror – and they question the medicalisation of wartime trauma, which, as an illness, implies deficiency in the organism, rather than experience that is unacceptable to the person. The finiteness they ask us to inhabit is not endless precisely because it is human, and it reasserts the human against the monumentality of death itself. Hence they offer comfort via a community of shared grief, but they also refuse to frame that grief for their viewers: what is shared remains open, implicit, to be made in an actual encounter. These memorials imply a sense of how history will be made, and remade, but, remarkably, they refrain from seeking to shape it in advance; what they demand, rather, is that the moment – of suffering, of grief, of empathy – remain alive while that history is in the making. Thus Tognasso clearly hoped that when we now see the Unknown Soldier memorial in Rome, we might also see his images and in particular grasp that one of the skeletons he shows us is most likely in the Vittoriano – and it is no different from the others, no less full of pathos, no more monumental.

How does this speak to our current memory boom? These memorials assert that the body cannot lie, but by foregrounding its finiteness they also recognise that history *must* be constantly rewritten. And they even warn us against a history that would be final, for such completeness would make for texts and images that are no longer performative. Increasingly, our archives, especially electronic ones, and thus also private ones, can grow to a size that gives the illusion of completeness and understanding. In contrast, these memorials remind us that to be alive, history must still speak to us, and that curatorship, not coverage, is key. Such curatorship can be that of the collector, or of the historian, or both, but, either way, it will introduce bias – the very bias a philosopher of history such as Wyschogrod asserts we cannot do without if we want to 'do justice' to what happened. Acknowledged bias, palpable bias, is also what can counter both trivialisation and a certain re-sacralisation of the past that the illusion of completeness implies. When the new *Historial* memorial, museum and archive at Péronne was inaugurated in 1992, the designers, who included the historian Jay Winter, made their bias clear: in particular, they placed 'fosses' or shallow dugouts in their museum to 'privilege horizontality' and to invoke a radical compassion that recalls the Unknown Soldier; 'to point downward', Winter asserts, 'is to recognize where most soldiers lived their lives when they came to the Somme.'[42] The angry, grieving woman sculpted by Auban leans her torso against the ground for the same visceral reason.

Moreover, the memorials I have discussed step away from the dualism whereby embodiment is personal and history is national by presenting us with different forms by which these forces engage with each other – and cannot fail to encounter each other.

Another way of putting this is that the work of remembrance forcefully reminds us that memorialisation takes place in many unusual forms, and that embodiment and empathy in particular can come alive in unexpected places. The use of the 'Hero's Journey' as defined by Joseph Campbell, based on (among others) the Homeric epics, in the narrations created by PTSD patients after our recent wars is reminiscent of d'Annunzio's Arengo, for it inserts suffering into a much longer history, but also depends on a personal encounter to keep it alive and give it its due. These narrations may seem private – and they are to a large extent unpublished – yet they are also memorials that need to be acknowledged as such to counter the memory boom's fragmentation, and its collapse into forms of memory that are increasingly empty.[43] These narrations, like the Arengo, and Tognasso's book most forcefully, produce disquiet because of what is left unsaid, consciously or unconsciously put in the shadows because it is too damaging or horrific to be made explicit. Vigilance against the memory boom's tendency to trivialise also means allowing such shadows to remain so that we can still be profoundly affected, by what is said, and by how little can be said.

## Notes

1. Annette Becker, 'From Death to Memory: The National Ossuaries in France after the Great War', *History and Memory*, 5.2 (1993), 38; Daniel Sherman, 'Bodies and Names: The Emergence of Commemoration in Interwar France', *The American Historical Review*, 102.2 (1998), 443–6; Annette Becker, 'Les Soldats Inconnus', *Historiens et Géographes*, 89.364 (1998), 135–9; Thomas W. Laqueur, 'Names, Bodies, and the Anxiety of Erasure', in Theodore R. Schatzki and Wolfgang Natter (eds), *The Social and Political Body* (New York: Guilford Press, 1996), pp. 123–41; Ken S. Inglis, 'Entombing Unknown Soldiers: From London and Paris to Baghdad', *History & Memory: Studies in Representations of the Past*, 5.2 (1993), 8–31, and 'War Memorials: Ten Questions for Historians', *Guerres mondiales et conflits contemporains*, 167 (1992), 5–21; Daniel W. Ingersoll and James N. Nickell, 'The Most Important Monument: The Tomb of the Unknown Soldier', in Gordon Bronitsky (ed.), *Mirror and Metaphor: The Material and Social Constructions of Reality* (Lanham, MD: University Press of America, 1987), pp. 199–225; Pierre Nora, *Les lieux de mémoire*, 3 vols (Paris: Éditions Gallimard, 1997); Patricia Dogliani, 'Redipuglia', in Mario Isnenghi and Ersilia Alessandrone Perona (eds), *I luoghi della memoria. Simboli e miti dell'Italia Unita* (Rome: Laterza, 1996), pp. 382–3.
2. Laura Wittman, *The Tomb of the Unknown Soldier, Modern Mourning, and the Reinvention of the Mystical Body*, Toronto Italian Studies (Toronto and Buffalo: University of Toronto Press, 2011); Alfredo Bonadeo, *Mark of the Beast: Death and Degradation in the Literature of the Great War* (Lexington: University Press of Kentucky, 1989). More recently, on the French Unknown Soldier, see Alain Gauthier, *1914–1918: La prise en charge des morts pour la France et l'invention du Soldat Inconnu*, Collection l'éveil de la mémoire (Albi: Un autre reg'art, 2014). On Unknown Soldiers all over the world, see François Cochet and Jean-Noël Grandhomme, *Les Soldats Inconnus de la Grande Guerre: la mort, le deuil, la mémoire* (Saint-Cloud: Soteca, 2012).
3. Jay Winter, *Remembering War: The Great War between Memory and History in the Twentieth Century* (New Haven: Yale University Press, 2006), Kindle edition, loc. 2,963 and 2,938.
4. Ibid., loc. 102, 586, 706.
5. Anne Harrington, *The Cure Within: A History of Mind-Body Medicine* (New York: W. W. Norton & Co., 2008).

6. Edith Wyschogrod, *An Ethics of Remembering: History, Heterology, and the Nameless Others* (Chicago: University of Chicago Press, 1998); James M. Mayo, *War Memorials as Political Landscape: The American Experience and Beyond* (New York: Praeger, 1998), p. 8; Winter, *Remembering War*, loc. 524. For a related argument on the relationship between history and individual death, see Paul Ricoeur, *Memory, History, Forgetting* (Chicago and London: University of Chicago Press, 2004).
7. Thomas Walter Laqueur, *The Work of the Dead: A Cultural History of Mortal Remains* (Princeton: Princeton University Press, 2015); Maureen Caroll, *Earthly Paradises: Ancient Gardens in History and Archaeology* (Los Angeles: Getty Publications, 2003); Vincenzo Cazzato, 'Le Sacre Rimembranze Dei Parchi', in Maria Luisa Margiotta (ed.), *Il giardino sacro: chiostri e giardini della Campania* (Naples: Electa, 2000).
8. On the organisation and changes at Verdun, see Jean-Paul Amat, Paola Filippucci and Edwige Savouret, 'The "Cemetery of France": Reconstruction and Memorialisation on the Battlefield of Verdun (France)', in Marie Louise Stig Sørensen and Dacia Viejo-Rose (eds), *War and Cultural Heritage: Biographies of Place* (Cambridge: Cambridge University Press, 2015); Anne-Sophie Anglaret, 'Le Mémorial de Verdun et les enjeux de la mémoire combattante, 1959–2011', *Revue Historique*, 669 (January 2014); Serge Barcellini, 'Mémoire et mémoires de Verdun 1916–1996', *Guerres mondiales et conflits contemporains*, 182 (1996), 77–98; Xavier Pierson, 'Le Mémorial de Verdun: "Le Mémorial des combattants"', *Guerres mondiales et conflits contemporains*, 235 (2009), 13–20; Antoine Prost, 'Verdun', in Lawrence Kritzman and Pierre Nora (eds), *Realms of Memory: The Construction of the French Past* (New York: Columbia University Press, 1998), pp. 377–400; 'Les cimetières militaires de la Grande Guerre, 1914–1940', *Le Mouvement social*, 237 (2011), 135–51; and 'Verdun: The Life of a Site of Memory', in *Republican Identities in War and Peace: Representations of France in the Nineteenth and Twentieth Centuries*, trans. Jay Winter with Helen McPhail, The Legacy of the Great War (Oxford and New York: Berg, 2002), pp. 45–72.
9. Barcellini, 'Mémoire et mémoires de Verdun 1916–1996', pp. 78, 81.
10. For this trajectory in general, see Wittman, *The Tomb of the Unknown Soldier*. For 'perpetually mobilized' soldiers, see Eric J. Leed, *No Man's Land: Combat and Identity in World War I* (Cambridge: Cambridge University Press, 1979). For its instantiation in the Italian Unknown Soldier's inauguration, see Vito Labita, 'Il Milite Ignoto: Dalle Trincee All'altare Della Patria', in C. Grottanelli and S. Bertelli (eds), *Gli occhi di Alessandro. Potere sovrano e sacralità del corpo da Alessandro Magno a Ceaucescu* (Florence: Ponte delle Grazie, 1990).
11. Historical postcards show that the machine guns were present at times, and in different configurations, until the 1960s. They do not appear in more recent images. For some examples, see the following: an undated postcard, with bayonets, from the website 'Picture Postcards from the Great War 1914–1918', titled 'The Trench of Bayonets', <http://www.worldwar1postcards.com/the-trench-of-bayonets.php>; another undated postcard, with bayonets, and with post-war visitors, from 'Armchair General', 'Bayonet Trench', <http://www.armchairgeneral.com/forums/showthread.php?t=103329&page=156>; a 1930s image, with bayonets, from 'Some WW1 Photographs', depicting 'The Bayonet Trench', <https://ww1photographs.wordpress.com/2012/02/27/the-bayonet-trench>; a 1950s image, with bayonets, but more orderly, from 'PriceMinister', postcard of 'Monument de la tranchée des baïonnettes', <http://www.priceminister.com/offer/buy/184067084/monument-de-la-tranchee-des-baonnettes-vue-interieure-ventre-architecte-editions-verdun.html>; current image from 'Verduntourisme', without bayonets, <http://en.verdun-tourisme.com/the-bayonet-trench-centenary-14-18.html> (all last accessed 7 November 2016).
12. On hands, see Jean Giono, *Le grand troupeau*, ed. Robert Ricatte, Œuvres Romanesques Complètes (Paris: Gallimard, 1971), p. 621; Blaise Cendrars, *La main coupée*, ed. Raymond Dumay and Nino Frank, vol. 10, Oeuvres Complètes (Paris: Club français du livre, 1968); *La vie et la mort du Soldat Inconnu*, Cahiers Blaise Cendrars (Paris: H. Champion, 1995).

13. Barcellini, 'Mémoire et mémoires de Verdun 1916–1996', pp. 83, 80.
14. Philippe Rivé (ed.), *Monuments de mémoire: Les monuments aux morts de la première guerre mondiale* (Paris: Ministère des anciens combattants, 1991), p. 106.
15. Barcellini, 'Mémoire et mémoires de Verdun 1916–1996'; Prost, 'Verdun: The Life of a Site of Memory'.
16. Lucia Re, 'Gabriele D'Annunzio's Theater of Memory: Il Vittoriale degli Italiani', *The Journal of Decorative and Propaganda Arts*, 3 (1987), 6–50.
17. Giovanni Dalla Pozza, *La fabbrica del Vittoriale* (Gardone Riviera: Edizioni del Vittoriale, 1980), p. 3; Attilio Mazza, *D'Annunzio et le Vittoriale: guide de la maison du poète* (Brescia: Editions du Vittoriale, 1987), p. 70; Annamaria Andreoli, *Il Vittoriale* (Milan: Electa, 1993), p. 71. There is also a 'throne' or special chair for d'Annunzio and a column that served as a book stand: Andreoli, *Il Vittoriale*, p. 72.
18. See images in Rivé (ed.), *Monuments de mémoire*, pp. 159 ff.
19. Gabriele d'Annunzio, *Notturno* (Milan: Garzanti, 1995).
20. Leed, *No Man's Land*.
21. For d'Annunzio's obsession with death and recourse to history, see Wittman, *The Tomb of the Unknown Soldier*, pp. 165–6.
22. On d'Annunzio and scale, and in particular its political implications, see Paolo Valesio, 'Pax Italiae and the Literature of Politics', *Yale Italian Studies*, 2 (1978), 143–67; 'Declensions: D'Annunzio after the Sublime', *New Literary History: A Journal of Theory and Interpretation*, 16.2 (1985), 401–15; and *The Dark Flame* (New Haven: Yale University Press, 1992). Winter notes memorials have a 'shelf-life': Winter, *Remembering War*, loc. 1,412.
23. See chapter on 'art de série' for common motifs, in Rivé (ed.), *Monuments de mémoire*. On mourning as a less frequent motif, see ibid., pp. 184 ff.
24. On Auban's memorial, see Susan R. Grayzel, *Women's Identities at War: Gender, Motherhood, and Politics in Britain and France during the First World War* (Chapel Hill: University of North Carolina Press, 1999). For his other similar sculptures, see 'Auban, Paul Ch. A., sculpteur' dossier, in 'Les Monuments aux Morts: France – Belgique' website, <http://monumentsmorts.univ-lille3.fr/auteur/530/aubanpaulcha/> (last accessed 7 November 2016).
25. See 'Châteauroux' dossier, in 'Les Monuments aux Morts: France – Belgique' website, <http://monumentsmorts.univ-lille3.fr/monument/14359/chateauroux-place/> (last accessed 7 November 2016).
26. This memorial is one of two at Châteauroux; the other is a mourning mother held by her son, presumably both mourning a dead father. It has a huge vertical stone inscribed with the words 'Patrie' and 'Paix'. Nivet, a local, also sculpted a remarkable *Homage to French Women during the Great War* – a figure also vertical, but equally surrounded by silence.
27. Winter, *Remembering War*, loc. 1,501 and 1,486. The parents kept Peter's room the same as when he died, kept his place at table, and found many ways to keep his presence alive for many years. Kollwitz aimed to express 'the *totality of grief*': Antonina Filonov Gove, 'The Modernist Poetics of Grief in the Wartime Works of Tsvetaeva, Filonov, and Kollwitz', in Roger Anderson and Paul Debreczeny (eds), *Russian Narrative and Visual Art: Varieties of Seeing* (Gainesville: University Press of Florida, 1994), pp. 148–72. For this totality as a form of prayer, see Susie Paulik Babka, 'Art as Witness to Sorrow: Käthe Kollwitz, Emmanuel Levinas, and Dorothee Solle', in Rosemary P. Carbine and Kathleen J. Dolphin (eds), *Women, Wisdom, and Witness* (Collegeville: Liturgical Press, 2012), pp. 25–44.
28. On the importance of framing, see Karsten Harries, *The Broken Frame: Three Lectures* (Washington, DC: Catholic University of America Press, 1989).
29. Winter, *Remembering War*, loc. 1,512.

30. 'Innocenza e memoria', in Giuseppe Ungaretti, *Vita d'un uomo: saggi e interventi* (Milan: Mondadori, 1974).
31. Alexandra Hudson, *Reuters*, Sunday 29 June 2014.
32. For the details of the Unknown Soldier's burial, in Italy, France and England, see Wittman, *The Tomb of the Unknown Soldier*, esp. pp. 154–66.
33. This book is rare enough that only four libraries in Italy have a copy. It was reprinted in 1962 in Milan by the Tipografia Zanoli, in an 'edizione fuori commercio', this time 'A favore della Casa militare veterani guerre naz. Umberto 1. e della erigenda Casa del combattente in Bovisa'.
34. On texts, see Winter, *Remembering War*; Amy Boylan, 'Maternal Images in Song, Bronze, and Rhetoric: Mercantini's "Inno di Garibaldi," Baroni's "Monumento ai Mille," and D'Annunzio's "Orazione per la sagra dei Mille"', *Italian Studies*, 66.1 (2011), 40–58, and 'Maternity, Mortality and Mourning in the Trench Poetry of World War I', *Forum Italicum*, 46.2 (2012), 380–402.
35. For details on the ten who were not chosen, and their association with the unconventional mourning rituals that took place at Fiume, see Wittman, *The Tomb of the Unknown Soldier*, pp. 38–9.
36. Laqueur, 'Names, Bodies, and the Anxiety of Erasure'; Wittman, *The Tomb of the Unknown Soldier*, pp. 58–63. I would also like to thank Professor Laqueur for discussing these unusual photographs with me, and confirming that to his knowledge no other nation allowed publication of exhumations.
37. Susan Sontag, *On Photography* (New York: Farrar, Straus and Giroux, 1977); 'Regarding the Torture of Others', *New York Times*, 23 May 2004. For an example of this from the First World War, see Winter, *Remembering War*, chapter 3.
38. For concern about decay, see Wittman, *The Tomb of the Unknown Soldier*, p. 135. More generally, for worry over families' reactions, see Quinto Antonelli, *I dimenticati della Grande Guerra. La memoria dei combattenti trentini (1914–1920)*, Orizzonti (Trento: Il margine, 2008), and *Storia intima della Grande Guerra. Lettere, diari e memorie dei soldati dal fronte*, Saggi Storia e Scienze Sociali (Rome: Donzelli, 2014).
39. Winter, *Remembering War*, loc. 843.
40. Ibid., loc. 841; Leed, *No Man's Land*.
41. Tognasso does mention the finding of a mass grave in the text, and how it was not possible to distinguish one body from another – making it all the more remarkable that he did not show any images of this. For what more recent archaeological finds yield (and the confusion of bodies), see Nicholas J. Saunders and Paul Cornish, *Contested Objects: Material Memories of the Great War* (London and New York: Routledge, 2009), esp. chapter 18 on human remains; Yves Desfossés, Alain Jacques and Gilles Prilaux, *L'archéologie de la Grande Guerre* (Rennes: Éditions Ouest France, 2008).
42. Winter, *Remembering War*, loc. 2,338. This strategy is in stark contrast to the one Fogu sees developing under Fascism, in which history is collapsed into the present: Claudio Fogu, 'Fare la storia al presente. Il fascismo e la rappresentazione della Grande Guerra', *Memoria e ricerca* (July 2001), 49–70.
43. Edward Tick, *War and the Soul: Healing Our Nation's Veterans from Post-Traumatic Stress Disorder* (Wheaton: Quest Books, 2005); Daryl S. Krippner and Stanley Paulson, *Haunted by Combat: Understanding PTSD in War Veterans, Including Women, Reservists, and Those Coming Back from Iraq* (Westport, CT, and London: Praeger Security International, 2007). Concern over the emptying of memory is voiced in Winter, *Remembering War*; Nora, *Les lieux de mémoire.*

# 10

# Posters, Advertising and the First World War in Britain

*James Thompson*

THIS CHAPTER EXAMINES how the media of posters and advertising responded to the First World War. It focuses principally upon Britain. Posters and adverts are conventionally seen as ephemeral forms, yet First World War posters have been preserved, and disseminated, in huge numbers, and have supplied some of the most enduring images of the Great War. The commercial adverts of wartime have not become similarly iconic, though in 2014 the Sainsbury's Christmas advert portrayed the 'Christmas truce' of 1914. The dominant interpretation of the war in popular culture – a composite of selected war poetry and *Blackadder Goes Forth* emphasising futility and disillusionment – renders much of the consumer advertising of 1914–18 ('Fashionable furs at War Prices') alien, bordering on the incomprehensible.[1] The Sainsbury's advert was made in partnership with the Royal British Legion but sharply divided viewers, with some finding the use of wartime events to advertise groceries offensive, though this was common practice during the war itself. War posters also now meet with deep scepticism, even derision; but the frequent appeals to duty can certainly be accommodated within the 'lions led by donkeys' narrative, and with a sense of the pathos of war; while the anti-waste campaigns of the home front chime with narratives about Britons' capacity for making do, envisioning the Great War through notions of shared sacrifice powerfully shaped by the cultural legacy of the next global conflict.[2]

While the posters of the war now have greater visual currency than the adverts of the time, debates about the former have long been shaped by attitudes to advertising. Jay Winter's description of the propaganda of 1914–18 as 'the most spectacular advertising campaign to date' perpetuates a view rooted in the conflict itself, with *The Times* noting the 'liberal use of advertising methods' less than a month into the war.[3] The involvement of advertisers in the production of propaganda was real, and, as we shall see, the visual vocabulary of posters was indebted to advertising. However, the established focus on advertising as an influence upon wartime posters has occluded the significance of other traditions of image-making, and obscured aspects of their reception and character. In particular, existing accounts pay insufficient attention to pre-war political postering. During a by-election in 1916, *The Times* referred to posters as one of 'the older, and ordinary, election methods'.[4] Posters were well established in British politics by 1914, with output in the dual election year of 1910 running into the millions.[5] As John Bourne noted a quarter of a century ago, election campaigning provided the model for much wartime propaganda, and this point can be extended to posters.[6]

This chapter reconstructs the relationship between posters and advertising by recognising the variety of early-twentieth-century visual culture in Britain, noting especially the rapid development of the political poster in the twenty years before the war. The neglect of pre-war postering has led some to present the First World War as the birth of the political poster.[7] This emphasis upon novelty can be found in accounts that stress the debt to advertising in wartime posters, reflecting a long-standing, though not unproblematic, identification between advertising and modernity. Important recent work on First World War posters provides a sophisticated analysis of continuity and change, but is hampered by inattention to peacetime political postering.[8]

The chapter argues that relating First World War posters to peacetime political practice reveals important continuities, as well as significant developments.[9] It shows how the exigencies of wartime could hark back to an allegorical register which political posters had largely jettisoned, and how fine art traditions came to seem more relevant in wartime than they had in peacetime politics. It analyses the ways in which the positive appeal, characteristic of many recruiting posters, drew upon commercial techniques less evident in pre-war political posters, but emphasises the complex and changing relationships between political postering, advertising and cartooning in British visual culture before and during the war.

The rest of the chapter is divided into three parts. The first section examines the history of First World War posters. It begins with production, placing war posters in the context of their pre-war precursors, reconstructing the visual vocabulary of wartime posters, investigating the relationship of word and image, and charting stylistic and rhetorical trends. It then turns to reception, exploring the contemporary response to war posters. The second section looks at commercial advertising. It notes how quickly advertisers adopted a patriotic appeal, seeking to sell goods by reference to the war. The response of contemporaries to wartime advertising is an elusive question, but some headway can be made. The chapter ends with brief reflections on the historical relationship between posters, advertising and the First World War.

## Poster History and Reception

Before the First World War, the political poster was flourishing in Britain. *The Times* noted that the January 1910 general election 'was characterised by a greater output of campaign publications of all kinds, posters, pamphlets and leaflets, than any which has occurred since the passing of the Reform Bill of 1832'.[10] There were more political posters than ever before, and those posters were larger, and increasingly colourful. Posters were produced in large numbers by political parties, but also by an array of extra-party organisations and pressure groups, from suffragists to the Union Defence League. Many posters, as they would be in the war, were purely textual, but picture posters were growing rapidly in number, encouraged by technical developments in printing.[11]

Pre-war political posters were controversial, accused by critics of compromising democracy with the methods of advertising. This view overstated the influence of advertising relative to that of political cartooning, which was the prime supplier of iconography and visual motifs. The relationship between word and image was central to pre-war political posters as text played an important role, typically more so than in commercial advertising posters. Many political posters were fiercely critical of the opposing side, as exemplified in G. R. Halkett's often shrill posters for the Conservative Party. The associational logic that characterised much advertising imagery – in which 'a bottle of sauce supports a reclining Shakespeare' – was widely present, but there was greater attention to the construction of pictorial argument than typically appeared in commercial imagery.[12] Advertising was certainly an influence upon the political poster, but it was far from the only or dominant one. Many working artists, such as John Hassall, drew both political and commercial posters, but they adopted differing approaches to each. Neither political cartooning nor commercial design was a static visual tradition; both responded to the emergence of cinema and its fascination with breaking the picture frame to engage the viewer.

A good way into these issues is provided by the most famous poster of the war, Alfred Leete's familiar image of Kitchener. Historians have differed sharply over the contemporary popularity of this image, and its 'unofficial' origins have been stressed.[13] There is good reason to think other posters were more heavily used at the time, but the question of its official status is perhaps less significant. As Andrew Thompson has noted, the propaganda machinery of 1914–17 operated not unlike that of the South African War of 1899–1902, with considerable reliance upon non-state organisations.[14] Furthermore, the Parliamentary Recruiting Committee (PRC) was built upon the expanded party apparatus that had developed in the previous thirty years alongside, and often working with, a panoply of extra-party organisations.[15] We will touch later on the afterlives of the image, but deal now with its visual character.

In a characteristically learned essay, Carlo Ginzburg has traced the long history of the key visual devices in the Kitchener image: the direct gaze towards the viewer and the foreshortened finger pointing out of the picture plane. He sketches a tradition of figures, usually all-seeing Christ images, but also archers, staring towards the viewer; he traces the foreshortened gesture through the work of Antonello da Messina, Michelangelo and, perhaps most obviously, Caravaggio. While such pictorial conventions are a necessary deep background to Leete's design, Ginzburg finds the more immediate and effective visual context is provided by 'the demotic language of advertisement'.[16] But such imagery was scarcely confined to advertising. Consider, in particular, the cartoonist and journalist Edward Huskinson's poster for the 1907 London County Council elections, 'It's Your Money We Want'.[17] This foreshortened finger and staring gaze were plastered around London in March 1907, and were the subject of much discussion, not least in Graham Wallas's *Human Nature in Politics* (1908).[18] The same image reappeared at the 1910 LCC elections ('It's Still Your Money We Want'). As A. G. Gardiner noted, it closely resembles an illustration from *Change for a Half-Penny* – a comic look at the Northcliffe press – drawn by the cartoonist George Morrow, with the very phrase 'It's Your Money We Want'.[19]

Figures gazing and reaching out of the picture frame were increasingly common in Edwardian political imagery, and informed the ways in which the posters of wartime were seen. In November 1914, the Conservative MP J. A. Grant recognised the relevance of pre-war politics to the reception of war propaganda, arguing that the credibility of the recruiting drive was undermined for many as 'for years they have listened to equally impassioned appeals from partisan, political platforms, and seen even more flaming posters on the same hoardings'.[20] Likewise, in its journey from magazine cover to poster, Leete's image described a trajectory common to pre-war political posters, and reflected a visual culture in which such migrations were common. Historians have long noted the frequent translation of press cartoons and illustrations into posters during the First World War, but this was simply business as usual.

The visual vocabulary of cartooning is apparent, for example, in the work of established *Punch* cartoonist Bernard Partridge. Partridge produced both political and commercial posters before the war, but it is the former, and the traditions of cartooning, upon which his wartime poster 'Soldiers All' draws, with its dependence upon text, dramatising a moment of conversation between soldier and workman.[21] The techniques of cartooning, not least caricature, were particularly relevant in the production of 'hate' posters, such as David Wilson's 1918 poster 'Once a German – Always a German', which began life in the pages of the British Empire Union's *Monthly Record* (Figure 10.1). Wilson's cartoons for the *Daily Chronicle* had been used as political posters in peacetime, and his work had a sharp edge. 'Once a German' contains multiple scenes spread across the picture plane, combined with a 'split screen' device in which the portrayal of the post-war German businessmen visually echoes that of the German soldier, with pipe and briefcase in place of knife and grenade. Its use of 'Remember!', placed in the largest font, rehearses an injunction repeatedly issued through the war to 'Remember Belgium',

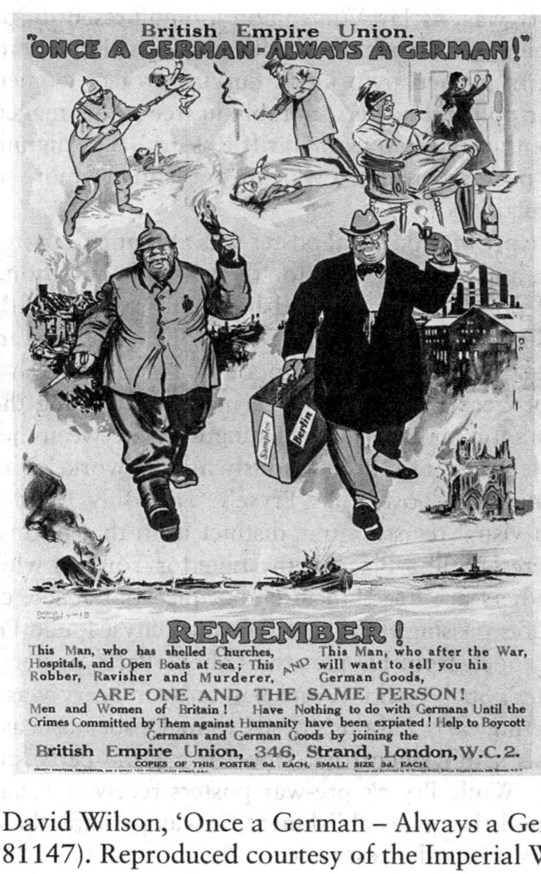


Figure 10.1 David Wilson, 'Once a German – Always a German' (1918). © IWM (Q 81147). Reproduced courtesy of the Imperial War Museum.

or 'Remember Scarborough'. In a nice instance of old and new technologies combining, the drawing of 'Once a German' was animated in a film, as were a number of cartoons and posters.[22]

The campaign against waste frequently recalled the pre-war imagery of the fiscal controversy, albeit now with messages about eating less bread rather than arguments over its size and price. 'Save the Wheat and Help the Fleet', now marketed by the Imperial War Museum as a jigsaw, displays a large loaf in the foreground on a background of battleships silhouetted against yellow.[23] The controversy over tariff reform and free trade had distributed images of loaves across the country before the war, and free traders especially had proclaimed the centrality, and sanctity, of bread to working-class life.[24] Echoing such imagery aided intelligibility, though the target audience in wartime very much included those accustomed to a more plentiful diet than that characteristic of pre-war working-class life.

As Adrian Gregory has recently reiterated, and a generation of historiography has demonstrated, links between soldiers and civilians were strong and concern for those in the trenches or at sea ubiquitous.[25] The demands of 'duty' were endlessly asserted in the war, invoking a widely and deeply held value, though for most Britons duties were multiple, with commitments to family looming large. A duty not to waste food was presented as a debt to seamen risking their lives to bring food to Britain. J. P. Beadle's 'A Message from our Seamen' proclaimed that 'it's up to you not to waste' food.[26] The language of morality was, as Jay Winter notes, omnipresent in publicity that sought to locate the demands of wartime above the messy world of politics.[27] However, the appeal to morality, in particular to men's duty to protect women and children, was apparent in pre-war political posters, notably in free trade imagery, in which viewers were urged to 'Save the Children from Tariff Reform'. The dignified 'manly' sailor of Beadle's anti-waste poster provided a wartime recasting of more positive pre-war representations of manual labour.

The legacy of the pre-war political poster was also apparent in those posters championed, at the time and subsequently, for their artistic ambition. In their influential post-war survey of posters 'distinguished by their artistic merit', Sabin and Hardie praised especially Frank Brangwyn and Gerald Spencer Pryse among British poster designers, while generally decrying the poor quality of British work compared to French or, more so, German posters.[28] Recent work stressing the preponderance of posters designed by anonymous printers distinguishes between their advertising-based designs and a smaller body of self-consciously artistic work, within which Pryse and Brangwyn are located.[29] A poster like Pryse's 'The Only Road for an Englishman' certainly adopted a visual register quite distinct from that of an image such as PRC poster no. 35, 'There Is Still a Place in the Line for You', in which identikit, almost mannequin-like soldiers are lined up in empty pictorial space, contrasting with the more animated figures passing through a damaged cityscape in Pryse's poster. Pryse's wartime work descended from his pre-war Labour Party posters, such as 'Forward! The Day Is Breaking'. Such positive, and painterly, imagery was unusual in pre-war party politics, reflecting early Labour's desire to make socialists as much as win votes, and its self-image as a movement that stood above the petty strife of conventional two-party politics.[30] While Pryse's pre-war posters received acclaim from within the labour movement and the art establishment, it was perhaps the context of war that first gave his imagery a broader resonance.

It is important to recognise that just as images were actively recycled, so poster designers often worked in a variety of media. Bernard Partridge's much-imitated 'Take Up the Sword of Justice' (Plate 6) was the work of a long-standing *Punch* cartoonist, who also produced advertising and political posters before the war. Partridge's poster of Lloyd George as a golfer impeded by a peer was gently humorous compared to many of the hoardings in 1910, but its visual vocabulary was in keeping with developments in political posters whereby allegorical figures, with the exception of John Bull, were becoming less common. The grandness – the pictorial and textual high diction of 'Take Up the Sword' – was a conscious choice, reflecting the circumstances of the sinking of the *Lusitania*. Jay Winter has famously argued, largely in dialogue with the work of Paul Fussell, that much of the cultural response to war was characterised by the revival of 'older languages', and this is certainly detectable in posters.[31] While medieval motifs are less evident in British than in German posters, an image like the PRC poster 'Britain Needs You at Once', with its intimation of stained glass and interlocking St George and the dragon, is closer in visual language to the murals of 1895 than 1910. Aspects of 'Britain Needs You at Once' – its font, the verticality of the overall design – can be seen as 'modern', but, like 'Take Up the Sword', its heightened visual rhetoric departs from pre-war trends in visual mass media, whether advertising or political posters. It is scarcely surprising to see images of nationhood in a time of conflict, but personifications of the nation were also a standard feature of pre-war political posters, which nonetheless saw a decline in the use of many traditional allegorical devices (Britannia, Justice, the British Lion) that was reversed in wartime.

The kinds of choices made by poster designers are illuminated by the work of John Hassall. Best known now for the 'Skegness Is So Bracing' image – one of a number he produced for seaside councils – Hassall was a prolific commercial artist who was also responsible for a series of anti-budget posters in 1909–10. His 'Electors Don't Ruin Your Country' pictured capital as the soil that nourished the tree of labour, with John Bull upbraiding Lloyd George for removing the soil. His recruitment poster 'Hurry Up! Boys Fill the Ranks', produced, as befits the illustrator of Henty, for the Public Schools Brigade – with its smiling, waving, open-collared soldier, surrounded by helmets of conquered Germans – was clearly closer in style to his commercial work. Compare, though, his 'Music in War-Time' concert poster of 1915 for the Professional Classes War Relief Council (Figure 10.2). This starkly dramatic black and white design, in keeping with its subject matter, was much more aesthetically high-minded, harking back to the 'artistic' theatrical posters of the 1890s. By contrast, his 1916 Belgium Canal Boat Fund appeal adopted a much more 'realistic' and detailed style, with greater use of perspective and corresponding depth, rather than the more flattened picture space of 'Music in War-Time'. The triangular arrangement of the mother and her two children recalls a kind of broken pietà, with the boy staring out of the picture, engaging sympathy and donations. Hardie and Sabin, who were largely dismissive of the advertising poster in Britain, found space for the Belgium Canal Boat Fund and 'Music in War-Time' as amongst the 'best' British posters of the war.[32]

As Hassall's range of commissions suggests, posters were employed in wartime for a range of causes. The output of the PRC has understandably attracted much attention, reflecting the sheer quantity of posters produced, though the widely quoted figure of 2.5 million in its first year was not dissimilar to the volume of postering across the two general elections of 1910. A focus on the PRC has tended to reinforce emphasis

Figure 10.2 John Hassall, 'Music in War-Time' (1915). Poster designed for the Professional Classes War Relief Council, lithograph on paper. © IWM (Art.IWM PST 8096). Reproduced courtesy of the Imperial War Museum.

upon the impact of advertising, since it was, as Hiley observed, within the PRC campaign that the most overt adoption of advertising tropes and techniques is apparent, especially in idealised and sanitised images of a single, often smiling, soldier.[33] Aulich and Hewitt have rightly drawn attention to the role of non-state actors, covering a wide range of organisations from charities to newspapers, whose output demonstrates the diversity of wartime posters. The National Mission of Repentance and Hope was the Church of England's response to the challenges and the opportunities of wartime, intended to revivify religion by harnessing the sense of duty and sacrifice it thought had been awakened by the conflict. The Literature Committee, persuaded that 'many of those whom the Church is seeking will perhaps be first reached by the appeal to the eye', released a poster by the war artist Eric Kennington (the son of T. B. Kennington, whose picture *The Battle of Life* had been turned into a pre-war Conservative poster). The Mission poster was set in an industrial town and pictured Christ opposite a large crowd, including 'a soldier, sailor, airman, Red Cross nurse, workmen, clergy, beggars, women and little children', above the text 'Jesus said, The Kingdom of God is at hand. Repent ye and believe the Gospel.'[34] The Church presented the Mission as 'war work of the highest kind', and the poster's release was reported in both *The Times* and New Zealand's *Poverty Bay Herald*.[35] The Mission was alive to the full range of visual media, noting that 'experience has proved the value of a badge in many great movements'.[36] The Mission did not eschew the textual appeal, casting its work as war work through placards quoting the imperial hero Lord Robert's words, 'What we want is the Nation on its knees'.[37]

The device of personifying groups, usually occupational ones, found in Kennington's poster was widely used in First World War posters. Baden-Powell's 'Are You in This?' offers a well-known example and includes a soldier, sailor, Boy Scout, nurse, woman munitions worker and male blacksmith. As Gregory has noted, it clearly pictures the shirker, and by implication the viewer, as middle class. Gregory reads the image as 'disturbingly modern' in its portrayal of the interlinking of civilian and combatant, men and women.[38] Yet its emphasis on active volunteering (most apparent in the figure of the Boy Scout) extended nineteenth-century ideals of civic participation into wartime circumstances, while its depiction of interdependence was compatible with communitarian currents in pre-war political thought. Its visual vocabulary was one familiar from pre-war imagery, notably that of the fiscal controversy, in which archetypes of different social groups (workmen, clerks) proliferated in posters and cartoons (Figure 10.3).

Figure 10.3 R. S. S. Baden-Powell, 'Are You in This?' (1915). Poster designed for the Parliamentary Recruiting Committee, lithograph on paper. © IWM (Art.IWM PST 2712). Reproduced courtesy of the Imperial War Museum.

As Susan Sontag noted long ago, visual shorthand, and references to other images, are central to the pictorial language of posters.[39] The German helmet, the *Pickelhaube*, was a recurring motif that developed both added meaning and familiarity through its repetition, coming to symbolise German 'militarism' in action. In some ways, this translated into wartime the role of hats as social signifiers, both as worn and as pictured in posters and cartoons. Paul Fussell compared the British helmet to the bowler hat 'with its familiar associations of normality and domesticity'.[40] In Partridge's 'Soldiers All', the Tommy's cap is visually paired with the workman's flat cap, conveying a shared democratic authenticity, albeit with the soldier positioned visually and rhetorically above the 'disaffected workman'. The accretion of meaning, not least through representations of hats, was a well-developed feature of pre-war visual culture. Gregory argues that the term 'profiteer' was pioneered by the Labour press before achieving wider circulation in 1915.[41] Similarly, it was the Labour press, especially Will Dyson in the *Daily Herald*, that first visualised the profiteer.[42] The appearance of the profiteer in his shiny top hat followed the Edwardian personification of the 'Trust' in W. K. Haselden's *Daily Mirror* cartoons attacking the 'Soap Trust', and in the cartoons and posters of the 1907 London County Council election.[43] Meaning became condensed, and the top hat came to signify the profiteer. In a *John Bull* cartoon of 1917, Frank Holland placed it on leeches shown attacking the British workman.

In their valuable study of wartime posters, Aulich and Hewitt pay particular attention to the physical location of posters and the symbolic ownership of urban space. They rightly observe that wartime posters entered civic space and town squares, and contrast this with the more specialised locations used by commercial bill posters. However, these civic spaces were much coveted by Edwardian political activists seeking to claim ownership of symbolically significant public spaces for their party. Contemporary statements about the omnipresence of war posters simply reiterate earlier comments about the ubiquity of electoral posters. Similarly, the use of posters as a backdrop for speeches, and their incorporation more generally into the visual theatre of wartime campaigns, was very much a continuation of pre-war political practices. This is unsurprising given the grounding of the PRC in the existing party machinery. In his letter donating the minutes of the PRC to the British Library, R. Humphrey Davies contrasted the collaborative work of the Committee with the situation 'prior to the war', when 'party feeling ran very high, not only in the Houses of Parliament, but also in the constituencies'.[44] Posters were very much part of the fiercely contested world of Edwardian politics, and were often ripped down, replaced or amended in the struggle for votes and for public space.

Historians have differed markedly in their accounts of the contemporary reception of First World War posters. In part, this reflects larger debates about the power of propaganda, and diverging assessments of voluntary recruitment. While many have seen the impact of advertising on war posters as increasing their influence, others have suggested that affinities with commercial imagery were unpalatable and reduced their impact. By relating wartime posters more closely than hitherto to pre-war political precursors, it is possible to clarify aspects of their reception. Liberal intellectuals who detected, and generally overstated, the influence of advertising upon pre-war political publicity attacked its allegedly debasing vulgarity. Wartime debates about the efficacy and morality of posters recall pre-war discussions. Important recent writing about the war stresses the role of events, notably German violation of Belgian neutrality and the bombing of the east coast, in shaping public attitudes, and argues that the level of distortion in British propaganda has been overstated.[45] Claims about the relative efficacy of visual propaganda in different countries are difficult to test, and there were significant commonalities in the character and content of propaganda. More frequent use of medieval motifs, such as Gothic scripts, in German posters may simply have reflected the greater resonance of the medieval past in Germany, while the story-telling tendencies of British posters – bemoaned by Hardie and Sabin – might just be an instance of a broader fondness for narrative, evident in other media, such as illustrated books. It does, though, seem plausible to argue, as Winter has for propaganda more broadly, that the civil society origins of many British posters, and the continuities with pre-war popular and political culture, made posters intelligible to their audience, and visually 'contained' some of the strains of wartime.[46]

Widespread patriotism, and the common conviction that Britain's cause was just, conditioned how war posters were received. However, pre-war traditions of disruption did not disappear, with posters in Glasgow subject to defacement, and Sinn Fein producing their own parodies of Irish recruiting posters.[47] Some bemoaned the 'shrieking' character of war posters, but others defended their tactics, arguing, as Tennant did in the House of Commons, that 'appeals must necessarily be addressed to meet the most varied tastes'.[48] As with product advertising, there is evidence to suggest that soldiers were more troubled by the often highly romanticised and deeply unrealistic portrayals of conflict, especially the persistence of cavalry posters. Over time, posters came to focus less upon securing volunteers for the forces. The arrival of Lord Derby, followed by the onset of conscription, redirected pictorial posters away from recruitment towards loans, and the home front more broadly.

First World War posters have become a mainstay of museum shops and websites.[49] They are presented and perceived as tokens of a culturally and emotionally distant past, full of naive appeals to duty. They can be consumed as kitsch or, as with Lumley's 'Daddy, what did YOU do in the Great War?', experienced by many as alien exercises in emotional blackmail. While institutions like the Imperial War Museum and the Victoria and Albert Museum have sought to historicise the imagery of war, First World War posters are still too often wrenched from the visual and political culture out of which they emerged.

## Commercial Advertising

The immediate response of commerce to the war was deep anxiety about the economy. Early evidence of rising newspaper circulations led to a revival, though advertisers argued for lower prices out of concerns that reach would not translate into sales. As it became clear that economic dislocation had been averted, demand for many goods came to exceed supply with much production geared to war, and firms found less need to spend on advertising. Paper restrictions grew over the course of the conflict, reducing the availability of space in newspapers and limiting the size of posters. Enhanced press readership, along with the higher cost of paper, and a smaller total volume of advertising space, intensified competition between posters and print to attract advertisers. As the war went on, competition from abroad for the domestic market in industries focusing on war production led to adverts encouraging consumers to defer purchases until the struggle was concluded.[50]

Advertisers swiftly sought to use patriotism to sell goods. Such adverts now seem culturally distant, and even bizarrely trivialising. 'Zog' paint cleaner, readers of *The Times* were told in April 1915, would 'Make Dirt Fly', and the accompanying illustration showed the miracle product removing dirt Zeppelins, and dirt German soldiers, easily identifiable from their spiked helmets.[51] The widely and deeply felt desire to help the troops – to be worthy of their sacrifice – was mined by advertisers. Female readers of *The Times* were alerted to the free postage through which Horlick's Malted Milk flasks could be sent direct to 'YOUR soldier' in the trenches (the only possible evidence of any fighting pictured at a safe distance), so saving 'the strength of the soldier when he most needs it'.[52] Bovril issued a poster with a single male munitions worker staring out of the picture frame, drink in one hand, hammer in the other. The persuasive power of the poster was attested in a newspaper advert with a quotation from, and photograph of, Arsenal employee Leon Clark. Clark is quoted as saying he had seen the poster the previous year, and had resolved 'to put it to the test', and, after twelve months of regular consumption of the branded drink, 'can safely say with the poster, "Bovril Gives You Strength to Win"'. The photograph showed an impressively muscled Clark in the precise pose of the poster. This 'patriotic' tribute to 'the body building power of Bovril' was a striking amalgam of science ('proved by independent scientific investigation'), photography and consumer voice, celebrating the power of advertising, and thus itself (Figure 10.4).[53]

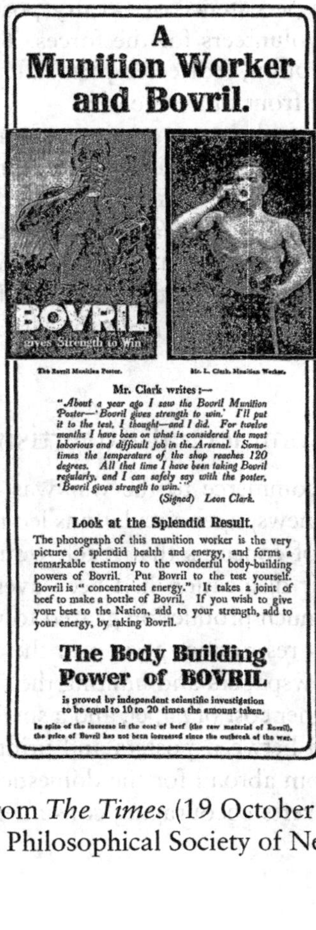


Figure 10.4 Bovril advert from *The Times* (19 October 1916). Reproduced courtesy of the Literary and Philosophical Society of Newcastle upon Tyne.

The unfolding realities of the war supplied numerous opportunities to remind consumers of the new relevance of a variety of goods. As early as October 1914, Heal's was emphasising that the 'hygienic' quality of their beds made them especially suitable for convalescents.[54] A year later Burberry was assuring readers of *The Bystander* that its 'Trench-Warm' coat was 'impenetrable, for excessively severe weather', 'a distinguished coat, a veritable safeguard', as sported by a dashing soldier standing jauntily in a trench with his head visible above ground level: trench warfare as Sunday stroll.[55] Charles Packer and Co., goldsmiths and silversmiths, enterprisingly marketed 'military badge brooches' in 15ct gold for the affluent readers of *The Bystander*.[56] Newspapers were alert to the opportunities offered by public interest in the conflict, with *The Graphic* in October 1915 advertising its pictorial map of the Dardanelles as 'the most striking and intelligent war map yet produced', available for 6d. Soap manufacturers were traditionally heavy advertisers, and this continued in wartime. Adverts, firmly aimed at women, proclaimed 'Send him Soap', in the words of Wright's. Combining a large bar of soap with images of fresh-faced soldiers, Wright's Coal Tar was the right choice whether 'your soldier friend is fighting in FLANDERS or the DARDANNELES [*sic*]'. Maps of both locations were helpfully provided, including the line of the trenches snaking from France into Belgium.[57]

Advertisers were adept at incorporating the war into their branding. 'Black and White' Scotch whisky referenced its name pictorially, not through the monochrome dogs used since the 1890s, but by a 'study in black and white' of a British destroyer whose searchlight picks out a looming black Zeppelin, with the brand name in white lettering in a modern font against the night sky.[58] John Walker and Sons of Kilmarnock proclaimed the quality of their blended whisky with the aid of the Johnnie Walker 'striding man' logo created in 1908 by the comic artist Tom Browne. Retaining the slogan 'Born 1820 – Still Going Strong', the war found Johnnie Walker presenting his passport to the French military, proving that 'he [can] go anywhere'.[59] Manufacturers in the motor industry were equally willing to link their products to the war, with Dunlop claiming to be 'the "make" that is doing the most for the nation, and will do the most for you'. Picturing the four national saints of the United Kingdom in the manner of stained glass windows, Dunlop hymned 'Nationality' as 'a vital thing these days for the country, individual and firm', insisting – heavy-handedly even by the advertising standards of 1915 – that 'if there is any merit in morality, if there is any merit in patriotism, if there is any merit in nationality, your tyres should be British and Dunlops' (Figure 10.5).[60] 'Noiseless Napier Motor carriages' were presented as the choice of the Prime Minister, the Minister of Munitions, the First Lord of the Admiralty, and the Chancellor of the Duchy of Lancaster – 'truly a happy combination of a British Cabinet and a British Car'. Photographic portraits of the four politicians – of the familiar oval, head-and-shoulders kind – surrounded a central image of the car, confidently described as 'the World's Proved Best Car'.[61] With slightly more modesty, Sunbeam announced that 'by gaining distinction in the present war by sheer force of achievement, the Sunbeam car has proved itself to be the equal of the highest class of cars and the superior of most'. Aimed at a less wealthy clientele, Sunbeam was already in 1915 suggesting that purchase would be considered 'when the war was over'. Consumers were expected to warm to the punning assurance that 'Sunbeam Coatalen Aircraft motors are helping to maintain the ascendancy which distinguishes the flying services of the Allied Forces'.[62]

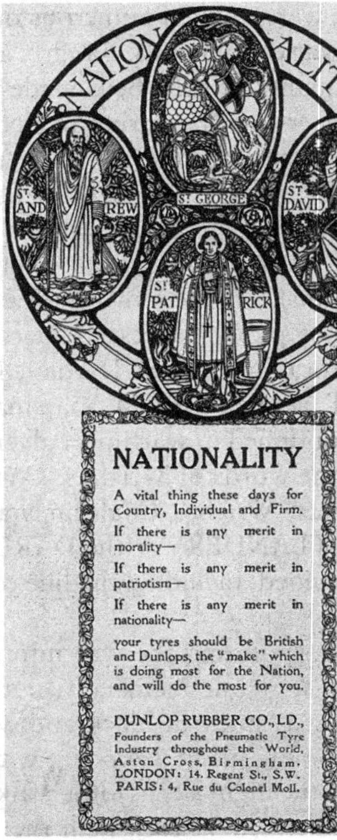


Fig. 10.5 Dunlop 'Nationality' car advert from *The Bystander* (13 October 1915). Reproduced courtesy of the British Library.

The use of politicians to sell goods was not a wartime innovation. Indeed, the war sorely tested political reputations, and not just those of individuals: in late 1915, when Napier was advertising in *The Bystander*, a columnist in the magazine asked 'Have the politicians failed?' before bemoaning the absence of 'super-men' like Gladstone or Disraeli.[63] The flow of ideas and influence between propaganda, including political propaganda, and advertising moved both ways, and this traffic continued into the war. 'Sanitas' disinfectant's advert, '<u>Your</u> House Should Be Made Sweet and Healthy', displayed an apron-wearing young woman, whose gaze and foreshortened finger clearly mimicked Alfred Leete's Kitchener poster.[64] The 'Bovril Gives You Strength to Win' poster, already touched upon, similarly referenced and appropriated the patriotic appeal of recruiting posters, seeking to convert consumption into a signifier of war-winning virtue. The new-found significance of the home front, and the importance attached to morale, in a war of such scale, character and duration, offered the possibility of casting cheerful consumption as appropriate non-combatant behaviour. It may not be fanciful to detect in the adverts for cleaning products, like Sanitas, an implied contrast with the mud of Flanders: maintenance of the cleanliness, and hence sanctity, of the home as recognition of the soldier's sacrifice.

Looking at the advertising of 1914–18, it is not hard to see why Niall Ferguson called the First World War a 'carnival of vulgarity'.[65] An image like the Pear's Soap advert 'An Incident of the Trenches' in which soldiers under fire retrieve a bar of soap – Tommy: 'Line up, we must have it', 'They got it, and had the wash of their lives' – seems to us offensively banal.[66] Yet it is not totally incomprehensible that those on the home front, distant from the immediate stench of trench warfare, perhaps guiltily aware of some of its tribulations, should wish to do something, however desperately inadequate, for those on the frontline. The willingness of business to adopt such marketing strategies reflects the pre-existing advertising culture of spectacle and bold assertion, along with the commercial imperatives and opportunities of wartime. The duration of the war, and the stalemate made visible in maps of the frontline, meant that it became a constant, everyday reality. The scale of loss was unintelligibly vast compared to previous conflicts. The very banality, and familiar boosterism, of advertising may have served to 'normalise' and to contain the unfolding reality of industrialised mass conflict. For instance, the tank made a powerful appeal in city centres as a backdrop for the war loans campaign; it was also a hugely popular toy.

It would, of course, be a mistake to assume that adverts necessarily found a ready response. Trench newspapers found them irresistible objects for satire. One asked, 'Are you going over the top? If so be sure to first inspect our new line of velveteen corduroy plush breeches. Be in the fashion and look like a soldier.'[67] The *Wipers Times* included mock notices for Christmas boxes and must-have items like 'Our Latest Improved Pattern Combination Umbrella and Wire Cutter'.[68] Conversely, *The Bystander* included Bairnfather's cartoons alongside adverts for cars and soap. These cartoons are generally seen as showing the 'stoical determination' of the ordinary soldier, and this is not wrong. There was, though, an edge to his 'Where to Live – advert'. It pictured a 'well-built dugout' helpfully located 'three minutes from the German lines', featuring 'all modern inconveniences – including gas and water' and standing 'one foot above water level, commanding an excellent view of the enemy lines'. The particulars of the late tenant, so the advert advised, were available at 'Room 6, Base Hospital'.[69] Similarly, the magazine featured cartoons by Sub-Lieutenant Arthur Watts, who had already begun his career with *Punch*, which punctured the claims of gossiping civilians to be in the know.[70] The perspective of soldiers was communicated in a host of ways, whether it be cartoons, or letters and visits, to those on the home front. Will Dyson sharply criticised bloodthirsty advertising through his *Daily Herald* cartoon.[71] The widespread hostility to profiteers that emerged from 1915, while principally driven by price rises, may have owed something to the making of outsized profits while insisting on the 'patriotic' duty of consumers to buy.

## Concluding Reflections

The effort to preserve and commemorate the posters of the First World War began during the conflict itself. It has, in many ways, been a greater success than its originators could possibly have hoped. Some of the images have become, to borrow an over-used word, iconic. The popularity of Leete's Kitchener image since the war considerably exceeds the original poster's visibility during the war. The advertisements of the war have not achieved the same level of recognition, however, and the 'lions led by donkeys' interpretation that became dominant in the 1960s has made First World War commercial advertising less celebrated than that produced in the more recent – and widely perceived as more justified – Second World War.

Both posters and advertisements need careful contextualisation. The posters have been understood through narratives about the birth of state propaganda and the modernising force of advertisements that underestimate the pluralism and complexity of British political and visual culture both before and during wartime. Neither the posters nor the adverts of Britain's war were wholly forward-looking, and aspects of what has been termed reactionary modernism need to be placed alongside genuine continuities with pre-war practices, and widespread appeals to tradition. In some respects, British visual culture was both more modern in 1914 and less modern in 1918 than is often realised. Contrasts between modern and older visual languages can distract from changes within and exchanges between visual languages. It is through a historical account of the relationships between the established, yet evolving, languages of advertising, the political poster and cartooning that we can best understand the popular visual culture of the war.

## Notes

1. Advertisement for the International Fur Store, *The Bystander*, 6 October 1915, p. vii.
2. On the impact of the Second World War on views of the First, see Adrian Gregory, *The Last Great War: British Society and the First World War* (Cambridge: Cambridge University Press, 2008), p. 6.
3. Jay Winter, 'Propaganda and the Mobilisation of Consent', in Hew Strachan (ed.), *The Oxford Illustrated History of the First World War* (Oxford: Oxford University Press, 2014), p. 216; 'Progress of Recruiting', *The Times*, 21 August 1914, p. 5.
4. 'The Mile End Contest', *The Times*, 19 January 1916, p. 5.
5. James Thompson, '"Pictorial Lies?" Posters and Politics in Britain, c. 1880–1914', *Past & Present*, 197 (2007), 175–200.
6. John Bourne, *Britain and the Great War* (London: Edward Arnold, 1989), p. 203.
7. Susan Sontag, 'Posters: Advertisement, Art, Political Artifact, Commodity', in Donald Stermer (ed.), *The Art of Revolution: 96 Posters from Castro's Cuba, 1959–1970* (New York: McGraw-Hill, 1970), pp. x–xi.
8. Jim Aulich and John Hewitt, *Seduction or Instruction? First World War Posters in Britain and Europe* (Manchester: Manchester University Press, 2007); Pearl James (ed.), *Picture This: World War I Posters and Visual Culture* (Lincoln: University of Nebraska Press, 2009).
9. On the war's relationship to pre-war political culture, see David Monger, 'Familiarity Breeds Consent? Patriotic Rituals in British First World War Propaganda', *Twentieth Century British History*, 26 (2015), 501–28.
10. 'Some Election Posters', *The Times*, 30 November 1910, p. 7.
11. Thompson, '"Pictorial Lies?"', pp. 191–4.
12. Clarence Moran, *The Business of Advertising* (London: Methuen & Co.), p. 51.
13. George Robb, *British Culture and the First World War* (Basingstoke: Palgrave, 2002), p. 106; Nicholas Hiley, '"Kitchener Wants You" and "Daddy, What Did You Do in the Great War?": The Myth of British Recruiting Posters', *Imperial War Museum Review*, 11 (1997), 40–58; James Taylor, *Your Country Needs You: The Secret History of the Propaganda Poster* (Glasgow: Saraband, 2013).

14. Andrew Thompson, 'Imperial Propaganda and the South African War', in Greg Cuthbertson, Albert Gundlingh and Mary-Lynn Suttie (eds), *Writing a Wider War: Rethinking Gender, Race and Identity in the South African War, 1899–1902* (Athens: Ohio University Press, 2002), p. 321.
15. Kathryn Rix, 'The Party Agent and English Electoral Culture, 1880–1896', unpublished thesis, University of Cambridge, 2001.
16. Carlo Ginzburg, '"Your Country Needs You": A Case Study in Political Iconography', *History Workshop Journal*, 52 (2001), 12.
17. Edward Huskinson, 'It's Your Money We Want' (1907), Guildhall Library.
18. Graham Wallas, *Human Nature in Politics* (London: Constable & Co., 1908), p. 109.
19. A. G. Gardiner, *John Benn and the Progressive Movement* (London: Ernest Benn, 1925), p. 356; Charles Graves and Edward Lucas, *Change for a Half-Penny* (London: Alston Rivers, 1905).
20. Letter from J. A. Grant, *The Times*, 25 November 1914, p. 9.
21. Bernard Partridge, 'Soldiers All', Imperial War Museum, Q 80318.
22. David Wilson, 'Once a German – Always a German', Imperial War Museum, Q 81147.
23. 'Save the Wheat and Help the Fleet', Imperial War Museum, Art.IWM PST 4470.
24. F. Trentmann, *Free Trade Nation: Commerce, Consumption and Civil Society in Modern Britain* (Oxford: Oxford University Press, 2009).
25. Gregory, *The Last Great War*, pp. 7–8.
26. J. P. Beadle, 'A Message from our Seamen', Imperial War Museum, Q 31443.
27. Winter, 'Propaganda and the Mobilisation of Consent', p. 216.
28. Martin Hardie and Arthur Sabin, *War Posters Issued by Belligerent and Neutral Nations 1914–19* (London: A & C Black, 1920), pp. 1–3.
29. Aulich and Hewitt, *Seduction or Instruction?*, p. 72.
30. James Thompson, *British Political Culture and the Idea of 'Public Opinion', 1867–1914* (Cambridge: Cambridge University Press, 2013); Jon Lawrence, *Speaking for the People: Party, Language and Popular Politics in England, 1867–1914* (Cambridge: Cambridge University Press, 1998).
31. Jay Winter, *Sites of Memory, Sites of Mourning: The Great War in European Cultural History* (Cambridge: Cambridge University Press, 1995); Paul Fussell, *The Great War and Modern Memory* (Oxford: Oxford University Press, 1975).
32. Hardie and Sabin, *War Posters*, p. x.
33. Philip Dutton, 'Moving Images? The Parliamentary Recruiting Committee's Poster Campaign, 1914–1916', *Imperial War Museum Review*, 4 (1989), 43–58; Hiley, 'The Myth of British Recruiting Posters', p. 48.
34. *Bulletin of the National Mission of Hope and Repentance*, 15 August 1916, pp. 2–3.
35. '"A Nation on its Knees"', *The Times*, 15 August 1916, p. 5; '"Nation on its Knees"', *Poverty Bay Herald*, 26 September 1916, p. 4.
36. *Bulletin of the National Mission of Hope and Repentance*, 15 August 1916, p. 3.
37. Ibid., pp. 3–4.
38. Gregory, *The Last Great War*, p. 71.
39. Sontag, 'Posters', pp. ix–x.
40. Fussell, *The Great War and Modern Memory*, p. 78.
41. Gregory, *The Last Great War*, p. 198.
42. Will Dyson, 'His Duty', *Daily Herald*, 7 November 1914, p. 1; Jean-Louis Robert, 'The Image of the Profiteer', in Jay Winter and Jean-Louis Robert (eds), *Capital Cities at War* (Cambridge: Cambridge University Press, 1997), p. 107.
43. W. K. Haselden, 'The Great Soap Trust Fight: Result', *Daily Mirror*, 27 November 1906, p. 7.
44. Letter from R. Humphrey Davies, British Library, Add. MS. 54192A.

45. Gregory, *The Last Great War*, pp. 44–5; Winter, 'Propaganda and the Mobilisation of Consent', p. 225; Niall Ferguson, *The Pity of War* (London: Allen Lane, 1998), p. 246; Trevor Wilson, *The Myriad Faces of War: Britain and the Great War 1914–1918* (Cambridge: Polity, 1985), pp. 744–7.
46. Winter, 'Propaganda and the Mobilisation of Consent', p. 218.
47. Robb, *British Culture and the First World War*, p. 125.
48. See the exchange in the House of Commons between L. G. Chiozza Money and H. J. Tennant reported in *The Times*, 11 June 1915, p. 10.
49. On the Imperial War Museum collection, see Leanne Green, 'Advertising War: Pictorial Publicity, 1914–1918', unpublished PhD thesis, Manchester Metropolitan University, 2015.
50. Terence R. Nevett, *Advertising in Britain: A History* (London: Heinemann, 1982), pp. 138–42; W. E. D. Allens, *David Allens: The History of a Family Firm* (London: John Murray, 1957), pp. 219–27.
51. *The Times*, 26 April 1915, p. 12.
52. *The Times*, 9 April 1915, p. 12.
53. *The Times*, 19 October 1916, p. 7.
54. *The Times*, 26 October 1914, p. 4.
55. *The Bystander*, 6 October 1915, p. viii.
56. Ibid., p. 41.
57. Ibid., p. 35.
58. *The Bystander*, 3 November 1915, p. 205.
59. *The Bystander*, 6 October 1915, p. 33.
60. *The Bystander*, 13 October 1915, p. 81.
61. *The Bystander*, 20 October 1915, p. 113.
62. Ibid., p. vii.
63. 'Have the Politicians Failed?', *The Bystander*, 27 October 1915, p. 125.
64. *The Bystander*, 27 October 1915, p. xvi.
65. Ferguson, *The Pity of War*, p. 234.
66. *The Bystander*, 3 November 1915, p. x.
67. Robb, *British Culture and the First World War*, p. 183.
68. Fussell, *The Great War and Modern Memory*, p. 66.
69. *The Bystander*, 6 October 1915, p. 14.
70. *The Bystander*, 13 October 1915, p. 57.
71. *Daily Herald*, 17 October 1914, p. 6.

# III.

# Music

# 11

# 'WE THINK YOU OUGHT TO GO': MUSIC HALL AND RECRUITMENT IN THE FIRST WORLD WAR

*Robert Dean*

## Music Hall and Patriotism (1890s–1910s)

IN THE TWO DECADES immediately preceding the First World War, music hall was at the centre of a burgeoning British popular entertainment industry. By 1892 there were approximately thirty-nine licensed music halls in London, with an estimated combined nightly capacity of 45,000, as well as another 160 outside London.[1] Later estimates place this figure at over 300 music halls in London alone.[2] Audience composition had become more and more varied during the nineteenth century, particularly in London, where patrons came from a range of diverse backgrounds. With this diversity came the need to ensure that the bill of fare satisfied the tastes of a broad demographic.[3] The segmented structure of music hall's variety programming, which drew together music, song, dance, comedy and novelty in a wide range of forms and combinations, was well suited to this task.

From the 1890s onwards the audience was increasingly populated by the middle classes.[4] In order to court and appease this clientele many music halls had introduced house rules to censor vulgarity and inappropriate satirical content.[5] Some even employed uniformed officials to eject hecklers, discourage chorus singing and limit encores.[6] Drinking and eating no longer took place in the auditorium, and as with traditional proscenium theatre venues the audience was 'stabilised in fixed seating facing the front'.[7] However, although the twentieth-century music halls emulated the theatre with regard to seating and stage, its performers connected with their audience in a way that actors seldom did. Performers, even those in character, would often address their audience directly. This practice was particularly prevalent amongst music hall singers, who would direct lyrics at spectators with a point or glance and share innuendoes with a nod or a wink.[8] Another convention that bridged the space between singer and audience was the sing-along chorus. This interaction formed a bond between the singers and their public as well as drawing together the various social strata of which the audience was composed into one unified voice.[9]

A theme that proved to be exceptionally effective at provoking such a reaction was patriotism. By 1914 the militaristic song with its patriotic sing-along chorus was already a music hall staple. In the previous century such songs had been particularly popular during periods of conflict when the public's appetite for such material was at its greatest. A report on music halls published in 1901 describes the effect of such performances as follows:

> In ordinary times politics plays no important part in these feasts of sensationalism, but the glorification of brute force and an ignorant contempt for foreigners are ever-present factors which at great political crises make the music-hall a very serviceable engine for generating military passion.[10]

In 1914 this engine was primed and ready to serve as a recruitment factory for the Western front.

## 'Your King and Country Want You' (1914–15)

On 28 September 1914 the Empire theatre in London began the evening's entertainment with an orchestral overture followed by a magic act and two comic mimes. Next on the bill was a troupe of jugglers, a female vocalist and the novelty animal act 'Lucky the Human Dog'. This demonstration of canine intellect was followed by that evening's sing-along segment:

> Miss ETHEL CADMAN
> Will Sing
> 'YOUR KING AND COUNTRY WANT YOU'
> Written and Composed by PAUL A. RUBENS
> *Published by CHAPPELL & CO., 90, New Bond Street.*
> Her Majesty the Queen has graciously permitted this song to be dedicated to her, and all Receipts and Royalties received from the sale of this song are being given to the Queen Mary's Fund.[11]

Cadman was a twenty-eight-year-old musical theatre actress with 'an exceptionally sweet voice',[12] while Rubens was a relatively well-known composer of songs for musical comedies. In August he was commissioned to write a recruitment song. There is nothing exceptional about this in itself. Composing to order was what a songwriter did, and at the beginning of the war military-themed songs were good business. Some songwriters even offered a 'war verse' service for which they would add a set of war-themed lyrics to existing songs.[13] On this occasion, however, the song was commissioned by a national newspaper in order to assist in the recruitment of Kitchener's New Army.

The song had been on the Empire's bill since 14 September 1914. Prior to Cadman taking over, a twenty-six-year-old opera singer called Maggie Teyte had been performing it.[14] However, it was not just the Empire that had the song on its programme. In fact, on the evening of 28 September 1914 the song was being officially performed by seventeen different singers in music halls across the country. As well as the singers on stage, audiences were also doing their bit. Only days after the first performances, the *Daily Mail*'s daily column on the song ran the headline 'EVERYBODY SINGING IT' and went on to report that

> The song had a splendid reception at the London music-halls last evening. Everywhere one went it was being sung. The audiences were delighted with it. The artists

> who volunteered to sing it were acclaimed, and before the second verse was well through people had caught up the air and were giving it chorus.[15]

Whether this is a factually accurate account of events or an example of media-hype is open to debate. Nonetheless, there were precedents of music hall songs being taken up by the populace in the manner the newspaper describes. Bailey offers a useful explanation of this phenomenon when he suggests that:

> The music-hall dealt in a new form of vocal shorthand, whose language operated like a cue or flash charge that needed the knowledge that was knowingness to complete its circuitry. When the circuit worked, as contemporary accounts show, the song went off like a rocket.[16]

In order to facilitate and accelerate this process the lyrics were printed in the *Daily Mail*, accompanied by an instruction for the reader to 'cut out the refrain of "Your King and Country Want You" and join in the singing at the various performances nightly'.[17] The song's first verse and chorus are given below:

> We've watched you playing cricket and every kind of game
> At football, golf and polo, you men have made your name,
> But now your country calls you to play your part in war,
> And no matter what befalls you, we shall love you all the more,
> So come and join the forces as your fathers did before.
>
> *Chorus*
> Oh! we don't want to lose you but we think you ought to go
> For your King and your Country both need you so;
> We shall want you and miss you but with all our might and main
> We shall cheer you, thank you, kiss (bless) you when you come back again.[18]

Rubens's composition was a 'Women's Recruiting Song' (Figure 11.1). Thus, while the song's title emulates the words and stateliness of the infamous Kitchener poster, its message and sentiment are more in line with recruitment posters such as 'Women of Britain say GO!'. Although there were alternate lyrics published so it could be sung by men (replacing 'kiss' with 'bless' etc.), the envisioned mouthpiece was female.

In performing the song, the singer is lyrically and visually positioned as a spokesperson for female opinion. At the start of the first verse she places herself and the 'we' she represents in the role of admiring spectators. The 'you' she addresses are the eligible recruits in the audience. After naming four sports that she and other women have watched the men compete in, she then adds the playing of 'war' to the list – a comparison that trivialises the realities of soldiering, and suggests that the penalties incurred on the pitch are comparable with those suffered on a battlefield. She goes on to explain that even if some unfortunate fate should befall them, as long as they take part in the fighting they will be loved 'all the more'. In the chorus, the singer further emphasises what the song asserts to be the female point of view on the question of recruitment, firstly stating their emotional dilemma – 'we don't want to lose you' – but nonetheless concluding that 'we think you ought to go'. At this moment the audience also assumes the position and opinion of the singer by

Figure 11.1 Cover of the original sheet music for Paul A. Rubens, 'Your King and Country Want You' (1914), cover design by John Hassall, Chromolithograph. © The Estate of John Hassall. Reproduced courtesy of the Victoria and Albert Museum, London (S.414–2013).

joining in with the chorus. This act of participation unites the potentially diverse crowd and affirms the notion that society and state are singing from the same hymn book. Finally, after reassuring the potential recruits that they will be wanted and missed while they are away, the promise is made of unreserved cheers, thanks and kisses upon their return.

Anecdotal evidence that at least one singer proved true to their word was reported by the *Daily Mail* in a story that begins with the headline 'RECRUITING SONG KISS. SOLDIER WHO CLAIMED HIS REWARD':

> An amusing incident occurred on Saturday evening [. . .] after Miss Kate Holbrook had finished singing the woman's recruiting song, 'Your King and Country Want You,' the chorus of which concludes 'We shall cheer you, thank-you, kiss you When you come back again.' A soldier, bearing the traces of having been wounded, stepped and challenged Miss Holbrook with the remark, 'I've come for my reward.' Miss Holbrook, seizing the situation, immediately leant over the platform rails and kissed the blushing soldier amid the delighted cheers of the audience.[19]

Songs about the average soldier's or sailor's allure to women were a well-established convention in music hall. In these songs, however, women were passive and only referred to as 'objects of attraction or as dependants left behind'.[20] The songs were often sung by male impersonators like Vesta Tilley ('Jolly Good Luck to a Girl who Loves a Soldier', 1907) and Hetty King ('All the Nice Girls Love a Sailor', 1909), both of whom performed costumed in the appropriate military uniform. However, the point of view adopted in Rubens's song precludes the singer from adopting such attire – a soldier would ask them to 'come' whereas a civilian would tell them to 'go'.

Two eyewitness accounts of two separate performances of the song refer to the type of outfits worn by the singers. One remembers the singer being 'beautifully dressed in a lovely gown of either gold or silver' over which she had draped the Union Jack.[21] The other description has the singer in full costume 'attired as Britannia, with a colossal Union Jack for background'.[22] In both cases the costume visually highlights the song's patriotism, with one singer sporting the British flag and the other dressed as the embodiment of the British nation. The wearing of such insignia lends the performer further significance and authority as an emblem of empire around which the audience could rally in song.

In contrast to the glamour and regalia of the costumes described above, the sheet music to Rubens's composition featured a very different female image. The woman depicted appears to be in some type of uniform. She is dressed in a plain long skirt and equally simple blouse with the sleeves rolled up. This outfit bears a striking resemblance to the T-shaped tunics worn by female munitions workers, who would improve their shapeless smocks by adding a belt and wearing their 'blouse collars showing outside the neckline'.[23] The image of a woman dressed and ready for work is also consistent with the remit of the charitable fund that sales and performances of the song were intended to benefit.

The bottom two lines of Cadman's billing in the Empire's programme notes state that 'Receipts and Royalties received from the sale of this song are being given to the Queen Mary's Fund'. This organisation, also known as the Queen's Work for Women Fund, was established to tackle the problem of female unemployment. In 1914 Queen Mary released the following statement about the situation facing women and the central principle informing the cause:

> In the firm belief that prevention of distress is better than its relief, and employment is better than charity, I have inaugurated the 'Queen's Work for Women Fund'. Its object is to provide employment for as many women as possible who have been thrown out of work by the war. I appeal to the women of Great Britain to help their less fortunate sisters through this fund.[24]

The fund proved to be extremely successful and the monies collected were used to pay for the running of workrooms where women could be retrained in skills that would give them an income and simultaneously enable them to contribute to the war effort.[25] Based on the reported sales figures of the sheet music for 'Your King and Country Want You', the song would have contributed greatly to the fund's effectiveness as well as its continued promotion. Even before its release, advance orders had already exceeded 15,000.[26] By 7 November 1914 sales had reached 80,000.[27] It was available from multiple retail outlets, including music dealers, bookshops and newsagents.[28] It could also be purchased at the venues where the song was being performed. Sometimes the singer would even sign copies to promote sales.[29] Gramophone recordings of the songs were also produced.[30] However, the song was not the sole preserve of the music hall and parlour.

At the end of September, the newspaper began publishing lists of Kinemas where it was also being performed. One of the *Daily Mail*'s updates includes a reader's letter offering magic lantern slides to accompany the song:

> Dear Sir, – I can supply sets of magic lantern slides (21 photographs in set) illustrating incidents in the song, also the words of the chorus. These slides have been produced in a very artistic manner by Graystone Bird, the well known art photographer of Bath, and can be supplied to vocalists, picture theatre proprietors etc.[31]

The song was interpolated into theatrical productions, performed at charity concerts, and played by '[m]any of the orchestras of the leading London restaurants', and it was also sung in hospitals.[32] Unsurprisingly, hospital audiences proved harder to rally. A report in *The Encore* on one woman's attempt to entertain hospitalised soldiers with the song concludes with the observation that the 'faces of the crippled heroes were several studies'.[33] Presumably the spirit of enthusiasm the song intended to motivate had already been extinguished in those with first-hand experience of where it was they were being told to go.

Some of the young men targeted in music halls also resented the song's manipulative purpose and message. A lengthy and particularly damning interpretation of the song is given by Coningsby Dawson in his 1917 book *The Glory of the Trenches*, which contains the following account of an evening he spent at the Empire Music Hall in Leicester Square:

> We had reached the stage at which we had become intensely patriotic by the singing of songs. A beautiful actress, who had no thought of doing "her bit" herself, attired as Britannia, with a colossal Union Jack for background, came before the footlights and sang the recruiting song of the moment, '*We don't want to lose you / But we think you ought to go.*' [. . .] The effect of such urging was to make me angry [. . .] I pictured the comfortable gentlemen, beyond the military age, who had written these heroic taunts, had gained reputation by so doing, and all the time sat at home in suburban security. The people who recited or sung their effusions, made me equally angry; they were making sham-patriotism a means of livelihood and had no intention of doing their part.[34]

Although Dawson doesn't name the singer billed on the night he saw the act described, the music hall he refers to is the same venue where Ethel Cadman and Maggie Teyte performed the song. While every singer may have had their own theatrical interpretation of the song, it is also possible that the performance details Dawson gives were the Empire's set house style. If this was the case, the format of the song's nightly performance would remain the same, but the singer would be interchangeable. Dawson is particularly scornful of what he perceives as the hypocrisy of those who write and perform recruitment songs. His account also gives voice to a sense of persecution – a feeling that would have no doubt been calcified by the handing out of white feathers which he also refers to later in his account.

In August 1914 Admiral Charles Fitzgerald had established the Order of the White Feather as a means of increasing recruitment. A white feather was a symbol of cowardice and therefore to be handed one was to be branded as such. The feather campaign was reported on positively in the *Daily Mail* and other newspapers.[35] Women were encouraged to hand them out to men who were not wearing military uniform in the hope that this would shame them into enlisting. Indeed, just as there were poster campaigns and adverts that addressed the young male population, other propaganda pressurised young women into persuading potential recruits to join the army. The *Daily Mail*'s listings also enabled the Order's members to attend performances of 'Your King and Country Want You' and hand out white feathers to young men in the audience who didn't act upon the song's directive:

> From mid-September a list of venues where it would be sung and the relevant artistes appeared in the paper – arguably this alerted the White Feather distributors, as the performance ended with those who did not show themselves ready to enlist being handed a feather, frequently by children.[36]

Instructing (and rehearsing) a child to distribute feathers was exploitative on a number of levels, taking advantage of both the child's pliability and the recipient's susceptibility. The children, like the feathers, were used because of what they symbolised – innocence and defencelessness. This adds an intentionally humiliating dimension to the performance. Firstly, the young male civilians in the audience are directly addressed and told to 'go' by the singer. The audience echoes this sentiment by joining in with the chorus. Finally, they are singled out and publicly labelled a coward by a child.

Another contemporary account, this time from a soldier who made the mistake of going to a music hall show out of uniform, describes how the judgements and taunts started before the performances even began:

> On the Saturday I went to the music hall in civilian clothes and as I lined up outside a lady came along and put a white feather into my hand. I looked at it and felt disgusted, but there wasn't much I could do about it. I felt small enough over the white feather incident outside, but as I went into the gallery a chap came out in naval uniform [. . .] and said that no girl should be sitting with a chap unless he was in uniform. No man should be out of uniform he went on – if he was out of uniform he was nothing more than a worm and a skunk [. . .] I just sat there on my own, while people looked at me and I looked at them.[37]

This recollection is taken from Max Arthur's anthology *Forgotten Voices of the Great War*, which is made up of transcribed interviews with soldiers and civilians recounting their experiences during the First World War. Another interviewee who describes a music hall performance of the song is Kitty Eckersley, who attended a show at the Manchester Palace with her husband. She describes the recruitment segment of the evening's entertainment as follows:

> Vesta Tilley was on stage. She was beautifully dressed in a lovely gown of either gold or silver. But what we didn't know until we got there was that also on stage were Army officers with tables all set out for recruiting. She introduced those songs, 'We Don't Want To Lose You, But We Think You Ought To Go' and 'Rule Britannia', and all those kind of things. Then she came off the stage and walked all around the audience [. . .] she put her hand on my husband's shoulder – he was on the end seat – and as the men were all following her, he got up and followed too. When we got home that night I was terribly upset. I told him I didn't want him to go and be a soldier – I didn't want to lose him. I didn't want him to go at all.[38]

In 1964 Kitty recounted her story in an interview for the BBC. During this she elaborated on a few details, recalling that Tilley 'had a big Union Jack wrapped round her' and that the uptake was so great the 'boys [. . .] couldn't really get on the stage'.[39] The song's effectiveness was also reported on in the *Daily Mail*. Indeed, if the figures they published are accurate, Phyllis Dare's appearance at Reading Town Hall led to the enlistment of thirty-nine recruits. This was just a little less than the forty-seven who had signed up after her performance in Newbury the previous week.[40] As such, it is fair to assume that a performance from Vesta Tilley would prompt a similar response from the men in the audience, particularly given that she was nicknamed 'Britain's best recruiting sergeant'.[41]

Tilley's association with the song has been reiterated and reinforced in a wide range of texts that make reference to music hall recruitment. Books, teaching materials and numerous web pages single out Tilley as a frequent performer of the song.[42] Nevertheless, the connection may be more presumptive than accurate. Tilley is not referred to in any of the *Daily Mail*'s frequent reports on the song's popularity and performances. Considering Tilley's celebrity status and the fact that all the other singers are listed, it seems odd that the newspaper neglected to promote or report her performance. Furthermore, Tilley does not make any mention of the song in her autobiography, despite writing fairly extensively on her recruitment activities and the songs she performed for this purpose.[43]

Tilley's repertoire was made up of her own songs, which she performed dressed as a range of male characters. Her act was billed as 'Songs of Masculinity'[44] and during the first years of the war the recruiting song she became best known for was 'The Army of Today's Alright'.[45] Therefore, although Tilley contributed greatly to the recruitment drive, it may have been her commitment to the campaign rather than any actual performances of 'Your King and Country Want You' that led to her being associated with the song. Indeed, it is worth noting that in Eckersley's interview she refers to Tilley 'introducing' the song rather than her actually singing it. However, regardless of whether Tilley sang it or not, Eckersley's appropriation of the song's lyrics at the end of the citation highlights the difference between what the song posits as female opinion ('We don't want to lose you but we think you ought to go') and the actual opinion of a wife whose husband did enlist ('I didn't want to lose him. I didn't want him to go').

Eckersley's account also offers further insight into how the song was performed and the environment it created. Not only did the music hall performance style allow the singer to directly address the audience with points, nods and gestures; on this occasion the singer actually left the stage and moved amongst the audience. From this position she was able to make direct physical contact with spectators who appeared eligible for enlistment. In doing so the young men she touched on the shoulder became the focal point of both the singer and the audience. Being singled out in public in this way further pressurises the recipient of such personal attention to accept the invitation. If they follow the singer up on to the stage they can share in the applause and appreciation of the audience; if they decline then they will be judged on their unwillingness, with all the cowardice and lack of patriotism it intimates.

## 'Your King and Country Want You' (1930s–1990s)

Music hall's role in persuading young men to enlist and the position 'Your King and Country Want You' occupied in its repertoire of recruitment was satirically referenced in the Theatre Workshop's stage production *Oh, What a Lovely War!* (1963). When the play was being developed, BBC radio producer Charles Chilton was employed by the company to help with the musical selections.[46] Chilton's recent production work on a radio show called *The Long, Long Trail* (1961 and 1962) had featured many of the songs that would be used in the production, including 'Your King and Country Want You'. In the play the song begins just after the 'Newspanel' (a translucent projection screen positioned above the stage) gives the headline 'AUG 4 BRITAIN DECLARES WAR ON GERMANY'. The subsequent stage directions are given below:

> The **Band** plays a chorus of 'Your King and Country', during which the **Pierrots** go off one by one, as slides of the coming war in different countries are shown, ending up with the Kitchener poster.[47]

During the slideshow 'The Girls sing' the first verse and chorus of 'Your King and Country Want You'. In the next chorus a 'mime of recruiting' is enacted: 'The Men hand in their Pierrot hats and kiss the girls goodbye, marching off behind the screen. They reemerge wearing uniform caps and marching off saluting.'[48]

Richard Attenborough's cinematic interpretation of the scene in the film version of *Oh! What a Lovely War* (1969) followed more realistic conventions. In the film the recruiting segment begins with images of a deflated music hall audience who have just found out that Belgium has been taken by the Germans. At this point a single voice sings out the first line to 'Are We Downhearted?'.[49] The song is quickly taken up by the audience and band. With the spectators revived, the stage curtains open and the stockinged calves of eight chorus girls dance on to the stage. They are costumed in frilled yellow dresses and pose with golden lacrosse sticks as they sing the opening lines to 'Your King and Country Want You'. As well as resonating with the sporting theme of the first verse, the sticks also double as rifles later in the song and are used to frame the entrance of the next act. The song that follows is the innuendo-laden 'I'll Make a Man of You',[50] performed by a provocatively dressed music hall star. Towards the end of the song the singer interjects recruiting poster phrases and an army officer marches on to the stage. He then proceeds to single out male members of the audience from all classes who eagerly accept his summons, clambering from the boxes and the stalls to join the girls on stage. The volunteers are then led off into the wings, each on the arm of a chorus girl. Once off-stage the young men are harangued by a recruiting sergeant and immediately transported to fight in Belgium. Although the film does incorporate some theatrical devices, such as the MC's knowing looks to camera and the use of a merry-go-round sequence to depict the ill-fated charge of the French cavalry, for the most part it follows a fairly standard form of cinematic realism.

In contrast, the Theatre Workshop's production of *Oh, What a Lovely War!* disregarded realism in favour of a multimedia approach. Song, dance, dialogue and mime were inter-spliced with rolling headlines on the 'Newspanel' above, while photographs, recruitment posters and maps were projected on a screen at the back of the stage. Paget refers to the play as '[a] new multi-media theatre' and compares this merger of components to the principles set out by Eisenstein in his essay on the 'Montage of Attractions'.[51] Eisenstein used the term 'attraction' to refer to aspects of theatrical performance that had a sensual or psychological impact on the audience. He proposed that these attractions could be arranged or montaged to guide the viewer's discovery of an otherwise hidden ideological conclusion. Eisenstein identifies the multifarious acts of the music hall and circus as being exemplary of this approach. However, Eisenstein's theories have become more commonly associated with cinematic montage, a technique Ian Aitken describes as follows:

> Eisenstein's initial theory of montage was premised on the belief that a film's structure should be built up through the juxtaposition of contrasting elements. Eisenstein believed that this form of collision montage would generate more powerful filmic effects, and consequently, would also have a more forceful impact upon the audience.[52]

From this perspective, the performance of 'Your King and Country Want You' in the Theatre Workshop's stage production can be viewed as a single component (or 'attraction') in a larger multimedia restaging of 1914 music hall hucksterism, the pomp and promise of which is juxtaposed by later scenes that use similar techniques to convey the grim realities of war. However, the Theatre Workshop was not the first to use Rubens's song as part of a montage. Noël Coward also featured the song in his 1931 play *Cavalcade* during a scene in which he attempted to summate the entire duration of the war in a single sequence.

*Cavalcade* begins on New Year's Eve 1899 and finishes on New Year's Day 1930. It focuses on the trials and tribulations of two English families during this period. Real-world events such as the Second Boer War, Queen Victoria's death and the sinking of the *Titanic* are all integrated into the narrative. The First World War is represented on stage in the following way:

> Above the proscenium 1914 glows in lights. It changes to 1915–1916, 1917 and 1918. Meanwhile, soldiers march uphill endlessly. Out of darkness into darkness. Sometimes they sing gay songs, sometimes they whistle, sometimes they march silently, but the sound of their tramping feet is unceasing. Below, the vision of them brightly-dressed, energetic women appear in pools of light, singing stirring recruiting songs – 'Sunday I walk out with a soldier,' 'We don't want to lose you,' etc., etc. With 1918 they fade away, as also does the vision of the soldiers, although the soldiers can still be heard very far off, marching and singing their songs.[53]

There are immediately apparent similarities between the compositional elements of Coward's scene and the techniques used in *Oh, What a Lovely War!*. Female singers perform the same recruiting songs. In place of the 'Newspanel' Coward has a lighting effect above the stage that tracks the passage of time. Both texts suspend theatrical realism in favour of multimedia and montaging. However, in *Cavalcade* the impact of the scene is generated through a more direct collision between juxtaposing attractions.

Coward creates this counterpoint both aurally and visually. The drab khaki uniform of the soldiers is contrasted by the colourful costumes of the female singers, who are also spatially separated from the continuous stream of recruits. While the lights above them show the passing of time, the soldiers' monotonous movement remains constant and unchanged, giving the scene an absurdist Sisyphean quality. The upbeat marching rhythm of 'Your King and Country Want You' is merged with the percussive beat of the soldiers' 'tramping feet' to which they add whistles and snatches from songs. The merging of these songs and noises creates a piece of haphazard polytonal underscoring which owes more to Expressionism and the avant-garde than mainstream middle-class musical theatre.

When *Cavalcade* was made into a film in 1933, the director, Frank Lloyd, followed Coward's lead and used similar montaging techniques to encapsulate and summarise the war on screen. The montage begins with troops singing 'It's a Long Way to Tipperary',[54] accompanied by marching drums. This steady rhythm and buoyant mood is juxtaposed with the sporadic sound of bombs exploding. The first sequence shows an endless stream of troops leaving a town. This is overlaid with more closely captured shots of happy soldiers marching and unpopulated townhouse windows. The next segment mixed with these images and sounds alludes to an earlier scene in which 'Your King and Country Want You' was performed by a young woman as part of a floorshow at a restaurant. The singer wears a frilly white dress topped with an army officer's peaked cap. She carries a framed photograph of a man in uniform that she looks at occasionally while singing. Her performance follows on from a rendition of 'I'll Make a Man of You' and is succeeded by a song with the refrain 'Mary, how she loved the military'. Both songs are sung by women wearing dresses and military headgear – one a side cap and the other a wide-brimmed ANZAC hat. At the end of their individual segments the three singers perform their respective choruses contrapuntally. In the film's montage sequence images of the three girls singing together are reintroduced alongside headshots of individual performers. The refrains of the three recruitment songs are also mixed into the soundtrack. As the scene continues, the close-ups of soldiers' smiling faces are replaced with shots of them grimacing in pain and dropping to the ground as if dead. A patchwork of non-diegetic[55] orchestral underscoring is also introduced which ultimately dominates the soundtrack as images loop round over and over again, punctuated by inter-titles indicating that another year has passed.

A more recent film that uses 'Your King and Country Want You' to provide a musical and thematic counterpoint is *Regeneration* (Gillies MacKinnon, 1997). The film is based on Pat Barker's novel of the same name and is set in the Craiglockhart hospital for shell-shocked soldiers. A storyline running through both texts follows semi-fictional meetings between Siegfried Sassoon and Wilfred Owen during which Sassoon tutors Owen on his poetry. One of these sessions takes place in a hospital dayroom where

Helen Clark's 1914 recording of the song is being played. The recording starts at the close of the previous scene just after a patient has questioned his therapist's mental state with the line 'maybe you're the one who's ill?'. In the next shot the music's source is established as coming from a gramophone and the camera pans across the room to a table where the two poets are seated. While the song plays in the background, Sassoon recites the opening lines to Owen's poem 'Greater Love'.[56] Sassoon then suggests that Owen amend the title he has given to an early draft of his poem 'Anthem for Doomed Youth'. A transcription of this moment is given below. The approximate positioning of the song lyrics in relation to the dialogue is shown in italics:

| | |
|---|---|
| Sassoon: | And this one [Pause] Dead Youth. I thought anthem. |
| | [. . .] *forces as your fathers did before. Oh! we don't want* |
| Owen: | This one. |
| | *to lose you, but we think you* |
| Owen: | Anthem for d-dead youth. |
| | *ought to go.* |
| Sassoon: | Well work at it then bring it back and we'll have a go on it together. |
| | *For your King and your Country* |
| | Is it traumatic for you? |
| | *both need you so;* |
| Owen: | No. Writing is like exorcism. |
| | *We shall want you and miss you* |
| Sassoon: | Well, if you ever go back to the front |
| | *but with all our might and main* |
| | at least it will be good for your poetry. |
| | [Sassoon exits outside through to large doors.] |
| Owen: | Yes. Yes, it would. |
| | *We shall cheer you, thank you, kiss you . . .* |

At this point the song fades out and is replaced by plaintive non-diegetic orchestral underscoring.[57] While this plays in the background Owen edits his poem 'Dulce et decorum est' (1917), reciting it as an internal monologue as he writes. Flashbacks of Owen's experience on the front and his earlier interaction with a traumatised blood-covered patient are intercut with the poet writing. The poem directly addresses and confronts the reader with a dark and graphic description of the physical effects of a gas attack, informing them that if they witnessed this themselves they would not be so enthusiastic about instructing the young men of England to 'go'.[58]

## Conclusion

The recruiting programme that developed during the First World War was a unique phenomenon of its time. Whether by chance or design, it harnessed the advertising potential of cross-media promotion, as Kitchener's call to arms was echoed across multiple forms. The campaign played an integral role in forging popular opinion, stoking patriotic fervour, and binding the emerging strands of the mass media, as well as convincing thousands of men to enlist. The network of music halls across the country had already proven to be extremely effective at popularising the songs they featured. As Hobson observed in his report on music halls at the turn of the century, 'words and melodies pass by quick magic from the Empire or the Alhambra over the length and breadth of the land, re-echoed in a thousand provincial halls, clubs, until the remotest village is familiar with air and sentiment'.[59] This transmission was to an extent organic, in that the popularity of the song and its relative success was largely dependent on it own merits. For instance, the success of a composition may have been because it captured the current cultural zeitgeist or it could have simply been due to the catchiness of its chorus.

The *Daily Mail* attempted to manufacture this phenomenon by commissioning and promoting its own hit song. For the most part this endeavour proved extremely successful. For months 'Your King and Country Want You' featured on the bills of music halls and numerous other venues up and down the country. Thousands of copies of the sheet music were sold so it could be played in the home. Gramophone records were released, and magic lantern slides produced, and a national newspaper reported on and revelled in the song's ever-increasing popularity. In some ways the song could even be regarded as a forerunner of the charity singles that have frequently topped the British charts since the 1980s. After all, it was conceived as a response to an emergency, it was sung by the popular artistes of the day, and all proceeds went to a charitable cause. However, while the song may have entered the public vernacular and brought people together around a common cause (and chorus), it did so at the expense of those at whom its message was aimed. Consequently, it is for this insidiousness that the song has been remembered by those who experienced its performance first hand and those who have used it to highlight how popular entertainment can be commandeered to sell a positive image of a bloody conflict to the public.

## Notes

1. Michael Booth, *Theatre in the Victorian Age* (Cambridge: Cambridge University Press, 1991), p. 11.
2. Paul Maloney, *Scotland and the Music Hall, 1850–1914* (Manchester: Manchester University Press, 2003), p. 100; John Lewis Stempel, 'Great War Centenary (1914–2014) – Part 13: Music Halls', *Daily Express*, 30 March 2014, <http://www.express.co.uk/news/world-war-1/467674/Great-War-Centenary-1914-2014-Part-13-Music-halls> (last accessed 9 November 2016).
3. Penelope Summerfield, 'Patriotism and Empire: Music-Hall Entertainment, 1870–1914', in John MacKenzie (ed.), *Imperialism and Popular Culture* (Manchester: Manchester University Press, 1986), pp. 17–48 (p. 24).
4. Dave Russell, *Popular Music in England, 1840–1914: A Social History* (Manchester: Manchester University Press, 1987), pp. 81–2.
5. Peter Bailey, *Popular Culture and Performance in the Victorian City* (Cambridge: Cambridge University Press, 2003), p. 141.
6. John Archer, '"Men Behaving Badly"?: Masculinity and the Uses of Violence, 1850–1900', in Shani D'Cruze (ed.), *Everyday Violence in Britain: Gender and Class* (Harlow: Longman, 2000), pp. 41–54 (p. 51).
7. Bailey, *Popular Culture and Performance*, p. 141.
8. Peter Bailey, 'Conspiracies of Meaning: Music-Hall and the Knowingness of Popular Culture', *Past & Present*, 144 (1994), 138–70 (143–4).

9. Barry J. Faulk, *Music Hall and Modernity: The Late-Victorian Discovery of Popular Culture* (Ohio: Ohio University Press, 2004), p. 62.
10. John Hobson, *The Psychology of Jingoism* (London: Grant Richards, 1901), p. 3.
11. Theatre Programme, The Empire, 28 September 1914 (V&A Theatre and Performance Archive, Blythe House, Kensington Olympia, London).
12. *The Theatre*, vol. 11 (New York: Meyer Bros. & Company, 1910), p. xii.
13. *The Encore*, 13 August 1914 (cited in Stempel, 'Great War Centenary').
14. Cadman had previously been performing the song at Boscombe Hippodrome before she moved to the Empire on 21 September 1914.
15. *Daily Mail*, 15 September 1914, p. 3.
16. Bailey, 'Conspiracies of Meaning', p. 148.
17. *Daily Mail*, 14 September 1914, p. 3.
18. Paul A. Rubens, 'Your King and Country Want You' (London: Chappell & Co. Ltd, 1914).
19. *Daily Mail*, 5 October 1914, p. 3.
20. Summerfield, 'Patriotism and Empire', p. 38.
21. Max Arthur, *Forgotten Voices of the Great War* (London: Random House, 2012), pp. 14–15.
22. Coningsby Dawson, *The Glory of the Trenches* (Brookfield, WI: First Rate Publishers, 2015), p. xxii.
23. Lucy Adlington, *Fashion: Women in World War One* (Stroud: The History Press Limited, 2014), p. 27.
24. A. M. de Beck, *Women of the Empire in War Time: In Honour of their Great Devotion and Self-Sacrifice* (London: Dominion of Canada News Company, 1916), p. 5.
25. The products made in these workrooms were only intended to replace the loss of German imports and were prohibited from competing with the British manufacturing industry; see Deborah Thom, *Nice Girls and Rude Girls: Women Workers in World War I* (London: I. B. Tauris, 2000), p. 30.
26. *Daily Mail*, 17 September 1914, p. 3.
27. *Daily Mail*, 7 November 1914, p. 3.
28. *Daily Mail*, 29 September 1914, p. 3.
29. *Daily Mail*, 1 October 1914, p. 3.
30. *Daily Mail*, 6 October 1914, p. 3.
31. Wallington, *Daily Mail*, 19 September 1914, p. 3.
32. Ibid., p. 3; *Daily Mail*, 2 October 1914, p. 3; *Daily Mail*, 16 September 1914, p. 3.
33. *The Encore*, 25 March 1915; cited in Matthew Crampton, 'War Sketches: Recruiting Blackmail', No Glory in War 1914–1918, 12 November 2013, <http://noglory.org/index.php/articles/war-sketches/79-recruiting-blackmail> (last accessed 10 January 2017).
34. Dawson, *The Glory of the Trenches*, p. xxii.
35. Vivien Newman, *We Also Served: The Forgotten Women of the First World War* (Barnsley: Pen and Sword, 2014), pp. 14–15.
36. Ibid., p. 15.
37. Arthur, *Forgotten Voices*, p. 49.
38. Ibid., pp. 14–15.
39. Kitty Eckersley, 'Sound Recordings 4089', Imperial War Museum, London. Broadcast in 'Palace Theatre, Manchester: Vesta Tilley, the Music Hall Recruiter', *World War One At Home*, BBC Radio, 20 January 2014, <http://www.bbc.co.uk/programmes/p01q7yp8> (last accessed 9 November 2016).
40. *Daily Mail*, 30 January 1915, p. 7.
41. John Mullen, *The Show Must Go On! Popular Song in Britain during the First World War* (Farnham: Ashgate, 2015), p. 152.

42. Kate Adie, *Fighting on the Home Front: The Legacy of Women in World War One* (London: Hodder & Stoughton, 2013), n.p.; Peter Forster, *Play the Ball* (London: Eyre & Spottiswoode, 1967), p. 186; David Lodge, *A Man of Parts* (London: Random House, 2012), p. 458; Stempel, 'Great War Centenary'; 'The Importance of Music in WW1', Music of the Great War, <http://musicofthegreatwar.org/music-ww1/> (last accessed 9 November 2016); 'Vintage Audio – Your King and Country Want You', Firstworldwar.com: A Multimedia History of World War One, <http://www.firstworldwar.com/audio/yourkingandcountrywantyou.htm> (last accessed 11 November 2016); 'Britain's Best Recruiting Sergeant: Teacher Resource Pack', Unicorn Theatre, <https://www.unicorntheatre.com/files/1-BRITAIN'S%20BEST%20RECRUITING%20SERGEANT%20teacher%20resources.pdf> (last accessed 9 November 2016). Eckersley's interview was also dramatised for the stage in Malcolm McKay's play *Forgotten Voices* (London: Oberon Books, 2007), p. 16.
43. Lady de Frece, *Recollections of Vesta Tilley* (London: Hutchinson & Co., 1934), pp. 136–42.
44. Theatre Programme, The Coliseum, 14 December 1914 (V&A Theatre and Performance Archive, Blythe House, Kensington Olympia, London).
45. Fred W. Leigh and Kenneth Lyle, 1914.
46. Derek Paget, 'Case Study: Theatre Workshop's *Oh What a Lovely War*, 1963', in Baz Kershaw (ed.), *The Cambridge History of British Theatre* (Cambridge: Cambridge University Press, 2004), pp. 397–411 (p. 399).
47. Theatre Workshop, *Oh What a Lovely War* (London: Methuen Drama, 2000), p. 12.
48. Ibid., p. 13.
49. Worton David and Lawrence Wright, 1914.
50. Arthur Wimperis and Herman Finck, 1914.
51. Paget, 'Case Study: Theatre Workshop's *Oh What a Lovely War*', pp. 401–4.
52. Ian Aitken, *European Film Theory and Cinema* (Edinburgh: Edinburgh University Press, 2001), p. 27.
53. Noël Coward, *Cavalcade* (London: William Heinemann Ltd, 1932), p. 105.
54. Jack Judge, 1914.
55. Non-diegetic music refers to underscoring that the audience perceives as emanating from a position outside the diegesis or story world, as opposed to diegetic music, which is established as existing within the diegesis or story world. See Claudia Gorbman, *Unheard Melodies: Narrative Film Music* (London: British Film Institute, 1987), p. 3.
56. 'Red lips are not so red / As the stained stones kissed by the English dead.' Wilfred Owen, *The Collected Poems of Wilfred Owen* (London: Chatto & Windus, 1963), p. 42.
57. Mychael Danna, 'Gas', *Regeneration Soundtrack* (Varese Sarabande Records, 1918).
58. Owen, *The Collected Poems*, p. 55. The last two lines of the poem – 'Dulce et decorum est / Pro patria mori' – can be roughly translated into English as '[I]t is sweet and glorious to die for one's country'.
59. Hobson, *The Psychology of Jingoism*, pp. 3–4.

# 12

# British Soldiers' Songs

*George Simmers*

IN AUGUST 1914, as soldiers marched through Portsmouth before embarkation, an observer admired

> the spontaneous, hearty almost joyous way in which the troops, knowing full well that they were leaving the next day for 'the front', from time to time burst into a rolling chorus of some popular air, whilst anxious listening relatives stood sobbing and breathless, realizing perhaps more fully than the soldiers themselves, that every note and every step carried some of them nearer their inevitable doom.[1]

These soldiers were part of the regular army, a force tiny in comparison with the huge conscript armies of the Continent. They would soon be reinforced by a massive citizens' army, first of volunteers and later including conscripts, that was unprecedented in British history. The future was uncertain, but newspapers were keen to allay fears by telling the nation that its soldiers were singing cheerfully. All armies throughout history have sung songs, to while away weary hours on the march, to bolster flagging spirits or to express group solidarity; few armies, however, can have had their singing studied more keenly than the British Expeditionary Force of 1914–18, by those (during the war and in later decades) eager to understand the soldiers and assess their morale. This chapter will investigate the extremely varied ways in which their songs have been interpreted over the succeeding century. During the war itself, singing was generally taken as an indication of the soldiers' high morale, and their choice of song an indication of their spirited independence; after the war, its songs became a focus for memories, whether nostalgic or bitter. In more recent decades, those who have represented the Great War soldier as a figure of pathos have found in his songs a meaning directly contrary to the most common wartime one, and his cheerful improvisations have been interpreted as signs of his victimhood and helplessness, and as, at best, weak protests against the war's futility.

## 'Are we downhearted? No!'

Especially during the war's first year, when no reporters were allowed near the front, newspapers satisfied their readers' eagerness for war news by publishing letters from serving soldiers and interviews with those returning wounded. The accounts selected (by editors mindful of the Defence of the Realm Act) were generally cheerful, with singing frequently mentioned as a sign of buoyant morale. When wounded soldiers of the Black Watch arrived home from Mons, they told listeners that 'it was a terrible bit of work, but our fellows stuck to their ground like men':

> We stuck there, popping off Germans as fast as we could, and all around us the German shells were bursting. And in the thick of it all we were singing Harry Lauder's latest, 'Roamin' in the Gloamin' and the 'Lass of Killiecrankie.'[2]

Singing signified fearlessness; another returning soldier praises his officers: 'The coolness they displayed when in a tight corner had a great effect on the men. In fact, whilst in the trenches, they played cards and sang popular songs.'[3] Even the singing of an adopted canary could be used to indicate morale. A soldier wrote home from the trenches: 'Our canary is sticking it like a brick. He is quite cheerful and has been singing beautifully all morning. Really, it gets so black with smoke that it's a job to distinguish him from a sparrow.'[4] Since singing contributed much to the image of the carefree British soldier, some commentators preferred to believe that the enemy sang only when forced to: 'It is well known that German soldiers are commanded to sing in battle under "Army Orders,"' reported a journalist writing in the *Musical Herald* in December 1914.[5] When British and German lines were close, however, soldiers knew differently, and songs could give an idea of enemy morale; after a bout of fighting, a soldier told the *Daily Mail* with satisfaction: 'Our friends in front have not been singing or shouting so much to us of late.'[6]

In such accounts of musical morale-building, singing is presented as a communal activity, bringing the battalion together; only rarely do there appear hints to the contrary. A critic from the *Musical Times*, arguing that soldiers needed musical instruction, noted that, though there were exceptions, 'according to my general observation about one in four appear to sing when marching, and the rest look bored'.[7] Some soldiers had reason to resent those who sang; in 1914 a Kitchener recruit complained to Edward Thomas: 'I have had a cement floor for a bed, and some of them singing till three in the morning. We have to be out at six.'[8] As for the Germans, British frontline troops sometimes realised that musically the two sides had much in common: 'We frequently give our friends the enemy a song in the trenches at night, and it seems funny to hear two rival armies singing the same hymn.'[9]

British civilians liked to hear of soldiers singing, and some had definite ideas about what songs were appropriate. Publishers were not slow to produce collections of high-minded patriotic words set to stirring tunes, such as the *Marching Songs for Soldiers* by A. C. Ainger, a retired Eton schoolmaster, who provided topical words for old songs ('D'ye ken John French, with his khaki suit', for example).[10] When some of these were printed in *The Times* on 29 September 1914, a reader signing himself 'H. L.' pointed out that they were unlikely to find favour with soldiers, because their language was not the soldiers' language. He drew particular attention to a couplet: 'Here's to Lord Kitchener, brown with the sun, / Gentle, persuasive and balmy.' 'Balmy', he suggested, 'is a word which has no place in the dictionary of Tommy Atkins, but he knows uncommonly well a word of a similar sound.' To show what soldiers actually liked marching to, 'H. L.' reports 'the latest popular marching song from Aldershot' (whose words, he believed, were 'the work of a sergeant of the Gordon Highlanders'):

> Send out the Army and the Navy,
> Send out the rank and file.
> (Have a banana!)
> Send out the brave Territorials,
> They easily can run a mile.
> (I don't think!)
> Send out the boys of the girls' brigade,
> They will keep old England free;
> Send out my mother, my sister and my brother,
> But for goodness' sake don't send me.[11]

Men responsible for defending Britain in this most terrible war were singing with merry irresponsibility, as though announcing their utter independence from the pieties of public discourse. Another *Times* reader worried that 'H. L.' had 'unconsciously placed a weapon in the hands of the German Press' by quoting this 'picture of cowardice and callousness'. Germans, he feared, would take it literally, failing to understand that 'here we have an admirable illustration of the difference between a nation which has a sense of humour and one which has not'.[12] As it became clear that most soldiers preferred to avoid explicit patriotism in their songs, it became usual for commentators, perhaps anxious that some Britons too might fail to appreciate humour, to insist that this avoidance must be taken to signify a deeper commitment in the soldier to the ideals of freedom, and to the fight against an enemy characterised by unthinking militarism. A writer in the *Manchester Guardian* explained:

> [T]he British soldier does not trouble so much about giving his patriotism in song; he uses music to show his cheerfulness and readiness to do whatever duty lies before him [. . .] You ask a soldier what he likes to sing, and he replies, 'Anything but a military song.' [. . .] When marching to battle he will sing his favourite song, and he naturally resents any interference with this shred of his liberty.[13]

Some songs that soldiers sang were handed down from the regular army; even 'I Want to Go Home', often cited as a typical song of 1914–18, dated from the Boer War.[14] Kitchener's Army added to this repertoire, bringing to the task skills developed in civilian life. As John Brophy would point out:

> Most units included at least one man with some literary experience: a small journalist, a writer of Christmas card verses or parish magazine poetry, or someone with a gift for personal abuse, who would produce, for the battalion concert-party, jests and ditties about the topics of the moment or outstanding personalities of the unit.[15]

In the first months of the war, when the scale of recruitment outstripped the ability of the army to equip recruits, soldiers sang (to the tune of the hymn 'There Is a Happy Land') 'Where are our uniforms? / Far far away.'[16] When recruits found themselves stranded somewhere for reasons known only to army bureaucracy, they sang (to 'Auld

Lang Syne') 'We're here because we're here / because we're here because we're here.' Songs or variations with a common application soon spread. John Brophy writes: 'This rapid and thorough propagation was due to the intermingling of men from different units in billets or in estaminets behind the line, and even more in hospitals, base camps and troopships.'[17]

Most of the songs with which soldiers made long marches more bearable were not particularly topical, and were generally less subversive than the one heard at Aldershot; they were current hits like 'Tipperary' (though that particular song was probably not as popular as journalists thought it) or repetitive catches that whiled away dreary miles. A *Daily Mail* correspondent took a condescending view of soldiers' musical choices: 'Soldiers like marching songs that do not over-burden the mind with meaning. That is the chief merit of "Tipperary".'[18] Even meaningless songs, however, could be opportunities for harmonic creativity. F. T. Nettleingham, whose 1917 anthology is the best source for many of the song texts, wrote:

> In the first place, these songs and chanties are *always* harmonised, and I should judge that an average of one in five or six men can improvise a harmony easily – and all harmony in the Army is improvised. Most of the songs [. . .] would be will-o'-the-wisp creations were it not for their harmonic rendering.[19]

Lance-Corporal J. Russell Warren, writing on soldiers' songs for the *Daily Mail*, remarks of that most banal of marching songs 'One Man Went to Mow':

> Senseless and monotonous as this refrain is, there is a remarkable swing in it, and fifty men, reiterating, 'Seven men, six men, five men, four men, three men, two men, one man,' produce a most curious vocal effect, something like an orchestra of jew's harps.[20]

Sometimes songs could be enjoyed precisely for their meaninglessness, but at other times soldiers could make them very useful conveyors of meaning, especially meaning that was not very respectable, as Warren pointed out in his article:

> An entire company, I blush to say, will lightheartedly hail a pretty girl who passes with the refrain:
> You're my baby, you're a wonderful child.
> I'd like to have you round to make a fuss over me.
> I'd like to bounce you up and down upon my knee.[21]

Songs could also convey the troop's opinion of other units. 'Colonel Bogey' was mostly hummed, except for the musical phrase that encouraged a shouted 'Bollocks! To the Manchesters!' (or another regiment whose name fitted the rhythm).[22]

Officers often encouraged singing to lift morale, though on one long, rainy night an officer of the Royal Welch noted: 'The march was a depressing affair, which C Company tried to enliven by a constant repetition of "China, China, Chinatown," but without great success.'[23] Songs could be used, however, to communicate communal opinion to officers. The parody song 'Grousing, Grousing, Grousing' (to the tune of the hymn 'Holy, Holy, Holy') could include a verse: 'Marching, marching, marching, /

Always ruddy well marching. / Marching all the morning, / And marching all the night.' Nettleingham writes: 'I have heard of this being sternly suppressed by company commanders, where men have spent long hours on the march, as being detrimental to good discipline.'[24] Singing could even be a way of communicating with the enemy; when Germans in the opposite trench sang Ernst Lissauer's rabidly anti-English 'Hymn of Hate', the British responded with a 'ragtime' version that provoked the Germans to a bombardment.[25]

Typically, though, the soldier's improvised song was to a familiar tune, from the common musical culture of the time. This would mean either a hymn tune or a hit from the music hall. The adaptation was not necessarily intended as criticism of the original. Lance-Corporal Warren told the *Daily Mail*:

> You will often hear us swinging along to the tune of a well-known hymn. I regret to say that the words were *not* those associated with the air in the hymn book. For instance, to one beautiful refrain we chant the words of 'Sing a Song of Sixpence,' ending up with
>
> And wasn't that a *dainty* dish,
> And wasn't that a *dainty* dish,
> And wasn't that a *dainty* dish,
> To set before a king.
> Let me assure you, though, that we mean nothing irreverent.[26]

There may have been no irreligious intent, but there is always an element of subversion in improvising trivial or inappropriate words to solemn tunes. Soldiers whose lives were otherwise rigidly controlled could let themselves go in verbal excesses, and the practice could even lift spirits in battle:

> It's wonderful how some of them start an appropriate song even during the heaviest fire. While this affair was going on they were singing 'We'll post up his number, we'll post up his number, we'll bring him to his knees' to 'Get out and get under.' It was very good considering they made up their own words.[27]

Such battlefield singing was probably rare, but the war presented plenty of musical opportunities. As well as singing to make long marches more bearable, there were sing-songs in estaminets, and concert parties of several kinds. Edmund Blunden later recalled how soldiers who had returned from the front, 'with clay and with death no longer striving', threw themselves into enjoyment of a battalion entertainment:

> How they crowded the barn with lusty laughter,
> Hailed the pierrots and shook each shadowy rafter,
> Even could ridicule their own sufferings,
> Sang as though nothing but joy came after![28]

Battalion concert parties gave scope for those with a knack for topical parody or the ability to compose 'gibes at quartermaster-sergeants and men in "cushy" jobs'.[29] In 1916 the *Invicta Gazette*, journal of the 20th Londons, regretfully noted the death of a machine-gunner called Walkley whose adaptations of music hall songs livened battalion concert parties. He used, for example, 'Any Old Iron' to comment on an incident where men in the line had been punished for eating their iron rations when not authorised to:

Where's your iron, where's your iron,
Where's your iron ration?
It's not for use, that's no excuse;
Your iron rations you must produce.
It's only meant for ornament,
You must be in the fashion,
But you'll have it hot if you haven't got
Your iron, iron ration.

After he was killed at Loos, the article notes, 'other comedians arose to take Walkley's place'.[30]

## Tommy's Tunes

Many fragments of song had appeared in newspapers and magazines during the first years of the war, but the first published collection aiming at anything like completeness was *Tommy's Tunes* of 1917, edited by F. T. Nettleingham, an officer in the Royal Flying Corps.[31] The book's subtitle indicates its scope: *A Comprehensive Collection of Soldiers' Songs, Marching Melodies, Rude Rhymes and Popular Parodies, Composed, Collected and Arranged on Active Service with the B.E.F.* Its ninety-seven songs range from trivial catches to highly developed parodies. Some songs are included in several versions, since 'all these marching songs differ slightly, according to the Unit singing, a little local colour being invariably added'.[32] The well-known hymn 'The Church's One Foundation' provides the tune for a mocking piece of self-denigration which compared the singers' unit to Fred Karno's chaotic troupe of music hall comedians: 'We are Fred Karno's Army, / A jolly fine lot are we: / Fred Karno is our Captain, / Charlie Chaplin our O.C.'[33] In Nettleingham's own branch of the service this becomes: 'We are the ragtime army, / We are the R.F.C. / We do not fight, we cannot fly, / So what earthly use are we?'[34] An ANZAC version develops the song, giving both a good idea of the Australians' own self-image and a demonstration of how a song could accommodate shifts of tone and ambiguities of attitude:

We are the ragtime army,
The A.N.Z.A.C.s,
We do not shoot, we won't salute,
What bally use are we?
And when we get to Berlin,
The Kaiser he will say:
Hoch! Hoch! Mein Gott!
What a jolly fine lot
Are the A.N.Z.A.C.s
We are the only heroes

Who stormed the Dardanelles,
And when we get to Berlin,
They'll say, 'What bally sells.'
You boast and spite from morn to night
And think you're bally brave,
But the men who really did the job
Are dead and in their graves.[35]

Over a quarter of the songs included by Nettleingham mention his own unit, the Royal Flying Corps; some of these adapt songs common elsewhere, while others seem very specific to the RFC, containing and celebrating their technical jargon. Later collections have concentrated on the songs commonest among all units of the BEF, and *Tommy's Tunes* is a useful corrective to these, reminding us that soldiers mostly sang in the company of men from their own battalion, who would have understood local nuances and references meaningless to outsiders.

Nettleingham bowdlerises some of the more ribald songs, such as 'Skibboo!' ('Two German officers crossed the Rhine')[36] and regrets that he 'found it impossible to present even a purged version' of songs like 'Kafoosalem, the Harlot of Jerusalem'. Most of the obscene songs (and John Brophy will claim that obscenity makes up only a small portion of the soldiers' repertoire) are versions of old regular army songs. They are reminders that, in Kipling's words, 'single men in barricks don't grow into plaster saints',[37] but also suggest how, though some may have been disturbed by obscenities and some disgusted by them, enlisting must for many young men have been an intriguing entry into a very masculine community where things unmentionable at home were boldly said and sung. These reminders of their shared animal nature could bond men together. A popular legend of the war tells of a platoon whose junior officer was lustily lending his voice to an obscene song. The men see a senior officer coming and fall silent, but the junior officer continues blithely unaware.[38] Soldiers doubtless enjoyed telling this tale of an officer as human as themselves.

Nettleingham's collection begins with 'When this Ruddy War Is Over', and many of his inclusions echo its fed-up longing for an end to the military life. Some, though, are more warlike ('Nevertheless, I want to be there. / I want to hit there / A certain someone with a bomb. / That's why I wish that I was back again, / Down on the Somme'),[39] and one song jauntily encourages soldiers to commit a war crime by shooting prisoners:

If it's a German – Guns Up!
If it's a German with hands up,
Don't start taking prisoners now,
Give it 'em in the neck and say 'Bow-wow.'
If it's a German – Guns Up!
Stick him in the leg – it is sublime.
If he whispers in your ear
'Kamerad! Kamerad!'
Guns Up – every time.[40]

Prisoners were indeed sometimes shot. Stephen Graham wrote that the unofficial ethos of his regiment, the tough-minded Scots Guards, was that 'a good soldier was one who would not take a prisoner'.[41] Soldiers who sang 'Guns Up!', however, might not necessarily have put its advice into practice; songs like this allowed soldiers to play at brutality, just as songs like 'For Gawd's Sake Don't Send Me' allowed them both to express and to mock defeatist sentiments.

Reactions to Nettleingham's anthology varied. Many reviewers conveyed the mixture of respect, admiration and slight condescension with which it was customary to speak of 'Tommy'. *The Spectator*'s reviewer, for example, acknowledged the songs' power, while seeing in them no trace of literary merit:

> In none of these verses is the true note of poetry sounded; we could not expect it; but in many, under cover of a rough cynicism and brutal humour, there is suddenly revealed something inexpressibly affecting and pathetic which touches us all the more closely because it is ostensibly intended to make us laugh.[42]

J. C. Squire in the *New Statesman* acknowledged even more strongly the emotive power of these 'queer, unique songs – whimsical, ironic, grumbling':

> The most famous of these [. . .] is *I Want to Go Home*, with its utter fed-upness. It was pretty early. I remember the first time I heard of it. A gunner officer (he is dead now) sent it to me, with the tune roughly dotted down. He said that his men would sing that melancholy tune very quietly and slowly when grooming their horses, and that he had never heard anything in his life which moved him more.[43]

The *Musical Herald*'s reviewer was less impressed; he disliked the songs' cursing and swearing, and touched on a subject sensitive to some musicians when pointing out that '[f]rom the infrequency of folk-tunes in the strict sense we may judge that folk-songs have not contributed much to Tommy'.[44] Early in the war, Sir Charles Stanford had campaigned to have soldiers taught the 'great old folk songs' like 'Lillibulero' and the 'Song of Agincourt'.[45] He was voicing the enthusiasm of the serious musical world for Cecil Sharp's project of rescuing England's rural folk songs from oblivion, and defending them against the commercialised and therefore second-rate music of the halls. Hubert Parry had told the newly formed Folk-Song Society in 1898: '[T]here is an enemy at the doors of folk music which is driving it out, namely the popular songs of the day, and this enemy is one of the most repulsive and most insidious.'[46] The *Musical Herald* in 1916 had inveighed against the 'imbecile and deleterious shows' of the music hall, arguing that the 'relaxation of moral and intellectual fibre involved in such entertainments is a serious national evil'.[47]

Traditional songs were not absent from the musical soundscape of the war, however; the national songs of the Scots, Welsh and Irish were popular among the troops of those nations (and the Scottish 'Annie Laurie' was popular among English soldiers, too). As for the English, traditional songs were sometimes rendered in estaminets and at concert parties, and regional songs may have enlivened the marches of units with a strong local base. None, though, seem to have made it into the general repertoire, which used the tunes of the two musical genres common to the whole country: hymns and the hits of the halls.

Highbrow critics might see the songs as merely reproducing a debased popular culture, but they often reveal a critical attitude towards the works they adapt. Favourite targets for parodists were unrealistic recruiting songs, and syrupy efforts like 'Never Mind' ('Though your heart may ache awhile, never mind / Though your face may lose its smile, never mind / For there's sunshine after rain, and then gladness follows pain / You'll be happy once again, never mind'). Soldiers' versions mocked the song's sentimentality by bringing it in contact with real life. The most popular version was 'If the sergeant steals your rum, never mind', but other versions appeared in trench newspapers.

The relationship between music hall and soldiers' song was not entirely one-way. A bowdlerised adaptation of 'Mademoiselle from Armentières' became a civilian favourite, and the Aldershot song of 1914 ('For Gawd's Sake Don't Send Me') was adapted in 1917 as the chorus of Albert Lester's 'The Conscientious Objector'. The Aldershot song became the chorus between verses in which Lester acted the part of an effeminate and affected coward. Audiences were asked to laugh at, not with, him, and the ambiguity which teased original listeners was lost.

## Wartime Songs Remembered

After 1918, the war's songs would be remembered at ex-servicemen's get-togethers, and used by memoirists and novelists wanting to evoke wartime. C. E. Montague, in *Disenchantment*, suggested the innocence of early Kitchener recruits by recalling 'the silly little songs on the road that seemed, then, to have tunes most human, pretty, and jolly'.[48] Ernest Raymond, in *Tell England* (1922), conveys the undaunted morale of troops during the gruelling retreat from Gallipoli by including their parody of 'Redwing':

> The men groaned merrily and burst into a drawling song:
> 'Oh, the moon shines bright on Mrs. Porter,
> And on her daughter,
> A regular snorter;
> She has washed her neck in dirty water,
> She didn't oughter,
> The dirty cat.'[49]

Frederic Manning, in *Her Privates We* (1930), went deeper, suggesting that song was an outlet for feelings otherwise repressed:

> the greater the hardships they had to endure, for wet and cold bring all kinds of attendant miseries in their train, the less they grumbled. They became a lot quieter and more reserved in themselves, and yet the estaminets would be swept by roaring storms of song.[50]

Manning's hardened soldiers sing a sardonic parody to Ivor Novello's lush melody 'Keep the Home Fires Burning':

> Oh, they've called them up from Weschurch,
> And they've called them up from Wen,
> And they'll call up all the women,
> When they've fucked up all the men.[51]

In David Jones's poem-novel *In Parenthesis* (begun about 1927, published 1936), the soundscape of the war is presented to us through the consciousness of his hero, Private John Ball. Military orders and soldiers' chatter interweave with echoes of myth, and snatches of song recur, from 'The British Grenadiers' to 'I Want to Go Home', from 'Sospan Fach' to 'I Do Like a Nice Mince Pie'. More than any other writer, Jones gives a sense of how songs were part of the texture of army life. Songs connected with the war were part of the repertoire when a community-singing craze was encouraged by the *Daily Express* in the late twenties. The *'Daily Express' Community Song Book* of 1927 includes, among its hymns, sea shanties and traditional songs, wartime favourites, including 'Pack Up your Troubles' and 'The Last Long Mile', a 'Mademoiselle from Armentières' without obscenity, and even the saucy 'Après la Guerre Fini' ('Après la guerre fini / English soldier parti. / Mam'selle Français beaucoup picaninny / Après la guerre fini').

There was a revival of interest in the war around the tenth anniversary of the Armistice (characterised by reunions and community commemorations, as well as by the books and plays of the late-twenties 'war books boom'). The *Daily Express* followed the fashion by publishing a new songbook, *Songs that Won the War* (1930). A foreword by Edward, Prince of Wales, defined the songs as part of a shared and sanctified national experience:

> The songs we sang in France, and wherever British troops fought from 1914 to 1918, will be found in this book. They bring back, as nothing else can, days we can never forget and faces we shall see no more. These songs, trivial as many may be, are historic. They are like no other songs. They are forever hallowed by association.[52]

For the Prince, the songs symbolise national unity and community:

> Perhaps the most important thing about these songs is that we sang them as choruses. We all took part in them. And when we sing them now they will remind us of that splendid comradeship of the Great War which united us through the darkest chapter of our history.[53]

The collection includes many wartime songs from the theatre and music hall, from 'Sister Susie' to 'Oh! It's a Lovely War', but also the anonymous songs of endurance: 'I Want to Go Home' and 'If you want to find the old battalion, / I know where they are – / They're hanging on the old barbed wire'. This songbook aims to rekindle nostalgia, not hatred; the nearest it comes to an aggressive spirit is a parody of 'If You Were the Only Girl in the World': 'If you were the only Boche in the trench, / And I had the only bomb, / Nothing else would matter in the world today, I would blow you up into eternity . . .'[54]

Also published in 1930 was a book with a very different agenda from the Prince's: *Songs and Slang of the British Soldier, 1914–1918*, edited by Eric Partridge and John Brophy. Both editors had served as private soldiers, and the war they remembered was not the Prince's war. Partridge (an Australian) had served on the Somme and at Passchendaele, while Brophy had been accepted into the army in September 1914, aged only fourteen; his 1927 autobiographical novel *The Bitter End* thinly fictionalises his growing dissatisfaction with army life. *Songs and Slang* is a collection speaking for the men in the ranks, the ones who bore the brunt of war's hardships, and of the 'absurdities and irritations' of military life.[55] The book includes caustic comments about officers, chaplains and MOs, and highlights the dark humour of soldiers' songs as a means of self-help. Men 'cheated hysteria with songs making fun of mud and lice and fear and weariness' and 'the very knowledge of such songs reduced the emotional disorganisation caused by fear, and aided [a man], after the experience, to pick his uncertain way back to sanity'.[56]

Partridge and Brophy's aim was to collect the songs that spread throughout the army, and therefore '[p]urely regimental ditties [were] excluded'.[57] Unlike Nettleingham, these editors rarely suggest local variants of the songs, and there are no songs like the 'Iron Rations' parody, specific to one particular occasion. The decade between the war and the collection of the songs must also have worked against recollection of the one-off jokes and skits that contributed much to the soldiers' culture of spontaneity in song. Obscenity, too, is probably under-represented. Brophy asserts, probably correctly, that 'only a small proportion of the songs are improper in subject or in language', but he and Partridge bowdlerise some songs that Nettleingham printed more boldly; notably absent from the collection is General von Kluck (whom A. G. Macdonell described as 'the subject of so many admirable rhymes').[58]

The book went into several editions, and was generally well received, often in a spirit of nostalgia. V. S. Pritchett, for instance, wrote in the *Fortnightly Review* that

> such a compilation as this, with its songs about the sergeant-major and its reminder that we once 'wangled,' 'scrounged,' 'swung the lead,' 'went on the binge,' and concealed a terror of 'pushing up daisies,' is calculated to stir the 'sentimental Tommy' in all of us.[59]

Pritchett's further comments show him interpreting (or perhaps over-interpreting) the songs in the 'anti-war' spirit of the 'war books boom' of the late twenties: 'They sprang out of the weary argument with life; their coarseness was a protest against coarseness forced upon them – their sardonic appropriation of hymn tunes, their blasphemy, was a protest against the blasphemy of the war.'[60] John Brophy claimed that the songs were 'genuine "folk-songs", and as such they stand alone in the modern world',[61] but there was still resistance to this classification. In *Scrutiny*, a literary magazine whose philosophy included the belief that commercial mass civilisation was incomparably poorer than traditional rural culture, John Speirs added a footnote to his essay praising traditional Scottish ballads: 'Mr Robert Graves is interested in the "ballads" that came into existence among the British troops during the war, but these are the merest drivel, as he would agree.'[62]

Despite such academic disapproval, wartime songs held their place in the public memory and affection. In September 1939, the popular double act Flanagan and Allen recorded a song which referenced an older one to remind young soldiers heading for France that they were following in their fathers' footsteps: 'If a grey-haired lady says "How's your father?" / That's mademoiselle from Armentières!'[63] During the Second World War, some of the old songs were revived or adapted; new versions appeared of 'I Want to Go Home' and 'We Are Fred Karno's Army'.[64] The tradition of defiant musical self-denigration continued, for example in the Eighth Army's song based on an insulting nickname (sung to the tune of 'Lili Marlene'): 'We're the D-Day Dodgers out in Italy – / Always on the vino, always on the spree.'[65]

## The Sixties and After

The urgencies of the Second World War eclipsed the First in the popular imagination until the early sixties, and the fiftieth anniversary of the Great War. A BBC producer, Charles Chilton, whose father had been killed in the Battle of Arras (and was one of the 35,492 who fell there and had no known grave), took the opportunity to devise a radio programme, *The Long, Long Trail*, in which the mellifluous BBC Singers told the story of the war through its songs. Gerry Raffles, manager of the Theatre Royal, Stratford East, heard and liked the programme; he and Theatre Workshop's director Joan Littlewood commissioned playwrights Ted Allan and Gwyn Thomas to turn Chilton's research into a play. The result was *Oh, What a Lovely War!*,[66] about a young woman disguising herself as a soldier to infiltrate Douglas Haig's headquarters. Littlewood disliked the play but liked the title. She discarded the script and told her cast to start researching their own show, telling the history of the war. The tone of *The Long, Long Trail* had been elegiac, but Littlewood's play, made up of short sketches interspersed with songs, had the tough-minded vigour of a political cartoon. Much of the first act showed Europe tumbling into a war that nobody intended – a topical and disturbing theme in the year after the Cuban Missile Crisis of 1962, when the world seemed on the brink of nuclear war. In Littlewood's play, music hall songs stereotyped the home front as inanely optimistic, while the earthier songs of the soldiers provided ironic commentary. Early in rehearsals Littlewood spent a day ensuring that her cast would not sound like the BBC Singers; instead she told them to 'sing the songs as if they were making them up, as if they were in those *circumstances*, not just BLOODY SINGING!'.[67]

The main sources for the show's songs were *Tommy's Tunes* and the Brophy and Partridge anthology, and the latter's emphasis on the songs of endurance and irony was even more evident in the songs included in the play. Littlewood's soldiers sang no anti-German sentiment (no 'If It's a German, Guns Up!') and did not vaunt their own unit at the expense of others. The songs were presented as expressions of the shared experience and fellow-feeling of the working-class privates, and to stress their sardonic realism in the face of industrialised war, capitalism and upper-class indifference. The 1969 film version, directed by Richard Attenborough, included most of the same songs, and had as strong an emotional impact, but muted the class antagonism. In *Oh! What a Lovely War* soldiers sing their mockery of the war they are forced to endure, but take no steps to alter their situation. The left-wing poet and critic Randall Swingler, reviewing the 1965 reissue of Brophy and Partridge's *Songs and Slang* (as *The Long Trail*), saw the soldiers' songs as embodying an inert false consciousness: '[T]he songs the soldiers sang, though universally ribald and contemptuous of the army and every aspect of the war, carry a tone, in tune and words, of stoical resignation, never of militant rebellion.'[68]

## A Hundred Years On

By the time of the war's centenary in 2014, the Great War's poetic canon had become, in Andrew Motion's words, a 'sacred national text',[69] with an established role in school curricula, and in each November's rituals of remembrance. In the margins of this national text, soldiers' songs had their place, though it was sometimes a humble one. Brian Gardner's influential 1964 anthology *Up the Line to Death*, for instance, which stayed on school examination set-book lists for fifty years and ordered the war's poems to demonstrate a thesis about the war's increasing horror and futility, paid a slightly condescending tribute to songs as 'the instinctive poetry of the troops themselves',[70] and Gardner used fragments of song to introduce each section of his anthology.

In the twenty-first century, new selections of soldiers' songs were published, including Max Arthur's *When this Bloody War Is Over* (2001) and Martin Pegler's *Soldiers' Songs and Slang of the Great War* (2014). Brophy and Partridge's book appeared in yet another guise as *The Daily Telegraph Dictionary of Tommies' Songs and Slang, 1914–18* (2008), a reprint of *The Long Trail* of 1965, with a new introduction by Malcolm Brown developing Brophy's comments about the private soldier's forced surrender of his personal liberty to claim that the songs 'might almost be seen as – of course on a far more modest scale – the equivalent of those more famous products of another society where there was a distinctive kept down underclass: the Negro Spirituals'.[71] In the early twenty-first century, the characteristic portrayal of the Great War soldier was as a hapless victim, and for Brown the songs signify this victimhood.

Tim Kendall's rigorously exclusive Oxford anthology *Poetry of the First World War* (2013) admits poems only on the grounds of literary merit, not mere historical interest; it acknowledges the vernacular muse, however, by including a final section of 'Music Hall and Trench Songs', mixing music hall songs like 'Good-Bye-ee!' and 'Pack Up your Troubles in your Old Kit Bag' with one of the more respectable versions of 'Mademoiselle from Armentières' and some of the more sardonic and self-mocking of the soldiers' songs, including, perhaps as an antidote to sentimentality, that incitement to war crime, 'If It's a German, Guns Up!'·

There are dangers, though, in treating soldiers' songs as poems. In 2013, the singer-songwriter P. J. Harvey contributed to a British Library celebration of war poetry by reading the words of songs like 'I Want to Go Home' in a sincere and thrilling poetic voice.[72] The result is an effective statement of her personal anti-war convictions, but the songs are stripped both of the music that gave them life and of the context that gave them richly ambiguous meaning. John Brophy pointed out that 'these songs satirised more than war: they poked fun at the soldier's own desire for peace and rest, and so prevented it from getting the better of him. They were not symptoms of defeatism, but strong bulwarks against it.'[73]

As time takes us further from the exceptional conditions in which men used these songs to grouse, to mock and to make dark jokes, but also to celebrate, to bond with their comrades, and for the sheer pleasure of fitting words to a tune, perhaps we can only fully understand them by an act of imaginative sympathy with the men who chose, and sometimes needed, to sing them. Then we will understand their strengths. Patrick MacGill, a private with the London Irish and also a poet and novelist, doubted in 1916 whether the songs would survive the war:

> None will outlast the turmoil in which they originated; having weathered the leaden storm of war, their vibrant strains will be choked and smothered in atmospheres of Peace. 'These 'ere songs are no good in England,' my friend Rifleman Bill Teake remarks. 'They 'ave too much guts in 'em.'[74]

But the songs have outlasted the war, and precisely because of the 'guts' that Rifleman Bill Teake admired. And in the future doubtless new meanings will be found in them, possibly ones that go beyond nostalgia or mere pathos, to help us to a fuller understanding of the lives and character of the soldiers who sang them.

## Notes

1. 'News from All Parts', *Musical Herald*, 1 September 1914, p. 311.
2. 'Soldiers' Stories', *Manchester Guardian*, 5 September 1914, p. 5.
3. 'Stories from the Front', *The Times*, 21 September 1914, p. 4.
4. *Daily Mail*, 11 February 1915, p. 8.
5. 'Music in the Soldier's Life: Our Interview with an Army Bandmaster', *Musical Herald*, 1 December 1914, p. 446.
6. 'Amusing Letter from a Trench', *Daily Mail*, 8 January 1915, p. 8.
7. S. Royle Shore, 'How to Help our Soldiers with their Songs', *Musical Times*, 1 November 1915, p. 671.
8. Edward Thomas, 'Tipperary', *English Review*, 18.71 (October 1914), p. 350.
9. '"Old Dad" to his Boy', *Daily Mail*, 8 December 1914, p. 8.
10. 'Marching Songs', *The Times*, 29 September 1914, p. 6. Ainger's songs were published as *Marching Songs for Soldiers. Adapted to well-known Tunes by A. C. Ainger. Arranged with new Pianoforte accompaniments by C. Courtenay, etc.* (London: Ascherberg, Hopwood & Crew, 1914).
11. H. L., 'Songs for Soldiers', *The Times*, 1 October 1914, p. 7. Most variants of this popular song have 'for Gawd's sake' in the last line.
12. C. S., 'Songs for Soldiers', *The Times*, 8 October 1914, p. 9.
13. 'Military Ballads', *Manchester Guardian*, 27 October 1914, p. 12.
14. Les Cleveland, *Dark Laughter: War in Song and Popular Culture* (Westport, CT: Praeger, 1994), p. 66.
15. John Brophy, 'Introduction', in John Brophy and Eric Partridge (eds), *Songs and Slang of the British Soldier, 1914–1918* (London: Eric Partridge, 1930), p. 5.
16. F. T. Nettleingham, *Tommy's Tunes: A Comprehensive Collection of Soldiers' Songs, Marching Melodies, Rude Rhymes and Popular Parodies, Composed, Collected and Arranged on Active Service with the B.E.F. by F. T. Nettleingham, 2nd Lt. R.F.C.* (London: Erskine Macdonald, 1917), p. 45.
17. Brophy, 'Introduction', pp. 6–7.
18. Charles E. Hands, 'Soldier Songs', *Daily Mail*, 3 December 1914, p. 4.
19. Nettleingham, *Tommy's Tunes*, pp. 15–16.
20. Lance-Corporal J. Russell Warren, 'What "Kitchener's Army" Sings', *Daily Mail*, 25 November 1914, p. 4.
21. Ibid., p. 4.
22. Brophy, 'Introduction', pp. 5–6.
23. Captain J. C. Dunn, *The War the Infantry Knew, 1914–1919* (London: Abacus, 1994), p. 152.
24. Nettleingham, *Tommy's Tunes*, p. 26.
25. 'Nights on the Ancre', *Daily Mail*, 10 May 1917, p. 3.
26. Warren, 'What "Kitchener's Army" Sings', p. 4. The adapted tune was perhaps 'Oh Come All Ye Faithful'.
27. 'As If Nothing Was Happening', *Daily Mail*, 9 October 1914, p. 8.
28. Edmund Blunden, 'At Senlis Once', in *Undertones of War*, rev. edn (London: Cobden Sanderson, 1930), p. 284.
29. W. J. Turner, 'A Concert at the Front', *New Statesman*, 5 January 1918, p. 332.
30. *Invicta Gazette: The Journal of the 20th Battalion, London Regiment*, December 1916, quoted in J. G. Fuller, *Troop Morale and Popular Culture in the British and Dominion Armies, 1914–1918* (Oxford: Clarendon Press, 1990), p. 101.
31. The book's success inspired a second volume, *More Tommy's Tunes*, in 1918.
32. Nettleingham, *Tommy's Tunes*, p. 21.
33. Ibid., p. 42.

34. Ibid., p. 43.
35. Ibid.
36. Ibid., pp. 22–3.
37. Rudyard Kipling, 'Tommy', in *The Complete Verse* (London: Kyle Kathie, 1990), p. 322.
38. One version of this story, collected in the *Guinness Book of Military Anecdotes*, casts Douglas Haig as the senior officer. The puritanical and abstemious Haig fits nicely into the story, but the anecdote pre-dates his taking command.
39. Nettleingham, *Tommy's Tunes*, p. 56.
40. Ibid., p. 59. This parodies 'If It's a Lady, Thumbs Up!', a 1914 song popularised by the music hall star Florrie Forde.
41. Stephen Graham, *A Private in the Guards* (London: Macmillan, 1919), p. 217.
42. 'Tommy's Tunes', *The Spectator*, 24 November 1917, p. 19.
43. 'Solomon Eagle' (J. C. Squire), 'Books in General', *New Statesman*, 13 October 1917, p. 40.
44. '"Tommy's Tunes" at First Hand', *Musical Herald*, 1 November 1917, p. 337.
45. 'Singing in the Ranks: Proposal to Revive Old Folk Songs', *The Times*, 13 January 1915, p. 6.
46. Hubert Parry, 'Inaugural Address', *Journal of the Folk-Song Society*, 1.1 (1899), 1–3. An interesting critical account of the English folk revival can be found in Georgina Boyes, *The Imagined Village: Culture, Ideology and the English Folk Revival* (Normanton: No Masters Co-Operative, 2010).
47. 'The Music-Hall a National Evil', *Musical Herald*, 1 September 1916, p. 315.
48. C. E. Montague, *Disenchantment* (New York: Brentano's, 1922), p. 11.
49. Ernest Raymond, *Tell England: A Study in a Generation* (London: Cassell, 1922), p. 313. A variant appears in another text of 1922, T. S. Eliot's *The Waste Land* (lines 199–201). In his note Eliot claims the song reached him via Australia without being sure of its origins. T. S. Eliot, *The Poems of T. S. Eliot, Volume I: Collected and Uncollected Poems*, ed. Christopher Ricks and Jim McCue (London: Faber, 2015), p. 74.
50. Private 19022 (Frederic Manning), *Her Privates We* (London: Peter Davies, 1930), p. 335.
51. Ibid., p. 92.
52. H. R. H. The Prince of Wales, 'Foreword', in *Songs that Won the War: 'Daily Express' Community Song Book No. 3* (London: Lane Publications, 1930), p. 5.
53. Ibid., p. 5.
54. *Songs that Won the War*, p. 96.
55. Brophy, 'Introduction', p. 9.
56. Ibid., p. 8.
57. Ibid., p. 3.
58. A. G. Macdonell, *England, Their England* (London: Macmillan, 1933), p. 19.
59. V. S. Pritchett, 'Songs and Slang of the British Soldier', *Fortnightly Review*, August 1930, p. 283.
60. Ibid., p. 284.
61. Brophy, 'Introduction', p. 4.
62. John Speirs, 'The Scottish Ballads', *Scrutiny*, June 1935, p. 39.
63. Ted Waite, *If a Grey-Haired Lady Says 'How's your Father': A Message from an Old Un of 1914 to a Young Un of 1939* (London: Chappell, 1939).
64. Cleveland, *Dark Laughter*, p. 61.
65. For a version of this song, see <https://en.wikipedia.org/wiki/D-Day_Dodgers> (last accessed 11 November 2016).
66. They took their title from a jauntily ironic 1917 song by J. P. Long and Maurice Scott, popularised in wartime by male impersonator Ella Shields, among others.
67. Quoted in Peter Rankin, *Joan Littlewood: Dreams and Realities* (London: Oberon Books, 2014), p. 149.

68. Randall Swingler, 'Arma Virumque: The Poetry of Three Wars', *Times Literary Supplement*, 10 March 1966, p. 186.
69. Andrew Motion, 'Introduction', in Motion (ed.), *First World War Poems* (London: Faber, 2003), p. xi.
70. Brian Gardner, 'Introductory Note', in Gardner (ed.), *Up the Line to Death: The War Poets 1914–1918*, rev. edn (London: Methuen, 1976), p. xxiii.
71. Malcolm Brown, 'After Ninety Years', in John Brophy and Eric Partridge (eds), *The Daily Telegraph Dictionary of Tommies' Songs and Slang, 1914–18* (London: Frontline Books, 2008), p. x.
72. The event took place on 12 December 2013. A video recording of the performance can be seen at <https://vimeo.com/82008449> (last accessed 11 November 2016). P. J. Harvey's 2011 album *Let England Shake* had commented emotively on the First World War and other conflicts.
73. John Brophy, 'Introduction', in John Brophy and Eric Partridge (eds), *The Long Trail* (New York: London House & Maxwell, 1965), p. 18.
74. Patrick MacGill, *Soldier Songs* (London: E. P. Dutton, 1917), p. 14.

# 13

# The First World War in Popular Music since 1958

*Peter Grant*

## Introduction

Since 1958 there have been over 1,600 newly composed songs 'about' the First World War in the different genres of popular music with numbers increasing significantly since the new millennium. By this I mean songs where the influence of the war is discernible, whether directly or through 'signifiers' or references, in the title or lyrics. Not surprisingly the largest number emanate from countries that were prominent in the fighting, with more coming from the victors than the losers, but there are also examples from as far afield as Armenia, Brazil, Colombia, Latvia, Malaysia, Mexico and Venezuela. The Great War was the first truly global conflict and its reflection in popular music has been equally universal.

National cultural perceptions of the First World War, which vary significantly, have a strong influence on popular musicians. The myth of the war as 'futile slaughter' persists in popular imagination in Britain and, though slightly modified, in the USA and Australia, greatly influenced by the war poets and the literature of the late 1920s. In Canada, whilst the Australian perception of 1914–18 as being the crucible of nationhood is shared, the war is not depicted as, to put it crudely, a British imperialist trick. Many Canadian songs are far more upbeat than those from either the United States or Australia. A good example is Bryan Adams's anthemic 'Remembrance Day' in which most of the soldiers, accurately, return from the conflict. In Germany it is the Second World War that is seen as senseless, the First 'as belonging utterly to the past', and in France, unlike in Britain, the idea of seeing the war through the eyes of war poets is a relatively new one.[1]

With notable exceptions, popular music often follows these dominant national cultural trends or myths which are, as Michel Tournier has observed, 'the history everyone already knows'.[2] Thus French songs about Verdun are as prolific as British ones about the Somme and the 1914 Christmas truce is a popular subject; best-selling examples include Jona Lewie's 'Stop the Cavalry' and The Farm's 'All Together Now'. Popular music thrives on references to popular imagination, although artists less interested in innovation simply endorse or reinforce myth by resorting to cliché whereas more creative ones approach myth in different ways: they add something new or different; they comment on myth or they directly refute it.[3] There are examples of all these approaches in popular music about the First World War.

## French *Chanson*, a Political Narrative

Though English folk music has a long tradition of comment on war it was French *chanson* that first began to look specifically at the First World War.[4] Larry Portis comments that 'popular music in France differs significantly from that of Britain and the United States'. He notes that 'its most striking peculiarity [. . .] is the prominence of overt political criticism and social comment' so that significant events in French history have always been marked with popular songs.[5] *Chanson* is also more narratival in construction than English folk song and *chanson* singers 'effectively "talk" their tunes.'[6] Lyrics are foregrounded and *chansons* are well described as dramatic monologues accompanied by music. The three singers usually considered the pinnacle of the *chanson*, Georges Brassens, Léo Ferré and, though Belgian, Jacques Brel, all recorded landmark songs about the war.

Unlike many songs from the war itself humorous or ironic popular songs are rare. It is as if there is an unwritten rule that one has to adopt a solemn or reverential tone in depicting the First World War. The finest humorous song, Georges Brassens's 'La Guerre de 14–18', translated into English as 'The War of 14–18' by Michael Flanders and Donald Swann, dates from the early 1960s. Like his contemporaries Brel and Ferré, Brassens was highly political and socially aware in his songwriting and between 1952 and 1964 almost half of his songs were banned from the airwaves in France by state broadcaster RTF, which is one reason he turned to satire in songs like 'La Guerre'.[7] Nevertheless, in a spirit of national contradiction, Brassens was awarded the prize for poetry by the Académie française in 1967, virtually the equivalent of being designated France's National Poet. Brassens rattles through a comparison of wars from the Trojan to the Napoleonic, the war of 1870 and the (then) current Algerian conflict before deciding that his favourite war is that of 1914–18.[8] Utilising a simple acoustic guitar accompaniment, which at times mocks a trumpet fanfare, Brassens's jaunty style only helps to reinforce the irony.[9] Flanders's version rewrites the song from an Anglo-Saxon perspective with comments on both Suez and, in one of the first references in popular song on either side of the Atlantic, Vietnam.

Léo Ferré's songs draw on an eclectic range of musical styles including classical, jazz, Latin American and rock and he took an overtly anti-nationalist stance that critically examined French national identity.[10] A self-declared anarchist, this led him into conflict with both the authorities and the right-wing paramilitary Organisation de l'armée secrète (OAS) who threatened his life and bombed a venue where he was due to appear.[11] However, Ferré was not a propagandist; he 'did not advocate a specific political program, but rather other, more progressive values, such as dignity, liberty and social responsibility'.[12] The words of Ferré's 'Tu n'en reviendras pas' (from the album *Les Chansons d'Aragon*, 1961, Barclay) are by the poet (and committed Communist) Louis Aragon. It is a notable forerunner of Eric Bogle's 'And the Band Played Waltzing Matilda', being partly about a disabled veteran 'sans visage, sans yeux'. But it also addresses issues such as the inadequacy, or hypocrisy, of memorials with 'un mot d'or sur nos places'.

As the war was fought on French soil, songs set behind the lines are more prevalent in French than in British songs. Born into a Parisian Jewish family who had to go into hiding during the German occupation, Barbara, whose real name was Monique Andrée Serf, recorded a version of Léo Ferré's 'Tu n'en reviendras pas' (on the album

*Barbara 1962*, Polygram). She also included the poignant 'Le Verger en Lorraine', devoted to all those who had shed their blood in Lorraine (not just in the First World War). One of her first recordings, in 1958 (re-released on the expanded *La Chanteuse de minuit*, EMI, 2001), was Marcel Cuvelier's song 'Veuve de guerre' which has a claim to be the earliest post-Second World War popular song about the First. Told from the point of view of a young widow it is a universal comment on both the tragedy of war and how life needs to go on despite its horrors and loss of life. Ultimately the song is one of fatalism and irony and yet there remains a strength to the narrator's character. As such it is something of an antidote to another well-trodden myth of the war, that of the 'lost generation'.

Jacques Brel is one of the few *chansonniers* to have made a lasting impact outside the francophone world. His songs have been recorded by a wide variety of English-speaking artists including Frank Sinatra, Ray Charles, David Bowie, Tom Jones and Marc Almond. Brel's 'La Colombe' ('The Dove') is based on a traditional French children's song, 'Nous n'irons plus au bois', and a poem by Théodore de Banville.[13] Recorded in 1959 it was covered several times in the context of opposition to the Vietnam War, notably by American singers Judy Collins and Joan Baez. Brel echoes the words of Wilfred Owen and 'the old lie' relating this to some of the grandiose memorials to war.[14] In line with Brel's less revolutionary political stance in comparison to Brassens the song suggests no positive solution; it views war as a depressing inevitability. One of Brel's last songs was 'Jaures', released in 1977 on his final album *Les Marquises* (Barclay/Universal). Jean Jaures, the anti-militarist leader of the French Socialist Party, was assassinated on 31 July 1914. The song asks why he had to die and, by implication, whether he might have been able to mitigate some of the war's excesses. However, it is primarily about the fate of the oppressed working classes Jaures represented. Brel suggests that though not slaves they were certainly not free. If they survived their terrible working conditions they got sent to war to die on the battlefield. Accompanied by a simple accordion tune 'Jaures' is a powerful and emotional song but again has a fatalistic tone, especially as Brel was already gravely ill with the lung cancer that killed him less than a year after the album was released. In comparing Brel to Brassens Larry Portis's criticism is that the latter was a 'tolerant anarchist' whereas Brel was a 'crusading preacher' whose songs are, at times, 'almost wearingly serious'.[15] Despite this there is no doubting either Brel's outstanding use of language or his emotional commitment, which evoke a politicised version of Leonard Cohen.

## Protest in Folk and Rock

As with many other subjects of protest and political comment, at least in the English-speaking world, Bob Dylan was one of the first to record an anti-war song that addressed the First World War. 'With God on Our Side' comes from his seminal 1964 album *The Times They Are A-Changin'* (Columbia). It set a tone that many others have followed and begins with a condemnation of the United States' genocide against Native Americans, before moving through verses about the American Civil War and the Spanish-American War to a verse about the First World War which has again been a model that many have copied, especially its ironic comments on religion.

In Britain songs appeared in the late 1960s featuring two of the country's most intellectually stimulating rock bands. The first was The Zombies' 'Butcher's Tale (Western Front 1914)' which, rather like the album on which it appeared, *Odessey and Oracle* (CBS, 1968), is slightly mistitled. As the lyrics make clear, with references to Gommecourt and Mametz Wood, it is set in 1916, not 1914, during the Battle of the Somme. The narrator, symbolically a butcher in civilian life, is a victim of shell shock and, though open-ended, its tone makes it clear that he did not get his wish of going home. Like the Dylan song, 'Butcher's Tale' takes issue with religion, specifically pro-war Anglican clergymen familiar from the poems of Siegfried Sassoon and the portrayal of the conflict in both stage and screen versions of *Oh! What a Lovely War*. The music is significantly different from the soft, psychedelic rock of the rest of the album. The most prominent instrument is an old-fashioned harmonium, the kind often used at battlefield services, and the song is sung not by their usual lead singer Colin Blunstone, but by the much harsher voiced Chris White, who also wrote the song.[16]

The following year The Kinks released their concept album *Arthur (or the Decline and Fall of the British Empire)* (Pye) which, as the title suggests, charts the story of post-war Britain. The songs describe the England that Arthur once knew, the promise of a new life in Australia for one of his sons, the emptiness of his superficially comfortable life, the resolve of the British people during the Second World War, the privations of austerity Britain and, in 'Yes Sir, No Sir' and 'Some Mother's Son', the death of his brother in the First World War. The former tells of the individuality that is left behind when the soldier volunteers, or is called up, but also displays a typical 1960s contempt for authority and hints at the supposed indifference of the higher command. The music has both a militaristic (drum rolls) and old-fashioned (a brass band backing) ambiance. 'Some Mother's Son' is a much more impressionistic, less direct or angry song than 'Butcher's Tale' or even 'Yes Sir, No Sir', concentrating on the theme of loss: the lost innocence of the soldiers; the sense of loss felt by their families and their memories of the deceased. As such it matches the overwhelming theme of nostalgia of both this album and that of The Kinks of this period more generally, being strongly evident on their previous release *The Kinks Are The Village Green Preservation Society*.

Following Dylan many other artists have written songs that are more specific in their engagement with the First World War. A notable example is the Scottish-Australian Eric Bogle whose songs 'And the Band Played Waltzing Matilda' and 'No Man's Land' (also known as 'The Green Fields of France' or 'Willie McBride') have been covered countless times.[17] 'And the Band Played Waltzing Matilda' is deservedly considered 'one of the greats, a song that has dug itself so far into the Australian consciousness in such a short time that it [. . .] feels like a memory'.[18] Conceived in 1971, it was meant as an anti-Vietnam War protest rather than a direct critique of the First World War and is the account of a young Australian volunteer in the ANZAC Corps, his experiences during the Gallipoli campaign where he loses his legs and his reflections many years later on what it means.[19] The reference to Banjo Paterson's original song (Australia's unofficial national anthem written in 1895) is a masterstroke. It acts as a refrain to the action, being played when the troops set sail, when they bury their dead after battle, when he returns from the war and at each ANZAC Day. The song concludes with a minor-key transposition of the original song and there is no doubting the overall tone of bitter irony. Despite this, the song is not without humour, particularly in its description of the speaker's being 'knocked [. . .] arse over head' ('tit' in The Pogues' version) by 'a big Turkish shell', a sense of comedy that makes 'And the Band Played Waltzing Matilda', along with the two versions of Brassens's contribution, conspicuous among modern songs about the war, displaying similarities with the 'black humour' of the trenches (see George Simmers's chapter). At the time he wrote the song Bogle was probably right that the veterans were 'forgotten heroes from a forgotten war' but since the 1970s interest in the war and participation in its remembrance have grown significantly in both Australia and Britain. Of all versions of the song it is The Pogues' 1985 recording (from *Rum, Sodomy and the Lash*, MCA/Stiff) that best captures its spirit. Shane MacGowan's loutish approach perfectly reflects the song's bitter tone, with some of the vocals almost spat out. Their arrangement begins with a simple phrase on the banjo, building to include other instruments and, ultimately, a brass section, giving a more epic, universal feel than Bogle's simple folk arrangement.

In comparison 'No Man's Land' is a more straightforward song. It reflects on the fate of a nineteen-year-old soldier, Willie McBride, who fell during the Battle of the Somme, told from the perspective of a battlefield visitor who sits down by his grave to reflect.[20] Bogle has told audiences that it is the favourite war poem of former British Prime Minister Tony Blair and that, although Blair knew the name of its author, he thought Bogle had died in the war. Bogle's Blair anecdote here serves as an example of how misinformation and myth can begin.[21] The chorus makes reference to two famous pieces of military music, 'The Last Post' and the Scottish lament for the dead of Flodden, 'The Flowers of the Forest'. It is one of many 'remembrance' songs, like 'Battleship Hill', but it is less complex than Harvey's and prone to cliché in places, as well as being unashamedly sentimental. These features make it less of an achievement than 'Waltzing Matilda', but they also serve to explain why it has been covered far more often; its clear statement that 'it was all done in vain' is a simpler idea to project and sits more comfortably with popular memory of the war as a futile conflict.

Lancashire folk singer Mike Harding has contributed two powerful songs about the war, recorded nearly thirty years apart. First, released as a single in 1977, came 'Christmas 1914', which looks at the famous truce between British and German troops near Ypres. Harding's songs are extremely detailed and he describes the exchange of presents, the football match and the soldiers' sharing food, drink and stories of their sweethearts. In 2005 Harding returned to the subject with 'The Accrington Pals' (on *Bombers' Moon*, Moonraker, which also contains a version of 'And the Band Played Waltzing Matilda'). Accrington is close to Harding's home town of Rochdale and provided perhaps the best-known of the 'Pals battalions' that formed part of Kitchener's New Army. Harding's song relates the innocence of the pre-war pals and the ordinariness of their lives but goes rather 'over the top' in his adherence to the myth of the war. In songs like 'Butcher's Tale' the historical errors are forgivable, being used for 'scene setting' and colour, but Harding ends up putting in too many clichés. In the sleeve notes and on his website Harding gives a wholly false explanation of how and why the Pals battalions were formed, saying that 'in 1916 the British Army, running out of cannon fodder for the trenches, introduced a policy of recruitment based on enticing men into the army from the same towns'.[22] The song concludes with Harding reading some of the names of the men who died and a brass band arrangement of the 9/8 retreat march 'The Battle of the

Somme'. Written by Pipe Major William Laurie of the Argyll and Sutherland Highlanders in 1916, this has been recorded many times including by Fairport Convention, on *House Full* (1977), the German 'krautrock' band the Peter Rübsam Group (1972) and The Albion Band (on *Battle of the Field*, Island, 1976). Another line-up of the Albion Band memorably incorporated the tune in their musical accompaniment to the National Theatre's 'promenade' adaptation of Flora Thompson's *Lark Rise to Candleford* in 1978 which also included a listing of local war dead, suggesting this was the source for Harding's idea. The listing of names is a technique often utilised to achieve psychological connections with the unknown dead. It is one also adopted by John Adams in *On the Transmigration of Souls* (written to commemorate the 9/11 attacks) and in *The Time Is Now* by Everybody's Children (a 1970 anti-Vietnam War single). The psychological impact of this device, giving individual reality to otherwise nameless victims, can provide closure and 'a conflict-averse path to catharsis in an age of instant gratification and short attention spans'.[23] It is clear that the link between folk song and the war is extremely strong. As part of their centenary commemorations the BBC have commissioned fifty new songs from 'the cream of British folk songwriters'. The idea of widening the remit to cover other genres appears not to have occurred to them.[24]

## Heavy Metal: The Unvarnished Truth?

Heavy metal began in the late 1960s in the English Midlands, notably Birmingham, from a fusion of blues and psychedelic rock with Led Zeppelin and Black Sabbath as its pioneers.[25] Confounding what many critics have suggested, it has proved an extraordinarily durable and flexible musical form, popular throughout most of the world, including much of the Far East and Latin America.[26] In the context of metal music and the First World War two subgenres are especially prominent. Collectively termed 'extreme' metal, death and black metal emerged in the late 1980s and early 1990s. They typically employ atonality, heavily distorted down-tuned guitars, tremolo picking, double-kick and blast beat drumming, and minor keys, and they often disrupt conventional ideas of musical development by rejecting the drive towards climax or resolution.[27]

In heavy metal the ensemble sound is privileged over any of its components and the voice is utilised more as an instrument than being distinct from the rest of the band, and this tendency is even more pronounced in extreme metal. Extreme metal lyrics also frequently emphasise the grotesque, a concept Kristeva explores as part of her interest in the 'abject', which disturbs identity, systems and order.[28] However, even though the specific meaning of extreme metal lyrics is often less important than their imagery they still play a significant role.[29] This is of particular relevance in songs about the First World War where there are so many recognisable symbolic images available to the lyricist. War is a significant theme in heavy metal and there are now distinctive strains of folk, Viking and battle metal based on the history, conflicts and mythology of northern Europe. In the mid-1980s together with bands such as Napalm Death and Carcass, Bolt Thrower 'combined punk and early death metal to develop an extreme sound that has been widely influential' and more than any other band built their career around songs relating to war in its varying forms, in both fantasy and history.[30] Laura Wiebe

Taylor suggests that they offer a '[c]oncentrated line of socio-political commentary, taking on the issue of widespread violence and the horrors of war, not in celebration but as a way of confronting and criticizing untamed aggression, lust for power and social and political oppression'.[31]

Two albums in particular, *For Victory* (Earache, 1994) and *Those Once Loyal* (Metal Blade, 2005), focus on the First World War.[32] Both contain highly graphic, though stylised, point-of-view songs, but with no identified protagonist and no sense of the ability of the individual to influence events. The title track of *For Victory* depicts the plight of battle survivors in no man's land, whereas 'At First Light' from *Those Once Loyal* describes the prelude to going over the top. Karl Willetts, the band's lyricist and singer, confirms that 'waiting and anticipation is a recurring theme throughout the music we create [. . .] It's about the psychological effects, the feelings.'[33] Both songs evoke the terrors and horrors of war, immensely magnified by the music, but paradoxically adopt a sober, neutral stance that does not condemn war outright, instead presenting the listener with its impact:

> We don't say war is a good thing, we don't say war is a bad thing, we don't glorify it [. . .] It's easy to go down that line to condemn or point fingers but we're not there to do that [. . .] We just say it as it is and try and put war in perspective.[34]

Bolt Thrower's contemplation of war in general and the First World War in particular is complex and distinctive. They avoid simple stereotypes and instead express the ambiguities of warfare: it is both horrifying and glorious, both insane and necessary. Similar ambiguities occur in the works of Siegfried Sassoon and Wilfred Owen, who both wrote of their utter contempt for the mindlessness of war but remained with their regiments and fought with distinction. Taylor also connects Bolt Thrower's vision with the works of authors such as H. G. Wells, Aldous Huxley and George Orwell, reading their songs in the context of a broader dystopian discourse.[35]

Over the last ten years Swedish power metal band Sabaton have rather assumed Bolt Thrower's mantle as commentators on war. Their songs cover all historical periods from ancient times through both world wars to modern conflicts including Iraq and the Falklands. 'Angels Calling' from *Attero Dominatus* (Black Lodge Records, 2006) is an impressionistic song, whose lyrics are like phrases from a memoir rather than a coherent narrative about a specific event. However, their next album, *The Art of War* (Black Lodge, 2008), which takes its title from Sun Tzu's military treatise of the same name, develops both musically and, especially, lyrically into a more comprehensive meditation on war and its impact. Each song is constructed around one of Sun Tzu's chapters, illustrated by reference to more recent conflicts. 'Cliffs of Gallipoli' is a song about the dead, with foe turning to friend in death.[36] In the booklet notes for the album, the band agree that the expedition was a badly planned disaster; however, they also praise the outstanding 'courage and competence' of some of the commanders, Monash and Chauvel on the Australian side and Mustafa Kemal on the Turkish. 'The Price of a Mile', like PJ Harvey's 'On Battleship Hill' or the paintings of Paul Nash, describes the rape of the countryside as well as the fate of the soldiers, scarring 'fields that once were green'. It is a fascinating song in that it is one of very few that describes the actual fighting, but the listener has no idea which side is being depicted. Set during the Battle of Passchendaele, it describes the horrific conditions from which the men have no way out. Both songs are set to Sabaton's driving, epic style of metal with stylistic flourishes including elaborate keyboards, guitar solos and female backing vocals that supply a high degree of drama, suggesting there is excitement in war among the death and destruction even though 'no glory has been won'.[37]

In its various forms heavy metal has made a highly distinctive contribution to songs about the war. By its very nature the music lends itself to a 'warts and all' depiction of war's brutalities and in its more extreme forms this verisimilitude is at its clearest. Phillipov emphasises the strength of extreme metal in approaching such complex and multifaceted subjects, highlighting the genre's 'emphasis on musical and lyrical disruption' which 'offers listeners fractured, ambivalent listening positions [. . .] in which [they] can explore alternative responses to, and experiences of, ordinarily contentious subject matter'.[38] As Karl Willetts puts it, 'the idea that there is no one version of the truth goes throughout my lyric writing; there are always alternative perspectives.'[39] Far from being the 'mindless' music many critics suggest, metal can be seen instead as a genre of depth, subtlety and intelligence in its complex portrayals of the First World War.

## *Let England Shake*

Polly Jean Harvey's *Let England Shake* represents a considerable effort. Written over a two-and-a-half-year period, she researched the history of war, notably the Gallipoli campaign, as well as more recent first-hand accounts from Iraq and Afghanistan.[40] The album marked a milestone in the history of popular music in the way it was received as a serious commentary on England's military past. Greeted with virtually unanimous acclaim, it went on to win the prestigious Mercury Prize in 2011.[41] At least three of its songs make general reference to the First World War whilst three others refer specifically to Gallipoli. 'All and Everyone' is one of the album's most explicit tracks, describing in detail the horrors of ANZAC Cove and Bolton's Ridge, using repetition to invoke the image of the relentless sun and its linkage to death. 'On Battleship Hill' describes the emotions of battlefield tourists. In a Proustian turn the song connects the scent of wild thyme with the recognition that the destruction wrought by the war is being eradicated by nature. It links time and remembrance in a complex dialectic: should we remember or make a conscious decision to forget? The song has a powerful resonance as it challenges the motives of such 'pilgrimages'. Do we visit the sites of former conflicts for positive or negative reasons? Are we 'bearers of the flame' or mere ghouls? Remarkably Harvey herself never visited the battlefields of Gallipoli, reflecting the ways an artist can 'think their way' into a subject.[42]

Throughout the album Harvey interweaves the theme of war with that of what England means for her and how the country's present is inextricably bound to its past. She explicitly excludes the other British nations, situating England at the heart of a former empire and all the historical 'baggage' that entails. Harvey's emotions range from ironic xenophobia in 'The Last Living Rose' to critical reflection on the violence that made England 'great' in 'The Glorious Land'. But her lyrics are always multifaceted. As well as condemning its violent excesses she expresses a deep personal attachment to England, its landscape and its people.

*Let England Shake* is also an example of how problematic genre is in popular music. To what genre or category does it belong? Is it 'rock' music at all? Harvey has stated that among her influences were the work of Harold Pinter, the poetry of

T. S. Eliot, the paintings of Salvador Dali and Goya, and music by The Doors, Velvet Underground and The Pogues.[43] For the album Harvey radically altered her image, a transformation at least as profound as that of David Bowie in the 1970s. Entirely absent was the husky-voiced, guitar-wielding 'rock chick' of the *Stories from the City, Stories from the Sea* era, replaced by a sombre figure playing an autoharp.[44] She also employs a high soprano which has a similar effect to other composers' usage of male countertenors. As in Philip Glass's *Akhnaten* or Thomas Adès's *The Tempest*, the high register evokes an unspecified past and an 'otherworldliness' helping to take the listener out of a specific time context. Harvey explained:

> If I used too much [. . .] breadth in my voice it made the songs too self-important, too dogmatic [. . .] So it was a very delicate balance to sing them in a way that was purely playing the role of a narrator and not trying to inflect the words with any particular bias.[45]

Her stance is perfectly demonstrated in the song 'The Words That Maketh Murder'. She never tells you what the words are, or who may have spoken them. For some they will be the orders of First World War commanders or those uttered in the pulpit by pro-war prelates; for others those of George W. Bush or Tony Blair, which is one reason she has been described as 'the first rock-and-roll war artist'.[46]

*Let England Shake* is an example of how popular music can approach the complexities of war. Its stance is undoubtedly anti-war even though its author has declared that 'I don't feel qualified to sing from a political standpoint'.[47] It memorably links the motivations behind and emotions within British conflicts of the last hundred years. It also evokes a positive picture of England and a lingering pride in the country's military achievements whilst questioning the role of memory and remembrance. It was little wonder that when Harvey premiered the work on *The Andrew Marr Show* in 2010 her fellow guest, Prime Minister Gordon Brown, appeared baffled by her performance.[48]

## Conclusion

Despite claims to the contrary, song lyrics are not poetry.[49] They are designed to perform a different function and this holds true even for those songs whose words can 'stand by themselves' for, once music is added, new meanings are produced. As Simon Frith suggests, it may well be that the very best songs 'can be heard as a *struggle* between verbal and musical rhetoric, between the singer and the song'.[50] For this reason direct settings of war poems by popular musicians are relatively rare. However, others, whilst not directly quoting the war poets, clearly take indirect inspiration from them. Karl Willetts acknowledged this, saying that 'the war poets, Wilfred Owen and Sassoon, they have inspired me. Even if it's not the words it's the rhyming structure; it helps me formulate a plan and a pattern.'[51] There are distinct similarities between Eric Bogle's 'And the Band Played Waltzing Matilda' and Wilfred Owen's 'Disabled', a poem about a legless young veteran that describes the protagonist's carefree pre-war life and lack of any patriotic motivation for enlisting, though the Owen character's freedom is depicted through football rather than trekking through the Australian outback. 'He was drafted out with drums and cheers' is reflected in Bogle's band playing the Patterson song. On his return, just as in Bogle, the cheers are absent and the women ignore him. He is left to 'take whatever pity they may dole' and 'spend a few sick years in institutes'.[52]

American indie band The Decemberists eschew the introspection common to modern rock for a more narrative approach and singer/lyricist Colin Meloy often paints 'historical scenes in faraway places, pluck[ing] literary references from dusty volumes and us[ing] multisyllabic words you may need a dictionary to define'.[53] In their 'The Soldiering Life' the easy-flowing indie-pop sound and Meloy's subtle lyrics conceal what is a ground-breaking song that updates some of Owen's themes in a modern context. Described by Meloy as a 'homoerotic love song', it has clear parallels with Owen's 'It Was a Navy Boy' and Meloy's 'bombazine doll' is at least as enticing as the poet's description of the young man he meets on a train.[54] 'The Soldiering Life' is arguably also the only popular song that has the temerity to suggest that, for some, the war was actually enjoyable and liberating, opening up new emotional experiences. As such it would be anathema to those who see the war as unremitting horror and its boldness does not simply confront the myth of the war but proposes an alternative, more human and radical interpretation.

One of the few books about music and the First World War, Glenn Watkins's *Proof through the Night*, concludes with an analysis of Benjamin Britten's *War Requiem* of 1961. Britten memorably fashioned nine of Wilfred Owen's poems into one of his greatest works and Watkins's concluding comment is that in the *War Requiem* 'the meaning as well as the meaninglessness of the Great War had found a new and resonant echo'.[55] This is, at best, an over-literal and incomplete interpretation of the work of both artists. Though Owen and Britten utilise the First World War in their imagery, they are aiming for a more universal message, an approach followed by many popular musicians. There is therefore more than a cursory link between popular music and the work of the war poets. Acknowledging this link, PJ Harvey noted that in writing the songs for *Let England Shake* she thought herself into the role of an officially appointed war songwriter 'like war poets or like any foreign correspondent but trying to do it through song'.[56] Harvey thus emulates one of the key approaches of *chanson* which, as Peter Hawkins points out, often resembles 'a kind of poetic and musical journalism'.[57]

Another achievement of the disillusioned war poets in particular was their professed abhorrence of euphemism. Paul Fussell suggests that Sassoon, Owen, Rosenberg and others decisively rejected the 'high flown' language that many previous poets had employed when writing about war. The danger of euphemism, as Richard Floeckher has noted, is that 'euphemistic language turns war crimes into mere abstractions', transferring 'culpability away from the aggressor and onto the victims'.[58] Popular music has been guilty of employing euphemism when dealing with the war. Mike Harding and Sting's 'Children's Crusade', which clumsily compares the 'innocents' of 1914–18 with modern victims of drug addiction, succeeding only in patronising both groups, are prime offenders in this respect. But other examples mirror the approach of the war poets, and the musical genre that lends itself more than any other to a non-euphemistic depiction of war is heavy metal. Metal speaks very directly in its lyrics, often utilising 'street language' or swearing:

> Blunt, confrontational, visceral and often as obscene as the suffering they describe, heavy metal lyrics look war in the face. They are the camera rolling in the middle of combat – an honest, fearless witness.[59]

Of all the metal bands who have recorded songs about the war, Bolt Thrower stand out in this regard. The listener is both horrified and fascinated by war and this ambiguity places them in a close relationship with the war poets. They quote from Kipling and, most memorably, Laurence Binyon. '. . . For Victory' ends with these newly composed lines prefacing those of Binyon:

> Now in death's glory
> Man's final destiny
> The final price to pay
> . . . For Victory

Despite the song's condemnation of the need for war and its terrible human cost there is recognition that there is pride as well. This is not at all a fashionable notion, but it has been part of the thinking of warriors throughout the ages and '. . . For Victory' is one of the few songs about the war that reminds us that, despite the bloodshed and horrors, Britain and her allies were victorious.

In the late 1950s in France and a few years later in Britain and the USA popular musicians began writing songs referencing the First World War. This timing corresponds with the emergence of new styles of music, the *chansons engagées* in the former, folk and rock protest music in the latter two countries. Moreover, they were written to reflect concerns and draw comparisons with contemporary political events – notably the wars in Algeria and Vietnam. Since then music about the war has spread globally and provides an ever-increasing source of inspiration. Many artists are seduced into repeating well-trodden myths, but others seek to bring a new perspective. Most recently the dub-reggae album *Empire Soldiers* was released as a two-CD set in 2013, with a live version recorded in 2015 (Yes High Tech/Jarring Effects). Representing one of the widest transnational collaborations to date in popular music about the war, the album's theme is that of the experience of Anglo-Caribbean and Franco-African soldiers and labourers. Its key collaborators are Steve Vibronics from the UK, Martin Nathan from France, Afro-Caribbean historian and poet Madu Messenger, British-born musician and DJ M. Parvez, who has Pakistani roots, Senegalese singer/lyricist Sir Jean, and French-Moroccan poet Mohammed el Amraoui. The collaborative range and inventiveness of this album demonstrates that in popular music the First World War shows no signs of losing its relevance.

## Notes

1. Rainer Rother, 'The Experience of the First World War and the German Film', in Michael Paris (ed.), *The First World War and Popular Cinema: 1914 to the Present* (Edinburgh: Edinburgh University Press, 1999), p. 217.
2. Michel Tournier, *Le Vent Paraclet*, quoted in Modris Eksteins, *Rites of Spring* (London: Black Swan/Bantam, 1990), p. 415. Comments by Christophe Didier, Deputy Director of the Bibliothèque nationale et universitaire, Strasbourg, 'War in the Archives' event, Institut Français, London, 19 June 2014.
3. John Street, *Music and Politics* (Cambridge: Polity Press, 2012), p. 103.
4. There are several surviving songs from the Thirty Years War of 1618–48; see Dorian Lynskey, *33 Revolutions Per Minute: A History of Protest Song* (London: Faber & Faber, 2012), p. 686. 'Babylon Is Falling' (recorded by the Home Service on *I'm Alright Jack*) is

a song of the English Civil War, as is 'The World Turned Upside Down' (recorded by Leon Rosselson and Billy Bragg among others); 'Lillibullero' dates to the seventeenth century; 'Heart of Oak' and 'The Girl I Left behind Me' to the eighteenth.

5. Larry Portis, *French Frenzies: A Social History of Pop Music in France* (College Station: Virtualbookworm Publishing, 2004), p. 3. See also Peter Hawkins, *Chanson: The French Singer-Songwriter from Aristide Bruant to the Present Day* (Aldershot: Ashgate, 2000), p. 3.
6. Simon Frith, *Performing Rites: Evaluating Popular Music* (Oxford: Oxford University Press, 1996), p. 170.
7. Chris Tinker, 'Anti-Nationalism in Postwar French Chanson', *National Identities*, 4 (2002), 133–43.
8. Chris Tinker, *Georges Brassens and Jacques Brel: Personal and Social Narratives in Post-War Chanson* (Liverpool: Liverpool University Press, 2005), p. 157.
9. Ibid., p. 13.
10. Chris Tinker, 'A Singer-Songwriter's View of the French Record Industry: The Case of Léo Ferré', *Popular Music*, 21 (2002), 147–8.
11. Ibid., pp. 148–9.
12. Portis, *French Frenzies*, p. 150.
13. Tinker, *Georges Brassens and Jacques Brel*, p. 158.
14. Wilfred Owen, 'Dulce et Decorum Est', in *The Poems of Wilfred Owen*, ed. Jon Stallworthy (London: Chatto & Windus, 1990), p. 117.
15. Portis, *French Frenzies*, p. 119.
16. The instrument used on the album is a mellotron, but in their reunion shows in 2008 Rod Argent played a real harmonium.
17. Though crowd-sourced and hence likely to be incomplete, Wikipedia lists a minimum of sixty-four recorded versions of the latter as of the date of access; see <https://en.wikipedia.org/wiki/No_Man%27s_Land_(Eric_Bogle_song)> (last accessed 9 January 2017).
18. Jon Casimir, 'Secret Life of Matilda', *Sydney Morning Herald*, 19 April 2002. His article includes an extensive interview with Bogle; see <http://www.smh.com.au/articles/2002/04/19/1019020705613.html> (last accessed 15 November 2016).
19. Ibid. There is some 'poetic licence' in the lyrics which say he enlisted in 1915 but was present at the Suvla Bay landings, which would mean he must have enlisted in 1914. They also refer to the troops being issued with steel helmets on enlistment, although steel helmets were not introduced until 1916.
20. The song was written following a trip Bogle made to the war cemeteries in 1976 and research has suggested that the real William McBride was a private in the Royal Inniskilling Fusiliers buried in Authuille Cemetery near Beaumont Hamel. See Commonwealth War Graves website, <http://www.cwgc.org/find-a-cemetery/cemetery/66101/AUTHUILE%20MILITARY%20CEMETERY> (last accessed 15 November 2016).
21. Eric Bogle concert at Weymouth, September 2009, YouTube, <http://www.youtube.com/watch?v=gqVGshDc-CM> (last accessed 15 November 2016).
22. Mike Harding's personal website, <http://www.mikeharding.co.uk/recordings/bombers-moon> (last accessed 15 November 2016).
23. Michael Kimmelman, quoted in Peter Tregear, 'For *alle Menschen*? Classical Music and Remembrance after 9/11', in Jonathan Ritter and J. Martin Daughtry (eds), *Music in the Post-9/11 World* (New York and London: Routledge, 2012), p. 161.
24. 'World War One: Marking the Centenary of World War One across the BBC', <http://www.bbc.co.uk/mediacentre/mediapacks/ww1/arts#heading-the-ballads-of-the-great-war> (last accessed 15 November 2016).
25. Critics dispute Led Zeppelin as being direct precursors of metal with Americans generally favouring their role and Britons dissenting. Deena Weinstein, *Heavy Metal: The Music and its Culture*, 2nd edn (New York: Da Capo Press, 2000), pp. 14–15.

26. Michelle Phillipov, *Death Metal and the Critics* (Lanham, MD: Lexington, 2012), p. xi; Weinstein, *Heavy Metal*, p. 113; Jeremy Wallach, Harris M. Berger and Paul D. Greene, *Metal Rules the Globe: Heavy Metal Music around the World* (Durham, NC: Duke University Press, 2011).
27. Phillipov, *Death Metal and the Critics*, p. 64.
28. Julia Kristeva, *The Powers of Horror: An Essay on Abjection* (New York: Columbia University Press, 1982). Phillipov relates Kristeva's ideas to death metal (pp. 107–13).
29. Phillipov, *Death Metal and the Critics*, p. 89.
30. Keith Kahn-Harris, *Extreme Metal: Music and Culture on the Edge* (Oxford: Berg, 2007), pp. 109 and 36–7. Bolt Thrower also have one of the relatively few female members in a death metal band, their bassist Jo Bench, who joined in 1987.
31. Laura Wiebe Taylor, 'Images of Human-Wrought Despair and Destruction: Social Critique in British Apocalyptic and Dystopian Metal', in Gerd Bayer (ed.), *Heavy Metal Music in Britain* (Aldershot: Ashgate, 2009), p. 95.
32. The artwork of *Those Once Loyal* depicts Gilbert Ledward's highly realistic frieze of an 18-pounder gun in action, which is part of the Guards Memorial in St James's Park, London.
33. Karl Willetts, interview with the author, 29 June 2014.
34. Ibid.
35. Taylor, 'Images of Human-Wrought Despair and Destruction', p. 91.
36. Suggesting another Wilfred Owen comparison, this time to 'Strange Meeting'. See Owen, *Poems*, p. 125.
37. Sabaton, lyrics for 'The Price of a Mile'.
38. Phillipov, *Death Metal and the Critics*, p. xix.
39. Willetts interview.
40. 'Local Rock Star PJ Harvey Talks to the News', *Bridport and Lyme Regis News*, 26 January 2011, <http://www.bridportnews.co.uk/news/8813041.Bridport__Local_rock_star_PJ_Harvey_talks_to_the_News> (last accessed 15 November 2016).
41. It was named 'album of the year' by sixteen publications and won the *Uncut* Music Award for 2011; see <http://www.metacritic.com/feature/music-critic-top-ten-lists-best-albums-of-2011?tag=supplementary-nav;article;2> (last accessed 15 November 2016). The album was not quite as successful commercially, peaking at number eight in the UK and number thirty-two in the US album charts.
42. Interview with Dorian Lynskey, *The Observer*, 24 April 2011, <http://www.guardian.co.uk/music/2011/apr/24/pj-harvey-england-shake-interview> (last accessed 15 November 2016).
43. 'Local Rock Star PJ Harvey Talks to the News'. Some of the references are more obvious than others, for example Goya's 'The Disasters of War', The Doors' track 'The End' and the Pogues' version of 'The Band Played Waltzing Matilda'.
44. The 'old' image is well captured in her performance at the V Festival in 2003; see <http://www.youtube.com/watch?v=A29BMj3v86w> (last accessed 15 November 2016). For the 'new' see <http://www.youtube.com/watch?v=fOV9e5eufMU> (last accessed 15 November 2016).
45. Interview with John Sellers, *GQ*, Music Issue 2011, <http://www.gq.com/entertainment/music/201111/pj-harvey-gq-music-issue> (last accessed 15 November 2016).
46. Neil McCormick, 'PJ Harvey: Masterpiece of the First Rock-and-Roll War Artist', *Daily Telegraph*, 20 July 2011, <http://www.telegraph.co.uk/culture/music/rockandpop features/8650329/P.J-Harvey-Masterpiece-of-the-first-rock-and-roll-war-artist.html> (last accessed 15 November 2016).
47. Interview on *The Andrew Marr Show*, BBC1, 18 April 2010, <http://www.youtube.com/watch?v=49BPRI0UbDo> (last accessed 15 November 2016).

48. See <http://www.youtube.com/watch?v=k0M5MFryU3c> (last accessed 15 November 2016).
49. Rob Woodard, 'Lyrics Poetry?', *The Guardian*, 19 December 2007, <http://www.guardian.co.uk/books/booksblog/2007/dec/19/lyricspoetry> (last accessed 15 November 2016).
50. Frith, *Performing Rites*, p. 182.
51. Willetts interview.
52. Owen, *Poems*, p. 152.
53. Devon Powers, review of *Her Majesty the Decemberists*, *Pop Matters*, 14 September 2003, <http://www.popmatters.com/review/decemberists-hermajesty/> (last accessed 15 November 2016).
54. Owen, *Poems*, p. 56.
55. Glenn Watkins, *Proof through the Night: Music and the Great War* (Berkeley and London: University of California Press, 2003), p. 429.
56. Interview with Miranda Sawyer on *The Culture Show*, BBC2, 10 February 2011, <http://www.youtube.com/watch?v=2Gqd-2Tz6cc> (last accessed 15 November 2016).
57. Hawkins, *Chanson*, p. 4.
58. Richard Floeckher, 'Fuck Euphemisms: How Heavy Metal Lyrics Speak the Truth about War', in Niall W. R. Scott and Imke von Helden (eds), *The Metal Void: First Gatherings* (Oxford: Inter-Disciplinary Press, 2010), pp. 233–44.
59. Ibid., p. 236.

# 14

# Requiems and Memorial Music

*Kate Kennedy*

The First World War is now remembered primarily through its literature. The response of classical musicians to the war, both during and after the conflict, is less familiar. It was more difficult (though not impossible) for composers to write music whilst on active service, and the majority of music written during the war was composed by those too old or unfit to serve. These pieces are a barometer of the needs of the time, serving a public need as well as being a vehicle for private emotion. Older composers who were not called upon to fight, such as Edward Elgar, Charles Villiers Stanford and Hubert Parry, felt strongly that they should write works that met the general populace's need to mourn, commemorate, celebrate and raise spirits. There were even calls in journals for composers to write 'the piece of the war' that might speak both for and to the British people, such as the *Musical Times*'s article in which a non-musician combatant called for a 'composer of genius' to write a Bugle-Call Symphony, which would create 'a work of real national importance by taking three or four of the most expressive [bugle] calls and enlarging symphonically on the meaning which they are supposed to convey'.[1]

Despite such appeals for a single musical utterance there were as many different musical responses to the conflict as there were varied and changing attitudes to the war. Pieces were, in the case of Arthur Bliss's *Morning Heroes* (1930), written to exorcise a deeply personal grief or guilt, whilst still serving a public purpose of bringing together large forces to mourn and contemplate loss en masse. Other composers wrote more intimate works, drawing on their own experiences of the war to create pieces that expressed their own very personal relationship to the event. They were not necessarily combatants; war compositions were inspired by civilians' losses as much as by the experience of fighting. Herbert Howells, who was too ill to fight, wrote an elegy for strings and viola in 1917 in honour of his friend Francis Purcell Warren, a budding composer and accomplished viola player, who had been killed. Frank Bridge was deeply affected by the war although he did not serve, and struggled to reconcile it with his pacifist beliefs. His *Piano Sonata* of 1921–4, dedicated to the memory of his friend the composer Ernest Farrar, is a stark contrast to his pre-war work. It ushered in a new era for Bridge's composition, just as the war itself altered the society around him irrevocably. At the expense of alienating his audience, he had written a work that was a dark and deeply turbulent reflection on the conflict. His *Sonata* was the result of years of condensation of thought, but his musical response to the war had also been immediate. In 1915 he had read about the torpedoing of the *Lusitania*, and had written a disturbing *Lament* dedicated to a girl who had been a passenger on board and who had drowned. It bears some resemblance to a distorted Brahms *Wiegenlied*, the sinister rocking of the boat in the waves shuddering to a halt as the torpedo finds its target. In the same year, the public embraced Elgar's hearty setting of Rudyard Kipling's nautical *The Fringes of the Fleet*. The two are musical and ideological worlds apart. A year later Elgar came closest to meeting the *Musical Times*'s demand for a war composition for the public to take to their hearts with *The Spirit of England* (1916–17), dedicated 'To the memory of our glorious men, with a special thought for the Worcesters'. The imperative to write a musical work of remembrance was one recognised by composers, not simply articulated by the general public or by journals, and yet the musical responses were far from uniform in their message and approach. They included works as diverse as Bliss's *Morning Heroes*, John Foulds's *A World Requiem* (1921), Holst's *Ode to Death* (1919) and Delius's *Requiem* (1913–16), to name a few.

These works, in their different ways, set the standard for the shape of musical mourning in the twentieth century.[2] Rather than list all the major works written in connection with the war, this chapter will trace the musical legacy of the war through an examination of an unlikely pairing of two key works: Ivor Gurney's song cycle *Ludlow and Teme*, written in 1919 in the immediate aftermath by an ex-combatant, and Benjamin Britten's *War Requiem*, written decades later by a pacifist composer. Although Britten was young enough that he barely remembered the First World War, it had a deep impact on him, and his *War Requiem* is one of the most iconic pieces of music written in the twentieth century in connection with war. Britten links it specifically to the First World War with his settings of Wilfred Owen, and acknowledges a debt to Bliss's *Morning Heroes* (which included the first setting of Owen's verse). Gurney's *Ludlow and Teme*, for tenor and piano quartet, is far less well known and rarely associated with the war and its aftermath. However, the works share striking similarities in their complex and troubled relationships to the texts they set, and an examination of how these deeply ambivalent settings function can shed light on some of the complexities faced and expressed by composers using music to articulate their relationship to war.

As cultural historian Jay Winter tells us, it is a misconception to think that societies can learn. They can simply contain individuals who remember a traumatic event such as a war, and whose memories will, for the time in which they are living, overlap with those of others. As Winter argues, '[f]or this overlap to become a social phenomenon, it must be expressed and shared. In this sense, and in this sense alone, can one speak, again metaphorically, of collective memory.'[3] This sharing takes the form of conversation and of expression, most prominently through the arts. Each sculpture, composition, memoir or painting alters or reaffirms what we believed we knew as a society about the war. Each generation, from those returned from the trenches to those learning about the war a century on, will have a different and changing understanding of what the war meant, and of how it ought to be understood and represented. How might we interpret the multifarious ways in which collective remembrance has played out through music? It is an art form which requires a particular collectivity, bringing together audience and performers to share the same experience. Music has a particular role to play in remembrance. No funeral or memorial ceremony would be complete without some form of music appropriate for the occasion, and resonant with memory and connection for the congregation or audience. Music has a Proustian power to return the listener to a past event or time, and so is a powerful tool in the process of both remembering and healing. The journalist H. V. Morton testified to this in 1927, when he witnessed a packed Royal Albert Hall during one of the first Festivals of

Remembrance after the Armistice, in which demobilised combatants came together to sing the songs that had sustained them in the trenches and at sea. An ex-combatant himself, he found the power of the event overwhelming:

> We did not realize until last night that the songs we sang in the Army were bits of history. In them is embalmed the comic fatalism which carried us through four years of hell. How easily we slipped back into it! Cynicism was blown clean out of us. We were young once more as we can never be again and we went deeper into our memories [. . .] Thirteen years fell from us. We ceased to see the Albert Hall and the thousands of faces white in the arc lights; we looked into an abyss of memories where long columns passed and repassed over the dusty roads of France, where grotesque, unthinkable things happened day and night – the brief joys, the sharp sorrows of those days, the insane injustices of fate, and above it all the memory of the men we knew so well [. . .] It seemed to me that we had caught the only decent thing in the war – the spirit of comradeship. We had come to the hall as individuals; we were now once more an army marching in our imagination to the old music.[4]

In the context of a memorial service or event, music is placed strategically between the specifics of the spoken word. It both complements text and serves an alternative purpose, creating mood, helping to stir the emotions of the congregation, and allowing an often wordless space in which to contemplate readings and testimonies. Grief, when recent, can be overwhelming and boundless. Music acts as a delineated space in which to remember and mourn. It is experienced in real time, unlike a text, which, when read on the page, can be scanned at a glance, interrupted, or re-read. Music carries its listener at its own speed, and the listener must relinquish control as it is dictated to them, whilst also being given the opportunity to pursue their own thoughts within this controlled but emotionally resonant space.

Even whilst he was still in the trenches, Ivor Gurney wrote songs that explored death and mourning from a range of different angles, from the glorious and mystical to the understated and wistful.[5] In songs such as his setting of John Masefield's 'By a Bierside' and Walter Raleigh's 'E'en Such is Time', he combines a musical enhancement of the text with space around it in the form of striking silences, or moments of musical stasis for contemplation. They function, in effect, as microcosmic requiem masses – spaces for contemplation and remembrance that combine in one event silence, text and music. Gurney had suffered episodes of poor mental health before the war, and enlisted in part because he hoped army life with its routine would have a beneficial effect. He served for fifteen months on the Western front, interrupting his studies at the Royal College of Music. Gurney survived the war and returned to chamber music and songs, and his war experience continued to influence and shape his work, prompting his decision to write a large-scale commemorative piece. An orchestral *War Elegy*, written in 1920, was intended as a public memorial and was no doubt partially inspired by the wealth of commemorative works that were performed at the Royal College of Music that same year. The Patron's Fund concerts on 1 June and 9 July 1920 had included Ernest Farrar's *Heroic Elegy*. If Gurney attended the choral class that July, he would have performed in the chorus for two pieces written by the older generation before the war, but appropriated as works of commemoration: *Dirge for Two Veterans*, a setting of Gurney's beloved Walt Whitman in 1901 by Charles Wood, and Stanford's 1910 *Songs of the Fleet*, the final song 'Fare Well' being reminiscent of a funeral oration. Gurney had spent many hours playing in a marching band during the war, and the experience stood him in good stead to write his own commemorative march.

There was one particular procession that took place in November 1920 as Gurney worked on his own march: the interment of the Unknown Warrior. Representing the repatriation of all those who would never return, it provided a locus for grieving relatives who had no body to bury. It was a moment of pure theatre that captivated the nation and its composers, poets and artists. Marion Arkwright composed 'Through the Mist', a musical account of the anonymous body returning on HMS *Verdun*. The poet Alfred Noyes quickly wrote 'The Passing of the Unknown Warrior' for the *Daily Mirror* to publish the day after the event. Gurney's own views on Armistice Day were, like many others', a complex combination of anger, sorrow and anxiety for the future. He had already begun to write a number of poetic responses to the Armistice, from his 1918 poem 'The Day of Victory' onwards. Now, two years later, he could write in music about the contradictory emotions the event inevitably triggered.

Since the Armistice, Gurney had felt that he wanted to write a musical memorial, a commemorative piece that would be his elegy to the war. He had his eye on *The Song of Roland* for a possible text, a medieval French poem based on the Battle of Roncevaux Pass in 778. Had he completed it, the work would have pre-dated Bliss's *Morning Heroes* by eleven years, and it is striking that both composers were drawn to poetic accounts of other historical battles to reflect on the war in which they had recently taken part. Gurney finally decided to write a purely orchestral piece, and *War Elegy* was the result. He had in fact begun work on the *War Elegy* in 1919, under the more generic titles 'Funeral March' and then 'March Elegy', before deciding to link the work directly to both war and mourning. It is a work that could have been written in response to Elgar's *Spirit of England*. It shares with Elgar's work, and in particular with his *First Symphony*, a processional march, a sweeping, lyrical melody underpinned with a solid bass line. Gurney even doubles the lower instruments with a contrabassoon to give the depth of dignity and gravitas he intends the work to convey, trying on Elgar's shoes, so to speak, to see if they fitted. At this point Gurney was already relatively secure in his identity as war poet, and now, as the Cenotaph was being unveiled and the Unknown Warrior interred, he had turned his hand to a musical war memorial.

Alongside the public, formal gesture of the *War Elegy*, Gurney also explored his personal emotional response to the conflict through more subtly war-related works, such as his 1919 song cycle *Ludlow and Teme*. The cycle, a setting of poems from A. E. Housman's *A Shropshire Lad*, achieves something similar to Gurney's own finest war poetry. Both in words and in music Gurney found ways to explore the psychological complexity and deep ambiguities at the heart of his relationship to the war. Housman's verse had accompanied Gurney through the trenches as he had often carried a copy of *A Shropshire Lad* with him in his kit. Now, Gurney turned to the deceptively simple verse, just as families turned to the deliberate simplicity of the Cenotaph. Both poetry and monument represent structures to contain and explore anger, grief, confusion and nostalgia.

It is here that the similarity stops. Edwin Lutyens's Cenotaph, a study in muted understatement, is a world apart from Housman's verse. Housman had written *A Shropshire Lad* in 1896 before the first Boer War, when war was at enough of a distance that a poem could endorse the validity and purpose of death in battle without having to trouble its conscience. Gurney's first-hand experiences of modern warfare at its very worst prompted him to engage with Housman's poetry in a troubling and often contradictory manner. His settings – as in the third song of *Ludlow and Teme*, which begins 'The lads in their hundreds to Ludlow come in for the fair' – juxtapose Housman's delicate, unassuming text with an unwarrantedly relentless accompaniment that echoes the sounds of marching feet and of guns firing. Despite the necessarily different outlook on war taken by Gurney and Housman, their work shares a preoccupation with images of a quintessential Englishness. Gurney's own ambivalent feelings towards the war and army life are exposed in his own poetry, which shows the life of a soldier to be both potentially therapeutic and stultifying, and this troubled perception is also reflected in his setting of Housman's poetry. In his setting of 'On the Idle Hill of Summer', Gurney begins the song with a distant military drum, in the form of a pizzicato cello. Throughout, other rhythms are explicitly associated with the military: a repeating triplet figure, a brisk fanfare-like dotted figure. At the rare moments when the glamour palls, and Housman allows a brief foray into what the cost of militarism might be (such as the line 'lovely lads and dead and rotten, none that go return again'), Gurney's musical language becomes nothing short of hysterical. The instruments break down, any reference to the first beat of the bar or to the harmonic progression is temporarily lost, and it is only by a concerted effort in the strings to impose order in the form of the militaristic rhythmic motifs that the song regains its footings.

Gurney's song settings offer more than a simple translation of poetry into sound: his decision to set Housman's texts creates a complex dialogue between composer's and poet's ideologies.[6] The brutal ending of 'On the Idle Hill of Summer' almost literally shoots down Housman's claims for glamourising 'the lads who will die in their glory'. The singer practically shouts the line 'and never be old', and the song is cut off abruptly by a biting, *fortissimo* figure redolent of a sudden burst of machine-gun fire. This is a song that understands and holds up to the light the true implications of dying in one's glory. In setting Housman to music, Gurney examines and questions Housman's assumptions, whilst also harnessing the poems' associations with the pastoral, England and nationhood. Gurney's music explores his own complicated post-war relationship to beauty, loss and anger in a way that a setting of a text with which he was in complete sympathy, such as Sassoon's righteous anger, or his own verse, would not have allowed.

Gurney's ambivalent words and music spoke for and on behalf of the wartime experiences of his fellow soldiers, but it was Benjamin Britten, a pacifist civilian, who became the musical elegist of the Second World War. He had wanted to write a major work relating to war for some years, when the opportunity presented itself in the form of a commission to mark the consecration of the new Coventry Cathedral, built next to the burnt ruins of the medieval cathedral that had been destroyed in the bombing. Britten inherited something of a contradiction: on the one hand, a rich musical tradition of memorialising war, and a cultural expectation that a composer would respond to such an event; on the other, post-war culture seemed to frown upon anything that tended towards the monumental. Britten did not see fighting at first hand, but visited the newly liberated concentration camps at Bergen-Belsen on a recital tour with Yehudi Menuhin in 1945. On his return, he faced the awesome responsibility and the urgent personal need to respond in music to what he had seen. He rarely talked about the visit, at the time or afterwards, writing to Peter Pears only that 'we stayed the night in Belsen, and saw over the hospital – and I needn't describe that to you . . . I don't know why we should be so lucky, in all this misery.'[7] Other journalists who visited the camp felt they were still inarticulate with shock years after.[8] All Britten ever said in an interview was 'we gave two or three recitals a day – they couldn't take more. It was in many ways a terrifying experience.'[9]

Belsen unlocked Britten's righteous fury, and it poured out in a song cycle, *The Holy Sonnets of John Donne*. It was a historical act of displacement, moving centuries away from the modern atrocity he had witnessed to explore his thoughts on death, evil, religion and the possibility of redemption in parallel to his modern-day experience. In doing so, he was in keeping with the feeling amongst historians and creative artists in every genre that 'the Nazi past is too massive to be forgotten, and too repellent to be integrated into the "normal" narrative of memory'.[10] One way to avoid integration was to side-step it historically, and the Donne poems afforded just such an opportunity.

When he came to work on his *War Requiem*, Britten built on this experiment, exploiting the possibilities that the traditional Latin Mass for the dead offered for considering death and resurrection without any connection to the war. The addition of the poems of Wilfred Owen, however, meant that war in the twentieth century could be addressed, but still at one remove from the war that had finished in 1945. It was a move towards subjectivity, strongly at odds with the collective impersonality of the Latin mass. This dichotomy between private and public, unresolved personal anger and collective memorial, is one that Britten shares with First World War composers such as Bliss and Gurney and which has a particularly strong parallel in the compositions of Britten's teacher Frank Bridge, whose drastic musical change in direction from well-behaved Edwardian chamber music to harmonic language pushed to its limits corresponded with the First World War. For Britten after his visit to Belsen,

> [t]he unclouded childlike optimism for which he had sometimes striven was no longer an option in his music, although (and quite logically) he would come to value it even more in children. Creatively, a time when 'all went well' was from now on only available to him as a barely accessible memory. There are very few easy resolutions in Britten's later work, and ease, when it is attempted, is always troubled by ambiguity.[11]

Britten's *Holy Sonnets of John Donne* were written in the heat of his return. They marked the trajectory his war-related works would take for the coming decades, but his most enduring utterance on war, written from the more objective distance of the early 1960s, was to be the *War Requiem*. It offers no easy resolutions, and its very structure embodies ambiguity, vacillating between the certainty of the Latin text, the innocence represented by the inclusion of a boys' choir, and the unresolved anger that pours from the poems of Wilfred Owen.

*War Requiem* was written for the consecration of the new Coventry Cathedral in 1962. Everything about the newly built cathedral is steeped in symbol. The tall stained glass windows of the nave represent a journey from darkness to light. As the audience looked about them during the first performance, they would have found themselves inside an emotionally charged space that was in itself a memorial, designed to lead them towards forgiveness, to a new world of hope and light. As we might expect,

Britten's *War Requiem* is itself deeply interested in symbolism, but neither Britten nor Owen was on the same trajectory as the cathedral. This is a work that can, at best, only offer an uncomfortable, ambiguous possibility of resurrection. The cathedral rises, phoenix-like, from the ruins, but Owen's poems cannot allow the ancient Latin text to do the same. The liturgy does not represent a shining beacon of hope to counter Owen's desolate trench landscape. What it does offer, like Gurney's cycle, is a painfully honest probe into the darker aspects of the human condition – the attractiveness of destruction and violence, the constant pull between darkness and light.

Britten wrote that 'I suppose [*War Requiem*] is the piece I hope will be remembered longest. But that is not because of the music, it is because of the message contained within, which I hope will be used for many years to come.'[12] But what is this message? Britten was a lifelong pacifist, and had grown up both in the shadow of the First World War and in the musical shadow of composers such as Elgar who had had the specific responsibility of responding to the war of 1914–18 through their music. Britten wrote of his specific debt to Frank Bridge:

> A lot of feeling about the First World War, which people seem to see in my War Requiem, came from Bridge. He had written a Piano Sonata in memory of a friend [the composer Ernest Farrar] killed in France and although he didn't encourage me to take a stand for the sake of a stand, he did make me argue and argue and argue [. . .] we had very serious and interesting arguments.[13]

Britten's thinking about the first war, which, as he notes, translated directly into his *War Requiem*, began as a result of these intellectual tussles. It is a work riven with struggle – from the disconcerting tritone that hangs unresolved over the whole work until the very last bars, to the strategic placing of the Owen texts alongside the Latin, embracing and attacking their meaning, or at the very least throwing them into a different relief. Both the musical and the textual structure of the *Requiem* enact an attempt to understand and to reconcile, without coming to any trite or comforting conclusions.

A requiem's purpose is to console the living, and to bury the dead. Through the structure of the Latin text, it traditionally offers an emotional journey from contemplation of the fearsome possibilities of the *Dies Irae* to the relief and assurance that our lost ones, and we ourselves, might end up *in paradisum*. However, the quotation with which Britten prefaces his *Requiem* is one of warning, not reconciliation: 'My subject is war and the pity of war. The Poetry is in the pity . . . All a poet can do today is warn.'[14] Owen's words are not just antithetical to the Latin text. It is not as simple as Owen versus the church. In fact, Owen considered a religious career and had a strong faith, although it became a belief in the sacredness of humanity more than an orthodox denominational faith. As Owen's letters show, he put his religion in dialogue with his war experience: 'For 14 hours yesterday I was at work – teaching Christ to lift his cross by numbers and how to adjust his crown: and not to imagine he thirst till after the last halt. I attended his Supper to see that there were not complaints: and inspected his feet that they should be worthy of the nails.'[15]

Britten put a great deal of thought both into the selection of the Owen poems and into their positioning within his libretto.[16] After much deliberation, he selected nine of Owen's poems to act as commentary on the text of the Latin mass. The section of the *Dies Irae* known as the *Lacrimosa* is one of the rare moments at which the Owen text is incorporated within the Latin; generally, the poems are juxtaposed with the mass text, each offering a commentary on the other. Here, however, the poem 'Futility' is interpolated into the *Lacrimosa*, whispered by the tenor and accompanied by low, murmuring flute tremolos and sustained strings, whilst the soprano sobs the Latin above them. The tenor's vocal line transforms the soprano's keening from a generalised, unspecific loss to the very particular death being mourned in Owen's poem – the tenor echoes the contours of her phrase for the words 'was it for this the clay grew tall?'. If a requiem could be said to frame grief and indeed death, and offer them a sense of purpose, then this moment of interrelated texts dashes it in the most understated, devastating manner. The poem describes the epitome of futility, as its title promises – a plea to move a corpse into the sun in the hope that its warmth will awaken the dead. We know, as does the speaker of the poem, that such an act is futile. In fact, it is as futile as living – 'what made fatuous sunbeams toil to break earth's sleep at all?' If a requiem traditionally moves from darkness to the beams of heaven, like the design of Coventry Cathedral itself, then here the fatuous sunbeams are pointless: 'If anything might rouse him now the kind old sun will know.' The kind old sun, a god-like figure who has the power to wake the dead, refuses to do so. What, then, Britten asks as he interleaves this bitter poem with a religious text promising resurrection, is the point of prayer?

Britten chooses Owen's 'Parable of the Old Man and the Young' to set alongside the lines from the Offertorium, '*quam olim Abrahae promisisti, et semini ejus*'. The poem is a powerful, dystopian version of the biblical story. Whereas the Latin text offers Abraham's promise as a reassurance, in Owen's version we find that Abraham wilfully slaughters his own son, and 'half the seed of Europe one by one'. Owen's anti-parable is written in quasi-religious language, its familiarity lulling us into a false sense of expectation, making the subversion of Abraham's actions the more jarring. Only at the point of Abraham binding the youth are we awakened to the possibility that this is not all that it seems; Abraham does not stop at tying up his son, but inexplicably builds 'parapets and trenches there'. This is not one father's pact with God, but every father who had failed to stop the political situation that created the war, and then encouraged their sons to fight.

As Abraham stretches forth his knife, the bassoon, horn and percussion all recall motifs from Britten's previous setting of Owen's 'Anthem for Doomed Youth'. We do not yet know the bloody conclusion of the 'Parable', but even to the most optimistic ear, the musical reference to doomed youth bodes ill. Isaac, like the generation of 1914, is destined for tragedy. God, and his angel's appearance to intervene, is irrelevant – Isaac's fate has already been sealed by his father. And so, again, Britten forces the listener to question where such tragic inevitability leaves us, if we have any faith at all. The tenor and baritone repeat the line 'and half the seed of Europe, one by one, one by one, half the seed of Europe, one by one', perpetually out of sync with each other. Their disjointed insistence on the repeated line is something akin to a jaunty dance of death – a fragment of a remembered soldiers' song, transmuted into a neurotic muttering condemned to continue for eternity, enacting the endlessness of the slaughter. Over this Britten places the innocent voices of the boys, the next generation's sacrifice. The boys sing the offertory, unconscious of the irony inherent in their recalling the memory of dead souls when the tenor and baritone are seemingly unable to relinquish them:

'*Hostias et preces tibi Domine laudis offerimus: tu sucipe pro animabus illis, quaram hodie memoriam facimus: fac eas, Domine, de morte transire ad vitam*' ('We offer unto Thee, O Lord, this sacrifice of prayer and praise: do thou receive it on behalf of the souls of those whose memory we this day recall: make them O Lord, to pass from death unto life'). According to Owen and Britten, God's pact with Abraham and his seed is worthless not because God himself is malevolent, but because Abraham, and men in general, are. If God is impotent, and cannot intervene to save Isaac, then how can we find reassurance in the promise he made Abraham?

Britten's settings of the Owen text reflect both poet and composer's discomfort with organised religion as they scrutinise the apparently unending capacity for evil inherent in human beings. Controversially for a Cathedral-commissioned work, Britten chose to set 'At a Calvary near the Ancre', one of Owen's few poems that directly attacks the Church's conduct during the war: 'The scribes on all the people shove / And bawl allegiance to the state.'[17] Whilst organised religion is critiqued, Christ's example, it seems, is embraced. The poem, which Britten places at the opening of the *Agnus Dei*, ends, 'But they who love the greater love, / Lay down their life: they do not hate.' Christ, shell-torn and hanging from his cross at one of the innumerable calvaries that mark crossroads in France, is supported not by his disciples, but by the men, their twentieth-century equivalents – flawed, weak-willed, but ultimately blessed and set apart, like their early predecessors:

> One ever hangs where shelled roads part.
> In this war He too lost a limb,
> But His disciples hide apart;
> And now the soldiers bear with Him.

After this verse, the choir sings the *Agnus Dei*, the Latin for once offering clarification of the Owen. 'He' who 'lost a limb' is of course the lamb of God. For the only time in the *Requiem*, Britten gives the tenor some Latin text; he substitutes what should be '*dona eis requiem sempiternam*', the final line of the *Agnus Dei*, for '*dona eis pacem*', a plea for peace. This moment is as near to the reconciliation and consolation that we might expect from a requiem as Britten allows us to get, but it stops short of a message of hope. As the tenor climbs the octave, as if his prayer for peace ascends to heaven, the intervals are altered from a C sharp to a natural so the 'mourning motif', the uneasy tritone with which the requiem began, is built into his scale (C to F sharp).

The requiem might have ended here with a prayer for peace, but to qualify any reassuringly optimistic ending *in paradisum*, we have the masterpiece 'Strange Meeting'. Here, in fantasy or nightmare, two dead soldiers from either side meet. Owen's experience of the Western front meant that he of all people understood that no simple restoration of peace could be adequate or possible. These soldiers have escaped war to find themselves ostensibly in hell, 'down some profound dull tunnel, long since scooped / Through granites which titanic wars had groined' – the absolute antithesis of paradise, where sleepers groan rather than rest for eternity. Fittingly, the musical landscape is barren; apocalyptic, rather than celestial. Just in case we are in any danger of missing the irony of this, and of labouring under the misapprehension that this meeting is one of hope and reconciliation, the baritone's answer to the tenor's statement that 'here is no cause to mourn' is about as pathetic as the attempts to warm the dead soldier in the sun in 'Futility': 'None, save the undone years, the hopelessness. Whatever hope is yours, was my life also.' Under these words, the oboe plays the *dona nobis pacem* motif.

The poem ends, 'I am the enemy you killed, my friend [. . .] Let us sleep now . . .' Owen had made the enemy more specific in an early draft, in which the line read 'I was a German conscript, and your friend', but this is too limiting; he must be everyman, the German equivalent of the Unknown Warrior, for the poem to have maximum impact. As the tenor and baritone sing 'Let us sleep now', the final line of their text, the boys' choir sing *In Paradisum*, its context lending their words an air of pathos. Their melody is almost identical to that sung for the words '*quam olim Abrahae*' – a symbolic return to the flawed pact between God and Abraham that the dead might pass from death to life. Can it be possible to interpret this significant reference as supporting a message of consolation? Critic Alec Robertson, wanting to read the *War Requiem* from a Christian perspective, finds that at this point God's promise is 'gloriously fulfilled'.[18] And yet the music is resolutely inglorious and understated. There is barely a climax before the procession to paradise is halted, and the requiem with its tolling bell is reinstated. And we might remember that the dead soldiers ask only to 'sleep now', not to be resurrected in paradise. Britten's *War Requiem* was commissioned by the clergy of the new cathedral, a musical war memorial to mark the opening of a living, architectural war memorial. Coventry Cathedral rises from the ashes of its destroyed predecessor with a wall of glass so that the ruins of the medieval building can be visible from everywhere inside. And yet for the consecration of a building created with the intention of offering hope and reconciliation, Britten wrote a requiem that questions the possibility of resurrection even as it offers it.

The purpose of many public memorials was to 'maintain war's immediacy and personal reality, [. . .] preserve the realness of its violence, [. . .] whilst simultaneously enfolding that trauma into a larger sense of continuity and community'.[19] *War Requiem* creates a sense of musical community, through its use of the traditional Latin text, and Britten's conscious decision to align it within the tradition of great musical memorials through reference to Mozart's and Verdi's *Requiems*. In a sense, to return to Jay Winter's theories on collective memory, Britten is both articulating the traumatic memories of those still alive who hold memories of war, and making a musical link to the collective musical memory of memorial music over the centuries. As Heather Wiebe puts it, *War Requiem* both recalls wartime disruption and contains it 'within a musical and religious tradition. It thus grapples with some of the central problems of commemoration: the mediation between private mourning and public expression.'[20] The central problem of the purpose of a monument, whether it is musical or architectural, is, according to Jay Winter, its need to serve two perhaps conflicting interests – the desire to keep alive the memory of particular events or actions, and the anxiety about sanctifying, glamourising or condoning violent death. As monuments to various conflicts multiply over the decades, so the assumption grows that violence and trauma are an unavoidable part of our culture, as the markers of individual events unwittingly create a sense of continuity. Once names have been carved into a monument to the war dead of the First World War and others added for the Second, it would come as no surprise to see the names of the Third on the same pedestal. This leaves composers, architects and writers with the perennial problem, if they believe war to be unnecessary and undesirable, of how to commemorate it without sentimentalising, celebrating or normalising it.

Stefan Goebel writes that '[f]rom the ruins of Coventry emerged a new mode of war commemoration, a mode which focused on the future rather than the past, a mode which invested the act of remembrance (that is reconciliation) rather than death on the battlefield with meaning'.[21] It united the ancient and the modern, and looked to the future. For the composers who wrote the First World War into their music, creating musical memorials that were both private and public spaces for grieving and reflection, the relationship between old and new was more often a representation of their own struggles than a happy reconciliation. Gurney embraced and simultaneously wrestled with the pre-war sentiments of Housman, and explored them in the light of his own trauma, anger and bereavement. Building on the examples of the previous generation, Britten brought into dialogue the ancient and the modern in his two texts. Whether or not the result was a forward-looking gesture of reconciliation is a matter perhaps for individual interpretation. What Britten has certainly given us is a work that could not have been possible without its First World War forebears; a work that dramatises the psychological complexity of our response to war, holding in tension the horror, fascination, respect and deep sadness with anger, disgust and trauma, offering a space in which to mourn, without the comfort of consolation.

## Notes

1. Robert Lorenz, 'Suggestions for a 'Bugle-Call Symphony', *Musical Times*, 1 July 1917, pp. 308–11.
2. For more detailed discussion of works inspired by the war, see my chapter 'Silence Recalled in Sound: British Classical Music and the Armistice', in Kate Kennedy and Trudi Tate (eds), *The Silent Morning: Culture and Memory after the Armistice* (Manchester: Manchester University Press, 2013).
3. Jay Winter and Emmanuel Sivan, *War and Remembrance in the Twentieth Century* (Cambridge: Cambridge University Press, 2000), p. 16.
4. H. V. Morton, *Daily Express*, 12 November 1927, p. 2.
5. For more detailed discussion of Gurney's musical engagement with the war and with A. E. Housman, see Kate Kennedy, 'Ivor Gurney – Embracing and Attacking Housman', in Delia da Sousa Correa (ed.), *The Edinburgh Companion to Literature and Music* (Edinburgh: Edinburgh University Press, forthcoming).
6. For a detailed examination of Gurney's settings of Housman, see my 'Ambivalent Englishness: Ivor Gurney's Song Cycle Ludlow and Teme', in Kate Kennedy and Trudi Tate (eds), *The First World War: Music, Literature, Memory* (London: Routledge, 2011).
7. Letter from Britten to Pears, 1 August 1945, letter 505, in *Letters from a Life: The Selected Letters and Diaries of Benjamin Britten, 1913–1976*, vol. 2, ed. Donald Mitchell (London: Faber & Faber, 1998).
8. See for instance *Vogue* editor Lee Miller's account of her visit and her enduring sense of shock, as referred to in Paul Kildea, *Benjamin Britten: A Life in the Twentieth Century* (London: Allen Lane, 2013), p. 255.
9. Britten in an interview with Murray Shafer, in R. Murray Shafer (ed.) *British Composers in Interview* (London: Faber & Faber, 1963), p. 231.
10. Saul Friedlander, *Memory, History and the Extermination of the Jews of Europe* (Bloomington: Indiana University Press, 1993), p. 2.
11. Neil Powell, *Benjamin Britten: A Life for Music* (London: Hutchinson, 2013), p. 244.
12. Quoted in Michael Foster, *The Idea Was Good: The Story of Britten's War Requiem* (Coventry: Coventry Cathedral Books, 2012), p. 19.

13. 'Britten Looking Back', *Sunday Telegraph*, 17 November 1963, p. 9.
14. Part of Owen's draft preface to his poems, probably written in Ripon, May 1918. See *The Poems of Wilfred Owen*, ed. Jon Stallworthy (London: Chatto & Windus, 1990), p. 192.
15. Wilfred Owen to Osbert Sitwell, July 1918, quoted in Jon Stallworthy, *Wilfred Owen* (Oxford: Oxford University Press, 1974), p. 265.
16. It is possible to trace, from the lists he made in notebooks and in the fly leaf of his collection of Owen's poems, the genesis of the final libretto. All are held in the Britten Pears Archive, Aldeburgh.
17. Wilfred Owen, 'At a Calvary near the Ancre', lines 9–10.
18. Alec Robertson, *Requiem: Music of Mourning and Consolation* (London: Cassell, 1967), p. 284.
19. Heather Wiebe, *Britten's Unquiet Pasts: Sound and Memory in Postwar Reconstruction* (Cambridge: Cambridge University Press, 2012), p. 198.
20. Ibid., p. 196.
21. Stefan Goebel, *The Great War and Medieval Memory: War, Remembrance and Medievalism in Britain and Germany, 1914–1940* (Cambridge: Cambridge University Press, 2007), p. 301.

# IV.

# Periodicals and Journalism

# 15

# Popular Periodicals: Wartime Newspapers, Magazines and Journals

*Kate Macdonald*

On 4 August 1914, on the announcement of the outbreak of war with Germany, John Buchan put aside his manuscript of *The Thirty-Nine Steps*, which he had begun writing a few days before, and wrote to his business partner George Brown, the production manager of the Edinburgh publishing house Thomas Nelson & Sons. They exchanged several letters a day to discuss how Nelson's could keep its business going in the new and unknown wartime conditions. They were anxious about keeping their recently upgraded printing presses running and their staff in work, as their usual printing orders from German publishers, on which they had relied strongly, were now cut off.[1] They also expected an immediate drop in domestic sales of books, and other publishers had the same fears. Cassell, a large publisher of books as well as of many successful periodicals, announced to its staff at the outbreak of war that it 'might well be obliged to close down. Heavy cuts were to be made in wages and salaries', although these were refunded a few months later.[2]

Nelson's agreed to try publishing a new magazine, one which Buchan called 'a budget of war news, articles and illustrations, sold at some price like 3d', 'what the ordinary man likes to read', though he was anxious to include a 'women's page' as well.[3] Nelson's called it *The War*, though Buchan felt that this title wasn't right: 'you ought to call it "Nelson's News of the War". Every one of these publications has got "The War" as the chief part of the title, and we want to identify our weekly with the firm.'[4] At least seven other weekly war-focused periodicals were springing into life during August 1914, so Buchan was right to press for a strategy to keep the Nelson's publication distinctive in the market. *The War* was brought out as a fortnightly magazine, in the event, but only lasted a few months before being quietly discontinued in March 1915. By attempting to offer news as well as features in issues each two weeks apart, *The War* was poorly conceived, demonstrating an ambitious but limited understanding of the periodicals market. Newspapers wouldn't buy *The War* as a supplement, so it had to go.[5] It was one of many opportunist magazines that disappeared in a crowded and increasingly specialised market. The Amalgamated Press's *Penny War Weekly* was another that also failed in the first few months of war, even though it originated from a well-established magazine publisher. The *Illustrated War News*, which was rushed into print at the beginning of the war as a weekly magazine from the publishers of the daily newspaper the *Illustrated London News*, only lasted until 1918.[6] *War Illustrated* was published from August 1914 to February 1919, and then resold in bound volumes as a war souvenir. The appearances and disappearances of periodicals are an important aspect of the pattern of popular periodical publishing during the war.

This chapter is intended to restore awareness of the importance and scale of the periodicals market in wartime Britain. It indicates the range of subjects covered and the trends over time in the movement of titles, and traces the evidence that the periodicals market offers for how and what the British population read during wartime. It gives an overview of the ebb and flow of magazine publishing in Britain during the First World War, looking at the periodicals that catered for leisure interests as well as for information and instruction. The publication and reading of periodicals is a culturally inflected practice, so while many aspects of the British experience will be shared by other countries, it should be remembered that this discussion only applies to British periodicals during the First World War. By looking at one market in depth, this chapter offers the fine detail of a discrete period in British reading history. Since wartime conditions made this period of periodical publishing history particularly volatile, the statistical evidence presented here shows how the war affected the way people read, and the extent to which the market changed.[7]

The magazines analysed for Figure 15.1 were sold to all classes and conditions of the population. Their survival in straitened economic circumstances is material evidence of sustained purchase and readership, and they were influential in recording and shaping the effects of war on public taste. We can read them now as repositories of literary taste and social history, while acknowledging that to their original readers they were an essential part of the national cultural ecosystem that supplied entertainment in weekly and monthly instalments, delivering encouragement, interest, sentiment, romance, adventure, pathos, intrigue, information, opinion, reassurance, amusement and innovation.

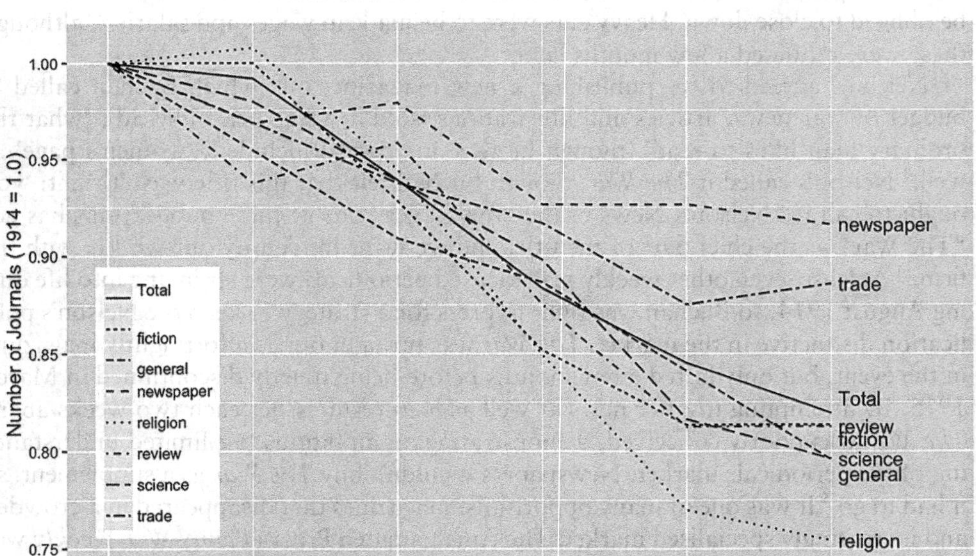


Figure 15.1 The relative changes in numbers of periodicals, as a total, and by the seven most numerous categories, from 1914 levels.

There are several sources to determine which periodicals were in print during the war years. Newspaper directories were published annually as business resources for potential advertisers, and in part as legal and fiscal evidence of a periodical's existence. However, their focus on the publisher and the advertiser (both commercially inclined) does not give a clear sense of the consumer's (as opposed to the producer's) perspective. The British Library, a statutory repository for registered periodicals, only contains those which were deposited; many (including *The War*, above) either were not received or have been lost. The unregistered periodicals of the war are an important example of magazine and newspaper ephemerality. To look at the market from a reader's perspective, rather than that of the producer, I used the annual editions for 1914–19 of A & C Black's *Writers' and Artists' Yearbook* (W&AY) as a basis for a corpus of British periodical titles for the war years. The W&AYs were (and still are) an annual almanac and directory to help writers and artists to identify buyers for their work. Since each edition is published in advance of the year it covers, the inclusion of a title on the list of periodicals in any year should be understood as an indication of activity in the previous year and the expectation of its continued existence, in the absence of any evidence to the contrary. However, like all other records of British periodicals history, the W&AY lists are not comprehensive. In the editorial to the 1915 edition the editor noted that

> owing to the war a few journals have suspended publication; these are left in [the lists] with a note appended as they will probably revive. As to the large number of ephemeral war publications, consisting mostly of pictures or the reports of special war-correspondents, these contain no opening for the unattached journalist and so are not mentioned.[8]

These lists are the basis for the corpus on which the findings of this chapter draw, the most comprehensive quantitative representation of the British domestic periodicals market during the years of the First World War.[9] Other titles found in other sources were added to the corpus, including little-known publications like *The Golfing Gentlewoman*, *The Landswoman* (for women working on the land) and *The Ringing World* (for bell-ringers).[10]

The aim of this chapter is to describe the periodicals that were available for the ordinary people of Britain to read during the war as they went about their usual lives and occupations. Thus the corpus does not include 'trench' journals, or refugee periodicals not in English, but it does include four well-known US magazines which were widely available in Britain: *The Atlantic Monthly*, *Munsey's Magazine*, *Scribner's Magazine* and *The Smart Set*. It excludes periodicals published for and by units or regiments, and by temporary military associations formed during the war. The corpus consists of 1,065 titles, with a range of between 968 (1914) and 793 (1919) titles in print in any one year (see Figure 15.1). Seventy-two per cent of this corpus can be categorised as magazines, with journals representing fifteen per cent and newspapers thirteen per cent of the total. However, the differences between a newspaper, journal and magazine were fluid in an era when the form of what one read was being challenged by avant-garde experimentation and market innovations.

To set the study of wartime periodicals in context, I want to discuss briefly the literary historiography for this period, although this chapter covers all periodicals, not just those publishing fiction. Samuel Hynes's magisterial history of the literary culture of the First World War, *A War Imagined* (1990), has been for decades the leading critical source on what was read during the war, succeeding Paul Fussell's *The Great War and Modern Memory* of 1975. The present chapter reconsiders the territory that Hynes examined, which is also discussed in Mary Hammond and Shafquat Towheed's edited collection *Publishing in the First World War* (2007), Randall Stevenson's *Literature and the Great War 1914–1918* (2013), and Shafquat Towheed and Edmund G. C. King's essay collection *Reading and the First World War* (2015).

Hynes's otherwise detailed and far-reaching analysis of English (not British) culture during the war is problematic in that it applies selective criteria. When discussing, for example, wartime music and art, Hynes uses critical judgements from that period to guide his assessments. He does not do this for his survey of literary production, though he does quote some contemporary reviews for individual texts. In contrast, he uses the assumptions of literary quality from the 1980s to select the texts and authors he considers to comprise 'English' wartime writing. As an example, he disparages poets included in anthologies published during the war because they are now no longer known: 'who today has heard of Henry Chappell, "the Bath Railway Porter"? Or of Harold Begbie? [. . .] But there they all are, among the war poets.'[11] His blinkered consideration of wartime literary output does not assess the work of these writers, who had been considered as good as 'the war poets' during the war, and does not consider that they, too, could be 'war poets' themselves. He thus overrides the judgement of the editors, publishers and readers who originally selected the poems, paid for the printing, and bought and read these anthologies. He misses the opportunity of considering contemporary evidence in assessing the value and nature of these texts. He also claims that 'the great Edwardians seemed to have lost their voices', arguing that the war did not produce major works of fiction because the older writers could not engage with it: a further assumption from a modern critical hegemony that privileges the views of the present over those of the past.[12]

There are three objections to this approach. The first is that of selective citation: it is dubious practice to use some contemporary authorities for one cultural field, but not for all. A consistent methodology must be used to consider all the available evidence, and Hynes does not do this. The second objection is economic. When examining a period of economic uncertainty, the contemporary commercial imperatives for what was published and bought are sound evidence for understanding the reading practices and standards of those times, but Hynes ignores this. A third objection is that Hynes does not recognise the importance of serialised fiction as constituting a significant share of the reading market in this period. His discussion of wartime fiction makes the assumption that all novels appeared first as books. He does not consider the vast amount of fiction that first appeared as serialised episodes in a periodical, before being published separately.[13] Serialisation was essential because it was the most lucrative form of publication for the author, not least because the same story could be sold to different markets, unlike books. In many cases serialisation was an inescapable part of the publication process for fiction, because publishers would test an author's selling power this way. The power of periodicals as distributors of reading material to the population (one person might buy one issue of a magazine, and five others might read that copy) is crucial when considering readership, access, literacy levels and the dissemination of the text. Hynes does mention the serialisation of Ian Hay's novel *The*

*First Hundred Thousand* (1915) in *Blackwood's Magazine*, as a one-off example,[14] yet he does not mention *The Thirty-Nine Steps*, which was published alongside Hay in that issue of *Blackwood's*, appeared in book form one month earlier than Hay's novel, and achieved far greater fame: it has never been out of print, whereas Hay's novel disappeared.

In March 1916, the Royal Commission on Paper was established in response to enemy action with the intention of reducing 'imports of paper and paper-making materials by one-third of their 1914 levels'.[15] The consequent rationing of stocks and paper components from this date means that all periodicals were obliged to print on continually coarsening paper and, as time went on, to reduce the size of their type and ration the number of pages for each issue. George Locke notes that the quality of paper stock for the very popular *Pearson's Weekly* was maintained until the middle of 1917, when 'paper shortages began to hit hard'.[16] By 1918 'paper economies had reduced the pagination to 12 pages per issue', and from the 11 May issue 'the magazine was further squeezed down to eight pages' until mid-July.[17] *The Strand Magazine* maintained its pre-war standards in paper quality and page numbers until 1917, but thereafter, as Reginald Pound records, as 'the submarine campaign intensified that year, a thinner magazine became inevitable. A smaller body type was used. The rule of "a picture on every page" was dropped, and with it colour printing "for the duration", and the print run was held at 500,000.'[18] From June 1917 Fry's Metal Foundry placed regular full-page announcements on the front page of *The Publishers' Circular and Booksellers' Record* asking publishers and printers to sell their spare stocks of 'old stereos, old electros, old type etc' for ammunition and other munitions.[19] Later in 1917 smaller appeals for waste paper appeared as well. This response to shortages for the war effort would draw on printers' stocks of plates and paper, affecting the quality of their products. Such reductions in quality could affect whether the public would continue to buy.

Unlike the opportunist publications, long-established periodicals with a large readership, like the highly successful fiction magazines *The Strand Magazine* and *The Story-Teller*, survived because they understood what the market required and delivered it well. These steady sellers retained their wartime buyers despite doubling their cover prices and printing on increasingly inferior paper stock over time. Well-established periodicals could survive even while their sales figures went down. The magazines that endured until 1919 and after did so because they had established themselves reliably in what they offered their readers, and because they had created a lasting identity for their readers. The weekly *War Illustrated* maintained its circulation well, with sales of three-quarters of a million recorded by the end of the war. It also managed to hold its inevitable overall price increase at fifty per cent, or a penny, which was far less than many established magazines could manage.[20] The *Illustrated War News*, on the other hand, stopped publication before the end of the war due to paper shortages.[21] Some journals, like *The Athenaeum*, survived by publishing monthly rather than weekly.[22] *The Book Monthly* went quarterly in late 1915, then produced only four issues in the next three years. Periodicals with an established market profile also retained their advertisers throughout the war, something which the new titles often could not do. Stephen Colclough has shown that 'the amount of money generated by newspaper sales increased significantly during the war', almost doubling the turnover at, for instance, W. H. Smith outlets from £1,529,687 in 1913–14 to £2,825,256 in 1918–19.[23] However, much of this income derived from increased cover prices, and the number of periodical titles distributed by W. H. Smith decreased overall during the war.[24] The evidence from W. H. Smith as a distributor is important because, as was recognised during the war, Smith's newsagent shops were an important point of purchase for a mass readership rather than for a specialist, single-interest elite.[25]

Present-day definitions of magazines and newspapers make distinctions between form, periodicity and content, but these are fluid across titles and time. For the Victorian period, which directly influenced the periodicals in print during the First World War, Margaret Beetham defines magazines as 'publications characterized by the variety and heterogeneity of their constituent genres and by a diversity of voices'.[26] In the Victorian period journals can be separated from magazines by their degrees of specialism. Beetham cites sporting, academic, literary and family journals, whereas magazines and 'miscellanies' contained a wide range for the casual or general reader. Examples of these would include *Punch*, which published humour and satirical commentary; *The Field*, which focused on country sports; *The Spectator*, which aligned itself with the Conservative and Unionist Party; and *The Nation* and *Land and Water*, which were bought for their quality fiction and serious journalism.[27]

In the twentieth century, the demand for scholarly publications from the proliferating research communities of the professions and the universities made the scholarly journal a more defined market presence. Learned and specialist journals, whose content had a narrow focus and were often sponsored by an institution or an organisation, were also undeniably popular in the sense that they continued to sell. *The Athenaeum* (learned critical thinking), *The Homiletic Review* (philosophy and religion), *The Gardeners' Chronicle* (for professional horticulturalists)[28] and the *Nursing Mirror and Midwives' Journal* (specialist clinical information) are examples of the type of periodical not usually considered under the heading of wartime magazines, but their commercial consistency is a strong argument for their inclusion in a discussion of the periodicals that were read widely during the war.

On the definition of the newspaper, Andrew King and Matthew Taunton note that the news presented in newspapers is defined by its topicality and the rapidity of the vehicle's turnover, with each number or edition of a newspaper being replaced frequently. Journals replaced their issues much less frequently, perhaps as slowly as once or twice a year.[29] Issues of a magazine and a journal are thus published weekly, monthly or quarterly, but not daily, whereas the editions of a newspaper are printed daily, or weekly. The content of a newspaper is primarily news and topical features, bulked up with advertising and non-time-sensitive features, whereas a magazine's contents are focused thematically on a particular kind of reader or that reader's tastes or requirements.

Whereas a magazine's or a journal's illustrations could be central to its identity (*Punch* would not be *Punch* without its cartoons, for instance), a newspaper's were not. In 1917, the publisher H. Simonis made trade-based distinctions between a newspaper, a 'picture paper', an 'illustrated paper' and a journal.[30] The 'picture papers' such as the *Daily Mail* used the new photographic journalism, but were differentiated from 'illustrated papers' (such as the *Illustrated London News*) by the assumed class of their readers (advertisements indicate this most clearly) and the tone and characters in their fiction. *The Sphere*, *The Graphic* and *The Sketch* are categorised in the corpus discussed here as magazines, since they were as near to being magazines as a weekly periodical can be, offering a 'pictorial record' of the news with photographs and illustrations alongside feature articles, and carrying fewer news stories than feature articles.[31] With the upmarket *Tatler* and *The Bystander*, these illustrated papers attracted readers with their photographs of society figures, and articles and adverts aimed at the upper classes and at officers.

The illustrations in periodicals could be crucial for retaining purchasers' loyalty. Rudyard Kipling had recognised this by 1918, when he observed to Lord Beaverbrook that 'the munition worker' (Kipling's example of the consumer of wartime popular fiction) 'is too tired or lazy to read about anything that requires thought after the work is done: they want something exciting [. . .] they are trained to go to cinemas: and they can be made to think through their eyes'.[32] Visual entertainment was certainly available in lavish illustrations and photomontages. At the beginning of the war, the elegant cover art that gave *Nash's and Pall Mall Magazine* its sophisticated appearance was exchanged for sumptuous images of muscular servicemen embracing fleshy young women. In *Punch* Mr Punch was restyled to represent the concerned citizen advising the nation, no longer in traditional *commedia dell'arte* costume, but in a decent mackintosh and suit. The traditional patriotic stance of *John Bull* was soon transformed into what David Reed calls 'nationalistic belligerence', taking the John Bull character on the cover out of his eighteenth-century top-boots and curly-brimmed hat and putting him into a sword-bearing Jolly Tar outfit, flanked by a bulldog and the Union Jack.[33]

A single publisher would often offer a stable of publications, whose agglomerated print-buying and other overheads helped keep production costs down. Cassell's published *Little Folks* and *Chums* (for children), *Cassell's Magazine*, *The Story-Teller*, *The New Magazine*, *The Quiver* (for Sunday reading), *Cassell's Saturday Journal* and *The Penny Magazine*. These titles were differentiated by their prices and the quality of the fiction they printed, but were advertised by the same publisher.[34] *Answers* was the 'principal publication' of the Amalgamated Press during the war years, which also produced *Woman's World*, *The Family Journal*, *The London Magazine* and *War Illustrated*.[35] C. Arthur Pearson Ltd published *Pearson's Weekly*, *Home Notes*, *Smith's Weekly* and *The Royal Magazine*. Joseph McAleer observes that periodical publishers in wartime revived the Victorian market in novelettes and Victorian publishing practice in their marketing strategies: 'popular magazines were grouped together in advertisements and marketed as series. The Amalgamated Press, for example, promoted *Fashions For All*, *Horner's Penny Stories*, *Forget-Me-Not*, *Woman's Weekly*, *Home Circle* and *Mother and Home* as "The Essential Six" in 1915.'[36]

Amalgamations between titles, especially in the fiction and light entertainment sector, happened throughout the war.[37] The youth market, in particular, was very quick to drop a title and replace it with a spin-off, often allowing a new title no more than a few issues to develop enough sales to justify its survival.[38] The fiction magazine *Penny Pictorial* was combined with the women's weekly *Home Circle* in 1914, as were the children's titles *Big Comic* and *Sparks*. In January 1915 the boys' magazine *Dreadnought* amalgamated with the *Boys' Journal*, and then with *Boys' Friend* in June.[39] In 1916 the more upmarket periodical *Vanity Fair* merged with *Hearth and Home*, and the Christian weeklies *Young Man* and *Young Woman* joined forces to become *Young Man and Woman*. In 1917 the girls' magazine *Girls' Realm* amalgamated with *Woman at Home*. Three successful children's story magazines, *Fun*, *Ally Sloper's Half-Holiday* and *Illustrated Bits*, came together as *Bits of Fun* in 1919. These were undoubtedly business decisions made to retain sales and reader loyalty while reducing production costs. They are also an indication of the shrinkage in those sectors. One exception is the convoluted wartime history of *T. P.'s Weekly* and *To-day*, which Louise Kane unpicks to show that this journal's existence in multiple guises depended on the strategic pursuit of different readers.[40]

In analysing the numbers in the corpus, I am focusing on trends, and the rise and fall in the numbers of titles in different categories, rather than the absolute numbers. I allocated many titles to more than one category, since they might, for example, be equally aimed at 'women' and 'flight' (e.g. *The Aerial Observer*), or 'cinema' and 'trade' (e.g. *Bioscope*). Overall, the total number of periodicals in the corpus reduced by eighteen per cent from 1914 to 1919, which gives us a baseline against which we can measure how individual categories of periodical weathered the war. Figure 15.1 shows the trajectory of the number of titles in print from 1914 to 1919, with the solid line representing all titles in the corpus. It also shows the top seven categories of periodical, those categories with the largest number of titles over the period. Almost every category lost titles by 1919, but some lost more than others. I discuss some of these in more detail below.

This general market depression is important to remember when considering the cases of individual periodicals during the war, and when considering circulation. David Reed's work on British and US popular magazines treats *John Bull*'s decline in circulation as particular to that title, while this was probably an industry-wide experience.[41] Yet Joseph McAleer shows that there was volatility in the war years for individual titles and publishers. In the domestic fiction market, D. C. Thomson's *Red Letter* experienced a dramatic rise in circulation during the war years, compared to barely perceptible increases from Thomson's *The People's Friend* and *Weekly Welcome*.[42] Net profits for the Religious Tract Society's *The Girls' Own Paper* were much higher than those for *The Boys' Own Paper* and for *Sunday at Home*, a religious fiction weekly, but the profits from all three titles rose and fell during the war, followed by a fast recovery in 1919–20.[43] The possible causes of this movement, discussed below, are various but can be broadly attributed to (1) rising production costs which restricted the products on offer in number and in quality and size; (2) a radically changed consumer profile, with men and women experiencing very different occupations and incomes by 1919 than they had at the beginning of the war; and (3) the rising prices of the wartime domestic economy, which restricted readers' purchasing power.

The largest single category in the corpus is fiction magazines, with 209 titles in 1914. This reduced by nineteen per cent to 169 titles by 1919. The next largest category was religious titles, which began the war with 126 titles, increasing by one in 1915, and then reducing by twenty-seven per cent to ninety-five titles. The only other category of over fifty titles was trade, the periodicals catering for manual and craft professions, and commercial suppliers, which began the war with ninety-seven titles, reducing by twelve per cent to eighty-five in 1919. The fifth of the corpus represented by fiction magazines must be considered as a result of source bias. The W&AY was marketed to people who wrote fiction to sell to magazines, and thus would have been more likely to include publishing opportunities for this readership, rather than, say, for periodicals that did not accept fiction (although many titles on the W&AY lists are noted as not accepting unsolicited submissions). Nonetheless, it is no surprise that fiction was so popular: many of the fiction magazines from this period are still familiar names today for the authors they first published (for instance, Arthur Conan Doyle and P. G. Wodehouse in *The Strand Magazine*, Dornford Yates in *The Windsor Magazine*, William Le Queux in *The Premier Magazine*, and Sax Rohmer in *The Story-Teller*), and have attracted a minor industry in critical and bibliographical attention. These, and less familiar fiction titles from this period, such as *Answers' Library*, *Cassell's Saturday Journal*, *Everyday*, *The Indiaman*, *Lady's Pictorial*, *The Nelson Lee Library*, *The People's Journal*, *Red Magazine*, *Tit-Bits' Novels*, *The Weekly Friend* and *Young Folks' Tales*, sold well because wartime conditions created a new readership of servicemen and women who were newly in need of cheap, portable, disposable or transferable entertainment. This was also true for the workers in wartime occupations at home, in factories, farms and in hospitals. The fiction magazine was ideally suited to all their needs for distraction, escape, comfort, reassurance, amusement, stimulation and pleasure. *The Strand*'s biographer observes that 'wartime readers wanted diversion from the over-riding theme. The editorial policy was re-defined with the accent on entertainment.'[44] However, this category's nineteen per cent reduction during the war years suggests how it weathered economic conditions, by shedding the weakest. The largest net losses of fiction titles happened in 1915–16 and in 1916–17. The subsequent years lost fewer titles, which suggests that the crisis of the middle years of the war, which expressed itself in other ways in other categories (discussed below), caused most damage.

The need in wartime for reading material that delivered consolation and reassurance as well as a strengthening of the spirit can be seen in the size of the religious periodical market. Many of these titles were sponsored by individual churches or denominations, and the *Aldersgate Primitive Methodist Magazine*, the *British Congregationalist and Examiner*, *The Catholic Fireside*, the *Free Church Chronicle* and *The Jewish Express* are examples of periodicals with guaranteed sales from such congregations. Some of the religious periodicals were professionally religious: *The Hibbert Review* was an academic theological journal, *The British Missionary* and *Indian Church Magazine* catered for Christian evangelists overseas, and *The Preachers' Magazine* for evangelism at home. There was reading for followers of a wide range of religions in periodicals such as *The Catholic Herald*, *The Jewish Chronicle*, *The Buddhist Review*, *The Church Times*, *The Friend*, *Moslem World* and *The Zionist Review*. Other periodicals categorised as 'religious' were more general in their scope, such as *Dawn of Day* (religious fiction), *Dublin Review* (a religious review), *Golden Rule* (religious reading for older children) and *Golden Sunbeams* (religious reading for the young). Despite this strong presence, religious periodicals reduced overall by twenty-seven per cent, a bigger reduction than for the fiction category, and experienced more losses later in the war, in 1916–17 and 1917–18. The reason for so many titles disappearing must be their dropping sales that could not accommodate rising production costs.

The third largest category, the trade periodicals, includes titles for the professions, trades and commerce. The lines of work indicated by the titles of *The Accountant*, *Bazaar*, *The Bookseller*, *Building World*, *The Colliery Guardian*, *Exchange and Mart*, *Iron and Coal Trades Review*, *Library World*, *Machinery Market*, *Photographic Dealer*, *Stone Trades Journal* and *World Carriers and Carrying Review* illustrate the variety of trades which supported this sector of the market. Again, as with some of the religious periodicals, a large number of these titles would have been read as a professional requirement as well as to satisfy personal interests, yet this does not deny them their popularity. They clearly served their readers' needs, and gave value for money in increasingly straitened times. This category had a smaller reduction in titles, only twelve per cent, suggesting that business continued steadily during the war, and that the trades needed their periodicals. Their relatively robust market presence indicates the basis for the post-war economic recovery in 1919.

While a handful of categories showed an overall increase in their numbers, many more experienced a definite rise in demand before succumbing to the cross-category slump by 1919. Periodicals on children, China, domestic subjects, gardening, humour, India, law, music, politics, religion, Russia, sport and women's interests all increased by at least one title in the middle years of the war, suggesting that opportunistic publishing ventures were spurred on by more than simply selling news about the war. The agriculture, animals, culture, literature and stamps categories ended the war with more titles than they had had in 1914. This reflects the stability of these subjects as leisure interests, as well as the probable stimulation by wartime food rationing of animal husbandry (hens, pigeons and pigs were kept by many families).

The establishment of the Ministry of Munitions in 1915 brought hundreds of women into salaried employment, enabling them to live independently away from home if they chose, or if their job took them. Women were targeted by publishers and advertisers through periodicals because of their increased spending power.[45] The money and leisure time introduced into their lives by employment would attract them to women's magazines, and to other reading areas, both professional and personal. Women's periodicals experienced very little reduction in titles, rising from forty to forty-three titles in 1916, and then only falling to thirty-five by 1919. This was considerably less than the total reduction in titles over all periodicals in the corpus, indicating that women's periodicals maintained the healthiest sector.

Subject categories showing a static performance can be regarded as positive evidence of the popularity of the subject, if not the titles themselves, holding their market share during challenging economic circumstances. These include the niche areas of bee-keeping (*The Bee-Keepers' Record* and *British Bee Journal*), the occult (*Light* and *The Occult Review*), fashion and nursing. These categories have relatively small numbers of titles – under ten each, and in some cases fewer than four – but demonstrate that these sectors of the market were clearly not shrinking, compared to much larger sectors. The steady demand for nursing periodicals in particular is directly attributable to evolving clinical and surgical practice during the war, and the entry into the profession of hundreds of British women and men.

The contemporary observer H. Simonis noted in 1917 that the 'sporting daily' was hit very hard by the war, by which he meant sports newspapers such as *The Racing Times*.[46] This observation is supported by evidence from the corpus showing that the weekly and monthly sporting magazines *Fox-Hound*, *Fry's Magazine of Sport*, *Hockey*, *Hockey Field*, *Ladies' Golf*, *Lotinga's Weekly*, *Sports Library*, *Swimming Magazine* and *World of Golf* all ceased publication during or by the end of the war. In addition, the thirty-six sporting periodicals published in 1914 had reduced to twenty-eight by 1919, a reduction of a little under a quarter.[47] This shrinking of the readership of sporting periodicals was presumably caused by the removal of most of their readers into the army and other wartime services, and also overseas, with less free time and fewer opportunities to take part in sport. Clearly the sector had to shrink to cope with reduced demand, and some magazines barely survived at all. In 1918 *The Golfing*

*Gentlewoman* was printed on the two sides of a single magazine page, a sad but brave shadow of its eight-page existence from only two years earlier.

Naturally, when war broke out, periodical publishers responded in different ways. War news emerged as a separate category, with the opportunist publication of eight periodicals at the outbreak of war, as mentioned above. Some of these were amalgamated or changed their names, responding to the public taste. The *Penny War Weekly* became the *Vivid War Weekly* in January 1915, and then was incorporated into *War Illustrated* in 1916.[48] The changing focus in its name from price and accessibility to sensation to simple illustration, which we can assume were publishing decisions to maximise sales, suggests the support of a readership participating in the construction of the war as a movement in history rather than merely observing the passing show.

We can see more clearly how the war affected periodical publishing in new technologies by looking at the numbers for groups of magazines selected by theme. It might be assumed that the military category (for example, *The War Office Times*, *Army and Navy Gazette*, *Bluejacket and Soldier*, *Broad Arrow* and *Fleet*) would have been likely to have increased its market presence as the war went on, but although it peaked at fourteen titles in 1917, it experienced the same reduction by 1919 as most other categories, ending the war with ten. There is only one radio periodical listed in the corpus, *Wireless World*. Until 1913 this was called *The Marconigraph*, published by the Marconi Company for their professional wireless operators from 1911 to 1913, but it remained the only magazine for radio amateurs and professionals alike during the war years, suggesting that it fulfilled all the needs of this new technical readership.[49] The periodicals marketed to driving enthusiasts reduced in number by nearly a quarter to thirteen by 1919, and sailing magazines dropped to three, whereas magazines about flying dropped to three in 1916, but were up to nearly pre-war levels at five by 1919. There were, however, twice the number of driving magazines than sailing or flying titles on the market, reflecting its accessibility as the more affordable sector, with titles like *Autocar*, *Autocycle* and *Automobile Engineer* surviving the war along with *King's Highway*, *Light Car and Cycle Car* and *Motor News*.

The direct effects of the war on periodical publishing can be seen most dramatically in the category of 'youth' magazines. Despite the use of 'boy' or 'girl' in the titles of many of these, they published fiction for a readership made adult by war responsibilities. The numbers of 'youth' magazine titles experienced a notable reduction by 1919 of forty-three per cent, with fourteen lost out of thirty-two – more than twice the overall reduction. *The Magnet* advertised its availability via Hachette et Cie in France throughout the war years,[50] hoping to attract buyers from British servicemen posted there. But the boys and young men who had been reading the *Boys' Journal*, the *Boys' Own Library* and the *Boys' Realm* were dying in large numbers, and those three titles, as an example, disappeared from the market. As well as this reduction in readership numbers, many servicemen would have developed different tastes once they had joined the armed forces.

Randall Stevenson points out that 'censorship and suppression by the military and the Press Bureau, along with often-bellicose patriotism in newspapers' was heavily influential in determining what the public would read. Magazines as well as newspapers would offer 'only a carefully sanitised description [. . .] through the rhetoric of "deathless deeds"'.[51] The Defence of the Realm Acts (DORA) of August and November 1914 prevented the publication of explicit imagery in mass-market print, along with anything else diminishing morale. Samuel Hynes observes that 'DORA gave the State unlimited power to control the instruments of communication and the transmission of information'.[52] 'Likely to cause disaffection' was the key phrase that could be applied to anything written or expressed:

> [In] 1916 amendments made the power of DORA over the arts more explicit: no one should either by word of mouth or in writing or in any newspaper, periodical, book, circular, or other printed publication, spread reports or make statements intended or likely to cause disaffection, or to prejudice recruiting or training, or produce any play or picture or film that would do any of these things.[53]

Cate Haste has shown that under the influence of the Acts, the Press Bureau exercised censorship and negative propaganda, suppressing information as well as propagating misleading or false information. It issued 700 sets of instructions to editors, and 'was asked to admonish individual editors for indiscreet publications as often as three times a week'.[54] Fiction magazines could avoid non-compliance with the Act by paying close attention to the romances, thrilling stories and sentimental plots that they published. In concert with incomplete and slanted information appearing in wartime periodicals was what Stevenson calls the 'dis-integrity' caused by adverts, fiction and commentary that avoided any reference to war.[55] This would have been compounded by the relentlessly cheerful visual messages given by advertisements for foodstuffs and equipment marketed to servicemen and their families. Adding a military kilt or a jaunty service cap to illustrate an advert for a tin of Mackintosh's toffee valorised the product through solely heroic terms, and perpetuated the disassociation that servicemen felt for civilians.

The serviceman's inability to speak about his experiences under fire was exacerbated by civilians on the home front who assumed that their normal lives were universal. Rose Macaulay's *Non-Combatants and Others* (1916) is exceptional for a novel published in wartime for delineating the dislocation between servicemen's experiences. Macaulay has a clergyman character discuss three real-life religious periodicals to indicate the range of opinions that enabled the British periodicals market to flourish in wartime:

> 'I came home and read the *Church Times*, the *Challenge* and the *Cambridge Magazine*. All interesting in their way, and quite different [. . .] People write to the *Challenge* every week asking "Are Christianity and War compatible?" and come to the conclusion that they are not, but that Christians may have to fight. People write to the *Church Times* saying that they have found a clergyman who won't wear a chasuble, and what shall they do to him? People write to the *Cambridge Magazine* saying that every one over forty should be disenfranchised and interned, if not shot.'[56]

Macaulay also emphasises the ephemerality of the periodical press in this novel. Titles of books, magazines and newspapers, invented and real, appear briefly throughout the narrative, causing different degrees of impact on the characters, but ultimately functioning as a backdrop to their lives. The *Evening Thrill* and the *Daily Message* are euphemisms for the daily newspapers that Macaulay pillories for their propaganda.[57] The leading protagonist goes to visit the clergyman, and walks past a newspaper stall with an alarming banner headline about war losses. The narrator observes: 'Evening papers, of course, are interesting, and should not really be missed; they often contain so much news that is ephemeral and fades away before the morning and into the light of common day.'[58] The effect of their news is also ephemeral, and can be rejected if war is too much for the person waiting, impotent to act, at home. The protagonist's younger brother and particular friend are in the trenches, so she needs to forget bad news about the war: '"Special. War Extra. British driven back . . ." The cries, the placards, were like lost ships tossed lightly on the top of wild waters. They would soon sink, if one did not listen or look . . .'[59] The protagonist does not want to think about what her menfolk might be suffering, but she also does not want to trust the newspapers, or believe what the magazines say.

Other characters in Macaulay's novel positively relish their daily reading of magazines and newspapers, because they reflect their daily lives. This represents the human enjoyment of reading one's life 'in the papers', which would validate the novel experience of wartime conditions, and provide reassurance that this was part of a larger experience. As an example of a popular wartime fiction magazine, *Betty's Magazine* was marketed to working-class girls working in mills and munitions factories, and offered novelette fiction, articles on handicrafts, advice, and explicit instruction on how best to support the troops. In its 1916 issues it published stories entitled 'A Shell-Maker's Sweetheart', by Grahame Fellowes, 'Sacrifice and Reward: A Thrilling Romance in a Munitions Factory', by M. C. Ramsay, and 'Keep the Home Fires Burning: Bessie, the Girl Chauffeur', 'Mary the Car Conductor' and 'Eileen the Commissionaire', by Hilda M. K. Neild, all realistic and mildly sentimental narratives about wartime service by women.

Other readerships were similarly protected from unpleasantness and supported in their wartime service during the war. David Finkelstein has shown how *Blackwood's Magazine* required its contributors of fiction and non-fiction alike to 'conform to the literary mould established by Beith's work', referring to Ian Hay (the pen-name of John Hay Beith) and *The First Hundred Thousand*, mentioned above. This 'mould' ensured that the war was 'humanized and made relevant to readers'.[60] Michael Joseph noted that when writing fiction for 'a particular and restricted market like the magazines it is [. . .] necessary to conform to type'.[61] Conformity becomes homogeneity, since 'what editors want are [. . .] stories of the same pattern which has hitherto found favour with their readers'.[62]

There is an obvious propagandist dimension to fiction written around topical situations and the profiles of its readership in wartime. None of the stories in *Betty's Magazine* advocated a walk-out from a munitions factory on health and safety grounds, or attempted to disseminate a pacifist message (unlike Macaulay's novel). Like the more serious war news periodicals, fiction magazines that propagated the details of wartime life in their content articulated propaganda and gave necessary information to their readers. The didacticism delivered through wartime periodicals was direct instruction for how readers should behave, and training in how they could conduct themselves. There is a sense of choice, but a limited one. It would be impossible to find a popular wartime periodical whose fiction or features encouraged soldiers to desert, workers to strike, or those serving in war industries to refuse to contribute any more to the war effort that was killing their friends and relatives, and in many cases themselves. Pacifist material was largely disseminated through pamphlets or books. Thus it should be remembered that while the war periodical is a widely sourced reflection of popular opinion, it was limited by politics and by statute, a partial reflection of the historical record that should be used with caution, in context, in research and study.

## Notes

1. Kate Macdonald, 'Translating Propaganda: John Buchan's Writing during the First World War', in Mary Hammond and Shafquat Towheed (eds), *Publishing in the First World War: Essays in Book History* (Basingstoke: Palgrave Macmillan, 2007), pp. 181–201 (pp. 182–7).
2. Simon Nowell-Smith, *The House of Cassell 1848–1958* (London: Cassell & Co., 1958), p. 206.
3. Letter from John Buchan to George Brown, 6 August 1914, Thomas Nelson papers Gen 1728/B/5/69, and letter from John Buchan to George Brown, 20 August 1914, Gen 1728/B/7/82a and 82b, Edinburgh University Library Special Collections (EUSC).
4. Letter from John Buchan to George Brown, 20 August 1914, Gen 1728/B/7/82a, EUSC.
5. Letter from George Brown to John Buchan, 4 February 1915, Gen 1728/B/5/228, EUSC.
6. *The Illustrated First World War*, <http://www.illustratedfirstworldwar.com/the-titles/the-illusted-war-news/> (last accessed 18 November 2016).
7. I owe many thanks to David Marsh for his assistance with statistical analysis, and for creating Figure 15.1 from my data.
8. Anon., 'Preface', *The Writers' and Artists' Yearbook 1915* (London: A & C Black, 1915), pp. v–vi (p. vi).
9. Kate Macdonald, *British First World War Periodicals 1914–1919*, University of Reading, doi: <http://dx.doi.org/10.17864/1947.46> (last accessed 18 November 2016).
10. Other sources used to construct the corpus were the British Library catalogue; SOLO, the online catalogue of the Bodleian Library, University of Oxford; the Reading Experience Database hosted by the Open University (<http://www.open.ac.uk/Arts/RED>); H. Simonis, *The Street of Ink* (London: Cassell & Co., 1917); Joseph McAleer, *Popular Reading and Publishing in Britain, 1914–1950* (Oxford: Oxford University Press, 1992); Michael Ashley, *The Age of the Storytellers: British Popular Fiction Magazines, 1880–1920* (London: Oak Knoll Press and the British Library, 2006); Patrick Belk's Pulp Magazine Project (<http://www.pulpmags.org>); the digitised periodicals in Stephen Donovan's Conrad First site (<http://www.conradfirst.net>); and the Fiction Mags Index, edited by William B. Contento and Phil Stephensen-Payne (<http://www.philsp.com/homeville/fmi/0start.htm>). All websites last accessed 18 November 2016.
11. Samuel Hynes, *A War Imagined: The First World War and English Culture* (London: Bodley Head, 1990), p. 28.
12. Ibid., p. 104.
13. Ibid., p. 47.
14. Ibid., pp. 48–9.
15. McAleer, *Popular Reading and Publishing in Britain*, p. 52.
16. George Locke, *Pearson's Weekly: A Checklist of Fiction 1890–1939* ([London]: Ferret Fantasy, 1990), p. 52.
17. Ibid., p. 53.
18. Reginald Pound, *The Strand Magazine, 1891–1950* (London: Heinemann, 1966), p. 127.
19. Front page advertisement, *The Publishers' Circular and Booksellers' Record*, 106.2660 (23 June 1917), 597.
20. Jonathan Rayner, '"Where 'Daddy' and Danger Were": The Portrayal of Children in *War Illustrated*, 1914–16', *Childhood in the Past: An International Journal*, 7.1 (May 2014), 14–34 (15).

21. *The Illustrated First World War*, <http://www.illustratedfirstworldwar.com/the-titles/the-illustated-war-news> (last accessed 18 November 2016).
22. Anon., 'The Publishers' Circular', *The Publishers' Circular and Booksellers' Record*, 103.2582 (25 December 1915), 643.
23. Stephen Colclough, '"No such bookselling has ever taken place in this country": Propaganda and the Wartime Distribution Practices of W. H. Smith & Son', in Hammond and Towheed (eds), *Publishing in the First World War*, pp. 27–45 (p. 29).
24. Ibid., pp. 30–1.
25. Ibid., p. 37.
26. Margaret Beetham, 'Magazines', in Laurel Brake and Marysa Demoor (eds), *The Dictionary of Nineteenth-Century Journalism in Great Britain and Ireland* (Ghent and London: Academia Press and the British Library, 2009), pp. 391–2 (p. 391).
27. Simonis, *The Street of Ink*, pp. 257–75.
28. Ursula Buchan, *A Green and Pleasant Land: How England's Gardeners Fought the Second World War* (London: Windmill Books, 2014), p. 23.
29. Andrew King and Matthew Taunton, 'News', in Brake and Demoor (eds), *The Dictionary of Nineteenth-Century Journalism*, pp. 448–50.
30. Simonis, *The Street of Ink*, p. vi.
31. Ibid., pp. 238–56.
32. Letter from Rudyard Kipling to Lord Beaverbrook, 25 February 1918, in *The Letters of Rudyard Kipling, Volume 4: 1911–19*, ed. Thomas Pinney (Basingstoke: Macmillan, 1999), p. 485.
33. Cartoon of John Bull, in David Reed, *The Popular Magazine in Britain and the United States 1880–1960* (London: British Library, 1997), p. 139.
34. Simonis, *The Street of Ink*, p. 277.
35. Ibid., p. 296.
36. McAleer, *Popular Reading and Publishing in Britain*, p. 55.
37. Brian Braithwaite and Joan Barrell, *The Business of Women's Magazines: The Agonies and the Ecstacies* (London: Associated Business Press, 1979), p. 11.
38. Robert J. Kirkpatrick, *From the Penny Dreadful to the Ha'Penny Dreadfuller: A Bibliographic History of the Boys' Periodical in Britain, 1762–1950* (London: British Library, 2013), chapter 10.
39. Ibid., p. 388.
40. Louise Kane, '"Chippy Bits Periodicals" and the Middlebrow: Holbrook Jackson, *T. P.'s Weekly* (1902–1916) and *To-day* (1917–1923)', *The Journal of Modern Periodical Studies*, 6.1 (2015), 23–43.
41. Reed, *The Popular Magazine in Britain and the United States*, p. 140.
42. McAleer, *Popular Reading and Publishing in Britain*, pp. 174–5.
43. Ibid., pp. 216, 218.
44. Pound, *The Strand Magazine*, p. 127.
45. McAleer, *Popular Reading and Publishing in Britain*, p. 53.
46. Simonis, *The Street of Ink*, p. 121.
47. These were: *Badminton Magazine*, *Baily's Magazine of Sport and Pastimes*, *Court Journal*, *Cycling*, *Cyclists' Touring Club Gazette*, *The Field*, *Golf Illustrated*, *Golf Monthly*, *Golfing*, *The Golfing Gentlewoman*, *Health and Strength*, *Horse and Hound*, *Illustrated Sporting and Dramatic News*, *The Ladies' Field*, *Land and Water*, *Lawn Tennis and Badminton*, *Mirror of Life*, *Referee*, *Rifleman*, *Scottish Country Life*, *Scottish Field*, *Shooting Times and British Sportsman*, *Sporting Life*, *Sporting Times*, *Sportsman*, *Topical Times*, *Town Topics* and *Vanity Fair*.
48. British Library Catalogue, '*Vivid War Weekly*'.
49. My thanks to Elizabeth Bruton for this information.

50. This was done throughout the war; an example may be seen at *The Magnet Library*, 12.525, p. 15; see <http://www.friardale.co.uk/Magnet/1918/Magnet%200525-A.pdf> (last accessed 18 November 2016). Thanks to George Simmers for this information.
51. Randall Stevenson, *Literature and the Great War 1914–1918* (Oxford: Oxford University Press, 2013), p. 24.
52. Hynes, *A War Imagined*, p. 79.
53. Ibid., p. 80.
54. Cate Haste, *Keep the Home Fires Burning: Propaganda in the First World War* (London: Penguin Books, 1977), pp. 30–1.
55. Stevenson, *Literature and the Great War*, p. 41.
56. Rose Macaulay, *Non-Combatants and Others* (1916; London: Methuen, 1986), pp. 48–9.
57. Ibid., p. 53.
58. Ibid., pp. 41–2.
59. Ibid., p. 51.
60. David Finkelstein, 'Literature, Propaganda, and the First World War: The Case of *Blackwood's Magazine*', in Jeremy Treglown and Bridget Bennett (eds), *Grub Street and the Ivory Tower: Literary Journalism and Literary Scholarship from Fielding to the Internet* (Oxford: Clarendon Press, 1998), pp. 91–111 (pp. 103–4).
61. Michael Joseph, *The Magazine Story, With Ten Examples Analysed* (London: Hutchinson & Co., 1928), p. 10.
62. Ibid., p. 17.

# 16

# Evolving Wartime Print Cultures of the Anglo-American Modern Literary Renaissance

*Christopher J. La Casse*

Scholars have depicted the First World War as a watershed event for modernism, but within this broad narrative of historic rupture, the local histories of 'little magazines' provide opportunities to re-envision the many underlying factors and nuances that are crucial to a more complete understanding of how this formative moment shaped literary history. The Anglo-American modern literary renaissance emerged and developed across 'little magazines' – a term referring to the small circulation and often short-lived (or irregular) appearances of low-budget non-commercial publications. Writers and artists could consolidate into collectives to exchange innovative art, experimental literature, and modern socio-political views that challenged the status quo. While some magazines were financially backed by patronage, other print communities existed in mutually supportive counter-cultural networks, sharing advertisements, readers and even regular contributors. Once the First World War erupted across Europe, these precarious publications faced several challenges that tested their commitment to avant-gardism. Economic, political and cultural pressures caused many editors to adopt mainstream nationalism or to adapt as they laboured through adversity while still using their publications as forums to advance political and cultural change. The interdisciplinary methods of periodical scholarship can be used to re-envision this formative moment by enabling scholars to understand the relationship between little magazines and the wider Anglo-American public spheres.

Current historiographies in print culture and periodical studies have examined how experimental aesthetic programmes were brought into the hands of broader readerships through various 'institutions of modernism'.[1] 'Periodical codes' – which range from format and materiality to distribution practices, networks and readerships – enable scholars to study the publication and public contexts through which modernism circulated to reconstruct how modernist culture and aesthetics were uniquely institutionalised.[2] Even though the field has become productively interdisciplinary, many revisionary histories still offer under-explored political contexts, failing to consider, for instance, how the vibrant radical political activism of the prewar avant-garde was disrupted across print communities and usually disappeared entirely from editorial agendas. This chapter briefly surveys the trajectories of several periodicals. The list consists of familiar names, but it also looks beyond the canonical modernist little magazines. British titles include *The English Review*, *Poetry and*

*Drama*, *Georgian Poetry*, *Blast* and *Wheels*, with *Poetry*, *The Little Review*, *The Masses* and *Mother Earth* from across the Atlantic. Some of these little magazines were avant-garde, with heterogeneous forms that encouraged a cross-pollination of literature and an assortment of radical politics that posed multiple oppositional stances to the mainstream; there were also mainstream versions of modernism produced for general audiences as well as ventures that were coterie modernist, with purely literary interests distributed in forms that resembled anthologies. By exploring an inclusive set of titles that assumed a range of periodical formats, this overview recovers a fuller picture of literary history that takes into account the diverse range of institutional channels that uniquely disseminated modernism while adapting to evolving wartime climates.

Several British and US magazines went out of print or changed between 4 August 1914 and 11 November 1918, but the timeline and circumstances that influenced the British and American print cultures differed. Editorial staff and contributors grew thin as many young modernists volunteered or were later conscripted; government suppression compromised free speech; patrons withdrew support for political reasons; and paper shortages posed additional financial difficulties. In 1915, British mills experienced increased operating costs due to price hikes for coal, imported pulp, shipping costs and wages.[3] One estimate claimed that labour and material shortages had decreased the operations of British mills to approximately fifteen to twenty per cent of their pre-war production levels.[4] By the late months of the war, the American paper and publishing industries began to endure similar circumstances, which induced the War Industries Conservation Board to create regulations and mandatory conservation pledges that publishers and stationers were required to sign before receiving one ton or more of annual paper stock.[5]

In Britain, political pressures also came immediately. Only four days after joining the war, the government passed the Defence of the Realm Act (DORA). DORA was written and revised to prevent 'disaffection or alarm' – a broadly applicable measure intended to repress dissent.[6] In America, the literary scene still flourished – perhaps nurtured by the sudden lull in Britain. Ezra Pound, an American expatriate living in London, sent many international literary luminaries abroad (particularly to *Poetry* and then *The Little Review*), helping British modernism endure while adding to a growing critical mass of American modernists who appeared in new periodical ventures.[7] US editors had an additional two years to establish their little magazines, but shortly after their nation's 1917 entry into the war, the Selective Service Act and a culture of volunteerism drew many writers away while editors faced a particularly repressive period in American history. Editors with potentially obscene material already drew scrutiny under the Comstock Law. With the introduction of the Espionage Act of 1917 and the Sedition Act of 1918, editors with pacifist agendas also faced possible suppression. Included in the selection of US titles examined here are socialist and anarchist little magazines that were forced to fold or dramatically change once the US Postmaster General impounded issues from publications already barely in the black. Taking a broad and quantifiable view of lower circulation numbers or suspended operations captures an unsurprising decline in counter-cultural activities.

The disappearance or silence of print communities affiliated with the pre-war avant-garde was not the only change. Alongside political and economic pressures, wartime culture altered the course of the literary renaissance. Before the political climate produced sudden divisions, British modernist, Georgian and Edwardian writers appeared together in periodicals that straddled generational and aesthetic differences. After war broke out, Edwardians and Georgians were largely responsible for producing cultural politics and literary tastes that were popularised in Great Britain and exported abroad. While Rupert Brooke's death made him an icon, spurring a demand for soldier-poet collections, the popular British Edwardian writers incited a war on German *Kultur*. Almost every little magazine from this selection contested or absorbed these trends from their unique national, aesthetic or political perspectives – launching oppositional narratives through literature and political commentary or adopting popular wartime tastes. Modernism's historiography is incomplete without scholarship that examines how wartime duress reshaped editorial agendas and policies, dissolved alliances, and reconfigured transatlantic print networks, as editors realigned their magazines within counter-cultural and/or nationalist mainstream networks.

British modernism first emerged in the pre-war years in eclectic periodicals with inclusive editorial policies. One such venue, *The English Review*, was a monthly with middle- and upper-class appeal in Edwardian London.[8] The original editor, Ford Madox Hueffer (later Ford), helped launch the career of modernists Ezra Pound, Wyndham Lewis and D. H. Lawrence while also consolidating his popular peers of the Edwardian generation, such as H. G. Wells, Arnold Bennett, Thomas Hardy, John Galsworthy, Henry James and Joseph Conrad. Ford devised the periodical to assume a central, rather than fringe, position in the public sphere.[9] In its content, material form and editorial vision, *The English Review* emulated the prominent monthly reviews that emerged during the mid-Victorian era.[10] For 2s. 6d., readers could purchase the 200-page publication, with its heterodox contents printed in single columns on thick quality paper.[11] Ford outwardly called for 'no party bias', and attempted to maintain heterodoxy to create a 'disinterested' space that encouraged debate.[12] His tenure, however, was short-lived. The £5,000 endowment provided by Arthur Marwood only produced four issues, and, moreover, Ford was woefully inept in financial and organisational matters.[13] The planned print run of 5,000 rarely exceeded 1,000 readers, and he quarrelled with contributors, whom he rarely paid in full or at all.[14] In 1910, Alfred Mond, a Liberal MP, purchased *The English Review*, replacing Ford with Austin Harrison, who increased advertising to about twenty-four pages and lowered the price to a shilling to reach more readers, which increased circulation to 15,000.[15] Harrison provided some continuity by publishing forty-six of the old guard; even Ford would appear fourteen times in eleven years.[16] The editorial vision nonetheless changed, as Harrison assumed an unambiguously partisan agenda through his 'diatribes' against Conservative and Unionist policies.[17]

Many of Austin Harrison's Edwardian peers and contributors heeded the national call in the autumn of 1914 by lending their pens to Wellington House, the building that housed Britain's Propaganda Bureau. C. F. G. Masterman received pledges of support from notables including John Galsworthy, J. M. Barrie, Arthur Conan Doyle, H. G. Wells, Arnold Bennett, Robert Bridges, Ford Madox Ford, Joseph Conrad and Rudyard Kipling.[18] The British war on *Kultur* derived, at least partly, from earlier tensions. Pre-war Germany had risen to become Britain's economic rival, expanding its colonies across Africa and rapidly modernising its fleet. During the early weeks of the war, the German army bypassed French fortifications by invading neutral Belgium, a manoeuvre that proved a costly political misstep. British newspapers increasingly printed unsubstantiated atrocity reports of Prussian war crimes while propagandists alleged that the conflict was caused by 'German militarism and lust for conquest'.[19] The destruction of Louvain marked an important development in this narrative. According to Adrian Gregory, the press began to focus on property destruction, especially cultural monuments. The term 'Hun' subsequently became synonymous with vandal. Following Louvain, Kipling was the first to use 'Hun' in the *Daily Mail* in his poem 'For All We Have and Are'.[20] After German artillery shelled Reims Cathedral, the *Daily Mail* produced photographs and captions that claimed to verify the accusation that Prussians were the enemies of civilisation.[21] In addition to newspapers, British and American critics advanced the claim that militarism was pervasive in German *Kultur* by arguing that Nietzsche's *Übermensch* concept was the 'martial ideal of imperial Germany'.[22] Edwardian writers were among those who drew a connection between the philosopher's 'vision of power and mastery' and accusations that Germany was pursuing 'Bismarck's imperialist blood-and-iron vision of [national] ascendancy'.[23]

In their November 1914 issues, *Poetry* and *The Little Review* contributors refuted British propaganda and viewed Europe's conflict from unique political perspectives. In *Poetry*'s 'War Number', Alice Corbin Henderson suggested that US exceptionalism was reflected in its citizens' cultural expressions: 'No future historian of the United States will be able to use quotations from her twentieth-century poets in support of an imperial policy of conquest and slaughter.'[24] Unlike American poets, who naturally celebrated democracy, she claimed that Hardy, Kipling, Bridges and Masefield were composing 'inadequate' patriotic verse because they were subconsciously 'better democrats than imperialists'.[25] Since Nietzsche was widely read and important to the revolutionary political and aesthetic conceptions of *The Little Review*, several contributors refuted Edwardian vilification of the German philosopher. Margaret Anderson's short editorial expressed exasperation that even John Galsworthy had joined the campaign in his *Scribner's Magazine* article that racially essentialised the 'Prussian superman of Nietzsche's Cult'. In the same issue, George Soule's 'Zarathustra Vs. Rheims' attributed Thomas Hardy's misreading of Nietzsche to the highly interpretative nature of the philosopher's aphoristic style. *The Little Review*'s early regulars fashioned versions of philosophical individualism by combining Nietzsche's anti-foundationalist principles with anarchism. For that reason, Soule refuted the common conflation of Nietzsche and imperialism from an anti-capitalist perspective: 'It is a pathetic absurdity to think that Nietzsche would have found the good war in the present struggle for territory and commercial supremacy.'[26]

Despite his generation's political leanings, Harrison maintained *The English Review*'s independence by remaining critical of government policy, refusing to print atrocity reports, and refuting the demonisation of Nietzsche.[27] Still, Harrison's early editorials echoed his pre-war warnings of German militarism, and as the stalemate continued into 1915, he called for conscription and increased munitions production.[28] Although some contributors were critical of the first year's surge in nationalistic jingles, the selection of contents also reflected the wider public's mood: contributors glorified death in the abstract, memorialised war heroes, fixated on martyr poets, and added to the revival in English pastoral verse.[29] As the conflict dragged on, British culture began imagining the filth and horror of trench warfare. *The English Review*'s poetry reflected this bleaker perspective while Harrison found reason for optimism. Following the Russian Revolution and the US entry into the war, his editorials began to envision a new world order formed by the working class aligning across national differences to sue for peace.[30] Once restricted to nationalist perspectives and networks, late-war editorials instead suggested *The English Review* was imagining wider, more idealistic, international relationships.

Harold Monro's editorial ventures also included pre-war publications that exemplify early British engagement in a growing international network for the arts. Innovative art movements had recently emerged on the Continent: while Henri Matisse's use of colour was revolutionary, Pablo Picasso reimagined how to draw a line. In 1909, the Parisian newspaper *Le Figaro* featured F. T. Marinetti's Futurist manifesto that called for artists to celebrate technology, industrial capitalism and the automobile.[31] In 1912, Monro began editing *The Poetry Review* (1912–15), a monthly with an array of critical commentary on modern poetry. Ezra Pound contributed one of his earliest statements that took to task the 'blurry' language of the nineteenth century while calling for more 'austere' and 'direct' poetic technique.[32] Monro's readers were also informed about international modern art movements, for example in the August 1914 issue, which was primarily devoted to F. S. Flint's article on the various experimental French schools practising *vers libre*. Unfortunately, the magazine was financially backed by an institution that did not share this modernising cosmopolitan vision, and by the year's end the Poetry Society seized control and replaced Monro as editor.[33]

Monro's Poetry Bookshop remained a headquarters where poets could rent rooms or meet twice weekly for poetry readings.[34] The Poetry Bookshop also produced *Georgian Poetry*, an anthology containing poets who shared Pound's rebellion against Victorian sentiments and rhetoric, but who often featured the natural world in pastoral verse. Futurism, Imagism and the Georgians appeared together once more in Monro's second editorial venture, *Poetry and Drama* (1913–14), but by the end of 1914, he suspended production while he waited out the war. The conflict persisted, however, meaning that the December issue was his last.[35] Dominic Hibberd has suggested that Monro's ventures were doomed because these schools had irreconcilable differences.[36] The heterogeneity of Monro's editorial policy may have made these emergent transnational modernisms aware of their differences, but it was the war that heightened tensions between these various aesthetic factions.

Feeling that Amy Lowell had usurped Imagism, Ezra Pound began assisting Wyndham Lewis's efforts to shake up the nation's cultural establishments. Vorticism borrowed generously from Futurism and Cubism in its use of perspective, subject matter and urgent rhetoric to proclaim that the cultural revolution had arrived. The movement combined the visual arts and literature, with its diverse members including Ford Madox Ford, T. S. Eliot, Rebecca West, Henri Gaudier-Brzeska, C. R. W. Nevinson and William Roberts. Kate Lechmere, a fellow painter and Lewis's romantic partner, provided funding towards a new magazine, and on 20 June 1914, the inaugural issue of *Blast* reached the public's hands.[37] The pink cover's diagonal block lettering announced the expletive title in a typographical shout similar to the advertising posters outside Leveridge & Co., where the magazine was printed. For 2s. 6d., readers could purchase the hefty 160-page quarterly printed on large (12" × 9") pages. These material markers indicated that *Blast* was intended to assume the prestigious cultural authority associated with the quarterly magazines. Although it was substantial in size for a little magazine, *Blast* had a small circulation and it lasted a mere two issues.

The manifestos were provocative denunciations of cultural authorities – or 'blasts' – as well as verbal-visual texts: using alternating typeface size and erratic justifications, Lewis produced an abstract representation of the vortex that would stir up decades of stagnant British culture. Machinery, factories and the technologies of modernity would replace the idyllic past. Readers of the second issue were invited into the lonely and seedy cityscapes of T. S. Eliot's 'Preludes' and 'Rhapsody of a Windy Night'. Nearly every visual contribution eschewed realistic representation. Wyndham Lewis, Edward Wadsworth, Frederick Etchells, William Roberts and Jacob Epstein executed their illustrations in aggressive angularities. *Blast*'s promotion of hyper-urbanised machine-aesthetics that celebrated a militarised modernity proved an ill-timed cultural revolt. Industrial warfare's overwhelming scope and horror arguably provoked a need for citizens to gaze back nostalgically to simpler times, resulting in a revival of traditional modes of aesthetic expression that connected readers with their past while 'mediat[ing] bereavement' to encourage healing.[38] Meanwhile, propagandists, such as H. G. Wells, called Germany a nation of 'blood and iron' – an image that conjured up pre-war industrial and military rivalries. One critic, who reviewed an exhibit showcasing the work of three Vorticist painters, even characterised their use of 'rigid' line patterns and geometric angles as 'Prussian' in essence.[39]

With sixty fewer pages than the previous issue, the long-delayed second (and final) instalment, entitled 'War Number', was released in July 1915 to a public in thrall to nationalist wartime ideology. Even before the war, *Blast*'s avant-garde status was questionable. Its editorial agenda did not advance an overtly political programme.[40] Pound always envisioned his enterprises as coteries, so rather than pursuing the avant-garde mission to restore art to the realm of life and the service of social change, his projects tended to reflect artistic individualism. By the second issue, the magazine's only oppositional stance – its assault on the British cultural establishment – had become far more subdued in tone. Several contributions featured the war, but their responses were either ambivalent or aligned with nationalism.[41] It is worth adding that Wyndham Lewis's cover art, *Before Antwerp*, was an abstract representation of Belgium's defensive position against imminent invasion. In the context of wartime propaganda, Antwerp signified the civilised world's duty to resist German aggression. If the first cover sought to 'blast' the establishment, the second positioned Vorticism in support of the Allies.

What compromised the magazine's claim to avant-gardism even more than its conformation to cultural nationalism was the fact that several of its contributors laid down pens and brushes to don uniforms and take up arms. Wyndham Lewis, Henri Gaudier-Brzeska, Ford Madox Ford and Williams Roberts were all bound for the trenches. *Poetry* co-editor Alice Corbin Henderson wrote to Pound requesting a report on the literati serving at the front.[42] According to Pound, the article would have been no more than a 'bulletin of names'.[43] 'What can one say?' he replied to Henderson, mentioning a few of *Blast*'s regulars: William Roberts was in trouble for abandoning his observation post to 'clean himself' and Ford was invalided with shell shock. Henri Gaudier-Brzeska witnessed half his squad killed. Between assaults and reconnaissance missions, the French sculptor busied himself by carving a German Mauser rifle into a 'gentler order of feeling'.[44] He, too, would soon die, and Pound's private correspondence reflected a lone expatriate in a wartime London where the energies that once fuelled the modern literary renaissance had been directed elsewhere. A populist revival in poetry was instead just over the horizon.

One of the Georgian poets, Rupert Brooke, was largely responsible for producing a demand for war poems on both sides of the Atlantic. In 1915, Brooke had died of sepsis aboard a French hospital ship, and his idealistic war sonnets became a prophetic elegy to his youthful sacrifice. Winston Churchill's letter to *The Times* eulogised him as a 'poet-soldier' and one of 'England's noblest sons' who 'expected to die' during a time when 'no sacrifice but the most precious is acceptable'.[45] Not only did many 'young subalterns' wish to 'emulate their national poet-patriot hero', but Brooke's death whetted the appetite of a reading public that became eager to consume patriotic jingles. 'Almost alone,' Robert H. Ross has claimed, 'Brooke's death resuscitated the lagging poetic revival [. . .] [I]t also opened the gates to a flood of sentimental poetry from the amateurs, the stay-at-home patriots, and the soldier-poets.'[46] Booksellers in England reported a spike in sales for war poems by the middle of 1916.[47] Almost simultaneously, the jingoistic craze also swept through America. In 1915, the successful anthology editor William Braithwaite was among the first to compile and distribute soldier-poet collections that exclusively featured American and British responses, a juxtaposition that reinforced Wellington House's goal of convincing American readers of their shared cultural heritage with Britain. Moreover, the poems tended to eulogise the deceased and denounce 'Germany's misdeeds'.[48] Similar collections were produced in the following year, and according to Mark Van Wienen, Braithwaite set in motion a cultural trend as the first critic to confer 'literary accomplishment as well as the mantle of historical significance' on war anthologies.[49]

Compared to modernists, Brooke's fellow Georgian poets were widely read. Under the editorship of Edward Marsh, *Georgian Poetry* had exceptional early sales, with the first two instalments reaching circulations of 15,000 and 19,000 copies respectively.[50] Their poems were accessible, allowing for immediate comprehension, but as a result, modernists saw them as 'pander[ing] to the public's tastes for "easy" and reassuring poetry'.[51] Their popularity may have also stemmed from their pastoral settings that harkened back to calmer times. As Vincent Sherry has observed, Rupert Brooke's lines have a 'steady grace of verbal music and the deep appeal of the pastoral's imaginative prospects'.[52] If the pre-war 'golden summer' of 1914 was remembered by that generation as especially idyllic – given to garden parties, leisure walks in the countryside, and 'tea served from a white wicker table under the trees' – then the popular Georgian poets best captured that age of innocence.[53]

The anthologies spanned several years (1912, 1915, 1917, 1919 and 1922) and reflected a range of styles. The first two volumes included realist poets, with the third annual welcoming a darker shade of realism. While overseas, Robert Graves, Siegfried Sassoon and Isaac Rosenberg shared correspondence with Edward Marsh, and the letters captured how their views on war were changing. Another *Georgian Poetry* reached the public in 1917 and featured poems that represented the front through immediate, unflinching and sometimes harrowing depictions. *Georgian Poetry*'s third instalment may have been an important departure from the glut of abstract nationalistic jingles, but the anthology's reputation is overshadowed by the final two collections – mainly comprising what Robert Ross has called the 'Neo-Georgians', a cohort of mostly conservative poets affiliated with J. C. Squire.

One modernist publication sustained an oppositional stance against these cultural attitudes and anticipated the post-war mood of disillusionment. Printed annually, *Wheels: An Anthology of Verse* (1916–21) showcased the creativity of the eccentric, aristocratic Sitwell siblings, with Edith as editor and her brothers Osbert and Sacheverell as recurrent contributors. Other poets featured across the annuals or 'cycles' were Aldous Huxley, Iris Tree, Nancy Cunard and Helen Roothman, Edith's former governess, who supplied translations of French Symbolist works. William Roberts and Laurence Atkinson provided cover art, adding Vorticism's disruptive visual perspective to the literary content. The first three instalments sold at 2s. 6d. and contained about ninety pages of poems, with an additional dozen pages of reprinted reviews found in the back matter under the sections 'Press Notices' and 'Bibliography'. The first *Cycle*'s run of 500 sold out, so a second printing of 500 was ordered.[54] Despite their annual's limited circulation, the Sitwells were savvy promoters, which enhanced *Wheels*'s public presence. Aaron Jaffe has explored how the anthology format bestowed an aura of canonicity on contributors, producing early pathways for modernism's institutionalisation.[55] Yet he has characterised the annuals, including *Wheels: A Fourth Cycle* that memorialised Wilfred Owen, as out of sync with 'post-war anomie', claiming that the Sitwells' use of 'aggression, violence, and war' was a mere 'rhetorical strateg[y]'.[56] In reality, the memorial number was a culmination of growing anti-war sympathies shared by the group.

Although *Wheels* did not explicitly promote a political programme, the Sitwell siblings felt the war was a 'Great Catastrophe'. Their wartime 'purpose' was to defy 'Edwardian absurdities', including the 'herd-instinct with its patriotic call to duty'.[57] Having seen combat, Osbert was the most outspoken. After meeting Sassoon in 1917, his pacifism was 'strengthened and confirmed'.[58] Appearing in *The Spectator* and *The Nation* under the pseudonyms 'Miles' (soldier) and 'Armchair', Osbert satirised the 'profiteers, the generals, the complacent patriotic public and the glib journalists and politicians'.[59] Importantly, Osbert also attacked *Georgian Poetry* for 'pretending that the larks were singing in the trenches'.[60] Memorialising Wilfred Owen was certainly an editorial response to the third *Georgian Poetry*, which Marsh had dedicated to Rupert Brooke. More than a publicity stunt, though, *Wheels: A Fourth Cycle* signalled a broader critical commentary on war anthologists, particularly the Georgians, who were in step with the escapist tendencies of popular representations that included benign depictions of conflict, jingles proclaiming abstract values, and celebrations of martyred poets.

*Wheels* gathered a considerable critical mass of trench poets and fellow pacifists. Those who served included Osbert Sitwell, Victor Perowne, Sherard Vines, Wyndham Tennant, William Roberts, Robert Nichols and Wilfred Owen, with Owen included posthumously. Recalling the pacifism he shared with Owen, Osbert stated that 'a link of nonconformity [. . .] in those years bound together the disbelievers with almost the same force with which faith had knitted together the early Christians'.[61] Amid wartime nationalism, the group clearly felt marginalised, but the fourth instalment intensified and amplified their fringe voices. After reading 'The Deranged', the Sitwells requested work from Owen; tragically, he died just one week before the Armistice. Still seeking to print his poems, both Osbert and Edith sent letters to Owen's mother; Edith called her son's work the 'finest war poetry', which brought her to tears while reading.[62] At the centre of *Wheels: A Fourth Cycle* appeared seven of Owen's poems:

'The Shoe', 'A Terre', 'Strange Meeting', 'The Sentry', 'Disabled', 'The Dead-Beat' and 'The Chances'. The significant increase in price to six shillings leant weightiness, if not gravitas, to this 1919 post-war issue. William Roberts's 'Gun Drill' and series of paintings, which featured men throwing darts, enshrouded the contents in a haunting aura, as his Vorticist technique rendered human subjects through mechanised and depersonalised representations. *Wheels: A Fourth Cycle* memorialised Owen, promoted his emergent brand of wartime aesthetics, offered an alternative to the sentiments Brooke's death had spread, and ultimately functioned as a bible for this small band of disbelievers. *Wheels* consequently became more than a self-absorbed coterie. Reviewers had typically puzzled over the poems. A reviewer from the *New Statesman* remarked: 'Miss Sitwell can write Fêtes Galantes and perverted nursery rhymes as well as any poet alive.'[63] Another from the *Pall Mall Gazette* described the poems as 'conceived in morbid eccentricity and executed in fierce factitious gloom'.[64] *Wheels: A Fourth Cycle* aligned these often-misunderstood contributions with Owen's tortured wartime visions, signalling a crucial gathering of voices that represented an early stage of post-war disillusionment.

Across the Atlantic, American little magazines also criticised wartime culture, yet their responses came from unique political and national positions, producing conflict and realignment across transatlantic modernist and mainstream networks. The American literary renaissance began with the birth of *Poetry: A Magazine of Verse* (1912–present), edited by Chicagoan Harriet Monroe with considerable assistance from Alice Corbin Henderson. Monroe recognised that poetry was a neglected genre with little presence in American print culture. Taking the advice of her friend H. C. Chatfield, she enlisted one hundred patrons in a five-year contract, each promising $50 per year to fund her vision for a magazine dedicated solely to poetry.[65] Designed in the fine arts printing tradition of thick paper with deckle edges, the monthly magazine dedicated the first thirty pages to poems, relegating criticism, reviews and editorials to the second half. Though *Poetry* only reached a couple of thousand readers, it survives today with a rich legacy distinguished by discovering notable modernists as well as introducing readers to European and regionally diverse US poets.[66]

*Poetry* consistently framed wartime art within a shifting conception of American exceptionalism. In the September 1914 issue, Monroe claimed that the old war epics functioned ideologically by fashioning the populace's collective imagination to support conflicts waged by kings. Using the magazine as a forum to initiate change, the editors hosted a war poem contest, with noteworthy submissions later printed in the November 'War Number', an issue almost entirely comprising US poets calling for peace. Shortly after Rupert Brooke's death, the US reading public also began to demand war collections. Although Brooke was a friend and had contributed to Monroe's magazine, she and Henderson disputed his sudden popularity, criticising Yale University's decision to award the Henry Howland Memorial, a prize of $1,500, to his family. Calling Brooke's poems 'bound to the past' in expressing a 'mediaeval ideal of heroism', she characterised his work (and Yale's decision) as out of touch with the modern trends of American poets like Edgar Lee Masters and Robert Frost.[67]

After President Woodrow Wilson and Congress declared war in April 1917, *Poetry*'s isolationist pacifism vanished, replaced by editorials and bibliographic changes that aligned the magazine and its content with the pro-war sentiments of an increasingly nationalist public. By October 1917, Monroe paid more for low-grade paper and faced the end of her five-year contract with financial guarantors. With daily living costs rising, many did not commit to another contract, and the magazine's revenue dropped from $5,990 to 4,605.[68] Despite these challenges, Monroe felt obliged to continue publishing after reading 'thousands' of manuscripts from mobilised soldiers who answered her call for modern American war poems.[69] By making changes to format and circulation strategies, Monroe realigned *Poetry* in support of nationwide programmes – practising what Christopher Capozzola has called a 'culture of obligation' and outright 'coercive volunteerism'.[70] Enlisting readers and contributors to create promotional poems for Liberty Loans and a militarist organisation called the Vigilantes were two additions to *Poetry*'s new allegiances with wartime institutions. *Poetry* also participated in the Burleson magazines initiative, a nationwide effort to fill camp libraries with used periodicals. From November 1918 to October 1919, 'NOTICE TO READERS' appeared in the top right corner of the front cover, asking subscribers to place a one-cent stamp on used issues so *Poetry* could be recirculated to soldiers and sailors overseas.

During the years of US involvement in the war, *Poetry* featured an exceptional number of war poems while editorials spotlighted poets in uniform. Monroe was even at the forefront of a hero-making culture when she memorialised American poets Alan Seeger and Joyce Kilmer while also publishing 'Vernon Castle', her own short poem commemorating the dancing icon and army aviator.[71] After the Armistice, Monroe reframed her 'open door' editorial policy to echo Wilsonian idealism, characterising the magazine's interest in regionally diverse and multinational submissions as a model for the League of Nations. By promoting modern American poetry as central to democratic progress on a global stage, realigning modernism with a nationalist public, and literally placing *Poetry* in the hands of men in the trenches, Monroe employed strategies that helped the new verse gain entry into mainstream readerships and institutions.

Another Chicago-based publication, *The Little Review*, repositioned itself across very different networks while charting its own path for modernism. *The Little Review* was a sixty-four-page heterogeneous monthly featuring the political and cultural avant-gardism that reflected the pre-war Chicago 'Renaissance'. After hearing Emma Goldman speak, Margaret Anderson devoted her editorial agenda to promoting applied anarchist values through reports on labour issues as well as philosophical individualism in articles explaining how Nietzsche's teachings could challenge complacent mainstream and bourgeois assumptions. Three regulars (George Burman Foster, Alexander Kaun and George Soule) were also engaged in cultural politics through their debates with the Edwardians who placed articles in American publications that intentionally misrepresented the German philosopher.[72]

*The Little Review*'s political alienation and shift in philosophical individualism can be traced across major historical moments. A German U-boat sank the *Lusitania* in May 1915, and in the next issue, Anderson responded to how nationalism began to consolidate pro-war public opinion. That month, her editorials were derisive of 'the masses' while she advanced an exclusive or 'aristocratic' reading of Nietzschean individualism that many anarchists rejected. Support for syndicalist labour issues actually increased in 1915, but by the late summer of 1916, the editorial agenda began to retreat from an advanced guard position of printing radical politics and political art. The growing public demonisation of anarchism most likely prompted this editorial shift. A roadside bomb had killed ten bystanders at a pro-war Preparedness Day parade in San Francisco. Around this time, Anderson and her new co-editor Jane Heap had disputed Goldman and Berkman's stance that art must cultivate a social conscience. A few weeks following the parade episode and debate, the September 1916 issue appeared with thirteen of its twenty-eight pages left blank to represent a 'Want Ad' for 'real art' akin to aestheticism. Amid the blank pages, Anderson featured one last counter-narrative to the mainstream press – Robert Minor's 'The San Francisco Bomb Case', which claimed that the press and Chamber of Commerce were using the incident to demonise organised labour. In a final editorial gesture of promotional support for the magazine's former counter-cultural network, Anderson also included 'Facts about the Preparedness Bomb', an advertisement for donations to the International Workers' Defence League.[73] 'The Reader Critic' columns carried debates for several months, as subscribers' reprinted letters protested against the editors' sudden apolitical direction.

In 1917, at the exact time Monroe lost part of her financial support and aligned *Poetry* with the wider nationalist mood, Pound vaguely resigned as Foreign Correspondent at *Poetry* to join Margaret Anderson.[74] The April 1917 issue's only protest against America's mobilisation was a nearly blank page entitled 'The War'. Anderson had dissolved the magazine's heterogeneous 'marriage' of political and artistic counter-cultural activism, the distinguishing feature of the avant-garde, to make way for a purely literary enterprise. As the new Foreign Editor, Pound began featuring criticism and his coterie: W. B. Yeats, T. S. Eliot, Ford Madox Ford, Wyndham Lewis and James Joyce. With *The Little Review* stripped of its affiliations with radical agendas, no longer embedded in counter-cultural networks, and now supported by patronage, Pound could realise his 'aristocracy of the arts' by marketing *The Little Review* through rarity and coterie status.[75] Despite costs, the August 1917 issue featured Yeats in a deluxe edition with thick deckle-edged paper. These material changes and Pound's mailing list targeted a transatlantic readership of 'establishment figures', potential wealthy patrons, bibliophiles and university professors across major metropolitan cities, including London, Paris and New York.[76] *The Little Review* was sold as a high modernist literary coterie across a cosmopolitan audience.[77]

*The Little Review* had previously publicised publications such as *The Masses* and *Mother Earth*, as well as lectures delivered by Goldman and Berkman, and their essay collections and pamphlets that bore the Mother Earth Publishing Association imprint. A series of arrests dissolved that radical modernist network in 1917. *The Masses* (1911–17) was a popular socialist monthly that cost five cents (later ten cents) and reached between 20,000 and 40,000 readers.[78] From the bohemian space of Greenwich Village, Max Eastman edited the magazine, attracting writers such as Carl Sandburg, Sherwood Anderson, Mable Dodge, Jack London, Amy Lowell and Sinclair Lewis. Aside from socialism and labour issues, the magazine's socio-political causes included racial equality, women's suffrage, free love and birth control. A 'plutocratic subsidy' funded the high-quality large 'tabloid format', where political cartoons often appeared on double-page spreads.[79] The magazine's artists, who were later associated with the Ashcan School, conveyed their social realism through graphic satire that both entertained and instructed subscribers. Recurrent images of muscular soldiers and bloated profiteers codified the socialist message that capitalist greed fuelled wars. In bold print on the back cover of the September 1917 issue, Eastman drew attention to free speech violations, and eventually, the Espionage Act prevented circulation through the mail.[80]

Just three months later, Eastman resurrected his editorial agenda under a new title, *The Liberator*.

Emma Goldman's *Mother Earth* (1907–15) was based out of her various apartments across New York City.[81] For ten cents, readers could purchase the 5" × 8" journal, originally printed on sixty-four pages before dropping to around thirty due to financial struggles.[82] The contents featured mostly international anarchist political thinkers, with some notable writers and artists, including Hippolyte Havel, Eugene O'Neill, Mable Dodge, Ben Hecht and Maxwell Bodenheim; Man Ray, Adolf Wolff and Manuel Komroff produced cover art.[83] Though Goldman was the publisher, Alexander Berkman edited the magazine until he left for San Francisco to cover labour issues from his own bi-weekly eight-page newspaper, *The Blast*. For a decade, Goldman embarked on arduous lecture tours around the USA and Canada, delivering hundreds of speeches and reaching up to an estimated 75,000 spectators yearly.[84] 'Red Emma' – America's most famous anarchist – was periodically arrested and her mainstream notoriety boosted her own promotional efforts. Editorials consistently publicised her lectures, commented on people she met during her travels, and promoted fundraising events and activities that financially sustained and helped create a sense of community across her substantial audience of 10,000 readers.[85]

Much like Eastman, Goldman and Berkman opposed militarism and spoke out against the draft. The two formed the American No-Conscription League and, on the same day the Espionage Act was signed, their respective editorial offices were raided: both were arrested for protecting draft dodgers whom vigilante citizens and the general national hysteria deemed 'slackers'.[86] The June and August issues were seized by the Post Office, but *Mother Earth Bulletin* struggled on with the help of Goldman's niece, Stella Comyn, and Berkman's lover, Eleanor Fitzgerald.[87] At this time, little magazines and their counter-cultural networks could prove a liability; during the raid, federal agents seized *Mother Earth*'s card index of subscription lists – records that exposed the identities of and incriminated readers who were part of the print community.[88] During the months before their eventual deportation from Ellis Island to Bolshevik Russia, Goldman and Berkman nonetheless enjoyed the company of Anderson and Heap, who were by their side at court, invited them into their home, and even privately summoned support through a letter asking correspondents to protest against the trial in the name of individualism.[89] That protest never found print in *The Little Review*.

Revisionary histories have explored modernism's institutionalisation, with periodical scholarship shedding light on how modernism was marketed, sold and distributed across varied readerships to target new and wider audiences. There is a missing chapter to the story of how experimental aesthetic programmes endured and even attained canonisation. Wartime magazine issues offer opportunities to view processes at work when the political and economic stakes were raised. The surge of mainstream nationalist discourses and cultural trends drew many little magazines into a common arena of debate. Editors either intensified their oppositional stances to the mainstream or succumbed to the pressures of a divisive political climate – silencing their dissidence or even adopting nationalism. By studying periodical formats and material practices, scholars can recover how editors positioned their publications in nationwide disputes as well as how they employed survival strategies and publicity tactics. This brief comparative overview has also traced commonalities and differences across Anglo-American print cultures. Occasionally, these cosmopolitan relationships were challenged as editors adapted their agendas within national frameworks. In other cases, editors formed alliances out of their mutual opposition to the wartime culture. Future histories of wartime magazine issues might reveal the particularities of how experimental aesthetic programmes, which became a transatlantic phenomenon, emerged out of a variety of counter-cultural spaces that evolved under wartime duress to reach different readers across new networks that spread within and across national boundaries.

## Notes

1. Lawrence Rainey, *Institutions of Modernism: Literary Elites and Public Culture* (New Haven: Yale University Press, 1998). This phrase is borrowed from Rainey's book title.
2. Peter Brooker and Andrew Thacker, 'General Introduction', in Brooker and Thacker (eds), *The Oxford Critical and Cultural History of Modernist Magazines, Volume I: Britain and Ireland, 1880–1955* (Oxford: Oxford University Press, 2012), pp. 1–26 (p. 6).
3. Thomas J. Keenan, 'British Paper Mills in War Time', *Paper: Weekly Technical Journal*, 10 November 1915, p. 18; S. C. Phillips, 'The Sulphite Pulp Situation in Canada', *Wood Pulp Maker: Supplement to The Paper-Maker and British Paper Trade Journal*, 1 November 1916, p. 435.
4. R. R. Bowker, 'Paper Goes Up: Digest of Address by H. H. Reynolds, of the B. D. Rising Paper Co., to the N. Y. Master Printers' Association', *Publishers' Weekly: American Book-Trade Journal*, 17 August 1918, p. 510.
5. Alan R. Thomson, 'The Paper Conservation Pledges', *Geyer's Stationer*, 19 September 1918, p. 14. For a more detailed account, see Christopher J. La Casse, '"Scrappy and Unselective": Rising Wartime Paper Costs and *The Little Review*', *American Periodicals*, 26.2 (Fall 2016), 208–21.
6. Samuel Hynes, *A War Imagined: The First World War and English Culture* (New York: Athenaeum, 1991), p. 80.
7. Ellen Williams, *Harriet Monroe and the Poetry Renaissance: The First Ten Years of* Poetry, *1912–1922* (Chicago: University of Illinois Press, 1977), p. 168.
8. Mark S. Morrisson, *The Public Face of Modernism: Little Magazines, Audiences, and Reception, 1905–1920* (Madison: University of Wisconsin Press, 2001), p. 53.
9. Ibid., p. 33.
10. Ibid., p. 32. Morrisson has argued that Ford modelled *The English Review* on the *Mercure de France* (p. 42). The periodical also shared characteristics with the *Fortnightly*, *Contemporary* and *Nineteenth Century*, which Morrisson has claimed 'rose to cultural prominence' by speaking with authority on 'political, social, and literary affairs' (ibid.).
11. Ibid., p. 43.
12. Ibid., p. 19.
13. Cliff Wulfman, 'Ford Madox Ford and *The English Review* (1908–1937)', in Brooker and Thacker (eds), *The Oxford Critical and Cultural History of Modernist Magazines*, pp. 226–39 (p. 235).
14. Morrisson, *The Public Face of Modernism*, p. 51.
15. Martha S. Vogeler, *Austin Harrison and the English Review* (Columbia: University of Missouri Press, 2008), p. 86.
16. Ibid., pp. 4, 66.
17. Morrisson, *The Public Face of Modernism*, p. 52.
18. Mark Wollaeger, *Modernism, Media, and Propaganda: British Narrative from 1900 to 1945* (Princeton: Princeton University Press, 2006), p. 14.
19. Peter Buitenhuis, *The Great War of Words: British, American and Canadian Propaganda and Fiction, 1914–1933* (Vancouver: University of British Columbia Press, 1987), p. xvi.

20. Adrian Gregory, 'A Clash of Cultures: The British Press and the Opening of the Great War', in Troy R. E. Paddock (ed.), *Call to Arms: Propaganda, Public Opinion, and Newspapers in the Great War* (Westport: Praeger Publishers, 2004), pp. 15–49 (p. 31).
21. Ibid., pp. 30–1.
22. Jennifer Ratner-Rosenhagen, *The American Nietzsche: A History of an Icon and his Ideas* (Chicago: University of Chicago Press, 2012), p. 116.
23. Ibid., pp. 132–3; Modris Eksteins, *Rites of Spring: The Great War and the Birth of the Modern Age* (Boston: Houghton Mifflin, 1989), pp. 76–80, 116. Both studies explore propagandist uses of the term 'Kultur'.
24. Alice Corbin Henderson, 'Comments and Reviews: Poetry and War', *Poetry: A Magazine of Verse*, November 1914, p. 84.
25. Ibid., pp. 82–4.
26. George Soule, 'Zarathustra Vs. Rheims', *The Little Review*, November 1914, pp. 4–5.
27. Vogeler, *Austin Harrison*, p. 195.
28. Ibid., p. 213.
29. Ibid., pp. 198–9.
30. Ibid., p. 221.
31. Michael Levenson, *Modernism* (New Haven: Yale University Press, 2011), pp. 45–6.
32. Ezra Pound, 'Prolegomena', quoted in Dominic Hibberd, 'The New Poetry, Georgians, and Others: *The Open Window* (1910–11), *The Poetry Review* (1912–15), *Poetry and Drama* (1913–14), and *New Numbers* (1914)', in Brooker and Thacker (eds), *The Oxford Critical and Cultural History of Modernist Magazines*, pp. 176–96 (p. 181).
33. Hibberd, 'The New Poetry', p. 188.
34. Ibid., p. 191.
35. Ibid., p. 196.
36. Ibid., p. 182.
37. Mark Morrisson, '*Blast*: An Introduction', Modernist Journals Project, <http://modjourn.org> (last accessed 18 November 2016); Lisa Tickner, 'Men's Work: Masculinity and Modernism', in Norman Bryson, Michael Ann Holly and Keith Moxey (eds), *Visual Culture: Images and Interpretations* (Middletown: Wesleyan University Press, 1994), pp. 42–82 (p. 63).
38. Jay Winter, *Sites of Memory, Sites of Mourning: The Great War in European Cultural History* (New York: Cambridge University Press, 1995), p. 115.
39. Paul Peppis, *Literature, Politics, and the English Avant-Garde: Nation and Empire, 1901–1918* (Cambridge: Cambridge University Press, 2000), pp. 100, 103.
40. Ibid., pp. 84–5. Peppis characterised *Blast* as the 'apex' of English avant-gardism, yet neither issue stated a clear oppositional political stance.
41. Ibid., p. 105.
42. Alice Corbin Henderson to Ezra Pound, 17 February 1917, in *The Letters of Ezra Pound to Alice Corbin Henderson*, ed. Ira B. Nadel (Austin: University of Texas Press, 1993), p. 193.
43. Ezra Pound to Alice Corbin Henderson, 9 March 1917, in *Letters*, pp. 200–1.
44. Henri Gaudier-Brzeska, 'Vortex Gaudier-Brzeska (Written from the Trenches)', *Blast*, 2 (July 1915), 34.
45. Robert H. Ross, *The Georgian Revolt: Rise and Fall of a Poetic Ideal* (Carbondale: Southern Illinois University Press, 1965), pp. 140–1.
46. Ibid., p. 141.
47. Ibid., p. 143.
48. Mark Van Wienen, *Partisans and Poets: The Political Work of American Poetry in the Great War* (Cambridge: Cambridge University Press, 1997), p. 115.
49. Ibid., p. 117.
50. Aaron Jaffe, *Modernism and the Culture of Celebrity* (Cambridge: Cambridge University Press, 2005), p. 143.

51. Myron Simon, *The Georgian Poetic* (Berkeley: University of California Press, 1975), p. 8.
52. Vincent Sherry, 'Introduction', in Sherry (ed.), *The Cambridge Companion to the Literature of the First World War* (Cambridge: Cambridge University Press, 2005), p. 4.
53. Paul Fussell, *The Great War and Modern Memory* (1975; Oxford: Oxford University Press, 2000), p. 24.
54. Michael Cotsell, '*Wheels*: An Introduction', Modernist Journals Project, <http://modjourn.org> (last accessed 18 November 2016).
55. Jaffe, *Modernism and the Culture of Celebrity*, pp. 148, 154–5.
56. Ibid., pp. 157–8.
57. John Pearson, *Façades: Edith, Osbert, and Sacheverell Sitwell* (London: Macmillan, 1978), p. 104.
58. Ibid., p. 114.
59. Ibid., p. 115.
60. Ibid., p. 116.
61. Osbert Sitwell, *Noble Essences* (London: Macmillan, 1950), p. 89.
62. Jaffe, *Modernism and the Culture of Celebrity*, p. 158.
63. 'Bibliography', *Wheels: A Fourth Cycle* (1919), p. 103. The review originally appeared in the *New Statesman*: 'Recent Verse', *New Statesman*, 14 December 1918, p. 222.
64. 'Bibliography', *Wheels: A Fourth Cycle* (1919), p. 99. The public's contentious reception of *Wheels* echoed into the post-war period. In the 1922 novel *Patchwork*, Beverley Nichols's character Ray Sheldon, an army veteran who attends Oxford, admits to disliking 'whining poems' and quotes the *Pall Mall Gazette*'s attack on *Wheels*. Beverley Nichols, *Patchwork* (New York: Henry Holt and Company, 1922), pp. 199–200.
65. Harriet Monroe, *A Poet's Life: Seventy Years in a Changing World* (New York: Macmillan Company, 1938), p. 243.
66. Williams, *Harriet Monroe and the Poetry Renaissance*, p. 114.
67. Harriet Monroe, 'Colonialism Again', *Poetry*, May 1915, p. 97.
68. Williams, *Harriet Monroe and the Poetry Renaissance*, p. 295. These figures are provided in Williams's Appendix: Figures on *Poetry*'s Income, Expenditures, and Circulation.
69. Harriet Monroe, 'Emerson in Loggia', *Poetry*, September 1917, p. 314; Harriet Monroe, 'These Five Years', *Poetry*, October 1917, p. 41.
70. Christopher Capozzola, *Uncle Sam Wants You: World War I and the Making of the Modern American Citizen* (Oxford: Oxford University Press, 2008), p. 10.
71. Harriet Monroe, 'Comment: Joyce Kilmer', *Poetry*, October 1918, pp. 31–4; Harriet Monroe, 'Vernon Castle', *Poetry*, March 1918, p. 311.
72. Soule, 'Zarathustra Vs. Rheims', p. 4; George Burman Foster, 'A Hard Bed', *The Little Review*, February 1915, pp. 44–5; Alexander Kaun, 'My Friend the Incurable: On Germanophobia; on the Perils of Monomania; on Raskolnikov and Alexander Berkman; on Surrogates and Sundry Subtleties', *The Little Review*, December 1914, pp. 10–11.
73. Robert Minor, 'The San Francisco Bomb Case: What Can a Poor Executioner Do against a Man Who Is Willing to Die?', *The Little Review*, September 1916, pp. 16–17; 'Facts about the Preparedness Bomb', *The Little Review*, September 1916, p. 29.
74. Williams, *Harriet Monroe and the Poetry Renaissance*, p. 212.
75. James Longenbach, *Stone Cottage: Pound, Yeats, and Modernism* (Oxford: Oxford University Press, 1988), p. 109.
76. Ezra Pound, *Letters of Ezra Pound to Margaret Anderson: The Little Review Correspondence*, ed. Thomas L. Scott, Melvin J. Friedman and Jackson R. Bryer (New York: New Directions Publishing Corporation, 1988), p. xxvii.
77. For a more detailed account, see Christopher J. La Casse, 'From the Historical Avant-Garde to Highbrow Coterie Modernism: *The Little Review*'s Wartime Advances and Retreats', forthcoming in *Criticism*, 57.4.

78. Morrisson, *The Public Face of Modernism*, p. 177.
79. Rachel Schreiber, *Gender and Activism in a Little Magazine: The Modern Figures of the* Masses (Farnham: Ashgate, 2011), pp. 3–4.
80. See ibid., pp. 7, 133.
81. Peter Glassgold, 'Introduction: The Life and Death of *Mother Earth*', in Glassgold (ed.), *Anarchy!: An Anthology of Emma Goldman's* Mother Earth (Washington, DC: Counterpoint, 2001), p. xxii.
82. Ibid., pp. xviii, xxx.
83. Ibid., p. xix.
84. Ibid., p. xxviii.
85. Ibid., p. xxiv; Kathy E. Ferguson, *Emma Goldman: Political Thinking in the Streets* (Lanham, MD: Rowman & Littlefield, 2011), p. 69. See Ferguson for a detailed account of Goldman's counter-public networking.
86. Capozzola, *Uncle Sam Wants You*, p. 41. Vigilantes conducted sweeping 'slacker raids' across major cities.
87. Glassgold, 'Introduction', p. xxxiii.
88. Glassgold, 'Introduction', p. xxi.
89. Newark, University of Delaware Special Collections Library, MSS 258, 'Florence Reynolds Collection Related to Jane Heap and *The Little Review*, 1908–1977', f. 7.

# 17

# Pamphlets and Political Writing

*Matthew Shaw*

## Introduction

Analogies with the machinery of war are hard to escape in any discussion of writing and the First World War, and pamphlets are no exception. They may be likened to the constant barrage of artillery or the fizzing of angry shrapnel across the lines of no man's land. Pamphlets appeared in their hundreds of thousands, making use of the technologies of cheap print and paper, the mass literacy of soldiers and those on the home front, and operating within the still-functioning and sophisticated networks of postal and commercial distribution. They were cheap, affordable, and also often closely associated with a specific organisation, including trade unions, political parties, religious organisations and interest groups, such as animal-welfare charities or vegetarian societies (for example, Partridge and Conklin's 1918 publication *Wheatless and Meatless Days*). Few could ignore the 'war question' in their literature. Ranging from vanity publications to national propaganda campaigns, pamphlets and other political writing, such as contributions to newspaper and magazine comments or letters pages, offered views on a host of issues, from pacifism to the exposure of foreign atrocities, from H. N. Brailsford's attack on militarism and imperialism in *Belgium and the Scrap of Paper* (1915) to B. H. Streeter's justification in *War – This War and the Sermon on the Mount* (1915). But against the noise of war, was the purpose and argument of the pamphlets easily drowned out? How was meaning to be found in the confusion of the war years? For what were the armies fighting, and for what kind of world were such sacrifices being called?

## Types of Writing

The first industrial war was marked not only by the coordination of *matériel* and human power, but by the mass production, dissemination and control of information. Put simply, the war could not have been fought in the way it was without the coordinating and persuasive – as well as resistive – power of print. As H. G. Wells argued, 'the ultimate purpose of this war is propaganda, the destruction of certain beliefs, and the creation of others. It is to this propaganda that reasonable men must address themselves.'[1] All sides in the conflict required the ability to record, exhort and systematise the information needed for millions of men and women, leading to the creation of an army of scribes, the rationing of paper and printing, and the development of publication networks. The mass of printed written records from this period, then, is the work of the state, offering advice on all aspects of life, from home economics to the correct method of cleaning a rifle or mucking out an army stable, and preserving for the historian a record of the anonymous voice of officialdom. But such works also co-existed with alternative voices, ones that raised concerns about the course of the war. As both a format and a genre, pamphlets presented a picture of the world that posited both the notion of a uniform, shared outlook and a cacophony of dissenting voices. Pamphlets could be greyly official, firmly putting the record straight, or the literary equivalent of a flare or tracer, lighting up the public realm with intense debate.

Here, 'pamphlets' refer to shorter printed texts, bound in paper or at most card, typically a few dozen pages long, but sometimes as short as a single sheet. In Britain, they had their origins in the disputes between various religious sects in the seventeenth and eighteenth centuries, and are marked in tone by their argumentative or polemical fervour. Occasionally, pamphlets would run longer, resembling modern-day paperbacks of a hundred or so pages, but the majority were deliberately small enough to slip into a jacket or top pocket as well as inexpensive enough to be easily purchased or given away. They also benefited from being quick to write, print and distribute, making them the perfect vehicle for responding to current events or attempting to shape opinion. Such materials were clearly ephemeral, with an immediate aim in mind, and designed to be read, discussed and perhaps passed along to another reader, rather than designed for a long life on the shelves of research or personal libraries. Certainly, few were sent to legal deposit libraries or were collected by the second-hand book trade, and in consequence the bibliographic record is something of a matter of happenstance rather than of design. Yet, because of the numbers produced, and perhaps the tendency to retain items connected to the 'Great War', numerous individual items can be found within the collections of most major research libraries, as well as amongst various archival repositories. There are also a number of major collections of materials, such as those held by national libraries like the National Library of Scotland, the Bibliothèque nationale de France, the British Library and the Library of Congress. Other collections are to be found at Senate House Library, London (the Playne Collection), Willikin University, Illinois, Princeton University (the Rodman Wanamaker and First World War pamphlet collection), the Joseph M. Bruccoli Collection at the University of Virginia, as well as the extensive collections held by the Imperial War Museums, Columbia University Libraries, the New York Public Library, and at the National World War I Museum and Memorial in Kansas City. All of these contain materials in French and German as well as English. Such collections provide a broad reflection of the types of pamphlets and other political writings produced at the time, but are not exhaustive and do not, perhaps, always reflect what was most popular or most widely read.

Many pamphlets also had a special relationship with newspapers. The original text often began as a letter or article in a newspaper or journal, but was then worked up into a standalone pamphlet, often sold alongside the newspaper, making use of those distribution channels, as well as networks of political sympathy. Newspapers reciprocated by republishing pamphlets, either in full or gutting them for their choicest polemical or literary meat. Just as books have a special relationship with the web of publisher, reviewer, bookshop and reader which constitute the life of such texts, pamphlets did not exist in isolation as solitary shorter pieces of prose. Their authorship, distribution and reception was highly pertinent to their message and helped in many ways to shape it. As texts with polemical or persuasive intentions, pamphlets were often produced not just by a solitary author, but by an organisation of some kind (or even an individual purporting to be a larger organisation in order to validate their text). Pamphlets responded to other pamphlets, in either support or rejection, and often referred to other publications for sale, or in exchange for postage, in a plethora of advertisements in their endpapers. In terms of their distribution, they found their readers not through the neutral route of the bookshop, but via a host of interested parties, from church groups to political parties, labour unions or women's organisations. They consciously existed in relation to the world around them, seeking to shape people's views and thereby the world itself. As such, they attracted the attention of the state in terms of its legislators, judiciary and police force.

## Censorship and Propaganda

Governments recognised that they were confronted with a delicate balance in terms of censoring materials. At the outbreak of war, the state had limited access to a range of legal instruments or institutional arrangements to bar publications that might undermine the war effort, despite being acutely aware of the need for restraint, in terms of general morale as well as protecting military secrets. In August 1914, for example, the Earl of Selborne asked if the police could control the night-time cries of newsboys, since 'it needs little imagination to realise what the effect may be in a few days or in a few weeks' time of the words "Awful slaughter" resounding through the streets in the early hours of the morning'.[2] Clearly the establishment was aware of the need for a certain public delicacy at such a time. This said, the Boer War had been conducted without any form of official British censorship, and a draft bill proposed by Prime Minister Balfour in 1904 failed to make it on to the statute book. However, by 1914, a form of self-censorship had begun with the introduction of the Joint Standing Committee, which brought together officials from the War Office and Admiralty with newspaper proprietors to suppress sensitive information on a voluntary basis.[3] On 7 August 1914, the government established a new Press Bureau to control the supply of information to the press as well as to review the telegrams and cables sent and received by each newspaper. A network of editors who could be used to disseminate suitable information was formed, and the press was asked to submit voluntarily other information for scrutiny. The Bureau could impose a voluntary 'D-Notice' (Defence Notice) on items it wished not to be reported. A pamphlet was issued offering guidance on the controls. Winston Churchill, as First Lord of the Admiralty, hoped that the Bureau would supply 'a steady stream of trustworthy information' to papers irrespective of their 'class or party', while avoiding 'irresponsible rumours'. The press, it was hoped, would also avoid over-optimism.[4] Nor were these controls restricted to newspapers: in November 1914, the Solicitor General Sir Stanley Buckmaster confirmed that press censorship extended to pamphlets, magazine articles and books.[5]

Although at first the Press Bureau's control of the 'steady stream' ensured that its non-statutory censorship largely worked, such gentlemanly agreements could not survive the test of the war, and by 1915 over thirty socialist and pacifist newspapers removed themselves from the system of D-Notices and oversight by the Bureau. In 1915, the Defence of the Realm Act shored up the system with a clause preventing the spreading of false reports and in subsequent regulation prohibited the unauthorised obtaining and dissemination of military and naval intelligence. Alongside general suppression of sharing military or naval information, the Act could also be used against works likely to cause 'disaffection'. This regulation was interpreted generously, and used broadly in prosecuting dissidents and allowing suspected premises to be entered and searched: between September and November 1917, at least twenty-four raids took place, leading to the seizure of leaflets and pamphlets, some of which were returned, but some of which were reviewed and destroyed by the police.[6] Labour agitation and pacifist materials often fell foul of such legislation. Seven thousand pamphlets that called for the avoidance of the production of war materials or otherwise contravened the Defence of the Realm regulations were destroyed in Salford in August 1915, the Independent Labour Party offices in Manchester and London were raided and pamphlets and leaflets seized, while several people were arrested in London and fined £100 merely for circulating a pamphlet entitled *Repeal the Act*, an attack on the Compulsory Military Service Act.[7] Such censorship was not accepted uncritically: the stipendiary magistrate heard from the various parties, and allowed some pamphlets to be returned. In a discussion of the matter in the Commons, Sir William Byles MP noted that 'the suppression of honest opinion is often more dangerous than the expression of it'.[8] Byles continued to take an interest in the suppression of materials, the following month asking whether pamphlets and other documents that were destroyed 'in camera [. . .] without their contents or even their titles being known to the public' always contained 'information of military value to the enemy'.[9] He was not the only person to be concerned: the seizure of a number of pamphlets in Penarth in 1916 led to the rumour that the police had confiscated a pamphlet on the Sermon on the Mount by the Bishop of Oxford. In reality, the owner of the left-wing pamphlets had just pointedly handed a copy to the police inspector and asked that he read it, and the Liberal MP Richard Holt took advantage of parliamentary privilege to read out the contents of *Repeal the Act*.[10]

The Press Bureau continued to review pamphlets throughout the war. For example, in December 1917, a pamphlet submitted by Arnold Lupton, 'Our Armies and Navies and Vaccination', was not passed as it was, the Home Secretary noted, 'likely to prejudice the training and discipline of the forces'.[11] In 1918, the regulations changed, meaning that leaflets did not have to be sent to the Bureau, but the Home Secretary still took measures to ensure that this pamphlet did not circulate.[12]

Regulations were even stricter in Britain's Empire, with the authorities more concerned about independence movements than support for the war or enlisting. The India Press Act (1910) had suppressed over twenty newspapers by 1914, and over 800 other publications including pamphlets. As the Liberal MP Philip Morrell noted, the Act's requirement that the supplicant demonstrate that 'his pamphlet does not contain words which fall within the all-comprehensive provisions of the Act, is an almost hopeless task'.[13] Closer to home, Parliament was informed in 1915 that 'it would be against the public interest to set out the steps taken to prevent the dissemination of treasonable literature in Ireland'. Members might have been reassured, however, that 'the efforts [. . .] have already led to a very great decrease in the circulation of offensive pamphlets'. Nonetheless, attention was still drawn to a pamphlet circulating 'in which it is stated that Lord Kitchener is confident he can entrap, cajole, gull, and force 100,000 Irishmen to enlist in the demoralised, decadent, crime-stained, blood-sodden British Army'.[14]

## Government Information, Propaganda and Wellington House

Pamphlets could support governments, as well as undermine their policies. The government recognised that the foreign powers were clearly producing their own propaganda. At the outbreak of the war, the German government published a pamphlet in English, *Germany's Reasons for War with Russia*, and sent it to prominent Americans. This, as a debate in the House of Commons noted, had been republished by British newspapers, along with many other 'explanations of the origin of the War'. Rather belatedly, it was wondered if the Parliamentary Library should collect such materials.[15] Such a laissez-faire approach would not last the war.

Other pamphlets were deployed as a major component in the national recruitment campaign. It was widely believed that pamphlets were an important inducement to serve (alongside posters and cinema advertisements), and they included works such as Rudyard Kipling's anti-conscription and pro-enlistment *To Arms!* (1914). Belief in the efficacy of such tracts was widely held, as can be seen by the strident opposition expressed towards any text that might undermine the military call: a pre-war pamphlet by the future Parliamentary Secretary to the Board of Education critical of military service, which compared it to slavery, was debated in parliament.[16] Official pamphlets were seen as important means of explaining the numerous regulations created by a government at war. For example, when questioned in November 1914, the Prime Minister pointed to the 'large number of pamphlets and leaflets in circulation' explaining the details of civilian service.[17] Paying attention to such materials had financial importance: in 1915, numerous soldiers and dependants complained that they had missed out on their allowance of 6d. a day, as they had failed to complete Army Form 1,838, despite it being 'clearly stated in the War Office pamphlets of October and January last that "Application should be made at once"'. The government was unable to make any payments to those unaware of this procedure.[18]

Other pamphlets explained army allowances and pensions, rationing, restrictions on the sale of liquor, regulations relating to livestock, and other advice on 'various agricultural processes' or details of War Loans.[19] Pamphlets were also prepared offering advice on

> the best means of arresting the prevalent waste long existent in the domestic arrangements of the homes of the poorer classes, and for furnishing reliable information as to the nutritive value of certain vegetables highly esteemed on the Continent but little known in the United Kingdom, and for instruction as to the proper mode for cooking vegetables generally in a palatable form, and thus placing within the reach of all at a reasonable cost additional nourishing food, and thus averting any privations which may arise from high prices and scarcity of the ordinary supplies of food during the continuance of the War.[20]

Alongside such official material produced by central government, the nation was saturated by texts emanating from a more secretive source, the government's propaganda unit, based at Wellington House, under the direction of the Liberal MP and writer Charles Masterman. Wellington House produced over 1,100 items of printed propaganda in the years 1914 to 1918, the great majority of which were pamphlets, considered to be a means of quickly disseminating views.[21] Masterman himself also took up his pen and wrote a number of political or more clearly propagandistic pamphlets, such as *The Triumph of the Fleet* (1915), reprinted from *The Nation* of 6 November 1915. Masterminded under conditions of great secrecy, the Propaganda Bureau's work, which made use of many of the leading writers and academics of the day, profoundly shaped the way in which the war was discussed in print. Largely avoiding crude propaganda, Wellington House's techniques were subtler, yet it too also ran the risk of stoking the fires of political debate and dissent, even contributing to what has often been termed the 'pamphlet war' which erupted in 1915 about the cause of the war. Until 1918, the focus of the propaganda network was foreign opinion, and a list of over 30,000 American names was maintained, to whom were sent relevant materials.[22]

Propaganda could backfire more profoundly, however. Ernst Haeckel and Rudolph Eucken, for example, two professors at the University of Jena, published a defence of Germany's position that is credited with unwittingly turning many leading American thinkers, academics and writers against Germany by its biased and subjective scholarship. Such works contrasted with the seemingly objective and measured materials largely emanating – without acknowledgement – from Wellington House. Reports of German atrocities were detailed with lawyerly precision and dryness in the Bryce Report, for example, and profoundly affected American public opinion. To these atrocity reports, which had been encouraged by Theodore Roosevelt, who advised on how to influence America, the Bureau could also add poignant and emotive accounts of the martyrdom of Edith Cavell, executed by German firing squad in October 1915.[23]

## What Men of Letters Say

'The time has now come to pluck up courage and begin to talk and write soberly about the war.' With this sentence, George Bernard Shaw began the major serious debate about the war. In a vigorous pamphlet, *Common Sense about the War*, which first appeared as a supplement to the *New Statesman* on 14 November 1914 and was reprinted in the *New York Times* the following day, he suggested that the British were as culpable for the war as the Germans and Austrians, and proposed a negotiated peace. Composed during a retreat to a hotel in Torquay accompanied by a mound of diplomatic communiqués, it sold 75,000 copies in the first year of publication, and earned Shaw widespread ignominy and criticism in parliament.[24] It was, as the Marxist critic Granville Hicks noted in 1939, 'only his position as licensed court jester [that] saved him from serious retaliation'.[25] The debate took on international dimensions, with the *New York Times* publishing *Current History*, an ongoing magazine about the war, which began with a collection of pamphlets titled *What Men of Letters Say*, and which drew in a series of literary and intellectual heavyweights, from Bertrand Russell to H. G. Wells.

Shaw was answered by Arnold Bennett's squib 'Shaw's Nonsense about Belgium', along with a series of attacks by H. G. Wells. To these, Bennett, who later became the director of propaganda for France at the Ministry of Information, added *Liberty! A Statement of the British Cause* (1914), alongside numerous newspaper articles and a long-running series ('War Journal') in the *London Daily News*, which argued that despite the hellishness of war 'we have a silly, sentimental, illogical objection to being enslaved [. . .] It is for liberty we are fighting.'[26] Like many such pamphlets, Bennett's text began as a newspaper article before being republished in standalone form (*Saturday Evening Post*, 17 October 1914). The *Times Literary Supplement* reviewed the article, which made the case against the German 'challenge to civilisation', and it received brief notices in the *New York Times* and *Outlook*.[27] Strictly speaking, *Liberty! A Statement of the British Cause* crossed over from pamphlet to book form: rushed into print by the Propaganda Bureau at Wellington House, using a commercial publisher to disguise its origins, the text was bulked up to fifty-eight pages and generously bound. Like many patriotic works, Bennett's text does not glorify war or revel in jingoism, but states the case of German aggression and the need to defeat an uncivilised and cruel foe. And like many such works, it had one eye on American opinion, warning that 'the Metropolitan Museum, and the Pennsylvania Railway Station, not to mention the Metropolitan Tower, would go the way of Louvain'.[28] Wellington House ensured that such material was read in the United States, making use of the services of an agent, who placed at least £2,000-worth of copy in American publications.[29]

Bennett, who subsequently expressed his own misgivings about the war in his novel *The Pretty Lady* (1918), was by no means the only man of letters to be involved.[30] Perhaps the most famous figure to produce such works, Rudyard Kipling was strongly supportive of the British war effort, producing a stream of articles, speeches and pamphlets. In 1915, the War Office sent him on a tour of the army in France, leading to the publication of *The New Army in Training* (1915; published as *New Army* in the USA), a sixty-four-page text that sold for sixpence and portrayed a young, 'beautifully fit' collection of Canadians, cockney cyclists and Indian troops, all living 'in these high days'. For Kipling, the war was at first an adventurous crusade, yet a crusade conducted in a decidedly English, understated manner: 'But having chosen to do his bit, he does it, and talks as much about his motives as he would of his religion or his love-affairs.'[31] Kipling also posed a challenge to those not heeding the bugle call: 'But what will be the position in years to come?' he asked, reminiscent of Savile Lumley and Arthur Gunn's Parliament Recruiting Committee poster, 'Daddy, what did YOU do in the Great War?'[32]

Kipling was not the only popular author to assist the Bureau. Anthony Hope Hawkins, playwright and author of the 'Ruritanian romance' *The Prisoner of Zenda*, reviewed thousands of novels and pamphlets to see if, as Masterman said, these were 'desirable to use [. . .] for publicity purposes'.[33] He also penned several pamphlets in the early years of the war, including a suite of works that attacked General Friedrich von Bernhardi, who had argued that the Germans were unsuited to democracy, and had to be governed by 'Powerful Personalities'. Ignoring Bernhardi's true (and limited) pre-war influence in Germany, such pamphlets proved very successful and were viewed as being exceedingly effective in shaping American opinion.

Literary writers were joined by historians. Seemingly without government encouragement, the History School of Oxford University published what they believed to be the authoritative account of the origins of the war in a series of 'Oxford Pamphlets', written by some of the university's best-known dons and begun by *Why We Are at War*. It was later claimed by Admiral Sir Reginald Hall that 'the printed page never played so important a part in war'.[34] Indeed, *Why We Are at War* (and the patriotic volume *War Songs*) almost completely occupied the syndic's presses for all of 1914.[35]

The series argued that Britain was at war in obligation to France as much as in defence of Belgium, and arguably played a substantial role in shaping public opinion.

'Oxford Pamphlets' also expanded its roster of authors to include hugely popular writers, including John Buchan, whose *Britain's War by Land* was number sixty-six in the series and sold around a quarter of a million copies. In 1916, Buchan asked for an estimate for printing 100,000 copies of 'a pamphlet by me on the battle of Jutland' to be sold at a price of 'no more than 1/-'.[36] Not only was the print run very high but the cost was deliberately kept reasonable to ensure the broadest circulation, which also gives some idea of the potential reach of pamphlets. Buchan, along with other members of the propaganda services, was keen for such works to find an international audience and, like many other of Buchan's works, his pamphlet was translated into several other languages (variously Dutch, French, Danish, Spanish, German), again a reminder that the work of propaganda was focused as much on foreign public opinion as it was on promoting morale on the home front. Indeed, it was sometimes felt that some materials should be just for foreign consumption: notably Buchan's account of the Somme, which – inaccurately but evocatively – depicts rows of Tommies slowly marching in line into the fire of the German machine guns.[37]

Propaganda was not, of course, limited to male writers or audiences. The English suffrage campaigner Christabel Pankhurst, for example, was a strong supporter of the war in Britain's 'hour of need', and turned from the cause of suffrage at the outbreak of the war. She toured the States in the autumn of 1914 seeking support, and the Women's Social and Political Union published at least one of her speeches for a British audience as *America and the War: A Speech at Carnegie Hall, New York* (London, 1914). Such works promoted both causes: they made the case for Britain's war aims and need for US support, but also demonstrated that a woman could act on the international political stage. These pamphlets took pains to appear reasoned and authoritative, with clear typography, but also with a good use of headings (in this case in bold), which guide the reader through the argument: 'Will not Submit to Arbitration [. . .] Brewing for Years [. . .] Fighting for Democratic Government [. . .] Britain Fighting for her own National Existence [. . .] Belgium the Suffragette Nation [. . .] Germany a Male Nation [. . .] American Women: Hold Hands with Great Britain!'

## Pacifism

A quartet of publishers, some with Quaker connections, but all with independent financial support, ensured that pacifist pamphlets, or texts supportive of such a position, found their way to market, producing 'a diverse body of literatures [. . .] which amounted to a chorus of dissent'.[38] Equally importantly, they were able to plug into British and indeed international networks vital for the supply of ideas, support and sense of community. The obstacles facing the production and dissemination of such materials should not be underestimated, and make their preservation in collections such as the Playne Collection (Senate House Library, University of London) all the more remarkable.

Much opposition revolved around conscription, and the authorities were particularly attentive to dissent along these lines, making full use of the regulations connected to the Defence of the Realm Act to prosecute and imprison those writing, printing and distributing leaflets, as well as ordering the destruction of such materials. While the Home Secretary had expressed a view that people were not to be prosecuted for voicing an opinion that did not incite violence or illegal action, it was clear that the dissent clause of the Act was being used to stifle debate. For example, in Northampton, two women were fined £50 or sentenced to three months' imprisonment for distributing anti-conscription and anti-war leaflets. One of them said: 'I plead guilty to trying to create a public feeling to stop the War.' The texts they were distributing contained reprints of speeches made by Richard Cobden in 1854 and an 1813 article by the Revd Sydney Smith, which Holt quoted in the House: 'there is more misery inflicted upon mankind by one year of war than by all the civil peculations and oppressions of a century.'[39] The issue was raised in Parliament, where Holt suggested that the pamphlets 'are almost punishable on the grounds of their literary inadequacies. I shall be glad to lend them to any Member in order that he may see for himself how absolutely trumpery are the grounds of these persecutions.'[40] Other writings, he noted, were taken from *Liberalism: Its Principles and Proposals* (1912), a work prefaced by the Prime Minister, Herbert Asquith. Thus Holt argued that '[f]or making extracts from the very juvenile writings of the Home Secretary people absolutely are being imprisoned at present'.[41] Texts clearly took on new, and often dangerous, meanings within the context of pamphlets.

## Post-War Pamphlets

The ending of the war did not curtail the output of pamphlets, but rather encouraged their production in order to discuss the post-war settlement, as did the ending of the rationing of paper and ink and the ending of censorship. Many of these pamphlets were acts of commemoration. Such materials had, of course, begun during the war, such as *St Andrews University in the Great War*, a twenty-eight-page roll of honour and list of members of the university on naval and military service, published in December 1915. Such works were often finely produced, with coloured covers and a range of inks (such as red and blue borders), fonts and printer's ornaments, as befitted their commemorative nature. Producing and collecting them was an act of remembrance, and could often also serve to raise funds for military charities. Pamphlets could also point to other intersections of commemoration and commerce, such as the *Catalogue d'affiches françaises illustrées, Guerre 1914–19* (Paris, 1919), which was produced to be sold by the 'Musée de la Guerre', a bookshop and journal that had operated commercially throughout the war. The Musée also sold military-themed stamps, maps and postcards as well as posters, and had begun as a vehicle for the journalist and writer John Grand-Carteret (1850–1927). For those seeking to contact the deceased, Spiritualist pamphlets offered one possible path, as well as advertising the services of mediums. More practical aid was offered by the Red Cross, whose various organisations were responsible for numerous pamphlets, such as the Red Cross Institute for Crippled and Disabled Men, which published Douglas McMurtrie's *Aidons les mutilés de la guerre à devenir de bons ouvriers de metiér* in 1918; like many such pamplets, this was published in several languages, including Norwegian, Spanish and Italian.

Pamphlets also reveal the radicalisation of politics, ranging from communism to proto-fascism. Socialist opposition to the war now found full voice, as the general tone of debate became more internationalist.[42] Nationalism was also well represented, for example in the *Red Book: Red Easter in the Dodecanese* (Manchester, 1919), which argued for the return of the Dodecanese to Greece from Italy. Such works offered solutions to the problems confronting citizens of the post-war world, such as the journalist and moderate trade-unionist Ralph Easley's (1856–1939) prosaic-sounding *After-the-War Problems* (New York, 1918, twenty-six pages), which offered the New York working class an alternative to communism and socialism along the lines of improvements to wages and working conditions, rather than the state ownership of factories.

The 'war to end all wars' – a phrase used mostly sardonically after the war, rather than idealistically during it – did not, of course, bring harmony, but only more strife. While some pamphlet and political writing sought to bring balm, relief or escapism, whether through acts of remembrance, a focus on the domestic or personal (such as the publications focusing on hobbies, gardening and other domestic pursuits), or the religious, mystical or superstitious, pamphlets continued to develop the political ideologies and conflicts that governments, with only limited success, attempted to suppress during the time of war. Cheap to produce, able to call on a wide distribution network, and difficult for governments to control, pamphlets sought to find someone to blame, whether corrupt politicians, the forces of capitalism and Empire, or, even more insidiously, racial and ethnic groups. As such, pamphlets set the stage for the great debates of the next decade, shaping memories of the Great War, defining political extremes, and helping to give birth to increasingly virulent forms of nationalsm.

## Notes

1. H. G. Wells, 'The War That Will End War', *Daily News*, 14 August 1914, reprinted as H. G. Wells, *The War to End All War* (London: Frank and Cecil Palmer, 1914).
2. *Hansard*, House of Lords Debates, 7 August 1914, vol. 17, column 469.
3. Deian Hopkin, 'Domestic Censorship in the First World War', *Journal of Contemporary History*, 5.4 (1970), 151–69 (153).
4. *Hansard*, House of Commons Debates, 7 August 1914, vol. 65, column 2,155.
5. 'Mr. KING asked whether a Press Censorship is exercised over pamphlets, magazine articles, and books, or whether the censorship extends only to newspaper publications? The SOLICITOR-GENERAL (Sir Stanley Buckmaster): The answer to the first part of the question is in the affirmative; consequently, the answer to the latter part of the question is in the negative.' HC Deb, 18 November 1914, vol. 68, column 417.
6. HC Deb, 17 January 1918, vol. 101, columns 482–3.
7. HC Deb, 16 September 1915, vol. 74, columns 148–9; HC Deb, 1 June 1916, vol. 82, column 2,978.
8. HC Deb, 16 September 1915, vol. 74, columns 148–9.
9. HC Deb, 12 October 1915, vol. 74, columns 1,168–9.
10. HC Deb, 26 June 1916, vol. 83, columns 509–10.
11. HC Deb, 23 January 1918, vol. 101, columns 1,004–5W.
12. Ibid.
13. HC Deb, 24 February 1914, vol. 58, columns 1,568–9. See also HC Deb, 23 July 1918, vol. 108, column 1,632.
14. HC Deb, 4 March 1915, vol. 70, column 947.
15. HC Deb, 27 August 1914, vol. 66, column 123.

16. 'Of all forms of subservience short of positive slavery, military subservience is by far the worst.' HC Deb, 23 April 1914, vol. 61, columns 1,253–60.
17. HC Deb, 26 November 1914, vol. 68, columns 1,303–4.
18. HC Deb, 19 May 1915, vol. 71, column 2,335.
19. HC Deb, 10 March 1915, vol. 70, columns 1,413–14; HC Deb, 7 July 1915, vol. 73, columns 357–9: 'Sir GODFREY BARING: Will the right hon. Gentleman embody all this valuable information he has given in pamphlets sent to the post offices so as to be accessible to the public?'
20. HC Deb, 5 July 1915, vol. 73, columns 28–9.
21. Peter Buitenhuis, *The Great War of Words: British, American and Canadian Propaganda and Fiction, 1914–1933* (Vancouver: University of British Columbia Press, 1987), p. 21.
22. Stuart Robson, *The First World War* (London and New York: Longman, 1998), p. 44.
23. Buitenhuis, *The Great War of Words*, p. 57.
24. HC Deb, 25 November 1914, vol. 68, columns 1,095–6.
25. Granville Hicks, 'Literature and the War', *College English*, 1.3 (1939), 199–207 (201).
26. Quoted in Harold Orel, *Popular Fiction in England, 1914–1918* (Lexington: University Press of Kentucky, 1992), p. 203.
27. Bennett received the sum of £200 for the article (James Hepburn, *Arnold Bennett: The Critical Heritage* (London: Routledge & Kegan Paul, 1971), p. 71). He was later asked, by an unwitting editor, to edit Shaw's *Common Sense about the War* for book publication (Buitenhuis, *The Great War of Words*, p. 40).
28. Arnold Bennett, 'Liberty – A Statement of the British Case', *Saturday Evening Post*, 17 October 1914, p. 32.
29. Buitenhuis, *The Great War of Words*, p. 42.
30. See *The Collected Papers of Bertrand Russell, Volume 13: Prophecy and Dissent, 1914–1916*, ed. Richard A. Rempel (London: Routledge, 1988).
31. Rudyard Kipling, *The New Army in Training* (London: Macmillan, 1915), chapter 6, section 4, 'The Secret of the Services', accessed via the Kipling Society, <http://www.kiplingsociety.co.uk/rg_newarmy_chapter6.htm> (last accessed 9 January 2017).
32. Rudyard Kipling, *The New Army in Training* (London: Macmillan, 1915), p. 62.
33. Buitenhuis, *The Great War of Words*, p. 31.
34. Quoted in Lynda Mugglestone, *Lost for Words: The Hidden History of the Oxford English Dictionary* (London and New Haven: Yale University Press, 2005), p. 194.
35. Ibid.
36. Kate Macdonald, 'Translating Propaganda', in Mary Hammond and Shafquat Towheed (eds), *Publishing in the First World War: Essays in Book History* (Basingstoke: Palgrave Macmillan, 2007), pp. 181–201 (p. 192).
37. See Benedikt Stuchtey and Peter Wende (eds), *British and German Historiography, 1750–1950: Traditions, Perceptions, and Transfers* (Oxford: Oxford University Press, 2000), p. 361.
38. Grace Brockington, 'Translating Peace: Pacifist Publishing and the Transmission of Texts', in Hammond and Towheed (eds), *Publishing in the First World War*, pp. 46–58 (p. 47).
39. Sydney Smith, 'Note to Article Reprinted from "Edinburgh Review," 1813', quoted in HC Deb, 1 June 1916, vol. 82, column 2,982.
40. HC Deb, 1 June 1916, vol. 82, column 2,983.
41. Ibid., columns 2,953–3,050.
42. Brockington, 'Translating Peace', p. 47.

# 18

# 'The whole of war is an atrocity': Morgan Philips Price and First World War Reporting in the Ottoman/Russian Borderlands

*Jo Laycock*

## Introduction

> From the heights which had been captured we could see, spread out before us like a chess-board, the whole region which was to be the field of battle that day for the other wing of advance. Could any battlefield in all the European theatres equal this one?[1]

By the end of 1915, *The Observer* reported, land battles were raging along a front stretching from 'the low countries to Ararat'.[2] Ararat, on the borders of the Russian and Ottoman Empires, was the mountain where Noah's Ark was believed to have come to rest after the flood and as such was evocative of the origins of Western, Christian civilisation. Its use here as a geographical reference point thus created a connection between conflict on the far-flung Caucasus front and the British readership of *The Observer*. During the First World War Ararat was at the heart of the clash between the Ottoman and Russian Empires, a conflict characterised by 'battles on an epic – and tragic – scale on a front more than 700 miles in length and pocked by high mountain ranges blanketed in snow and sub-zero temperatures'.[3] Beyond this front the region experienced mass population displacement, atrocities against combatants and civilians, and the implementation of genocidal policies which resulted in the deaths of around one million Armenians and the displacement of thousands more.[4]

Morgan Philips Price, a 'special correspondent' for the *Manchester Guardian*, was the only British correspondent on the Caucasus front. He is well known as a witness of the Russian Revolution and for his controversially sympathetic reporting of the early years of Bolshevik rule.[5] His writing on the war in the Caucasus, in contrast, has received relatively little attention. In November 1914 Philips Price travelled to Russia, spending the first part of his journey in St Petersburg (Petrograd), Warsaw and behind the lines on the Eastern front. He then travelled to the south to Tbilisi (Tiflis), where he remained for almost two years, before travelling to Moscow. During his time in Russia he sent 141 dispatches as well as many private memoranda.[6] Many of his later dispatches were censored and Philips Price's increasingly obvious support for the Bolsheviks meant that C. P. Scott, editor of the *Manchester Guardian*, ended his association with the newspaper in 1919.[7]

In 1918 Philips Price published an account of his experiences in the Caucasus, *War and Revolution in Asiatic Russia*.

Examining Philips Price's writings offers important insights into the way the British press engaged with the war beyond the Western front and confronted the representation of mass displacement and violence against civilians on an unprecedented scale. This chapter focuses on the first two and a half years of the war, before the Russian revolutions radically reshaped both the situation on the Caucasus front and the future of the region. The first part of the chapter focuses on the ways in which Philips Price represented and made sense of war in a region long considered to be an unstable fracture-line between Europe and Asia. The second focuses more closely upon his place in the British reporting of violence against civilians, especially the genocide of the Ottoman Armenians.

## Contexts: War and Genocide in an Imperial Borderland

Over the course of the last decade historians have challenged the conventional geographical boundaries of the First World War, demonstrating that the war was not only fought for imperial ends, across imperial territories, but that it also relied on the mobilisation of colonial resources and populations.[8] Nonetheless, while Jay Winter has suggested that the current generation of scholarship is characterised by its transnational approach, any transnational 'turn' has been uneven.[9] Erik Jan Zürcher has argued that 'with the single exception of the issue of the Armenian genocide [the First World War] remains the most understudied period in twentieth century Turkish history'.[10] Joshua Sanborn, meanwhile, has observed that whilst the names of the battlefields of the Western front have attained an iconic status for European and American audiences, the sites of violence of the Eastern front are much less familiar.[11] The war in Europe has also dominated collective memories of the First World War, with centenary commemorations, in Britain at least, focused on the trench warfare of the Western front. If the Russian Empire figures in popular memory at all, it is the image of an ill-equipped soldiery and social unrest on the home front which comes to the fore. In the case of the war in the Ottoman Empire, it is a highly romanticised vision of the Gallipoli campaign and the exploits of 'Lawrence of Arabia' which have captured the public imagination.[12] The clash of the Ottoman and Russian Empires in the Caucasus rarely figures in such popular representations.[13]

Over the course of the nineteenth century, as Russia had pushed south, the Caucasus and eastern Anatolia had become the site of multiple conflicts between the Ottoman and Russian Empires.[14] These imperial borderlands were home to a multi-ethnic, religiously diverse population of Turks, Armenians, Kurds, Greeks and other minorities. In the decades before the First World War entwined processes of Ottoman decline and the rise of nationalism amongst minority populations had led to social upheaval and inter-ethnic tension. In particular, Armenians became the targets of increased suspicion and hostility from Ottoman authorities, who questioned their loyalty and place in the Empire.[15] Between 1894 and 1896 these tensions had erupted into violence and around 100,000 Armenians were killed in a series of massacres.[16] These events prompted an international outcry. In Britain, 'Armenophile' networks of scholars, travellers, journalists and church leaders, many of them associated with the Liberal Party, lobbied on behalf of the Armenians. Their protests echoed the 'Bulgarian atrocities' agitation in which Gladstone had railed against the abuse of Christian minorities by 'the Turk'.[17] The Armenians were adopted as a deserving moral cause in Britain and the 'Armenian Question' continued to pose a geopolitical problem for the European powers.[18]

The outbreak of the First World War wreaked new kinds of violence on the Ottoman/Russian borderlands. The conflict was played out in the inhospitable highland terrain of eastern Anatolia and the Caucasus along a front extending south-east from the Black Sea to north-western Persia. On 22 December 1914 the Ottoman Third Army launched the first major offensive. Freezing weather, harsh terrain, supply problems and the poor condition of Ottoman forces led to a devastating defeat by the Russian Caucasus Army at Sarikamish. In the months that followed, whilst the Ottoman military struggled to recover from this defeat, the Russians pushed west, eventually occupying swathes of eastern Anatolia.[19] In April 1915 the Ottoman authorities were faced with an Armenian uprising in the city of Van, which exacerbated existing fears of Armenian disloyalty. As Ronald Grigor Suny has explained, 'fear and a profound sense of insecurity compounded by defeats in the winter of 1915 and the threats from Allied forces had combined into a toxic perception of all Armenians as an internal subversive force allied to the Russians.'[20] A systematic series of massacres and deportations, intended to rid the Empire of its Armenian population in its entirety, followed.[21] The fate of the Armenians once again caused an international outcry, but Allied protestations did nothing to halt a genocide perpetrated behind Ottoman lines. The Caucasus front, meanwhile, became the site of a refugee crisis as around 300,000 Armenians fled Ottoman violence.

## Reporting the War in the Caucasus

On the eve of the First World War, British relations with the Ottoman and Russian Empires were in flux. Stereotypes of Russian and Ottoman backwardness and despotism were still contrasted unfavourably with the progressive and civilising virtues of British rule. However, complexities lay below the surface. During the nineteenth century, the Ottoman Empire had been viewed as an essential ally, a bulwark against aggressive Russian expansionism. Britain's alliance with the Ottomans had, however, been rendered precarious by the crises provoked by the persecution of Christian minorities in the Empire's borderlands.[22] The Balkan Wars of 1912–13 had further reinforced images both of Ottoman barbarism and of the Empire's peripheries as sites of endemic violence and instability.[23] During the war these well-worn stereotypes were mobilised in order to reconstruct the Ottomans as an archetypal enemy. A propaganda pamphlet by Arnold Toynbee, for example, claimed that the Ottoman Empire was 'a pretension, enforced by bloodshed and violence whenever and wherever the Osmanli government has power'.[24] The image of the 'terrible Turk' was utilised to vilify not only the Ottoman Empire, but also Germany. *The Times* declared that the 'union of German Kultur and old fashioned Turkish barbarism has created a real Frankenstein monster'.[25]

Claiming Russia as an ally in a war framed by the British government as a defence of the freedom of small nations was more complex. Over the course of the nineteenth century Russian imperialism had been presented as a threat to the British Empire. Whilst attitudes began to change in the latter decades of the century, 'the tradition of Russophobia continued to flourish, both amongst radicals appalled by the brutality of the tsarist regime and imperially minded Conservatives who fretted about the threat posed to India.'[26] Even after the Anglo-Russian entente of 1907 negative perceptions of autocratic, oppressive tsarist rule lingered.[27] After the outbreak of war, efforts were made in the British press to 'rehabilitate' Russia. This went beyond praise of the might of the Russian military 'steamroller' and its importance for the defeat of Germany. In *The Times* and the *Daily Mail* the journalist and traveller Stephen Graham expounded the virtues of 'Holy Russia' and praised the 'Russian soul'.[28] These images of Britain's new ally were by no means universally accepted, especially by the radical left. In *War and Revolution*, Philips Price, by then sympathetic to the Bolshevik regime, recalled critically the 'sentimental travellers who wrote in the Northcliffe press' and 'babbled of the "new era" in "Holy Russia"; of a people on their knees to God and their little Father Tsar'.[29]

The progress of the war *between* the Russian and Ottoman Empires occupied the British press to a much lesser degree than the images and roles of the two empires as ally and enemy. Philips Price himself claimed that most of the British press had been 'inclined to turn the whole of their attention toward Europe', neglecting other theatres of war.[30] His own presence in the Caucasus arose from somewhat unlikely circumstances. He was not a professional journalist and his visit to the Ottoman/Russian borderlands came about because of existing connections with the region and the *Manchester Guardian*. His family's business had led him to travel extensively in the peripheries of the Russian Empire and he spoke fluent Russian. In 1912, based on his experiences during his travels, he had reported on the situation in the Russian occupied areas of Persia for the *Manchester Guardian*.[31] At the end of November 1914 he wrote to C. P. Scott offering his services as a correspondent:

> As you said you thought the *Manchester Guardian* would be able to receive some articles from me from Russia, I wonder if you could give me a letter describing me as your special correspondent like you did last year when I was in Turkey [. . .] I should probably get down into the Caucasus and try to see something interesting there, as I know that country very well.[32]

In *War and Revolution*, Philips Price claimed that it was his desire to give an honest account of the war which led him to the Caucasus front: 'I could not write and say that all was well, or join the chorus of those who conceived it their duty to hide the truth. Rather than bury my conscience in Europe I decided to betake myself to Asia.'[33] This tension between 'truth telling' and supporting the war effort permeated Philips Price's wartime reporting. His support for the war was reluctant and conditional. He was a member of the Union of Democratic Control, a pressure group established in the early days of the war which called for parliamentary control of foreign policy, open diplomacy and a just settlement for the war. In 1914 he authored their *Diplomatic History of the War*.[34] In a sense the *Manchester Guardian* was a natural home for his views. In the lead-up to August 1914 the paper had also espoused anti-war views, but upon the outbreak of war Scott, like Philips Price, had reluctantly come to support the war effort.[35]

The First World War ushered in unprecedented restrictions on the movements of war correspondents as well as intensified monitoring and censorship.[36] Kitchener infamously banned war correspondents entirely from the Western front until June 1915 before appointing just five accredited correspondents for the Press Bureau, while voluntary cooperation between the leaders of the British press and the state blurred the boundaries between reporting and 'official' propaganda.[37] Whilst a few journalists found fame exposing the realities of war, most correspondents found their activities curbed and their experiences at odds with the adventurous image of the war correspondent which had emerged during the 'golden age' of the late nineteenth century.[38] Philips Price presented himself in opposition to this trend, as the last of a dying breed of authentic, adventurous war correspondents, travelling bravely across unchartered terrain. He described setting off to the front from Tabriz:

> I bought three horses and hired one Persian Armenian to come with me [. . .] Thus equipped like war correspondents used to be in the Crimea and the Russo-Turkish war of 1877, I could pitch my tent anywhere, carry my own supplies and cook my own food. I must have been one of the last war correspondents of this type. They had already disappeared from the European front.[39]

He was, he claimed, 'the first person from the outside world' to visit the battlefield around Dilman (north-western Persia) and the first to 'make any investigations as to the effects of the war's ravages upon the native populations of these regions'.[40]

By emphasising his status as a lone reporter on a remote front, unbound by the restrictions placed on those closer to home, Philips Price presented himself as an authentic source of information. In Phillip Knightley's analysis, Philips Price's honesty about the situation in Russia rendered him 'the best British war correspondent to emerge from this period'.[41] Yet although Philips Price's writing was far removed from the approach of the Northcliffe press, it would be naive to view him as the source of untainted, objective 'truth', for he was well aware of the need to self-censor. For example, in the aftermath of the Russian taking of Erzerum, lauded in much of the press as a great victory and evidence of the endurance and strength of the Russian military, Philips Price described meeting Russian soldiers who told him they thought the war was 'very stupid and wrong' and they 'had no quarrel with the Turkish peasant'. But he did not 'sit down and write an article to my paper; for I knew that the wise controller of news and opinion, the censor, would regard any description of this conversation as "prejudicial to the interests of the state."'[42]

## Representing the Caucasus: Landscape, Population and Violence

In *War and Revolution*, Philips Price contrasted the Caucasus front with the modern warfare of the Western front: 'Campaigning on the Caucasus front and in Armenia is very different from that in Europe [. . .] the methods used are the old ones [. . .] The old maxim of "making a flank and turning it" has to be followed.'[43] He attributed the differences in part to the harsh geographical environment of the region.[44] He also suggested that Turkish and Russian methods of waging war were less advanced than those of their counterparts in Western Europe: he claimed one of the reasons for the failure of a Turkish advance in north-western Persia was because their 'only method of transport was by camels and mules'.[45] This was not simply a matter of decrying the strength of the enemy. Philips Price also observed that the Russians, despite their military might, 'did not move with the rapidity of *western* armies'.[46] Yet even if warfare in the Caucasus was less 'modern', it appeared, in Philips Price's narrative, to be more authentic. In 1915 he had joined a Red Cross detachment following the Russian army as they advanced past Van. From his vantage point in the mountains, he presented a deeply romanticised vision of the front at odds with the anti-war sentiments he expressed elsewhere:

> The beautiful scene of mountain, lake and plateau was not sullied, but rather embroidered by the sights of war, by the ant-like chains of infantry on the hills, and the white jewels of bursting shrapnel on the azure lake.[47]

His description of the beauties of battle recalls what Mary Louise Pratt has termed the 'monarch of all I survey scene', common to nineteenth-century travel writing, in which Europeans discover and describe from on high, in a manner which implied their 'power if not to possess then at least to evaluate' a landscape.[48] Philips Price certainly claimed for himself a viewpoint inaccessible to those taking part in the action.[49] He was able to position himself as both insider, uniquely close to the action, and outsider, maintaining a sense of difference and distance from the events unfolding around him. Matthew Farish has suggested that the spatial conditions created by trench warfare on the Western front obscured the war correspondent's traditional view from 'on high'; that on the Western front 'there was no untainted higher ground, no god's eye view to invoke in the name of science or civilisation'.[50] On the Caucasus front, the 'higher ground' still seemed to exist. Philips Price's later writings suggest that he felt the mountains of the Caucasus had provided him with a vantage point and distinctive understanding not only of the region but of the war on a global scale. In February 1917 he wrote to his uncle from Tbilisi:

> For my part living as I am on the threshold between east and west, I can look with dispassion on the ruin of European civilisation and I am only surprised at the extraordinarily rapid rate at which it totters to its fall.[51]

His analyses of the origins of the violence he witnessed were not based on well-established stereotypes of the region as the site of a clash between Europe and Asia or Christianity and Islam.[52] Instead he focused on geography and economics. Much of the region's *internal* conflict, he suggested, was the result of pressure on the sedentary populations by nomadic 'tribes' seeking land. These nomadic populations were not inherently bloodthirsty, but had become 'predatory by instinct' because of their harsh conditions of life.[53] However, he understood the more serious cause of conflict to be imperialism – 'the struggle of outside influences for the possession of trade routes and spheres of influence'.[54] Yet this kind of rational, structural analysis and anti-imperialist reasoning was interspersed with orientalist tropes and exotic, romantic vignettes. In the Russian army encampment at Lake Van, he claimed, he fell asleep 'to the sound of passing caravan-bells and the camels' plaintive moan, while the waves on the lake splashed gently on the pebbled beach'.[55] Similarly, his representation of the people he encountered varied between evocations of common humanity and clichéd ethnic and orientalist stereotypes. Reporting from the Eastern front, he abandoned historical or economic analysis for popular stereotypes of the war, describing 'my friend the Russian soldier, in his fur-lined, mud-covered coat, looking westward from his rampart in Poland, facing his century old enemy the Teuton'.[56] This image of the inherent fatalism of both Russian and Ottoman peasants, and his description of the piety of wounded Russian soldiers who 'bore their sufferings with the stoic fortitude of the Slav', recalled the popular images of 'Holy Russia' that he critiqued elsewhere.[57]

In March 1916 Philips Price arrived in Erzerum. The Russian taking of this fortified city had caused a sensation in the British press and Price was the first Western correspondent to arrive in the aftermath of the battle.[58] In his dispatch Philips Price seemed once again to resort to orientalist stereotypes as he observed that 'nowhere could the philosophy of the East be more plainly exhibited than on the calm and dignified faces of the 25,000 civilian Turks who stayed behind' in the city.[59] Yet his discovery of the bodies of several young Russian and Ottoman soldiers outside the city provoked a rather different response: 'In their homes in the Caucasus and Anatolia', he imagined, 'they had lived as neighbours peacefully together, with probably no thought of hatred to one another. War came and they were called and now they sleep together and the snow and frost were covering up all relics of the struggle.'[60] Such evocations of common humanity and the shared suffering of ordinary people in wartime regardless of their ethnic background would characterise Philips Price's response to the violence he encountered beyond the battlefield.

## Engaging with Atrocity in the Ottoman/Russian Borderlands

Before he arrived in the Caucasus, Philips Price travelled behind the Russian lines on the Eastern front in Galicia, the site of widespread attacks on the local Jewish population by occupying Russian forces. Due to Russian censorship he was unable to reveal what he had encountered.[61] During the First World War civilians were widely targeted as part of wartime state practice and military strategy as well as in spontaneous acts of violence. According to Philips Price, the European attempt 'to separate civilians from combatants' had failed and the world had descended into the 'primitive' methods of warfare in Asia.[62] In the Caucasus he witnessed violence against civilians of an even more widespread and extreme nature, including the state-sponsored massacre and deportation of the Ottoman Armenian population. In contrast to his experience in Galicia, he not only reported this violence for the *Manchester Guardian*, he also became involved with efforts to provide relief for those displaced and dispossessed as a result of it. He worked with the Tbilisi representatives of the British relief organisation the Lord Mayor's Fund for Armenian Refugees to start an 'industry' for the 200,000 Armenian refugees in the Caucasus, and distributed relief amongst remote villages in 'Lazistan'.

News of the fate of the Ottoman Armenians began to reach the British press in May 1915. On 24 April 1915, in the aftermath of the resistance at Van and on the eve of the Gallipoli landings, the leaders of the Armenian community in Istanbul were arrested. Over the following months the sporadic violence and insecurity which had characterised the first months of the war was replaced by a systematic campaign of massacre and deportation across the Empire. The genocidal process varied from region to region, but in general men were removed from their homes and killed outright, whereas women and children faced deportation marches. Thousands died of starvation and exposure during the marches; others were subjected to theft and sexual violence. Many Armenian women and children were taken into Turkish and Kurdish homes and forced to convert to Islam. Those who survived the marches found themselves in concentration camps in Syria lacking access to food, shelter or medical care.[63]

If total war created the conditions in which genocide became possible, it also created a 'cover' for the actions of the Young Turk government and meant that the interior of the Ottoman Empire was inaccessible to most British observers.[64] News trickled back to Britain via the Armenophile networks which had emerged there in the aftermath of the massacres of the 1890s. In Britain, Viscount James Bryce, veteran of the Armenian cause, played a central role in communicating the news to both the government and the press. Bryce had a long-standing relationship with C. P. Scott at the *Manchester Guardian*, and both were veterans of the 'pro-Boer' movement and a number of other liberal 'humanitarian' causes.[65] In August 1915 Bryce offered Scott accounts of 'massacres perpetrated by the Turks in Armenia' for publication.[66] A few days later the paper published a report from a 'trustworthy source' describing the removal of Armenian families from the Zeitun and Marash regions.[67] Over the course of the war the *Manchester Guardian* reported regularly on the fate of the Armenians, drawing on dispatches from Philips Price as well as accounts from Scott's contacts in Armenophile networks and other correspondents on the fringes of the Ottoman Empire.[68]

Recurring protests regarding the Ottoman persecution of minorities in the nineteenth-century press had made the notions of Turkish barbarism and Christian victimhood familiar to British readers. In his influential *Bulgarian Horrors* pamphlet, Gladstone had spoken of the 'unbounded savagery' of the Turks, whilst graphic, sensationalist reports of violence against Bulgarians, Armenians and other minorities were a staple of the crusading 'new journalism' of the late nineteenth century.[69] W. T. Stead, amongst others, helped to consolidate an image of 'the Turk' as the perpetrator of sadistic forms of violence, especially against women and children. In 1915 these images of Armenian victimhood and Ottoman barbarity resurfaced and were incorporated into state-sponsored propaganda intended to vilify the enemy and convince neutral countries that the war was both necessary and moral.

The fate of the Armenians in 1915 was recognised by British observers to be of a different order to previous acts of Ottoman violence. There was a widespread understanding that the massacres and deportations represented an attempt to 'exterminate' or 'destroy' the Armenian nation. 'There had never been', the *Manchester Guardian* claimed, 'so resolute an attempt to *exterminate* a whole race, never one which promised to be so successful.'[70] In the context of war, violence against the Armenians acquired new meanings. The 'extermination' of the Armenian population was understood not simply as a manifestation of inevitable Ottoman barbarism. It was also framed as an 'atrocity', an act of enemy violence which transgressed the rules of civilised warfare, directly comparable to the sinking of the *Lusitania*, the use of poison gas, the execution of the British nurse Edith Cavell, and, perhaps most significantly, the acts of violence committed by German troops during the invasion of Belgium.[71] Reports of atrocities played an important role in propaganda, but also had a broader social and cultural significance for making meaning from the war. They were, in the words of Horne and Kramer, an 'expressive and creative act. They vented fear and trauma and helped impose some kind of narrative order on what were usually chaotic experiences.'[72]

Atrocity narratives usually centred on violence against civilians, usually women and children. In 1915 the *Manchester Guardian* generally shied away from the graphic accounts of sexualised violence which had been characteristic of reports of Ottoman violence in the late nineteenth century.[73] Rather, they emphasised the intent, scale and implementation of the massacres and deportations. The majority of the massacres of Armenians in the interior of Anatolia, the deportation marches, and the camps of the Syrian desert, were beyond Philips Price's view from behind the Russian lines; however, he witnessed the aftermaths of this violence. On his journeys with the Russian army around Kars, for example, he witnessed around 180,000 Armenian refugees from Van and Bitlis 'pour' into the Kars plateau and the Erivan plain.[74] On the coast at Trebizond, he reported that the Armenian population were subjected to savage and inhuman treatment, and were annihilated within a very few days, whilst the Armenians of the Mush plain took to the mountains and were 'almost exterminated during fighting over the next two months'; in Erzerum, meanwhile, he reported that the Armenians 'were mostly put on their way on the road to exile'.[75]

Through Philips Price the *Manchester Guardian* became involved in the British campaign for aid for Armenian refugees. In March 1916 he wrote to Scott, 'I am very interested in the Armenian and Assyrian refugees in the Caucasus and want to write an appeal for more funds for their assistance.'[76] Later that year the newspaper would publish further appeals by Bryce and Harold Buxton, secretary of the Lord Mayor's Fund for Armenian Refugees.[77] These charitable appeals were a product of the newspaper's close connections to Armenophile circles and helped define the Armenians as a 'worthy' cause in Britain. Like atrocity stories, such appeals provided a way for the public to make sense of the conflict and engage with suffering on distant fronts, either through donating funds, joining local committees or venturing into the field of relief. These blurred boundaries between press, propaganda and relief bore a strong resemblance to previous 'agitations' on behalf of minorities in the Ottoman Empire which had established a 'template' for popular humanitarian politics based on the exposure of atrocity and the provision of relief which endured even in the rather different context of the First World War.[78]

Philips Price's engagement with the fate of the Armenians crossed these porous boundaries between war correspondence, propaganda, political advocacy and humanitarian concern. In 1916 he provided an account of his encounters with refugees for the official British 'blue book' of eyewitness testimonies, *The Treatment of the Armenians in the Ottoman Empire*, which was intended, at least in part, as propaganda to win support for the war in neutral countries.[79] Philips Price did not cast doubt upon the scale, intent or centrally planned nature of the Armenian massacres. In November 1916 he stated in a report for the *Manchester Guardian* that the Russian capture of Van was the 'signal for putting in to force the exile order, an excuse for which the Young Turks had long been waiting'. In the same article he suggested that after the Armenians had been 'removed' the Young Turks would turn on the Greeks as part of a plan for 'the elimination of all unassimilable Christian elements from these regions'.[80]

Much of his other writing on the subject, however, complicates the binary of Turkish barbarism and Armenian victimhood. The reports that Philips Price provided raised questions regarding the exclusive narrative of Armenian victimhood and Turkish depravity by drawing attention to other victims of violence in the region. At Dilman, for example, he witnessed the fate of 'thirty thousand starving and ragged' Assyrian refugees.[81] The Muslim populations of the region, he also stressed, were victims as well as perpetrators of mass violence. In *War and Revolution* he argued that the 'massacres of Moslems on the Asiatic fronts [perpetrated by the Russian army] were no less criminal, if less extensive, than the Turkish massacre of the Armenians'.[82] Earlier in the war, when Russia was an ally, he would perhaps not have been able to be so frank in his assessment. Philips Price also identified civilian Christian populations as the perpetrators of violence and massacre. In the aftermath of the Turkish invasion and retreat from the regions around Kars, he claimed that when 'Christian bands began to be formed, and to march into Moslem villages, there would be some pillaging, a few shots would be fired, and then would begin a general massacre'.[83]

Philips Price was reluctant to apportion blame for the violence in the Caucasus to any single ethnic group and emphasised that the various populations of the region had lived peacefully alongside one another until the war. The true cause of the plight of the region's population, he suggested, was imperialism in general rather than the particular nature of Ottoman rule.[84] Philips Price's purpose, made more explicit in *War and Revolution* than in his dispatches for the *Manchester Guardian*, was to demonstrate the horrors of war for all 'ordinary people' in the Caucasus (and, by implication, throughout the world): 'The whole of war is an atrocity [. . .] wherever it comes hunger, disease, massacres and burnings come in its train.'[85] It was therefore, he argued, 'impossible to charge any one government' with the 'crime' of the destruction wrought by war in the Caucasus.[86] In the context of the Turkish denial and in the light of new scholarship which has demonstrated the Ottoman state's orchestration of the Armenian Genocide this statement seems somewhat reductive, failing to differentiate between the genocidal intent of the violence directed at the Armenians and the multiple other patterns of violence against civilians which occurred in this region. However, in the context of his other writings, the statement appears less an exoneration of the Young Turks and more an expression of Philips Price's growing belief in the collective culpability of the imperial powers for the horrors wrought by the war on civilians.

## Conclusions: Forgotten Violence, Forgotten Fronts?

The Caucasus front was 'one of the areas of most intense and extended violence in the First World War'.[87] Yet histories of violence in the Russian and Ottoman borderlands remain isolated from both broader historiographies and the popular memory of the First World War. This is principally due to post-war developments in the Soviet Union and the Turkish Republic, neither of which experienced the 'memory boom' which followed in the aftermath of the First World War in Western Europe.[88] In Russia and the USSR, the significance of the First World War in popular memory and collective identity was displaced by the Russian Revolution and the Civil War.[89] In the Turkish Republic it was overshadowed by the War of Independence and the foundation myth of the Turkish nation. The experience of civilians on the Ottoman home front in general is still not well understood, whilst the Armenian experience has been deliberately silenced through a state-sponsored campaign of denial and has only recently been integrated into the wider historiography of the First World War. Paying attention to Philips Price's reporting and analysis provides a valuable reminder of the complexity of the patterns of violence which engulfed this region during the First World War and the inadequacy of exclusive or monolithic national narratives in explaining these processes.

The reporting of the war in the Caucasus in the European and American press has most frequently been analysed in terms of its value as 'evidence' of the treatment of the Ottoman Armenians. A close examination of Philips Price's writing not only provides details of the deportation and massacre of the Armenians, it also reveals some of the ways in which these events were represented for British audiences and the important role of atrocity narratives (even from distant fronts) in making sense of the war. As the only British reporter on the Caucasus front, Philips Price had a unique perspective on the war in the region. He positioned himself as both expert witness and bold adventurer, blurring the boundaries between journalism, travel writing and humanitarianism in a manner which had become typical of the British liberal engagement with the 'Eastern Question'.

His writing demonstrates how understandings of the war in the Caucasus were shaped not just by wartime priorities, but also by pre-war understandings of violence in Europe's peripheries and by orientalist tropes and assumptions which pervaded even his anti-imperialist rhetoric. Whilst his writing for the *Manchester Guardian* was never directly critical of the British government or Britain's role in the war, in *War and Revolution* he implied that he was well aware of the need to self-censor. Yet geographical and imaginative distance between the Caucasus and Britain, it seems, allowed Philips Price scope to infuse his reports with his own anti-war, anti-imperialist sentiments which would be made explicit in his subsequent reporting from Bolshevik Russia.

## Notes

1. M. Philips Price, *War and Revolution in Asiatic Russia* (London: George Allen & Unwin, 1918), p. 150.
2. 'The World War', *The Observer*, 8 November 1914, p. 8.
3. Kristian Coates Ulrichsen, *The First World War in the Middle East* (London: Hurst, 2014), p. 53.
4. The denial of the Armenian Genocide is beyond the scope of this chapter. Whilst the Turkish state continues a campaign of denial there is a growing scholarly consensus that the fate of the Armenians constituted genocide. The key debates are addressed in Norman M. Naimark, Fatma Müge Göçek and Ronald Grigor Suny (eds), *A Question of Genocide: Armenians and Turks at the End of the Ottoman Empire* (Oxford: Oxford University Press, 2012). On the historiography see Joanne Laycock, 'Beyond National Narratives? Centenary Histories, the First World War and the Armenian Genocide', *Revolutionary Russia*, 28.2 (2013), 93–117.
5. Some of his writings on the revolutions are collected in M. Philips Price, *Dispatches from the Russian Revolution*, ed. Tania Rose (Durham, NC: Duke University Press, 1998). See also his memoir, *My Three Revolutions* (London: George Allen & Unwin, 1969).
6. Tania Rose, 'Introduction', in Philips Price, *Dispatches*, p. 2. Rose suggests that twenty-four pieces in *The Economist* can also 'reasonably be attributed to him' (p. 7).

7. Ayerst claims that after a scandal regarding Price's contributions to a Bolshevik publication Scott asked him to send no more messages: 'it doesn't do for you as our correspondent to be carrying on Bolshevik propaganda.' David Ayerst, *The Guardian: Biography of a Newspaper* (London: Collins, 1971), p. 401. See also Charlotte Alston, 'British Journalism and the Campaign for Intervention in the Russian Civil War 1918–20', *Revolutionary Russia*, 20 (2007), 38, and Jonathan D. Smele, 'What the Papers Didn't Say: Unpublished Dispatches from Russia by M. Philips Price, May 1918–January 1919', *Revolutionary Russia*, 8 (1995), 129–65.
8. For example, Robert Gerwarth and Erez Manela (eds), *Empires at War: 1911–23* (Oxford: Oxford University Press, 2014).
9. Jay M. Winter, 'General Introduction', in Winter (ed.), *The Cambridge History of the First World War*, 3 vols (Cambridge: Cambridge University Press, 2014), p. 6. See also Alan Kramer, 'Recent Historiography of the First World War (I)', *Journal of Modern European History*, 12 (2014), 9.
10. Erik Jan Zürcher, *The Young Turk Legacy and Nation Building* (London: I. B. Tauris, 2010), p. 153.
11. Joshua Sanborn, *Imperial Apocalypse: The Great War and the Destruction of the Russian Empire* (Oxford: Oxford University Press,2014), p. 1.
12. On the memory of Gallipoli see Jenny Macleod, *Reconsidering Gallipoli* (Manchester: Manchester University Press, 2004).
13. The historiography is limited, with the notable exception of Michael A. Reynolds, *Shattering Empires: The Clash and Collapse of the Ottoman and Russian Empires, 1908–18* (Princeton: Princeton University Press, 2011). See also Ozan Arslan, 'The "Bon pour l'Orient" Front: Analysis of Russia's Anticipated Victory over the Ottoman Empire in World War I', *Middle East Critique*, 23 (2014), 175–88.
14. See W. E. D. Allen and Paul Muratoff, *Caucasian Battlefields: A History of Wars on the Turco-Caucasian Border 1828–1921* (Cambridge: Cambridge University Press, 2011).
15. On the Armenian position in the late Ottoman Empire see Ronald Grigor Suny, *They Can Live in the Desert but Nowhere Else: A History of the Armenian Genocide* (Princeton: Princeton University Press, 2015), chapters 1 to 3.
16. Most historians agree that these massacres were not the first stage in the Armenian Genocide, but rather an attempt by the Ottoman authorities 'to maintain the old order'. Richard Hovannisian, 'The Armenian Question in the Ottoman Empire', in Hovannisian (ed.), *The Armenian People from Ancient to Modern Times, Volume II: Foreign Dominion to Statehood* (New York: St. Martin's Press, 1997), p. 226.
17. On the 'Armenian Question' see Akaby Nassibian, *Britain and the Armenian Question* (London: Croom Helm, 1984), and Donald Bloxham, *The Great Game of Genocide* (Oxford: Oxford University Press, 2005). On the Balkans see Rebecca Gill, *Calculating Compassion: Humanity and War in Britain, 1870–1914* (Manchester: Manchester University Press, 2013), Part II, and James Perkins, 'The Congo of Europe: The Balkans and Empire in Early Twentieth-Century British Political Culture', *The Historical Journal*, 58 (2015), 565–87.
18. Joanne Laycock, *Imagining Armenia: Orientalism, Ambiguity and Intervention* (Manchester: Manchester University Press, 2009), esp. pp. 77–85.
19. A summary is provided in Ulrichsen, *The First World War in the Middle East*, pp. 53–72.
20. Suny, *They Can Live in the Desert*, p. 281; see also Donald Bloxham, 'The Armenian Genocide of 1915–1916: Cumulative Radicalization and the Development of a Destruction Policy', *Past & Present*, 181 (2003), 141–92.
21. The best surveys of this contested history include Suny, *They Can Live in the Desert*, Uğur Ümit Üngör, *The Making of Modern Turkey: Nation and State in Eastern Anatolia, 1913–1950* (Oxford: Oxford University Press, 2011), and Raymond Kevorkian, *The Armenian Genocide: A Complete History* (London: I. B. Tauris, 2011).

22. On European intervention in the Ottoman Empire see Davide Rodogno, *Against Massacre: Humanitarian Interventions in the Ottoman Empire, 1815–1914: The Emergence of a European Concept and International Practice* (Princeton: Princeton University Press, 2012).
23. On atrocity and the Balkan Wars see Alan Kramer, *Dynamic of Destruction: Culture and Mass Killing in the First World War* (Oxford: Oxford University Press, 2007), pp. 132–44. On violence and representations of the Ottoman peripheries see Laycock, *Imagining Armenia*, chapters 1 and 2, and Maria Todorova, *Imagining the Balkans* (Oxford: Oxford University Press, 1997).
24. Arnold Joseph Toynbee, *Turkey: A Past and a Future* (London: Hodder & Stoughton, 1917). Toynbee, a historian, was working for the British Propaganda Bureau at Wellington House.
25. *The Times*, 24 August 1916, p. 6.
26. Michael Hughes, 'Searching for the Soul of Russia: British Perceptions of Russia during the First World War', *Twentieth Century British History*, 20.2 (2009), 199.
27. Charlotte Alston, *Russia's Greatest Enemy? Harold Williams and the Russian Revolutions* (London: I. B. Tauris, 2007), chapter 3; Hughes, 'Searching for the Soul of Russia', pp. 201–2.
28. *The Times* had supported Anglo-Russian rapprochement in the years before the war. Hughes, 'Searching for the Soul of Russia', pp. 214–16.
29. Philips Price, *War and Revolution*, p. 271.
30. Ibid., pp. 50–1.
31. M. Philips Price, 'The Future of Persia', *Manchester Guardian*, 4 December 1920, p. 6. These travels were also the subject of a lecture to the Persia Society. M. Philips Price, *A Journey through Asiatic Persia and Khurdistan* (London: Hogg, 1913).
32. Philips Price to Scott, 30 October 1914, John Rylands Library, Guardian Archive, Philips Price Correspondence, A/P53/1–38.
33. Philips Price, *War and Revolution*, p. 5.
34. Marvin Swartz, *The Union of Democratic Control in British Politics during the First World War* (Oxford: Clarendon Press, 1971). The UDC had been founded by Philips Price's cousin, the Liberal MP Charles Trevelyan.
35. This echoed the approach of the *Manchester Guardian* more generally. Nicholas Owen states that by the 1930s, 'Practically alone, [the *Manchester Guardian*] had sought to preserve the educative ideal of mid-Victorian journalism, repeatedly stating its willingness to speak truth to power, its commitment to hearing every voice, and the importance of moral obligations in imperial policymaking.' Nicholas Owen, '"Facts Are Sacred": The *Manchester Guardian* and Colonial Violence, 1930–1932', *Journal of Modern History*, 84 (2012), 662.
36. Matthew Farish, 'Modern Witnesses: Foreign Correspondents, Geopolitical Vision, and the First World War', *Transactions of the Institute of British Geographers*, 26 (2001), 273–87.
37. Censorship, as Pennell has observed, was less a top-down imposition than a matter of voluntary participation, as editors, journalists and cartoonists often shared the views of the politicians. Catriona Pennell, *A Kingdom United: Popular Responses to the Outbreak of the First World War in Britain and Ireland* (Oxford: Oxford University Press, 2012), p. 7. Cooperation between the Northcliffe press and the British government is well documented, for example in J. Lee Thompson, *Politicians, the Press, and Propaganda: Lord Northcliffe and the Great War, 1914–1919* (Kent, OH, and London: Kent State University Press, 1999).
38. Those who established reputations through transgressing the new rules of censorship included Charles Repington, who exposed the 'shell scandal' in *The Times* in May 1915, and Ellis Ashmead-Bartlett, who, with Keith Murdoch, reported the failures of the Gallipoli campaign; on Gallipoli reporting see Macleod, *Reconsidering Gallipoli*, chapter 5 ('The Journalists' Response'). This 'golden age' is evoked by Phillip Knightley in *The First Casualty: The War Correspondent as Hero and Myth Maker from the Crimea to Iraq* (Baltimore: Johns Hopkins University Press, 2004), chapter 3.

39. Philips Price, *My Three Revolutions*, p. 38.
40. M. Philips Price, 'The Story of the Battle of Dilman', *Manchester Guardian*, 27 October 1915, p. 9, and Philips Price, *War and Revolution*, pp. 228, 215.
41. Knightley, *The First Casualty*, p. 151.
42. Philips Price, *War and Revolution*, pp. 181–2.
43. Ibid., p. 147.
44. M. Philips Price, 'The Armenian Campaign', *Manchester Guardian*, 12 September 1916, p. 6.
45. Philips Price, 'The Story of the Battle of Dilman', p. 9.
46. M. Philips Price, 'The Russian Army at Work', *Manchester Guardian*, 3 February 1915, p. 4 (italics added).
47. Philips Price, *War and Revolution*, p. 153.
48. Mary Louise Pratt, *Imperial Eyes, Travel Writing and Transculturation* (London: Routledge, 1992), p. 204.
49. Philips Price was unwilling to trust 'local' knowledge. When told about a massacre in Urmiah, he says he knew 'to discount the Eastern imagination in war-time'. *War and Revolution*, p. 99.
50. Farish, 'Modern Witnesses', p. 285.
51. Quoted in Rose, 'Introduction', in Philips Price, *Dispatches*, p. 27.
52. Laycock, *Imagining Armenia*, chapter 2.
53. Philips Price, *War and Revolution*, p. 23.
54. Ibid., p. 38.
55. Ibid., p. 138.
56. M. Philips Price, 'In Russian Trenches', *Manchester Guardian*, 22 January 1915, p. 8.
57. Philips Price, 'The Russian Army at Work', p. 4.
58. The Russian occupation of Erzerum was also the subject of John Buchan's novel *Greenmantle* (London: Hodder & Stoughton, 1916).
59. M. Philips Price, 'Erzerum Visited', *Manchester Guardian*, 7 April 1916, p. 10.
60. Ibid.
61. Philips Price, *War and Revolution*, p. 5. On the Russian occupation of Galicia see Peter Gatrell, 'Tsarist Russia at War: The View from Above, 1914–February 1917', *Journal of Modern History*, 87 (2015), 68–9. On atrocities see Alexander Victor Prusin, *Nationalizing a Borderland: War, Ethnicity, and Anti-Jewish Violence in East Galicia, 1914–1920* (Tuscaloosa: University of Alabama Press, 2005).
62. Philips Price, *War and Revolution*, p. 141. In the words of Alan Kramer, 'for all sides in the war, enemy civilians and other non-combatants came to be regarded to a greater or lesser degree as targets of war policy, even as legitimate objects of violence.' Kramer, *Dynamic of Destruction*, p. 3.
63. On the genocidal process and attention to regional differences see Kevorkian, *The Armenian Genocide*, and Üngör, *The Making of Modern Turkey*.
64. Jay M. Winter, 'Under Cover of War', in Winter (ed.), *America and the Armenian Genocide of 1915* (Cambridge: Cambridge University Press, 2007), pp. 37–51.
65. On liberal humanitarian networks and the 'pro-Boers' see Gill, *Calculating Compassion*, pp. 143–67.
66. Bryce to Scott, 4 August 1915, John Rylands Library, Guardian Archive, Bryce Correspondence, A/B108/1–6.
67. 'Turkish Outrages in Armenia', *Manchester Guardian*, 6 August 1915, p. 8.
68. Edmund Candler, for example, was a representative of the press with the British Expeditionary Force in Mesopotamia and later reported on Armenian refugees in Baghdad. 'Armenian Survivors: Episodes in the Turkish Massacres', *Manchester Guardian*, 21 June 1917, p. 3.
69. William Ewart Gladstone, *Bulgarian Horrors and the Question of the East* (London: John Murray, 1876); William Thomas Stead, *The Haunting Horrors in Armenia* (London: 'Review of Reviews', 1896).

70. 'Exterminating the Armenians', *Manchester Guardian*, 11 September 1915, p. 8. The term 'genocide' was not developed by Raphael Lemkin until after the Second World War.
71. There was much speculation about Germany's complicity in the Armenian massacres; see for example 'The Armenians in Turkey', *Manchester Guardian*, 26 May 1916, p. 6.
72. John Horne and Alan Kramer, *German Atrocities: A History of Denial* (New Haven: Yale University Press, 2001), p. 230.
73. Philips Price wrote, 'The deportations which began on June 26th 1915 and the abominable massacres that followed have been so fully described in the official British Blue-book that I will not weary the reader with the tale of horror.' *War and Revolution*, p. 247.
74. Ibid., pp. 185–6.
75. M. Philips Price, 'Turk and Armenian: A Chapter of Secret History', *Manchester Guardian*, 16 November 1916, p. 4. See also M. Philips Price, 'The Armenians in Trebizond: The First Photographs of their Fate', *Manchester Guardian*, 27 June 1916, p. 5. Two blurred images show women and children 'being driven out of the town with fixed bayonets' and the only surviving Armenian woman, who had survived by wearing Turkish costume.
76. Philips Price to Scott, 12 April 1916, John Rylands Library, Guardian Archive, Philips Price Correspondence, A/P53/1–38.
77. James Bryce, 'Repatriating the Armenians', *Manchester Guardian*, 8 June 1916, p. 6, and Harold Buxton, 'Armenia's Immediate Need', *Manchester Guardian*, 21 August 1916, p. 6.
78. Gill, *Calculating Compassion*, p. 76.
79. Azerbaijan: 'Statement, dated Tiflis, 22 February 1916, by Mr. M. Philips Price, War Correspondent for various British and Americas newspapers on the Caucasian Front; communicated to Aneurin Williams, Esq., M.P., and published in the Armenian journal "Ararat," of London, March 1916', in James Bryce and Arnold J. Toynbee (eds), *The Treatment of the Armenians in the Ottoman Empire* (London: Hodder & Stoughton, 1916). This volume was produced under the auspices of Wellington House.
80. Philips Price, 'Turk and Armenian: A Chapter of Secret History', p. 4.
81. Philips Price, *War and Revolution*, p. 122. See also 'War and Massacre in North-Western Persia', *Manchester Guardian*, 28 October 1915, p. 8.
82. Philips Price, *War and Revolution*, p. 271.
83. Ibid., p. 185.
84. The importance of the context of imperialism as a cause of the Armenian Genocide is stressed in much of the recent scholarship, for example in Bloxham's *The Great Game of Genocide*.
85. Philips Price, *War and Revolution*, p. 234.
86. Ibid.
87. Peter Holquist, 'Forms of Violence during the Russian Occupation of Ottoman Territory and in Northern Persia (Urmia and Astrabad), October 1914–December 1917', in Omer Bartov and Eric D. Weitz (eds), *Shatterzone of Empires: Coexistence and Violence in the German, Habsburg, Russian, and Ottoman Borderlands* (Bloomington: Indiana University Press, 2013), p. 334.
88. On the 'memory boom' see, for example, Jay M. Winter, *Remembering War: The Great War between Memory and History in the Twentieth Century* (New Haven: Yale University Press, 2006).
89. On the memory of the Great War in the Soviet Union see Karen Patrone, *The Great War in Russian Memory* (Bloomington: Indiana University Press, 2011).

# V.

# Film and Broadcasting

# 19

# Official War Films in Britain: *The Battle of the Somme* (1916), its Impact Then and its Meaning Today

*Toby Haggith*[1]

At 11am on 1 July 2016, at the Thiepval Memorial on the Somme, an hour-long commemorative ceremony was held to mark the centenary of the start of the Battle of the Somme. By 11am one hundred years earlier, the battle had already been in progress for three and a half hours and the ground around Thiepval and elsewhere along a sixteen-mile stretch was strewn with the dead and wounded of the British Army. By the end of the day it was clear that the losses of the British Army had been heavy; as it transpired, they amounted to nearly 60,000 casualties, the bloodiest day in British military history.[2] The battle evolved into a brutal campaign of attrition which lasted nearly five months and resulted in one million casualties.

The scale of the campaign, the number of casualties, the tactics employed by the generals, and the negligible territorial gains for the British Army have meant that this remains one of the most important and controversial battles in British history. Reflecting this importance, the 2016 commemorative ceremony at Thiepval was a large event with approximately 8,000 attendees, including an array of politicians, royalty and senior military figures representing all nations that had fought in the battle.

The official ceremony was preceded by the screening of a shortened version of *The Battle of the Somme* (1916), a remarkable British film that had been made to record the opening stages of the campaign. For this screening, *The Battle of the Somme* was accompanied by the BBC Symphony Orchestra, which played a score by Laura Rossi, commissioned by the Imperial War Museum for the ninetieth anniversary of the battle. The film and accompanying music had a great impact on the audience. Andrea Potts, one of the ceremony's organisers, recalled that when the screening began, 'the atmosphere at Thiepval changed quite dramatically – it really did seem to engage and move people and set the tone for the rest of the event.'[3] The screenings at Thiepval and elsewhere on and around 1 July 2016 were the first public screenings of the film that had been allowed for nearly two years, and were the start of a series of hundreds held in Britain and around the world that were a central feature of the Imperial War Museum's programme of commemorative events to mark the centenary of the battle.[4] To those at the IWM, such as myself, who had been involved in the restoration of *The Battle of the Somme* and had helped with the preparation of this film for the centenary programme, there is a pleasing circularity to these screenings as, when the film was

Figure 19.1 Film still from the re-enacted sequence at the start of part three of *The Battle of the Somme* (1916), preceded by title 31: THE ATTACK. AT A SIGNAL, ALONG THE ENTIRE 16 MILE FRONT, THE BRITISH TROOPS LEAPED OVER THE TRENCH PARAPETS AND ADVANCED TOWARDS THE GERMAN TRENCHES, UNDER HEAVY FIRE OF THE ENEMY. © IWM (Q 70169). Reproduced courtesy of the Imperial War Museum.

Figure 19.2 Film still from *The Battle of the Somme* (1916). A British soldier carries a wounded comrade along a trench. © IWM (Q 79501). Reproduced courtesy of the Imperial War Museum.

released in August 1916, many commentators instantly recognised the film's historical value, predicting that

> In years to come, when historians wish to know the conditions under which the great offensive was launched, they will only have to send for these films and a complete idea of the situation will be revealed before their eyes – for we take it as a matter of course that a number of copies of them will be carefully preserved in the national archives.[5]

Although the IWM's film curators were confident that *The Battle of the Somme* would be well received, there were those who were sceptical that a black and white period documentary feature could hold the attention of contemporary audiences, particularly younger viewers. As a result, requests were received for shortened versions of the film and the IWM developed a project to produce a completely new film about the Somme battle, giving a director, possibly of feature films, the freedom to rework creatively and technically the original archive film to engage new audiences. Perhaps none of us should have doubted the power of *The Battle of the Somme*, because this film and its less well-known sequel *The Battle of the Ancre and Advance of the Tanks* (1917) are landmarks in the history of cinema. They are the first feature-length documentary records of a military campaign that were shot in the frontline as a battle took place. They are long, for any film of the period, running at about seventy minutes each. Although they do contain re-enacted scenes, most of the footage is an actuality recording of the battle, and the films were recognised as setting a new standard in the realistic coverage and representation of armed combat.

The films had a tremendous impact at the time, being seen by millions in Britain and around the world. As a result of the importance of the films' subject matter and their success with audiences, film gained a new credibility with the political and cultural elites in Britain. Some suggested that it was 'the Somme battle films which first established the position of the cinematograph as a necessary adjunct of any government scheme of publicity'.[6] After the war this new status led to the establishment of the world's first properly funded film archive at the IWM (in which the Somme films were deposited) and serious discussions about the creation of a permanent government department to create a film record of national life. The first event to be filmed for this national cinematic record was, appropriately, the unveiling of the Cenotaph in Whitehall.

The long-term impact of the Somme campaign films has been even greater, with certain sequences being endlessly recycled in film and television programmes whenever there is a need to convey the nature of fighting on the Western Front, or even warfare in general. Some of these sequences (notably the mine explosion under Hawthorn Ridge, the 'over the top' attack, the 'piggy-back' rescue, and the field of dead) have become synonymous with the First World War and form part of our collective memory. However, until recently, the source of these memorable sequences has not been widely known, as the Somme battle films have been rarely broadcast or screened publicly in their entirety and in anything close to the manner in which they so impressed audiences in 1916 and 1917: at full length, on a big screen, at the correct speed and with an appropriate musical accompaniment.

In fact, after the First World War the Somme campaign films were largely forgotten. Firstly, until 1966 the IWM did not have a cinema of its own to showcase the collection, and so it had to rely on other organisations to borrow the films and show them. There was also the difficulty of showing films from the silent era in cinemas fitted for sound films; silent films are projected at a frame rate of 15 to 18 frames per second, while sound films are run at 24fps (or 25fps when broadcast on television). Showing First World War films at sound speed produces a comical effect of rapid movement that undermines the serious purpose of the films. The absence of a recorded soundtrack on the film also discouraged the screening of the film except at specialist venues such as the National Film Theatre, where screening silent films with a live piano accompaniment was an established practice.[7] Until 1990, apart from those people who had the rare opportunity to watch the film at the NFT or at a specialist film festival devoted to silent films, most people's experience of the Somme battle films was watching them in a poorly darkened classroom from mute 16mm or VHS copies. Appreciation of the Somme battle films was also hampered by the physical condition of the copies themselves. Although archivists and curators at the IWM had ensured the preservation of the masters, the originals were scratched and damaged (a sign of their original popularity), with occasional frame instability and flicker. Successive copying had only preserved these distracting blemishes and also led to a darkening of the image, a process which conceals details.

At the same time scholarly neglect of the Somme battle films meant they were omitted from a range of studies of British and international cinema.[8] The first published reference did not appear until 1950, when Rachel Low covered them in the First World War volume of the BFI/BAFTA *History of the British Film*. This reflects the generally low opinion that British filmmakers and writers held of films from their own country and of First World War official films in particular. For example, while acknowledging their popularity at the time, Low only gave them a paragraph of analysis:

> The success of these films must have been due to the material itself rather than to its arrangement. The editing was very elementary. The order in which shots followed each other had little meaning, and the structure of the films seems to have depended almost entirely on the titles.[9]

Wider awareness of the films began in the 1980s, spurred in part by historical cataloguing of the IWM's First World War film collection and the VHS release of the films in 1987 and 1990.[10] In 2005, the importance of *The Battle of the Somme* received significant recognition when it was accepted into UNESCO's 'Memory of the World Register' – the first British document of any kind to be accepted, and at the time one of only a handful of films to be included. But wider ignorance of the films remains striking. *The Battle of the Somme* was overlooked in a recent list, compiled in *The Observer*, of the fifty best documentaries ever made.[11]

Partly in an effort to redress this situation, in 2006 the IWM completed a major digital restoration of *The Battle of the Somme*, which also encompassed the recording of two music tracks: Laura Rossi's commissioned score and a revival of the musical medley which had been recommended to be played to the film when it was first screened in 1916. Scholarly interest in the films has concentrated on *The Battle of the Somme* (very little has been written about *The Battle of the Ancre*) and its value as a record of the fighting. Historians have shown particular interest in the 'fakes'[12] and the scenes of the wounded and the dead, elements of the film often framed within a wider question of truth.[13] Researchers have also examined the film's impact on audiences and the phenomenon of recognition of soldiers appearing in the film.[14] *The Battle of the Somme* is rarely studied as 'cinema', Kevin Brownlow being one of the few to write about the film and the camerawork in terms of art and in a manner commonly found in studies of film.[15] Many studies of *The Battle of the Somme* attempt to categorise the film variously as 'documentary', 'reportage', 'newsreel', 'educational' or as a kind of 'primitive' or 'transitional' form between these genres.[16] These scholarly perspectives are also reflected in widespread popular assumptions about the film still prevalent today: notably that all the action was 'faked' for the camera or that it is a sanitised record of the Battle of the Somme, mere government propaganda to conceal the terrible casualty figures.

## Government Film Production

By the First World War the cinema had become the most popular form of entertainment in Britain: in March 1916 eighteen million tickets were being sold per week in the country's 4,500 cinemas.[17] Despite the importance of film to national life, the state was slow to realise the value of film to the war effort. It was not until August 1915 that a body existed to organise government filming (Wellington House Cinema Committee) and not until December 1915 that the first official film, *Britain Prepared: A Review of the Activities of His Majesty's Naval and Military Forces*, was released. But this film only dealt with Britain's armed forces at home as from September 1914 photography and filming were forbidden on the British sector of the Western Front, reflecting official concerns about maintaining military secrecy and protecting the image of the army. This general objection to photojournalism was compounded in the case of film by the lack of respectability of the cinema industry in the eyes of the upper-class military authorities.

By 1915, attitudes in the Army and War Office were beginning to change, as more progressive minds recognised the propaganda potential of film. This change was hastened by the need to respond to German official films of the war being distributed to neutral countries such as Romania and the USA and even being shown in Britain. After lengthy negotiations between the cinema industry and the War Office, an arrangement was made for official filming to be overseen by a War Office-created committee of leading commercial newsreel and topical companies. The committee was given the right to film on the Western front in return for giving a share of the profits from film rental to War Office charities. Finally, on 2 November, the cameramen Geoffrey H. Malins (Gaumont Graphic) and William Tong (Jury's Imperial Pictures) were sent to France. Once appointed, the War Office ensured that the former newsreel cameramen were controlled and fully inculcated into the ethos of the British Army. They were given the military uniform of an officer, billeted and fed at GHQ and given a salary of £1 per day. The cameramen were transported around by a military car and were assisted by a soldier who helped carry their camera equipment. They were also always escorted by a Conducting Officer, usually Captain Faunthorpe of Military Intelligence and the Director of Kinematographic Operations, who told them where and what they could film.

Films for and about the military took priority in government production, reflecting the aims of propaganda policy which was to promote the British and Allied cause to neutrals and the dominions. The IWM holds nearly 600 films produced for the armed forces, but only sixty or so made purely for domestic audiences. Government films designed for the home front were not produced until 1917, and it was not until the creation of the Ministry of Information in February 1918 that large numbers were made with the purpose of directing people to assist with the war effort. Most films for the home front were short, ten to fifteen minutes long, and in contrast to the documentary-type military films that had dominated the official output, they employed the techniques of cinema entertainment – dramas, cartoons and hybrid forms. To give an indication of the themes that were tackled in these films, among the collection held at the IWM twelve promote the sale of war bonds, eighteen promote measures to maximise the nation's food resources (rationing, garden farming, communal feeding, discouraging waste, etc.), four champion the contribution of women to the war effort, four exhort shipbuilders, three encourage recycling, two focus on munitions workers, and three are anti-German.

*With the Indian Troops at the Front* (17 January 1916) was the first film to be shown in Britain made from the footage shot on the Western front by the War Office cameramen. The twenty-six 'episodes' of the *Official Pictures of the British Army in France* were released in six batches on a monthly basis until the end of July. The films were short, no more than ten minutes long, and although initially well received, they were generally shot far behind the frontlines and concentrated on scenes of soldiers in non-combat roles (fixing and draining trenches, undergoing training, marching, playing football, etc.), views of war-damaged French villages, the visits of VIPs, and other topics. There was little of men actually fighting (unless re-enacted or on exercise) or of the realities of war such as shells exploding, the wounded or the dead (unless in marked graves). Partly this was due to tight restrictions on the cameramen, leading to complaints from the British Topical Committee for War Films that the cameramen were 'unduly restricted in their activities'.[18] But for the British Army's offensive on the Somme, the cameramen were allowed much greater access, embedded in the frontline as the battle unfolded. The resultant film was longer, more dramatic, more comprehensive and much more candid in its coverage of battle than anything the War Office had released previously.

The summer offensive on the Somme was Britain's contribution to a coordinated Allied strike across Europe to defeat the Central Powers after the setbacks of 1915. The war had not been going well for the Allies, and 1916 had been a particularly bad one for the British; lack of progress on the Western front was compounded in the spring by the Easter Uprising, the Battle of Jutland and the death of Lord Kitchener, which were traumatic events in themselves, but also blows to the nation's self-confidence. 1916 also saw the war brought ever closer and more directly to British civilians, with Zeppelin raids and an intensification of the U-boat attacks on merchant shipping. The growing impact of the war on people's lives, and the pressures brought by the increasing incursions into work and private affairs as the state mobilised for total war, met with resistance and public protest, with labour strikes, large demonstrations against conscription and even isolated attacks on members of the Royal Flying Corps for failing to protect civilians from air raids.

While it cannot be said that British society was breaking down or that support for the war had diminished greatly, evidence suggests that the government could no longer assume the unanimous support of the people for the war effort or the way it was being conducted. In this context, the success of the Somme offensive was paramount and the desire to give that success full publicity prompted the production of a film that would bring the realities of the war to the people. *The Battle of the Somme* represents an important shift in government thinking about film propaganda. Lloyd George, who was to prioritise propaganda when he became Prime Minister, clearly saw the value of this film, attending a private screening on 2 August, after which he wrote the letter of introduction that was read out at the press show on 10 August and widely published.

The exact purpose of *The Battle of the Somme* or the reason it took the form it did remains unclear because few documents survive, partly as a consequence of the government being covert in the creation of propaganda. There were plans to release the footage as single-reelers, but the power of the rushes combined with unhappiness with the tired format of official war films encouraged the War Office to produce a five-reel feature which it was hoped would be more entertaining, better propaganda and more suitable for overseas distribution.[19]

## The Purposes of *The Battle of the Somme*

Firstly, the film was to record and publicise a British military victory. Those in charge of the film must have assumed the offensive on the Somme would be a success; otherwise, they would not have given cameramen access to the frontline to record it. This in turn was to raise the morale of the British people after a year of military defeats and setbacks. *Kine Weekly* encouraged every showman to screen the film 'with as little delay as possible. It will do more to hearten the people and hasten the day of the final and complete victory over our enemies than all the newspapers and all the books ever printed.'[20] As Lloyd George expressed it in his letter of 10 August, it was hoped that the example of the bravery and stoicism of the soldiers at the front would rally civilian support behind the war effort:

> I am convinced that when you have seen this wonderful picture, every heart will beat in sympathy with its purpose, which is no other than that everyone of us at home and abroad shall see what our men at the Front are doing and suffering for us, and how their achievements have been made possible by the sacrifices made at home.[21]

Lloyd George's desire that the film would forge a link between the civilians at home and the soldiers in France was especially designed to impress upon industrial workers the need to increase the production of war material; shells were particularly important, the 'shell scandal' of 1915 having led to a government reshuffle. This message was directly conveyed in title eight ('Along the Entire Front the Munition "Dumps" Are Receiving Vast Supplies of Shells; Thanks to the British Munition Workers'), the words 'shell', 'shelling' and 'munitions' occurring a further twelve times in the intertitles. There are also sixteen shots of shells and shell dumps, which occupy 195 seconds of screen time. The importance of this message was reinforced during introductions to screenings of the film and in articles in the press.[22] The film's Supervising Editor, Charles Urban, declared it was this issue that led Prime Minister Asquith and members of the cabinet to release the film, despite their misgivings about the scenes of the 'awful horribleness' of modern warfare:

> One of the principal reasons for their arrival at this conclusion was the fact that it wanted the thousands of workers in the munitions factories to appreciate as keenly as possible the absolute dependence of the boys in the trenches upon a constant and ever increasing supply of guns and ammunition.[23]

Another key purpose was to reassure civilians that the soldiers were being well fed, clothed and equipped and that their mail was reaching them. Equally important in the minds of the public was to know that casualties were treated promptly and effectively, and so the care of British casualties features prominently in parts three and four. The lesser and subsidiary aims of *The Battle of the Somme* were to show that the British soldier behaved with honour and chivalry towards enemy prisoners, to raise money for military charities, and to promote the sale of war bonds.

*The Battle of the Somme* was moreover used to aid recruiting in Ireland and in Dominion and Empire countries where conscription had not yet been introduced and was a controversial issue.[24] As conscription had been in place for five months when the film was released (three months for married men), its recruiting value in Britain is usually not considered. However, Malins boasted that '[t]he Somme film had proved a mighty instrument in the service of recruiting'.[25] Although Malins may be referring to the value of the film overseas, there is evidence that screenings of *The Battle of the Somme* were considered valuable in applying pressure on those British men who had not yet responded to their call-up papers.

## The Making of *The Battle of the Somme* and its Characteristics

The War Office cameramen Geoffrey H. Malins and J. B. McDowell filmed between 25 June and 9 July 1916, and they covered the preparations and opening of the Battle of Albert, as this phase of the Somme campaign was called. Although the cameramen were given greater access than previously, there were numerous practical and official constraints that limited the scope of their filming. Firstly, reaching the places to film was difficult as the army cars could not cope with the terrain, so beyond the road the cameramen had to walk many miles through trenches to reach their final destination, carrying film, a tripod and a camera which weighed around 40lbs. They were also in danger from shelling, and anyone within five miles of the frontline was vulnerable: McDowell talked about being 'under fire several times' and Malins was blown sideways by the blast from a shell and was injured in the back and foot.[26] When the camera was mounted on the tripod it could draw fire from snipers, which made filming difficult and the soldiers nervous, and on one occasion an officer stopped Malins filming for this reason.[27] As this episode indicates, the official control exercised by the army went beyond that of the cameramen's regular minder, Captain Faunthorpe, as presumably there were numerous occasions when the camera team had to defer to those in local command.

With only two cameramen covering a sixteen-mile front and unable to move freely or direct the action in front of the camera, Malins and McDowell tended to film from one position and survey what could be seen of the battle directly in front of the camera. As a result, they often resorted to panning: slow pans across the landscape like a guide pointing out scenes of interest to the tourist, or of soldiers standing in front of or walking past the camera. But the pan was not just a compensatory framing device, as it also demonstrates the scale of the battlefield, and in one memorable moment (part one, title eight) this shot is employed to show the number of shells amassed for the offensive, the cameraman tracking nearly 360° to reveal boxes of shells stacked under sheets of tarpaulin which are removed by the soldiers as the camera sweeps round. As a technique the pan is also thought to reinforce the authentic nature of the scenes being filmed.

## Editing and Censorship

The cameramen returned from the Somme with 8,000ft of 35mm black and white film. The rushes were screened in London on 12 July and the editing was supervised by the film producer Charles Urban (who had made *Britain Prepared*), assisted by Malins, with Faunthorpe in overall charge. Once the footage had been edited, a rough cut was screened to War Office officials and then sent to GHQ in France for more scrutiny and censorship. Any cuts identified by the Chief Censor were made when the film returned to London. Malins records that the Somme battle films were prone to even more oversight than the other official films, and he hints at the constraints this imposed on the filmmaking process:

> I am not sure that the functions of the film editor – at least in the case of a picture such as the Somme Film – do not call for a greater exercise of discretion, diplomacy and tact; for so many interests have to be taken into account; so much has to be left out for so much is at stake.[28]

Exactly what was censored is difficult to tell as the IWM does not hold the rushes, and there are no notes of what was excised. Examination of censored sections from other official war films is not very revealing and does not always indicate why certain scenes were considered sensitive. An entry in General Henry Rawlinson's diary (commander of the Fourth Army at the Somme) records that he watched a version of the film in France and ordered cuts of the 'horrors in dead and wounded' – a report supported by an account of another British officer who claimed that the version he had seen in Amiens had been 'very much watered down' by the time it was shown in London.[29] Moreover, Malins wrote about filming the horrors of Trones Wood, which do not appear in the film. About 3,000ft of the original rushes were excluded to produce the final version, although it is unlikely that all the cuts were removed to satisfy the censors. There were also various rumours, some covered in the press, that the film was censored before reaching certain audiences and territories. Lack of candour in films from the First World War cannot solely be attributed to the intervention of the military and official propagandists, however, as the cameramen practised a good deal of self-censorship. When Malins described the scenes of dead that had been included, he noted that 'It is only a very mild touch of what is happening day after day [. . .] There never was such dearly bought land since creation [. . .] The place reeks with the horrible stench of countless decaying bodies, and every minute adds to their number.'[30]

## Structure and Inter-Titles

Due to the practical difficulties of filming a battlefield and the limitations of the camera equipment, the film concentrates on the build-up and aftermath of the offensive, bringing men and material up to the frontline, artillery firing, soldiers eating, donning uniform, and so on. Parts one and two record the artillery barrage and other preparations for the infantry offensive. Part three covers the offensive, and begins with the climax of the film, the scene of men going 'over the top' to attack the German trenches. The rest of the reel and part four record the immediate aftermath of the attack, the treatment of casualties, the burial of the dead and the rounding up of prisoners. Part five shows troops resting, captured German trenches and war booty, then the army making its preparations for the next stage of the battle. But the film does not just follow a chronological structure, as there is an implicit narrative flow to the ordering of the scenes, with the broad triptych of preparation for battle, infantry attack and aftermath being supplemented by numerous individual stories, notably that following the rescue of the wounded man from 'no man's land' to the trenches and his being 'stretchered' away for treatment.

It was a condition of the contract struck between the War Office and the Topical Committee for War Films that the titles and inter-titles would be written by the state, which in most cases meant Captain Faunthorpe. These sixty-three titles (also known as inter-titles or subtitles) are crucial to organising the film and conveying its meaning. Firstly, they provide the commentary for the action seen on the screen. Mostly one action is described, but twenty-five of the titles describe two actions and two of them three different episodes. Using a single title card to convey this amount of information seems unusual for filmmaking at the time: one American reviewer suggested that this was too much information for a viewer to absorb, and in at least two British newspapers there were complaints that the titles sped by too quickly.[31] Secondly, the titles outline military strategy, for example, 'Just before the attack. Blowing up Enemy Trenches by a Huge Mine . . .' The titles also provide information about objectives, impressing upon the viewer the weight of shells dropped on the German positions and detailing the specific function of each type of shell. Thus the titles, in combination with the images, ensured that the film provided a visual glossary for a mass of features of the Western Front which would have been unfamiliar to civilian audiences. They also name the regiments or service units that appear (without identifying the division or battalion), thus helping audiences to establish a connection with the men on the screen.

In a mute film without a recorded soundtrack, the titles help to convey the noise of battle, notably of the guns (for example, title 13: 'The vicious bark of the Canadian 60 pounders adds to the din of gun fire'), and to make sense of those innocent-looking clouds of white smoke bursting on the horizon (38: 'One of five unsuccessful counter attacks at La Boisselle'). Finally, the titles explicitly promote propaganda messages, for example by encouraging greater efforts by workers in the munitions industry, and more subtly by ensuring that the viewer responded appropriately to images which might present an ambivalent message, as for example in title 41 ('. . . Wounded awaiting attention at Minden Post. Showing how quickly the wounded are attended to'). Title 50 ('The Manchesters' Pet dog fell with his master charging Danzig alley') is a strikingly propagandist use of the titles, as these words frame not just the first scene of death in a heroic tableau, but the following scenes of British dead and their burial in common graves, which are more graphic and depressing than the opening shot of the fallen beagle and his master.

Along with the scenes of the landscape of battle and of the artillery in action, it is the faces of the soldiers looking directly into the camera which is the most familiar motif of the film. Anticipating the desire of the audience to spot their loved ones on the screen, the cameramen captured as many faces as possible, often encouraging the men to turn and acknowledge the camera. Keen to be spotted in the cinemas at home and to secure their place in history, the soldiers needed little encouragement to grin, wave and even bow to the camera. As the noise of the camera being cranked was quite loud, British soldiers often spontaneously acknowledged the lens and can be seen sneaking into shot or returning to a line of men to be recorded again. British soldiers can sometimes be seen urging German prisoners to be filmed as well, a comradely gesture which reflects the broader humanity of the Somme battle films and helps to explain their continuing appeal.

## Staging and Re-Enacting, and Coverage of the Dead and Wounded

Because of the difficulties of filming actual combat, some scenes were staged for the camera, the first and most well known being the attack or 'over the top' sequence at the start of part three in which a group of soldiers climb out of a trench and advance into no man's land. The second is the scene of a group of 'battle police' led by an officer, checking for the enemy hiding in an area of ground captured by the British. The third comprises three separate scenes of artillery shells exploding in no man's land (following titles 17, 27 and 29), in which the explosions all neatly appear within the static frame. The first and the last cases of staging are believed to have been set up for the camera at a British military training school in France between 12 and 19 July 1916.[32] The second incidence of staging is better described as a re-enactment, as the scene, following title 46, of soldiers 'clearing the battlefield of snipers and hidden machine guns' and 'routing Germans from dugouts', although unconvincing as a record of such a dangerous action, features frontline troops and was filmed during the battle.[33]

*The Battle of the Somme* is unique in the history of British news and documentary filming to show scenes of British dead and wounded and of men being buried on the battlefield. We see the dead, we see men who we are told died later, and we even see men being killed. In the IWM's collection of First World War films, there are only three other scenes in which the corpses of Empire or British soldiers are shown and this footage was not released to the public. In fact, this was the first and last time this has happened to the present day. Just as striking about *The Battle of the Somme* is that views of the British corpses are presented without ambiguity as they are identified as such in the titles (37 and 50).[34]

## The Release and Screenings of *The Battle of the Somme*

The completed film was shown to an invited audience on 10 August 1916. It was initially released, on 21 August, to thirty-four cinemas in London, followed on 28 August by one hundred copies sent out across the country. Distribution of *The Battle of the Somme* was managed by William Jury's Pictures, prints being rented at £20 a day, reduced in October to £6 for three nights, so that it could be screened in town halls and other smaller venues. The film was distributed internationally to at least eighteen countries across Europe, the Americas, Australasia, India and Russia. Despite its length, there was heavy demand from cinema renters. In the first two months the film secured 2,000 bookings, and in Britain alone the rental fee raised £30,000 for military charities. It is estimated that by the end of October it had been seen by twenty million people and, as it was in distribution for at least five months, it is quite possible that it was seen by as many as twenty-two million people, over half the population of the UK at the time. This makes it one of the most successful films in British history, achieving far higher audiences than popular television shows today.[35]

The popularity and importance of the film meant that normal cinema practices were modified to meet demand. For example, owners of large rival cinemas were willing for the film to be screened simultaneously in some towns and it was not unusual for it to be booked for a second run at the same cinema a month or so later. *The Battle of the Somme* proved so popular at the Polytechnic Hall in Regent Street that in late September 1916 it was decided to hold screenings indefinitely.[36] In towns serving large rural populations, such as Cork, Derry, Dublin and Douglas, cinemas ran extra matinee screenings so that people could catch trains home after the film had been shown.[37] Such was the demand in Derry that extra trains were scheduled to ensure people could get home to Buncrana and Limavady after the last screening.

Because *The Battle of the Somme* was unusually long, a special programme had to be created to accommodate it, which meant that many cinema owners had to forgo shorter films that had already been booked. Although the film was generally run in one sitting as a continuous feature, it was quite often shown in a serial format over a few programmes. The difficulties the film's length presented for cinemas probably explains the arrangement of the reels into five distinct parts with their own start and end titles. This meant that *The Battle of the Somme* was often screened within a programme of comedies and serials that many regarded as inappropriate. Screening the film in part form was particularly likely to occur when *The Battle of the Somme* was shown in variety halls where live acts dominated the bill.

Most people paid to see *The Battle of the Somme* in their local cinemas; however, special screenings were arranged so that members of the armed forces and key groups connected to the war effort could see the film for free. For example, a free screening was arranged at the Picture House in Huddersfield for wounded soldiers, sailors, nurses, officials, and managers and off-duty workers from local munitions factories. In February 1917, arrangements were even made for convicts serving sentences in Dartmoor, Parkhurst and Maidstone prisons to see the film instead of the usual monthly lecture. There were also screenings arranged for men on active service to see the film and makeshift cinemas were set up on the Western front, in Mesopotamia and on Royal Naval vessels and hospital ships.

## Audience Responses

Everywhere *The Battle of the Somme* was shown there were reports of packed cinemas and long queues, and of people returning to see the film a second time. Audiences were reported to be 'intensely interested' in the film, following the action with 'keen attention' and engaging with the film by applauding, cheering, shouting out and gasping.[38] These voluble reactions were typical of film audiences at the time; cinemas were communal spaces where there was a great deal of collective and often rowdy interaction between the projected films and the audience. But the character of Somme screenings was even noisier and more highly charged than usual. Firstly, screenings of *The Battle of the Somme* were what the historian Michael Hammond has described as 'special event' screenings, endorsed by the King, Lloyd George and other leading political and military figures: to attend the film was seen as a patriotic gesture.[39] Secondly, many members of the audience were personally connected to the events on the screen and the people who appeared on the film. Screenings in military towns were often dominated by uniformed men and elsewhere it was common for cinema managers to arrange special screenings for fit and convalescent men to watch the film for free or at reduced admission.[40] Reviewers attending these military screenings recorded the men cheering scenes of the victorious soldiers and even overheard private mutterings when the artillery was fired or German prisoners were brought in.[41] In addition, it was common for civilians to spot, or think they had spotted, relatives and loved ones among the men on the screen; invariably people shouted out when they saw someone they knew. At a screening in Hammersmith, for instance, 'One boy recognised his brother in the picture, an officer: "Look, look," he cried, "that's my brother"'.[42]

It was noticed that viewers were moved, even humbled, by the bravery and cheerful stoicism of the 'Tommies' in the face of discomfort and danger. British audiences were also impressed with the chivalry of the soldiers, and scenes of them giving drinks and cigarettes to the German prisoners were greeted with applause.[43] As the climax in the film, the reaction of audiences to the 'over the top' sequences was often recorded, generally people watching it in awed silence or with a collective gasp, but it was also reported that sometimes individuals reacted audibly to the men being struck down by enemy fire, one woman screaming out, 'Oh God, they're dead!'[44] We have these impressions of how audiences responded to the film because this was a recurring feature of press reports. Such an account of a screening, which turns the focus away from the film itself and on to the audience (reminiscent of the work of Mass Observers nearly thirty years later), underlines just how special the atmosphere of these 'event screenings' must have been, but it also reflects a curiosity with how people reacted to scenes in which real battle action was shown or those depicting the wounded, the dead and those being killed.

## Accompanying Music

Music is an important factor to consider when evaluating how *The Battle of the Somme* was received by audiences. Four days before the film was released, a cinema musician, J. Morton Hutcheson, published a list of forty-one pieces that he recommended be played to accompany the film. Morton Hutcheson was given access to the film by the official distributor, so it is correct to describe this medley as the 'official score'. We know this medley was used on at least eleven occasions and similar selections, with some substitutions, were used elsewhere. The score, revived by the IWM, has been performed live to accompany numerous screenings of *The Battle of the Somme* and is the alternative track on the DVD release. It comprises military music, selections from the great and 'light' classical composers, folk tunes and popular songs of the era. Loud and vigorous overtures were suggested for the scenes of artillery firing, uptempo marches for the men moving up to the front or engaging in action, and folk tunes and songs for scenes of the casualties or for the images of men resting, washing and eating. The musical selections were chosen to amplify the film's propaganda messages and, to modern sensibilities, some can seem jingoistic. Particularly striking is the choice of Suppé's 'Light Cavalry Overture' to accompany the 'over the top' scenes and following action, an uptempo piece, which seems crudely martial, even jaunty, for the moment of violence it is to support. More offensive is the choice of Stuart's 'Soldiers of the King' which is suggested to accompany a scene of horse-drawn artillery moving over ground in which the dead of the Gordon Highlanders and Devon regiments can be seen clearly. However, not all of the choices seem designed to deflect the emotions of the viewer, because Morton Hutcheson was himself deeply moved by the film and was perhaps unsure of exactly what messages he should be using the music to convey. For example, he confessed that he was haunted by the scenes of the men going over the top and of 'our hero carrying his wounded brother to safety' and even believed he had seen a man he knew among the soldiers.[45] Indeed, most of his musical recommendations for the scenes of the casualties, of the dead and other moments of the aftermath of battle, are sympathetic and very moving, increasing the distress that the viewer feels.

As the music was rarely mentioned in accounts of screenings, except in general terms, it is difficult to assess how the pieces worked with the film to affect viewers' responses to *The Battle of the Somme*. However, the martial and patriotic character of many of the pieces would not have surprised audiences in 1916. Many viewers, perhaps the majority, would have shared the patriotic sentiments expressed in the music. But we also know from reviews that some who watched the film found it supported their own views about the war which verged on the pacifist; such people may have found Morton Hutcheson's more martial musical selections distasteful. Those pieces of music which amplify the distressing scenes of the casualties and the dead for viewers today (e.g. Schubert's 'Serenade') would have had the same impact on viewers in 1916, except that the impact was likely to have been intensified as so many audience members had a direct personal connection to the war. Thus we can be sure that screenings of *The Battle of the Somme* were even more emotionally charged than we suppose, and also noisier and more rowdy, as it is likely that many joined in with familiar songs, such as 'Keep the Home Fires Burning', and hummed along to the well-known melodies in Morton Hutcheson's selection. Lastly, observations of screenings with the medley music today have shown that it increases the film's impact as a spectacle (notably by creating sound effects for the action) and gives it more coherence and narrative drive. This helps us to understand why the film was so successful with audiences.

## Critical Responses to *The Battle of the Somme*

The most common critical assessment of the film was its realism: 'the real thing at last' was a phrase that appeared repeatedly in reviews. Firstly, this was a comment on the coverage of the fighting, stressing that this film was unprecedented in showing genuine fighting, or 'actual fighting', as it was frequently termed.[46] The other aspect of the film's realism was the candid view it gave of the wounded and the dead. These scenes were widely commented on and people were clear that men of the British Army were among the dead shown in the film.[47] Many claimed that the realism of *The Battle of the Somme* was not just unusual for film, but that this characteristic made it superior to any previous efforts in capturing the truth of war, written, drawn or performed.[48] Reviewers also commended the visual glossary of the battlefield that titles and images provide for civilian viewers: 'To see these pictures, will enable one to follow the war with greater interest and better understanding.'[49]

The 'over the top' sequence was widely regarded as the climax to the film and was often described in detail, with some writers so transfixed by the action that their own description of it followed the camera, even into the German trenches. This scene and the images of the wounded and dead led to a debate about the appropriateness of showing such candid details of the horrors of war. But despite some opposition, it was generally felt that it was people's duty to see these scenes.[50]

This 'realism', and the importance of the event the film recorded, raised the status of *The Battle of the Somme* to that of 'history', as when *The Times* referred to the film as 'a drama which instead of being mimicry is a fragment of history'.[51] Looking more widely, there were those who argued that modern warfare was so technologically advanced that only the aviator or the film cameraman could really cover the action. An article in *Country Life* heralded the cameramen who had filmed 'some of the hottest fighting' on the Somme and at Verdun, for producing a historical record of these battles that was not only comprehensive but unimpeachable:

> The film pictures tell their own tale. They have been taken on a very large scale during this war, and to future historians they will be of more value than they are to us, because on many a disputed point their evidence will be unimpeachable. Never in history has a war been so recorded.[52]

Part of the impact of the film can be explained by the relative shortage of images of the British fighting. Significantly, *The Battle of the Somme* was regarded as more realistic than the previous official film releases, but also more realistic than the photographs of the front that had been published, as a Belfast writer put it: 'In the absence of anything better they were accepted as "live" pictures but when compared with the production now being shown they are as dead as the proverbial door nail.'[53] In fact, there were few images of any kind in the newspaper reports of the opening of the Somme offensive, with the exception of the *Daily Mirror*, which made a feature of photographs in general, with the front page of the edition of 3 July dominated by a photo of a British heavy gun in action. The power of the film's imagery is indicated by the fact that stills from the film were blown up for an article about the Somme offensive in the *Illustrated London News* and printed just before a highly romanticised illustration of the battle, in the tradition of military painting, where all the action was held within the frame.[54]

## Wider Issues Arising from the Film

Many who attend screenings of *The Battle of the Somme* argue that the film conceals the scale of the casualties suffered by the British Army and that it was a deliberate effort by the government to sanitise the sacrifice of war. This was not, however, how the film was received in 1916, when the images of the dead, of killing, and of the battlefield burials traumatised audiences and were regarded as candid and unprecedented in their honesty. This even extended to those in the military, as one officer, who was otherwise unimpressed with the film, still acknowledged that it would probably impress those at home: 'Certainly they are not spared the horrors of war. Personally I thought there was too much of the wounded soldier – the whole thing might quite well have been done on Salisbury plain.'[55] Some military authorities considered the film so revealing of the horrors of war that it would be a disincentive to recruiting. For this reason, the Board of Film Censors in British Columbia considered banning the film altogether.[56]

There is even a degree of frankness in title 31, which precedes the 'over the top' sequence, which while not giving actual casualty figures alludes to the fact that the German positions had not been quietened by the artillery bombardment (the title notes that British troops had 'advanced towards the German trenches, under heavy fire of the enemy'). The scenes that follow, re-enacted and actuality, then show a number of British soldiers falling, shot, presumed dead or badly wounded, scenes which produced awestruck silence among audiences.

This candid content meant that the film could play to audiences who by August and September 1916 were painfully aware that there had been tremendous bloodshed during the great offensive on the Somme. Thousands of unfortunate families had received official notification that their loved ones were missing or dead, and casualty lists were also published in newspapers. One diarist who himself watched *The Battle of the Somme* kept a daily tally of the officers and men whose deaths were reported in *The Times*.[57] When *The Battle of the Somme* was screened in Derry in October 1916, the review of the film in the *Londonderry Sentinel* on 17 October was printed alongside a casualty list of local men from the Royal Inniskilling Fusiliers and Royal Irish Regiment who had been involved in the opening phase of the Somme campaign. If the film had been less candid, less sobering, and thus less truthful, it surely would have been a less credible film and not as popular. Indeed, Malins argued that only the film camera had been able to convey the indescribable horrors of the battlefield.[58] As a writer in *Screen* put it, when commenting on those who were critical of *The Battle of the Somme* for its coverage of the wounded and dead,

> After two years of a dreadful war the British people are not supposed to be able to stand looking at the effects of it. Nobody in these days thinks war is a delightful romance. It is a horrible nightmare, and everybody nowadays knows it, and why they should desire to be hoodwinked we cannot tell. As a matter of fact we don't believe it. One opinion is that the public are tired of being kept in the dark. They

> want to know what is the actual state of affairs. They want to see what our boys are suffering on our behalf. This picture shows them all they wish for, and we hope it will be shown to the public as it was shown to the trade – in its entirety.[59]

Such a robust demand for journalistic openness, with all its connotations of democracy, was repeated by many other commentators and in a manner that feels very contemporary.

It is also significant that the film conveyed the truth of war to those who were highly critical of the war, even people who expressed a pacifist position.[60] Moreover, the ability to convey the unfamiliar world of the battlefield and the experience of the soldiers had a profound importance to those who had lost a loved one, and in this sense the 'over the top' sequence, even though it was traumatic, helped those who were grieving by providing context. Frances Stevenson, who had lost her brother Paul, observed that the film helped her visualise her brother's last hours, and concluded: 'I felt something of what the Greeks must have felt when they went in their crowds to witness those grand old plays – to be purged in their minds through pity and terror.'[61]

## Responses Then and Now: Documentary, Reportage or Propaganda?

Today, one of the most common assertions made about the film is that it is 'propaganda'. But as we have seen, this perspective differs from that which was recorded in 1916. The film possesses strong factual and documentary credentials, even though its overall message is propagandist. For example, the titles contain factual information which identify units (Manchesters, Devons, etc.), give dates and timings for actions, and list some of the locations where the battle took place (Picardy, Bray, Mametz, etc.). The film's documentary integrity has also been bolstered by the extensive research into the issue of the 'fakes', it now being concluded that only about seventy-two seconds of the action was not 'genuine'.[62] Moreover, the consensus is that such filming should be called 'staged', 're-enacted' or even 'improved', to confer a certain ethical justification on the filmmakers and to reinforce the point that the majority of the action in the film is what it is claimed in the titles.

There was also a clear attempt to edit the film so that the recorded scenes were broadly faithful to the chronology of the battle. For this reason, Roger Smither has suggested that the film is really more like a 'bulletin' or even 'dispatches from the front', words that ally *The Battle of the Somme* with a television news report from a war zone. Indeed, close examination to establish when and where the footage of the battle was actually shot shows that the action of each successive scene is broadly chronological and the film is a generally faithful record of the progress of the battle.

Given this brief analysis, a better way to answer the question 'Is this a documentary or a propaganda film?' is to say that it is both; it is a film that betrays the tension between the aims of these two types of filmmaking, between the cameramen's desire to show the truth of war and its brutality and the propagandist's imperative to boost support for the war effort and promote the image of the victorious British Army. These two conflicting aims lead to a tension in the film. The difficulty was that the War

Office was inexperienced in filmmaking, and also a film of this nature had never been produced. This helps to explain why the film includes such candid footage of the dead and wounded, in retrospect a naive action given the public outcry and controversy that resulted. While the claims made in 1916 for its impartiality must be challenged, the scope of the coverage of a battle remains unique in the history of the British moving image. Despite the propagandist and often heroic overtones of the 'packaging', the footage contained within *The Battle of the Somme* is a soberingly honest account of key aspects of warfare: the strenuous and unglamorous nature of soldiering; the brutalised landscape of the Western front; and the effect of war on the minds and bodies of men.

Judging from the well-attended public screenings and feedback gathered at these events, it is clear that the film is well received today; when asked to rate *The Battle of the Somme* on a simple scale of 1–5 (where 1 is poor and 5 is excellent), the vast majority of respondents rated the film a 5 or a 4.[63] Observation of audience behaviour and analysis of comments in the feedback forms show that the film engages and captivates audiences as it did in 1916, and that viewers are struck by those aspects of the film, such as the realism, which so impressed spectators a hundred years ago. In some respects, today's screenings share the character of those held in 1916. They are 'special events'; organised with or by the IWM, they have an official stamp about them, and watching the film might even be seen as a patriotic gesture. However, not all those who attend the film do so for such motives, and many are moved by the film's universal message about war's destruction of man, nature and settlements.

Since the premiere of the digitally restored version of *The Battle of the Somme*, held to coincide with the ninetieth anniversary of the battle, public screenings of the film have taken on a memorial character not fully anticipated by commentators in 1916. One might describe each screening of *The Battle of the Somme* as an act of memorialisation, with the cinema as a kind of darkened chapel; some screenings are actually held in churches.[64] Even when the screenings are held in secular spaces, the content of the film and the numerous personal family connections people have with the Somme campaign and the First World War in general make the Somme screenings deeply moving occasions. Caught up in the memorial atmosphere of the screening in Chester, one member of the audience suggested that 'the Last Post could have been played at the end of the film in memory of the fallen'.

## Notes

1. I would like to thank Roger Smither, former Keeper of the IWM's Film Archive, and Fiona Kelly, IWM Film Curator, for their comments on a draft of this chapter.
2. The precise casualty figure for the British Army is 57,470, including 19,240 killed.
3. Andrea Potts, First World War Centenary Commemorations, Department for Culture, Media and Sport, in an email to Toby Haggith of 15 July 2016.
4. There were also screenings at IWM London (night of 30 June 2016), Southend, Berkhamstead School, an open rehearsal at Cheethams School of Music in Manchester, and a screening in the Docklands performed by the Docklands Sinfonia.
5. *The Times*, 11 August 1916, p. 3.
6. 'First Day of the "Tanks" Film', *The Times*, 16 January 1917, p. 4.

7. Such a screening of *The Battle of the Somme* and *The Battle of the Ancre* was held at the National Film Theatre in July 1962, as part of the programme marking the tenth anniversary of the NFT. In 1990 the IWM released a VHS double pack of the 'Somme' and 'Ancre' films with a piano accompaniment performed by Andrew Youdell.
8. For example, *The Battle of the Somme* is absent from such important British-based studies of documentary cinema as Paul Rotha, *Documentary Film* (London: Faber & Faber, 1938), and Forsyth Hardy (ed.), *Grierson on Documentary* (London: Collins, 1946); general studies of cinema, such as Paul Rotha, *The Film Till Now: A Survey of World Cinema* (London: Spring Books, 1967), and Basil Wright, *The Long View: An International History of Cinema* (New York: Alfred A. Knopf, 1974); and international studies of documentary and films in general, notably Eric Barnouw, *Documentary: A History of the Non-Fiction Film* (Oxford: Oxford University Press, 1993), Brian Winston, *Claiming the Real: The Documentary Film Revisited* (London: BFI, 1995), *Halliwell's Film Guide*, 8th edn (New York: HarperCollins, 1992), and Pam Cook (ed.), *The Cinema Book* (London: BFI, 1990). Notable exceptions are Clyde Jeavons, *A Pictorial History of War Films* (Secaucus: Citadel, 1974), Ivan Butler, *The War Film* (New York: Barnes, 1974), and Kevin Brownlow, *The War, the West and the Wilderness* (New York: Alfred A. Knopf, 1979).
9. Rachel Low, *The History of the British Film, 1914–1918* (London: Allen & Unwin, 1950), p. 158.
10. In addition, there are two doctoral theses on British First World War filming: Nicholas Reeves, 'Official British Film Propaganda during the First World War' (University of London, 1981), and Nicholas Hiley, 'Making War: The British News Media and Government Control, 1914–1916' (Open University, 1985). Reeves's thesis led to the publication, in association with the IWM, of his book *Official British Film Propaganda during the First World War* (1986), which included the first detailed analysis of the Somme battle films.
11. '50 Documentaries You Need to See', *The Observer*, 27 March 2016, <https://www.theguardian.com/film/2016/mar/27/50-best-documentaries-alex-gibney-joshua-oppenheimer-james-marsh> (last accessed 24 November 2016).
12. Roger Smither, '"A Wonderful Idea of the Fighting": The Question of Fakes in "The Battle of the Somme"', *Historical Journal of Film, Radio and Television*, 13.2 (1993); Alastair Fraser, Andrew Robertshaw and Steve Roberts, *Ghosts on the Somme: Filming the Battle, June–July 1916* (Barnsley: Pen & Sword, 2009).
13. See Nicholas Reeves, '"The Real Thing at Last": *The Battle of the Somme* and the Domestic Cinema Audience in the Autumn of 1916', *The Historian*, 51 (1996).
14. Roger Smither, '"Watch the Picture Carefully, and See If You Can Identify Anyone": Recognition in Factual Film of the First World War Period', *Film History*, 14 (2002); Matt Lee, 'How IWM Is Trying to Identify the Man in this Film', <http://www.iwm.org.uk/history/how-iwm-is-trying-to-identify-the-man-in-this-film> (last accessed 24 November 2016).
15. Brownlow, *The War, the West and the Wilderness*, p. 64.
16. Butler, *The War Film*, p. 24; Michael Hammond, 'The Battle of the Somme', in Michael Hammond and Michael Williams (eds), *British Silent Cinema and the Great War* (Basingstoke: Palgrave Macmillan, 2011).
17. Nick Hiley, 'The British Cinema Auditorium', in Karel Dibbets and Bert Hogenkamp (eds), *Film and the First World War* (Amsterdam: Amsterdam University Press, 1995), pp. 160, 162.
18. Nick Hiley, 'Introduction', in Geoffrey Malins, *How I Filmed the War: A Record of the Extraordinary Experiences of the Man Who Filmed the Somme Battles etc.* (1920; London: Imperial War Museum, 1993), p. xxii.
19. 'Urban Tells How "Battle of the Somme" Was Obtained', *Motion Picture News*, 14 October 1916, p. 2,395.
20. *The Kinematograph and Lantern Weekly*, 10 August 1916, p. 7.

21. *Bioscope*, 17 August 1916, p. 576.
22. See *Bioscope*, 10 August 1916, p. 476, and Geoffrey Malins, speaking at the Finsbury Cinema on 21 August 1916, *Hornsey Journal*, 25 August 1916, p. 2, quoted in Hiley, 'Introduction', pp. xxvi–xxvii.
23. 'Urban Tells How "Battle of the Somme" Was Obtained', p. 2,393.
24. On 23 April 1918, the Irish trade unions held a one-day strike against the threat of conscription.
25. Malins, *How I Filmed the War*, p. 177.
26. John Benjamin McDowell in *Kinematograph Weekly*, 10 July 1916, quoted in Fraser, Robertshaw and Roberts, *Ghosts on the Somme*, p. 58.
27. David Laing, Aberdeen, to Tony Essex, BBC, undated letter (probably 1964). IWM.
28. Malins, *How I Filmed the War*, p. 178.
29. General Henry Rawlinson, diary entry of 26 July 1916. Churchill Archives Centre: RWLN/1/5. The supporting account appears in a diary entry of 26 August 1916, by 2nd Lt Frank Wollocombe, 9th Battalion, Devonshire Regiment, held in the IWM, Documents Reference 95/33/1.
30. Malins, *How I Filmed the War*, p. 183. See also his reflections on his own practice on p. 303.
31. See *Variety*, 44.6 (6 October 1916), 27.
32. Doubts about the authenticity of these sequences along with likely locations for the filming can be found in Roger Smither (ed.), *The Battles of the Somme and Ancre* (London: DD Video, 1993), pp. 19–20, 24–5. A more detailed study by Andy Robertshaw has confirmed these suspicions and suggested plausible accounts for the context of the staging. See Fraser, Robertshaw and Roberts, *Ghosts on the Somme*, pp. 156–7, 161–71.
33. Believed to have been filmed at Montauban by Geoffrey Malins, 5–6 July 1916.
34. An example of a press review in which the viewer clearly noticed the British dead referred to in the inter-titles is found in the Irish paper *Freeman's Journal* of 12 September 1916.
35. For example, an episode of *Coronation Street* broadcast on 23 February 2009 was seen by ten million viewers. The last episode of the 2015 series of *The Great British Bake Off*, broadcast on BBC1, was seen by 13.4 million viewers.
36. *The Observer*, 24 September 1916, p. 5.
37. *Evening Herald* [Dublin], 13 September 1916, p. 2.
38. *Irish Independent*, 12 September 1916, p. 4.
39. Hammond, 'The Battle of the Somme', p. 25.
40. In Glasgow on 31 August 1916, hundreds of wounded soldiers attended a screening of *The Battle of the Somme*, with some men even brought to the cinema by Red Cross ambulances.
41. See, for example, 'Crumlin Picture House: Matinee for the Military: The Battle of the Somme', *Belfast Telegraph*, 13 September 1916, front page.
42. Article in the *Evening Standard* from August 1916, quoted in Marie Seton, 'War', *Sight and Sound*, 6.24 (Winter 1937–8), 184.
43. 'Theatre Royal Hippodrome', *Irish Times*, 12 September 1916, p. 3.
44. *Bioscope*, 24 August 1916, p. 671.
45. When Morton Hutcheson reported back from a tour he made of the Midlands and Scotland, accompanying *The Battle of the Somme* on the piano, he related how '[t]he two thoughts, scenes visions call them what you like, made a very deep impression upon me, and I find some difficulty in placing these scenes in the back of my brain box and carrying on as usual'. *Bioscope*, 31 August 1916, p. 816.
46. 'Urban Tells How "Battle of the Somme" Was Obtained', p. 2,393.
47. 'Battle of the Somme: War Battle Pictures at the Theatre Royal', *Freeman's Journal*, 12 September 1916, p. 7.

48. See, for example, comments in the *Freeman's Journal*, 12 September 1916, p. 7.
49. *Londonderry Sentinel*, 19 October 1916, p. 2.
50. 'The Somme Pictures', *Irish Times*, 12 September 1916, p. 4.
51. 'War Realities on the Cinema: Pictures of the "Push"', *The Times*, 22 August 1916, p. 3; see also *Daily Express*, 11 August 1916, p. 6.
52. *Country Life*, 28 October 1916, p. 511.
53. *Belfast Evening Telegraph*, 12 September 1916, p. 3.
54. '"An Epic of Self Sacrifice and Gallantry": British War Films: The Most Wonderful Films Ever Taken of the British Offensive', *Illustrated London News*, 26 August 1916, pp. 240, 241.
55. IWM Collection: Documents Archive, the papers of Lt Col. Sir Cuthbert Headlam, Intelligence Officer, VIII Corps, writing to his wife on 13 February 1917.
56. *Irish Limelight*, January 1917, p. 14.
57. The diarist Frederick Robinson is quoted in Malcolm Brown, *The Imperial War Museum Book of the Somme* (London: Sidgwick & Jackson, 1996), pp. 264–5.
58. Malins, *How I Filmed the War*, pp. 183–4.
59. 'Editorial Notes', Northern Section, *Screen*, 6.11 (26 August 1916), i.
60. 'The Battle of the Somme Pictures', *Mona's Herald*, 13 September 1916, p. 4.
61. From *Lloyd George: A Diary by Frances Stevenson*, ed. A. J. P. Taylor (London: Hutchinson, 1971), p. 112, entry for 4 August 1916.
62. Fraser, Robertshaw and Roberts, *Ghosts on the Somme*, p. 170.
63. At the 22 October 2006 screening at the Queen Elizabeth Hall, out of 116 feedback forms, seventy-four respondents (63.8%) rated the film a 5 and thirty rated it a 4 (25.9%). This means that 89.7% of the audience rated the film excellent or very good.
64. Among the Somme 100 screenings that took place in a church are Manchester Cathedral (5 July), Christ Church Spitalfields (9 July), St George's Church, Cambridge (10 September) and Leicester Cathedral (1 October).

# 20

# Too Colossal to Be Dramatic: The Cinema of the Great War

*Michael Paris*

In 1917 the British government invited the celebrated American filmmaker D. W. Griffiths to make a propaganda film about the war that would enthuse a war-weary public with renewed anti-Germanism and provide the incentive to the people to 'carry on' to victory. Griffiths and his crew were given unprecedented access to take their cameras into the frontline and film whatever they wished. After some initial shots, however, Griffiths decided instead to recreate the Western front on Salisbury Plain. As he later explained in an interview,

> Viewed as drama, the war is in some ways disappointing, everything is hidden away in ditches. As you look over No Man's Land [. . .] there is literally nothing that meets the eye but an aching desolation of nothingness. It is too colossal to be dramatic![1]

It beggars the imagination to accept the idea that the site of the greatest war in history was not sufficiently dramatic for a Hollywood director. Of course, what Griffiths meant was that from the trenches little could be seen of the war; it was out of sight below the parapet or buried underground in the troglodyte world of the trenches. Given the difficulties, then, of attempting to capture the Great War on film, it is remarkable that so many filmmakers have made so many feature films set on the Western front or in the other theatres of war. This chapter is an attempt to survey the main themes and trends of the Great War film.[2]

From its creation at the end of the nineteenth century, the cinema quickly became one of the most powerful forms of mass communication yet devised. The short primitive actuality films of the 1890s soon gave way to longer narrative films which, by 1914, were increasingly complex, technically sophisticated and enormously popular, particularly with the working classes. Films operate on the emotions. In the darkened auditorium and without distractions, the audience becomes a part of the unfolding drama on the screen – the world represented there becomes their world, and they are drawn into the unfolding narrative. They identify with those portrayed upon the screen, and share, if only temporarily, the protagonists' struggles, fears and aspirations. Even in today's visually literate society, this can still happen, but for the unsophisticated audiences of the early decades of the twentieth century, what was on the screen was often believed to be 'real'. It is this quality – what we might call 'the magic of cinema' – that makes film such a powerful form of mass persuasion. But film was

Figure 20.1 Film poster for *All Quiet on the Western Front* (1930, dir. Lewis Milestone). Author's collection.

Figure 20.2 Film poster for *Gallipoli* (1981, dir. Peter Weir). Author's collection.

also a source of information for the audience, by interpreting great events, making sense of the world in which the audience lived and its past; and film is particularly effective in recreating and interpreting the past. Films, then, are not just entertainment but an important factor in shaping the worldview of the viewer, which can, of course, be manipulated for political purpose.

War was always a good subject for the filmmaker: dramatic, exciting and popular with jingoistic audiences. The short imaginative accounts of contemporary wars or colonial conflicts created in studios were soon overtaken by coverage of real events, and when the British Army went to South Africa to fight the Boers filmmakers went with them. But constrained by the limitations of their equipment, they recorded only posed groups of soldiers or passing columns of men and guns going into action. For the face of battle audiences at home had to turn to representations of war made by filmmakers eager to exploit the public's interest. Films like *The Attack on the Red Cross Tent* (1900) and *The Sneaky Boer* (1901), both from the Mitchell & Kenyon studio, posed scenes of plucky Britons and vicious Boers fighting, man-to-man, in close detail – detail which cameramen filming the 'real' war were unable to match.[3] But in 1914, despite the ever-increasing popularity of the cinema, and the general enthusiasm for the war, the British, like other European governments, saw no place for filmmakers in the national effort. The cinema was too frivolous; an indulgence for the lower classes. In the early months of the war, the political and military leadership had little sense of just how powerful film could be as an agent of mass communication and persuasion, and filmmakers found their offers of assistance rejected again and again. In September 1914 *Kine Weekly*, the foremost British trade paper, argued that film was uniquely placed to 'arouse patriotism'; a few days later its rival, *Bioscope*, suggested that citizens had the right to be informed about the conduct of the war, and cinema, with its ability to record the 'actual likeness of events', was well placed to play this role – but all with little effect.[4] Yet in those early months footage of the war did appear on the screen. The newsreels were full of scenes at recruiting offices, of soldiers, laughing as they accepted cigarettes and flowers from the onlookers who cheered them on their way to the front. Filmmakers even found their way to France with the British Expeditionary Force, and recorded more smiling, laughing columns as they trudged along country roads looking for the enemy. But as soon as the armies came into contact and the retreat from Mons began, the generals sent the cameras home, fearful they would record information 'of value to the enemy'.

By the end of 1914, the trench system ran from the Channel to the Swiss frontier, effectively dividing the continent. For the British public most information about the fighting came from War Office dispatches and the artists' impressions of battle in newspapers and magazines, usually heroic figures gallantly charging the German lines, struggling hand-to-hand with the wicked Hun and performing heroic and courageous deeds. These images, of course, drew upon the experience of colonial warfare and confirmed the public imagining of battle. Meanwhile, filmmakers, determined to demonstrate their patriotism, set about recreating the war in their studios, and what followed were a number of short, heroic tales. But recreating the Western front in leafy Surrey, or in the Parisian suburbs, with a handful of actors provided audiences with a very limited and sanitised idea of what it might be like in France. By early 1915 even the most hidebound generals had begun to realise that this was not the war that had been expected and victory would require all the nation's resources and the full cooperation of all citizens. Their efforts would have to be encouraged and thus it would be necessary to inform them about the war and of the demands for ever more men and material. And what better way to inform the public than through film, a medium that reached millions and which was widely regarded as a very picture of reality? Positive images of war, then, could raise public morale, encourage war production, denigrate the enemy and persuade the neutral nations that the Allied cause was just. In mid-1915, the government finally conceded and appointed the first official war artists, and even allowed photographers to go to the front.[5] With them went two army cinematographers, Lieutenants Geoffrey Malins and J. B. McDowell. The footage they shot would be released to the newsreels and thus, for the first time, cinema audiences would be allowed to see what this war was really like, or rather what the movie camera could record of it. But when these 'pictures from the Front' did appear on the screen, they were certainly not what the public expected. Filmmakers, as non-combatants, were positioned in a relatively safe position behind the frontline. With heavy, unwieldy cameras, rapid movement was impossible, and without the advantages of telephoto lenses or fast film, it was impossible to record the detail of war. Filmed reports from the battlefields show only a distant view of tiny figures moving towards the enemy before they are obscured in smoke. Film, then, was disappointing to an audience weaned on graphic, detailed images of war created by the artist and popular illustrator. In April 1916, the *Manchester Guardian* complained that the footage that had so far been released 'offered such little access to life at the front' that it might as well have been taken in this country.[6]

This attitude changed, however, in August 1916 with the release of the War Office film *The Battle of the Somme*: a detailed account of the preparations and opening phase of the Somme offensive of July, one of the war's bloodiest and still most controversial battles. The film had a tremendous effect on spectators and added a new dimension to the visual imagery of the war. While many of the scenes would have been familiar to audiences – columns of smiling troops moving up to the front, preparations behind the lines and so on – it included a short sequence of British troops going 'over the top', taking casualties, but advancing on the German frontline. This twenty-one-second sequence had considerable impact on audiences for here was the 'real war' at last. As we now know, but which contemporary audiences did not, the attack sequence was faked, filmed in Britain. The real footage of British troops going into action was filmed from such a distance as to be almost meaningless. Yet the scenes of British soldiers climbing the parapet and then falling, apparently dead or dying, profoundly shocked the audiences; women fainted, men cried, others swore they had seen their sons or brothers fall.[7] But the film also distorts the truth in other ways as well. Scenes of German prisoners trudging back under guard or of the enemy dead appeared to suggest that the opening phase of the battle had been successful; indeed, the film's captions about 'objectives taken' reinforce this idea, though in reality, of course, 1 July 1916 was the most disastrous day in the history of the British Army in terms of casualties. Yet while the film evades the truth in some ways, the camera cannot disguise the horrors of combat, for *The Battle of the Somme* also includes unprecedented footage of the pain and trauma of war captured on the faces of the survivors, and longer sequences that show graphic images of the dead – slow panning shots across a heap of bodies at the bottom of a crater, and later the unceremonious mass burials of the enemy dead. As *The Cinema* put it, 'This is war, rich with death.'[8] The German Command were greatly impressed with the film and the same year made their own version of *The Battle of the Somme*, *Bei Unseren Helden an der Somme* ('With our Heroes of the Somme') (Plate 7), but with somewhat less success. Nevertheless, in Germany film propaganda was judged to be so important by the High Command that the government secretly took control of the film industry – thus creating the conglomerate UFA, which by the 1920s had become the second largest film producer in the world after Hollywood.[9]

The Somme film broke all box office records: Prime Minister David Lloyd George wrote a dedication that was read aloud in many cinemas, and audiences across the country were shocked and horrified at the conditions at the front, far more horrible than they could ever have imagined. Nothing could disguise the suffering of the combatants, but it also introduced audiences to a new factor – that modern industrialised warfare destroyed not only men, but the physical environment as well. It is impossible to view *The Somme* without becoming aware of what the war had done to the gentle landscape of northern France – a theme that would be developed by many of the war artists, most notably Paul Nash in his aptly titled canvas *We Are Making a New World*, or C. R. W. Nevinson's *Harvest of Battle*. Cooperation between the government and the film industry was now considered desirable and the War Office Cinematograph Committee was created in 1916. Chaired by the press baron Lord Beaverbrook, the committee became responsible for all film propaganda. After a somewhat shaky start, 1917 saw British film propaganda become an effective political weapon. Interestingly, many Americans later blamed this propaganda for pulling them into the war, but after they did enter the war in April 1917 they set up their own film propaganda department, organised by the US Signal Corps, remarkably quickly.

The films sponsored by the British government were surprisingly varied, from feature-styled documentaries like *The Somme* to short animations by the illustrator Lancelot Speed like *The U-Tube* (1917), which made fun of the Kaiser's ambitions, or *Britain's Effort* (1918), which lauded the manner in which all classes had come together in a united war effort. *The Somme* was followed by several other feature-length films in the same style – *The Battle of Ancre* in early 1917 being the first – but these actuality films often had a depressing effect on the public, perhaps as they were just too real after such a long diet of sanitised images. Nor did audiences identify with the documentary format in the same way as they did with narrative film – they preferred to be drawn into the story, to become part of the drama in a way that was impossible with actuality footage.[10]

It was Beaverbrook also who in 1917, perceiving that war-weariness was having a debilitating effect on public morale, invited the distinguished American director D. W. Griffiths to make a narrative film about the war that would increase anti-German sentiment and provide the public with an incentive to 'carry on' to victory. The Cinematograph Committee even partly financed the film. *Hearts of the World – The Story of a Village* is set in a village in eastern France. It begins in 1912; the villagers are happy, peaceful and content. All that spoils this idyll is an unpleasant German tourist, Von Strohm, who displays a curious interest in the strategic position of the village. In August 1914 the village is occupied. Von Strohm now reappears in his true colours as an arrogant Prussian officer. The villagers suffer under the occupation but eventually the village is liberated by French and American troops who drive out the Germans – a typically naive Griffiths scenario, but one which had great appeal for audiences, and one in which the 'Huns' were legitimate targets for the audience's anger. To establish the authenticity of the film, it opened with a prologue of Griffiths in France looking for locations and later meeting Lloyd George. However, as we have seen, Griffiths actually preferred to recreate the Western front on Salisbury Plain using British and Canadian troops, and it was these scenes which provided the necessary 'realism' of close combat that audiences expected to see in pictures of the 'real' war. But whether or not *Hearts of the World* would have been great propaganda was never really tested, for the war ended before it was widely shown.

The part played by women in the war effort was largely ignored by filmmakers until the last years of the war but from 1917 a number of films paid tribute to women workers. *A Day in the Life of a Munitions Worker* (1917) focused on the contribution of the women who worked in highly dangerous conditions at Woolwich Arsenal. *Sisters in Arms* (1918) paid tribute to women in the armed forces, but showed little detail of their routine. However, in summer 1918, *With the Women's Royal Air Force: Life on a British Aerodrome* provided a fairly comprehensive picture of the duties performed by servicewomen. The film opens with airwomen launching an anti-submarine patrol airship, and carrying out minor repairs while rigging the vessel. However, the film soon cuts to 'Mid-Morning Recreation', a cosy scene in which the airwomen have tea and gossip. After 'Cleaning Aeroplanes', the lunch break again shows the women at leisure, before scenes in which they sew new canvas for aircraft and clean things. In fact, the whole emphasis of the film seems to be suggesting that recruits would find the work remarkably familiar and that in the WRAF they would find sociable companionship while helping the war effort.

The war, of course, had considerable impact upon cinema and created an enormous public demand for visual entertainment while also revealing the value of film as a political weapon. The involvement of governments in film production helped legitimise what had been before the war something of a fairground attraction, and as Furhammer and Isaksson point out, through the war cinema managed to 'shake off its cultural inferiority complex [. . .] and attained a significance far beyond that of cheap entertainment'.[11] We should not be surprised, then, that in the immediate post-war years the fledgling totalitarian regimes in Russia and Germany began to make use of film as a major channel of mass persuasion. The war also contributed to the development of national cinemas and created an understanding that patriotism could go hand in hand with profitability. Yet in the long term, the concentration on the war effort among European nations was to the detriment of their film industries, the closing of national frontiers and the rapid growth of the American film industry enabled the United States to establish dominance in the production and distribution of films that has never been seriously challenged.

Until recently it was common among historians to claim that with the Armistice, the war disappeared from the screen; this, of course, is nonsense. It is certainly true that fewer films were made, but the impact of the Great War on British society and on Europe generally was so great that it became an ever-present influence on all the arts, not least on cinema. Between 1919 and 1939 more than thirty major feature films about the war were made by British studios alone; Hollywood produced three times that number; and if we add European productions to the list, it becomes clear that the Great War was a major theme in cinemas throughout the period. Nor does that include those films that referenced the war in some way or another – films about war widows, disillusioned or damaged veterans and so on. It has become equally commonplace to argue that after the mid-1920s, British society turned against the war, recognising it as a futile struggle that achieved nothing but the death of a generation. This disillusionment was allegedly reflected in all forms of cultural production – particularly literature, and by implication film. But viewing the films made in those years today reveals a far less determinist picture. Between 1919 and 1929, British war films reflected a positive, almost heroic interpretation of the war. As far as cinematography was concerned, the war was certainly horrible, the suffering great, and many young men died, but it was a justified struggle that ended in a significant victory for the British Empire and its Allies. It ended the menace of Prussian militarism, ensured the freedom of Europe, and enlarged the British Empire – it was, in fact, one of the Empire's 'finest hours'. Typical of this group of laudatory films were British Instructional's series of reconstructions of famous battles, created by Harry Bruce Woolfe, himself a veteran of the trenches. Beginning with the commemorative *The Battle of Jutland* in 1921, these included *Ypres* (1925), *Mons* (1926) and *Blockade* (1932). Woolfe used actuality footage, models and re-enactments to tell his stories and received considerable assistance from the War Office in the form of men and equipment.

These films were, as Samuel Hynes has suggested, concerned with telling the story of the war in 'heroic, value-affirming terms'; they were testaments to courage, patriotism and the nobility of sacrifice. Not everyone agreed. The critic 'Bryher' (Winifred Ellerman), writing in the avant-garde journal *Close Up*, suggested the films suffered from a romantic and sentimental approach that ignored the disease, discomfort and horror of the war, and she equally disliked their strident militarism.[12] But in Woolfe's films the war was a justified crusade against tyranny, in which those who gave their lives found immortality in the memory of the nation. These films largely employ pre-1914 images of war and the language of G. A. Henty and Henry Newbolt – 'valorous', 'heroic' and 'brave'. Extremely popular with British audiences, these films reinforced the official view of the war and offered another form of commemoration – a testament to justified loss such as the public memorials and remembrance ceremonies. Moreover, they were exactly what bereaved families wanted to hear: that their loved ones had not suffered and died in vain but had given their lives for something fine and noble. Understandably, such an interpretation eased the pain of loss. This docu-drama style of filmmaking also had appeal for European filmmakers. In France Léon Poirier produced *Verdun: Visions of History* (1928), a reconstruction of the epic battle, while Germany produced *Douamont: The Hell of Verdun* (1931) and *Tannenberg* (1932), both directed by Heinz Paul. However, the intentions of the filmmakers were very different. While Poirier reconstructed the battle to show the 'obscene folly of war', Heinz Paul created interpretations of the conflict that are clearly heroic, which glorify individual soldiers, and support the 'stab in the back' argument of the political right.[13]

In British feature films, from Maurice Elvey's *Comradeship* in 1919 to Walter Forde's *Forever England* (1935), while the horror of the trenches and the suffering of the soldiers were not minimised, most films continued to find a positive interpretation of the war – as a justified conflict in which stoic British 'Tommies' served God, King and Empire and did their duty. A useful example here is Walter Summers's 1930 production *Suspense*, interestingly one of the few films where the focus is on enlisted men, not officers. An infantry company takes over a sector of the line and the men explore their new home; strange sounds from beneath the trench suggest that German sappers are tunnelling beneath them. Two German prisoners later confirm this. Now all the men can do is wait for the digging to stop, a signal the enemy mine will be exploded. When the tunnelling does cease, their anxiety becomes intense but they can only wait to be relieved and pray. Finally their relief comes, but as they reach the rear an explosion tells them the mine has been exploded. This is a war of chance, a gamble on who will live and who will die. But the Tommies are enduring, and there is never any doubt that they will do their duty and hold the trench until relieved or killed. A similar storyline was used in the recent Australian film *Beneath Hill 60* (Jeremy Sims, 2010). However, in the growing anti-war climate of inter-war Britain some filmmakers attempted to play both sides. Adrian Brunel (1892–1958), director of the highly successful *Blighty* (1927), candidly explained his position:

> It fulfilled the requirements of a popular patriotic film, in that it showed a decent English family behaving decently [. . .] They refused to join in the singing of either 'Land of Hope and Glory' or 'The Hymn of Hate' [. . .] It also fulfilled the requirements of a 'war' picture, although we never showed the war [. . .] And it was quietly, an anti-war picture rather than a pro-war picture.[14]

By the later 1930s even the 'war as adventure' film was back in fashion in British studios, in productions like Victor Saville's fine account of Belgian patriot Marthe Cnockaert, *I Was a Spy* (1933), one of the very few films made to feature a female protagonist, as well as *Forever England* and *Secret Agent* (Alfred Hitchcock, 1936).

But after 1930 British films about the war began to fall out of step with their European and American counterparts, which were by now becoming unanimous in their condemnation of the war. This trend had emerged in the mid-1920s in America with King Vidor's *The Big Parade* (1925) and was continued with *Dawn Patrol* (Howard Hawks, 1930), as many Americans began to question exactly why they had become embroiled in a war that had caused such great suffering. The key film in this context was almost certainly Lewis Milestone's *All Quiet on the Western Front*, released in 1930, still one of the most powerful anti-war films ever made. This American-produced version of a German novel by the veteran Erich Maria Remarque had an international appeal that spoke to veterans of all sides and to anyone who had lived through the war. Its powerful narrative, which tells of the inevitable fate of all its young protagonists, its brilliant direction and exceptional visual qualities made it the benchmark for later Great War films. *All Quiet* and its European-made counterparts established an uncompromisingly negative interpretation of the war.[15] In France, Abel Gance had completed the first version of his anti-war epic *J'accuse* in 1919, but it was Poirier's *Verdun* that amply illustrated the horrors of the conflict and, as Pierre Sorlin has pointed out, 'encapsulates the pathetic mood typical of the few French films dealing with the Great War',[16] a mood that would be fully explored in narrative films such as *The Doomed Battalion* and Raymond Bernard's *Wooden Crosses* (both 1932).

*All Quiet on the Western Front* appeared to have considerable international appeal, but in Germany, where the novel had already been heavily criticised by the political right, it ran into trouble for its pacifist message. The initial promotion for the film even carried *Variety* magazine's original endorsement of the film:

> The League of Nations could make no better investment than to buy up the master print, reproduce it in every language, to be shown to every nation every year until the word 'war' is taken out of the dictionaries.[17]

This was hardly the message the growing nationalist movement wanted to hear. The distributors arranged for a specially edited version to be premiered in Berlin in December 1930. But Josef Goebbels, the Nazi leader of Berlin, saw this as an opportunity to flex his growing political muscle and claimed that the film's anti-war messages were Jewish lies that slandered German soldiers, while his brown-shirted thugs disrupted the screening. The subsequent riots persuaded the German censors to ban the film.[18] After 1933, with the Nazis now in control of the film industry, German filmmakers soon started to produce a series of militarist propaganda films which encouraged martial spirit, some of which dealt with the Great War. *Shock Troop 1917* (1934) and *Operation Michael* (1937) focused on just how effective German soldiers were, but how they were denied victory by other factors. *Pour le Merite*, directed by Karl Ritter in 1938, pays tribute to the German air service and shows how fighter pilots had never really been defeated by the Allies, but betrayed by alien elements at home. In the film these heroes of the Fatherland have transferred their allegiance to the Nazis – the real successors of the brotherhood of the trenches.[19] At the end of the 1920s, however, a handful of anti-war films had been made in Germany, of which G. W. Pabst's *Westfront 1918* (1930) (Plate 8) is perhaps the most important. The film mirrors both *All Quiet* and *Wooden Crosses* in that it deals with the fate of a single company on the Western front. However, the rise of Nazism and the rebirth of militarism prevented other anti-war films from being made.

The only non-German film that even remotely resembled the pro-war vehicles made in Nazi Germany was Howard Hawks's 1941 production *Sergeant York*, in which farm boy and confirmed pacifist Alvin York goes into the mountains to pray for guidance when he is drafted in 1917. By 1940, with Europe already at war, the mood was changing. American interventionists (including Hawks) were now calling for American rearmament and a commitment to the Allied cause and *Sergeant York* was another element in that propaganda campaign. It is not surprising, then, that in the film God gives Alvin the go-ahead to join up and kill in the Allied cause. Not only does he become a soldier, but he takes to his new role so well that he becomes the hero of the Argonne in 1918 and wins the Congressional Medal of Honour.[20]

The two British films that are often assumed to be anti-war are *Journey's End* (1930), directed by James Whale and based on R. C. Sherriff's acclaimed stage play, and the 1931 screen version of Ernest Raymond's best-selling novel *Tell England*, directed by Anthony Asquith. Sherriff and Raymond had both served in the war, the former as an infantry officer and the latter as a chaplain at Gallipoli. The war is a horrible and brutal business in these films, but both are really studies in the idea of duty, sacrifice and heroism; specifically, that extraordinary sense of duty and understated everyday heroism found among the junior officers that formed the backbone of the newly raised Kitchener battalions. In both these films the war is cruel and deeply unpleasant, but the young protagonists must carry on and do their duty for a justified cause even if it requires the ultimate sacrifice.[21] The only British film that really came close to an unqualified anti-war position was Norman Lee's documentary *Forgotten Men* (1934), which highlighted the plight of many veterans, the 'forgotten men' of the title. Introduced by the popular historian Sir John Hammerton, it largely consists of a group of veterans, led by the disabled Major Bernard Cohen of the British Legion, recalling their experiences against a background of archive footage. The film's title, of course, evokes the memory of the wonderful musical number 'Remember My Forgotten Man' in the 1933 Busby Berkeley musical *Gold Diggers of 1933*:

Remember my forgotten man,
You put a rifle in his hand;
You sent him far away,
You shouted, 'Hip, hooray!'
But look at him today!

We see the unemployed veteran wandering the streets looking for work, moved on by the police, his medals just so much scrap metal. He is the forgotten man, who put his life on the line for his country but who is now unwanted, an embarrassment. The disillusioned veteran of this futile war had by the 1930s become a staple character in Hollywood movies: 'Eddie Bartlett' (James Cagney) in the classic gangster movie *The Roaring Twenties* (1939), for example, who, unable to find work after his war service, turns to crime.

It is curious that through the later 1930s, the British film industry, which was built around reflecting populist opinion for success, did not echo the strong public anti-war sentiment more powerfully if indeed such opinions were so widespread. Historian Jeffrey Richards has suggested that censorship may have had something to do with it, as 'the subject of pacifism and anti-war feeling came within the realm of British Board of Film Censorship's "controversial politics" and so no film on the subject was permitted'.[22] But censorship in France was equally sensitive to the national interest, yet this did not prevent films like *The Doomed Battalion* or *Wooden Crosses* from being produced. It seems more likely, then, that the majority of British people may well have wanted to remember the war as a cruelly fought but justified conflict for which the sacrifice had been worthwhile. This view, however, was certainly to change with the Second World War.

Between 1939 and 1945 the Great War was rarely mentioned in films; there were a few passing references in several productions such as the Boulting brothers' *The Dawn Guard* (1941) and Leslie Howard's *The Gentle Sex* (1943), but always to point to its futility or because those who survived it felt betrayed by post-1918 governments. In comparison, the war against Hitler was seen as a great moral crusade and after 1945, as more was revealed about the Nazi occupation of Europe, this belief was greatly strengthened. Against this conviction, the waste of the Great War appeared even more pointless, and the films that have been made since 1945 have all reflected this negative view. In fact, it was only the approach of the fiftieth anniversary in 1964 that appears to have reawakened public interest in the Great War at all. The sixties saw a number of popular critical studies published, while the British Broadcasting Corporation produced its monumental and enormously popular documentary series *The Great War* (1964).[23] One might have expected that British filmmakers would be tempted to exploit this renewed interest in the war but only four war films were made in Britain between 1960 and 1976: David Lean's epic *Lawrence of Arabia* (1962), *King and Country* (directed by Joseph Losey in 1964), Richard Attenborough's 1969 version of the stage show *Oh, What a Lovely War!*, a cynical and very bitter commentary on the brutality and waste, and *Aces High* (1976), yet another version of *Journey's End* but this time set in a Royal Flying Corps squadron in France. Each of these films interpreted the war as a bloody and brutal experience which dehumanised its victims; even *Lawrence*, which could so easily have become a paean to heroism, demonstrated that war can not only bring out the best in its participants, but also encourage the very worst excesses.

The single exception to these anti-war texts was the 1971 adventure story *Zeppelin* – a 'Boys' Own' style romp which included giant airships, double agents, beautiful spies and fanatical German officers. But it was much the same story with world cinema. In France *King of Hearts* (Philippe de Broca, 1966) and Bertrand Tavernier's powerful but bleak *Life and Nothing But* (1989) were typical; and even in Poland, where the war had once been seen as the key to Polish independence, the 1982 film *Austeria* (Jerzy Kawalerowicz) concentrated on the futility and waste. In Australia Peter Weir produced *Gallipoli* (1981) as his moving testament to 'mateship' and heroism in this story of the ANZAC Turkish expedition, while in America almost the only filmic references to the war were Stanley Kubrick's *Paths of Glory* (1957) and Dalton Trumbo's stark *Johnny Got His Gun* (1971). At the end of the twentieth century, several other films were made including the critically acclaimed British film *Regeneration* (Gillies MacKinnon, 1997), based on the novel by Pat Barker, a fictionalised account of the meeting between Siegfried Sassoon and Wilfred Owen at Craiglockart Hospital in 1917, and the peculiar *Deathwatch* (Michael Bassett, 2002), a horror film in which a group of infantrymen are destroyed by an 'evil presence' in the trenches. Since then, there have been a handful of films made by the combatant nations. Yet despite considerable public interest in the Great War in the twenty-first century and especially around the centennial, surprisingly few films about the war have been produced.[24]

This would seem mainly due to the high cost of such productions and diminishing cinema audiences – the recent European co-production *Joyeux Noël* (Christian Carion, 2005) involved financing from no fewer than six nations. However, it may also be due to the fact that since the 1970s television has become the most significant provider of films about the war, beginning with the documentary series *The Great War* (BBC, 1964) and prestigious adaptations like *Testament of Youth* (BBC, 1979), *All the King's Men* (BBC, 1999), imported series like *ANZAC* (Australia, 1983), and the recent *Parade's End* (BBC, 2012). But over the last few years, filmmakers have had access to a whole range of constantly improving computer-generated images which have opened unlimited opportunities for lavish productions at a more reasonable cost. Unfortunately, and whatever the filmmakers' original intention, all too often these productions finish up looking like rather poor computer games – particularly those films that deal with the hardware of battle, especially war in the air, like *Flyboys* (2006) or *The Red Baron* (2008). However, what is perhaps most evident in all these productions, whether made for cinema or television, is that since the 1930s at least, on the screen the war is always seen as a futile struggle in which a generation of patriotic young men and women, led by dull-witted and unsympathetic senior officers, endure a cruel and bloody experience for very little purpose. These films have also been almost exclusively set in Europe, or very occasionally the Middle East. A rare exception is John Huston's *The African Queen*, in which Humphrey Bogart and Katherine Hepburn take on the enemy in East Africa.[25] The conventions of the filmic Great War story were established by the influential anti-war texts written in the later 1920s by the young survivors of the trenches, a narrative in three acts: the patriotism of youth; the suffering of the trenches; and inevitably death or disillusionment. This interpretation of the war is, it seems, international and constant, while historical revisionism, however persuasive, makes not a scrap of difference. As the French historian Pierre Sorlin has perceptively written,

> In pictures, the War has been turned into myth. It is like a Greek tragedy: we can tell the same story again and again; we can create new characters and circumstances; but we can change neither the plot nor the symbols which define the period.[26]

This Greek myth syndrome has also, it seems, persuaded filmmakers to focus on a limited number of texts usually taken from the canon of English war books. It is worth noting here that R. C. Sherriff's *Journey's End* has been filmed or televised no fewer than five times since it was written in 1927, and that the story BBC Films chose to mark the centennial of 2014 was another version of Vera Brittain's *Testament of Youth* (2014), that classic of dashed dreams, suffering and the 'lost generation'.[27] It seems that only French filmmakers have attempted to find something more in their exploration of the Great War with subjects that have hardly been touched upon in British film: loss and bereavement in *Life and Nothing But* (1989) and *A Very Long Engagement* (2004); disfigurement in *Officers' Ward* (2001); shell shock in *Fragments of Antonin* (2006); and desertion and the role of women other than as nurses in *La France* (2006).[28] But overall it would seem that even now, almost one hundred years after the last guns fell silent, this entrenched and limited view of one of the twentieth century's most dramatic events has become the dominant interpretation of the war in popular cinema.

## Notes

1. Karl Brown, *Adventures with D. W. Griffiths* (London: Faber & Faber, 1986), p. 195.
2. The literature of Great War cinema is not vast but includes: Karel Dibbets and Bert Hogenkamp (eds), *Film and the First World War* (Amsterdam: Amsterdam University Press, 1995); Peter Rollins and John E. O'Connor, *Hollywood's World War I* (Bowling Green: Kentucky University Press, 1997); Andrew Kelly, *Cinema and the Great War* (London: Routledge, 1997); Leslie Midkiff DeBauche, *Reel Patriotism: The Movies and World War I* (Madison: University of Wisconsin Press, 1997); Michael Paris (ed.), *The First World War and Popular Cinema* (Edinburgh: Edinburgh University Press, 1999); Bernadette Kester, *Film Front Weimar: Representations of the First World War in German Films of the Weimar Period, 1919–1933* (Amsterdam: Amsterdam University Press, 2003); Daniel Reynaud, *Celluloid Anzacs: The Great War through Australian Cinema* (Melbourne: Australian Scholarly Press, 2007); Michael Williams, *British Silent Cinema and the Great War* (London: Palgrave, 2011); Lawrence Napper, *The Great War in Popular British Cinema of the 1920s: Before 'Journey's End'* (London: Palgrave, 2015); Mark Connelly, *Creating Celluloid Memorials for the British Empire: British Instructional Films and the Great War* (Exeter: Exeter University Press, 2015).
3. See Stephen Badsey, 'War Correspondents in the Boer War', in John Gooch (ed.), *The Boer War: Image, Experience and Direction* (London: Frank Cass, 2000).
4. *Kine Weekly*, 27 August 1914, p. 63; *Bioscope*, 3 September 1914, p. 859.
5. Nicholas Reeves, 'Official British War Propaganda', in Paris (ed.), *The First World War and Popular Cinema*, p. 27.
6. *Manchester Guardian*, 19 April 1916, p. 3.
7. Questions of fakes and reception are examined in Roger Smither, 'A Wonderful Idea of the Fighting: The Question of Fakes in "The Battle of the Somme"', *Historical Journal of Film, Radio and Television*, 13.2 (1993), 149–69, and Nicholas Reeves, 'Cinema, Spectatorship and Propaganda: "The Battle of the Somme" (1916) and its Contemporary Audience', *Historical Journal of Film, Radio and Television*, 17.1 (1997), 5–28.
8. *The Cinema*, 11.200 (10 August 1916), 26.
9. Peter Jelavich, 'German Culture in the Great War', in Aviel Roshwald and Richard Stites (eds), *European Culture in the Great War* (Cambridge: Cambridge University Press, 1999), p. 42.
10. On the documentary films produced during the war see Nicholas Reeves, *Official British Film Propaganda during the First World War* (London: Croom Helm, 1986).
11. Leif Furhammer and Folke Isaksson, *Politics and Film* (London: Studio Vista, 1971), p. 12.
12. Samuel Hynes, *A War Imagined: The First World War and English Culture* (London: Pimlico, 1992), pp. 445–6; 'Bryher', 'The War from Three Angles', *Close Up*, 1.1 (July 1927), 45. On Woolfe and British Educational see Connelly, *Creating Celluloid Memorials for the British Empire*.
13. See Clement Puget, 'Verdun . . . de Leon Poirier', *1895: Mille huit cent quatre-vingt-quinze. Review de l'association française de recherche sur l'histoire du cinema*, 45 (26 February 2007), 5–29; Rainer Rother, 'The Experience of the First World War and the German Film', in Paris (ed.), *The First World War and Popular Cinema*, p. 233; and Kester, *Film Front Weimar*. On television docu-drama see Michael Paris, 'The Great War and British Docudrama: "The Somme", "My Boy Jack" and "Walter's War"', in Martin Löschnigg and Marzena Sokolowska-Paryz (eds), *The Great War in Post-Memory Literature and Film* (Berlin: Walter de Gruyter, 2014).
14. Quoted in Adrian Brunel, *Nice Work: The Story of Thirty Years in British Film Production* (London: Forbes Robertson, 1947), p. 47. On early British cinema see Kelly, *Cinema and the Great War*, Williams, *British Silent Cinema and the Great War*, and Napper, *The Great War in Popular British Cinema*.

15. On *All Quiet on the Western Front* see Andrew Kelly, *Filming 'All Quiet on the Western Front'* (London: I. B. Tauris, 1998).
16. Pierre Sorlin, 'France: The Silent Memory', in Paris (ed.), *The First World War and Popular Cinema*, p. 128.
17. Quoted on the 1989 Universal DVD release.
18. See Modris Eksteins, 'War, Memory and Politics: The Fate of the Film "All Quiet on the Western Front"', *Central European History*, 13 (1980), 345–66.
19. On Nazi cinema see David Welch, *Propaganda and the German Cinema, 1933–1945* (Oxford: Oxford University Press, 1983).
20. A similar function might have been intended by Australian filmmaker Charles Chauvel in his 1940 production *Forty Thousand Horsemen*. See Reynaud, *Celluloid Anzacs*, pp. 142–59. Unfortunately, many of the early Australian films about the war have been lost or exist only in fragments. See Reynaud, *passim*.
21. See the comments by R. C. Sherriff in 'The English Public Schools in the War', in George A. Panichas (ed.), *Promise of Greatness: The War of 1914–1918* (London: Cassell, 1968). On the commitment of junior officers see John Lewis-Stempel, *Six Weeks: The Short and Gallant Life of the British Officer in the First World War* (London: Orion, 2011).
22. Jeffrey Richards, 'The British Board of Film Censors and Content Control in the 1930s: Foreign Affairs', *Historical Journal of Film, Radio and Television*, 2.1 (1982), 45.
23. Among the most critical were Leon Wolff, *In Flanders Fields* (London: Longmans Green, 1959), Alan Clark, *The Donkeys* (London: Hutchinson, 1961), and A. J. P. Taylor, *The First World War: An Illustrated History* (London: Hamish Hamilton, 1963).
24. They include the completely predictable *The Trench* (UK 1999), *The War Game* (UK 2002), an animation based on the 1914 Christmas truce, *In Love and War* (US 1996), based on Ernest Hemingway's experiences in Italy, a film version of his novel *A Farewell to Arms* (1929), *The Lost Battalion* (US 2001), and the New Zealand production *Chunuk Bair* (1992).
25. One might also mention the brief sequence set during the East African campaign in *Out of Africa* (1985). It should also be pointed out that with the exception of H. Bruce Woolfe's *Jutland* and Walter Forde's 1935 production *Forever England* (remade by the Boulting brothers in 1953), there are almost no films dealing with the war at sea.
26. Pierre Sorlin, 'Cinema and the Memory of the Great War', in Paris (ed.), *The First World War and Popular Cinema*, p. 22.
27. *Journey's End* was filmed in 1930, televised by the BBC in 1937, 1960 and 1980, and filmed in 1976 as *Aces High* – this time set in a Royal Flying Corps squadron. *Testament of Youth* was first televised by the BBC in 1979 with a brilliant Cheryl Campbell as Vera Brittain, and filmed again in 2014 (dir. James Kent). To mark the centenary, the BBC also televised two series, *Crimson Fields* (2014) and *ANZAC Girls* (NZ 2015), both of which dealt with volunteer nursing units.
28. It is also perhaps worth mentioning here Christian Carion's brave attempt at creating a multinational war film with his retelling of the story of the Christmas 1914 truce on the Western front (*Joyeux Noël*, 2005). That the film descends into cliché at its climax can perhaps be blamed on the operation of Sorlin's 'dominant myth'.

# 21

# Representations of the First World War in Contemporary British Television Drama

*Emma Hanna*

British television programmes about 1914–18 are generally produced, broadcast and received as memorials: small-screen alternatives to stone and bronze.[1] Across the drama and documentary genres, from the landmark epic series *The Great War* (BBC, 1964) through to the avalanche of commemorative programming for the centenary, British television output has worked to parallel significant anniversaries of the war. The act of making and watching a programme about the First World War is an act of remembrance in its own right. This commemorative impulse, the visceral need to remember the war at significant points in time, means that small-screen representations of the conflict are expressions of grief and consolation which continue to utilise established tropes of remembrance in their visual, aural and historiographical design. British television dramas, driven by emotive narratives which are heightened by the wartime context, continue to be a powerful and influential platform for representations of 1914–18.

This chapter will provide a survey of representations of the First World War in contemporary British television dramas. As the essence of cultural history is to examine the signifying practices which indicate how societies make sense of the world in which they live, it will place the programmes in their cultural, social and political context. Any cultural history of British society in the years after the Second World War cannot ignore television output. The television medium is such an all-pervasive part of twentieth- and twenty-first-century life that any such history would be incomprehensible without it. Moreover, in the period 2008–14, drama – including series, soaps and single plays – was the second most popular television genre, which accounted for a 16.7 per cent share of the available audience. Documentaries achieved 12.2 per cent, followed by films (9.7 per cent), news/weather (9.6 per cent) and sport (9.4 per cent).[2] From the development of new broadcast technologies in the 1960s, through the 'memory boom' of the 1990s, and the centenary commemorations from 2014, the media, publishing and tourism industries have broadened the public space of remembrance in contemporary British culture.[3] The study of televisual representations of the First World War is especially important because the historiography of the conflict bears the mark of two crossing vectors: one lies inside the historical profession and the other outside of it.[4] The site where these two vectors form a very public interface is on the television screen. Many historians now recognise that it is imperative to understand and analyse television output as influential pieces of public history. Despite being the prevalent medium for information and entertainment in most developed countries since the 1960s, however, until the contemporary period remarkably few studies embraced television as a primary source. George Brandt's edited collection *British Television Drama* (1981) was the first examination of the genre, followed by a second volume, *British Television Drama in the 1980s* (1993). Other academic studies have been published by Lez Cooke and Jason Jacobs in addition to several edited volumes such as Erin Bell and Ann Gray's *Televising History* (2010) and Jonathan Bignell and Stephen Lacey's *British Television Drama: Past, Present and Future* (2014).[5]

Contemporary television dramas about the First World War can be divided into five types: dramatic series made about the war, such as *The Monocled Mutineer* (BBC, 1986), *The Unknown Soldier* (BBC, 1996), *The Red Baron* (BBC, 2012), *The Crimson Field* (BBC, 2014), *The Passing Bells* (BBC, 2014), *37 Days* (BBC, 2014), *Our World War* (BBC, 2015) and *ANZAC Girls* (Channel 4, 2015); dramatic series which include episodes/wartime narratives such as *Upstairs, Downstairs*, series four (LWT, 1974), *Downton Abbey*, series two (ITV, 2011), *The Village*, series one (ITV, 2012) and *Life in Squares* (BBC, 2015); literary adaptations such as *My Boy Jack* (ITV1, 2007), *Birdsong* (BBC, 2012) and *Parade's End* (BBC, 2012); comedies such as *Blackadder Goes Forth* (BBC, 1989), *Chickens* (Sky, 2013) and *The Wipers Times* (BBC, 2013); and finally dramatic series set in the immediate post-war period, for example *Peaky Blinders*, series one and two (BBC, 2013–14). The majority of these dramatic narratives engage with the themes of loss and futility that are well established in Britain's modern memory of the First World War. Indeed, although new programmes emerge, televisual output about the First World War still refers back to images and ideas which resonate with the accepted stories of the conflict: the established tropes of mud, blood and poetry, that the majority of women served as nurses, and at least one case of a character suffering from shell shock executed on the orders of an idiotic 'donkey' from the High Command.

## Television Drama: A 'Golden Age'?

It has been said that British television experienced a 'golden age' of drama in the 1960s and 1970s, when television dramatists were allowed greater freedom and creativity compared to 'the more subservient roles played by their counterparts today'.[6] By the late 1990s British television drama was believed to be experiencing difficulties with the quality of its output. In 1999 a report commissioned by the Campaign for Quality Television offered a comparative analysis of the content of selected dramas from the late 1970s, 1980s and 1990s. *'A Shrinking Iceberg Travelling South . . .': Changing Trends in British Television*, by Steven Barnett and Emily Seymour, interviewed senior industry figures involved in commissioning and producing television drama, and performed a content analysis exercise on television output. This showed the extent to which the single play, traditionally the outlet for original drama, had disappeared from the schedules between the late 1970s and the late 1990s, with the number of such productions declining by more than half.[7] Series drama, particularly relating to crime, and soaps had both increased, but there was, in the words of one unnamed television executive, 'no long term commitment to anything – no Lew Grade type character developing great pools of talent, nowhere for writers and directors to grow up. The quality end is a shrinking iceberg travelling south.'[8] The report also found that

British-produced drama dominated BBC1 and ITV while imported (especially American) drama was mostly found on minority channels like BBC2 and Channel 4. The authors further underlined that there was greater commercial pressure to maximise ratings and audiences.[9]

One of the flagship dramatic series of the 'golden age' is *Upstairs, Downstairs* (LWT, 1971–5), featuring the lives of the Bellamy family, residents of 165 Eaton Place, who are loyally served by a team of domestic staff, described in the national press as the nation's 'favourite household'. The fourth series, which is set in the period of the First World War, was first broadcast in September 1974 during the sixtieth anniversary of the start of the conflict. *Upstairs, Downstairs* closely followed the accepted narrative line of the British war experience. The eldest son goes off to join his battalion, the butler is horrified by the arrival of Belgian refugees, the elder daughter signs up to be a VAD, and the footman is handed a white feather before returning from the trenches with shell shock. *Upstairs, Downstairs* deployed the 'nostalgia mode', where the costume drama is a 'heritage product' aimed towards a female middle-class audience which 'tends towards cultural conservatism and enshrines particularly erroneous myths about historical identity'.[10] The series had a warm reception. As an established and popular prime-time entertainment programme, *Upstairs, Downstairs* did not set out to challenge the perception of the conflict's memory in 1970s Britain, but it was acknowledged that the setting of the fourth series in the First World War gave added power to its narrative drive.

*Downton Abbey* (ITV, 2010–15) is the natural heir to *Upstairs, Downstairs*. As the popularity of the series testifies, even in the 2010s it remains the case that 'the British usually look back [to] the trenches as a lost Edwardian Eden'.[11] The second series of *Downton Abbey* is set against the backdrop of the second half of the war, from the Battle of the Somme in 1916 to the 1918 flu pandemic. The storyline details how many of the town's men go off to fight in the war, as Downton Abbey is converted into an officers' hospital. Matthew, the heir to the estate, enlists as an officer in the British Army, with Downton's footman William Mason as his batman. William dies from his war wounds after a deathbed marriage, the cook discovers her nephew has been shot for cowardice, and several characters suffer during the Spanish influenza epidemic. The first series of *Downton Abbey* had already established itself as a national Sunday evening favourite with approximately twelve million viewers.[12] Reviewers understood that the war

> will irrevocably change the genteel world of Downton Abbey's refined inhabitants. From the opening scene, the stark contrast in tone is apparent. Instead of seeing Carson the butler (Jim Carter) ironing his master's newspaper, the audience is greeted by the noise, mud and chaos of the Somme.[13]

However, the usual clichés which accompany the wartime narrative did not sit well with other members of the press, who accused the programme of being

> (unintentionally?) funny. Even die-hard fans [. . .] have struggled to keep a straight face through 99% of this season [. . .] Poor Hugh Bonneville (the Earl of Grantham) had to give a whole speech looking into the middle-distance about how – guess what? – a lot of men had died in the first world war. It was insulting to him as an actor.[14]

Nevertheless, when the final episode of series two was broadcast on Remembrance Sunday, *Downton Abbey* was watched by approximately 12.15 million viewers. This placed the episode as the ninth most popular programme of 2011, as measured by the Broadcasters Audience Research Board (BARB), just 1.5 million viewers short of the number who watched the BBC coverage of the Royal Wedding (13.59 million), and the finals of *Strictly Come Dancing* (13.34 million) and *The X Factor* (12.92 million).[15] Series five of *Downton Abbey* (ITV, 2014) went on to feature the planning and erection of the Downton war memorial as part of the post-war storyline. By that time, however, viewing figures had dipped below 11 million and the series did not make the BARB's top ten programmes for that year.[16]

Nursing drama *The Crimson Field* (BBC, 2014) was dismissed as '[a]nother posh period drama', and television critic Sam Wollaston asked, 'Could those be Downton Abbey girls nursing the wounded soldiers?' Making further comparisons with the BBC's flagship Sunday night success *Call the Midwife* (BBC, 2012), Wollaston decided that

> it looks a bit as if they've looked at what's done really well recently, Sunday night period drama-wise [. . .] and made a kind of amalgam. Which happily also ties in with a major anniversary [. . .] But the figures will be good, of course, because this country loves a posh polished period soap for a Sunday night [. . .] a rare story of women among all the men and mud. I certainly wouldn't bet on The Crimson Field being over by Christmas.[17]

The *Independent* thought that *The Crimson Field* was disappointing in that 'the series is unable to decide exactly what it wants to be. It's not an amusing *Downton* romp, but it lacks the emotional pull of the BBC's other forays into the same period.'[18] With 6.327 million viewers watching the final episode, *The Crimson Field* was placed twenty-fifth in BBC1's top thirty programmes.[19] The *Telegraph* read the series through the lens of the war poets:

> The events of 100 years ago still lacerate our emotions and we are still susceptible to the shocking power of the poetry it produced. When we have read in Sassoon's Golgotha how 'mirthless laughter rakes the whistling night' and of the 'vile, incurable sores on innocent tongues' in Owen's Dulce et Decorum Est, any contemporary attempt at drama seems futile. It is impossible to improve on the compassionate realism of Sassoon and Owen and of Rosenberg and Thomas, impossible to replicate what they had seen at first hand [. . .] The forgotten women of the First World War deserve our attention, but they also deserved better than this.[20]

*The Crimson Field* employed several historical advisers, among them the nursing historian Professor Christine Hallett. In response to a question after a plenary lecture at the Institute of Historical Research in July 2014, Professor Hallett underlined that she was glad the series had brought nurses to people's attention, but that she found some elements of the drama, particularly the Edith Cavell-type storyline of the final episode, 'rather melodramatic'.[21] Indeed, *The Crimson Field* perpetuated many wartime clichés. Members of the High Command were portrayed as unfeeling, stubborn and at times psychopathic, and a high number of men were portrayed as suffering from shell shock. It was regularly commented upon in the press that one of the lead actresses was a direct descendant of Charlie Chaplin, the British servicemen's favourite star. However, in the wake of *The Crimson Field*'s failure to capture the hearts of the viewing audience, it was reported in June 2014 that a second series would not be commissioned by the BBC.[22]

Continuing the nursing theme, the Australian series *ANZAC Girls* (Channel 4, 2015) was broadcast during the centenary commemorations of the Gallipoli landings. The six-part series tells the rarely heard true stories of the nurses serving with the Australian Army Nursing Service at Gallipoli and the Western front during the First World War. The programme follows five Australian nurses serving in Egypt, the Dardanelles and Lemnos. Their portrayal was based on a book by the journalist Peter Rees, which drew on actual AANS nurses' wartime diaries. Reviewers were critical of the 'pristine modern eyebrow shaping' and 'the unlikely general Australian accents', but despite its shortcomings 'it's always refreshing to see stories of women at war [. . .] there's still lots more to discover about [. . .] Anzac history more broadly, and isn't that really the point of period dramas?'[23] *ANZAC Girls* was watched by a much smaller audience than *The Crimson Field*[24] and it may be argued that, particularly so close to the release of a new film adaptation of Vera Brittain's 1933 memoir *Testament of Youth* (UK, 2014), viewers were tired of dramas which perpetuated the idea that the majority of women in the First World War were nurses.

One drama series which did portray a wider variety of female characters was *The Village* (ITV, 2013). Set in a Derbyshire village, the first six-episode series covered the years 1914 to 1920. The story is narrated by the character of Bert, a twelve-year-old boy in a working-class farming family who are experiencing hard times. His brother Joe Middleton is encouraged to go to war by his mother Grace as an opportunity to leave the village, but he returns with shell shock having fought on the Somme and been subjected to the harsh military punishment of being tied to a stake and exposed to enemy fire overnight. When he fails to return to his regiment he is caught in the village by the military police and executed for desertion. Other storylines include the women of the village going to work in a new factory which makes boots for the army, and a man from the village is imprisoned as a conscientious objector. *The Village* opened with an audience of 8.17 million viewers.[25]

The majority of television critics welcomed the series, saying that it was 'a proper, grown-up period drama'.[26] Several reviewers pointed to the series being the British version of *Heimat*, a thirty-episode German drama featuring a century of rural life, and that it was 'a welcome relief from those McCostume dramas (mentioning no names) that offer little more than a game of "dress-up" with a host of posh frocks and a repertoire of above/below stairs shenanigans'.[27] Striking cinematic shots of the vast panoramas of the English countryside provided a counterpoint to the microcosm of village life, albeit during a period of intense suffering and trauma. The nature of the series was 'unremittingly grim, and offered few moments of escapism'.[28] The programme's audience decreased throughout the series, the final episode being watched by 5.48 million viewers.[29] This implies that the events of the wartime narrative were not enough to keep viewers' interest, or that they may have found the series too harrowing. Television critic Ben Lawrence suggested that the scheduling of the programme was an issue:

> Viewers tend not to want challenging fare on Sunday nights. The costume dramas that have succeeded on Sundays – *Lark Rise to Candleford*, *Downton Abbey*, *Mr Selfridge* – have seduced audiences by rejecting any sort of reality and aiming for a cosy candlelit view of the past, or big, bold storylines with a soap-like quality.[30]

Lawrence surmised that *The Village* was flawed because 'in its quest to add dramatic tension [it] ended up playing God with the past', and asserted that the village's reaction to Joe Middleton's shell shock and 'the way in which everybody spoke with astonishing emotional articulacy' when the war memorial was unveiled 'felt unlikely and therefore dishonest'.[31] When one character questioned the models of soldiers' helmets on the memorial, stating they were merely there for pathos, Lawrence felt that 'if *The Village* itself had been less concerned with creating pathos it might have won more viewers round'. However, he also noted that 'only the most stone-hearted of critics would fail to feel the dramatic power of last night's closing scene as the villagers united to commemorate the dead at the 11th hour'.[32]

## Portraying Violence

In relation to portrayals of combat during the First World War, *Our World War* (BBC, 2015) was perceived as the most realistic. Billed as a '[t]ense combat drama series revealing experiences of British soldiers in World War One', *Our World War* was made for BBC3, which is aimed at a young adult audience. *The Guardian* saw this as an opportunity to provide a summary of each channel's approach to the centenary:

> You may have noticed, there's a big anniversary – a centenary – going on, which the BBC has been covering extensively and impressively, divvying it up as you'd imagine. BBC2 gets the history and the arguments: Ferguson, Hastings, Paxman, poppies etc. BBC4 gets the art and the poetry. And BBC3 gets left with the difficult task of selling the first world war to its target audience, 16- to 34-year-olds. It could have gone badly wrong. They might have done *Little Europe*, or *Snog, Marry, Machine Gun*. Instead, they've made Our World War.[33]

*Our World War* is a drama based on the accounts of real soldiers who served on the Western front. Some of these sources were being used for the first time, and several of the soldiers who featured in the dramatisation were decorated for bravery. The blueprint for the series was a documentary, *Our War* (BBC, 2011), about British soldiers serving in modern-day Afghanistan, a programme which had been awarded the British Academy Television Award for Best Factual Series. Combat footage from cameras placed on soldiers' helmets and gun barrels, as seen in *Our War*, was reused and reimagined as the fighting might have appeared to soldiers on the Western front. The language used by the soldiers is recognisably modern, and the soundtrack featured music by P. J. Harvey. The *Guardian* reviewer thought it was 'a 1914/2014 mashup for a new audience and hopefully a new relevance'.[34]

Each of the three episodes of *Our World War* centres on a key battle: Mons (1914), the Somme (1916) and Amiens (1918). Episode one, 'The First Day', is set two weeks after war is declared when the 4th Battalion of the Royal Fusiliers set up defences around the Belgian town of Mons. They expect to march beyond the town's bridges the next morning, but they soon discover the German army has already reached the other side of the canal. In the second episode, 'Pals', a group of office workers from Levenshulme, Manchester, join a local Pals battalion, the 18th Battalion Manchester Regiment. They soon find themselves facing the Germans at the Somme. Months later, Paddy Kennedy, another real soldier whose records can be found in the Imperial War

Museum, pleads with the battalion chaplain to let him off the firing-squad duty that will see him killing one of the friends he made on his journey. The final episode, 'War Machine', is set four years into the war when the British deploy tanks along the German border in an attempt to break the stalemate at the Battle of Amiens. The military historian Paul Reed wrote that 'with rumours of indie pop, odd camera angles and "Call of Duty" style graphics I had feared the worst', but he 'really rather enjoyed it' and thought it was 'a fitting addition to their WW1 Centenary season'.[35] Other reviews found the series to be intense and

> almost unbearable. There's something of *Saving Private Ryan* about it, though less grand and cinematic, more intimate and personal. Helmet cam, machine-gun cam, in-front-of-the-face cam, the jitteriness and the narrow field, all give it a claustrophobic, visceral intensity. Not so much bringing Mons into your living room maybe, as dropping you into Mons, having first blasted away a hundred years with heavy artillery. By the end, you're left exhausted, dazed, shell-shocked, with the rat-a-tat of the machine gun still ringing in your ears.[36]

The programme also gave viewers to opportunity to 'play' interactive episodes on the BBC iWonder website.[37] However, some commentators questioned whether or not this was a suitable programme to be shown in a period of national remembrance:

> Such up-to-the-minute technology and techniques are likely to look dated this time next year. Not what you want from First World War television. To make matters worse, faux helmet-cam footage and slow-motion tracking of bullets were also included, which at times gave the thing an unintentional and unwelcome whiff of spoof. And much of the acting was palpably ham, with slain German soldiers dropping to the ground like children in a school play. Having said all this, if you put the anachronisms to one side, the first episode was both entertaining and gripping. But in this year of solemn remembrance, that's not quite the point, is it?[38]

A more traditional take on the soldiers' experiences of war was seen in *The Passing Bells* (BBC, 2014). This series attempted to follow the wartime narratives of one young British soldier in parallel with a German soldier of a similarly young age. Very few representations of the First World War in British film or television have taken a comparative route, and in doing so *The Passing Bells* can be placed alongside the international cinematic interpretation of the Christmas truce, *Joyeux Noël* (2005). The five-part series was produced and broadcast as part of the BBC's centenary season, and was a joint venture between British and Polish production companies. It features scenes on both the Western and Eastern fronts, and also includes the American Expeditionary Force in its storylines. In this way *The Passing Bells* has been rather more ambitious than other Anglocentric productions in its storytelling about the war as a worldwide event. Nevertheless, the use of Wilfred Owen's 'Anthem for Doomed Youth' was somewhat disingenuous. The series was written for young adults 'with little knowledge of world events between 1914 and 1918' by a former lead writer on *EastEnders* who wrote the series with a pre-watershed audience in mind. One reviewer commented that 'this makes sense. After all, many soldiers were little more than children when they signed up to fight in the Great War.'[39] Recognising that a realistic depiction of the horrors of war would be too violent for the 7pm timeslot, 'there's not enough to distinguish the reality of the trenches from the derring-do adventure that Tommy/Michael had childishly imagined. And let's not imagine we're sparing the sensitivities of today's teenagers by omitting it. Most of them probably have games on their smartphones more graphic than this.'[40]

The different attempts at portraying the fighting on the Western front in *Our World War* and *The Passing Bells* harks back to more realistic First World War dramas such as *The Monocled Mutineer* (BBC, 1986).[41] The series was caught in the crossfire between the Conservative government and the allegedly over-liberal BBC, and when exaggerated claims of historical accuracy were made by advertising executives – particularly about the alleged British mutiny at Étaples in September 1917 – politicians, journalists and historians engaged in a very public battle which at the very least called into question the nature of historical and institutional transparency. Despite it being seen by up to ten million viewers, the violent nature of the series jarred with the accepted narrative of Britain's modern memory of 1914–18, and there was little empathy for the swearing, robbing, raping and mutinous soldiers of *The Monocled Mutineer* in the stormy social, political and economic challenges of the Thatcher era.

More palatable to the British audiences of the 1980s was the irreverent sitcom *Blackadder Goes Forth*, a programme which is now ingrained in Britain's modern memory of the First World War. The six-episode pastiche drew from a selection of First World War literature, with large helpings of *Journey's End* (1928), *Biggles* (1932) and *Oh, What a Lovely War!* (1963). The first broadcast run was watched by an average of 11.7 million viewers. The series is now a regular feature on BBC2 and satellite channels because it still resonates as historical truth about Britain's war experience. When *Blackadder Goes Forth* was repeated during the Armistice's eightieth anniversary in 1998, it entered the weekly list of the top twenty most watched programmes with 4.12 million viewers.[42]

Any discussion of Britain's modern memory of the First World War is drawn back to *Blackadder Goes Forth*. The series was the subject of renewed controversy when, in January 2014, the then Secretary of State for Education, Michael Gove, wrote an article for the *Daily Mail* about the place of *Blackadder Goes Forth* in the history and memory of the First World War. Gove said he had little time for the view of the Department for Culture and the Foreign Office that the commemorations should not lay fault at Germany's door. He pointed out that the conflict has been seen 'through the fictional prism of dramas such as *Oh! What a Lovely War*, *The Monocled Mutineer* and *Blackadder* as a misbegotten shambles – a series of catastrophic mistakes perpetrated by an out-of-touch elite' and he criticised '[l]eft-wing academics all too happy to feed those myths by attacking Britain's role in the conflict'.[43]

## Comedies

While the Second World War has provided ample material for comedy programmes, the sacred nature of Britain's war memory means that *Blackadder Goes Forth* was the only television comedy about the First World War until *Chickens* (Sky, 2013) and *The Wipers Times* (BBC, 2013). *Chickens* features three idiosyncratic young men who avoid serving in the First World War, and who live in fear of being labelled as cowards by the women who now dominate their village. With viewing figures ranging between 301,000 and 199,000 – above Sky 1's slot average of 121,000 viewers[44] – it was still very poorly received. One reviewer thought that 'it was almost like a historical version of *The Young Ones*. But not a hysterical one, sadly [. . .] the humour is clumsy, the plotlines are laboured and it just isn't funny enough.'[45] Most reviewers could not overlook the fact that two of the writers and performers, Simon Bird and Joe Thomas, had previously starred in a successful teen comedy:

> Much of the pre-publicity for the show has focused on the risky nature of its situation and the way it hopes to invert sexual stereotypes by placing three non-combatant men as a minority in a village run by women. Save that for a dinner party conversation, because Bird and Thomas are basically playing their *Inbetweeners* characters.[46]

*The Wipers Times*, a true story based on the publication of a satirical trench magazine, fared much better. Written by *Private Eye* editor and television star Ian Hislop, the ninety-minute drama was watched by two million viewers and was well received in the press. One broadsheet reviewer found it '[f]unny, sad, and peculiarly British' and observed that it was 'told with an affectionate twinkle',[47] while another felt that despite 'countless species of exploding shells (crumps, pipsqueaks, whizz-bangs and so on), the mud, the rats, gas and death, we saw reflected in the pages of *The Wipers Times* a heroic habit of resolute cheerfulness'.[48]

## Literary Adaptations

Lez Cooke has underlined that in the field of literary adaptation, 'Britain has been able to capitalise on its cultural heritage, producing costume dramas which have no peers [. . .] [and are] not only popular with viewers but also replete with quality in their writing, acting and production values.'[49] Jerome de Groot has added that literary adaptations have 'an instant cultural value conferred by their source material' and that they 'convey a sense of the depth and richness of British literary history [. . .] [which] works to establish the cultural hegemony and standing of the BBC [and] and is subsequently part of a worldwide strategy to sell a particular type of "British", classic product'.[50]

*Birdsong* (BBC, 2012) and *Parade's End* (BBC, 2012) are prime examples of what is perceived as the best of British television in the contemporary period. The former is based on Sebastian Faulks's best-selling novel of the same name, published in 1993, and the latter was adapted from Ford Madox Ford's tetralogy (1924–8) by the revered British playwright and screenwriter Tom Stoppard. *Birdsong*, starring Eddie Redmayne as Stephen Wraysford, was watched by an average of seven million viewers, while Benedict Cumberbatch's portrayal of Christopher Tietjens in *Parade's End* was seen by approximately two million viewers. Some reviewers wondered if 'we're fast approaching saturation point when it comes to early 20th-century drama' and whether the elitist tone of *Parade's End* was exacerbated by its being scheduled on a Friday night in the middle of August.[51] *Birdsong* was understood in the now traditional cultural references of the war, with Sam Wollaston commenting that in watching the adaptation 'we yo-yo [. . .] between Claude Monet and Siegfried

Sassoon', and that the 'tableaux of the battlefield [. . .] looked like Paul Nash's paintings. When Wraysford's near-expired body was rescued [. . .] it looked like a scene from the Deposition of Christ.'[52] What both series seemed to offer was 'a war at one remove, where we could stand back and contemplate the abstract – its tragedy, its alienation, its despair – without getting too mired in the filth'.[53]

## The Past War in the Present: *Peaky Blinders* (BBC2)

Tunnelling and filth featured in series one and two of the post-war drama *Peaky Blinders* (BBC, 2013–14). An epic gangster drama set in the lawless streets of 1920s Birmingham, the series was compared to the American *Boardwalk Empire* (HBO, 2010–14) and was voted number one in *The Guardian*'s 'Best TV Shows of 2014: Readers' Picks'.[54] Exceeding levels of violence seen in *The Monocled Mutineer*, the behaviour of the rival gang members is in part explained and contextualised by the men's wartime experiences, and the assumption that most British veterans 'were not hypersensitively reflective about their own manhood, sexuality or even suffering'.[55] Opening scenes include a line of men blinded in the war begging for pennies, singing 'Molly Malone', and in the home of the gang leader, Thomas Shelby, a close-up shows a photograph of the three brothers (Arthur, Thomas and John) smiling in the khaki uniform of the Warwickshire Yeomanry with a freshly dug trench behind them. During the war, we learn, Thomas Shelby was awarded the King's Medal for gallantry, but he is now suspected of robbing a factory of firearms to supply to Irish dissidents.

The war is ever present in the interplay between the characters. Freddie Thorne, a Factory Union organiser and former wartime comrade of Thomas Shelby, admits that 'there are days when I hear about the cuttings and beatings that I wish I'd let you take that bullet in France'. Thomas is privately amused and retorts almost instantly, '[t]here are nights I wish you had.' Shell-shocked veteran Danny 'Whizz Bang' has episodes where he believes he is a bomb and destroys the local pub. The script directs that

> *Thomas and Freddie swap a half amused glance before silently resolving to act [. . .] in restraining the madman, we see that they are used to working together in violent situations [. . .] Thomas hisses in Danny's ear.*
>
> 'Danny, you're home. You're home. We're all home in England.'
>
> *Both Freddie and Thomas see the comedy of all this. Danny growls out a furious mantra . . .*

| | |
|---|---|
| Danny: | 'Had to go bang, had to go bang, had to go bang.' |
| Thomas: | 'You're not an artillery shell, Danny, you're a man.' |
| | *Danny roars and struggles some more.* |
| Thomas: | 'You're not a whizz bang. You're a human being. Now get yourself together for Christ's sake.' |
| | *After a moment Danny takes a huge breath and then takes this on board* [. . .] |
| Danny: | 'Ah hell. Did I do it again?' |
| | [. . .] |
| Thomas: | 'Yeah you did it again Danny. Got to stop doing this, man [. . .] Go home to your wife, Danny. Try to get all that smoke and mud out of your head.'[56] |

When Danny 'Whizz Bang' murders a man shouting 'fix bayonets!', he tells Thomas, 'I died over there [. . .] I left my fucking brains in the mud.' Thomas Shelby, likewise, has a number of flashbacks to hand-to-hand fighting in underground tunnels during the war. He habitually uses opium and imagines that he can hear tapping on his wall and that people are digging through it. When Thomas's gang require reinforcements against a London gang, he calls on fellow veteran and criminal Billy Kitchen's Black Country Boys:

> Billy Kitchen: [to Thomas] Ready for active service.
> Thomas: That's alright Billy, you don't have to stand in line for us, you're just the man we're looking for, but you'll have to pass the medical first [. . .]
> Thomas: It's been a long time, eh, Billy? What did you do with your medals?
> Billy: I threw them in the cut, same as you.
> Thomas: It was never a hardship having you black country boys on our left flank.
> Billy: You Brummies did alright on our right.
> John: Damn right.
> Thomas: I want you to be the head of a brigade, Bill. You'll be Brigadier Kitchen from now on, you'll have a hundred men under your command [. . .] Go home Bill. Round up any good men you can trust and put the word out. Black country boys and Brummie boys are on the same side again.[57]

This sense of wartime camaraderie among the criminals is seen in how they relate to Thomas's brother Arthur, another man suffering acute psychological damage as a result of the war. He is addicted to drink and drugs, and prone to murderously violent outbursts, and one reviewer underlined that this might '[provoke] viewers to consider how many other men like him went on after the Somme to kill and kill again in pub fight, gang battle and prison brawl [. . .] it became difficult to know if he believed the war was truly over.'[58] The 'ghosts of war' also dominate the war widow, May Carleton, an aristocrat racehorse trainer who becomes romantically involved with Thomas Shelby.

## Conclusion: The Centenary Onwards

The centenary is unsurprisingly proving to be a boom time for television programmes about 1914–18. All British channels, particularly ITV and the various BBC outlets, have concentrated their resources on producing a wide variety of programmes in which drama features heavily. This is particularly true of the BBC. In October 2013, the BBC announced an unprecedented broadcasting project in its commemoration of the First World War: 2,500 hours of programming across all platforms, to be transmitted throughout 2014–18.[59] Certainly, 'it is pertinent to consider how commemoration of events key to national identity are [filtered] through broadcasters' preconceptions of audience preferences and their own institutional identities.'[60] Rowan Aust has suggested that the self-billed 'four-year season' goes much further than the BBC's fulfilment of its Public Service Broadcasting Charter in the Reithian sense of informing, educating and entertaining. In the wake of a tumultuous period of crisis, where trust in the BBC has declined, and where the corporation must compete with a wider range of formats which have proliferated in the digital era, the commemorative season is 'the BBC's attempt to bolster and secure its own place as a repository for public history and public memory'.[61]

It has been suggested that the BBC's four-year-long project is excessive, and that the commemoration will be longer than the war itself.[62] Nevertheless, the centenary period of the First World War has given British television drama opportunities to return to its former glory, although this is not always reflected in the viewing figures for each programme. No drama about the First World War appeared in the BARB top thirty viewing figures on BBC1 or BBC2 in November 2014: the viewing figures are dominated by *Strictly Come Dancing* and *EastEnders*, attracting between 7 million and 11.5 million viewers each. When blockbuster series such as *Downton Abbey* and *The Village* have incorporated wartime storylines the viewing figures can be seen to have decreased through each series. In August 2014, the start of the commemorative period, BBC1 was dominated by *The Great British Bake Off* with up to 10.2 million viewers, and no war-related drama or documentary featured in the top thirty most watched programmes.[63]

Despite the fact that the Tommies of 1914–18 are now 'as far away from us as Wellington's redcoats of 1815 were from them', that so many television dramas have been made for the centenary period shows that the First World War 'endures because of the continued human presence of the past'.[64] While the emotive storylines afforded by a wartime context naturally lend themselves to the genre of television drama, the persistent dominance of the tropes of mud, blood and poetry means that the programmes continue to buttress Britain's traditional memory of 1914–18. It is still the case in Britain that the act of watching any programme about the First World War is an act of remembrance.

## Notes

1. See Emma Hanna, 'A Small Screen Alternative to Stone and Bronze: "The Great War" (BBC, 1964)', *European Journal of Cultural Studies*, 10.1 (February 2007), 89–111, and *The Great War on the Small Screen: Representing the First World War in Contemporary Britain* (Edinburgh: Edinburgh University Press, 2009).
2. 'Shifting Genres', Broadcasters Audience Research Board (BARB) report. For BARB data for this and subsequent notes, please visit the Broadcasters Audience Research Board website at <http://www.barb.co.uk/> (report last accessed 14 September 2015).
3. Jay Winter, 'The Generation of Memory: Reflections on the "Memory Boom" in Contemporary Historical Studies', *Bulletin of the German Historical Institute*, 27 (2000), *passim*; Jay Winter and Emmanuel Sivan, *War and Remembrance in the Twentieth Century* (Cambridge: Cambridge University Press, 1999), pp. 2–3.
4. Jay Winter and Antoine Prost, *The Great War in History: Debates and Controversies, 1914 to the Present* (Cambridge: Cambridge University Press, 2005), p. 3.
5. Jonathan Bignell and Stephen Lacey (eds), *British Television Drama: Past, Present and Future* (New York: Palgrave Macmillan, 2014); Erin Bell and Ann Gray (eds), *Televising History: Mediating the Past in Post-War Europe* (Basingstoke: Palgrave Macmillan, 2010); James Leggott and Julie Anne Taddeo, *Upstairs and Downstairs: British Costume Drama*

*Television from 'The Forsyte Saga' to 'Downton Abbey'* (Lanham, MD: Rowman & Littlefield, 2015).

6. Lez Cooke, *British Television Drama: A History* (London: BFI Publishing, 2003), p. 4.
7. Ibid., p. 191.
8. Unnamed 'television insider' quoted in Steven Barnett and Emily Seymour, *'A Shrinking Iceberg Travelling South . . .': Changing Trends in British Television: A Case Study of Drama and Current Affairs* (London: Campaign for Quality Television, 1999), quoted in Cooke, *British Television Drama*, p. 191.
9. Barnett and Seymour, *'A Shrinking Iceberg Travelling South . . .'*, quoted in Cooke, *British Television Drama*, p. 191.
10. Jerome de Groot, *Consuming History: Historians and Heritage in Contemporary Popular Culture* (Oxford: Routledge, 2009), p. 184.
11. David Reynolds, *The Long Shadow: The Great War and the Twentieth Century* (London: Simon & Schuster, 2013), p. 430.
12. BARB Top 10 Programmes 2011 (last accessed 28 November 2016).
13. Ceri Radford, '*Downton Abbey* second series: first review', *The Telegraph*, 30 July 2011, <http://www.telegraph.co.uk/culture/tvandradio/8670941/Downton-Abbey-second-series-first-review.html> (last accessed 28 November 2016).
14. Viv Groskop, '*Downton Abbey* on PBS: season two, the verdict', *The Guardian*, 20 February 2012, <http://www.theguardian.com/tv-and-radio/tvandradioblog/2012/feb/20/downton-abbey-series-two-pbs> (last accessed 28 November 2016).
15. BARB Top 10 Programmes 2011 (last accessed 28 November 2016).
16. BARB Top 10 Programmes 2014 (last accessed 28 November 2016).
17. Sam Wollaston, '*The Crimson Field* – TV review', *The Guardian*, 7 April 2014, <http://www.theguardian.com/tv-and-radio/2014/apr/07/the-crimson-field-tv-review> (last accessed 28 November 2016).
18. Rose Troup Buchanan, 'A BBC drama that can't decide what it's about', *The Independent*, 13 April 2014, <http://www.independent.co.uk/arts-entertainment/tv/reviews/the-crimson-field-tv-review-a-bbc-drama-that-cant-decide-what-its-about-9256610.html> (last accessed 28 November 2016).
19. BARB Monthly Top 30, May 2014 (last accessed 28 November 2016).
20. Ben Lawrence, 'Soapy and disappointing', *The Telegraph*, 11 May 2014, <http://www.telegraph.co.uk/culture/tvandradio/tv-and-radio-reviews/10820129/The-Crimson-Field-final-episode-review-soapy-and-disappointing.html> (last accessed 28 November 2016).
21. Christine E. Hallett, 'Veiled Warriors: Allied Nurses in the First World War', plenary lecture at the 'Great War at Home' Anglo-American conference, Institute of Historical Research, 4 July 2014.
22. Ben Dowell, 'BBC1 axes First World War drama', *Radio Times*, 10 June 2014, <http://www.radiotimes.com/news/2014-06-10/bbc1-axes-first-world-war-drama-the-crimson-field> (last accessed 28 November 2016).
23. Eleanor Robertson, 'A TV history of Gallipoli that focuses on women', *The Guardian*, 21 April 2015, <http://www.theguardian.com/tv-and-radio/tvandradioblog/2015/apr/21/anzac-girls-more4-gallipoli-war> (last accessed 28 November 2016).
24. This series was watched by fewer than 1.79 million viewers as it does not appear in the BARB Monthly Top 30 programmes for the month it was broadcast, April 2015 (last accessed 28 November 2016).
25. BARB Monthly Top 30 for BBC1, March 2013 (last accessed 20 April 2013).
26. Arifa Akbar, '*The Village* gives viewers – finally – a proper grown-up period drama', *The Independent*, 1 April 2013, <http://www.independent.co.uk/arts-entertainment/tv/reviews/tv-review-the-village-gives-viewers-finally-a-proper-grown-up-period-drama-8555619.html> (last accessed 28 November 2016).

27. Ibid.
28. Ben Lawrence, '*The Village*: episode six, BBC One, review', *The Telegraph*, 5 May 2013, <http://www.telegraph.co.uk/culture/tvandradio/10036702/The-Village-episode-six-BBC-One-review.html> (last accessed 28 November 2016).
29. BARB Monthly Top 30, March 2013 (last accessed 20 April 2013).
30. Lawrence, '*The Village*: episode six, BBC One, review'.
31. Ibid.
32. Ibid.
33. Sam Wollaston, '*Our World War* review – excellent, innovative and moving television', *The Guardian*, 8 August 2014, <http://www.theguardian.com/tv-and-radio/2014/aug/08/our-world-war-review-first-world-war-bbc3-cuckoo-siblings> (last accessed 28 November 2016).
34. Ibid.
35. Paul Reed, WW1 Centenary website, <http://ww1centenary.net/2014/08/09/bbc-our-world-war-review-of-ep1-mons> (last accessed 28 November 2016).
36. Wollaston, '*Our World War* review'.
37. BBC iWonder, *Our World War*, interactive episode, <http://play.bbc.co.uk/play/pen/gc58xjnzp5> (last accessed 28 November 2016).
38. Jake Wallis Simons, '*Our World War*, BBC Three, review: "a whiff of spoof"', *The Telegraph*, 7 August 2014, <http://www.telegraph.co.uk/culture/tvandradio/tv-and-radio-reviews/11018605/Our-World-War-BBC-Three-review-a-whiff-of-spoof.html> (last accessed 28 November 2016).
39. Ellen E. Jones, '*The Passing Bells*, BBC1, TV review: The First World War drama for children', *The Independent*, 6 November 2014, <http://www.independent.co.uk/arts-entertainment/tv/reviews/the-passing-bells-bbc1-tv-review-the-first-world-war-drama-for-children-9844991.html> (last accessed 28 November 2016).
40. Ibid.
41. See chapter 5 in Hanna, *The Great War on the Small Screen*.
42. *Broadcast*, 6 November 1998, p. 28.
43. Michael Gove, 'Why does the Left insist on belittling true British heroes?', *Daily Mail*, 2 January 2014, <http://www.dailymail.co.uk/debate/article-2532930/MICHAEL-GOVE-Why-does-Left-insist-belittling-true-British-heroes.html> (last accessed 28 November 2016).
44. See <http://www.broadcastnow.co.uk/ratings/chickens-scares-off-one-third-of-audience/5059778.article> (last accessed 28 November 2016).
45. Terry Ramsey, '*Chickens*, Sky1, review', *The Telegraph*, 22 August 2013, <http://www.telegraph.co.uk/culture/tvandradio/10260397/Chickens-Sky1-review.html> (last accessed 28 November 2016).
46. John Crace, '*Chickens*: TV review', *The Guardian*, 22 August 2013, <http://www.theguardian.com/tv-and-radio/2013/aug/22/chickens-poaching-wars-tom-hardy> (last accessed 28 November 2016).
47. Sam Wollaston, '*The Wipers Times* – TV review', *The Guardian*, 12 September 2013, <http://www.theguardian.com/tv-and-radio/2013/sep/12/the-wipers-times-tv-review> (last accessed 28 November 2016).
48. Christopher Howse, '*The Wipers Times*, BBC Two, review', *The Telegraph*, 12 September 2013, <http://www.telegraph.co.uk/culture/tvandradio/10303282/The-Wipers-Times-BBC-Two-review.html> (last accessed 28 November 2016).
49. Cooke, *British Television Drama*, p. 195.
50. De Groot, *Consuming History*, p. 185.

51. Ben Dowell, 'Have you been watching . . . *Parade's End*?', *The Guardian*, 20 September 2012, <http://www.theguardian.com/tv-and-radio/tvandradioblog/2012/sep/20/have-you-been-watching-parades-end> (last accessed 28 November 2016).
52. Sam Wollaston, 'TV review: *Birdsong*', *The Guardian*, 22 January 2012, <http://www.theguardian.com/tv-and-radio/2012/jan/22/birdsong-tv-review> (last accessed 28 November 2016).
53. Serena Davies, '*Birdsong*, part one, BBC One, review', *The Telegraph*, 22 January 2012, <http://www.telegraph.co.uk/culture/tvandradio/9028774/Birdsong-part-one-BBC-One-review.html> (last accessed 28 November 2016).
54. Marta Bausells, 'The best TV shows of 2014 – readers' picks', *The Guardian*, 30 December 2014, <http://www.theguardian.com/tv-and-radio/tvandradioblog/2014/dec/30/the-best-tv-shows-of-2014-readers-picks-peaky-blinders> (last accessed 28 November 2016).
55. Reynolds, *The Long Shadow*, p. 431.
56. *Peaky Blinders*, episode one, 'Blue Amends', p. 17, <downloads.bbc.co.uk/writersroom/scripts/Peaky-Blinders-S1-Ep1.pdf> (last accessed 28 November 2016).
57. Ibid.
58. Grace Dent, 'Grace Dent on TV: *Peaky Blinders* needs a third series', *The Independent*, 7 November 2014, <http://www.independent.co.uk/arts-entertainment/tv/reviews/grace-dent-on-tv-this-gangland-tale-needs-a-third-series-9845780.html> (last accessed 28 November 2016).
59. 'BBC reveals 2,500-hour World War I season', <http://www.bbc.co.uk/news/entertainment-arts-24552194> (last accessed 28 November 2016).
60. Erin Bell and Ann Gray, *History on Television* (London: Routledge, 2013), p. 20.
61. Rowan Aust, 'The Presentation of the First World War: History, Crisis and Recovery at the BBC', conference paper delivered at CATH conference, De Montfort University, Leicester, 4 June 2014.
62. Clarissa Tan, 'Jeremy Paxman's Great War is great. But is 2,500 hours of WW1 programming too much?', *The Spectator*, 1 February 2014, <http://www.spectator.co.uk/arts/television/9126702/is-war-the-bbcs-safe-zone/> (last accessed 28 November 2016).
63. BARB Monthly Top 30, August 2014 (last accessed 28 November 2016).
64. Reynolds, *The Long Shadow*, pp. 433–4.

# 22

# The Sound of War: Audio, Radio and the First World War

*Richard J. Hand*

When we consider the First World War, the first things that spring to mind are probably *visual*. We might think of propaganda posters, including the iconic image of Earl Kitchener wanting the spectator to enlist. It may be more in the realm of the perceived verisimilitude of photographic technology as in, for example, the monochromatic images of soldiers: military portraits of uniformed men; troops marching joyfully to the front; doomed youth bedraggled and haggard in filthy trenches; the wounded and maimed in hospital; and corpses, hanging on the old barbed wire of no man's land. In addition, we might think of motion photography: the First World War was the first consistently filmed war and 'silent' newsreel footage of all aspects of the conflict continues to define our perception of this century-old conflict. In this regard, the Great War is captured for us by the technological culture of the camera. Remarkably, perhaps even disturbingly, the power of the technical media of visual culture had a direct impact on First World War military life itself. Joanna Bourke cites the example of a Royal Fusilier who ordered a group of entrenched machine-gunners to imagine they were filming rather than aiming at the enemy: 'cinematograph the grey devils' and take 'as many pictures as possible'.[1]

However, the camera was not the only new technology with an indelible impact on the documentation and cultural legacy of the First World War. Sonic cultures are as important as the visual to our understanding of the conflict. Along with the cinematograph, one of the last great inventions of the nineteenth century was the gramophone. The gramophone enabled the circulation of music and popularised sentimental, jingoistic or comical songs. But the gramophone also captured other sounds including examples of documentation and the spoken word. People purchased recordings of recitations and political and militaristic speeches. There are also unique audio documents that are as striking or revealing as any photograph or prose account. These include remarkable eye-witness accounts told by survivors and even interviews with British prisoners of war recorded by their German captors. There are also examples that are effectively audio drama before the invention of radio. The theoretical basis for radio was established in the late nineteenth century, with its practical implementation coming in the early twentieth century. The burgeoning wireless technology had an important role in military activity and it is this practical use that paved the way for broadcast radio. In addition, the diverse sonic content of gramophone recordings (from music to documentation to drama) was eventually reflected in the content of radio transmission. This chapter will look at examples of 'pre-radio' drama produced during the First World War as well as a survey of how radio drama has presented the First World War in the hundred years since the conflict. However, before we analyse and evaluate these aspects of audio culture and technology, it is important to explore the concept of *sound* itself.

## The Sound of War

During the First World War, if the weather over London promised clear skies and moonlight, many people would take to trains to escape the city. This was because moonlight brought the threat of enemy bombing raids. With this new era of warfare in which civilians in their own homes became 'legitimate' targets, people learned how to *listen* – because their lives might depend upon it. Virginia Woolf recounts a raid in December 1917:

> Nothing was further from our minds than air raids; a bitter night, no moon up till eleven. At 5 however, I was wakened by L. to a most instant sense of guns: as if one's faculties jumped up fully dressed [. . .] [The guns] fired very quickly, apparently towards Barnes. Slowly the sounds got more distant, & finally ceased; we unwrapped ourselves & went back to bed. In ten minutes there could be no question of staying there: guns apparently at Kew [. . .] Servants apparently calm & even jocose. In fact one talks through the noise, rather bored by having to talk at 5 a.m. than anything else. Guns at one point so loud that the whistle of the shell going up followed the explosion. One window did, I think, rattle. Then silence. Cocoa was brewed for us, & off we went again. Having trained one's ears to listen one can't get them not to for a time; & as it was after 6, carts were rolling out of stables, motor cars throbbing, & then the prolonged ghostly whistlings which meant, I suppose, Belgian work people recalled to the munitions factory. At last in the distance I heard bugles [. . .] it struck me how sentimental the suggestion of the sound was, & how thousands of old ladies were offering up their thanksgivings at the sound.[2]

Woolf's diary entry is significant for its prevalent sense of the auditory. Her vivid description takes us through the detected sense of impending peril that can rouse one from the darkness of sleep; the aural mapping of the targeted zones; the chatting and joking through the noise; the rattling window in the immediate domestic space; the acute silence before the eerie whistling drifting over from Belgian factories; and the bugles heralding that the skies were clear. This was a war in which, for many people, more was *heard* than *seen*. For Woolf and other people in southern England during aerial bombing raids, they needed to shelter in the relative security of dark basements or ground-floor rooms. They were hidden out of view, deprived of vision, but nothing could stop the permeation of sound. Such testimony makes us realise how important sound was (and is) in the experience of warfare. Throughout the First World War, while the public might see carefully mediated newsreels, press coverage and censored correspondence, nothing could prevent the sound of the guns from being heard in the south of England and London.

The uncontrollable auditory signifiers of conflict can challenge the very sanity of the listener, especially a former combatant. For example, in the final, poignant verse of Siegfried Sassoon's 'Repression of War Experience' the peaceful summer of home is invaded by the far-off thudding of guns, which drives the listening soldier demented.[3] The sound of the guns is so distant – a mere whisper – yet able to crawl beneath the skin and send the listener insane. For the combatants in the First World War, it would seem that sound and its close association with anamnesis (in other words, the intense recollection of memory) could send someone insane as much as the desperation of the circumstances or the horrors the eyes beheld. The military historian Richard Holmes informs us that during the bombardment of the Verdun forts in 1916, although the garrisoned troops were 'safer' than the more exposed soldiers in shell-holes, 'the sheer din of shells smashing into the forts [. . .] and the agony of waiting for the arrival of the next shell drove men stark mad'.[4]

Richard Holmes has done much to capture the visceral dimension of the experience of war. He reveals how for the soldiers fighting on the front the auditory is as acutely important as it is (literally) resonant. The First World War introduced a cacophony the world had never encountered before, as is captured in this description:

> These small knots of men, scuttling hunched against the fire, or sheltering behind such cover as can be found, are assailed by noise which is often, as [Field-Marshall] Alanbrooke said of that at the Battle of the Somme, 'unimaginable'. The sounds of battle fill a broad spectrum from the soft moan of a wounded man to the ear-splitting crash of a shell-burst.[5]

With experience of the front, soldiers could chart a taxonomy of sounds: Holmes quotes Charles Carrington's vivid description of how every gun and projectile had its own sonic 'personality', and Charles Sorley heard within the gunfire what seemed like the noise of motorbikes and trains or even the sounds of cows and buffaloes.[6] These mechanical projectiles may have sounded like modes of transport or bucolic animals, but they were designed to maim and kill. Moreover, when they succeed in attaining their designed effect, this too has a number of distinct sounds:

> Sometimes the impact of bullet or shell fragment is clearly audible. Bullets make a solid thud or, more rarely, a metallic shriek as the spinning round is deflected by bone.[7]

If the listener was not killed by projectiles, a new field of distinct sounds opened up, as revealed in Passchendaele survivor Edwin Campion Vaughan's description of the (significantly) lightless battlefield:

> From the darkness on all sides came the groans and wails of wounded men; faint, long, sobbing moans of agony, and despairing shrieks.[8]

It is hardly surprising that this panoply of sounds imbedded itself into the memory of the war's survivors. Robert Graves nearly died from shrapnel wounds at the Battle of the Somme and suffered shell shock. He would remain terrified of loud or sudden noises, which would cast him back to the trenches: 'I couldn't face the sound of heavy shelling now; the noise of a car back-firing would send me flat on my face, or running for cover.'[9]

During the First World War, shell shock was often formally described as 'neurasthenia' or, in other words, exhaustion-induced weakness of the physical nervous system. Looking at Graves and other veterans now, they would seem to be clear victims of 'hyperacusis', or extreme sensitivity to noise. Contemporary science closely associates hyperacusis with post-traumatic stress. There is evidence that heightened stress levels at the time of acoustic trauma expose the cochlea to acoustic damage and therefore heighten the likelihood of developing hyperacusis.[10] In this regard, we see that sound – so often as uncontrollable as it is unstoppable – can have a physical *and* a psychological impact. The eardrum-tearing blast of detonation or impact, the mechanised rhythm and retort of weaponry or the sickening sounds of demise and injury, all permeating through total darkness or blinding light, imbed themselves in the memory and sometimes even the physiognomy of combatants.

The intensely potent effect of sound on the emotional and physical levels makes it no surprise that sound is recurrently important in First World War poetry. For poets such as Sassoon, the auditory is a consistent element of his poetic language. In 'Before the Battle', Sassoon finds solace in silence and the natural sounds of birdsong and brooks, which offer the speaker safety and strength to scorn the noises of battle.[11] Elsewhere, Sassoon juxtaposes music against cacophony;[12] but for some other poets there is horror in the stillness and silence after conflict, as in Margaret Sackville's 'A Memory':

> There was no sound at all, no crying in the village,
> Nothing you would count as sound, that is, after the shells;
> Only behind a wall the low sobbing of women,
> The creaking of a door, a lost dog – nothing else.[13]

What remains for Sackville is 'Silence', a silence that can be felt and is '[h]orrible' and 'soft like blood'.[14] In contrast to the acute auditory sensibility of Sassoon and Sackville, some poets are dominated by the *visual*. Isaac Rosenberg is a particularly striking example in this regard, his poetry imbued with a sense of the visual – but he was a trained artist, after all. Nevertheless, one of Rosenberg's most accomplished poems, 'Dead Man's Dump', concludes its powerful vision-dominated journey with a haunting irony revealed through sound as a dying soldier shifts from *heard* life to *beheld* death:

> We heard his weak scream,
> We heard his very last sound,
> And our wheels grazed his dead face.[15]

## Recording the War

Ironically, the onslaught of battle sounds, from deafening, mechanised blasts to the frailty of human utterance, was counteracted with *melody*. Richard Holmes informs us that the German military (re)introduced the use of bugles in March 1918 in an attempt to boost morale. For the German soldier Alfred Bruntsh, weeping in terror, the shifting auditory experience seems to be the cause of and the (near) cure for his state of mind:

> I was emotionally finished and glad in my heart when, after the four-hour barrage, the signal 'spring up' sounded. This ancient call blown by our trumpeter helped me to get rid of my tears but the fear still remained.[16]

As well as the martial sound of bugles or other armies' drums or bagpipes, popular songs were an indelible part of the soldier's experience. Almost certainly, the First World War has more songs associated with it than any other conflict in history (as George Simmers's contribution to this volume testifies). Troops on both sides were encouraged to sing songs to boost morale and build an *esprit de corps*. As well as in the trenches, songs were popularised in music halls, sheet music and recordings. These gramophone and phonograph recordings were not just for listening by the home fires: gramophones were actively encouraged in both the British and German armies. Indeed, as Fred Gaisberg (who was a sound recordist during the First World War) notes, the gramophone was more than just encouraged; it was regarded as a 'vital necessity' for troops, and these listening habits led to a post-war boom in the gramophone industry.[17] The gramophone permitted multiple versions of favourite and new songs to be spread, working in close relationship to the oral circulation of rumours, stories and jokes.

For writers during the First World War, popular song and the gramophone could have a powerfully ironic position. In the poem 'Gramophone Tunes' by the wartime nurse Eva Dobell, we experience a poignant observation of severely wounded and traumatised patients in the ward as they play gramophone records over and over again. Although the tragic patients seem to find solace in the music, for Dobell 'these common tunes / Can never sound the same again' for all she can hear in the 'nasal melodies' is, 'clear and plain', the 'laugh of death and pain'.[18] For one such patient, Sassoon in 'Dead Musicians', the great German and Austrian composers who once inspired him have lost all relevance; it is only in listening to gramophone recordings of popular songs that his fallen comrades are brought to mind. However, what may have brought solace and remembrance eventually brings panic: when the song finishes the poet realises that he is as alone as his comrades are dead.[19] The powerful impact of recordings was not just understood by individuals but recognised by the military authorities: the aforementioned Fred Gaisberg was tasked by the British Army to record prisoners and deserters singing traditional folk songs and heartfelt messages to urge their erstwhile trench comrades to desert. These recordings were then played across no man's land to apparently great if localised effect.[20]

Although synonymous with music, the gramophone had always been used to capture the spoken word. There were spoken word recordings of Lloyd George and other politicians and military figures. There were also recorded testimonies by active soldiers such as Edward Dwyer. This nineteen-year-old Victoria Cross winner was recorded giving fascinating eye-witness accounts of life in the frontline. As Tim Crook signals, the recordings of Dwyer – ostensibly produced as 'rallying' propaganda – are notable for their sense of realism, revealing in honesty that aspects of the war were 'agonizing' and a 'nightmare'.[21] The fact that Dwyer returned to the front and was killed in action at the Battle of the Somme adds to the poignancy of the recording. Indeed, Crook has detected the 'haunting' quality this has had in reception, a particularly potent example of Derridean 'hauntology' wherein the present only exists in relation to the ghosts of the past.[22] In this regard, audio artist Greg Whitehead's description of listening to radio voices as hearing 'a whole chorus of death rattles', voices 'severed from the body',[23] is never more apt than when applied to spoken word recordings from the First World War. The disembodied voice in recordings can be an uncanny experience. Certainly, listening to the voice of Edward Dwyer chatting to us – vividly and humbly, colloquially and accented (he came from Fulham) – and singing 'We're Here Because We're Here' can be an eerie, poignant experience. Audio has an uncanny power; the disembodied voice can be so full of vitality, not least because, in stark contrast to photographs, it is time-based. Sound is invisible and, like life, ephemeral and yet recordings can capture it.

It is not only recordings of voices that can be uncanny: voices, too, can be uncanny. This is revealed in contemporaneous poetry of the First World War. In Mary Symon's poem 'A Recruit for the Gordons' (written in Aberdeenshire dialect), the poet gives voice to an enthusiastic young man enlisting into the Gordon Highlanders, but his keenness to join is tempered by a haunting final verse:

It's laich, laich noo, in Flanders' sod,
An' I'm mairchin' wi' the drum,
'Cause doon the lang La Bassée road,
There's dead lips cryin' 'Come!'[24]

A similar uncanny sound of the voices of the recently fallen is heard in Sassoon's 'The Return' where the ghosts are auditory, haunting the dark and the ruins of war.[25] Significantly, it is death that seems to have given them voice: when alive, the soldiers spoke in actions; now dead, they converse in an enmeshed, unseen voice.

It can be a small step from the uncanny to the disturbingly absurd. If we return to Edward Dwyer's rendition of 'We're Here Because We're Here', crackling from its gramophone recording, we find a song that was a popular favourite amongst the British 'Tommies'. It is a song that has a disconcerting quality of repetition and futility. This was demonstrated to great effect in the launch of the Europeana Collections 1914–18 project. This enormous digital project features a portal of several hundred thousand First World War items from numerous pan-European collections. At the British Library launch event in London in December 2013, the musician P. J. Harvey recited the lyrics to several popular First World War soldier songs to haunting effect, as a British Library blog recounts:

> Stripped of the accompanying music, the cold absurdity of their lyrics was laid bare [. . .] [W]hen you listen to the lyrics – really listen – they are jaw-dropping in their calm horror. The biggest revelation among the lyrics that Polly read was the song 'We're here because': originally sheltered behind the tune of 'Auld Lang Syne', that night the lyrics opened up a Beckettian no man's land of senseless repetition. 'Here because we're here because we're here because we're here': on it went, that tortuous, clinically neat, anti-logic.[26]

## Audio Drama during the First World War

Amongst the many examples of non-music recordings on gramophone, there are pioneering examples of audio drama. Although the technology of radio had been invented by the First World War, its use was primarily for shipping: the death toll on the *Titanic* in 1912 would have been even higher if it had not been for the ship sending an emergency call. By the time of the First World War, wireless had also become an important communication tool for the military and it determined the course of the conflict. Following this, and the gradual uptake of radio technology by amateur enthusiasts, the development of network radio broadcasting began in the 1920s. Early in the evolution of radio, examples of drama can be detected, and eventually the genre of 'radio drama' became an extremely important part of its provision. In his pioneering research into radio, Tim Crook argues that the First World War is a key era in the development of audio drama. Effectively, wartime dramatic recordings are examples of audio drama in an emphatically pre-radio era.

Convincingly, Tim Crook cites a Boer War era (1899–1902) recording, 'The Departure of the Troopship', as an important precursor to the First World War audio drama recordings. In this popular record, the listener hears a melding of departing troops, emotional well-wishers, military bands (playing songs including 'God Save the Queen') and the whistle of the departing steamship. This (re)constructed soundscape permits the listener to experience an auditory moment that is simultaneously dramatic, patriotic and sentimental, and 'The Departure of the Troopship' sets a template for First World War recordings. As Crook reveals, as well as a huge number of popular music and spoken word recordings, First World War phonograph records included a wealth of 'mini-plays':

> The mini-plays dramatize a wide range of narratives including a German bombing raid on a seaside town, embarkation by the troops to France and a mother's tearful farewell, heroic Victoria Cross winning action in the trenches, a re-enactment of the Great War myth of the Angels of Mons – the ghosts of angels said to have saved British troops from the German advance, and the sinking of the Lusitania by U-boat off the coast of southern Ireland. These are also supplemented by clear evidence of early sound documentary, journalism and actuality recording.[27]

In regard to actuality, sometimes 'Gas Shells Bombardment, Lille, 1918' has been cited as the only actual sound recording of the frontline, but argument persists as to whether this is really a studio recording created with kettle drums and whistles.[28]

A particularly important collection unearthed by Crook is the 'On Active Service' series released by Columbia Records. This 1917 series of phonograph recordings produced by the British soldier Major A. E. Rees (and based on his own experiences) comprises six three-and-a-half-minute dramatised sketches titled 'Leaving for the Front', 'In the Trenches', 'The Night Attack', 'The Big Push', 'For Valor!' and 'Back Home in Blighty'.[29] Crook has analysed 'In the Trenches' in some depth, convincingly arguing that it demonstrates a remarkable ability to present 'complex, sophisticated and highly entertaining performance by a large cast with a range of synthesised sound effects that create a clear sound design'.[30] In its succinct three minutes twenty-eight seconds duration, 'In the Trenches' is a powerfully directed piece of audio drama which features a background soundscape of machine-gun and shelling sounds with foregrounded dialogue. As Crook notes, there is much to impress us about this pioneering example of audio drama:

> A balance between the foreground dialogue and background sound of larger numbers of soldiers and atmospheric and spot effects has been clearly arranged. The

> result is that here is a propagandist and popular drama being communicated with clarity on a wax phonograph and predating production techniques which were to become standard five to six years later.[31]

Rees's series remains an exciting and pioneering collection of recordings that capture the intense experience of the soldier. Other contemporaneous recordings can be somewhat disturbing. Just as the print media spread propaganda myths about German atrocities perpetrated against babies and children, and the industrial extraction of fat from dead soldiers,[32] some recordings are surprising in their emphatically uncompromising approach. As an example of what he terms 'the Sound of Hatred', Crook cites a 'chilling' December 1914 recording about the capture of a spy in a British trench:

> Listeners can hear the prisoner being searched, the discovery of a packet of papers including signal codes and military telegrams. His denials and refusal to answer questions are met by being blindfolded and stood up against a wall to be shot. The German's repeated and desperate cries of 'Mercy! Mercy!' fall on deaf ears. His crying and wailing continues as the Colonel is dramatized offering no due process of trial and coldly ordering his execution.[33]

Such recordings are evidently designed to shock the listener with an unsentimental sense of the desperate realities of war (and, of course, the dastardly conduct of the Hun). As Crook writes, the spectrum of recordings reveal the use of sonic technology 'to inform, motivate, comfort and amuse' and in so doing became a sound agency for recruitment, mourning, patriotism, religious observance and cultural anxiety as well as outrage.[34] Looking forward, Crook writes:

> The records provide audio textual evidence of a culture mobilized and emotionalized for total war. In addition, they also represent the foundations of broadcast radio drama and sound design for the talking film.[35]

Certainly in the genre of war films, the construction of effective sound design is immensely important. Even in theatre, the success of National Theatre Wales's site-specific epic *Mametz* (2014) owed as much to the rich and elaborate soundscape of distant and frontline combat tearing across no man's land and the adjacent forest as it did to the physically reconstructed trenches and landscape. However, as Crook suggests, the key significance of these pioneering recordings is in regard to broadcast radio drama. Once the war was over, cultural reflection and reminiscence began and, with the new technology of radio, this would take to – and never leave – the airwaves.

## The First World War and Radio Drama

With the inauguration of radio broadcasting in the 1920s, radio drama gradually came into being. In the British context, radio drama began with the recitation of stage plays by Shakespeare and other writers before the production of adaptations of fiction. Eventually, original plays began to be written for radio: the first British radio drama is usually credited as *A Comedy of Danger* by Richard Hughes in 1924. Radio has the potential to present an extraordinarily intimate dynamic. This is recognised in

Hughes's pioneering drama itself, which builds up suspense and claustrophobia: the play is set in a coalmine during a power cut. By the late 1920s, other plays would also seem to use the intensely personal nature of radio, such as Cecil Lewis's *The Night Fighters* (26 March 1928) and Mannin Crane's *The Howling Silence* (10 November 1928), both of which attempt to capture and recreate personal experiences of the First World War. These examples reveal the beginnings of what would become a subgenre of audio readings and radio drama related to the First World War.

BBC Radio has featured innumerable historical documentaries and audio readings of First World War writing, including in November 2006 a twice-daily series presenting *The Complete War Poems of Wilfred Owen*. Linked to this, there are a number of examples of biographical drama on British radio. In 1984, the BBC broadcast David Buck's *Her Privates We*, an adaptation of Frederic Manning's *The Middle Parts of Fortune: Somme and Ancre, 1916*, a powerful autobiographical novel originally published anonymously in 1929, with Manning's identity only formally acknowledged in 1977. In 2010, the BBC broadcast Louis Nowra's *The Light of Darkness*, a play about Leslie Davis, the American consul when Turkey entered the war in support of Germany in 1915, based on Davis's memoir *The Slaughterhouse Province: An American Diplomat's Report on the Armenian Genocide, 1915–1917* (1989). In 2014, BBC Radio 3 broadcast Iain Burnside's biographical drama *Music in the Great War: A Soldier and a Maker*, about the First World War writer and composer Ivor Gurney, which featured Gurney's songs and writings interwoven with original dramatic scenes.

Similarly, just as British radio has used biographical sources for its drama, it has also presented other ostensibly 'pre-existing' texts, including versions of classic First World War-themed stage plays such as R. C. Sherriff's *Journey's End* (1928) in 1956; Sean O'Casey's *The Silver Tassie* (1928) in 1966; and Somerset Maugham's *For Services Rendered* (1932) in 2013. In 1999, the BBC broadcast a four-hour version in two parts of Karl Kraus's anti-war drama *The Last Days of Mankind* (*Die letzten Tage der Menschheit*). Giles Havergal's audio adaptation captured the epic scope of this masterpiece of Austrian literature, using the atonal music of Arnold Schoenberg and his peers to capture the mood of Kraus's account of the collapse of a great civilisation into the insanity and horror of war.

However, given the traditional popularity of the adaptation of novels as a genre in radio drama, it is no surprise that radio has dramatised numerous examples of war fiction. In 2003, the BBC broadcast Robert Forrest's adaptation of Ford Madox Ford's *Parade's End* in a major production nearly three hours in duration. Similarly, BBC Radio 4's Classic Serial has permitted substantial adaptations of major but frequently neglected (at least by the screen media) examples of fiction. These include: in 2006, Robin Brooks's adaptation of Rebecca West's largely pre-war narrative *The Fountain Overflows* (1957); in the same year, Omar Sharif starred in Naguib Mahfouz's *Cairo Trilogy* (1956–7), an epic Egyptian family saga set at the end of the First World War and beyond; and in 2009, Gerda Stevenson's adaptation of Lewis Grassic Gibbon's *Sunset Song* (1932).

Jaroslav Hašek's epic satirical masterpiece *The Good Soldier Švejk* (1921–3) has enjoyed several significant adaptations on British radio with, seemingly, several generations readapting the work: R. D. Smith's dramatisation of Paul Selver's translation *The Good Soldier Schweik* appeared in 1962; Barry Campbell's adaptation of Cecil Parrott's definitive English translation of *The Good Soldier Švejk* appeared in an outstanding serialisation starring Richard Griffiths in 1981; and a two-part version by Christopher Reason was broadcast in 2008. The adventures of the happy-go-lucky Josef Švejk in the Austro-Hungarian army during the First World War works exceptionally well on radio. The picaresque escapades of Švejk with their rich panorama of characters, journeys and absurdity can create a particularly fulfilling audio experience, as dramatic as it is hilarious.

In 2002, Mike Walker adapted two examples of First World War-based fiction: Humphrey Cobb's account of a true-life court-martial of French soldiers for cowardice, *Paths of Glory* (1935), and Marc Dugain's novel about the life of a severely disfigured French lieutenant, *The Officers' Ward* (*La chambre des officiers*, 1998). Interestingly, both these anti-war books enjoyed increased popularity through film versions: Stanley Kubrick's 1957 version of *Paths of Glory* starring Kirk Douglas remains a classic First World War drama, and François Dupeyron's 2001 screen version of Dugain's novel was nominated for the Palme d'Or at the Cannes Film Festival. Undoubtedly, the popular film versions of the source novels were an impetus for audio adaptation. Similarly, First World War audio adaptation has extended into aspects of popular genre: in 1976, the BBC broadcast Alison Plowden's dramatisation of Anthony Price's novel *Other Paths to Glory* (1973), a popular 'crime' thriller about a historian who uncovers details about the Battle of the Somme that put his life at risk.

In regard to the scheduling of the aforementioned dramas, BBC Radio has aired its First World War dramas as standalone plays on Radio 4 and occasionally Radio 3, as well as in the form of Radio 4 serialised dramas in daytime or nighttime slots. It is evident that First World War radio drama is perceived as commanding a wide audience, from those interested in experimental literary adaptation on Radio 3 as much as those receiving a daily dose of fifteen-minute serial drama presented within the mid-morning Radio 4 *Woman's Hour* slot. Over the years, the organisation has also commissioned and premiered several examples of audio drama specifically for Remembrance Day (11 November). These include, in 1998, Peter Wolf's *Strange Meeting*, about the death of Wilfred Owen, and, in 2002, Charlotte Fyfe's biographical drama *The Tears of War*, about the First World War poet May Wedderburn Cannan and her relationship with the war hero Bevil Quiller-Couch, who survived the conflict but died in the 1919 influenza epidemic. On 11 November 2011, the BBC broadcast *Laurels and Donkeys* (based on Andrew Motion's collection of verse), which featured poems about war from 1914 to the contemporary conflicts in Iraq and Afghanistan. This assembled 'play' of new and historical texts is reminiscent of 1998's *The Girls They Left Behind*, which was presented as a journey through the battlefields of the First World War, seen through the eyes of teenagers from a high school in Edinburgh (using original poetry as well as First World War reminiscences).

Playwrights have repeatedly drawn on historical research to create original radio plays. Dave Sheasby's *Donkeys Led by Lions* (1999) is a powerful drama about the severe treatment of a conscientious objector; Gregory Burke's *Shell Shocked* (2002) portrays the different lives of two brothers separated in the trenches; and Adam Thorpe's *Devastated Areas* (2009) explores civilian grief through the interweaving stories of a German sculptress working on a memorial statue to the volunteers, a glazier repairing the blown-out windows of a church in the Somme, and a gardener in England.

The sheer output of BBC radio drama means that we can find works that take a unique or neglected angle in original pieces alongside those informed by in-depth historical research. *One Hot Summer* (1996) presents a dramatic account of the true story of the 1919 race riots in Liverpool and the tensions of the immediate aftermath of the war. Tina Pepler's docu-drama *The Silence of Memory* (1998) explores the 1920 burial of the Unknown Warrior in Westminster Abbey. Linked in theme, Stephen Wyatt's *Memorials to the Missing* (2007) is a play about the establishment of the Imperial War Graves Commission. *The Last Tsar* by Ian Curteis (2009) is a dramatic investigation of the apparent refusal of King George V to give sanctuary to his cousin Tsar Nicholas during the Russian Revolution.

As we can see, spoken word and drama on radio has produced a wealth of material, with topics and 'angles' ranging from the predictable to the surprising. Moreover, First World War radio has proved highly influential. One of the most famous productions in the history of British political theatre – *Oh, What a Lovely War!* (1963), devised by Joan Littlewood and the Theatre Workshop – is a play that has regular stage revivals and was adapted to the screen by Richard Attenborough in 1969. Interestingly, this landmark in British theatre finds its roots in British radio. The Theatre Workshop drew direct inspiration from Charles Chilton's *The Long, Long Trail* (1961), a BBC Home Service radio documentary that established a similar structure in its interweaving statistics, facts, reminiscences and songs (especially the ironic rewritings created by the troops). Chilton created *The Long, Long Trail* largely for personal reasons: his father had been killed during the Second Battles of Arras in 1918 aged nineteen, shortly after Chilton had been born. Chilton's mother died soon afterwards and he was raised by his grandmother. Although his father was acclaimed as a hero, Chilton knew very little about the actions of his father or the circumstances of his death. This enigma that determined the beginning of his life (and the lives of so many others) provided Chilton with a creative impetus: he interviewed war veterans in London pubs when he started working at the BBC in the 1930s. He also discovered a popular wartime book of songs called *Tommy's Tunes*. The songs, ranging from the morale-boosting and the sentimental to the bleakly ironic, provided Chilton with a highly successful way to structure his innovative radio documentary. In many respects, despite their unmistakable similarities in style and structure, the Theatre Workshop's reimagining of *The Long, Long Trail* creates a much more politicised drama than Chilton's reflective documentary. This is not least reflected in the titles themselves: although both directly allude to wartime songs, *Oh, What a Lovely War!* is a sardonically biting title compared to the pain and tragedy embodied in *The Long, Long Trail*.

With the centenary of the conflict BBC Radio has featured two ambitious team-written series, namely *Home Front* and *Tommies* (both 2014–18). *Home Front* charts the lives of a group of fictional characters through the First World War, presenting about twenty-five hours of drama each year (in three eight-week seasons) spread over the four 'centennial' years, with every well-researched episode set precisely one hundred years ago to the day. This is an interesting experiment in commemoration, a character-driven drama (in the tradition of *The Archers*) which can explore social change against a historical backdrop in a 'real' timespan.

While *Home Front* charts the impact of the war on those at home (initially in Folkestone), *Tommies* is a parallel series, also team-written, which focuses on the experience of the frontline. The central character is Mickey Bliss, a sergeant from the Indian army with a specialist skill in wireless signalling. Bliss's expertise is apt for radio: it is the technology that will supersede telegraphy and help to win the war; it is also the same technology which will go on to pave the way for broadcast radio. Hence, in *Tommies*, we have a work of radio about radio. Bliss is not the only character: *Tommies* has an epic range that captures the enormity of the conflict and the diverse people swept up into it. This scope is evident in the first broadcast episode (7 October 2014), written by Michael Chaplin. The ambitions of the play are immediately established, the Commentator providing an omniscient narrative that spans the past and the future: the play opens with Alphonse Minet, a French farmer, ploughing his land as generations of his family have done, only for the Commentator to tell us that Minet 'will be killed by a stray bullet fired by one of his own countrymen in January 1917'.[36] Although *Tommies* unfurls in 'real time' (inasmuch as, like *Home Front*, the episodes tie on to the respective centenary dates), the Commentator consistently contextualises the narrative with an overview that passes through, beyond and into the characters. In the space of the first half-hour episode, we encounter the British and German soldiers as well as the local farmers and nuns. The series is as dramatically exciting as it is well researched. Its historically accurate detail maps the work on to real locations and gives an account of the technological developments, not least in Bliss risking his life in his attempts to get the wireless to work. At the same time, Chaplin's script shows a social world that is changing (upper-class fox-hunting officers with swords drawn) and, already, the baptism of fire the young soldiers are experiencing just a few weeks into the conflict.

The ambition and scope of *Tommies* is reflected in the fact that in the second episode (14 October 2014), written by Nick Warburton, we follow Bliss and Walter Oddy (injured at the end of episode one) away from the frontline to the doctors and nurses at Boulogne. The episode is concerned with medical process and the equally desperate situation in which the medics find themselves. The treatment of the seriously injured Oddy is focal to the episode and Warburton uses audio to its full potential: the dialogue, the Commentator's narrative and sound effects take us up close to Oddy's infected wounds and linger there in a way at which the screen might have baulked. We hear the doctor Celestine's professional engagement:

> [She looks] down at Walter's ruined leg. It doesn't disgust her, it fascinates. To her this is a piece of nature. It's a fungus, it's a flower. That's Celestine. How she always was.
>
> She puts her fingers to the skin. It's so tight it shines under the lamplight.[37]

A few moments later, we have stark juxtaposition in Bliss's perception:

> There's no rifle-fire here, no bombardment, no glorifying touch of danger. This is a quiet table with lamps.
>
> It terrifies him.[38]

In this way, *Tommies* uses radio drama to the fullest degree, giving us the experiential as well as the meticulously researched. We find in this rolling series the heroic as well as the tragic and yet it is consistently *real* rather than idealistic, maintaining an effective drama without needing to become melodramatic or sermonising. It is an example of BBC contemporary radio drama at its most crafted and distinctive.

At the beginning of this chapter we saw how Virginia Woolf recounted the experience of an air raid in principally auditory terms. When peace came at last, Woolf describes her realisation:

> Twentyfive minutes ago the guns went off, announcing peace. A siren hooted on the river. They are hooting still. A few people ran to look out of windows [. . .] So far neither bells nor flags, but the wailing of sirens & intermittent guns.[39]

It is significant that although only a 'few people' ran to look outside, the aural signs were evident and understood. The horror of war can arrive in sound and its ending is first detected sonically. We can close our eyes or avert our gaze, but it is almost impossible not to listen. What's more, one hundred years of audio recording and radio broadcasting shows that we *want* to listen.

## Notes

1. Joanna Bourke, *An Intimate History of Killing: Face-to-Face Killing in Twentieth-Century Warfare* (London: Granta, 1999), p. 27.
2. Virginia Woolf, *The Diary of Virginia Woolf, Volume 1: 1915–19* (Harmondsworth: Penguin, 1979), pp. 84–5.
3. Siegfried Sassoon, *The War Poems* (London: Faber & Faber, 1983), p. 85.
4. Richard Holmes, *Firing Line* (London: Pimlico, 1994), pp. 166–7.
5. Ibid., p. 161.
6. Ibid., pp. 161–2.
7. Ibid., p. 177.
8. Ibid., p. 186.
9. Robert Graves, *Goodbye to All That: An Autobiography* (Harmondsworth: Penguin, 1960), p. 220.
10. M. Knipper et al., 'Advances in the Neurobiology of Hearing Disorders: Recent Developments regarding the Basis of Tinnitus and Hyperacusis', *Progress in Neurobiology*, 111 (December 2013), 17–33.
11. Sassoon, *The War Poems*, p. 39.
12. Ibid., p. 62.
13. Catherine Reilly (ed.), *Scars Upon My Heart: Women's Poetry and Verse of the First World War* (London: Virago, 1981), p. 95.
14. Ibid.
15. Isaac Rosenberg, *The Collected Works of Isaac Rosenberg* (London: Chatto & Windus, 1984), p. 111.
16. Quoted in Holmes, *Firing Line*, p. 164.
17. Quoted in Tim Crook, 'Vocalizing the Angels of Mons: Audio Dramas as Propaganda in the Great War of 1914 to 1918', *Societies*, 4.2 (2014), 180–221 (202).
18. Reilly (ed.), *Scars Upon My Heart*, pp. 31–2.
19. Sassoon, *The War Poems*, p. 114.
20. Crook, 'Vocalizing the Angels of Mons', p. 189.
21. Ibid., p. 190.
22. Ibid., p. 203.
23. Gregory Whitehead, 'Radio Art Le Mômo: Gas Leaks, Shock Needles and Death Rattles', Public, 4.5 (1990), 141–9 (145).

24. Leslie Wheeler (ed.), *Ten Northeast Poets: An Anthology* (Aberdeen: Aberdeen University Press, 1985), p. 139.
25. Sassoon, *The War Poems*, p. 73.
26. British Library, <http://britishlibrary.typepad.co.uk/english-and-drama/2014/01/fifty-years-after-its-first-productionand-marking-the-centenary-of-the-outbreak-of-the-first-world-war-oh-what-a-lovel.html#sthash.luXMUX1s.dpuf> (last accessed 28 November 2016).
27. Crook, 'Vocalizing the Angels of Mons', p. 192.
28. Ibid., p. 193.
29. Ibid., p. 194.
30. Tim Crook, *Radio Drama: Theory and Practice* (London: Routledge, 1999), p. 33.
31. Ibid.
32. Crook, 'Vocalizing the Angels of Mons', p. 191.
33. Ibid., p. 192.
34. Ibid., p. 215.
35. Ibid.
36. Michael Chaplin, *Tommies*, 7 October 1914 (Series 1, Episode 1), BBC Radio 4, <http://www.bbc.co.uk/writersroom/scripts/tommies> (last accessed 28 November 2016).
37. Nick Warburton, *Tommies*, 14 October 1914 (Series 1, Episode 2), BBC Radio 4, <http://www.bbc.co.uk/writersroom/scripts/tommies> (last accessed 28 November 2016).
38. Ibid.
39. Woolf, *The Diary of Virginia Woolf*, vol. 1, p. 216.

# VI.

# Publishing and Material Culture

# 23

# The British Publishing Industry and the First World War

*Jane Potter*

> In the *Grimmaische Strasse* there were thousands of people flowing up and down at midnight, and there were endless little knots and groups – mostly girls and women – eagerly discussing the topic of the hour – all of them grave and concerned. There was a complete absence of laughter and all faces seemed set, either with grim determination or with a curious look of vacant apprehension.[1]

So wrote William Heinemann as he recalled his experience on the evening of the declaration of war in August 1914. In Leipzig, visiting an international exhibition of books and graphic arts for the British Board of Trade, this successful, well-respected English publisher of German extraction (his father was from Hanover, his mother from Lancashire) did not find a bloodthirsty nation eager to go to war, as was stereotyped even before the outbreak by dire warnings promulgated in the popular press. Rather, he observed an uneasy and anxious people, thrown, like his fellow Britons, into an uncertain future.

For publishers, the uncertain future was of equal significance personally and professionally, individually and nationally. Heinemann would go on to publish some of the most important literary works of the Great War, including those by Robert Graves, Siegfried Sassoon, Enid Bagnold and Philip Gibbs. Yet he found himself in the position of many people with German surnames in England who faced everything from whispered suspicion to outright attack. Patriotically British yet fiercely proud of his German heritage, he loathed jingoism about 'the Hun' and his refusal to anglicise his name meant he endured the premises of his firm at 21 Bedford Street, London, being not infrequently pelted with rotten vegetables and horse manure. In 1929, Mrs C. S. Peel remarked retrospectively that

> By the autumn of 1914 about 500 of those who bore [forty-three] foreign names had changed them: Bernstein became Curzon, Steineke Stanley, Stohwasser Stowe—even British soldiers who were fighting but who had German names changed them. Business firms found it advisable to get rid of German partners and if the firm had a German name to change it. Later no unnaturalized foreigner was allowed to change his name. It was a popular act when in 1917 the King abolished German titles in his family and adopted the family name of Windsor.[2]

Heinemann was not alone in despising rabid anti-German sentiment. Another publisher, Stanley Unwin, whose own uncertain future was particularly acute since his firm George Allen & Unwin Ltd was founded on 4 August, equally loathed hyperbolic propaganda. Like many other publishers, he had honed his craft of bookselling and book production in Germany, at a time when Leipzig was the centre of the book trade and publishing was 'an industry that was already profoundly transnational'.[3] Only four days after the outbreak of war, *The Publishers' Circular* reflected on the 'very friendly relations which have always existed between the British and German book trades' and averred that 'we are sure that the German book-sellers regret as much as we do this sudden termination of business relations'.[4]

Although publishers' and booksellers' perspectives are not often counted amongst the literature and history of the First World War, these agents – or 'merchants of culture', to use John B. Thompson's phrase – played a crucial role in the production and dissemination of print.[5] Memoirs and 'house histories' of individual firms as well as trade and popular periodicals such as *The Bookman*, the *Times Literary Supplement*, *The Athenaeum* and the *Saturday Review* offer insights into not only the business of wartime book production, but the profound personal challenges and emotions of individuals who supported a wartime cultural economy, provided information and amusement, and at times assisted the government in disseminating its messages. All are invaluable sources of reviews, comments and opinions that lend important context to the literary texts usually studied. Supplying both the home and the fighting fronts with reading material, the book trade was an essential component in the war effort and helped to construct the public consciousness of war itself. Despite the fact that 'the Great War was a period of intense and unparalleled creative activity', Hammond and Towheed have highlighted how 'few have yet to consider in any sustained, systematic way *how* this outpouring of words – old and new – was printed and distributed, controlled or got around, to whom it was available and from whom it was withheld'.[6] Studies in the relatively recent discipline of book history have begun to fill this lacuna, contextualising the literary output of writers and poets into a wider network of production, distribution and reception, whether in examinations of particular genres such as the short story,[7] edited collections of selected themes,[8] or analyses of distinct time periods, especially the inter-war years.[9] Other countries' publishing and bookselling are also increasingly being studied.[10] As Vincent Trott cogently argues, 'with writers, publishers and readers – albeit in an increasingly digital context – set to play a prominent role in determining how the memory of the war continues to develop over the course of the centenary and beyond, it is important that we pay attention to how these agents have shaped the memory of the war over the last hundred years.'[11] This chapter is part of the project to bring the publisher and the bookseller into clearer focus and will reflect on how they were (and continue to be) central in shaping the memory of the Great War and embedding it in the national imaginary. It shows that despite involvement with national war aims, publishers of the time circulated a variety of ideas at a time of great personal and business difficulties and uncertainty. At the heart of such an activity lay concepts I identified in a previous study as those of country, conscience and commerce.[12] Whilst publishers kept their eyes on the market in order to decide the kind and the volume of war books they would publish, they were not just committed to profit. General trade difficulties were coupled with individual personal sacrifice and grief.

The years before the outbreak of war were a boom time for the publishing industry and for bookselling in Britain. Successive education acts of the nineteenth and early twentieth centuries helped to foster near-universal literacy. A thriving schoolbook market provided lucrative opportunities for publishers such as Nelson, Longman's and Macmillan, while an autodidact population made budget literature series such as J. M. Dent's Everyman's Library a profitable enterprise. Cheaper production costs and efficient distribution methods all added to the mix of success. This can be seen through the dramatic increase in the number of books published, from 7,000 in 1900 and 10,914 in 1911 to 12,379 in 1913, then an all-time high.[13] W. H. Smith was a particular beneficiary and agent of this development. As 'one of the great institutions of British print culture', this distributor and retailer of books, periodicals and newspapers owned, in 1914, 'over 1,500 stalls and 223 shops throughout England and Wales and controlled much of the trade on the London Underground', and its provincial wholesale houses put it 'in touch with several thousands of newsagents throughout the country'.[14] Together with Smith's and other booksellers, publishers reached a mass audience in what was truly a 'golden age' for the book trade. An expansion in the number of public libraries further contributed to making books more accessible.

The outbreak of war in August 1914 had, according to Iain Stevenson, a 'rather muted' impact on the trade, with publishers recognising new markets for 'patriotic tracts and accounts of German brutality' and facing 'the emergency with stoicism rather than panic'.[15] Yet there were real issues with which to contend. The practical challenges of a war economy were many. The Board of Trade placed restrictions on paper; the only area given unlimited supply was schoolbooks. Production, printing, binding and distribution were all hit by inflated prices and disruption of transport networks. As the *Saturday Review* noted,

> [p]ublishers were faced with a very serious crisis. They had somehow had to keep their businesses going till people recovered from the first shock of war and from their first absorption in its progress. Most publishers met the position with resource and skill. They contrived to avoid shutting down their enterprises – a proceeding which would have dislocated half a dozen allied industries and caused suffering and difficulty among thousands; and they hopefully waited for the moment when they could again induce the public to find time and inclination for literature.[16]

In 1914 the number of books published dropped to 11,537, although *The Athenaeum* did not think this necessarily a bad development, reflecting that 'over-production' had led to 'a host of inferior productions'.[17] In 'What of the Book Season?', published in *The Academy* on 26 September 1914, Alfred Berlyn had his own view of publishers, whom he likened to 'conies, a feeble folk': 'you would have had to go a long way to find a body of more hopeless pessimists than the publishers.'[18] They first viewed the war with despair; 'their occupation was as tragically gone as Othello's Postponements, cancellations, and closing down in all its branches.'[19] Rumours of the dismissal of employees and reductions in salaries abounded in the early days, as publishers 'became just as much the victims of momentary panic as the people who made haste to cram their cellars with canned provisions and sides of bacon'.[20] But within weeks, Berlyn argued, common sense and enterprise prevailed, with the new autumn lists showing that 'the spirit of the adage, "Nothing venture, nothing win," is visibly beginning to reassert itself among the bookmen'.[21] Firms adapted their output to cater to and anticipate public interest, so that by three months into the war there was 'already [. . .] a large library of books devoted to almost every phase of the campaign so far as anybody has been allowed to learn anything about it'.[22]

Hodder & Stoughton swiftly organised a War Book Department that produced some of the most profitable and popular books of the war. In addition, with *Princess Mary's Gift Book* (1914) and *King Albert's Book* (1914), which were issued for charity and sold in enormous numbers, Hodder & Stoughton 'became increasingly identified with reading for entertainment',[23] publishing novels by popular writers of the day such as Ian Hay, 'Sapper' (Herman Cyril McNeile), Ruby M. Ayres and Berta Ruck. The firm provided what Berlyn called a 'regular dose of that mental anodyne' that a book offered as a 'respite from the strain of patriotic anxiety'.[24] As the *Saturday Review* averred, '[w]e cannot live permanently with thoughts of war.'[25]

Nevertheless, publishers and authors knew well that at such a time it would be 'difficult to turn the attention of the public from the latest telegrams',[26] and adjusted their lists to reflect popular needs. This included the reissuing of older works, published before the war, but which tapped into and reinforced current anxieties and antipathies. Such *livres d'occasion* included General F. von Bernhardi's *Germany and the Next War*. Published originally in 1912 by Edward Arnold, it warned people to prepare for future conflict and turned 'a staid publisher's office into a good imitation of an evening newspaper's distribution department on Derby Day'.[27] The firm found it difficult to keep up with demand as the first edition of October 1912, priced at 10s. 6d., was quickly reprinted. In 1914, Arnold issued a 'New Popular Edition' at 2s. and a 'Popular Edition' in cloth at 2s. 6d. In doing so, 'Arnold showed a good publisher's awareness of the war and its implications' and went on to publish another thirty books on various aspects of the conflict.[28]

Macmillan had its share too of 'war books', including Mabel Dearmer's *Letters from a Field Hospital*, Edith Wharton's *The Marne*, F. S. Oliver's *Ordeal by Battle*, and three volumes from Kipling: *France at War*, *The New Army in Training* and *The Fringes of the Fleet*. But Charles Morgan, author of the house history of the firm, noted, 'it is of interest to observe how little the life of the firm depended on books arising directly from the war', and it continued to publish a variety of authors and topics that were far removed from the 'events in Europe'.[29]

Methuen & Co.'s 'flurry of titles' included poetry such as Alfred Noyes's *The Searchlight* (1914) and *A Salute from the Fleet and other Poems* (1915), a reprint of Bret Harte's *The Reveille* (1914), and Kipling's *Recessional*. The firm was especially foresighted in anticipating a shortage of materials and loss of staff, ordering 'enough paper for fifty thousand books' and taking on 'its first females as replacements' for men who had enlisted.[30] Yet its reaction at the outset was critical, as one of its authors, Marie Belloc Lowndes, recounted:

> [Mr Webster] is most unhappy with the literary outlook. He told me the slump continues, the cheap edition of my book *Barbara Rebell* was put off and nothing was moving at all. I did not tell him that Methuen were not going to have my next book. Their offer was incredibly less good than that of Hutchinson and that though they admitted that *The End of Her Honeymoon* had paid off its advance. I said what seemed to distress him very much, that I thought all fiction would be

> profoundly altered by the War, and I could not see writers going back to the kind of stories which, if not exactly popular, were highly praised before the War. He seemed to think that if a casual allusion to the War were thrown in, it would make them sell.[31]

J. D. Symon called this 'the novel of commerce', 'rudely twisted about so as to include men in khaki and Belgian refugees' and 'unabashed by the gravity of the present crisis'.[32] Novels were rebranded as 'action series',[33] and books routinely used war as a backdrop for thrilling adventure and love entanglements. Blackie's transformed its Edwardian school boys and girls into young patriots for the consumption of an adolescent readership: Angela Brazil, Captain Brereton and Bessie Marchant spun yarns about munitions workers and motor-scouts in the vein of G. A. Henty. Meanwhile, managers at its main rival in the education and young reader market, Nelson, made its mark on the wartime market for books with its twenty-nine-volume *Nelson's History of the War* (1915–19) by John Buchan, who had been key in revamping and extending the firm's brand image in the years before the conflict.[34]

Belloc Lowndes's early concern in the wake of her anxiety over earning money from her writing, 'no one will think of buying books',[35] was a theme taken up by the *Saturday Review*. Equating book buying with a patriotic act, it urged readers 'to cut off many another luxury before they cut off new and expensive books. The community owes a debt to the author transcending its debt to the fashionable tailor or wine merchant.'[36] Publishers, too, whether big or small, were seen to be 'doing their part in keeping contemporary literature alive at the present time', employing all their 'courage and enterprise' to ensure that 'all may yet be well with letters, even though the enemy is at the gate'.[37] Thus, '[w]e must buy the books we can afford without stint or grudge.'[38] As Susann Liebich has noted, organisations such as the National Home Reading Union 'were at pains to show that reading was crucial to keep up morale, and ultimately to uphold the values of civilisation', but also turned 'reading into an act of citizenship and patriotism'.[39] National Book Fortnight was inaugurated in 1915 by British publishers in order to 'quicken public interest in the use of books for reading solace and instruction as well as to encourage people at home to keep the fighting men well supplied in this respect on all fronts'.[40]

After three months of war, the bleakest predictions for the trade had not in fact materialised. The trade was beginning to recover. *The Bookman* took the temperature of the trade in early 1915 by interviewing George Tyler, Chief of W. H. Smith & Son's 230 bookshops. Books about the war, directly or indirectly, as well as fiction and new poetry were particularly in demand, all helped by publishers providing a big and wonderfully varied supply 'at lower [. . .] prices'.[41] Shilling books were being purchased 'in immense numbers', 'partly because in size they are admirably suited for sending out to our soldiers and sailors'.[42] The Camps Library, the Red Cross, the YMCA and the British War Library, among others, were instrumental in keeping the troops supplied with reading material.

Thus fiction and non-fiction, poetry and educational texts, political tracts and light-hearted comic sketches fed a reading public's desire for amusement and information. Medical and military memoirs provided first-hand accounts that complemented newspaper reports, while novels, whether in the form of detective stories, spy thrillers or romantic yarns, provided Berlyn's 'regular dose of that mental anodyne'. But of all the genres that flourished in the war years, it is poetry that has had the most lasting resonance.

Katharine Tynan observed in an article in *The Bookman* that '[i]t seems impossible, indeed, for the poets to get away from the heart-moving war'.[43] Publishers provided their platform, although poetry was often printed first in newspapers, magazines and journals before being taken up in collections and anthologies by publishers. One of the most respected firms was that of Sidgwick & Jackson. Best known for Rupert Brooke's *1914 and Other Poems* (1915), they also published volumes by Rose Macaulay, *Two Blind Countries* (1914), Herbert Asquith, *The Volunteer and Other Poems* (1915), John Drinkwater, *Swords and Ploughshares* (1915), Ivor Gurney, *Severn and Somme* (1916), and F. W. Harvey, *A Gloucestershire Lad at Home and Abroad* (1916) and *Gloucestershire Friends: Poems from a German Prison Camp* (1917). Both partners in the firm shared in the experiences of the soldiers that they published. R. C. Jackson was called up in 1916, the year that the firm's gross sales exceeded the sum of the preceding two years, mainly due to Brooke's volumes. With £5 out of every £7 coming from modern poetry, the trading profit rose from £660 in 1915 to £4,926. Frank Sidgwick was called up in 1917. He would survive the war, returning to the firm in December 1919. Jackson did not. He was killed in action during the Third Battle of Ypres in September 1917 whilst serving with the 223rd Company Machine Gun Corps.[44]

Despite the efforts of the Publishers' Association, publishing was not classified as a trade of national importance whose employees could be exempted from military service. Other publishers, including one of Unwin's own co-directors, Col. P. H. Dalbaic, either enlisted for or were later called up to active service. Thus beyond the professional uncertainties, those in the book trade faced the same anxieties over the fate of sons and colleagues fighting in the various theatres of war as every other person in the country. Daniel de Mendi Macmillan, who had enlisted in 1914, was invalided out in 1915. William Collins IV served in France as an officer in the Royal Army Service Corps and won the Distinguished Service Order, while his brother Godfrey also joined the RASC and served in France, Egypt, India, Gallipoli and Mesopotamia. Frederick Longman was killed in action eight weeks into the war,[45] and J. M. Dent, famous for his Everyman's Library,[46] was devastated by the loss of two of his youngest sons, Paxton and Austin, heirs apparent to the firm, who were killed on active service within weeks of each other in 1915, aged twenty-four and twenty-three respectively.[47] Edward Arnold's daughter Peggy, who had been nursing in France for nine months, died after two days' illness in March 1916. 'Death', as F. A. Mumby put it, 'was busy' amongst the book trade and Dent was not alone in finding work 'the only anodyne' for the grief and anxieties of war.[48]

Some publishers saw such grief as an opportunity, coupling the upsurge in the appeal of poetry with the young poets' desires for publication and the need of survivors to memorialise those they had lost. Galloway Kyle, under the guise of Erskine Macdonald Ltd, was one such publisher. Among the volumes that appeared under the Erskine Macdonald imprint were Edmund Blunden's *Pastorals* (1916) and Vera Brittain's *Verses of a V.A.D.* (1918), but also titles from Leslie Coulson (*From an Outpost and Other Poems*, 1917), Colin Mitchell (*Trampled Clay*, 1917), J. W. Streets (*The Undying Spendour*, 1917) and Gilbert Waterhouse (*Rail-Head and Other Poems*, 1916), all of whom were killed in the war. As Dominic Hibberd has shown, the Kyle-Macdonald enterprise perfected 'an ingenious racket' of publishing volumes of verse at the author's (or the author's family's) expense and being elusive when it came to royalties: 'Kyle well knew that his authors, if still alive, would be more interested in getting into print than in being paid.'[49]

Yet publishers provided an outlet not only for mainstream work, but for writers on the margins of a seemingly all-encompassing national voice of unity, especially pacifism. Grace Brockington has demonstrated the ways in which publishers helped to maintain 'a healthy (or troublesome) pacifist presence amidst the outpouring of printed propaganda', in spite of the not inconsiderable risks that they shared with pacifists, including prosecution, fines, imprisonment and social opprobrium.[50] Stanley Unwin was among those who 'persevered to produce a diverse body of literature [. . .] which amounted to a wartime chorus of dissent'.[51] A confirmed pacifist, when his exemption from national service ended in 1917, he decided he had 'to do whatever I could conscientiously do' and served with a London Voluntary Aid Detachment.[52] Not only did Unwin believe the war to be avoidable, unnecessary and 'stupid', but as a believer in the open forum of ideas, he was an outspoken critic of the Defence of the Realm Act and its enforcement of censorship. Publishing Bertrand Russell's *The Principles of Social Reconstruction* and Mrs Henry Hobhouse's *'I Appeal unto Caesar': The Case of the Conscientious Objector*, Unwin firmly demonstrated where his sympathies lay. Unwin avoided the most severe reactions of the censor, but others did not. The seizing and destruction of *The Rainbow* in 1915 under Lord Campbell's 1857 Obscene Publications Act effectively stigmatised D. H. Lawrence as a writer – he was already seen as suspicious both for his pacifist opinions and for his marriage to a German national – and rendered him 'practically unable to publish fiction'.[53] Over 1,000 copies of the novel, seized from his publisher Methuen's warehouse, were ordered to be destroyed by the judgement of Sir John Dickinson at Bow Street Magistrates' Court on 13 March 1915. With the novel branded 'a mass of obscenity of thought, idea and action',[54] Methuen offered no defence and stressed that he had asked Lawrence twice to revise offending passages, and Lawrence had refused. The judgement meant Lawrence lost his copyright and it took him three years to pay back his £300 advance to Methuen.

Lawrence was not the only author to suffer at the hands of the censor. The journalist who instigated the censorship of *The Rainbow* in 1915, James Douglas, turned his sights to Rose Allatini's novel *Despised and Rejected*, which under her pseudonym A. T. Fitzroy was published by C. W. Daniel in 1918, having first been turned down by Stanley Unwin. Its sympathetic portrayal of pacifism, conscientious objection and homosexuality led to its banning under the Defence of the Realm Act. Fined £400 and ordered to pay £60 costs, Daniel represents the undercurrent of protest that struggled against the tide of patriotic stoicism.[55]

But it was not all an 'us-and-them' relationship between publishers and the government. From the outset, there was a symbiotic, cooperative relationship that existed 'under the radar' of public attention and, for a time, of Parliament itself. The government Propaganda Bureau at Wellington House was initially set up soon after the outbreak of war to counter German propaganda abroad, especially in the United States, where a large immigrant population might find itself torn between loyalties. Under the leadership of Charles Masterman and with the declared support of numerous well-known authors and public figures from Mrs Humphry Ward and Arthur Conan Doyle to May Sinclair and H. G. Wells, all of whom signed the

Authors' Manifesto pledging support for the British war effort, published in the *New York Times* on 18 September 1914, Wellington House also enlisted the cooperation of British publishers.[56] Under the '5/5 arrangement', commercial publishing houses disseminated books and pamphlets for the government. Publishers received £5 for the cost of production and distribution and £5 for the use of their imprint on texts either commissioned or selected from existing lists by Masterman and his colleagues. It was felt that reading material with no outward connection to the government would appeal more widely to the target audience. Secrecy was further maintained by having the Stationery Office act as the official purchasing agent and A. S. Watt, the literary agent, carry out negotiations with the publishers on Wellington House's behalf. Steamship companies, labour organisations and peace societies, the Central Committee for Patriotic Organisations and even the Religious Tract Society all helped to distribute this material. Masterman acknowledged that there would be objections to such covert methods, but he was determined that the literature get 'into the hands of those who will read it' and not 'to thrust it or force it upon those who resent its gifts, or who will merely treat it as waste paper'.[57] Virtually all established publishing firms participated in the scheme. The Schedule of Wellington House Literature, strictly confidential at the time, shows exactly who these publishers were and what they produced.[58] Hodder & Stoughton published (or provided at 'the lowest terms') the most material for the bureau, over 130 pamphlets and books, including Arthur Conan Doyle's *The German War*, Ford Madox Hueffer's *When Blood Is Their Argument*, *J'accuse* by A German, and *The Front Line* by C. E. Montague with drawings by Muirhead Bone. Nelson and Macmillan produced eighteen texts each, Heinemann nine, Methuen six, and J. M. Dent two. Despite Stanley Unwin's avowed pacifism, George Allen & Unwin were also among those supplying Wellington House documents; thirteen texts, including *The Allies' Prospects of Victory*, *Dangerous Optimism*, *The Pan-German Programme* and *Three Aspects of the Russian Revolution*, were sponsored under the government auspices. Of this last text in particular Wellington House ordered – through the Stationery Office – 200 copies from Unwin. Masterman's desire to avoid rampant propaganda and to maintain secrecy worked against him, however. Many in the government did not even know of the true purpose of Wellington House and thus questioned the amount of money being spent on an agency that appeared to do little to further the British cause. As casualties mounted, the propaganda machine was reorganised and intensified under successive leaderships of John Buchan, Lord Beaverbrook and Lord Northcliffe and was renamed the Ministry of Information in 1918. But as this story of state-sponsored print culture demonstrates, '[t]here was no neat overlap between the political sympathies of publishers and the material they produced; publishers with known pacifist sympathies still worked for Wellington House, and enlisted publishers still attempted to maintain a diversity of opinion on their lists.'[59]

Booksellers too were part and parcel of this reciprocal government relationship. Stephen Colclough has examined the situation for W. H. Smith & Son from its bookselling enterprise to its involvement with the government's National War Aims Committee. Colclough argues that 'Smith's intervention into the battle for the home front had a huge impact upon the print culture of wartime Britain'.[60] Like their publishing counterparts, 1,200 of Smith's staff had joined up by 1915, and over 3,000 women would swell the workforce as more men went to war. As the report from

*The Bookman* noted, after the initial shock of the outbreak of war, when staff were urged to display copies of old and new books that had a war theme, the turnover picked up and 'some titles began to sell in record numbers as books directly related to the war effort were produced'. For instance, Smith's sold 120,000 copies of *Princess Mary's Gift Book* (priced at 2s. 6d.) and 150,000 copies of *King Albert's Book* (priced at 3s.), with 1s. of each copy going 'to aid occupied Belgium'.[61] *Germany and England* by Robert Blatchford sold 145,000 copies, with *Secrets of the German War Office*, *Quick Training for War* and *Pan-Germanism* selling 10,000 copies each. While cheap fiction remained Smith's 'main purchasing power', it could also make a profit 'from books that the Government wanted to see distributed as widely as possible'.[62] Yet as Colclough points out, reminding us of the link to Wellington House, '[i]t is not always easy to distinguish between private initiative and government intervention.'[63]

As the war dragged on, publishers and booksellers continued to face the uncertainties of a wartime economy and the competing demand of wartime culture. *The Bookseller* was filled with various news items as well as notices from publishing firms rueing the restrictions on paper and production materials and cataloguing the ensuing effects. Equally, however, there were reports that the trade was doing remarkably well considering all the obstacles, and the advertisements and reviews that appeared in all trade periodicals demonstrate that the publishing and bookselling trades, though challenged enormously by the war, held their own. Jacob Omnium, writing in his regular feature 'Under Cover' in *The Bookseller* in November 1916, noted in his grandiloquent style, perhaps in an attempt to boost morale, how

> On the whole, the autumn book-season in this third year of war seems to be showing a surprising amount of vitality. New works of interest – and by no means only those directly concerned with the one great subject – are doing well and attracting their due share of attention; and the trade is also being helped by the phenomenal run upon popular cheap editions and reprints, nowadays demanded by our Empire's defenders on land and sea, and by our wounded heroes in the hospital.[64]

The number of books published continued to decline, with 8,131 books in 1917 and just over 7,770 in 1918. But for some, events provided opportunities. Methuen, for instance, 'with the ever-growing demand for reading matter – especially on subjects related to the war', expanded its lists and the company's sales rose to more than £145,000 in 1917.[65] Odhams Limited, however, was less fortunate, as its offices in Long Acre in Covent Garden, designated as a shelter, were hit by a German bomb early in the morning of 29 January 1918. An estimated thirty-five people were killed and the damage caused amounted to more than £250,000.[66] And the death-toll of those in the trade on active service continued to mount, changing the character of the paternal business with brute force. Captain Tommy Nelson, a partner in the Nelson firm, was killed at the Battle of Arras on 9 April 1917. John Alexander 'Jack' Blackie, who died just after Armistice Day in 1918, had never fully recovered from the death of his only son, John Stewart Blackie, who was killed on the Somme, aged nineteen, in 1916. And the worst tragedy of the war for William Heinemann was the death in action at Ypres of his twenty-six-year-old cousin and heir apparent Captain John Heinemann. Rejected three times due to bad eyesight, John had eventually been allowed to enlist and gained a commission within a month. He was shot through the brain while superintending a wiring party and died as he was carried out of the trench. Those who knew William said he never got over John's death. 'Both in the initial enthusiasm for voluntary recruitment in 1914–15', writes John Feather, 'and in the later conscription to the forces, many good and essential men were lost.'[67]

When the Armistice finally came in November 1918, the book trade, like every other business and family, had to recover not only from economic challenges, but from personal bereavement and trauma. Trade periodicals and house histories rendered an upbeat image of a national industry that endured with stoicism and faith even as it was battered by losses of many kinds. Publishing and bookselling sought to reflect the mood of the country, catering to public demand for all sorts of books, for in the end they were businesses – the market and its needs and desires were what they existed for. In producing ideas that were mainly in tune with the government, but sometimes were radically opposed, publishers in particular responded to a larger development and dissemination of ideas that far exceeds the narrow range of First World War literature as it is now studied and 'understood'.

Publishers in the Great War created a legacy of print culture even as the war was being fought and they helped to construct a memory of stoicism and good humour amidst incredible tragedy and loss. Such a memory did not survive the inter-war years as it did after the Second World War, which was and is remembered in those terms, for Britain at least. There was no immediate cessation of war books in the months after the war, but publishers and booksellers were aware of war fatigue in their readers. As the *Saturday Review* asserted, '[n]ow that the war is over, we look to the publishers for less of the war book, and more literature of serious worth.'[68] The social, political and economic realities were far from the promised 'land fit for heroes' and literature about the Great War took its now well-known turn to anguish and bitterness in the late 1920s and 1930s, 'a crucial period during which the mythology of the war began to take shape', as Vincent Trott has illuminated.[69] This second 'war books boom' was immensely profitable as readers began to revisit the events of 1914–18 from a different perspective, responding to the trend in disillusioned war books established by the publication of and publicity for Remarque's *All Quiet on the Western Front*.[70]

Although a range of more positive interpretations did persist beyond the inter-war years, disillusionment undoubtedly began to replace confidence as the twentieth century progressed. The First World War generation was increasingly remembered as duped and naive, except for some lone, angry voices such as Wilfred Owen and Siegfried Sassoon, whose work came to define the mood in the inter-war period and has had lasting resonance. Their voices have come to be seen as the 'truth' of the Great War and its legacy. But a consideration of the book trade of the time reveals a very different picture.[71] Trade periodicals and publishers' house histories show how a broad range of print culture from different voices was disseminated and consumed, even in the midst of censorship, official and personal. Although forgotten now, these works were taken seriously and reviewed with attention, if not always favourably, by reviewers who were candid in their opinions and could be every bit as critical as commentators now about implausibility of plot, cashing-in on topics, and hyperbolic pronouncements about the 'evil Hun'.

Publishers continue to shape the memory of the Great War, particularly in the centenary, for readers whose awareness of the global cataclysm is increasingly removed, mediated and abstract. The publishing industry has created a new 'war books boom' with anthologies of poetry, editions of letters, biographies, reprints of 'classic' as well as forgotten or marginalised texts, and new historical studies that chronicle not just battles and military strategy, but life as it was lived on the home front. Both trade and academic publishers have created 'centenary lists', mirroring the extensive official, national commemorations in various countries. In a special report, Caroline Sanderson in *The Bookseller* noted that '[i]t is difficult to think of an anniversary that publishers have more wholeheartedly embraced than the centenary of the First World War'. Her keyword search on Nielsen BookData revealed that 'almost 1,000 titles themed on the Great War [were] to be published (or republished) over the next 12 months. And this is just the start [. . .] given that we have four years of important centenaries to come.'[72] As it was one hundred years ago, the print culture of the First World War is not only a literature of memory and remembrance and a potent creator of the wider cultural consciousness of 1914–18, it is also a lucrative commercial enterprise.

## Notes

1. J. St John, *William Heinemann: A Century of Publishing 1890–1990* (London: Heinemann, 1990), p. 159.
2. C. S. Peel, *How We Lived Then, 1914–18: A Sketch of Social and Domestic Life in England during the War* (London: John Lane – The Bodley Head, 1929), p. 42.
3. Mary Hammond and Shafquat Towheed, 'Introduction', in Hammond and Towheed (eds), *Publishing in the First World War: Essays in Book History* (Basingstoke: Palgrave Macmillan, 2007), p. 4. From 1903 to 1904, Unwin had worked six days a week in Leipzig for a bookseller and theological publisher, experience that augmented his time with his step-uncle T. Fisher Unwin's company.
4. *The Publishers' Circular*, 8 August 1914, p. 127.
5. See the title of Thompson's study, *Merchants of Culture: The Publishing Business in the Twenty-First Century* (Cambridge and Malden, MA: Polity, 2010).
6. Hammond and Towheed, 'Introduction', p. 2.
7. See, for example, Ann-Marie Einhaus, *The Short Story and the First World War* (Cambridge: Cambridge University Press, 2013).
8. See, for example, Shafquat Towheed and Edmund King (eds), *Reading in the First World War: Readers, Texts, Archives* (Basingstoke: Palgrave Macmillan, 2015).
9. See, for example, Vincent Trott, *Publishers, Readers and the Great War: Literature and Memory since 1918* (London: Bloomsbury Academic, forthcoming), and Ian Isherwood, 'The British Publishing Industry and Commercial Memories of the First World War', *War in History*, 23.3 (2016), 323–40.
10. See, for instance, Hazel Hutchison, *The War That Used Up Words: American Writers and the First World War* (New Haven and London: Yale University Press, 2015), and Thomas F. Schneider, '"The Truth about the War Finally": Critics' Expectations of War Literature during the Weimar Republic: The Reception of Erich Maria Remarque's *Im Westen nichts Neues* [*All Quiet on the Western Front*], 1928–1930', *Journalism Studies*, 17.4 (2016), 490–501.
11. Trott, *Publishers, Readers and the Great War*, p. 256.
12. See Jane Potter, 'For Country, Conscience and Commerce: Publishers and Publishing, 1914–18', in Hammond and Towheed (eds), *Publishing in the First World War*, pp. 11–26.
13. For comparison, the number of new and revised titles published in 2013 was 184,000.

14. WHSA 135/1: 'WHS to the Ministry of Food, 5 November 1917', quoted in Stephen Colclough, '"No such bookselling has ever before taken place in this country": Propaganda and the Wartime Distribution Practices of W. H. Smith & Son', in Hammond and Towheed (eds), *Publishing in the First World War*, pp. 27–45 (p. 29).
15. Iain Stevenson, *Book Makers: British Publishing in the Twentieth Century* (London: British Library, 2010), p. 37.
16. *Saturday Review* supplement, 24 October 1914, p. iii.
17. *The Athenaeum*, 2 January 1915, p. 11.
18. Alfred Berlyn, 'What of the Book Season?', *The Academy*, 26 September 1914, p. 333.
19. Ibid.
20. Ibid.
21. Ibid.
22. 'War – Past and Present', *The Bookman*, War Book supplement, November 1914, n.p.
23. J. Attenborough, *A Living Memory: Hodder & Stoughton Publishers, 1868–1975* (London: Hodder & Stoughton, 1975), p. 78.
24. Berlyn, 'What of the Book Season?', p. 333.
25. *Saturday Review* supplement, 24 October 1914, p. iii.
26. Ibid.
27. Bryan Bennett and Anthony Hamilton, *Edward Arnold: 100 Years of Publishing* (London: Edward Arnold, 1990), p. 39.
28. Ibid., p. 41. But the firm still found its output vastly reduced overall. In 1913, ninety-eight books were published; in 1914, fifty-one titles; in 1915, forty-five; in 1916, twenty-eight; in 1917, twenty-nine; and in 1918, sixteen – the lowest since 1890.
29. Charles Morgan, *The House of Macmillan (1843–1943)* (London: Macmillan & Co., 1944), pp. 209–10.
30. Dennis Griffiths, 'Methuen and Company', in *Dictionary of Literary Biography*, vol. 122, *British Library Publishing Houses, 1881–1965* (Detroit and London: Gale Research, 1991), pp. 211–20 (p. 214).
31. Marie Belloc Lowndes, *Diaries and Letters of Marie Belloc Lowndes, 1911–1947*, ed. Susan Lowndes (London: Chatto & Windus, 1971), p. 49.
32. J. D. Symon, 'The Novel under Commerce', *English Review*, 25.108 (November 1917), 421.
33. Stevenson, *Book Makers*, p. 43.
34. Kate Macdonald, 'The Symbiotic Relationship of Thomas Nelson & Sons and John Buchan within the Publisher's Series', in John Spiers (ed.), *The Culture of the Publisher's Series, Volume 1: Authors, Publishers and the Shaping of Taste* (Basingstoke and New York: Palgrave Macmillan, 2010), pp. 156–70 (p. 160).
35. Marie Belloc Lowndes, *A Passing World* (London: Macmillan, 1948), p. 22.
36. *Saturday Review* supplement, 24 October 1914, p. iii.
37. Ibid.
38. Ibid.
39. Susann Liebich, 'Reading as War Effort: The National Home Reading Union during the First World War', *First World War Studies*, 6.3 (2015), 219–38. Marcella P. Sutcliffe examines how 'the battle for "culture" saw its main theatre transferred from the heart of civic institutions – educational organisations and libraries – to the context of "war libraries"' in 'Reading at the Front: Books and Soldiers in the First World War', *Paedagogica Historica*, 52.1–2 (2016), 104–20. See also Towheed and King (eds), *Reading in the First World War*.
40. Frank Arthur Mumby, *Publishing and Bookselling: A History from the Earliest Times to the Present Day* (London: Jonathan Cape, 1930), p. 374; Potter, 'For Country, Conscience and Commerce', p. 16.
41. 'Books and the War', *The Bookman*, October 1915, p. 3.

42. Ibid.
43. Katharine Tynan, 'War Poets and Others', *The Bookman*, October 1916, p. 21.
44. Dorothy W. Collin, 'Sidgwick and Jackson Limited', in *Dictionary of Literary Biography*, vol. 122, pp. 307–15 (p. 314). The name of Robert Cameron Jackson, Second Lieutenant, is recorded on the Tyne Cot Memorial, West Flanders, Belgium.
45. Lieutenant Frederick Longman, 4th Battalion Royal Fusiliers, is commemorated on the Le Touret Memorial, Pas de Calais, France.
46. Jonathan Rose, 'J. M. Dent and Sons', in *Dictionary of Literary Biography*, vol. 122, pp. 81–94 (p. 88). Seven hundred volumes of the Everyman's Library had been published by 1914, but it then 'ground to a halt'. Wartime inflation had doubled the price of each volume from one shilling to two shillings.
47. Private Paxton Malaby Dent, 4th Battalion Seaforth Highlanders, is buried at Cabaret-Rouge British Cemetery, Souchez, Pas de Calais, France. His brother, Lance Sergeant Austin Campbell Dent, Royal Army Medical Corps 88th (1st/1st East Anglian) Field Ambulance, is buried at the Lancashire Landing Cemetery, Gallipoli Peninsular, Turkey.
48. A. Waugh, *One Hundred Years of Publishing, Being the Story of Chapman & Hall, Ltd* (London: Chapman & Hall, 1930), p. 270.
49. Dominic Hibberd, 'Introduction', in Dominic Hibberd and John Onions (eds), *The Winter of the World: Poems of the First World War* (London: Constable, 2007), p. xxii. See also Dominic Hibberd, 'A Publisher of First World War Poetry: Galloway Kyle', *Notes and Queries*, 32.2 (June 1986), 185–6, and 'Galloway Kyle and *The Poetry Review*', in *Harold Monro: Poet of the New Age* (Basingstoke: Macmillan, 2000), pp. 270–3.
50. Grace Brockington, 'Translating Peace: Pacifist Publishing and the Transmission of Foreign Texts', in Hammond and Towheed (eds), *Publishing in the First World War*, pp. 46–58 (p. 47).
51. Ibid.
52. Stanley Unwin, *The Truth about a Publisher* (London: George Allen & Unwin, 1960), p. 138.
53. John Worthen, 'D. H. Lawrence and the "Expensive Edition Business"', in Warren L. Chernaik, Warwick Gould and I. R. Willison (eds), *Modernist Writers and the Marketplace* (New York: St. Martin's Press, 1996), pp. 105–23 (p. 106).
54. Ibid.
55. Unwin refused to publish Allatini's novel on the grounds that its subject matter – of homosexuality and conscientious objection – would surely lead to them being prosecuted 'in the then state of public opinion'. When Allatini asked Unwin to suggest the name of another publisher, he told her that he didn't think anyone would dare take the novel on except C. W. Daniel: 'Daniel accepted the novel, was prosecuted for publishing it, and sentenced to three months' imprisonment or £460 fine (to which latter, having a guilty conscience for having mentioned his name, I contributed).' Potter, 'For Country, Conscience and Commerce', p. 17.
56. The Manifesto was reprinted in *The Times* in London the following month. For a fuller consideration of Wellington House and its activities see Peter Buitenhuis, *The Great War of Words: Literature as Propaganda, 1914–18 and After* (London: Batsford, 1987). Hazel Hutchison examines American involvement with particular attention in *The War That Used Up Words*.
57. *Second Report on the Work Conducted for the Government at Wellington House*, 1 February 1916, p. 6. Imperial War Museum and Public Record Office, London.
58. See Jane Potter, *Boys in Khaki, Girls in Print: Women's Literary Responses to the Great War 1914–1918* (Oxford and New York: Oxford University Press, 2005), pp. 227–8.
59. Hammond and Towheed, 'Introduction', p. 5.
60. Colclough, '"No such bookselling"', p. 27.

61. Ibid., p. 32.
62. Ibid., p. 33.
63. Ibid., p. 34.
64. Jacob Omnium, 'Under Cover', *The Bookseller*, November 1916, p. 599.
65. Griffiths, 'Methuen and Company', p. 214.
66. Ruth Panofsky, 'Odhams Press Limited', in *Dictionary of Literary Biography*, vol. 122, pp. 237–9 (p. 237).
67. John Feather, *A History of British Publishing* (London: Routledge, 1988), p. 196. Captain Thomas Arthur Nelson, Lothians and Border Horse Machine Gun Corps Awards, is buried at Faubourg d'Amiens Cemetery, Arras. Lieutenant John Stewart Blackie, 1st/5th Rifle Brigade, is commemorated on the Thiepval Memorial. Captain John William Heinemann, 20th Battalion Royal Fusiliers, is buried in the Cambrin Churchyard Extension, Pas de Calais, France.
68. *Saturday Review*, 15 March 1919, p. 248.
69. Trott, *Publishers, Readers and the Great War*, p. 21.
70. Schneider illustrates how both Remarque and his publisher Ullstein 'attempted to influence and change the dominant nationalist discourse on the First World War and its legacy from a democratic position', by creating 'a product – the text *Im Westen nichts Neues*' and conducting 'a highly professional marketing campaign'. In the context of 1930s Germany, however, and despite the novel's enormous success elsewhere, Schneider argues they 'ultimately failed'. Schneider, '"The Truth about the War Finally"', p. 498.
71. George Simmers has demonstrated how different fictions of the Great War look 'if, while acknowledging the appalling tragedy of slaughter on such a scale, one does not make Fussell's assumptions; if one does not take it for granted that the deaths were meaningless, and if one is willing to accept that the mass of writers, especially civilian ones, who produced work during the War and in the years immediately afterwards, and who actively endorsed the project of the War, were not necessarily naïve victims of false consciousness, or swayed by propaganda, or dishonest'. 'Military Fictions: Stories about Soldiers, 1914–1930', unpublished PhD thesis, Oxford Brookes University, 2009, p. 9. See also Simmers's blog Great War Fiction, <https://greatwarfiction.wordpress.com/> (last accessed 30 November 2016), for further analyses of and commentary on both canonical and now-forgotten texts.
72. Caroline Sanderson, 'In Depth: First World War Special', *The Bookseller*, 16 September 2013, <http://www.thebookseller.com/feature/depth-first-world-war-special> (last accessed 30 November 2016).

# 24

# Photography and the First World War

*J. J. Long*

The history of photography is a plural history: the medium operates across numerous institutional spaces, and is integrated into countless fields of social practice. This is nowhere more apparent than in the multiple photographic cultures of the First World War; from soldiers' mementoes to propaganda campaigns, from the news media to operational planning and execution, from control of information by the censor to constructions of cultural memory, few aspects of the war were left unaffected by photography.

## Soldiers

It is often argued that the First World War brought about a crisis of vision and a concomitant disorientation of the combatants.[1] In Paul Virilio's account of the parallel development of weapons and optical technology, the First World War functions as a turning point in the history of representation and perception. 'To the naked eye,' Virilio writes, 'the vast new battlefield seemed to be composed of nothing – no more trees or vegetation, no more water or even earth, no hand-to-hand encounters, no visible trace of the unity of homicide and suicide.'[2] This loss of the 'direct quality of sight' brought about several effects: it turned the war into an unprecedented spectacle of light emitted by gun blasts, flares and searchlights; soldiers felt deprived of sensory orientation, but paradoxically also felt constantly within sight of the enemy; and it necessitated the use of compensatory technologies such as aerial photography.[3] Ground-level photography was found to be incapable of capturing battlefield experience or the nature of modern warfare; commentators expressed disappointment that images from the front conveyed so little. This was not only a question of topography. The fact that strategy was now led from behind the lines, the sheer extent of the front and the tendency for the war to fragment into countless small-scale actions meant that conventional strategies for visualising combat were no longer available. There were also practical problems. Taking photographs during an assault was almost impossible, for as soon as the enemy was close enough to be seen, the act of photographing would have made any photographer a military liability as well as fully exposing him to enemy fire. Furthermore, the propitious conditions for offensive operations – poor light, fog or darkness – were not conducive to successful photography.

The crisis of vision, then, was allied to what Bernd Hüppauf has called a 'crisis of representation'. Hüppauf argues that although the First World War was widely understood as a war of mass armies, technology and economic strength,

> the images associated with it remained predominantly archaic images of individual suffering and heroism. The structural changes of the battlefield [. . .] were lost in a type of photography that maintained as its central object the fighting, running, resting, eating, laughing, dying soldier.[4]

This involved the reactivation of an image repertoire that had been established by war photographers of the previous century, which humanised war even as it captured the military technology that made conflict increasingly mechanised and *de*humanised. This humanisation went hand in hand with a taboo on representations of the dead and maimed, which persisted into the public photographic culture of the First World War in the form of a transnational iconography whose fundamental motifs comprised touristic or quasi-ethnographic images of foreign places, male friendship when off-duty, destroyed buildings and *matériel*.[5]

And yet, more photographs of the First World War were produced than of any previous war, largely because of the prevalence of camera ownership among soldiers themselves. Small-format, hand-held cameras such as the Vest Pocket Kodak, the Ensignette and the Goerz-Anschütz plate camera were marketed to military personnel and widely used by frontline soldiers. Despite prohibitions on trench photography in all the major belligerent armies, such prohibitions appear to have been rarely enforced, and the German, Austrian and American armies even operated a system whereby amateurs could seek permission to take photographs in the trenches. The result is a vast corpus of photographic material.

A striking thing about many collections of soldiers' photographs is the sheer diversity of subjects that servicemen felt worthy of representation and preservation. In some cases, the images left behind corroborate much of what is written about soldiers' war albums: there is an emphasis on camaraderie and life behind the frontlines, on military hardware, on destroyed buildings and landscapes, and on the people and places occupied by armies on the move. But apparently random motifs are surprisingly common, among them minor aircraft crashes, which are not trophy images – they generally capture friendly aeroplanes rather than enemy ones – but seem to betoken fascination with a new form of hardware, with perhaps a sense of ironic humour at the frailty and fallibility of flying machines.[6] A further notable aspect is that many servicemen collected and preserved their photographs in albums which structure the viewing experience in highly specific ways.

Exemplary in this regard is an album of Gunner T. N. Sutherland of the New Zealand Field Artillery, who was stationed at Gallipoli and in northern France. Of the four albums preserved in the Liddle Collection at the University of Leeds, the second starts with photographs of the equipment and personnel of Sutherland's field gun battery. Images of soldiers at leisure follow, in dugouts, tents or cooking shelters, or posing in front of the half-ruined buildings of an unidentified town. In some of the latter, the men depicted are in costume, as though putting on a play. But these light-hearted scenes are interspersed with churches and other public buildings that have been torn apart by artillery fire. The album ends with various photographs of ships, Turkish troops, a fortified coastline, Arab men trekking on donkeys across a beach, and a further group portrait of gunners beside their cannon. While the photographs do not fully shy away from war's destruction, they place it at a distance. Overall, the album suggests a narrative of soldierly companionship, and a passing quasi-ethnographic curiosity about local people in foreign lands.[7]

So far, so predictable. But the last of the Sutherland albums is quite different.[8] It begins with a photograph that shows seven men: three standing, three sitting in front of them, and one lounging in the foreground. In the background to the left is a receding group of conical tents and piles of kit, while to the right can be seen an orderly row of horses. A hand-written caption beneath says simply 'Gallipoli'. Beneath it is a coastal view captioned 'ANZAC Cove'. On turning the page, though, the viewer is confronted with three photographs of grave markers, accompanied by the hand-written names of the dead. The upper image on the verso page is that of P. Manby, the two in the lower image those of R. McRae and an indecipherable name. McRae's grave is depicted on its own on the next page, in portrait format, which requires the viewer to turn the album on its side in order to view it properly. Beneath McRae's grave is a trench photograph, showing a soldier apparently asleep, with others sitting athwart the trench behind him. The remainder of the album is devoted to the Gallipoli landscape and further images of off-duty soldiers, and the alternation of landscape and portrait orientation is preserved until about half-way through. The album is thus a complex memorial artefact, linking historically significant locations with the quotidian sociability of military life and the inevitable consequences of battle: death. It simultaneously marks major sites of cultural memory and national mythology (ANZAC Cove, Australian Valley), offers a resource for personal memory, and engages in mourning work by commemorating the deaths of fellow servicemen. The fact that it has to be held, and turned alternately on its side and the right way up, engages the viewer haptically as well as optically, one effect of which is to force a more protracted, contemplative engagement with the images and the things they depict.

The album of Flight Sergeant E. Vousden is similarly complex in terms of its contents and organisation.[9] More than most, it concentrates on male camaraderie, with many of the captions seeming to be in-jokes that have no information value for an uninitiated viewer; 'Six of Them / Lined up', 'Some who helped / In FORMATION', 'Sat for IT / daisy cutters' are captions attached to three small-format (4.2 × 6.5 cm) group portraits, for example. The captions construct the user-group of the album: Vousden himself and a small number of close confederates, who function as a closed homosocial community held together by a largely private language. Like Sutherland's album, Vousden's demands haptic engagement, for not all of the photographs can be accommodated in its pages and some have to be handled as loose leaves that both are and are not part of the album. Towards the end, we are presented with a pasted-in mass-produced discharge notice, in which the hope is expressed that Vousden's future career will allow him to look back to the years spent in the Royal Air Force 'with pleasure, and not to feel that the time so spent was wasted'. Beneath it, in Vousden's hand, is written 'PERHAPS / Feb. 1919'. The melancholy potential of this laconic remark carries over into the photographs, too; a larger (15.5 × 10.1 cm) group portrait is captioned 'Good Boy's [*sic*] / London / Colney / 1916', and beneath each of the men depicted is a name. It is further noted that four were killed in action in 1916 or 1917, and that the whereabouts of the remaining two is unknown. As with the Sutherland album, then, personal memories of comradeship in service are tempered by the inevitable 'posthumous irony' that attaches to photographs of the dead: they are dead and they are going to die, as Roland Barthes famously put it. But they are going to die young, and violently.

Sutherland's and Vousden's albums show how inconspicuous vernacular objects come to function in surprisingly complex ways, which cannot be reduced to a typology of motifs. Albums need to be read as visual-haptic ensembles, whose juxtapositions, layout and captioning require interrogation if their multi-dimensional memorial economies are to be fully appreciated.

## Propaganda and Censorship

Historians of the First World War argue that the conflict rapidly came to be understood as a total war that would determine the survival of nations. As a consequence, governments needed to mobilise 'hearts and minds', and thereby find ways of managing information so as to bolster civilian morale, and satisfy public demand for information without compromising military operations. They achieved this by means of concentrated propaganda campaigns and the military mobilisation of culture.[10] While there were differences between them, the major belligerents ended the war with highly organised censorship and propaganda agencies, with dedicated bodies for generating and regulating the supply of photographs for public consumption: the pictorial section of the War Propaganda Bureau in Britain, the Section photographique des armées in France, a subdivision of the G-2 Army Intelligence Section for the American Expeditionary Force, a dedicated photographic department of the Austrian Kaiserliche und Königliche Kriegspressequartier (KPQ; Imperial and Royal War Press Section), and the Bild- und Filmamt (BuFa) in Germany.[11]

Censorship was not a purely negative affair consisting of nothing but prohibitions: the military was reliant on the press for generating continued public support for the war, while the press was reliant on the military for a supply of images and access to combat zones. As Anton Holzer puts it, censorship was part of a complex media system: 'censorship did not merely explicitly prohibit and withhold images; it also – and in retrospect this seems to have been at least as effective – schooled the photographers' gaze, training the eye to see the war in the "right" way.'[12] Self-censorship by photographers and picture editors was central to the effective functioning of propaganda on the side of the Allies and the Central Powers alike. Beyond this, though, active and positive propaganda efforts were directed at influencing neutral opinion, and a major means of prosecuting this agenda was the photographic periodical.

The illustrated periodical press generally thrived during the war. Not only did established titles persist, such as *L'Illustration* in France, *Das interessante Blatt* and the *Wiener Illustrierte Zeitung* in Austria, the *Leipziger Illustrierte Zeitung* and the *Zeitbilder* photo supplement of the *Vossische Zeitung* in Germany, and the *London Illustrated News* and the *Daily Mirror* in Britain, but new illustrated periodicals were launched specifically to disseminate photographic views of war to a domestic audience.[13] Germany and Britain quickly realised the potential propaganda value of illustrated periodicals. Germany established the Überseedienst Transozean (transcontinental overseas service), which both acquired control of neutral newspapers and launched new ones, such as *Germania*, covering South America; a Chinese edition of the *Deutsche Zeitung*; the *Continental Korrespondenz*, designed to supply ready copy to the neutral press; and, most importantly, the *Staats-Zeitung*, a

New York-based paper that spearheaded a massive German propaganda campaign in the United States. In addition, a semi-official organisation, the Presse-Abteilung zur Beeinflussung der Neutralen, coordinated the production of numerous multilingual newspapers for European distribution.[14] By February 1916, the British Propaganda Bureau based at Wellington House was producing four international illustrated magazines: *America Latina*, distributed throughout Spain and South America; *O Espelho*, published in Portuguese and circulated in Brazil; *Al Hakikat*, published in Arabic, Persian and Hindustani; and *War Pictorial*, a monthly publication with commentary in English, French, Dutch, Spanish, Portuguese, Italian, Russian, Greek, Danish, Swedish and German. Further publications were circulated throughout and beyond the Empire, in Chinese, Japanese, Malay, Bengali, Hindi, Gujarati, Tamil, Urdu and Gurmukhi. Both the quality and the circulation of these increased, with *War Pictorial* attaining a monthly circulation of 750,000 copies.[15] This was a photographic propaganda exercise on a vast scale.

As the war drew on, propaganda was devoted not only to influencing international opinion and preventing communication of information of military value, but to the home front. In 1916, almost two years of positional warfare culminated in bloodshed and death on a colossal scale on the Somme and at Verdun, but neither side achieved a decisive breakthrough. The reality of an ongoing, drawn-out campaign of attrition necessitated active management of home-front morale and the ever-greater mobilisation of civilian labour to meet the demands of the war economy. In 1916 in Germany, prohibitions were issued regarding publication of images of hardship and hunger on the German home front,[16] and BuFa inaugurated a programme of lectures illustrated by lantern slides, which aimed at avoiding civil unrest and negotiating the changed social position of women, as well as celebrating German military achievements.[17] In Britain, as the war entered its third year, Wellington House likewise realised that it needed to devote propaganda attention to the civilian population on the home front, leading to the appointment of Horace Nicholls as the first official home-front photographer in July 1917. Among the functions of home-front propaganda was managing the new role of women within the war economy and the armed services, which was potentially disruptive of workplace culture, industrial relations and family structures.[18]

As part of this campaign, the War Office issued a large-format pamphlet entitled *Women's War Work* in September 1916.[19] The very title of this publication is noteworthy. Deborah Thom argues that in the years immediately preceding the First World War, the term 'women's work' had come to signify 'sweating' – that is, work that was not done in factories, was not protected by government agencies or trade unions, and did not provide a living wage. As such, 'women's work' was seen as a social problem that needed to be eradicated, if necessary by means of state intervention, and photography played a significant role in media-based campaigning to improve the lot of (sweated) women workers.[20] The decade leading up to the First World War had seen increasing agitation on behalf of and organisation of women's labour. In other words, women not only already constituted a large part of the British workforce, but were highly visible as such. Nevertheless, as Thom goes on to note,

> It was not in the Government's interest to remind employers that women were already workers, with workers' inconvenient attitudes and divisions. Women were thus pictorially characterised as novices, heroic workers motivated solely

> by patriotism [. . .] The image of women workers in wartime [. . .] is of a frail girl wrestling alone with a machine, working heroically against her nature for the duration of the war only.[21]

However, a closer look at *Women's War Work* suggests that the work of propaganda photography was more complex than this diagnosis implies.

The 'Preface' and the 'Introductory Note by the Adjutant-General to the Forces' make the publication's instrumental purpose explicit: 'the necessity of replacing wastage in our Armies' means that physically able men will need to be 'released' from all forms of civilian occupation that can be carried out by women.[22] The purpose was to reduce the number of men whose civilian work was deemed 'indispensable' and who were therefore exempt from military service at the front, thereby increasing the army's recruitment pool without detriment to Britain's economic productivity. And yet other concerns emerge that go beyond the question of so-called 'dilution' (the replacement of skilled men with unskilled or semi-skilled women). In the 'Preface' it is noted that 'domestic disturbance and the breaking-up of homes' can be avoided if women take over the work of the menfolk within their own family.[23] And in the 'Introductory Note', a further purpose of the publication is announced: 'this book is intended not only to indicate that women have shown themselves capable of successfully replacing the stronger sex in practically every calling, but is offered also as a tribute to their effective contribution to the Empire in its hour of need.'[24] Alongside its utility as a recruitment tool, then, *Women's War Work* also addresses the need to manage the altered family dynamics and social disturbances that women's presence in the industrial workplace will, it is assumed, produce, along with the need to champion the women themselves and their contribution to the war effort.[25] Its mode of address is thus multiple, and relies on photography for its power.

The substantive textual part of *Women's War Work* simply lists the 'Trades and Processes in which Women are successfully employed in temporary replacement of Men', and lest we miss the point, the subsequent part is entitled 'Photographs of Women Workers. Illustrating the successful employment of Women in temporary replacement of Men'. The inflationary use of the word 'temporary' can be read symptomatically, as revealing anxiety about the disruptions to economic and gender relations that women's dominance in the workplace necessarily brought about. The photographic section consists of eighteen double-page spreads, each containing four symmetrically arranged photographs, most from agency and press sources. The first eight depict women's agricultural work: harrowing, horse grooming and a variety of harvesting tasks.[26] After that, however, the images concentrate on urban and industrial work, from relatively light work such as cleaning windows and railway rolling stock to heavy work in flour mills, shipyards, gas works, coal mines and munitions factories. An immediate function of this is to bring women workers visually into contexts from which they had conventionally been absent: the industrial workplace.[27] Images of women operating heavy machinery, driving delivery vans and steamrollers, or hauling vast steel bars were an attempt quite literally to re-envision the gender of industrial labour. Captions are short, and often feature the present participle of verbs to convey ongoing action: harvesting, loading, feeding, shovelling, barrowing, cleaning, welding, driving, transporting and so on. The element of risk or difficulty is highlighted in several images: we are asked to note how arduous bakery work is, the height of the ladders in a photograph of window cleaners, or how the difficulty of lifting heavy objects has been overcome.[28] In other words, the images demonstrate the fact that very few occupations are beyond the physical capabilities of women.

The women in the photographs are depicted either fully absorbed by the task in hand or pausing to look up and (in most cases) smile or pose for the camera. Both are crucial to the rhetoric of *Women's War Work*, as can be seen in an image of 'Electric Train Cleaners': two women (clearly posed) are in a pit beneath the train, busily applying cloths to the couplings and axles, eyes trained on the task. Another woman is posing jauntily, one foot on the driver's access step, one on the buffer, leaning back and beaming into the lens (Figure 24.1). The image conveys a simultaneous sense of industrious concentration *and* pride and pleasure in the work, and this is replicated within the macro-structure of the volume as a whole. The photographs' mode of address, then, appears to correspond to that of the 'Preface' and 'Introductory Note': while making a case for the effectiveness of women workers for the benefit of tribunals, there is also a more generalised appeal here – to women themselves, to society at large – which seeks to reassure the viewer that women derive benefit from doing men's work, benefit that goes beyond the mere discharge of patriotic duty. The work of reassurance is

Figure 24.1 Page from *Women's War Work in Maintaining the Industries and Export Trade of the United Kingdom: Information Officially Compiled for the Use of Recruiting Officers, Military Representatives and Tribunals* (London: HMSO, 1916). Reproduced courtesy of Durham University Library Archives and Special Collections.

undertaken in a different way at other points, too, for while most images show women working without men, a number include men within their frames. Differentiated by dress, the men are almost always present as overseers: in the fields, a foundry, a grocery store, a railway goods yard, a shipyard, a flour mill.[29] There are a small number of photographs showing men and women workers as equals, but in the main, where the co-existence of the sexes in the workplace is thematised, *Women's War Work* upholds conventional hierarchies. Men are in charge – with one exception: when it comes to instructing army recruits in the use of a travelling field kitchen – a kind of extension of the domestic realm – a woman takes the lead.

*Women's War Work*, then, is a hybrid, advocating the integration of women into the workforce in ways that challenge the gendered divisions of labour that had evolved under industrial capitalism, while simultaneously attempting to contain the potentially subversive effects of the mass mobilisation of female labour. It seeks to fulfil this ostensibly contradictory task not only by repeatedly insisting on the temporary nature of 'women's war work', but by seeking, throughout the photographic section, to naturalise both women's work *and* the persistence of a gender hierarchy in which men remain superior. The fact that the work of persuasion is entrusted almost entirely to minimally captioned photographs demonstrates the confidence that the war authorities placed, here and more broadly, in the photographic image as a mode of propaganda.

## Reconnaissance

As we have seen, the free press did not, as a rule, need to be coerced into serving the state in the main belligerent countries. In July 1918, for example, the popular science periodical *Scientific American* published a short article on aerial reconnaissance on the Western front. Between 1914 and 1918, *Scientific American* carried numerous photographically illustrated features on the technological and strategic developments of wartime, representing a fascinating case of a putatively scientific publication serving a fundamentally propagandistic goal. The article begins hyperbolically:

> It is difficult to conceive of a photographic plate that holds the fate of hundreds of thousands of men, batteries of guns, and possibly the decision of a great battle, in its thin coating of emulsion. Yet there are numerous such plates made every day by intrepid airmen, which, after being developed in less than fifteen minutes of reaching the ground and then flashed on the stereopticon screen in the presence of skilled photograph readers and officers, sign the death warrant of numerous soldiers and the order for the destruction of extensive military works and equipment, so to speak.[30]

The aerial photograph is described as the 'eye and memory of the military airman', and the purpose of air combat, we are told, is to secure the safe arrival of exposed plates at the aerodrome. The author offers brief interpretations of the five photographs reproduced in the article. The first two depict the Belgian town of Zonnebeke before and after Allied bombardment, targeting having been effected by photographic reconnaissance. The central image shows a German supply station and is praised for its detail. The lower left image shows the effects of British barrage fire designed to cut off the rear German trenches and prevent the forward movement of reinforcements, while the lower right image highlights the near-impregnability of the Hindenburg Line (which, the article tells us, had nevertheless been breached by the Allies the previous year).

For all its brevity and sensationalism, 'The Eyes and Memory of the Military Airman' addresses most of the key features of photographic aerial reconnaissance as it developed in the First World War. It notes the significance of photography for tactical reconnaissance, targeting and damage evaluation; it recognises the fact that aerial combat developed in order to disrupt or prevent reconnaissance missions and the dangers to which aerial observers were exposed; it notes the speed with which aerial photographs were developed and disseminated; and finally it offers a little primer in the interpretation of aerial photographs, while stressing that, in reality, this work is done by trained personnel using a stereopticon.

Both the German and Allied armies were quick to mobilise aerial photography for reconnaissance purposes after the war broke out, even if the conservative and stereotyped thinking of military high commands and a variety of internal political and administrative factors militated against rapid high-level acceptance, coordination and standardisation. Over the course of the war, what began as ad hoc, local processes were transformed into a thoroughly organised intelligence operation on the Allied and German sides alike.[31]

As the *Scientific American* article suggests, aerial photography came to be regarded as a powerful weapon, and both aviation strategy and photographic equipment evolved in order to secure a constant supply of high-quality images. Aerial observation from two-seater aeroplanes accommodating a pilot and an observer was initially the fundamental function of the airborne units in all belligerent countries, with the development of single-seat fighter or pursuit aircraft a response to the unimpeded access to one's own airspace by enemy reconnaissance planes. The dangers posed by pursuit aircraft led to the adoption of formation flying at a tactical level as well as to the strategic doctrine of air superiority: whoever commanded the airspace had access to the most reliable intelligence. Meanwhile, as ground anti-aircraft defences improved, it became necessary to fly at ever-greater altitudes to escape flak. Not only did airframes and engines improve to facilitate this, but cameras of increasing focal length were required to photograph from high altitude with sufficient detail. Cameras with focal lengths of 120 or even 137 centimetres were invented. The size and weight made them unsuitable for manual operation if vertical photographs were required; cameras needed to be accommodated within the aircraft's fuselage. They also needed to have automatic or semi-automatic plate changers, as well as fast shutter speeds and suspension mechanisms to counteract the effects of engine vibration.[32] The photographic requirements of the military in the First World War did not fundamentally change chemical and optical technology, but they did stimulate innovation in camera design, airframe design, and the tactical and strategic conduct of aerial warfare.

The main military uses of aerial photography were (1) interpretation of the photograph to identify enemy works; (2) application of aerial data to map production; and (3) exploitation of the intelligence thus gained in operations against the enemy. While panoramic and oblique views were useful for general topographical orientation and tactical planning, the perpendicular aerial view was favoured as an intelligence source (Figures 24.2 and 24.3). Both sides quickly formalised training in photographic interpretation, and evolved large-scale, high-speed processing techniques that articulated with complex distribution channels in order to ensure that photographic intelligence was both accurate and timely. Photographic intelligence was vital for artillery targeting and damage evaluation, and for tactical reconnaissance in advance of offensives: photographs allowed identification of enemy defensive positions and fortifications, obstacles, machine-gun emplacements and so on. The French, in particular, pioneered the use of photography for strategic reconnaissance, flying missions tens of kilometres behind enemy lines in order to spot large-scale movements of men and material in the rear echelons. Reconnaissance of this kind enabled the Allies to predict the location and strength of enemy offensives up to a month in advance.[33]

Aerial reconnaissance also responded to the need for cartographic accuracy, which was essential for artillery targeting in particular. At the outbreak of hostilities, both the Allies and the Central Powers found that existing maps were wholly inadequate.[34] The onset of positional warfare led to the partial or total destruction of topographical landmarks; in some cases, entire forests disappeared and man-made structures such as buildings and roads were obliterated. The destruction of fixed points such as church steeples meant that traditional methods of trigonometric surveying were seriously

Figure 24.2 Oblique of Vieux Berquin, a village near Merville, from the west May 1918. It shows Ankle Farm and the Factory in the bottom left hand corner. Durham University Special Collections, WDL/G/20. Reproduced by permission of Durham University Library.

Figure 24.3 Vertical of the area slightly to the west of Figure 24.2, June 1918. Ankle Farm and the Factory are at top right. Both photographs were probably used in the planning of a small and very successful night-time operation on 28–29 June 1918, in which 93 Brigade, 31st Division took both Ankle Farm and the Factory. I thank Alastair Fraser for supplying this information. Durham University Special Collections, WDL/G/21. Reproduced by permission of Durham University Library.

impeded, and existing maps became obsolete as daily barrages transformed the landscape. As a result, aerial photography became a prized means of maintaining accurate maps within a shifting topographic environment.

Photo-maps were widely used. In their crude form, they consisted of a mosaic of overlapping perpendicular aerial photographs taken from the same altitude. The Germans pioneered the *Reihenbildner*, a camera that could sequentially expose long strips of 35mm film which, when aligned and abutted, gave wide coverage of territory at a consistent scale. *Reihenbildner* were of considerable tactical and cartographic utility.[35] The dominant method for the Allies was 'restitution' – the discipline of transferring information, on a daily basis, from a photograph to a map in a reciprocal process of cartography and photo-interpretation: vertical photographs of sections of the front 'became the primary template for the map. In turn, the map, augmented through the restitution process, guided the aerial photographic interpreter throughout his exploration of the photograph.'[36] Knowing the altitude and banking angle of an aeroplane at the moment the photograph was taken allowed cartographers to correct oblique distortion, and the Germans even developed an apparatus called the *Umbildner*, or 'image converter', for optically transforming oblique views into vertical ones. Using photographic data to enhance large-scale maps for artillery purposes and smaller-scale maps for tactical operations became an integral part of positional warfare.

The efficacy of aerial photography meant that anything visible from the air became a point of vulnerability. As a consequence, the art and science of camouflage rapidly became a major focus of military activity – an aspect of aerial warfare not mentioned by *Scientific American*. Before the First World War, camouflage was largely aimed at horizontal disappearance: making oneself apparently invisible to an eye-level observer. The view from above, however, negated the value of horizontal disguise; it became necessary to ensure invisibility not just from an aerial observer, but, more particularly, from the photographic eye of the camera. Indeed, the word 'camouflage' originated to mean 'systematic dissimulation for the purposes of concealment from photographic detection': photography produced camouflage.[37] This led, in turn, to a reconfiguration of the relationship between space, landscape and vision. As Paul K. Saint-Amour has shown, contemporary works on aerial reconnaissance convey a remarkable confidence in photographs, which were deemed to be unsurpassable in terms of their accuracy, information saturation, semiotic plenitude and legibility.[38] However, the intrusion of camouflage removed any certainty in a stable semiotics of landscape; rather than being simply surveyed, territory was now subjected to an active surveillance governed by the hermeneutics of suspicion; things were not necessarily what they seemed. Reconnaissance and camouflage developed through a mutually reinforcing dance of surveillance and counter-surveillance, deception and counter-deception.

Photography's challenge to camouflage was multifaceted. Not only did it reveal detail that would not be readily noticed by the naked eye, but it preserved views for later interpretation. This in turn facilitated the process that became one of the photo-interpreter's most valuable weapons: the ability to compare photographs sequentially, which allowed interpreters to decipher even the minutest changes over time. According to the British artist-turned-*camoufleur* Solomon J. Solomon, 'the elimination of shadow is the essence of invisibility',[39] but hue and texture were also captured on the photograph, and to an increasing extent, with the use of panchromatic film (black and white film that is sensitive to all wavelengths within the visible spectrum and whose greyscale tones closely approximate the brightness of the objects depicted) and the use of filters to detect anomalies between hues that ordinarily looked the same in a monochrome print.[40] Ever-more sophisticated camouflage was thus needed if it was to blend effectively with the environment. This blending had to be invisible not to the eye, but to the camera. Photography does not mimic natural vision, since it only captures reflected light, not 'actinic' light (photochemically active radiation such as that produced by sunlight). All involved in the production of camouflage therefore had to imagine themselves as embodying the view of the aerial camera, and both the Allies and the Germans took aerial photographs of their own camouflaged positions to gauge the effectiveness of the measures taken.[41]

The one technique of photographic intelligence that defied almost all attempts at camouflage involved the revivification of the stereoscope, which had had its heyday as a parlour toy in the 1850s. By enabling an observer to view two images of the same object taken from slightly different positions (typically with lenses about 2.75 inches apart, corresponding to the average distance between the pupils), the stereoscope created the illusion of three-dimensional space. Landscapes appear completely flat both in aerial photographs and to direct observation from aeroplanes – the latter because beyond an altitude of 1,500 to 2,000 feet, objects become too remote for the sight-lines of the naked eye to converge sufficiently to produce vision in three dimensions.[42]

If two photographs of the same territory were taken not 2.75 inches but 1,250 feet apart (the norm for Allied stereoscopic reconnaissance), and viewed side by side through a stereoscope, an effect of hyperstereoscopy was produced: vertical relief was massively exaggerated, allowing photo-interpreters to see what was presumed to be invisible, including objects under bridges or beneath camouflage netting. Placing photographs of the same terrain but taken on different days in a stereoscope, meanwhile, meant that any changes became visible as a 'disturbance' or 'flicker' in the image.[43] Though the process was more difficult and painstaking than the *Scientific American* suggests, the intelligence value of stereoscopy was enormous, and proved its usefulness in the Second World War as well, notably in the Allied search for V-1 'flying bomb' facilities. Indeed, the photographic reconnaissance methods that were developed in the First World War became a mainstay of intelligence operations throughout the remainder of the twentieth century.

## History and Memory

What photo-interpreters were seeking in aerial photographs was evidence: evidence of enemy activity and works that would materially affect the conduct of battle. As the above discussion has shown, however, evidence was very seldom self-evident: the status of the photograph as evidence was predicated on often-minute differences between one photograph and another, differences that could in many cases only be discerned by applying highly sophisticated interpretative protocols and with the help of prosthetic devices such as the magnifying glass or the stereoscope. As John Tagg argues, the evidentiary status of photography is discursively produced, not ontologically given.[44] This becomes apparent when we look at other ways in which the photograph was called upon to function as evidence.

One of the most striking uses of photography was in so-called atrocity propaganda produced during the war by the Allied powers. Its function was to discredit and stir up animosity towards the Central Powers by documenting alleged contraventions of the Hague Conventions, the destruction of cultural heritage, and violence meted out to civilians – including women and children – by Austrian and German soldiers. During the First World War, the French issued numerous books and pamphlets, through both official and commercial channels, photographically documenting the destruction of houses and churches, foremost among them being Arsène Alexandre's *Les Monuments français détruits par l'Allemagne*.[45] The most systematic and sophisticated use of photography as evidence of atrocity, though, was arguably made by Alphonse Reiss in his *Report upon the Atrocities Committed by the Austro-Hungarian Army during the First Invasion of Serbia*.[46] Reiss was a noted criminologist who had published a handbook of police photography in 1903.[47] His deployment of photography in the Serbia report is correspondingly forensic. In the opening chapter on explosive bullets, which detonate inside the body and were proscribed by international law, Reiss includes a cutaway drawing showing the mechanism of explosive bullets and their dimensions, alongside photographs showing the internal components of the ammunition as well as its side and base. The latter is engraved with the Austrian Eagle and bears the date 1912, ostensibly proving that the illegal ammunition was being manufactured in Austria in the immediate pre-war period.[48] This integrates photography into a rhetoric of pure documentation, and although this is an extreme case, the photographs elsewhere are endowed with the status of documentary evidence by the surrounding text, much of which consists of depositions by named Serbian witnesses and numbered Austro-Hungarian soldiers, or simply lists of sickening injuries inflicted on the civilian population of occupied Serbia. The photographs of destroyed buildings, piled-up corpses, hangings and the sites of civilian massacres become pieces of evidence within a judicial process, the result of which is the indictment of Austria-Hungary.

Reports on war damage and atrocities show that even during the war, photography was being mobilised to negotiate the war's meaning, establish responsibility and guilt, and record its depredations for posterity. As such, these reports and the photographic evidence they included were part of a wider concern to document the conflict. Most of the belligerent countries established institutions charged with collection and preservation, many of which were organised by the state but enlisted the support of the nation to supply material. The function of the collections was twofold: to cultivate patriotic allegiance and celebrate wartime achievements on the one hand, and to provide material for posterity on the other. The First World War was historicised as it happened.

Archival material was not only amenable to historical study by academics, however; in Germany in particular it was strategically deployed in the 1920s and 1930s in order to construct and contest the cultural memory of a lost war. Among many books of First World War photographs, two of the most noteworthy are *Krieg dem Kriege!* (*War against War!*), by the pacifist Ernst Friedrich, and *Das Antlitz des Weltkrieges* (*The Countenance of the Great War*), by the conservative nationalist Ernst Jünger.[49] Both mined archives of different kinds to produce highly polemical works that exploit, once again, the assumed evidentiary status of the photograph.

Friedrich had opened an Anti-War Museum in Berlin in the early 1920s, and included photographs prominently among the exhibits. The most contentious were those of war veterans with horrific facial injuries, and these were taken up in Friedrich's 1924 publication *War against War!* The images are disturbing because they represent the destruction of that which makes us most recognisably human, but also because facial wounds disrupt the cultural meaning of bodily orifices. The mouth, in particular, is always a troubling site for Western aesthetics, since it is the part of the body that offers access to, and has the capacity to display, the interior of the body. In classical aesthetics the open mouth was thus repudiated as a potential cause of disgust. The images in Friedrich's book, on the other hand, show mouths that are not just grotesquely open but shot away or, in the best-case scenario, surgically replaced by a stoma. Beyond this, though, the images engage critically with the discourse of physiognomy, which had undergone a renaissance in the Weimar Republic. The destroyed mouths and missing jaws trouble the hermeneutics of surface and depth on which physiognomic discourse depends, namely the assumption that inner moral character can be gauged from the surface features of the face. The crudely ironic point of these images within Weimar physiognomic thinking, then, is to show that all that is inside is animal flesh or a gaping void. Rather than being able to read the face as giving clues to moral character, to subjective interiority or 'soul', it is revealed that behind and beneath the face lies just more matter, which is as vulnerable to physical destruction as the face itself. If any text deserved the title 'The Countenance of the Great War', it is this section of *War against War!*[50]

But *The Countenance of the Great War* was in fact a book edited by Ernst Jünger, which has been seen as a direct riposte to Friedrich's provocation. The book is remarkable for its obsession not with dead people (of which there are many), but with dead horses, to which Jünger devotes an entire section. Bodily mutilation is largely displaced on to the horse:[51] we see one animal actually in the process of being shot, and other images of horses are characterised by corporal distortions, advanced states of decay, and a tendency to fill the frame. Within *The Countenance of the Great War*, horses function as a metonymic substitute for all that was destroyed not only by mechanised warfare, but by the technological innovations of modernity more generally. In this sense, the book attempts to provide a pictorial counterpart to Jünger's comment, in an essay of 1932, that '[t]he Great War was a battle not simply between two groups of nations but between two epochs, and in this sense there were both victors and vanquished to be found in our country'.[52] The First World War, on this reading, is little more than an epiphenomenon of a wider conflict between the comfortable culture of the nineteenth-century bourgeoisie and a modernity that embraces the possibilities and dangers of technology. In terms of the cultural memory of World War I, the advantages of Jünger's position are clear: if the war is reconfigured in terms of an epochal struggle, the damage to Germany's national interests that resulted from the Treaty of Versailles can be not only downplayed, but elided altogether. The war can thus be commemorated not as a national disaster, but as a necessary moment in the transition to modernity.

## Conclusion

This account of photography and the First World War cannot, of course, be exhaustive; photography certainly played other significant roles, including (among other things) in cultures of exhibition and display, the reinforcement of sentimental ties at times of separation and familial stress, the inter-war craze for spirit photography, the use of photographs in the discourse of post-war reconstruction, and contemporary use of aerial photographs to plot the history of the front using GIS technology. What this chapter highlights, though, is how many of the issues raised by First World War photography remain alive in the early twenty-first century: censorship and embedded photojournalists; the nature and role of soldier photography; atrocity photography and the claims of justice; the visual technologies of warfare; and the primarily visual construction of the cultural memory of conflict.

## Notes

1. Martin Jay, *Downcast Eyes: The Denigration of Vision in Twentieth-Century French Thought* (Berkeley and Los Angeles: University of California Press, 1993), p. 211.
2. Paul Virilio, *War and Cinema: The Logistics of Perception*, trans. Patrick Camiller (London: Verso, 1989), pp. 5–6.
3. Ibid., pp. 14–15, 70.
4. Bernd Hüppauf, 'Experiences of Modern Warfare and the Crisis of Representation', *New German Critique*, 59 (1993), 41–76.
5. Gerhard Paul, *Krieg der Bilder, Bilder des Krieges: Die Visualisierung des modernen Krieges* (Paderborn: Schöningh; Munich: Fink, 2004), pp. 79–115.
6. A rich source of air crash photography, which contains images of highly diverse provenance, is the University of Leeds's Liddle Collection. See, for example, LIDDLE/WWI/AIR/371, Items 9, 12d, 23, 36, 42, 48, and LIDDLE/WWI/AIR/167. A prominent German example of the same phenomenon is the photographic collection of the officer-turned-writer Ernst Jünger: Jünger, Ernst, 1. WK; DLA-Marbach B 1997.G 0395.
7. LIDDLE/WWI/ANZAC/NZ Item 3 (Album 11.5 × 15.5 cm).
8. LIDDLE/WWI/ANZAC/NZ Item 5 (Album 13.5 × 11 cm).
9. LIDDLE/WWI/AIR/371 Item 45: Album of Flight Sergeant E. Vousden, 56 Squadron (20 × 17 cm).

10. See, for example, Paul, *Krieg der Bilder, Bilder des Krieges*, pp. 103–4; M. L. Sanders and Philip M. Taylor, *British Propaganda during the First World War* (London: Macmillan, 1983), p. 2; Susan L. Carruthers, *The Media at War* (Basingstoke: Palgrave Macmillan, 2000), pp. 55–6; David Welch, 'Mobilizing the Masses: The Organization of German Propaganda during World War One', in Mike Connelly and David Welch (eds), *War and the Media: Reportage and Propaganda, 1900–2003* (London: I. B. Tauris, 2005), pp. 19–46 (p. 19); Alan Kramer, *Dynamic of Destruction: Culture and Mass Killing in the First World War* (Oxford: Oxford University Press, 2010), p. 4.
11. In addition to the works on propaganda cited above, see Jane Carmichael, *First World War Photographers* (London: Routledge, 1989), pp. 14–15, 36, 120, 131; Laurent Veray, 'Montrer la guerre: La photographie et le cinématographe', in Jean-Jacques Becker et al. (eds), *Guerre et cultures 1914–1918* (Paris: Armand Colin, 1994), pp. 229–38; Susan D. Moeller, *Shooting War: Photography and the American Experience of Combat* (New York: Basic Books, 1989), pp. 111–25; Christine Brocks, '"Unser Schild muss rein bleiben!" Deutsche Bildzensur und -propaganda im Ersten Weltkrieg', *Militärgeschichtliche Zeitschrift*, 67 (2008), 25–51.
12. Anton Holzer, *Die andere Front: Fotografie und Propaganda im Ersten Weltkrieg* (Darmstadt: Primus Verlag, 2007), p. 89; Carruthers, *The Media at War*, pp. 58, 63; Moeller, *Shooting War*, pp. 114–15.
13. This trend was particularly marked in France; see Veray, 'Montrer la guerre', p. 230.
14. Welch, 'Mobilizing the Masses', pp. 21–2.
15. Sanders and Taylor, *British Propaganda*, pp. 120–1.
16. Brocks, '"Unser Schild muss rein bleiben!"', pp. 36–7.
17. Ibid., pp. 41–2.
18. Katharina Menzel, '"Frauen helfen siegen": Frauenarbeit in der Fotopropaganda des Ersten und Zweiten Weltkriegs', in Anton Holzer (ed.), *Mit der Kamera bewaffnet: Krieg und Fotografie* (Marburg: Jonas, 2003), pp. 71–96.
19. *Women's War Work in Maintaining the Industries and Export Trade of the United Kingdom: Information Officially Compiled for the Use of Recruiting Officers, Military Representatives and Tribunals* (London: HMSO, 1916).
20. Deborah Thom, *Nice Girls and Rude Girls: Women Workers in World War I* (London: I. B. Tauris, 1998), pp. 82–3.
21. Ibid., pp. 88–9.
22. *Women's War Work*, p. 15.
23. Ibid., p. 6. Two images, one of a farmer's daughter, one of a pork butcher's wife and daughters, do indeed purport to show women carrying on the family business in the men's absence (ibid., pp. 42, 56).
24. Ibid., p. 7.
25. As noted by Katharina Menzel in '"Frauen helfen siegen"', p. 75.
26. *Women's War Work*, pp. 42–5.
27. Thom notes the tendency for pre-war images of women's work to be set in small workrooms rather than the factory floor (*Nice Girls and Rude Girls*, p. 86).
28. *Women's War Work*, pp. 57, 66, 62.
29. Ibid., pp. 42, 44, 49, 57, 68, 76, 77. Thom reproduces a striking counter-example that shows a young woman and an old man in a rope works, the woman's superior strength and competence clearly legible. Such images were not used in propaganda. See Thom, *Nice Girls and Rude Girls*, image section (unpaginated).
30. Anon., 'The Photographic Eye and Memory of the Military Airman', *Scientific American*, 119 (1918), 61.
31. For full details on the organisation of Allied and German aerial photography, see, respectively, Terence J. Finnegan, *Shooting the Front: Allied Aerial Reconnaissance in the First World War* (Stroud: Spellmount, 2014), and Helmut Jäger, *Erkundung mit der Kamera:*

*Die Entwicklung der Photographie zur Waffe und ihr Einsatz im 1. Weltkrieg* (Munich: Venorion VKA, 2007).

32. Finnegan, *Shooting the Front*, pp. 266–81; Jäger, *Erkundung mit der Kamera*, pp. 269–305.
33. Finnegan, *Shooting the Front*, p. 108.
34. See Finnegan, *Shooting the Front*, p. 131; Jäger, *Erkundung mit der Kamera*, pp. 205–6.
35. Jäger, *Erkundung mit der Kamera*, pp. 136–43. Good results with film were hard to obtain at altitude because of the difficulty of holding the film completely flat as well as film's sensitivity to electrical discharges prevalent in the upper atmosphere. Despite the best efforts of Kodak entrepreneur George Eastman, the Allies were reluctant to adopt film rather than glass-plate negatives (Finnegan, *Shooting the Front*, pp. 258–9).
36. Finnegan, *Shooting the Front*, p. 132.
37. See Hanna Rose Shell, *Hide and Seek: Camouflage, Photography, and the Media of Reconnaissance* (New York: Zone Books, 2012), p. 14.
38. Paul K. Saint-Amour, 'Modernist Reconnaissance', *Modernism/Modernity*, 10 (2003), 349–80 (355).
39. Solomon J. Solomon, *Visual Deception in Warfare*, April 1916, Public Record Office AIR1/530/16/12/89, p. 1, cited in Shell, *Hide and Seek*, p. 104.
40. Finnegan, *Shooting the Front*, pp. 232–3.
41. Ibid., p. 98; Jäger, *Erkundung mit der Kamera*, p. 167; Shell, *Hide and Seek*, p. 101.
42. Saint-Amour, 'Modernist Reconnaissance', p. 360.
43. See Jäger, *Erkundung mit der Kamera*, pp. 199–200; Holzer, *Die andere Front*, p. 136.
44. John Tagg, *The Burden of Representation: Essays on Photographies and Histories* (Basingstoke: Palgrave Macmillan, 1988), p. 76.
45. Arsène Alexandre, *Les Monuments français détruits par l'Allemagne. Enquête entreprise par ordre de M. Albert Dalimier, sous secrétaire d'état des beaux-arts* (Paris: Berger-Levrault, 1918).
46. R. A. Reiss, *Report upon the Atrocities Committed by the Austro-Hungarian Army during the First Invasion of Serbia*, trans. F. S. Copeland (London: Simpkin, Marshall, Hamilton, Kent & Co., 1916).
47. R. A. Reiss, *La Photographie judiciaire* (Paris: Mendel, 1903).
48. Reiss, *Report*, photograph facing p. 2.
49. Ernst Friedrich (ed.), *Krieg dem Kriege!* (Berlin: Freie Welt, 1924); Ernst Jünger (ed.), *Das Antlitz des Weltkrieges: Fronterlebnisse deutscher Soldaten* (Berlin: Neufeld & Henius, 1930). For discussions of these and other German photo books, see Paul, *Krieg der Bilder, Bilder des Krieges*, pp. 133–42; Dora Apel, 'Cultural Battlegrounds: Weimar Photographic Narratives of War', *New German Critique*, 76 (1999), 49–84; and Thomas F. Schneider, 'Narrating the War in Pictures: German Photo Books on World War I and the Construction of Pictorial War Narrations', *Journal of War and Culture Studies*, 4 (2011), 31–49.
50. Some of the images used by Friedrich had been previously published – see Bernd Ulrich, '"Als wenn nichts geschehen wäre": Anmerkungen zur Behandlung der Kriegsopfer während des Ersten Weltkriegs', in Gerhard Hirschfeld, Gerd Krumeich and Irina Renz (eds), *'Keiner fühlt sich hier mehr als Mensch': Erlebnis und Wirkung des Ersten Weltkrieges* (Frankfurt am Main: Fischer, 1996), pp. 140–56 – and some were reused in an American pacifist publication, *The Horror of It*, in 1932. See John M. Kinder, 'Iconography of Injury: Encountering the Wounded Soldier's Body in American Poster Art and Photography of World War I', in Pearl James (ed.), *Picture This: World War I Posters and Visual Culture* (Lincoln: University of Nebraska Press, 2009), pp. 340–68. Photographic propaganda did not start with Friedrich, nor was it a purely German phenomenon.
51. Janina Struk notes that dead horses play a similar role in soldiers' snapshots: *Private Pictures: Soldiers' Inside View of War* (London: I. B. Tauris, 2011), p. 68.
52. Ernst Jünger, *Der Arbeiter: Herrschaft und Gestalt*, in *Sämtliche Werke*, vol. 8 (Stuttgart: Klett-Cotta, 1979), p. 61.

# 25

# The Imperial War Museum and the Material Culture of the First World War, 1917–2014

*Alys Cundy*

## Introduction

In the closing years of the First World War the 'afterlife' of the material culture of the war was hotly contested. The need to determine the appropriate fate of the artefacts of this unprecedented conflict was both pressingly felt and problematic.[1] There was a sense that the public would want and need some material record of the fighting, but the exact nature of this record, its composition and meaning, and the form and function of its display were uncertain. This chapter focuses on the management and mediation of this contested material culture, as seen through the prism of the Imperial War Museum (IWM). The IWM was established in the penultimate year of the First World War.[2] Its founders aimed to form a permanent material record of the conflict then still raging across the globe. As the officers of the IWM came to construct and display their collection they faced criticism from those hostile to the very concept of the institution.

In negotiating the challenges of collecting, preserving and exhibiting the objects associated with its foundational conflict, the IWM has acted as a microcosm of wider cultural understandings of the material culture of the First World War. In its collections and displays can be traced the central themes that ran through the British relationship to the physical evidence of the First World War in its aftermath: the contested nature of the artefacts of war, the perceived democratic character of the conflict and items associated with it, and a sense of union between the objects that survived the war and the bodies that did not. However, after the onset of the Second World War, the relationship of the IWM and of wider memorial culture to the artefacts of the First World War shifted. The themes introduced in the inter-war years, with their democratic appeal and focus on the elision of body and object, were replaced with a more historical, straightforwardly educational approach. Thus the material culture of 1914–18 within the museum's collections is now used primarily to illustrate themes established by historians and curators.

Material culture is a distinct cultural resource and output. Like more straightforwardly artistic or literary media, such as visual art, and fictional and non-fictional texts, physical objects are products of their time and cultural context. They are thus imbued with the perceptions, priorities and systems of value of those who created, interpreted and responded to them. Christopher Tilley suggests that

> The material object may be a powerful metaphorical medium through which people may reflect on their world in and through material practice. Through the artefact, layered and often contradictory sets of meaning can be conveyed simultaneously.[3]

However, whilst material objects are imbued with the same cultural significance as other forms, they also differ from them. Susan Pearce has described physical objects as 'independent of words' because of their three-dimensional existence in space. As such, she argues, 'we must see them and perhaps touch them to understand them'.[4] This tangibility and physical fixedness mean that material objects and the treatment of them offer a unique insight into cultural mentalities. Exploring the material culture of the First World War is, therefore, important to any analysis of how people responded to and made sense of the conflict. In addition, while it is the case that, as Tilley notes, 'certain material forms – in particular, houses and the layout of villages or tombs and mortuary practices or art' have been 'privileged' in being considered 'sites for the objectification of cultural meaning', attention must also be paid to more everyday material worlds.[5] This chapter thus explores the collection, preservation and display of the array of physical remnants associated with the First World War; not only overtly symbolic pieces such as commemorative icons or trench art, but also weaponry, munitions and the ephemera of the trenches.

Material culture is particularly valuable as a means of understanding the response to the First World War as that conflict engendered significant shifts in people's material worlds. For soldiers, the battlefronts consisted of a bewildering array of new materialities.[6] Eric Leed has explained how those fighting were compelled to learn 'to recognise realities that were most often termed "material," "technological," or "mechanical"'.[7] He argues that the texture of this material reality was entirely new and wholly unnerving. Thus, the physical experience of the battlefield

> meant not just an array of weapons and tools, but the organisation of material and men. This organisation – freed from the nexus of use and wont that had made it ideologically comprehensible before 1914 as a means of progress and a system for the improvement of the human condition – took on the qualities of an abstraction, a unified system of force.[8]

This new material experience had a lasting impact. Even after the war ended, men continued to talk 'about technology in a way that was quite different than the discussions of mechanisation before 1914'.[9]

After the war, what was left of this bewildering material experience remained potent. Nicholas Saunders's description of objects associated with conflict is especially true of the First World War. 'The objects of war are not anonymous weapons, scrap or ephemera,' he argues, 'but rather different kinds of matter that can be seen as embodying an individual's experience and attitudes, as well as cultural choices in the varied technologies of production.'[10] As a result, '[s]uch objects occupy a dynamic point of interplay between animate and inanimate worlds, inviting us to look beyond physical form and consider the hybrid and constantly renegotiated relationships between material culture and people.'[11] Those who did not fight were also confronted with new physical worlds. The high casualty rates of the conflict prompted a heightened material culture of loss. Hallam and Hockney describe the important role that '[m]ementoes, memorials, words and artefacts' play in mediating grief. Such objects can, they note, 'be understood as external cultural forms functioning to sustain thoughts and images that are conceived as part of the internal states of living persons'.[12] This chapter draws on this understanding to analyse how people made sense of their war experience through things.

## Contested Culture

In a debate at the Museums Association annual conference of 1918, Henry Howorth, President-elect of the Association, warned against the establishment of war museums:

> A few years hence the generation that has this fearful thing in its dream-memory will be passed away, and you will come to another generation that will neither understand the weapons nor the machines that you show them. They are all ephemeral. You will have the galleries filled with objects of not the slightest interest to the people.[13]

Howorth's statement reveals that in the closing years of the conflict any object that possessed a physical connection to the war was a complex and contested icon. Charles ffoulkes, the IWM's first curator and secretary, recognised the problematic nature of the museum's purpose. He noted in 1918 in the *Museums Journal*:

> It may be urged by a certain section of the public that there is no need for the preservation and exhibition of trophies reminiscent of warfare, which some consider to be merely a form of authorized and organized murder, and that museums should only record constructive efforts of mankind.[14]

ffoulkes's prediction of criticism was correct, as Howorth's warning was not the only objection among members of the Museums Association.[15] Cecil Smith, Director of the Victoria and Albert Museum, argued against 'collecting a hideous set of atrocities which, as the years went on, would become dusty and moth-eaten'.[16]

Nor was the controversy over the IWM's collection limited to museum professionals. The Imperial War Museum Bill faced opposition when it was read in the House of Commons in 1920. Naval officer and vocal Liberal back-bencher Joseph Kenworthy objected to the war museum on the grounds that it was now necessary to 'let people forget about the War'.[17] It was vital, he argued, that 'the glamour and ceremony of war' be kept out of 'the minds of the people of this country, especially the younger generation'. In this context, the IWM could be seen as a dangerous reminder. He ended with a plea that the country 'should forbid our children to have anything to do with the pomp and glamour and the bestiality of the late War, which has led to the death of millions of men' and refused 'to vote a penny of public money to commemorate such suicidal madness of civilisation as that which was shown in the late War'.[18] Kenworthy was joined in opposition of the Bill by the Spen Valley Labour MP Thomas Myers. Like Kenworthy, Myers was particularly concerned about the 'effect upon the young mind' which, faced with artefacts of war, may be seduced by 'all the barbarism of warfare when we ought to be proclaiming the virtues of peace'.[19]

Some in the press also criticised the premise of a museum full of the material culture of war. The *Pall Mall and Globe* asked in 1922, 'What end is served by repetition of one machine-gun or minenwerfer after another, one steel helmet after another, merely because one was used at the Somme and the other in Flanders or elsewhere?', concluding, 'It is all confusing and – could anything be more depressing?'[20] An ex-serviceman wrote to the *Middlesex County Times* in 1926 to express his own frustration at the existence of the IWM. Such an institution was, for former soldiers like himself, unnecessary:

> At present, I have a museum of my own which is of sufficient interest to me – some photographs, for instance, in my own brain – and the paradox is that I have to look upon them much against my will, and I would gladly give more than twelve pence to be shown the way out.[21]

Thus as the founders and staff of the IWM came to construct and display their collection, they were required to demonstrate the purpose and the importance not only of collecting the material remnants of a national trauma but of displaying these remnants to a public still recovering in that trauma's aftermath.

The same challenges faced those attempting to establish museums of the war in local communities. In 1917, C. Reginald Grundy, editor of the journal *Connoisseur*, proposed the establishment of a network of local war museums. His plan was ambitious: he proposed the creation of a war museum in every population centre, which would contain rolls of honour, records of local regiments, press cuttings, photographs, uniforms, weapons, medals, decorations, swords, mementoes, trophies, and relics from previous wars.[22] Some steps were taken to achieve Grundy's aim. War material was distributed to provincial museums by the War Trophies Committee, on the understanding that the national collection at the IWM would always have priority.[23] However, despite Grundy's best efforts, his campaign for local war museums never became the large-scale movement for which he hoped. Gaynor Kavanagh argues that this was a result of the difficulty of presenting material culture associated with the conflict as a means of marking the event.[24] 'Museums that memorialised the war through its own destructive hardware', she notes, 'could not find public support.'[25] Instead, 'cities, towns and villages commemorated their dead either through dignified war memorials erected in prominent positions, so that all would see and remember, or through community facilities such as parks, halls and recreation grounds.'[26]

Neither was Britain the only country to experience controversy over artefacts of the war. Jay Winter has recounted how collections of war exhibits in Germany were 'criticized powerfully by the pacifist activist Ernst Friedrich'.[27] Just as Kenworthy and Myers had feared that the IWM would inevitably glorify war for younger generations, Friedrich criticised the German collections on the grounds that they sanitised the conflict by failing to represent it faithfully. In response he set up an Anti-War Museum in Berlin, where he 'showed everything the patriotic collections omitted' and in 'displays of savage images of the mayhem caused by war [. . .] pointed out graphically the dangerous selectivity of the patriotic collections of wartime memorabilia, documents and books'.[28] In countries dealing with the aftermath of a brutal conflict, its physical traces were deemed to be potentially dangerous and volatile reminders.

## Popular Appeal

In the face of such volatility the IWM authorities sought to establish the value of the objects within its collections. In doing so they translated aspects of the wider cultural climate of the First World War into the treatment of its material culture. Fundamental to this translation was an emphasis on popular appeal. The IWM was founded and opened at a time when all of its potential audience possessed personal war memories. The museum appealed to these memories by claiming to provide a physical site for their public validation. In seeking to understand why the IWM authorities emphasised their unique popular appeal it is important to note how the war museum differed from its predecessors. Before the foundation of the IWM the principal national collections of military material were restricted to weaponry or were associated with particular services or regiments.[29] The Royal Armouries had been housed in the Tower of London since the seventeenth century.[30] King George III had established the Museum of Artillery in 1778, and the Royal United Service Institution had been housed in Banqueting House in Whitehall since 1860.[31] The first British regimental museum was the Royal Engineers Museum, established in 1875.[32] All these institutions were limited in the access they gave to the general public. Furthermore, Peter Thwaites has argued that the focus and content of these collections were similarly limited.[33] These institutions were intended solely to 'record the bravery and hardship endured' by the members of a specific military community. Thus the objects collected were symbolic and heroic, rather than 'ugly, mundane or ordinary'.[34]

The IWM's founders sought to differentiate themselves from these more restricted collections by presenting the museum as a place where those who had experienced the war in any capacity could easily visit and see themselves represented. One of the earliest pieces of publicity material explained the special value of the newly founded institution: 'As the War has directly or indirectly touched nearly every family in the Empire, the Imperial War Museum should have a more intimate personal interest to the individual than any museum that has ever been contemplated.'[35] The same sentiment was echoed in a speech by Alfred Mond, the museum's first chairman, at its public opening in June 1920:

> It is hoped to make it so complete that every individual, man or woman, sailor, soldier, airman or civilian who contributed, however obscurely, to the final result, may be able to find in these galleries an example of an illustration of the sacrifice he made or the work he did, and in the archives some record of it.[36]

The IWM, its authorities argued, was meaningful to everyone in the country and the Empire.

This perceived universal appeal drove the choice of building to house the museum's first semi-permanent displays. Initially, the Tower of London was considered as a possible site.[37] Diana Condell has argued that the decision not to use the Tower was based at least in part on the realisation that

> the historical remoteness of the existing collections in the Tower ill-fitted it to be the home of an institution devoted to a contemporary event, the momentous nature of which had such a profound effect upon every section of the population.[38]

It was felt by the founders that '[t]he Tower exemplified the distant past' whereas 'the Museum was of the present'.[39] The IWM's first semi-permanent home was instead the Crystal Palace, a public recreational venue best known for its regular Handel festivals and associated with the hugely popular Great Exhibition of 1851 (Figure 25.1).[40]

In order to live up to their democratic rhetoric, the IWM's authorities collected and displayed a large number of familiar, even homely, objects of human scale and significance. These included personal equipment, as well as the material ephemera of life on the battle and home fronts (Figures 25.2 and 25.3). Ian Hay, in an article on the museum soon after it opened to the public at Crystal Palace in 1920, described such 'humbler exhibits' as 'trench-tools, trench-signs, trench-weapons, trench literature' displayed in galleries whose tone was 'less grim, more domestic, more characteristically happy-go-lucky'.[41] The inclusion of such objects continued into the 1920s. When the galleries relocated to South Kensington, a reporter for *Naval and Military Record* noted in particular his appreciation for the display of all 'the little things which meant so much to the sailor and soldier', adding that even the 'battered bully-beef' had 'not been forgotten'.[42] The *Western Morning News and Mercury* also praised the museum's collection of 'trench relics' which appeared to have 'been selected with a dramatic sense of what the war meant to the soldier'.[43]

Figure 25.1 The IWM's display at Crystal Palace 1920–4. © IWM (Q 31451). Reproduced courtesy of the Imperial War Museum.

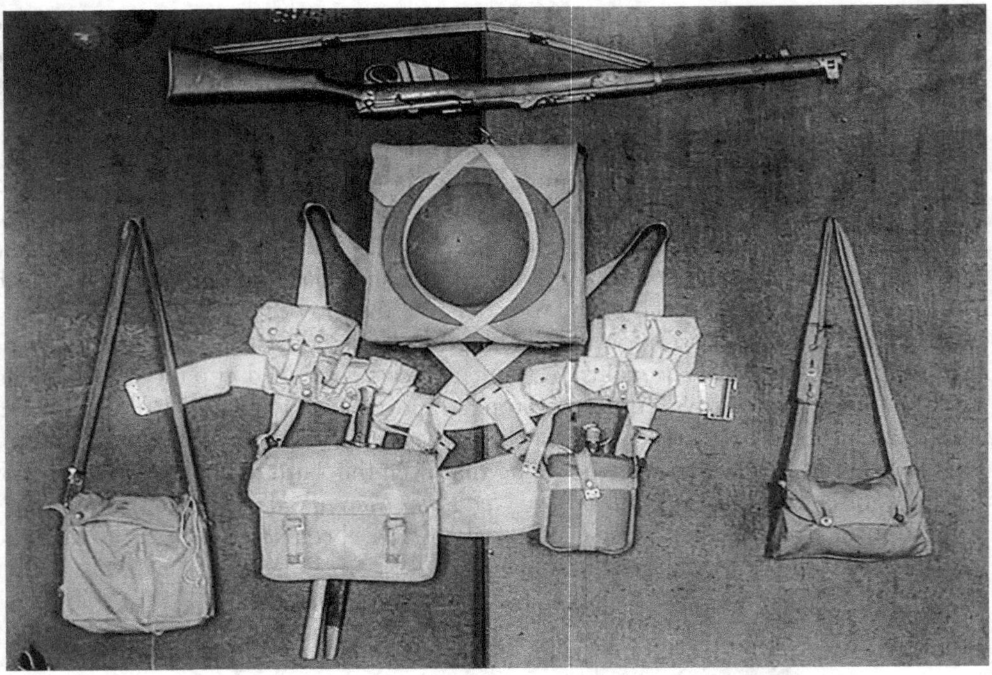

Figure 25.2 A soldier's personal equipment on display at Crystal Palace. © IWM (Q 30217). Reproduced courtesy of the Imperial War Museum.

Figure 25.3 Soldiers' charms, part of the IWM's collections on display at Crystal Palace. © IWM (Q 30177). Reproduced courtesy of the Imperial War Museum.

The IWM's presentation of itself as a popular collection was in tune with the wider discourse of the war and inter-war years. The mass nature of mobilisation meant the First World War was the first modern conflict to touch the lives of the whole population on an unprecedented scale. This meant that 'people were well informed about this war and wanted to know even more'.[44] The impact of the war on everyone in the country contributed to a widespread commitment that it be publicly marked. 'Regardless of the perspective taken of the war,' Kavanagh argues, it was accepted that 'it was a profound human experience and deserved an adequate and full record'.[45] This impulse to mark the universal nature of the fighting and its losses was reflected in the material culture of memorialisation. Alex King has described the democratic tone of commemorative projects in this period. The symbolic centre of many of the local memorials was the 'ordinary' soldier. A significant consequence of this, King notes, was the development of the practice of listing the dead just by name and not rank on these memorials. The implication was that all who had been involved in the conflict, in whatever capacity and of whatever status, had fulfilled their moral purpose and were thus worthy of valorisation. The dead were celebrated precisely for, not in spite of, 'their ordinariness'.[46] This democratisation of memorialisation extended to those who had not fought, but who nevertheless had contributed to the war effort.[47] By claiming to represent the war experience of all who had lived through the war, the IWM's authorities positioned the museum within this inclusive memorial context.

The far-reaching impact of the conflict also prompted other collections of war material. The inter-war period saw a marked growth in the number of regimental museums.[48] This was a result, Thwaites has argued, of the fact that by '1920 the vast majority of civilians had either first-hand experience of military service or had had members of their family in the armed forces'. Furthermore, these 'same armed forces had just played a major role in winning the greatest war the world had ever seen'.[49] As a result, 'there was often now an obvious bond of affection between the civilian population and their local regiments.'[50] In response, the number of regimental collections or museums grew from fourteen in the 1920s to fifty in the 1930s.[51] In addition, Britain shared this popular impulse with war collections in other Commonwealth countries. It was a characteristic particularly in evidence at the Australian War Memorial, a similar institution to the IWM, established during the war itself.[52] Tony Bennett has noted the democratic rhetoric and attention to the ordinary soldier embedded in the displays at the Memorial.[53] The Australian institution, he argues, 'genuinely did go further than its European counterparts in the respect that a demotic rhetoric provides the governing principle of its displays rather than being present merely interstitially'.[54] It was, he explains, 'there in the dioramas; in the listing of names alphabetically, without distinction of rank, in the Roll of Honour', as well as in 'the display of the incidental aspects of daily life in the trenches – the improvised cricket bats and bookmakers' plates through which life was normalised and made bearable'.[55]

## Objects: Bodies: Landscapes

The IWM may have reflected a universal conflict but it also related to its audience on a more intimate scale. The museum's treatment of its collections employed an elision of war objects with the war dead that mirrored wider memorial culture. Saunders writes of the diverse ways in which soldiers and civilians made sense and use of objects associated with the war, both during and after the conflict. One of the most significant of these was the practice of souvenir collecting and keeping, and the related trend for art made from the ephemera of the trenches.[56] Soldiers acquired and kept such ephemera as a physical reminder of their lives in wartime. Such objects functioned, writes Saunders, as 'narratives of the war experience inscribed in three dimensions'.[57] Furthermore, Fabio Gygi's work on war objects as relics has revealed how soldiers translated the material traces of their war experience into something that was 'both profane and potentially transcendent'.[58] This treatment of objects during the First World War reflected a practice that had been occurring in a regimental context for centuries. Thwaites describes the long tradition of regimental 'relics', consisting of objects that embodied the 'religious experience of the community', in this case the military regiment.[59] The mass mobilisation of men during the First World War made this regimental practice relevant to a much larger body of people.

It was not, however, just soldiers who placed importance on the artefacts of war. For the bereaved, too, material culture offered a means of establishing a connection with their loved ones and their wartime lives. Many of those who travelled to the former battlefields of the Western front returned with tangible reminders of their visit. Saunders has outlined the value placed on such objects. 'These items', he argues, 'help[ed] authenticate the pilgrimage experience and enabled pilgrims to take home a tangible link with the dead.'[60] In addition, once placed in the 'domestic space' of the home, such objects 'became an integral part of the house-worlds of their owners, reordering the symbolic terrain of memory'.[61] They were able to do so by acting as 'a constant reminder of missing loved ones – a presence of absence'.[62] In this capacity souvenirs stood in for the dead, whose own physical remains had not been returned to Britain.[63] The result was that, by acquiring and preserving '[d]ecorated shells on a mantelpiece, a bullet letter-opener on a desk or a shell dinner gong sounded at meal times', the bereaved engaged in an act of transference, 'where the memory of the body [was] replaced by the memory of the object'.[64]

There is evidence to suggest that the IWM intended to serve on a public scale the function that souvenirs did at a domestic level. Mond gestured towards the function of physical objects as a stand-in for missing bodies in his address on 9 June 1920. The museum, he declared, had endeavoured to select objects 'to which a definite honourable history can be attached' in order that these exhibits may 'serve as memorials of the heroic men who served on the field of battle and too often laid down their lives beside them'.[65] The exhibits, this speech suggested, had been present at the moment of death and thus body and object had become symbolically intertwined. Thus, Gabriel Koureas argues, the objects within the museum acted as 'a personification of the dead men as well as a vehicle for the memories of the survivors'.[66]

This is demonstrated by a letter to the IWM from a former naval officer of HMS *Chester*, in which the author requested to view and take a photograph of the naval gun at which his colleague, Jack Cornwell, had died. He went on to explain the particular value of the *Chester* gun:

> This gun as you know was the one which Jack Cornwell served & as I was his chum, was on the same gun & wounded by the same shell as he was [. . .] You will understand how much I should prize such a photo not only for the gun itself but for the memory of my dead chum.[67]

For this correspondent, the naval gun was more than itself. It had been transformed by its physical connection to the death of his fellow sailor into a 'War Relic'.[68] The gun in the museum replaced the dead friend just as the decorated shell-case replaced the dead husband or father in the home.

The IWM also bore a close connection to another form of inter-war material culture: battlefield landscapes. Such landscapes, like the objects of war, had an intimate relationship with the wartime past and its dead. The sites of the former fighting fronts possessed what David Lloyd has identified as a 'special relationship with the dead and with the memory of the war', whereby 'the men's sacrifice altered [that] on which they had shed their blood; they had made it sacred'.[69] The years after the Armistice saw a wave of people visiting these sacred sites and the cemeteries erected on them.[70] Correspondence between veterans' groups and the museum suggests that the IWM was perceived as a site of remembrance within this wider context. In a letter of June 1922, Colonel Heath of the British Legion wrote to ffoulkes in response to proposals for a Legion event at the museum. A visit to the museum, Heath felt, 'may easily be worked up into something in the nature of a Pilgrimage in connection, as you suggest, with Armistice Day'.[71] Furthermore, he declared that that IWM's collection was 'one of the most inspiring sights that I have seen for many a day, and I feel is one that should be seen by everyone in this country'.[72] Numerous local groups of the British Legion, as well as a delegation from the Ypres League, did make visits to the museum during the inter-war period.[73] In 1936 the museum's director, L. R. Bradley, made arrangements for groups from local British Legion divisions to visit the museum out of hours, during which time they were given guided tours,[74] and an article in the *British Legion Journal* in October of the same year predicted that the museum in its new home at Lambeth Road 'would assuredly be a popular pilgrimage'.[75]

## After the Inter-War Period

The inter-war period was a distinct moment in the understanding and treatment of the material culture of the First World War. This moment was reflected in the IWM. The onset of the Second World War profoundly altered the IWM's institutional purpose and its relationship to its First World War artefacts. The passing of time brought with it a crystallisation of public memory into what Samuel Hynes has referred to as 'catch-phrase identifiers: the Old Men, the Big Words, the Turning Point, Disenchantment – identities they still retain'.[76] Temporal distance also meant that fewer and fewer people had personal memories of the earlier global conflict. The impact of this change can be seen within the IWM's approach to its collections. When the IWM reopened in 1946, after being closed for most of the Second World War, the collections associated with 1914–18 were largely absent from the displays. The introduction of a new conflict, and wartime damage to the museum's buildings at Lambeth Road, resulted in much of the First World War collection being placed in storage or being allocated for disposal.[77]

When the First World War did return to the displays it was often in the form of comparison with the later conflict. As director, Bradley proposed 'comparison and contrast' as the 'general idea' of the post-1939 IWM.[78] He repeated this view to the *Sunday Express* in 1945, when he confirmed that while '[t]he 1914–18 war [would] not take a back stand', the 'two wars [would] be compared'.[79] In the galleries comparison appeared in a number of displays. These included a 'model showing the various branches of Civil Defence at their tasks after an air-raid incident at night, based mainly on the fire-bomb raid on London in December 1940', which was described as displayed by 'way of contrast with 1914–1918 models' in the Civil Defence gallery. Another example was the 'collection of miniature models of ships which illustrate the changes and variations in external appearance of ships of the navies and merchant navies of the world during the two World Wars'.[80] Basing the post-1945 representation of the First World War on comparison reflected wider cultural practices. Victoria Stewart has argued that in the literature of the Second World War the same process can be observed. In such writing, the war of 1914–18 was 'used as a means of attempting to grasp the import of a new, and in many respects very different, war', with the 'tension between difference and sameness' being noticeable and 'important'.[81]

In more recent decades, the passing of time and of the war generation has resulted in an interpretation of the material culture of the First World War that is very different from that of the 1920s and 1930s. No longer layered with perceptions of universality and of the elision of object and body, the objects have been used as three-dimensional representations of history. This was given particular emphasis by Noble Frankland, Director-General of the IWM from 1960 to 1982. From the outset, he made it clear to the staff that the collections, including those of the First World War, were to be interpreted according to their general historical relevance, rather than their specific individual significance. Thus he wrote in an exhibition planning note soon after his arrival that the main public galleries were to be 'concerned as far as possible to show the weapons themselves in chronological sequence 1914–45'. Within this scheme, '[s]ouvenirs could be included but not <u>as such</u>. Labels can point to souvenir interest but incidentally.'[82]

This revised understanding of the value of First World War material culture can be observed in the fate of one particular field gun. The gun served by 'L' Battery during the fighting at Néry in 1914 had been one of the centrepieces of the IWM in the inter-war period.[83] It had been treated as a commemorative icon, with an annual wreath-laying ceremony taking place on the September anniversary of the fighting.[84] However, by the mid-1960s this object was no longer integral to the IWM's perception of the value of First World War artefacts. A suggested exchange of material with the Royal Artillery Institution at Woolwich in 1966 led to the IWM considering the significance of the exhibit. In response to the Royal Artillery's request, Peter Simkins, Keeper of the Department of Exhibits, could 'see no reason to oppose [. . .] on principle' giving them the gun of 'L' Battery.[85] Whilst the museum would be losing one of its better-known objects, it would be 'obtaining new and fairly spectacular exhibits'. Furthermore, he thought, the absence of one of the field guns 'would not destroy our present display too much' and the '13-pdrs. have been in the Museum for over 40 years, and there is something to be said for rotations of exhibits of this kind'.[86] The result was that the 'Néry gun' was transferred on what was referred to as 'Permanent Loan' from the IWM to the Royal Artillery Institution.

By the time of the major redevelopment of the museum in 1989 the First World War had been explicitly condensed to certain key elements. The exhibition team behind the historical galleries, in which the First World War formed one section alongside the Second World War and post-1945 conflicts, established the themes and events that, for them, constituted the 1914–18 conflict.[87] Within this scheme, objects were selected for display according to the extent to which they illustrated these themes.[88] In the new First World War galleries created in 2014 the same principle has been applied. The First World War displays show the IWM continuing to work to its historical educational remit, a remit that drives the use of material culture. Roger Mann, one of the designers from the firm, Casson Mann, that created the galleries, noted that there were '2,000 deliberately chosen objects' in the exhibition and 'each one [was] "nested" into a carefully considered theme'.[89] James Taylor, the senior IWM curator for the galleries, explained to *The Guardian* that the exhibition was intended to give 'a shape and context' to a conflict that had just 'fallen from living memory'.[90] It was thus essential that the galleries did not 'use the objects as relics but ma[de] them speak'.[91] For the curators in the inter-war years, the value of the material objects in their collections stemmed from their status as 'relics'. By 2014 the IWM's curators felt that such an understanding of the artefacts of the First World War was insufficient for a museum whose purpose was to engage audiences with historical questions rather than personal memories.

The shift away from interpreting war objects as popular relics has reflected wider cultural shifts since the 1940s. Deborah Marshall argues that, while symbols and rituals associated with remembrance of 1914–18 have remained active, material heritage has had a more mixed fate.[92] While large numbers of people elect to wear red poppies during the period around Armistice Day, physical war memorials themselves often become invisible.[93] Furthermore, Marshall notes, the meaning of such memorials can be lost to audiences who no longer possess the same personal experience or knowledge of the First World War that the memorials' creators took for granted.[94] Thwaites has also noted that the British public's familiarity with the military, its traditions and its materiality has declined in the decades after 1918.[95] Particularly since the reorganisations of the army in the late 1950s and 1960s, which saw reductions in the number of regiments, the link between local communities and their military units has been diminishing.[96] This has threatened the resources and the funding of regimental museums. It has also prompted a different approach from such museums, which have in recent decades adopted interpretative strategies based to a greater extent on social and historical context rather than purely object-based display.[97] The IWM's focus on placing its collections within the explanatory framework of historical themes reflects the same impulse to engage with audiences no longer familiar with war history and the military.

## Conclusion

Exploring the history of the IWM can tell us much about how the material culture of the First World War was understood and used during and in the decades after the conflict. In turn, placing the IWM within its cultural context, both national and international, helps to illuminate the attitudes and approaches of its founders and staff. What the two aspects taken together reveal is a society ambivalent about the physical traces of the conflict. Such traces were understood to serve as tangible reminders. For the many who wanted to remember their war and their dead, these material prompts were a valuable externalisation of loss and a substitute for missing loved ones. However, for those like the Members of Parliament who spoke out against the Imperial War Museum Bill in 1920 and the soldier who objected to a physical museum when he had a gallery of horrors in his own mind, material objects associated with the war were best consigned to the past. According to this opinion, such objects were barriers to securing peace, whether political or psychological. Those who favoured preservation and display were largely successful because the universal reach of the conflict gave enough people enough of an investment in the material culture of the war to support its collection and public exhibition.

Over the decades since the 1920s and 1930s, the First World War has shifted in public understanding. With the diminution of living memory and the establishment of 'myths' and key images associated with the war, the understanding of the material culture of the conflict has been simplified. This has been reflected in the treatment of its collections by the IWM. Beginning with the introduction of comparison with objects of the Second World War and continuing with the establishment of history as the principle behind object display, education has taken the place of a value system that interpreted artefacts of the war as democratic totems of conflict and its losses. This shift in the IWM's treatment of the material culture of the First World War demonstrates the extent to which physical objects are subject to the same developments in interpretation as other artistic outputs. Whilst the material form remains largely the same, the ideas that this form is thought to embody change with shifts in cultural context and memory. The IWM offers an insight into these changes as they have been presented to the British public through material culture since 1917.

## Notes

1. I use the term 'artefacts' here to refer to movable objects originating from the war and its associated battle and home fronts. This definition encompasses both very large objects, such as artillery, as well as smaller-scale weaponry, military materials, such as maps and models, and personal belongings.
2. IWM, 'Minutes of the Meeting of the Imperial War Museum Committee', 29 November 1917, National War Museum Committee Minutes Mar 1917–Jun 1920, IWM Central Files.
3. Christopher Tilley, 'Objectification', in Chris Tilley, Webb Keane, Susanne Küchler, Mike Rowlands and Patricia Spyer (eds), *Handbook of Material Culture* (London: Sage, 2006), pp. 60–73 (p. 62).
4. Susan Pearce, *Museums, Objects, and Collections: A Cultural Study* (Washington, DC: Smithsonian Institution Press, 1992), p. 23. The centrality of tangibility to comprehension of material objects is called into question by digital museum projects. Initiatives such as the European Union-funded *Europeana 1914–1918* seek to make objects and archives widely accessible in digital form (Europeana Foundation, *Europeana Collections*, <http://www.europeana.eu/portal/> (last accessed 2 December 2016)). Initiatives such as these do

make collections available to those unable to view them in person. However, if Pearce is correct in considering physicality to be integral to the appreciation of material objects, then such projects must inevitably fail to capture an essential element of the potency of the collections uploaded to them. Nevertheless, digital projects have been a key element of First World War centenary projects. These have included *Europeana 1914–1918* and the IWM's own *Lives of the First World War*. For a consideration of this project in the context of the IWM's history see Alys Cundy, 'Thresholds of Memory: Representing Function through Space and Object at the Imperial War Museum, London, 1918–2014', *Museum History Journal*, 8.2 (2015), 247–68.

5. Tilley, 'Objectification', p. 70.
6. Nicholas Saunders, 'Material Culture and Conflict: The Great War, 1914–2003', in Saunders (ed.), *Matters of Conflict: Material Culture, Memory and the First World War* (London: Routledge, 2004), pp. 5–25.
7. Eric Leed, *No Man's Land: Combat and Identity in World War I* (Cambridge: Cambridge University Press, 1979), p. 29.
8. Ibid., p. 3.
9. Ibid.
10. Nicholas Saunders, 'Culture, Conflict and Materiality: The Social Lives of Great War Objects', in Bernard Finn and Barton C. Hacker (eds), *Materializing the Military* (London: NMSI Trading Ltd, 2005), pp. 77–94 (p. 78).
11. Ibid.
12. Elizabeth Hallam and Jenny Hockney, *Death, Memory and Material Culture* (Oxford: Berg, 2001), p. 4.
13. Henry Howorth, 'Discussion of the Papers', *Museums Journal*, 18.4 (1919), 68.
14. Charles ffoulkes, 'War Museums', *Museums Journal*, 18.4 (1919), 57–61 (57).
15. Howorth, 'Discussion of the Papers', p. 68.
16. Cecil Smith, 'Discussion', *Museums Journal*, 18.7 (1919), 109–24 (115).
17. *Hansard*, House of Commons Debate: Imperial War Museum Bill, 12 April 1920, vol. 127, column 1,467, <http://hansard.millbanksystems.com/commons/1920/apr/12/imperial-war-museum-bill#column_1465> (last accessed 2 December 2016).
18. Ibid., column 1,468.
19. Ibid.
20. Special Representative, 'Our Costly War Museum: Is It a Waste of Public Money and Without Present Utility? Suspension for 20 Years Urged', *Pall Mall and Globe*, 27 February 1922, IWM Documents Collection, EPH C I.W.M., Newscuttings, Nov. 1920–9.
21. W. R.,'Museums, Wars and Dodos', *Middlesex County Times*, 3 July 1926, IWM Documents Collection, EPH C I.W.M., Newscuttings, Nov. 1920–9.
22. See Gaynor Kavanagh, *Museums and the First World War: A Social History* (London: Leicester University Press, 1994).
23. Ibid., p. 107.
24. Ibid., p. 113.
25. Ibid.
26. Ibid.
27. Jay Winter, *Sites of Memory, Sites of Mourning: The Great War in European Cultural History* (Cambridge: Cambridge University Press, 1995), p. 81.
28. Ibid., pp. 81–2.
29. Peter Thwaites, *Presenting Arms: Museum Representation of British Military History, 1660–1900* (London: Leicester University Press, 1996), pp. 26–31.
30. Ibid.
31. Ibid.

32. Ibid.
33. Ibid.
34. Ibid., p. 26.
35. IWM, *The Imperial War Museum* (1917).
36. Alfred Mond, 'Chairman's Address', *Third Annual Report of the Imperial War Museum 1919–1920* (London: HMSO, 1920), pp. 2–3 (p. 3).
37. See Diana Condell, 'The Imperial War Museum 1917–1920: A Study of the Institution and its Presentation of the First World War', unpublished MPhil dissertation, Imperial War Museum, 1985.
38. Ibid., p. 30.
39. Ibid.
40. J. R. Piggott, *Palace of the People: The Crystal Palace at Sydenham 1854–1936* (London: Hurst and Company, 2004), p. 170.
41. Ian Hay, 'The Palace of Voices', *Daily Mail*, 8 June 1920, IWM Documents Collection, EPH C I.W.M., Newscuttings, March–Nov 1920.
42. Anon., 'Imperial War Museum: Features of the Reassembled Collection', *Naval and Military Record*, 19 November 1924, IWM Documents Collection, EPH C I.W.M., Newscuttings, Nov. 1920–9.
43. Anon., 'New Imperial War Museum', *Western Morning News and Mercury*, 11 November 1924, IWM Documents Collection, EPH C I.W.M., Newscuttings, Nov. 1920–9.
44. Thwaites, *Presenting Arms*, p. 32.
45. Kavanagh, *Museums and the First World War*, p. 171.
46. Alex King, *Memorials of the Great War in Britain* (Oxford: Berg, 1998), p. 184.
47. Ibid., p. 198.
48. Thwaites, *Presenting Arms*, p. 35.
49. Ibid., p. 42.
50. Ibid.
51. Kavanagh, *Museums and the First World War*, p. 157.
52. Tony Bennett, *The Birth of the Museum: History, Theory, Politics* (London: Routledge, 1995), p. 139.
53. Ibid.
54. Ibid.
55. Ibid.
56. Saunders, 'Culture, Conflict and Materiality', p. 89.
57. Ibid., p. 81.
58. Fabio Gygi, 'Shattered Experiences – Recycled Relics: Strategies of Representation and the Legacy of the Great War', in Saunders (ed.), *Matters of Conflict*, pp. 72–89 (p. 87).
59. Thwaites, *Presenting Arms*, pp. 14–16.
60. Saunders, 'Culture, Conflict and Materiality', p. 84.
61. Ibid.
62. Ibid.
63. Joanna Bourke has written of the disapproval that met the government's decision not to repatriate the remains of soldiers killed in action. Although 'equity and economy' made repatriation 'inappropriate', many objected to the state claiming possession over the bodies of dead loved ones, denying families the consolation of funeral practices. See *Dismembering the Male: Men's Bodies, Britain and the Great War* (London: Reaktion, 1996), p. 226.
64. Saunders, 'Culture, Conflict and Materiality', p. 84.
65. Mond, 'Chairman's Address', p. 3.
66. Gabriel Koureas, *Memory, Masculinity and National Identity in British Visual Culture, 1914–1930: A Study of Unconquerable Manhood* (Aldershot: Ashgate, 2007), p. 149.

67. Jack Robeson to Charles ffoulkes, 3 January 1923, EN1/1/GUN/29/1, IWM Central Files.
68. Ibid.
69. David Lloyd, *Battlefield Tourism: Pilgrimage and Commemoration in Britain, Australia and Canada 1919–1939* (Oxford: Berg, 1998), pp. 24–6, 117.
70. Ibid. For further discussion of the phenomenon of battlefield visiting see George Mosse, *Fallen Soldiers: Reshaping the Memory of the World Wars* (Oxford: Oxford University Press, 1990).
71. Colonel Heath (British Legion) to Charles ffoulkes, 12 June 1922, EN1/1/BLE/001, IWM Central Files.
72. Ibid.
73. For veterans' groups making arrangements to visit the museum see, for example, E. Robert (Secretary, British Legion, Darenth Branch) to IWM, 8 July 1928, EN1/1/MUS/22, IWM Central Files; H. Hardy (British Legion, Chelwood Gate and Danehill Branch) to IWM, 21 August 1931, EN1/1/MUS/22, IWM Central Files; J. Boughy (Hon Sec. London County Committee, Ypres League) to IWM, 8 April 1933, EN1/1/MUS/22, IWM Central Files; J. E. Stores (Salonika Re-Union Association, Redhill and Reigate Branch) to IWM, 17 May 1935, EN1/1/MUS/22, IWM Central Files.
74. L. R. Bradley to Captain Kingdon (British Legion, Metropolitan Area Chairman), 18 September 1936, EN1/1/BLE/001, IWM Central Files.
75. Denys Stanley, 'The War Museum Comes to Rest', *British Legion Journal*, October 1936, pp. 131–2.
76. Samuel Hynes, *A War Imagined: The First World War and English Culture* (London: Pimlico, 1992), Kindle edition, loc. 8,979.
77. IWM, 'Collection of Material Relating to the Present War', n.d., EN2/1/GOV/85, IWM Central Files.
78. Ibid.
79. Anon., 'Two Wars Will Be Compared', *Sunday Express*, 30 December 1945, IWM Documents Collection, EPH C I.W.M., Newscuttings, 1940–58.
80. IWM, *A Short Guide to the Imperial War Museum Lambeth Road, S.E.1 1914–1918 1939–1945*, 2nd edn (London: HMSO, 1956).
81. Victoria Stewart, 'The Last War: The Legacy of the First World War in 1940s British Fiction', in Jessica Meyer (ed.), *British Popular Culture and the First World War* (Leiden: Brill, 2008), pp. 259–81.
82. IWM, 'The New Exhibition', n.d., EN3/1/24/1, IWM Central Files.
83. Charles ffoulkes to A. H. Burne, 3 September 1922, EN1/1/GUN/22/1, IWM Central Files.
84. Correspondence between Officer Commanding, 'L' Battery and IWM, 1923–38, EN1/1/GUN/22/1–4, IWM Central Files.
85. Peter Simkins to Noble Frankland, 28 February 1966, EN3/2/3/003, IWM Central Files.
86. Ibid.
87. IWM, 'Imperial War Museum: Redevelopment Plan', n.d., EN4/41/CF/1/10/2, IWM Central Files.
88. Ibid.
89. Roger Mann, 'Shock: Bringing the First World War to Life at the Imperial War Museum', *The Guardian*, 17 July 2014, <http://www.theguardian.com/culture-professionals-network/culture-professionals-blog/2014/jul/17/first-world-war-imperial-war-museum> (last accessed 2 December 2016).
90. In interview with Stephen Moss. Stephen Moss, 'The Imperial War Museum: As Much a Relic as its Spitfires and Doodlebugs?', *The Guardian*, 10 July 2014, <http://www.theguardian.com/culture/2014/jul/10/imperial-war-museum-reopens-first-world-war> (last accessed 2 December 2016).

91. Ibid.
92. Deborah Marshall, 'Making Sense of Remembrance', *Social and Cultural Geography*, 5.1 (2004), 37–54.
93. Ibid., p. 40.
94. Ibid., pp. 39–40.
95. Thwaites, *Presenting Arms*, p. 49.
96. Ibid.
97. Ibid., pp. 55–7.

# 26

# The Evolution of First World War Computer Games

*Chris Kempshall*

The First World War has never appeared to be a natural setting for gaming or play. Why some conflicts and wars resonate more in a game session than others largely seems to be built around the relationship with the imagination of the player: can the player project themselves into the conflict in a sufficiently engaging way? Additionally, how suitable is the conflict for games and play to begin with? A conflict that is popularly known for both its brutality and its lack of movement does not immediately stand out as being an enjoyable experience for reproduction.[1] However, the First World War has had strong links to toys and games almost from the moment the conflict broke out. The famous First World War recruitment poster 'Daddy, what did YOU do in the Great War?' prominently features a young boy playing with toy soldiers at the feet of his father.[2] The war itself soon began to produce toys, and British children played with miniature tanks only six months after they first appeared in battle, while militarised versions of Monopoly were available in France, and toy artillery guns that fired peas were on sale in Germany.[3] In France wounded soldiers were given the opportunity to make toys for children. These *mutilé*-produced toys were highly popular during the war, but immediately began to lose a market after 1918.[4]

The desire to 'play' with conflicts is neither a new occurrence nor necessarily an implicit support for either the military or militarism. For as long as there have been soldiers there have been toys representing them. A stick is as good as a sword to a child with imagination, and the act of playing at soldiers has rarely been a focused consideration as to the realities of war. For video and computer games in particular, however, it is necessary for the war in question to be compelling enough for interaction. In regard to modern computer games the First World War has often been overshadowed by its more dynamic and morally satisfying successor. Since the 1990s the number of games which focus on the Second World War has dwarfed those of the First.[5] However, computer games set during the First World War largely pre-date those of the Second. The elements that appeared in these early First World War titles helped set the format for the future of war-focused computer games.

## Origins

The natural partner for games focused on the Second World War has always been cinema. Modern computer game portrayals of the war have incorporated the bravery and daring of films such as *Where Eagles Dare*, the desperate fighting of *A Bridge*

*Too Far* and *Battle of Britain*, and the brutal set piece action of *Saving Private Ryan* and *Enemy at the Gates*.[6] These sorts of films, spanning a time period from the 1960s to the modern day, have provided a body of reference that games have been able to mine for inspiration during what should probably now be termed the 'golden age' of Second World War games, running from the first *Medal of Honor* title in 1999 to the final *Call of Duty* instalment to focus on the conflict in 2008.[7] From this starting point Second World War games have been able to place the player in any number of situations and scenarios that, at the very least, feel familiar and in context with their players' understanding of the war, be it as a fighter pilot over the English Channel in 1940, an American infantry soldier storming Omaha Beach, or a Soviet sniper in the ruins of Stalingrad.

However, First World War games have never had as extensive a popular cinematic archive from which to draw their inspiration.[8] Instead, the First World War has always been far more literary in its popular associations. Today's social consciousness tends to process the war through the writings of particular war poets such as Wilfred Owen and Siegfried Sassoon and a select number of canonical memoirs and novels, both new and old. However, the very earliest First World War computer games owe a much greater debt to another type of popular writing – that is, pulp adventure books and comics.

The first recognisable First World War computer game was an arcade title known as *Red Baron* which debuted in 1980 and pre-dated by a year the first Second World War game, the original title in the Nazi occult series *Castle Wolfenstein*.[9] From 1980 to 1990 seven First World War games were created and all of them focused on aerial warfare. First World War flight simulator games have become a staple of the genre. Out of the forty-two games that Wackerfuss has identified as being focused on the conflict, twenty-four were piloting games, and nineteen of the fifty-eight identified by Chapman are similarly focused.[10]

This early preoccupation with the air war in these early computer games can be understood on multiple levels. Firstly, such tendencies must be considered alongside the limitations of technology and graphics of the time. The computing power of the 1980s and the modern day are worlds apart, particularly in regard to the difficulty of accurately representing human beings on screen. Flight simulator games neatly side-step this issue by replacing individual humans with individual planes. Whilst the original *Castle Wolfenstein* was able to render recognisable wire-frame human shapes just a year later, it could offer nothing comparable with the types of characters that appear in modern games. Nonetheless, the technology to attempt such characters did exist at the time of the original *Red Baron*, and as a result the decision to focus on flight simulator games suggests that it was not simply a decision based upon computing power, but rather one of editorial interest.

Flight simulator games set in the First World War tapped into an existing popular image of the chivalrous bravery of the First World War fighter pilot. Real-life pilots such as Manfred von Richthofen, the Red Baron himself, along with the fictional James Bigglesworth, the eponymous hero of the *Biggles* stories, combined to create a pseudo-world of airborne derring-do. To understand why this particular area of popular culture came to dominate early First World War computer games, it is necessary to understand both what these games portrayed and, equally, what they did not.

These games featured a much cleaner and loftier war than that which the infantry experienced. Above the mud and blood of the trenches, pilots came to embody airborne knights duelling for honour amongst the clouds. In fact, the durability of the chivalrous image of First World War pilots is readily notable in the names of various flight simulator games such as *Knights of the Sky* and *Wings of Glory*.[11] That this image is far removed from the reality of the air war becomes irrelevant; the myth is entertaining enough to become the focus for gameplay.[12] The air war becomes distant enough from the ground war to be almost an entirely separate conflict. It also lacks the last-ditch desperation of air combat in the Second World War and appears comparatively gentler and nobler for it. The wire-frame graphics of *Red Baron* moreover ensured that there was never any realistic impression that the offensive actions the player undertook would cause the death of a virtual pilot. Combat flight simulator games have always traded on the notion that the player fights against an opposition plane, an object, rather than an actual pilot.[13] The graphical limitations of *Red Baron* only added to this impression (Plate 9). Additionally, in comparison to the First World War, the relatively recent nature of the Second World War may well have made it more difficult to produce a computer game based around the latter conflict for fear of it proving distasteful. By the time that *Red Baron* was released, by contrast, sixty-two years had passed since the First World War Armistice. Indeed, by the 1980s the First World War was passing out of direct living memory in a manner which the Second was yet to do.

The foundations laid by *Red Baron* effectively set the rules for the First World War flight simulator genre for the following decades. The enduring simplicity of the game's design coupled with its playability meant it was often replicated. Improvements to graphics meant that it soon became possible to create actual representations of the inside of a plane's cockpit and, as a result, move the perspective of the game from third to first person. Whilst a seemingly simple innovation, this move allowed the player to take an extra step in the process of willing suspension of disbelief. By fighting in the cockpit itself, the games could become more immersive and increase the perceived skill of the player. Now navigating the skies and successfully shooting down an opponent became more difficult as the field of vision was restricted. However, later attempts to make these flight simulators easier to play, particularly in comparison with the actual difficulty level in piloting a First World War plane, were condemned as disrespectful to the memories of First World War pilots.[14]

Debates between playability and accurate reproduction of the conflict have caused an ongoing tension within historical games in general, but particularly those focused on the First World War. To an extent they represent the second reason that cinema has not been as strong an influence in the development of First World War games as it has on those focused on the Second. Whilst air combat novels provided the primary reference point for games such as *Red Baron*, it has been the relationship with table-top military games that has had the greatest influence on the other staple of First World War games, that is, those focused on strategy. The notion of the Western front as a strategic conundrum to be solved has helped create a cerebral aura around the First World War and assisted in the production of numerous strategy games set in the era both for the computer and for the table top. The originator of these in computer games is the 1992 title *History Line: 1914–1918* (Plate 10) which, much the same as *Red Baron*, helped construct many of the future rules for the genre.[15] For example, the use of hexagonal shapes within *History Line* to define each playing 'tile' has long been associated with table-top gaming as it increases the options of movement, attack and defence, and increases the tactical potential of any given situation. In computer games this system lives on in modern incarnations of the *Civilization* series, but is also present in such table-top games as *1914: Offensive à outrance* and more recently *The Great War*.[16] The enduring popularity of strategy games focused on the First World War can be largely rationalised through the power allotted to the player. Additionally, the turn-based nature of combat that grants each side a 'Movement' and a 'Combat' phase which alternate, allowing the player and computer to react to each other, continues to be a highly recognisable function of modern strategy gaming.

Whereas Second World War games have tended to place the player in the role of an individual soldier, until recently First World War games have avoided such a scenario. Much of this relates to common popular understandings of the different wars. With the Second World War popularly held as a war of democracy against an evil and uniform fascism, the existence and importance of individuality within the Allied armies gives the player an important role to inhabit. Individual men are seen to have the power to influence the outcome of the war. Conversely, the notion of the First World War being far more dangerous for the infantry means these men inhabit the role of 'Mass' rather than 'Individual' in a manner synonymous with popular constructions of First World War soldiers as cannon fodder.[17] Given that a role as an individual soldier was deemed unsuitable for engaging gameplay, the shift to strategy games gives the player the power to control directly all aspects of the military operation from above rather than below. The satisfaction the player gains from such a position is achieved through the act of 'solving' the military impasse in France and Belgium in more inventive, and by implication more 'correct', ways than the contemporary generals did. That achieving this requires the player to morph into the sort of heartless general who has become the caricature of First World War discussion is an uncomfortable reality not yet properly addressed.[18]

What is particularly interesting regarding First World War strategy games is their enduring popularity with players and, indeed, the demand for First World War versions of games from different sources or settings. The popular series of *Total War* strategy games has largely dominated the genre for the past decade. Whilst none of the official games released have interacted at all with the First World War, this did not stop members of the game's community from 'modding' the 2010 title *Napoleon: Total War* and changing virtually every aspect of the game to focus on the years 1914–18.[19] This *Great War Mod* is indicative of a wider movement at grass-roots levels to create engaging strategy games of the conflict.[20]

Similarly, the hugely popular table-top strategy game *Axis & Allies* has historically focused on the Second World War. However, following ongoing demand for a First World War version, one was finally released in 2013, entitled *Axis & Allies: WW1 1914*, to coincide with the lead-up to the centenary.[21] The principal designer of these games, Larry Harris Jr, had previously said he could not imagine a First World War version of his game being interesting enough to warrant creation.[22] Harris clearly revised his opinion, and popular demand has also sparked other

First World War modification to existing games. Another recent table-top game, *The Great War*, was a success through the crowdfunding website Kickstarter and was a variation on the existing format of 'Command and Colors', from the game's designer Richard Borg.[23] The power granted to players within strategy games thus seems only secondary to the power these players also now wield in creating the types of games they wish to experience. With this in mind it might seem likely that the First World War could become trapped in a repetitive cycle of flight simulators and strategy games. Whilst this has previously been true, recent developments in computer game depictions of the conflict have brought the war into new, and largely uncharted, territory.

## Modern Developments

The First World War of modern computer games has been changed not only by narrative and editorial developments, but also by technological ones. It is important to note that pre-existing genres and depictions of the First World War do not simply disappear. The war remains a fertile topic for strategy games and for flight simulators, but alongside these established formats, games developers have begun to explore the war in much more interesting and original ways. Some of these developments can be linked to evolutions in technology. For example, the emergence of 'Flash games', which are simple games that can be played on websites, has allowed developers to make easily contained games based around particular concepts or narratives. Many of these games follow already familiar trends such as the flight-based games *Dogfight* and *Dogfight 2*, which have a clear ancestry linking back to the original *Red Baron*.[24] Whilst the graphics have greatly improved and the action now takes place side-on rather than behind the plane, the basic details of the experience have not changed since the 1980s. The player still engages in combat with a variety of enemy fighters and Zeppelins within a self-contained war.

On first impressions, strategy games would not immediately appear suitable for this new technology. Games like *Napoleon: Total War*, upon which *The Great War Mod* is based, are renowned for their complexity and the heavy computing power they require to play. As a result, such games are never going to be fully compatible with lower specification websites. However, in a similar way to that in which *Dogfight* took the basics of *Red Baron* and moved it into a side-scrolling set-up, strategy games famed for their macro level of control were brought into this new era through a focus on the micromanagement of individual soldiers. What resulted were internet games such as *Warfare 1917* and the mobile phone and tablet-based *Trenches 2*.[25] These games adopt a similar side-on view to that found in the *Dogfight* titles, but instead engage the player in ground combat. Players fight out self-contained missions by ordering small groups of soldiers into battle in order to capture an enemy base. This then 'wins' the mission and advances the game. Additionally, like missions in *Dogfight*, these battles are almost entirely stripped of any connection to the actual events of the war. These games utilise the appearance of First World War military strategy and combat, but are devoid of its realities and locations.

It is this disconnection from the details of the war that helped produce a new wave of First World War computer games that dramatically changed the way players interact with the conflict. To understand the emergence of new First World War games it is first necessary to explore the different attempts to answer the wider question of what purpose these games serve. The first, and indeed best, place to begin this examination is with *Trench Warfare*, a game that used to be a feature of the BBC's education section on the First World War, before it was archived, but left accessible, in advance of the centenary. This game requires the player to fight their way through four missions, utilising three different tactics drawn from a wider pool, in order to complete each battle successfully. Despite this, *Trench Warfare* is peculiarly ahistorical in a manner which sees it confusing various technologies and tactics so that they do not work in keeping with the First World War context.

However, the main issues surrounding the game relate firstly to its purpose and secondly to its ending. Designed for school children, *Trench Warfare* is an educational game that cannot be won. The primary aim of the game is to highlight the 'futile' nature of First World War combat and then cast the player, in the role of general, as the villain of the piece for having attempted to win unwinnable battles. Some of these elements are certainly in keeping with particular strands of First World War historiography and, in gaming terms, strategy games rarely require the player to guard against the deaths of their own soldiers for anything approaching moral reasons.[26] As an educational tool, the actual purpose of *Trench Warfare* was to present a vision of the war that would be useful and engaging for children. Regardless of the actual politics behind the portrayal of the war, *Trench Warfare* serves a wider purpose than just entertainment, which is probably for the best because, in purely experiential terms, it is not much fun to play. Its ahistorical flaws and 'surprise' ending result in the game seeming unbalanced and faintly cruel. Its role in delivering an approved educational message, however, is something that has become a running trend in new First World War computer games.

In a move similar to that of the BBC, the Canadian War Museum incorporated an educational game into their website, entitled *Over the Top*.[27] This game allowed players to experience the war in the manner of a 'Choose Your Own Adventure' book, where every decision the player takes can lead to their untimely death. Again this is a game that uses the First World War as a vehicle to discuss the dangers of warfare and the risks that soldiers of the period faced. It is also far more playable and fun than *Trench Warfare* and possesses far smoother graphics and production. The dual package of playability and an educational message makes it a more successful proposition than *Trench Warfare* despite the fact that their general intentions are fairly similar.

What *Over the Top* demonstrates most of all, however, is that the First World War can be used as a narrative device, representing an opportunity for First World War games to depart significantly from the conventions of games revolving around the Second World War. Because of the more straightforward 'good versus evil' narrative that marks the Second World War in popular consciousness, the plots for World War II computer games have become increasingly repetitive. By contrast, the First World War already plays a different role, particularly within mainstream British society, but also in wider European understandings of the war, where the conflict is seen as a futile tragedy that, at best, cost the lives of millions for little gain and, at worst, heralded the rise of fascism.[28] As result the war has become a cautionary tale about the dangers of militarism and direct competition between powerful nations. A consequence of this societal understanding of the war as a universally futile tragedy is that it gives games designers a greater degree of freedom to tell engaging stories than they would now find within, for example, the Second World War.

The clearest proof of this is the 2014 game *Valiant Hearts: The Great War*.[29] This game represents the first cohesive narrative exploration of the war that is predominantly focused on particular characters. In most existing First World War games the players themselves have been either the primary protagonist or a basic substitute for different roles and individuals. *Valiant Hearts* creates a vision of the war that is largely transnational in its nature and scope and focuses on the lives of select characters and their experience of the First World War (Figure 26.1). The main 'cast' of *Valiant Hearts* is composed firstly of a French farmer named Emile who is called up for national service at the outbreak of war. Similarly, his son-in-law, Karl, is deported by the French and called up for military service by the Germans. An American soldier named Freddie, who seeks to avenge the death of his wife, is also a playable character, as is Anna, a Belgian medical student. The final playable character is Walt, a small dog who accompanies the various other characters through the game.

Whilst set in the period of the First World War, *Valiant Hearts* takes a very different approach to the topic than might be expected. It is, at heart, a puzzle-solving game

Figure 26.1 Cast of *Valiant Hearts: The Great War*, Ubisoft (2014), Emile, Anna, Freddie, Walt, Karl (left to right). 

that requires the player to move through fairly linear levels navigating the devastation caused by the war, saving the lives of civilians, and attempting to achieve military objectives. However, despite the setting and the military circumstances in which Emile, Karl and Freddie find themselves, this is not a game focused on combat. Rather it is the act of surviving the war that becomes the overriding objective. In this sense it is similar to *Over the Top*, where the player also had to navigate the dangers of the war in order to win the game by surviving. However, by placing the player in control of characters on both sides of the conflict, *Valiant Hearts* helps break down national barriers and creates an experience that is far more universal.

Whilst for part of the game there is a vaguely comedic 'villain' figure known as Baron Von Dorf, who was responsible for killing Freddie's wife on their wedding day, the real antagonist of the game is the war itself. To varying degrees each of the primary characters is attempting to get through the conflict with their lives and honour intact and return to their loved ones. Whilst this may at certain points lead them to partake in military operations, the game is carefully designed to ensure that the player never really undertakes any violent actions. Enemy planes and tanks can be blown up, but, similar to the trends initiated in *Red Baron*, these are always objects rather than vessels for people. The treatment of war machinery as devoid of human presence is in fact a concept that has spread from computer games to cooperative board games, too, with the release in 2015 of *The Grizzled*, a game where players work together as French soldiers to survive the war.[30]

In *Valiant Hearts* some enemy soldiers may be knocked unconscious, but the only actual act of targeted and deliberate killing occurs when Emile kills his own officer in retaliation for forcing French soldiers to attack at the Chemin des Dames. With this single exception, the characters go to great lengths to avoid inflicting death or violence on any other individuals they meet regardless of which 'side' they are supposed to be on. The war is seen as the disruption of normal relations between men, such as Emile and Karl, who are actually related and only set against each other by national forces. The desire to avoid combat and, where possible, simply to get through the war becomes the recurring thread of the game. It must be noted that, similar to other media portrayals of the First World War, this is a vision of the war that highlights the human cost and the destruction it produced. Similarly, the 2015 game *To Burn in Memory* (Orihaus) guides the player on a text-based narrative adventure through 'a city that never existed' to understand the lives of those in Europe in the days before the cataclysm of the First World War.

In this sense *Valiant Hearts* does stick to the narrative norms for the conflict within popular consciousness, eschewing an attempt to paint it in the same light as the Second World War. However, it is because of this embeddedness in the popular futility narrative that *Valiant Hearts* represents such an important shift in the portrayal of the First World War. Whilst it does not seek to reshape completely the overarching narrative of the war as a tragedy, it does present the tragedy as being equally spread across the various combatants and nations. There are no particular 'bad guys' (beyond Baron Von Dorf) in the game's representation of the war. All the characters are equally affected by the conflict and equally determined simply to survive. The notion of a Second World War game allowing the player to assume the role of a German soldier has been rendered largely unthinkable by the tight morality that binds popular perceptions of the conflict together.[31] However, no such obstruction prevents *Valiant Hearts* from portraying Karl as a fully rounded and relatable character who finds himself on the opposite side of an unfolding disaster. The different role the First World War plays in modern society as a parable of futility actually allows it room to be explored in a manner in which the Second World War cannot be.[32]

It is for a similar reason that the game *Verdun 1914–1918* is also interesting and important.[33] *Verdun* represents perhaps the biggest shift in the evolution of First World War gaming in that it places the player in the role of an individual infantry soldier in a war renowned for the vulnerability of such men. First Person Shooter (FPS) games have traditionally been the preserve of the Second World War genre because of the clearer sense of moral boundaries associated with this conflict, coupled with the idea that a single soldier can make a difference in the eventual outcome.[34] These notions have never really extended to include the First World War and, just as games creator Larry Harris Jr did not believe people would find a strategy board game of the First World War entertaining, it had long been felt that a First World War FPS would prove to be boring and frustrating as players would be killed within moments of going over the top.

*Verdun* benefits, once more, from significant technological developments that have moved FPS games online into large-scale multiplayer battles. By allowing players to participate in large battles both alongside and against other players, the game firstly ensures a sense of scale and danger in the combat system. Additionally, however, it also allows players the choice to participate as a soldier of either the Entente or Central Powers. As mentioned above, the possibility of doing this in a Second World War game is virtually non-existent, but because of the prevailing view that the First World War was a tragedy equally spread, there are no such restrictions on allowing the player to take on a role within the opposing army.

The emergence of games like *Valiant Hearts* and *Verdun* represents the modern evolution of the First World War in computer games. These games allow for the portrayal and exploration of the First World War in a far more imaginative and liberated manner than had previously been available. As outlined above, these shifts were partly made possible because of new developments in technology, but much is due to games designers realising that the First World War is a far more fertile topic for narrative exploration than the increasingly stale good-versus-evil narrative of the Second World War. Through this realisation has come a renewed sense of freedom to tell interesting stories within a First World War environment. The future success of this, however, may depend upon the ability of games designers and historians to collaborate in a mutually beneficial manner.

## The Future of First World War Games

Studies of computer games often focus on what games portray or what their purpose is. In addition to this it is necessary, particularly when it comes to First World War games, to understand what their very existence actually represents. The success of games like *Valiant Hearts*, which according to Creative and Audio Director Yoan Fanise has sold over three million copies, *Verdun 1914–1918*, which has been played over four million times, and *The Great War Mod*, which has been downloaded over half a million times, has to be understood in context.[35] Interest in military-focused computer games has been a virtual constant since the days of the first *Red Baron* and *Castle Wolfenstein* games. However, as discussed previously, the First World War has not been a natural setting for such games, and neither, until recently, has it appeared to have a substantial audience. That games focusing on this conflict now seem to have attracted fans in such numbers is highly significant for understanding where this genre is heading and what it means in regard to wider interest in the war.

The centenary of the First World War has undoubtedly increased public interaction with its memory as both governmental and media attention have been focusing on significant moments throughout the conflict.[36] This public engagement in Britain has been further fuelled by the creation of new structures between community groups and academic historians to assist in commemorations, such as the World War One Engagement Centres jointly funded by the Arts and Humanities Research Council and the Heritage Lottery Fund.[37] Academic interest in the First World War was already guaranteed even before the centenary, and given that a search on the website of online retailer Amazon revealed over 6,000 books apparently published on the topic between the start of 2014 and February 2016, this interest has clearly not diminished to date.

Despite all this interest, for the success of First World War-focused computer games to have moved beneath the radar of historians to such an extent belies the development and ingenuity that have gone into these games. Modern computer game representations of the First World War have grown increasingly sophisticated and interesting in their approaches. The failure of First World War scholarship to recognise this new emerging medium fully and to interact with these games properly is an issue that still needs to be addressed. The huge numbers of sales, plays and downloads for games like *Verdun* and *Valiant Hearts* would be impressive on their own and appear even more so when one understands that they were created with very little interaction with what would ordinarily be considered mainstream academic historical discourse. The research undertaken by the developers of these games was often entirely self-directed and took a grass-roots approach in utilising historical websites, Osprey military books and re-enactment literature as popular sources.[38]

What is most obvious when examining these games is the determination of the developers to approach the topic with as much diligence and historical accuracy as possible. The creation of the most successful First World War computer games has not been undertaken without at least some attempt towards realism and historical veracity. Despite all this, one might argue that links between the developers of these games and First World War historians are practically non-existent and that this should be a source of great concern: not because computer game developers are not sufficiently influenced by the most up-to-date research on the First World War, but because it suggests that historians either do not recognise this developing medium or do not understand the opportunity on which they are passing.

Research for the book-length study *The First World War in Computer Games* rapidly revealed that the developers of these games were extremely keen and at times flattered to have their work examined from an academic perspective. The developers often spoke of their desire to create the type of First World War game that they had always wanted whilst at the same time producing something as factually and historically sound as they could. Nonetheless, it is notable that although there is some interest in computer games, many academic historians do not fully realise quite how large a sector First World War-focused games titles have become.

However, it is not just by engaging with the developers that these games can be used to increase discussions of the First World War. A final project report, 'The First World War in the Classroom: Teaching and the Construction of Popular Memory', centred on English secondary-school classrooms, highlighted the dedicated and inventive approaches that teachers are already taking to make the First World War accessible to their students.[39] The emergence of this focus on the First World War in the computer games industry can provide new opportunities for both school and university study of the war. It is worth bearing in mind that these games have a huge potential reach and, additionally, an almost overlooked potential impact on the way young people in particular view the First World War. Educators at both schools and universities will inevitably use the media sources that they can access most easily for discussions about the representation of the First World War. Criticisms of the supposed over-reliance of teachers on *Blackadder Goes Forth* have often overlooked the simple fact that the series is incredibly easy to find both on home media and on internet platforms such as YouTube. However, the rise of mobile gaming for titles such as *Trenches 2* and the ability both to download games and to watch others play them online means that the actual audience for First World War games has increased beyond those who are prepared to purchase these games. *Valiant Hearts*, for instance, drew a great deal of its success through word-of-mouth testimony and 'Let's Play' videos on YouTube.[40]

As a result of these technological developments, computer games are already reaching a much wider and more diverse audience than previously considered possible. When films and documentaries can be utilised both in teaching and on reading lists for studies of the First World War, there must now surely also be room for computer games. For whilst documentaries, films, television comedies and poetry all provide legitimate artistic responses to the war and evidence of its continuing evolution in public memory, computer games are, by their very nature, far more interactive. They enable the viewer to move from being at least partially passive to being an active participant in proceedings and, depending on the nature of those events, a potential collaborator in any number of scenarios.

With this in mind the worlds of First World War research and First World War computer game development can no longer exist apart from each other and with no substantial contact or discussion. At an event discussing Franco-British commemoration of the First World War at the Institut français du Royaume-Uni, upon hearing Yoan Fanise explain that *Valiant Hearts* had sold over three million copies, several members of the audience commented that if any academic historian had sold that many copies of their own work they would, legitimately, never stop mentioning it. First World War computer games are selling in vast numbers, they are finding a growing audience of interested players, and groups of these people are then taking it upon themselves to create their own First World War-focused games and modifications such as *The Great War Mod*. An entire culture is growing up around First World War computer games, creating new and fascinating representations of the conflict, which in turn feed into the developing popular memory of the conflict. This alternative memory culture is grass-roots and independent whilst at the same time linked to some of the biggest games companies in the world, but much of it is taking place with very little interaction with academia or historians. If an enormous opportunity is not to be missed then these two groups have to start contacting one another, collaborating and conversing.

## Notes

1. Chris Kempshall, *The First World War in Computer Games*, Palgrave Pivot (Basingstoke: Palgrave Macmillan, 2015), p. 18.
2. 'Daddy, what did YOU do in the Great War?', British Library, <http://www.bl.uk/collection-items/daddy-what-did-you-do-in-great-war> (last accessed 2 December 2016).
3. Niall Ferguson, *The Pity of War* (London: Allen Lane, 1998), p. 229.
4. Mark Levitch, 'War by Other Means: Mutilé Toy Makers and French National Identity', conference paper delivered at the conference 'Other Combatants, Other Fronts: Competing Histories of the First World War', held in London, Imperial War Museum, 2009.
5. 'List of World War II Video Games', *Wikipedia, the Free Encyclopedia*, <https://en.wikipedia.org/wiki/List_of_World_War_II_video_games>; 'List of World War I Video Games', *Wikipedia, the Free Encyclopedia*, <https://en.wikipedia.org/wiki/List_of_World_War_I_video_games> (both last accessed 2 December 2016).
6. Brian G. Hutton, *Where Eagles Dare* (Metro-Goldwyn-Mayer, 1968); Guy Hamilton, *Battle of Britain* (United Artists, 1969); Richard Attenborough, *A Bridge Too Far* (United Artists, 1977); Steven Spielberg, *Saving Private Ryan* (DreamWorks Pictures and Paramount Pictures, 1998); Jean-Jacques Annaud, *Enemy at the Gates* (Paramount Pictures, 2001).
7. *Medal of Honor*, PlayStation (DreamWorks Interactive, 1999); *Call of Duty: World at War*, Microsoft Windows, PlayStation 2, PlayStation 3, Nintendo Wii, Nintendo DS, Windows Mobile, Xbox 360, Mobile, Mac OS X (Treyarch, Exakt Entertainment, Arkane Studios, 2008).
8. See Kempshall, *The First World War in Computer Games*, pp. 17–38.
9. *Red Baron*, Arcade (Atari, Inc., 1980); *Castle Wolfenstein*, Apple II, DOS, Atari 400/800, Commodore 64 (Muse Software, 1981).
10. Andrew Wackerfuss, '"This Game of Sudden Death": Simulating Air Combat of the First World War', in Matthew Kapell and Andrew B. R. Elliott (eds), *Playing with the Past: Digital Games and the Simulation of History* (New York: Bloomsbury Academic, 2013), p. 234; Adam Chapman, 'It's Hard to Play in the Trenches: World War 1 in Videogames', conference paper delivered at the conference 'Gotland Game Conference and Nordic DiGRA', held in Gotland, Uppsala University, 2014.
11. *Knights of the Sky*, DOS, Amiga, Atari ST (MicroProse, 1990); *Wings of Glory*, x86 (DOS) (Origin Systems, 1994).
12. Kempshall, *The First World War in Computer Games*, pp. 76–7.
13. Wackerfuss, '"This Game of Sudden Death"', pp. 235–41.
14. Ibid., pp. 237–8.
15. *History Line: 1914–1918* (Blue Byte Software, 1992).
16. *Sid Meier's Civilization V*, Microsoft Windows, Mac OS, Linux, OnLive (Firaxis, 2010); Michael Resch, *1914: Offensive à outrance* (GMT Games, 2013); Richard Borg, *The Great War* (PSC Games, 2015).
17. Chris Kempshall, 'Pixel Lions – The Image of the Soldier in First World War Computer Games', *Historical Journal of Film, Radio and Television*, 19 October 2015, pp. 656–72, doi: <http://dx.doi.org/10.1080/01439685.2015.1096665> (last accessed 5 December 2016).
18. Kempshall, *The First World War in Computer Games*, pp. 60–70.
19. *Napoleon: Total War*, Microsoft Windows, Mac OS X (The Creative Assembly, 2010).
20. *The Great War Mod*, Microsoft Windows (The Great War Dev Team, 2013).
21. Larry Harris Jr, *Axis & Allies: WW1 1914* (Avalon Hill (Hasbro) and Wizards of the Coast, 2013).

22. 'Harris Game Design – Axis & Allies Forums View Topic – A&A WWI', <http://www.harrisgamedesign.com/phpBB3/viewtopic.php?f=12&t=93> (last accessed 5 December 2016).
23. 'The Great War', Kickstarter, <https://www.kickstarter.com/projects/1992455033/the-great-war-0> (last accessed 5 December 2016).
24. *Dogfight: The Great War* (Rock Solid Arcade, 2008), <http://www.addictinggames.com/action-games/dogfight.jsp>; *Dogfight 2: The Great War* (Rock Solid Arcade, 2009), <http://www.addictinggames.com/action-games/dogfight2.jsp> (both last accessed 5 December 2016).
25. *Warfare 1917* (ConArtists, 2008), <http://armorgames.com/play/2267/warfare-1917> (last accessed 5 December 2016); *Trenches 2*, iPhone, iPod Touch, iPad (Thunder Game Works and Catapult Consulting, 2011).
26. Kempshall, *The First World War in Computer Games*, pp. 58–81.
27. *Over the Top* (Canadian War Museum, n.d.), <http://www.warmuseum.ca/overthetop/> (last accessed 5 December 2016).
28. Daniel Todman, *The Great War: Myth and Memory* (London: Hambledon, 2005), pp. 121–52.
29. *Valiant Hearts: The Great War*, Microsoft Windows (Ubisoft Montpellier, 2014).
30. Fabien Riffaud and Juan Rodriguez, *The Grizzled*, 2015. The original name for this game was 'Les Poilus', which translates literally as 'the hairy ones'.
31. Adam Chapman and Jonas Linderoth, 'Exploring the Limits of Play: A Case Study of Representations of Nazism in Games', in Torill Elvira Mortensen, Jonas Linderoth and Ashley M. L. Brown (eds), *The Dark Side of Game Play: Controversial Issues in Playful Environments*, Routledge Advances in Game Studies (London: Routledge, 2015), pp. 137–54.
32. Kempshall, *The First World War in Computer Games*, pp. 96–104.
33. *Verdun 1914–1918*, Steam (Mac, Linux, Windows) (M2H and Blackmill Games, 2013).
34. Kempshall, 'Pixel Lions', p. 663.
35. Yoan Fanise, 'Valiant Hearts', presentation given at the conference 'Observing the First World War: Franco-British Perspectives on the History and Memory of the Centenary', held at the Institut français du Royaume-Uni, London, 2015; and Kempshall, *The First World War in Computer Games*, p. 100.
36. See, for example, 'First World War Centenary', <https://www.gov.uk/government/topical-events/first-world-war-centenary>; 'World War One on TV and Radio', <http://www.bbc.co.uk/programmes/p01nb93y> (both last accessed 5 December 2016).
37. 'World War One Engagement Centres', <http://www.ahrc.ac.uk/research/fundedthemesandprogrammes/worldwaroneanditslegacy/worldwaroneengagementcentres/> (last accessed 5 December 2016).
38. Kempshall, *The First World War in Computer Games*, pp. 77–8.
39. Ann-Marie Einhaus and Catriona Pennell, 'The First World War in the Classroom: Teaching and the Construction of Cultural Memory', May 2014, <http://ww1intheclassroom.exeter.ac.uk/wp-content/uploads/2014/06/FWW-in-the-Classroom-final-project-report.pdf> (last accessed 5 December 2016).
40. Fanise, 'Valiant Hearts'.

# Contributors

**Katherine Isobel Baxter** is Reader in English Literature in the Department of Humanities at Northumbria University. She has published widely on Joseph Conrad as well as on colonial and postcolonial literature. Other research interests include literary multilingualism, and law and literature studies.

**Laura Brandon** is the former Historian, Art and War, at the Canadian War Museum, Ottawa, and currently a Research Associate. She is the author of *Art or Memorial? The Forgotten History of Canada's War Art* (University of Calgary Press 2006) and *Art and War* (I. B. Tauris 2007). An Adjunct Research Professor in the School for Studies in Art and Culture at Carleton University, Ottawa, she was appointed to the Order of Canada in 2015.

**Alys Cundy** completed a Collaborative Doctoral Award PhD with the University of Bristol and Imperial War Museums. The project explored the changing display policies and practices at the Imperial War Museum London since its foundation in 1917 up to its major redevelopment in 2014. Her research interests include material culture and commemoration, and difficult heritage. She has previously published on the use of objects and space in displays at the Imperial War Museum. She was a Goethe Institut 'Scholar in Residence' in 2013–14, working on emotional strategies in museum representations of twentieth-century conflict.

**Clara Dawson** is Lecturer in Victorian Literature at the University of Manchester. Her research focuses on the relationship between nineteenth-century poetic forms and reception history, particularly periodicals and gift annuals. She recently published a two-volume edition, *Critical Heritage: Elizabeth Barrett Browning*, anthologising periodical reviews of her poetry, and an article on '*Sordello* and the Poetics of Reception' in *Essays in Criticism.*

**Robert Dean** is a Principal Lecturer in Drama and Music at the University of Lincoln. He has published work that identifies and explores the parallels between nineteenth-century theatrical practice and contemporary dramatic conventions. This includes the representation of archetypal characters, the role of musical accompaniment, and the function of sound effects. His research into musical dramaturgy and the history of sound production has resulted in publications that reconsider the role of sonic material in the works of Ibsen, Chekhov, Boucicault and Shaw.

**Ann-Marie Einhaus** is Senior Lecturer in Modern and Contemporary Literature in the Department of Humanities at Northumbria University, Newcastle upon Tyne. Her main research specialism is short fiction of and about the First World War from 1914 to the present, and she has also published on links between teaching, literature and cultural memory of the war, on middlebrow fiction, and on Wyndham Lewis. Her monograph, *The Short Story and the First World War*, was published by Cambridge University Press in 2013.

**Peter Grant** is Senior Fellow in Grantmaking, Philanthropy and Social Investment at Cass Business School, City, University of London. His book, *The Business of Giving: The Theory and Practice of Philanthropy, Grantmaking and Social Investment*, was published in 2011. His latest book, *Philanthropy and Voluntary Action in the First World War*, was published by Routledge/Taylor Francis in 2014. His next book will be *National Myth and the First World War in Modern Popular Music* from Palgrave Macmillan. Peter is a Fellow of the Royal Historical Society, a Trustee of the DHL Foundation and of the Amy Winehouse Foundation, and former Chair of the Voluntary Action History Society.

**Toby Haggith** is a historian who joined the Film Department of the Imperial War Museum in 1988. His PhD in Social History, from the University of Warwick, examined British films advocating slum clearance and town planning in the period 1918–51. He has published various essays on history and film and is the co-editor with Dr Joanna Newman of *Holocaust and the Moving Image: Representations in Film and Television since 1933* (Wallflower Press 2005). He was part of the team that oversaw the digital remastering of *The Battle of the Somme* (1916) and co-led the project to restore *The Battle of the Ancre and Advance of the Tanks* (1917). Since July 2016 he has introduced numerous public screenings of *The Battle of the Somme* which have been held to mark the centenary of the battle.

**Richard J. Hand** is Professor of Media Practice at the University of East Anglia. He is the founding co-editor of the international peer-reviewed *Journal of Adaptation in Film and Performance* and his interests include interdisciplinarity in performance (with a particular interest in historical forms of popular culture) using critical and practical research methodologies. He is the author of three books on Grand-Guignol theatre (Exeter University Press 2002, 2007 and 2016), three books on radio drama (McFarland 2006, Continuum 2011 and Manchester University Press 2014), two books on Joseph Conrad (Palgrave 2005 and Rodopi 2009) and a book on Graham Greene (Palgrave 2015), and has published translations of plays by Victor Hugo (Methuen 2004) and Octave Mirbeau (Intellect 2012). He has co-edited academic volumes on Conrad (2009), Horror Film (2007) and Radio (2012). As a practitioner he has written and directed radio and stage plays in the UK and US.

**Emma Hanna** completed her PhD at Kent and worked at the University of Greenwich as a Senior Lecturer in History and History Programme Leader before returning to the School of History at the University of Kent in 2015. Emma is a Co-Investigator on Gateways to the First World War, an AHRC/HLF-funded project based at the University of Kent, one of five national centres working to enhance community research and engagement with the centenary of 1914–18. Emma's research interests include the memory and representations of the First World War in contemporary popular culture, the various modes of entertainment on the home and fighting fronts in the First World War, principally cinema, music and dance, and the work of organisations such as the YMCA and Talbot House.

**Alice Kelly** is the Harmsworth Postdoctoral Research Fellow in the History of the United States and the First World War at the University of Oxford, based at the Rothermere American Institute and Corpus Christi College. Her current book project seeks to rethink modernism from the perspective of war commemoration and to reassess the significance of the Great War for modernist culture. Alice's critical edition of Edith Wharton's First World War reportage, *Fighting France: From Dunkerque to Belfort* (1915), was published by Edinburgh University Press in 2015. She has previously published on Katherine Mansfield's First World War writings and deathbed scenes in Great War nurses' narratives.

**Chris Kempshall** has taught on the First World War and military history at the University of Sussex, the University of Kent and the University of Brighton. His recent book *The First World War in Computer Games* (Palgrave Pivot 2015) examines the representation of the conflict in the modern media and is a topic on which he has continued to publish. He is also the author of the forthcoming monograph *British, French and American Relations on the Western Front, 1914–1918* (Palgrave Macmillan) and is a member of the Academic Advisory Board to the Imperial War Museum.

**Kate Kennedy** has twice been awarded research fellowships at the University of Cambridge, and is now Weinrebe Fellow in Life Writing at Wolfson College, Oxford, supported by the Leverhulme Trust. She has published and broadcast widely on the BBC on First World War literature and music, and her biography of Ivor Gurney, *Dweller in Shadows*, is forthcoming with Princeton University Press. She is the editor of *The Silent Morning: Culture and Memory after the Armistice* (2012), and is working on a triple biography of Rupert Brooke and two composers, entitled *The Fateful Voyage*.

**Christopher J. La Casse** is an English Lecturer at the United States Coast Guard Academy. His research focuses on the influence of the First World War on modernist little magazines and modern periodicals. His articles include '"Scrappy and Unselective": Rising Wartime Paper Costs and *The Little Review*' (*American Periodicals*, 26.2) as well as 'From the Historical Avant-Garde to Highbrow Coterie Modernism: *The Little Review*'s Wartime Advances and Retreats' (*Criticism*, 57.4). He also served as project coordinator of the 2015 NEH Summer Institute 'City of Print: New York and the Periodical Press'.

**Jo Laycock** is Senior Lecturer in History at Sheffield Hallam University; prior to this she held a Manoogian Simone Post-Doctoral Fellowship in Armenian History at the University of Michigan, Ann Arbor. Her research focuses on the aftermaths of conflict and displacement in Armenia and the South Caucasus. She is the author of *Imagining Armenia: Orientalism, Ambiguity and Intervention* (Manchester University Press 2009). Recent publications include articles in *Cultural and Social History* and *History and Memory* on repatriations to Soviet Armenia following the Second World War and a review essay on the history of the Armenian Genocide in *Revolutionary Russia*.

**J. J. Long** is Professor of German and Visual Culture at Durham University. He is the author of *The Novels of Thomas Bernhard* and *W. G. Sebald: Image, Archive, Modernity*, and has published extensively on twentieth-century German writing and photography. His current research concerns the role of photography in Weimar Germany (1919–33), and includes a focus on the politics of representing the First World War in the inter-war period.

**Kate Macdonald** is a literary historian working on British twentieth-century publishing culture and book history, linking literature with social and political history, at the University of Reading. Her most recent book is *Novelists Against Social Change: Conservative Popular Fiction, 1920–1960* (Palgrave Macmillan, 2015), and she is the editor of *Rose Macaulay, Gender and Modernity* (Routledge 2017).

**Anna Maguire** recently completed a doctorate through the AHRC's Collaborative Doctoral Programme at King's College, London, and Imperial War Museums. Her research focuses on the experience of troops from New Zealand, South Africa and the West Indies, and their colonial encounters, during the First World War. She is also a member of the HERA-funded project 'Cultural Exchange in a Time of Global Conflict: Colonials, Neutrals and Belligerents', led by Dr Santanu Das.

**Andrew Maunder** is Head of English at the University of Hertfordshire. He is the editor of *British Theatre and the Great War, 1914–1919* (Palgrave 2015) and of the Pickering and Chatto anthology *British Literature of World War I* (2011). He is also the author of biographies of *Bram Stoker* (2006) and *Wilkie Collins* (with Graham Law, 2010). He is a member of the AHRC-funded Centre for Everyday Lives in War based at the University of Hertfordshire, where he also leads the World War I Theatre Project which revives forgotten wartime plays for modern audiences.

**Michael Paris**, PhD, FRHistS, is Emeritus Professor of Modern History at the University of Central Lancashire. Specialising in popular culture and war, he has published a number of books including *Warrior Nation: Images of War in British Popular Culture* (Reaktion 2000), *From the Wright Brothers to Top Gun: Aviation, Nationalism and the Movies* (Manchester University Press 1997) and *Repicturing the Second World War* (Routledge 2008). He is now working on a study of Liverpool in the Second World War.

**Jane Potter** is Reader in Publishing at Oxford Brookes University. Jane's research focuses on book and literary history. Her monograph *Boys in Khaki, Girls in Print: Women's Literary Responses to the Great War 1914–1918* (Oxford University Press 2005; paperback 2007) was joint winner of the 2006 Women's History Network Book Prize and she has published widely on many aspects of war literature, book history and women's writing. A Trustee of the Wilfred Owen Literary Estate, she is the author of *Wilfred Owen: An Illustrated Life* (Bodleian Library Publishing 2014) and is currently working on a new edition of Owen's *Selected Letters* for Oxford University Press. She is also editing *A Cambridge History of World War I Poetry* (forthcoming, Cambridge University Press) and, with Ralf Schneider (University of Bielefeld), *The Handbook of British Literature and Culture of the First World War* (forthcoming, de Gruyter).

**Matthew C. Potter** is an Associate Professor in Art and Design History at Northumbria University. His research focuses on the role played by visual culture in the construction of national identity and wider issues of international exchange predominantly in the period between 1850 and 1950. He is the author of *The Inspirational Genius of Germany: British Art and Germanism, 1850–1939* (Manchester University Press 2012), editor of and contributor to *The Concept of the 'Master' in Art Education in Britain and Ireland, 1770 to the Present* (Ashgate 2013), and has written numerous articles and chapters on the history of art within imperial and internationalist contexts.

**Matthew Shaw** is the Institute of Historical Research Librarian, and formerly a curator at the British Library, where he helped to lead the Europeana Collections 1914–1918 digitisation project and curated the library's First World War centenary exhibition, 'Enduring War: Grief, Grit and Humour'. He is a Visiting Research Fellow at the University of Northumbria.

**George Simmers** researched a PhD in the prose literature of the Great War at Oxford Brookes University after a career in teaching. He has published articles and chapters on Kipling, 'Sapper', Arnold Bennett, the fiction of the 1920s, P. G. Wodehouse and T. S. Eliot. He is currently an Honorary Research Fellow at Sheffield Hallam University.

**Marie Stern-Peltz** undertook her AHRC-funded doctorate at Newcastle University on contemporary representations of the First World War in adult and young adult fiction. She has an article forthcoming on Michael Morpurgo's *Private Peaceful* and has previously completed a downloadable reading guide on First World War fiction as part of the Catherine Cookson Foundation-funded project 'World War I and Trauma: Commemoration through Shared Reading Communities'.

**James Thompson** is Reader in Modern British History at the University of Bristol. He is the author of *British Political Culture and the Idea of 'Public Opinion', 1867–1914* (Cambridge University Press 2013). He is currently writing a book on the visual culture of British politics from the 1860s to the 1930s.

**Laura Wittman** is Associate Professor of French and Italian at Stanford University. She primarily works on nineteenth- and twentieth-century Italian and French literature from a comparative perspective. She is interested in connections between modernity, religion and politics. Much of her work explores the role of the ineffable, the mystical and the body in modern poetry, philosophy and culture. Her book *The Tomb of the Unknown Soldier, Modern Mourning, and the Reinvention of the Mystical Body* (University of Toronto Press 2011) was awarded the Marraro Award of the Society for Italian Historical Studies for 2012. Laura has (co-)edited special issues of the *Romanic Review*, *California Italian Studies* and *Futurism: An Anthology* (Yale University Press 2009). She has published articles on d'Annunzio, Marinetti, Fogazzaro, Ungaretti, Montale, Sereni and Merini, as well as on decadent-era culture and Italian cinema.

# INDEX

9781399546751